ANNUAL EDITIONS

Social Problems 13/14

Thirty-Ninth Edition

EDITOR

Kurt Finsterbusch
University of Maryland, College Park

Kurt Finsterbusch received a bachelor's degree in history from Princeton University in 1957 and a bachelor of divinity degree from Grace Theological Seminary in 1960. His PhD in sociology, from Columbia University, was conferred in 1969. Dr. Finsterbusch is the author of several books, including *Understanding Social Impacts* (Sage Publications, 1980), *Social Research for Policy Decisions* (Wadsworth Publishing, 1980, with Annabelle Bender Motz), and *Organizational Change as a Development Strategy* (Lynne Rienner Publishers, 1987, with Jerald Hage). He is currently teaching at the University of Maryland, College Park, and, in addition to serving as editor for *Annual Editions: Social Problems,* he is also editor of *Annual Editions: Sociology,* McGraw-Hill/CLS's *Taking Sides: Clashing Views on Controversial Social Issues,* and *Sources: Notable Selections in Sociology.*

ANNUAL EDITIONS: SOCIAL PROBLEMS 13/14,THIRTY-NINTH EDITION

Annual Editions is published by the **Contemporary Learning Series** group within The McGraw-
Hill Higher Education division.

2 3 4 5 6 7 8 9 0 QVS/QVS 16 15 14

MHID: 0-07-805119-3
ISBN: 978-0-07-805119-7
ISSN: 1093-278X(print)
ISSN: 2158-4141 (online)

Developmental Editor: *Dave Welsh*
Senior Permissions Coordinator: *Shirley Lanners*
Marketing Director: *Adam Kloza*
Marketing Manager: *Nathan Edwards*
Senior Project Manager: *Melissa Leick*
Cover Designer: *Studio Montage, St. Louis, MO.*
Buyer: *Nichole Birkenholz*
Media Project Manager: *Sridevi Palani*

Compositor: Laserwords Private Limited
Cover Image Credits: Brand X Pictures / Jupiterimages [Background]; Luiz Felipe Castro/Getty
Images [Inset]

www.mhhe.com

Editors/Academic Advisory Board

Members of the Academic Advisory Board are instrumental in the final selection of articles for each edition of ANNUAL EDITIONS. Their review of articles for content, level, and appropriateness provides critical direction to the editors and staff. We think that you will find their careful consideration well reflected in this volume.

ANNUAL EDITIONS: Social Problems 13/14
39th Edition

EDITOR

Kurt Finsterbusch
University of Maryland, College Park

Preface

In publishing ANNUAL EDITIONS we recognize the enormous role played by the magazines, newspapers, and journals of the public press in providing current, first-rate educational information in a broad spectrum of interest areas. Many of these articles are appropriate for students, researchers, and professionals seeking accurate, current material to help bridge the gap between principles and theories and the real world. These articles, however, become more useful for study when those of lasting value are carefully collected, organized, indexed, and reproduced in a low-cost format, which provides easy and permanent access when the material is needed. That is the role played by ANNUAL EDITIONS.

The reason we study social problems is so that we can do something about them. Corrective action, however, is not taken until the situation is seen as a problem and the fire of concern is kindled in a number of citizens. A democratic country gives those citizens means for legally trying to change things, and this freedom and opportunity is a great pride for our country. In fact, most college students have already given time or money to some cause in which they believe. This is necessary as each generation will face struggles for rights and justice. Daily forces operate to corrupt, distort, bias, exploit, and defraud as individuals and groups seek their own advantage at the expense of others and the public interest. Those dedicated to a good society, therefore, constantly struggle against these forces. Furthermore, the struggle is often complex and confusing. Not always are the defenders of the status quo wrong and the champions of change right. Important values will be championed by both sides. Today there is much debate about the best way to improve education. Opposing spokespersons think that they are serving the good of the children and of the United States. In a similar manner, conscientious students in the same college class and reading the same material will hotly disagree. Therefore, solving problems is usually not a peaceful process. First, it requires information and an understanding of the problem, and we can expect disagreements on both the facts and the interpretations. Second, it requires discussion, compromise, and a plan with majority support, or at least the support of the powerful groups. Third, it requires action. In a democratic society this process should involve tolerance and even goodwill toward one's opponents as long as they act honestly, fairly, and democratically. Class discussions should involve respect for each other's opinions.

In some ways the study of social problems is easy and in some ways it is hard. The easy aspect is that most people know quite a lot about the problems that this book addresses; the hard part is that solving those problems is very difficult. If the solutions were easy, the problems would have been solved by now, and we would not be studying these particular issues. It may be easy to plan solutions, but it is hard to implement them. In general, however, Americans are optimistic and believe in progress; we learn by our mistakes and keep trying until conditions are acceptable. For instance, the members of Common Cause, including myself, have worked for campaign finance reform since 1970. Our efforts failed until Watergate created a huge public demand for it, and both campaign finance reform and public-right-to-know laws were passed. The reform, however, led to the formation of PACs (Political Action Committees) to get around the law and buy influence legally.

Recently, new campaign finance reform laws were passed.

Nevertheless, I would speculate that while they will somewhat reduce the influence of money on politics, sooner or later moneyed interests will find a way to continue to have inordinate influence on policy decisions and eventually precipitate yet another reform effort. It could be that at the end of the twenty-first century, Americans will still be struggling with many of the same problems as today. But it is reasonable to believe that things will be somewhat better at that point because throughout this century people will mobilize again and again to improve our society; some will even do this at considerable cost to themselves.

The articles presented here were selected for their attention to important issues, the value of the information and ideas they present, and/or their ability to move the reader to concern and possibly even action toward correcting social problems. This edition of *Annual Editions: Social Problems 13/14* begins in Unit 1 by broadly describing the United States and recent changes in forces that affect our lifestyles. Unit 2 examines some big issues in the political and economic systems that have society-wide impacts. Next, Unit 3 examines issues of inequality and injustice that challenge basic American values. Unit 4 considers how well the various institutions of society work. Most institutions are being heavily criticized. These articles help to explain why. Then, Unit 5 studies the traditional problem of crime and law enforcement. Fortunately, there is some good news here. Finally, Unit 6 focuses on the future and problems of population, environment, technology, globalization, community, and long-term change.

To assist the reader in identifying issues covered in the articles, the topic guide lists the topics in alphabetical order and the articles in which they are discussed. A reader doing research on a specific topic is advised to check this guide first. A valuable resource for users of this

Contents

UNIT 1
Introduction: Clashing Values and Problematic Transformations of Social Life

Part A. Social Life

1. **The American Narrative: Is There One & What Is It?,** William H. Chafe,
   Daedalus, Winter 2012

   William H. Chafe shows that America has two major moral premises from the early
   Puritans until today: serving the public good and individual freedom. These more or less
   balance each other and over the long run serve us well. The current drive to undo the
   programs that assist the needy, including social security and medicare, may destroy that
   balance if unchecked and weaken the country.   2

2. **Still Bowling Alone? The Post-9/11 Split,** Thomas H. Sander and Robert D.
   Putnam, *Journal of Democracy,* January 2010

   Robert D. Putnam documented the decline in group activities and the associated loss
   of social capital since the 1960s in his article and book "Bowling Alone." Since society
   needs lots of social capital to run well, his book was a frightening warning. The question
   in Sander and Putnam's title points to increased volunteerism and greater connectedness since 9/11. Crises can pull us together.   6

Part B. Transformation of Influences on People and Culture

3. **Relationships, Community, and Identity in the New Virtual Society,**
   Arnold Brown, *The Futurist,* March/April 2011

   Arnold Brown argues against the declining community thesis. The explosion of communication technology has greatly increased connectedness. Contrary to most people's assumptions, Brown believes that virtual connections are becoming almost as strong as personal
   connections. These technologies will greatly impact society and individual psychologies. 11

4. **What Isn't for Sale?** Michael J. Sandel, *Atlantic,* April 2012

   Michael J. Sandel documents the increasing commodification of modern life. Market
   values are becoming more dominant in area after area. The subordination of important
   morals like caring for others to market values is corrupting our thinking and behavior to
   the detriment of the functioning of society.   15

UNIT 2
Problems of the Political Economy

Part A. The Polity

5. **The Rule of the Rich,** Bill Moyers, *The Progressive,* February 2011

   All sociologists to some extent accept the power elite theory that the economic elite

The concepts in bold italics are developed in the article. For further expansion, please refer to the Topic Guide.

UNIT 3
Problems of Poverty and Inequality

The concepts in bold italics are developed in the article. For further expansion, please refer to the Topic Guide.

The concepts in bold italics are developed in the article. For further expansion, please refer to the Topic Guide.

UNIT 4
Institutional Problems

The concepts in bold italics are developed in the article. For further expansion, please refer to the Topic Guide.

UNIT 5
Crime, Violence, and Law Enforcement

The concepts in bold italics are developed in the article. For further expansion, please refer to the Topic Guide.

UNIT 6
Problems of Population, Environment, Resources, and the Future

The concepts in bold italics are developed in the article. For further expansion, please refer to the Topic Guide.

The concepts in bold italics are developed in the article. For further expansion, please refer to the Topic Guide.

Correlation Guide

The *Annual Editions* series provides students with convenient, inexpensive access to current, carefully selected articles from the public press. **Annual Editions: Social Problems 13/14** is an easy-to-use reader that presents articles on important topics such as *poverty and inequality, the family, crime, law enforcement, terrorism,* and many more. For more information on *Annual Editions* and other *McGraw-Hill Contemporary Learning Series* titles, visit www.mhhe.com/cls.

This convenient guide matches the units in **Annual Editions: Social Problems 13/14** with the corresponding chapters in one of our best-selling McGraw-Hill Social Problems textbooks by Lauer/Lauer.

Annual Editions: Social Problems 13/14	Social Problems and the Quality of Life, 12/e by Lauer/Lauer
Unit 1: Introduction: Clashing Values and Problematic Transformations of Social Life	**Chapter 1:** Understanding Social Problems **Chapter 5:** Sexual Deviance
Unit 2: Problems of the Political Economy	**Chapter 9:** Government and Politics **Chapter 10:** Work and the Economy
Unit 3: Problems of Poverty and Inequality	**Chapter 6:** Poverty **Chapter 7:** Gender and Sexual Orientation **Chapter 8:** Race, Ethnic Groups, and Racism
Unit 4: Institutional Problems	**Chapter 11:** Education **Chapter 12:** Family Problems **Chapter 13:** Health Care and Illness: Physical and Mental
Unit 5: Crime, Violence, and Law Enforcement	**Chapter 2:** Alcohol and Other Drugs **Chapter 3:** Crime and Delinquency **Chapter 4:** Violence **Chapter 14:** War and Terrorism
Unit 6: Problems of Population, Environment, Resources, and the Future	**Chapter 15:** The Environment

Topic Guide

This topic guide suggests how the selections in this book relate to the subjects covered in your course. You may want to use the topics listed on these pages to search the Web more easily.

On the following pages a number of websites have been gathered specifically for this book. They are arranged to reflect the units of this Annual Editions reader. You can link to these sites by going to www.mhhe.com/cls.

All the articles that relate to each topic are listed below the bold-faced term.

Abuse
20. Human Sex Trafficking
34. License to Kill

Assimilation
18. Fear and Loathing of Islam

Business and the market
4. What Isn't for Sale?
9. Hard at Work in the Jobless Future
45. The Broken Contract: Inequality and American Decline

Capitalism
4. What Isn't for Sale?
6. Follow the Dark Money
45. The Broken Contract: Inequality and American Decline

Children and childhood
25. Good Parents, Bad Results
26. Introduction: The Next Wave of School Reform
27. Is $600 Billion Enough?

Cities
10. Urban Legends

Civil rights
12. The Invisible Ones
16. Somewhere between Jim Crow & Post-Racialism: Reflections on the Racial Divide in America Today
17. A More Perfect Union
18. Fear and Loathing of Islam
20. Human Sex Trafficking
21. Free and Equal in Dignity and LGBT Rights
32. Crime, Inequality & Social Justice
33. Wrongful Convictions
34. License to Kill
36. The Year in Hate & Extremism, 2010

Community
2. Still Bowling Alone? The Post-9/11 Split
3. Relationships, Community, and Identity in the New Virtual Society
4. What Isn't for Sale?
10. Urban Legends

Conflict
1. The American Narrative: Is There One & What Is It?
16. Somewhere between Jim Crow & Post-Racialism: Reflections on the Racial Divide in America Today
17. A More Perfect Union
18. Fear and Loathing of Islam
36. The Year in Hate & Extremism, 2010
38. The New Virology
45. The Broken Contract: Inequality and American Decline
46. The Democratic Malaise: Globalization and the Threat to the West
47. The Future of History: Can Liberal Democracy Survive the Decline of the Middle Class?

Crime
20. Human Sex Trafficking
30. Fighting Crime: An Economist's View
31. The Aggregate Burden of Crime
32. Crime, Inequality & Social Justice
33. Wrongful Convictions
34. License to Kill
35. Toward Fewer Prisoners and Less Crime
37. War in the Fifth Domain
38. The New Virology

Culture
1. The American Narrative: Is There One & What Is It?
2. Still Bowling Alone? The Post-9/11 Split?
3. Relationships, Community, and Identity in the New Virtual Society
4. What Isn't for Sale?
10. Urban Legends
11. Immigration Benefits America
15. The Myth of the "Culture of Poverty"
17. A More Perfect Union
18. Fear and Loathing of Islam
19. Why Women Still Can't Have It All
21. Free and Equal in Dignity and LGBT Rights
22. The End of Men
23. All the Single Ladies
24. Matches Made on Earth: Why Family Values Are Human Values
36. The Year in Hate & Extremism, 2010
46. The Democratic Malaise: Globalization and the Threat to the West
47. The Future of History: Can Liberal Democracy Survive the Decline of the Middle Class?

Demography
23. All the Single Ladies
39. The New Population Bomb: The Four Megatrends That Will Change the World
41. The World Will Be More Crowded—With Old People

Discrimination
16. Somewhere between Jim Crow & Post-Racialism: Reflections on the Racial Divide in America Today
17. A More Perfect Union
21. Free and Equal in Dignity and LGBT Rights
24. Matches Made on Earth: Why Family Values Are Human Values
32. Crime, Inequality & Social Justice
33. Wrongful Convictions
35. Toward Fewer Prisoners and Less Crime

Ecology and environment
10. Urban Legends
39. The New Population Bomb: The Four Megatrends That Will Change the World
42. Climate Change
44. Engineering the Future of Food

Economy
4. What Isn't for Sale?
5. The Rule of the Rich
6. Follow the Dark Money
8. The Withering of the Affluent Society

Internet References

The following Internet sites have been selected to support the articles found in this reader. These sites were available at the time of publication. However, because websites often change their structure and content, the information listed may no longer be available. We invite you to visit www.mhhe.com/cls for easy access to these sites.

Annual Editions: Social Problems 13/14

General Sources

The Gallup Organization
www.gallup.com

Open this Gallup Organization home page for links to an extensive archive of public opinion poll results and special reports on a huge variety of topics related to U.S. society.

Library of Congress
www.loc.gov

Examine this extensive website to learn about resource tools, library services/resources, exhibitions, and databases in many different fields related to social problems.

National Geographic Society
www.nationalgeographic.com

This site provides links to National Geographic's huge archive of maps, articles, and other documents. There is a great deal of material related to social and cultural topics that will be of great value to those interested in the study of cultural pluralism.

UNIT 1: Introduction: The Nature of Social Problems and Calls for Transforming Society

The American Studies Web
http://lamp.georgetown.edu/asw

This site functions as a search engine for resources in American Studies.

Anthropology Resources Page
www.usd.edu/anth

Many cultural topics can be accessed at this site from the University of South Dakota. Click on the links to find information about differences and similarities in values and lifestyles among the world's peoples.

Social Science Information Gateway
http://sosig.esrc.bris.ac.uk

This site provides access to online resources that have been evaluated and selected by subject specialists in the social sciences.

UNIT 2: Problems of the Political Economy

National Center for Policy Analysis
www.ncpa.org

Through this site, you can reach links that provide discussions of an array of topics that are of major interest in the study of American politics and government from a sociological perspective, including regulatory policy, affirmative action, and income.

Penn Library: Sociology
www.library.upenn.edu

This site allows you to research subjects and collections at the University of Pennsylvania's Penn Libraries.

UNIT 3: Problems of Poverty and Inequality

grass-roots.org
www.grass-roots.org

This site describes innovative grassroots programs in the United States that have helped people better their communities.

Immigration Facts
www.immigrationforum.org

Visit this site for press releases, facts on immigration and immigration reform, advocacy materials, and links to immigration reform resources.

Joint Center for Poverty Research
www.jcpr.org

Finding research information related to poverty is possible at this site. It provides working papers, answers to FAQs, and facts about who is poor in America. Welfare reform is also addressed.

SocioSite
www.pscw.uva.nl/sociosite/TOPICS/Women.html

Open this enormous sociology site of the University of Amsterdam's Sociological Institute to gain insights into a number of issues that affect both men and women. It provides biographies of women through history, an international network for women in the workplace, links to gay studies, affirmative action, family and children's issues, and much more. Return to the site's home page for many other sociological links.

William Davidson Institute
www.wdi.bus.umich.edu

The William Davidson Institute at the University of Michigan Business School is dedicated to the understanding and promotion of economic transition. Consult this site for discussion of topics related to the changing global economy and the effects of globalization in general.

WWW Virtual Library: Demography & Population Studies
http://demography.anu.edu.au/VirtualLibrary

Valuable information of interest to researchers in the field of demography can be found through the Demography Program at Australian National University. Visit this site for more information and links to various resources.

UNIT 4: Institutional Problems

The Center for Education Reform
http://edreform.com/school_choice

Visit this site to learn how the Center for Education Reform combines education policy with grassroots advocacy, working in over 40 states to better education for America's communities.

Go Ask Alice!
www.goaskalice.columbia.edu

Columbia University's Go Ask Alice! is a web resource that answers questions about relationships, sexuality, sexual health, emotional health, fitness, nutrition, alcohol, nicotine and other drugs, and general health.

Internet References

The National Academy for Child Development (NACD)
www.nacd.org

Peruse this site to see how NACD partners with parents to help children reach their full potential through activities, tasks, and training sessions.

National Council on Family Relations (NCFR)
www.ncfr.com

This site provides a forum for family researchers, educators, and practitioners to share knowledge about families and their relationships as well as establish professional standards in order to promote family well-being.

National Institute on Aging (NIA)
www.nih.gov/nia

Browse this site to see how NIA provides leadership in aging research, training, health information dissemination, and other programs relevant to aging and the elderly.

National Institute on Drug Abuse (NIDA)
www.nida.nih.gov

This site provides information and research results in an effort to improve the treatment, policy, and prevention of drug abuse and addiction.

National Institutes of Health (NIH)
www.nih.gov

Consult this site for links to extensive health information and scientific resources of interest to sociologists from the NIH, one of eight health agencies of the Public Health Service.

Parenting and Families
www.cyfc.umn.edu/features/index.html

This site describes how the University of Minnesota and Minnesota communities use research to influence policy and enhance practice in order to improve the well-being of Minnesota's children, youth, and families.

World Health Organization (WHO)
www.who.int/home-page

Access this site to see how the WHO provides leadership as well as monitors and assesses global health matters.

UNIT 5: Crime, Violence, and Law Enforcement

ACLU Criminal Justice Home Page
www.aclu.org/crimjustice/index.html

View this site to see how the ACLU is working to preserve all of the protections and guarantees of the Constitution.

Terrorism Research Center
www.terrorism.com

The Terrorism Research Center features definitions and original research on terrorism, counterterrorism documents, a comprehensive list of web links, and monthly profiles of terrorist and counterterrorist groups.

UNIT 6: Problems of Population, Environment, Resources, and the Future

Human Rights and Humanitarian Assistance
www.etown.edu/vl/humrts.html

This site provides links to sites and search engines associated with human rights and humanitarian assistance.

The Hunger Project
www.thp.org

Browse through this nonprofit organization's site to explore how it tries to achieve its goal: the end to global hunger through leadership at all levels of society. The Hunger Project contends that the persistence of hunger is at the heart of the major security issues threatening our planet.

UNIT 1

Introduction: Clashing Values and Problematic Transformations of Social Life

Unit Selections

1. **The American Narrative: Is There One & What Is It?** William H. Chafe
2. **Still Bowling Alone? The Post-9/11 Split,** Thomas H. Sander and Robert D. Putnam
3. **Relationships, Community, and Identity in the New Virtual Society,** Arnold Brown
4. **What Isn't for Sale?** Michael Sandel

Learning Outcomes

After reading this unit, you should be able to:

- Describe the key features of America in one paragraph. Identify what is distinctive about America.

- Present five major social problems in America.

- How much distance do you feel from people with very different interests, values, lifestyles, religions, races, ethnicities, and classes? What kinds of bonds do you feel with them? Explain your feelings and bonds.

- Discuss the strength of morals in America. What signs of moral decay in America do you observe? What signs of moral strength do you observe?

- Present your analysis of how aspects of modern life interfere with deep relationships and how aspects facilitate them.

Student Website

www.mhhe.com/cls

Internet References

The American Studies Web
www.lamp.georgetown.edu/asw
Anthropology Resources Page
www.usd.edu/anth
Social Science Information Gateway
http://sosig.esrc.bris.ac.uk

The first unit presents a very broad view of American society and the subsequent units look at specific social problems. William H. Chafe begins the first article with the question "Who are we?" and his article answers this question. Right now we are a deeply divided country, but we have always been a divided country. We have always pursued two competing sets of values. First, we should always act on behalf of the common good and serve others, and second, our individual freedoms should always be protected, and government often is the greatest threat to our freedoms. These themes are found in tension in Puritanism and in every period of American history. Usually the tension has been healthy with the two emphases balancing each other. Chafe argues that the polarization today is unparalleled and may jettison the balance between the two narratives of America.

The second article by Thomas H. Sander and Robert D. Putnam attempts to document the decline in social capital in America. The significance of this decline is that social capital is essential to the effective functioning of democracy, of key institutions, and of society. This article updates Putnam's earlier article and subsequent book "Bowling Alone: America's Declining Social Capital." Critics have found some social capital that Putnam overlooked, but his thesis has stood up and generated considerable concern about the future of America. Then 9/11 occurred and the crisis reversed the declining social capital trend (at least for a time) among certain sectors of society. In addition new technologies facilitate connectedness, but the authors are agnostic about whether web connections generate social capital like face-to-face connections do. However, new communication technologies provide hope.

The next article focuses on how the new communications are and will alter our futures. This topic is very dynamic, and therefore, very uncertain. Some of my students have pointed out to me that it is already outdated in some of its details. Nevertheless, it helps us explore the future of social life. Arnold Brown is more optimistic about the future of community in America than Sander and Putnam, because of the positive impacts of communication technologies that he predicts. He argues in "Relationships, Community, and Identity in the New Virtual Society," that "relationships made in virtual space can be just as powerful and meaningful as those formed in the real world. . . . Distinctions between real and virtual identity will become less sharply defined." From these judgments he draws out numerous interesting implications about future social and psychological life including increasing identity confusion.

© BananaStock/Punchstock

In the next article Michael J. Sandel documents the increasing commercialization of life and then explores the ramifications or hidden costs of this trend. Much of this trend is not subtle as in the expansion of for-profit schools, hospitals, prisons, and local and international security forces. More subtle is the increasing dominance of economic or market thinking in decisions and the declining importance of moral considerations. This process subtly corrupts our thinking and behavior. We can fall into the trap of thinking that if something is economically sound that it is morally right. We are drifting from being a market economy to being a market society.

The American Narrative: Is There One & What Is It?

William H. Chafe

Who are we? Where have we been? Where are we going? Can we even agree on who "we" includes? At no time in our history have these questions been more relevant. The American political system seems dysfunctional, if not permanently fractured. A generational gap in technological expertise and familiarity with the social network divides the country to an even greater extent than the culture wars of the 1960s and 1970s. Soon, more "Americans" will speak Spanish as their first language than English. For some, access to health care is a universal right, for others, a privilege that must be earned. Rarely—and certainly not since the Civil War—have we been so divided on which direction we should be heading as a country. How can there be an American narrative when it is not clear what it means to talk about an American people or nation? Two overriding paradigms have long competed in defining who we are. The first imagines America as a community that places the good of the whole first; the second envisions the country as a gathering of individuals who prize individual freedom and value more than anything else each person's ability to determine his own fate.

When the Puritans arrived in the Massachusetts Bay Colony in 1630, their leader, John Winthrop, told his shipmates aboard the *Arabella* that their mission was to create a "city upon a hill," a blessed society that would embody values so noble that the entire world would admire and emulate the new colony. Entitled "A Modell of Christian Charity," Winthrop's sermon described what it would take to create that beloved community: "We must love one another. We must bear one another's burdens . . . make others' conditions our own. We must rejoice together, mourn together, labor and suffer together, always having before our eyes a community [where we are all] members of the same body."

Consistent with Winthrop's vision, Massachusetts was governed in its early decades by a sense of communal well-being. While the colony tolerated differences of status and power, the ruling norm was that the common good took precedence. Thus, "just prices" were prescribed for goods for sale, and punishment was imposed on businesses that sought

excess profits. Parents who mistreated their children were shamed; people who committed adultery were exposed and humiliated.

Soon enough, a surge of individualism challenged the reigning norms. Entrepreneurs viewed communal rules as shackles to be broken so that they could pursue individual aspirations—and profits. The ideal of a "just price" was discarded. While religion remained a powerful presence, secularism ruled everyday business life, and Christianity was restricted to a once-a-week ritual. Class distinctions proliferated, economic inequality increased, and the values of *laissez-faire individualism* displaced the once-enshrined "common wealth." Aid to the poor became an act of individual charity rather than a communal responsibility.

Not surprisingly, the tensions between those who put the good of the community first and those who value individual freedom foremost have reverberated throughout our history. Thomas Jefferson sought to resolve the conflict in the Declaration of Independence by embracing the idea of "equal opportunity" for all. Note that he championed not equality of results, but equality of opportunity. Every citizen might have an "inalienable" right to "life, liberty and the pursuit of happiness," but what happened to each person's "equal opportunity" depended on the performance of that particular individual. Success was not guaranteed.

Throughout American history, the tensions between the value of the common good and the right to unbridled individual freedom have resurfaced. The federal government sought to build roads and canals across state lines to serve the general good. The nation fought a Civil War because slavery contradicted the belief in the right of equal citizenship. In the aftermath of the war, the Constitution guaranteed all males the right to vote, and its Fourteenth Amendment promised each citizen "equal protection" under the law.

But by the end of the nineteenth century, rampant economic growth had created myriad enterprises that threatened the common good. In *The Jungle*, Upton Sinclair highlighted the danger of workers falling into vats of boiling liquid at meat-packing plants. The influx of millions of immigrants brought new dangers of infectious disease. As sweatshops, germ-filled tenements, and unsafe factories blighted American cities, more and more Americans insisted on legislation that fostered the general welfare. Led by women reformers such as Jane Addams and Florence Kelley, social activists succeeded in getting laws passed that ended child labor, protected workers from injury from dangerous factory machines, and created standards for safe meat and food. The Progressive Era still left most people free to pursue their own destiny, but under President Theodore Roosevelt, the government became the ultimate arbiter of minimal standards for industry, railroads, and consumer safety.

The tensions between the two narratives continued to grow as the nation entered the Great Depression. Nearly a million mortgages were foreclosed, the stock market crashed, 25 percent of all American workers were chronically unemployed, and banks failed. When Franklin Roosevelt was elected president, he promised to use "bold, persistent experimentation" to find answers to people's suffering. The legislation of the first hundred days of his presidency encompassed unprecedented federal intervention in the regulation of industry, agriculture, and the provision of welfare payments to the unemployed. The good of the whole reemerged as a dominant concern. By 1935, however, the American Liberty League, a political group formed by conservative Democrats to oppose New Deal legislation, was indicting **fdr** as a socialist and demanding a return to laissez-faire individualism. But the New Deal rolled on. In 1935, Congress enacted Social Security, the single greatest collective investment America had ever made, for all people over sixty-five, and the Wagner Labor Relations Act gave unions the right to organize. Roosevelt ran his 1936 reelection campaign on a platform emphasizing that "one third of [our] nation is ill-housed, ill-clothed and ill-fed."

This focus on the good of the whole culminated during World War II, a time when everyone was reminded of being part of a larger battle to preserve the values that "equal opportunity" represented: the dignity of every citizen, as well as the right to freedom of religion, freedom from want, and freedom of political expression. For the first time since Reconstruction, the government acted to prohibit discrimination against African Americans, issuing an executive order to allow blacks as well as whites to be hired in the war industries. Similarly, it supported policies of equal pay to women workers while leading a massive effort to recruit more women into the labor force to meet wartime demands. From wage and price controls to the universal draft, government action on behalf of the good of the whole reached a new height.

After the war ended, the tension between the competing value systems returned, but, significantly, even most Republicans accepted as a given the fundamental reforms achieved under the New Deal. Anyone who suggested repeal of Social Security, President Dwight Eisenhower wrote to his brother Milton midway through his term in office, was "out of his mind." Eisenhower even created a new Cabinet department to oversee health and welfare.

The stage was set for the revolutions of the 1960s: that is, the civil rights movement, the women's movement, the student movement, and the War on Poverty. Blacks had no intention of accepting the status quo of prewar Jim Crow segregation when they returned from serving in World War II. Building on the community institutions they had created during the era of Jim Crow, they mobilized to confront racism. When a black woman was raped by six white policemen in Montgomery, Alabama, in the late 1940s, the Women's Political Council, organized by local black women, and the Brotherhood of Sleeping Car Porters, an all-black union, took on the police and forced a trial. That same network of black activists sought improvements in the treatment of blacks at downtown department stores and on public transport. Thus, when one of their members, Rosa Parks, was arrested in 1955 for refusing to give up her seat on a city bus to a white person, both groups took action. By initiating a phone tree and printing four thousand leaflets, they organized a mass rally overnight. Held at a local Baptist church to consider a bus boycott, the rally featured an address by Martin Luther King, Jr., who later became the embodiment of the movement (though it should be noted that the movement created King and not vice versa). After that night, Montgomery's black community refused to ride the city buses for 381 consecutive days, until the buses were desegregated.

A few years later, four first-year students at the all-black North Carolina Agricultural and Technical College in Greensboro, North Carolina, carried the movement a step further. Although they had come of age after the Supreme Court outlawed school segregation, little had changed. Now that their generation was reaching maturity, they asked what they could do. The young men had gone to an all-black high school where their teachers had asked them to address voter registration envelopes to community residents and encouraged them to think of themselves as first-class citizens. They had participated in an **naacp** youth group in which weekly discussions had centered on events such as the Montgomery Bus Boycott. They attended a Baptist church where the pastor preached the social gospel and asked for "justice now." Embittered by how little the status of black Americans had improved, they sought new ways of carrying forward what they had learned.

Their solution was simple: highlight the absurdity of segregation by going to a downtown department store and acting like regular customers. At the Woolworth's in Greensboro, they bought notebooks at one counter, purchased toothpaste at another, then sat down at the lunch counter and ordered a cup of coffee. "We don't serve colored people here," they were told. "But you served us over there," they responded, showing their receipts. Opening their school books, they sat for three hours until the store closed. The next day, they returned to the lunch counter with twenty-three of their classmates. The day after there were sixty-six, the next day one hundred. On the fifth day, one thousand black students and adults crowded the streets of downtown Greensboro.

The direct-action civil rights movement had begun. Within two months, sit-ins occurred in fifty-four cities in nine states. By April 1960, the Student Nonviolent Co-ordinating Committee (sncc) had been founded. Soon, *The New York Times* was devoting a special section each day to civil rights demonstrations in the South. On August 28, 1963, a quarter-million people came together for the March on Washington. There, Martin Luther King, Jr., gave his "I Have a Dream" speech, a contemporary version of what John Winthrop had said 238 years earlier that celebrated the same idea of a "beloved community" where "neither Jew nor Gentile, black man or white man" could be separated from each other.

At long last, the government responded. The Civil Rights Act of 1964 ended Jim Crow. The Voting Rights Act of 1965 restored the franchise to black Americans. The War on Poverty gave hope to millions who had been left out of the American dream. Medicare offered health care to all senior citizens, and Medicaid offered it to those who could not otherwise afford to go to the doctor. Federal Aid to Education created new and better schools. The Model Cities Program offered a way for blighted neighborhoods to be revitalized.

The narrative of progress toward the common good reached a new crescendo. With the civil rights movement as an inspiration, women started their own movement for social equality. Access to previously closed careers opened up under pressure. By 1990, half of all medical, law, and business students were women. Young girls grew up with the same aspirations as young boys. Latinos, gay Americans, and other minorities soon joined the march demanding greater equality. It seemed as though a permanent turning point had occurred.

B ut the counternarrative eventually rediscovered its voice. Millions of white Americans who might have supported the right of blacks to vote or eat at a lunch counter were appalled by affirmative action and demands for Black Power. When the war in Vietnam caused well-off students to take to the streets in protest against their country's military actions, thousands of ordinary workers were angered by the rebellion of the young against authority. Traditional families were outraged when feminists questioned monogamy and dared to challenge male authority.

By 1968, the nation was divided once more, and the events of that election year crystallized the issues. Incumbent Lyndon Johnson withdrew from the presidential race at the end of March. Martin Luther King, Jr., was assassinated in April, with riots spreading like wildfire across the country in response. Student protestors took over Columbia University in May, making a mockery of the idea of civil discourse and respect for authority. Robert F. Kennedy was assassinated in June, just as he seemed ready to move decisively toward the Democratic presidential nomination. And when the Democratic party met for its convention in Chicago, thousands of protestors were pummeled by police as they demonstrated against conventional politics.

At the same time, Richard Nixon was nominated by the Republican party on a platform of "law and order" and respect for authority. Adopting a "Southern strategy," he appealed for white Southern votes by opposing forced desegregation of schools. Lambasting students who protested the war, he pleaded for a return to respect for traditional institutions. Nixon claimed to speak on behalf of "the silent majority" who remained proud to be American citizens, who celebrated the flag rather than mocked it, and who affirmed the rights of individuals to do as they wished.

Richard Nixon's election in Fall 1968 launched the resurgence of a conservative consensus in American politics. Though on issues such as the environment Nixon pursued many policies consistent with the "good of the whole" framework, on most issues he moved in the opposite direction. He opposed busing as a tool to create greater school desegregation, started to dismantle War on Poverty programs, based his 1972 reelection campaign on attacking the "collectivism" of the Democratic party, and insisted on defending the values of "traditional" Americans against attacks by the young, minorities, and women.

As social issues provided a rallying point for those set against further social change, the conservative narrative gained new proponents. Those opposed to gay rights mobilized to curtail further efforts to make sexuality a civil rights issue. Evangelical Christians joined groups such as Jerry Falwell's Moral Majority or Pat Robertson's "Praise the Lord" clubs to lobby against advances for minority rights. Direct mail campaigns and the use of cable television helped the Right galvanize new audiences of potential supporters.

Presidential politics also continued on a conservative path. Even though Richard Nixon was compelled to resign in shame over his illegal activities in the Watergate scandal, each of his successors—even Democrats—advanced the conservative agenda he initiated. Gerald Ford vetoed more legislation in two years than most presidents veto in eight. Jimmy Carter, though a liberal on gender equality and black civil rights, proved conservative on most economic issues. Ronald Reagan personified the conservative revival. He not only celebrated patriotism, but also revived the viewpoint that the best America was one without government intervention in the economy, and one that venerated the ideal of individualism.

Even Democrat Bill Clinton, excoriated by the Right as a demonic embodiment of counterculture values, was in practice more a Dwight Eisenhower Republican than a Lyndon Johnson Democrat. Dedicated to cultivating the political mainstream, he achieved legislative victories primarily on traditionally Republican issues: deficit reduction; the North American Free Trade Agreement; an increased police presence on the streets; welfare reform that took people off the public dole after two years; and the use of V-chips to allow parents to control their children's television viewing habits. Only his failed health care proposal acted in tune with the ideology of fdr and lbj.

George W. Bush simply extended the conservative tradition. With massive tax cuts, he created lower rates for the wealthy than had been seen in more than a half-century. His consistent support of deregulation freed up countless companies and investment capital firms to pursue profits without restriction. He made nationalism a cherished part of his political legacy, including the pursuit of a doctrine that emphasized unilateral initiatives defined as in the best interests of the United States, and downplayed multilateral co-operation that would subject America to constraint by the wishes of its partners and allies.

From 1968 to 2008, the American political and ideological trajectory hewed to a conservative narrative that celebrates individualism over collective action and criticizes government activity on behalf of the common good.

I n recent years, the tension between the two narratives has escalated to an alarming degree. Barack Obama's 2008 election appeared to revitalize a focus on the common good. More people voted, embracing the idea of change, and elected a black American who seemed to embody those values. The fact that Obama became the first president in one hundred years to successfully pass national health care reform–albeit without the provision of a public alternative to private insurance companies–appeared to validate that presumption.

But with the midterm elections of 2010, the rejection of Democratic politics–especially state intervention on behalf of the common good–resulted in the most dramatic electoral turnaround since 1946, when President Harry Truman's Democrats lost eighty-one seats in the House of Representatives. "Tea Party" Republicans not only stood for conservative positions on most social issues, but most dramatically, they insisted that all taxes should be cut, that federal expenditures for Medicare, Social Security, and other social programs must be slashed, and that it is preferable for the government to default on its financial responsibilities than to raise the national debt ceiling.

A backward glance through United States history would reveal no clearer example of the tension between the two competing American narratives, existing side by side, seemingly irreconcilable. The moment is historic, particularly at a time when climate change, stalled immigration reform, and a depressed global economy cry out for action. Thus, the conflict between the good of the whole and the ascendancy of individualist freedom has reached new heights. The choice that voters make in the 2012 presidential election will define our country's political future. Which narrative will we pursue? Are health care and quality education universal rights or privileges reserved for only those with the means to pay? Do we wish to bear "one another's burdens . . . make others' conditions our own . . . mourn together [and] labor and suffer together?" Or do

we wish to make each individual responsible for his or her own fate? These questions are not new. But now, more than ever, they challenge us to find an answer: Who are we? In which direction do we wish to go?

D espite the trend over the past three-and-a-half centuries toward legislation that creates a safety net to protect the larger community, millions of Americans appear committed to dismantling government, slashing federal spending, and walking away from previous commitments to the good of the whole. A number of candidates running for the Republican presidential nomination in 2012 wish to curtail federal responsibility for Social Security for senior citizens. Every Republican candidate seeks to repeal Obama's national health insurance program. Cutting taxes has become a holy mantra. While it is true that in the coming decades demographic change will dramatically increase the number of Latino voters, who historically have favored legislation on behalf of the common good, it is not inconceivable that a reversal of social welfare legislation will happen first.

The tension between these two narratives is as old as the country itself. More often than not, it has been a healthy tension, with one set of values checking and balancing the other. But the polarization of today is unparalleled. The decisions the electorate makes in 2012 are of historic importance in determining which direction the country will take.

Critical Thinking

1. What values best capture the American spirit?
2. What two ideologies are strong in America?
3. Should one ideology dominate over a long period?

WILLIAM H. CHAFE, a Fellow of the American Academy since 2001, is the Alice Mary Baldwin Professor of History at Duke University. His publications include *Private Lives/Public Consequences: Personality and Politics in Modern America* (2005) and *The Rise and Fall of the American Century: The United States from 1890 to 2008* (2008). His current project is titled *Behind the Veil: African American Life During the Age of Segregation.*

From *Daedalus*, Winter 2012, pp. 11–17. Copyright © 2012 by MIT Press Journals/American Academy of Arts and Sciences. Reprinted by permission via Rightslink.

Still Bowling Alone? The Post-9/11 Split

Thomas H. Sander and Robert D. Putnam

Exactly fifteen years ago, the *Journal of Democracy* published in its fifth anniversary issue an article by Robert D. Putnam entitled "Bowling Alone: America's Declining Social Capital."[1] The essay struck a chord with readers who had watched their voting precincts empty out, their favorite bowling alleys or Elks lodges close for lack of patrons and members, and their once-regular card games and dinner parties become sporadic. Marshaling evidence of such trends, the article galvanized widespread concern about the weakening of civic engagement in the United States. But it also roused deep interest in the broader concept of "social capital"—a term that social scientists use as shorthand for social networks and the norms of reciprocity and trust to which those networks give rise. No democracy, and indeed no society, can be healthy without at least a modicum of this resource.

Even though Putnam's article and subsequent book-length study *Bowling Alone: The Collapse and Revival of American Community*[2] focused on the United States, scholars and political leaders around the world were seized by the question of how to foster the growth and improve the quality of social capital.[3] This interest was not altogether surprising, as research in a variety of fields was demonstrating that social capital makes citizens happier and healthier, reduces crime, makes government more responsive and honest, and improves economic productivity.[4]

The trend that "Bowling Alone" spotlighted was alarming: By many measures, since the 1960s or 1970s Americans had been withdrawing from their communities. Attendance at public meetings plunged by nearly half between 1973 and 1994. The family dinner seemed at risk of becoming an endangered species. Trust in strangers took a sharp drop: In the early 1960s, more than half of all Americans said that they trusted others; fewer than a third say the same thing today. In the 1990s, as Americans' social connections withered, they increasingly watched *Friends* rather than had friends. Sociologists who had once been skeptical of Putnam's findings found to their dismay that over the last two decades the incidence of close friendships had declined.[5] As of 2004, a quarter of those polled in the United States reported that they lacked a confidant with whom to discuss important personal matters (the 1983 figure had been less than half that), and nearly half of all respondents reported being only one confidant away from

social isolation. Since social isolation (that is, the lack of any confidants) strongly predicts premature death, these are sobering statistics.

Both *Bowling Alone* and a 2001 Harvard report known as *Better Together*[6] argued that America could be civically restored in two ways: by encouraging adults to socialize more, join more groups, or volunteer more; and by teaching the young, whose habits are more malleable, to be increasingly socially connected.

Americans need only look back two generations to see just how committed to civic life a generation can be. The "Greatest Generation" celebrated by Tom Brokaw's book of that name grew up amid the sense of solidarity generated by the Second World War and before the rise of television and its civically noxious influence. In comparison with their grandchildren, Americans born before 1930 were twice as trusting, 75 percent more likely to vote, and more than twice as likely to take part in community projects.[7] But the Greatest Generation, who viewed helping others as downright American, never managed to pass their civic traits on to their "Baby Boomer" children (born between 1946 and 1964) or their "Generation X" grandchildren (born during the late 1960s and the 1970s). As its older civic stalwarts have died off, America's population has become less engaged year by year.

Nevertheless, surveying the landscape of the late 1990s, *Bowling Alone* spotted one hopeful trend: an increase in youth volunteering that potentially heralded broader generational engagement. Putnam noted that the task of sparking this greater engagement "would be eased by a palpable national crisis, like war or depression or natural disaster, but for better and for worse, America at the dawn of the new century faces no such galvanizing crisis."[8]

Newly Engaged? The Rise of the Post-9/11 Generation

Just a year after those words were written, a massive national crisis struck. The terrorists who carried out the 9/11 attacks were aiming to ruin America's confidence and resolve, but the roughly three-thousand days that have passed since that fateful day seem instead to have strengthened the civic conscience of young people in the United States.

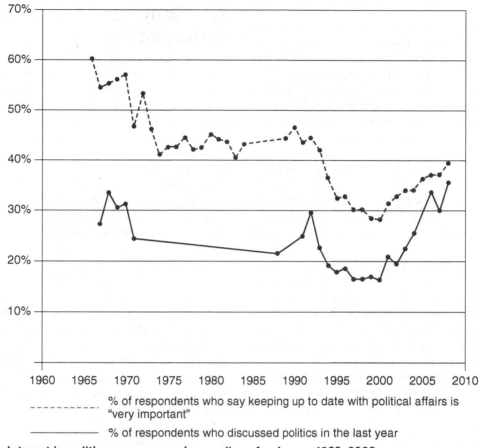

--------- % of respondents who say keeping up to date with political affairs is "very important"

——————— % of respondents who discussed politics in the last year

Interest in politics among american college freshmen, 1966–2008

whether they were in college, high school, or even grade school when the twin towers and the Pentagon were hit, the members of the 9/11 generation[9] were in their most impressionable years and as a result seem to grasp their civic and mutual responsibilities far more firmly than do their parents. While the upswing in volunteering that Putnam observed in the mid-1990s may have been largely an effect of school-graduation requirements or the desire to gain an edge while seeking admission to selective colleges,[10] the years since 9/11 have brought an unmistakable expansion of youth interest in politics and public affairs. For example, young collegians' interest in politics has rapidly increased in the last eight years, an increase all the more remarkable given its arrival on the heels of thirty years of steady decline. From 1967 to 2000, the share of college freshmen who said that they had "discussed politics" in the previous twelve months dropped from 27 to 16 percent; since 2001, it has more than doubled and is now at an all-time high of 36 percent.

First-year college students also evince a long-term decline and then post-2001 rise in interest in "keeping up to date with political affairs."[11] Surveys of high-school seniors show a similar and simultaneous decline and then rise in civic engagement.[12] Moreover, between 2000 and 2008, voting rates rose more than three times faster for Americans under age 29 than they did for Americans over 30.[13] The turning point in 2001 is unmistakable. On college campuses nationwide, this

civic engagement "youth movement" has evoked the spirit of the early John F. Kennedy years.

While the post-9/11 spike in community-mindedness among adults was short-lived, the shift appears more lasting among those who experienced the attacks during their impressionable adolescent years.[14] Why? As we wrote four years after 9/11:

The attacks and their aftermath demonstrated that our fates are highly interdependent. We learned that we need to—and can—depend on the kindness of strangers who happen to be near us in a plane, office building or subway. Moreover, regardless of one's political leanings, it is easy to see that we needed effective governmental action: to coordinate volunteers, police national borders, design emergency response preparedness, engage in diplomacy, and train police and firefighters. Government and politics mattered. If young people used to wonder why they should bother to vote, Sept[ember] 11 . . . gave them an answer.[15]

If this effect persists among young people who lived through 9/11, the inevitable turnover of generations will provide the cause of civic engagement with a powerful following wind. Amid such generational change, even if no present-day *adults* deepen their community engagement, the United States may witness a gradual yet inexorable reversal of the civic decline that *Bowling Alone* chronicled.

The final size of the "Post-9/11 Generation" remains unclear, however, since its lower age boundary is still a mystery. How likely is it that those who were grade-schoolers in 2001 will be counted as members of this generation? One less than encouraging hint may be gleaned from anecdotal evidence suggesting that those born in the early to mid-1990s increasingly say that they cannot remember 9/11.[16] How decisive can that day be for those who never had or no longer possess a vivid firsthand memory of it? Educators are experimenting with programs to freshen the memory of 9/11 among younger Americans, but a solitary lesson plan is likely to have far less impact than the raw immediacy of the suicide attacks and the pervasive discussions and reflection that followed. This suggests that while the 9/11 Generation is real, the attack's effects may be most concentrated among Americans born in the 1980s.

In his 2008 campaign for the U.S. presidency, Barack Obama ably surfed this wave of post-9/11 youthful civic engagement. Though the initial ripple had been visible years before he became a national figure, he and his campaign mightily amplified it. Some credit Internet-based social networking for bolstering youthful interest in politics and community life, but the advent of the well-known social-networking sites Facebook (2004) and Twitter (2006) occurred years after the initial upturn in civic engagement by young people. Nonetheless, the Obama campaign adroitly deployed classic organizing techniques to expand the impact of such new technologies. For example, the campaign created an iPhone application to enable Obama supporters to rank-order the campaign phone calls that they should make to friends, based on whether their friends lived in swing states; it also compiled millions of mobile-phone numbers and e-mail addresses to mobilize citizens for old-style, face-to-face politicking during the campaign and after. Campaign workers exploited cutting-edge technology to find volunteers, decide which wards to visit, and record people's political leanings, but relied on old-school door-knocking as the chief means of actually connecting with voters.

The Obama campaign, with its heavy use of young volunteers and workers, not only counted on an upwelling of youth civic engagement, but contributed to it as well. In the United States, the share of those aged 18 to 29 who avowed complete agreement with the claim that "it's my duty as a citizen to always vote" rose by almost 50 percent between 1999 and 2009. During the same years, the comparable rate among those older than 30 stayed flat. A closer look at trends among the 18-to-29 group, moreover, reveals a spike in agreement during the years surrounding the Obama campaign.[17]

The long-term civic effects of the Obama campaign on the 9/11 Generation remain uncertain. If Obama's campaign promises on issues such as health care, financial reform, and equality of opportunity go unrealized, young voters could become politically dispirited. Or perhaps such failure would only strengthen their political resolve. As Yogi Berra observed, prediction is hard, especially about the future.

Are Only the Young "Haves" Engaged?

The emergence of the 9/11 Generation since 2001 is undoubtedly to be cheered. But it is only part of an ominous larger and longer-term picture whose main feature is a growing civic and social gap in the United States between upper-middle-class young white people and their less affluent counterparts. (A similar gap has not appeared within the ranks of black youth, though an overall black-white gap in engagement remains wide and troubling.)

Over the last thirty years, and with growing intensity over the latter half of that period, white high-school seniors from upper middle-class families have steadily *deepened* the degree to which they are engaged in their communities, while white high-school seniors from working- or lower-class backgrounds have shown a propensity to withdraw from (or never undertake) such engagement.[18] Advantaged kids increasingly flocked to church, while working-class kids deserted the pews. Middle-class kids connected more meaningfully with parents, while working-class kids were increasingly left alone, in large part because single parenting has proliferated among lower- and working-class whites, while becoming rarer among upper-middle-class families. Among "have-not" high-school seniors, trust in other people plummeted, while seniors from the "right side of the tracks" showed no decline at all in social trust. On indicator after indicator—general and academic self-esteem, academic ambition, social friendships, and volunteering—the kids who could be described as the "haves" grew in confidence and engagement while their not-so-well-off contemporaries slipped farther into disengagement with every year.[19] Among other things, this means that the overall rise in youth political engagement and volunteering since 9/11 masks a pair of subtrends that are headed in different directions, with lower-class youth growing less involved while better-off youngsters become more involved. Since public discussion in the United States often tends to conflate class and race, it is important to emphasize that *this* growing gap among different groups of young people is about the former and not just the latter.

If the United States is to avoid becoming two nations, it must find ways to expand the post-9/11 resurgence of civic and social engagement beyond the ranks of affluent young white people.

If the United States is to avoid becoming two nations, it must find ways to expand the post-9/11 resurgence of civic and social engagement beyond the ranks of affluent young white people. The widening gaps that we are seeing in social capital, academic ambition, and self-esteem augur poorly for the life chances of working-class youngsters. If these gaps remain unaddressed, the United States could become less a land of opportunity than a caste society replete with the tightly limited social mobility and simmering resentments that such societies invariably feature.

The basic, if unstated, social contract in America is this: We generally do not worry about how high the socioeconomic ladder extends upward (even to the heights scaled by Bill Gates and Warren Buffett), as long as everyone has a chance to get on the ladder at roughly the same rung. Of course, the image of exact equality of opportunity has never been entirely realistic, but as a statement of our national aspiration, it has been important, and as the discrepancy between aspiration and reality grows, a fundamental promise of American life is endangered. The growing class gap among high-school seniors erodes this promise.

Having noted above that greater engagement on the part of adults is another path toward civic restoration, we may ask how adult Americans are behaving on this score. Are they becoming more civically engaged? While there is no convincing evidence of such an encouraging trend over the last decade, adult Americans are engaging *differently*. Graduates reconnect with lost classmates on Facebook. Stay-at-home moms befriend each other through Meetup. Americans can locate proximate friends through BeaconBuddy. Brief posts on Twitter (known as "tweets") convey people's meal or sock choices, instant movie reactions, rush-hour rants, and occasionally even their profound reflections. Measured against the arc of history, such technological civic invention is in its infancy. In a world where Facebook "friendship" can encompass people who have never actually met, we remain agnostic about whether Internet social entrepreneurs have found the right mix of virtual and real strands to replace traditional social ties. But technological innovators may yet master the elusive social alchemy that will enable online behavior to produce real and enduring civic effects. If such effects do come about, they will benefit young and adult Americans alike—and fortify the civic impact of our new 9/11 Generation.

Notes

1. Robert D. Putnam, "Bowling Alone: America's Declining Social Capital," *Journal of Democracy* 6 (January 1995): 65–78.

2. Robert D. Putnam, *Bowling Alone: The Collapse and Revival of American Community* (New York: Simon and Schuster, 2000).

3. The year 1994 saw the publication of a dozen scholarly articles on social capital. For 2008, that figure was nearly fifty times greater, with a comparable rise in press mentions of the concept.

4. See Putnam, *Bowling Alone,* section 4. While much of the work on social capital is correlational, some work done since 2000 consists of panel data suggesting that social capital *causes* these beneficial outcomes.

5. Miller McPherson, Lynn Smith-Lovin, and Matthew E. Brashears, "Social Isolation in America: Changes in Core Discussion Networks over Two Decades," *American Sociological Review* 71 (June 2006): 353–75. For a subsequent methodological debate about this study, see

Claude Fischer, "The 2004 GSS Finding of Shrunken Social Networks: An Artifact?" *American Sociological Review* 74 (August 2009): 657–69, plus the original authors' rejoinder, "Models and Marginals: Using Survey Evidence to Study Social Networks," *American Sociological Review* 74 (August 2009): 670–81.

6. Available at *www.bettertogether.org/thereport.htm.*

7. Putnam, *Bowling Alone,* 253.

8. Putnam, *Bowling Alone,* 402.

9. It is worth noting that at any *single* instant, one cannot differentiate *life-cycle patterns* (how frequently people do something at one age or another) from *generational patterns* (the variation in how frequently people born in different periods do something). In our discussion of age differences, we rely on evidence gathered over many years and emphasize differences between one generation and another rather than lifecycle-related differences.

10. Such motivations may matter little, however: Those who are introduced to volunteerism while they are young typically volunteer more often throughout their lives.

11. From 2000 to 2008, the share of first-year U.S. college students who responded to a survey taken by the United States Higher Education Research Institute by saying that they considered keeping up with political affairs to be "essential" or "very important" rose from 28.1 to 39.5 percent. That was still below the all-time high, which came in 1966, when 60 percent of college first years said that they considered keeping up with politics to be "essential" or "very important." See www.gseis.ucla.edu/heri/pr-display.php?prQry=28.

12. The data are from "Monitoring the Future," an annual survey of more than fifty-thousand U.S. high-school seniors that has been taken under the auspices of the United States National Institutes of Health since 1976. The survey's main focus is drug use, but there are also many questions on social attitudes, social capital, self-esteem, ambition, materialism, and so on. For more information, see www.monitoringthefuture.org. This class gap was discovered by Rebekah Crooks Horowitz in her 2005 Harvard College senior thesis, "Minding the Gap: An Examination of the Growing Class Gap in Youth Volunteering and Political Participation."

13. According to U.S. Current Population Survey data compiled by the U.S. Census Bureau and Labor Department, 60 percent of U.S. registered voters aged 30 or older actually cast ballots in 1996 and 2000, while only 36 percent of those aged 18 to 29 did so. In 2008, turnout among the over-30s rose modestly to 68 percent even as it shot up to 51 percent for those aged 18 to 29. Since 2000, campaign volunteering has risen at an average rate of about 5.5 percent per presidential election among Americans over 30, and by almost 20 percent among those from 18 to 29 years old.

14. During the first six weeks after 9/11, Americans in general reported rising trust in government, rising trust in the police, greater interest in politics, more frequent attendance at political meetings, and more work on community projects. Among adults surveyed, all these increases had vanished by March 2002. See Robert D. Putnam, "Bowling Together," *American Prospect,* 11 February 2002.

15. Thomas H. Sander and Robert D. Putnam, "Sept. 11 as Civics Lesson," *Washington Post,* 10 September 2005.

16. Sarah Schweitzer, "When Students Don't Know 9/11," *Boston Globe,* 11 September 2009.

17. See the report by the Pew Research Center for the People and the Press, "Trends in Political Values and Core Attitudes: 1987–2009: Independents Take Center Stage in Obama Era,"

21 May 2009, 75. Available at people-press.org/reports/pdf/517 .pdf. Statistics also from crosstabs conducted by Leah Christian at the Pew Research Center for the People and the Press, 25 September 2009.

18. Social class in this analysis is measured by parental educational levels, so by "upper middle class" we mean kids with at least parent who has a postgraduate education, whereas by "working [or lower] class" we mean kids whose parents have not gone beyond high school, if that.

19. These results come from our unpublished analyses of "Monitoring the Future" data.

Critical Thinking

1. What is the importance of social capital?

2. What are the trends in social capital and why?

3. What can increase social capital?

THOMAS H. SANDER is executive director of the Saguaro Seminar: Civic Engagement in America at the John F. Kennedy School of Government, Harvard University. **ROBERT D. PUTNAM** is Peter and Isabel Malkin Professor of Public Policy at Harvard University.

From *Journal of Democracy*, January 2010, pp. 9–16. Copyright © 2010 by National Endowment for Democracy and The Johns Hopkins University Press. Reprinted with permission of The Johns Hopkins University Press.

Relationships, Community, and Identity in the New Virtual Society

As we spend more of our social lives online, the definitions of relationships and families are shifting. A business futurist offers an overview of these trends and what they imply for organizations in the coming years.

ARNOLD BROWN

In India, where for centuries marriages have been arranged by families, online dating services such as BharatMatrimony.com are profoundly changing embedded traditions.

MyGamma, a Singapore-based mobile phone social networking site, has millions of users throughout Asia and Africa, giving social networking capability to people across continents—no personal computer necessary.

In China, individuals have been participating in *wang hun* (online role-play marriages). These gaming sites are causing actual married couples to get divorced on the grounds that this constitutes adultery—even though no face-to-face meetings ever took place.

And Web sites such as GeneTree.com and Ancestry.com, which offer inexpensive cheek-swab DNA tests, link up people throughout the world who have similar DNA, thus combining genealogy, medical technology, and social networking.

Clearly the Internet has radically reshaped our social lives over the span of just a couple of decades, luring us into a virtual metaworld where traditional interactions—living, loving, belonging, and separating, as well as finding customers and keeping them—require new protocols.

Relationships Take on a Digital Dimension

The future of falling in love may be online. Dating sites, once considered a gimmicky way to meet and connect with new people, have grown immensely in popularity, thanks in part to the convergence of information technologies and digital entertainment. Facilitating and managing relationships online is projected to become close to a billion-dollar industry in the United States in 2011.

In the new Virtual Society, we will see an increasing transition from basic matchmaking sites to sites that enable people to actually go out on online "dates" without ever leaving their desks. While face-to-face dating will never entirely disappear, the process—and even relationships themselves—will happen more and more in virtual space.

Especially for young people, relationships made in virtual space can be just as powerful and meaningful as those formed in the real world. Additionally, as more people gain access to broadband technologies, an increasing number are seeking social connectivity this way. There are already at least 500 million mobile broadband users globally. The speed and flexibility with which people communicate and socialize online will likely only continue to increase.

Technology doesn't just bring people together, though. As Douglas Rushkoff points out in *Program or Be Programmed* (OR Books, 2010), cyberspace creates a temporal and spatial separation from which it becomes seemingly easier to accomplish unpleasant interpersonal tasks. Hence, the *techno brush-off*: breaking up with a significant other via e-mail or text message.

This will increasingly be a dominant fixture of the global youth culture. Young people everywhere link up through IM, Twitter, blogs, smart-phones, and social networking sites that are proliferating at an accelerating rate. This is a critical point for businesses to understand. The emerging generation is part of what is, in essence, a vast new cross-border empire. It is marked by an instant awareness of what's new, what's hot, what's desirable—and what's not. This is the group that pollster John Zogby, in his book *The Way We'll Be* (Random House, 2008), calls the First Globals. His research shows that their expectations of products and services will be vastly different and that they will force businesses to redefine their offerings.

Young people will not, as their elders did, simply adapt to the technology. The new youth cyberculture will continue to find ways to adapt the technology to their needs and desires. For example, Ning, created in 2005 by Netscape co-founder Marc Andreessen, enables people to create their own individual social network—not join a preexisting world but actually build their own. A website called paper.li creates a personalized newspaper for you everyday based on whom you follow on Twitter and whether or not they said anything particularly important in the last 24 hours (as measured by retweets). Your friend's brilliant blog post about last night's St. Patrick's Day party could appear directly next to Tim O'Reilly or Bruce Sterling's most recent missive on China's Internet policy. It's hard to imagine a local newspaper providing that sort of personalized content.

But online relationships are not exclusively reserved for young people. As the elderly become more comfortable with the Internet, they will increasingly turn to alternative spaces, such as virtual worlds, to find company or meet people with similar interests. By 2008, more than 20 million social networkers in the United States were over the age of 50, according to a study by Deloitte. There have been a slew of media reports playing up the fact that many seniors are joining Facebook and Twitter, as well as becoming an increasingly significant part of the growing commercial activity in virtual worlds.

Commercializing Communities

More and more people regard the virtual world as a place where they can establish and maintain safer, less demanding relationships on their own time. Ease, flexibility, and relative anonymity will continue to be three key components of dating online. Monetization will happen quickly, as virtual restaurants, movie theaters, concerts, and even wedding chapels are established.

In addition to using virtual worlds as test markets for real-life products and services, as is done now, businesses will offer a much wider variety of virtual products and services. Having these options would give a substantive feel to online relationships. The more real and satisfying these relationships can be made to seem, the more they will attract and hold people, and the more money they will generate.

Commercialized virtual venues such as upscale bars and coffeehouses could even be looked to as testing grounds to develop the social skills necessary to form meaningful human relationships. Businesses could use game applications like Mall World or Café World on Facebook as platforms to advertise various specials that occur in virtual space, ranging from coupons for those aforementioned simulations of bars and coffeehouses to discounts for two to "live" streaming concert events. Advertising boards could promote online activities and events such as speed dating in a virtual nightclub setting. All this will dramatically change the nature of relationships.

As social researchers have pointed out, the Internet is programming us as well, starting at an early age. For example, there are combination social networking and gaming sites for children such as Disney's Club Penguin. Children are developing social skills within these virtual worlds. What this will mean in terms of how they will start, maintain, and end "real" friendships and relationships in the future is anyone's guess.

But the Internet can also strengthen family ties because it provides a continuously connected presence. In Norway, for example, one study showed that college students were in touch with their parents on average 10 times a week. Young people use mobile devices to Skype, text, upload photos and videos to Facebook, and more, with increasing frequency. Cyberspace enables families and friends to converse, in effect, as if they were in the same room. This is part of the reason that the Millennial generation reported feeling closer to their parents than did their older siblings during adolescence, according to the Pew Internet and American Life Survey.

So what does all this tell us? For one thing, the temporal and spatial "here-and-now" limitations that formerly characterized social interactions such as dating and family get-togethers have broken down. The composition of, and behavior in, relationships and households in the future will therefore change seriously. These trends are powerfully affecting how companies and organizations will design, sell, and market a wide range of products and services to consumers, with a growing emphasis on individualization and personalization. For instance, if relationships and families are more virtual, we should see an increase in the construction of new kinds of single-person housing units or dual sleeping quarters.

Family formation will need to be flexible and adaptive. The nuclear family was a response to the Industrial Age, in large measure replacing the extended family that characterized the Agricultural Era. It spurred vast economic shifts and led to new multibillion-dollar industries, from autos to washing machines to personal telephones. We are already seeing indications that the family is morphing into other forms as the Virtual Age approaches. Employers and governments will see their social, human resources, financial services, and benefits programs challenged, as the new economy takes great advantage of these multiple, newly unfolding personal relationships. For instance, should a "virtual spouse" be able to claim the Social Security benefits of a partner? The easy answer is, of course not. But what if it's the virtual spouse who is charged with monitoring the health of an aged parent remotely? What if he or she does the household bill-paying, or even contributes half of the household income? In other words, what if the virtual spouse performs many if not all of the tasks associated with a traditional spouse? And should the same polygamy laws applied to regular marriages also apply to virtual marriages? Should such marriages be subject to the same taxation laws?

With the advent of an electronic era, many social scientists and other "experts" decried what they saw as a loss of social capital—the so-called "Bowling Alone" theory—because people were supposedly decreasing their participation in such things as bowling leagues. The big mistake that the fearful always make is to equate change with destruction. The social turmoil of the 1970s was heralded by such observers as "the destruction of the family." But the family did not die; it just changed—and it is still changing.

Similarly, social capital is not going away; it is too intrinsic to human nature, although aspects of it may well be changing, and it is important that you view these changes objectively if you want to understand what they are and what they mean to you.

Social ties are being created, strengthened, and—yes—weakened in an almost unbelievable variety of ways. This has to entail, as well, the remaking and establishing of both a

The Reality of Virtual Feelings

Advances in brain research and multisensory perception could play an important role in the development of virtual relationships. Neural devices already allow people to control electronic equipment such as wheelchairs, televisions, and video games via brain–computer interfaces. One day soon, avatars may also be controllable this way.

Virtual reality may become so advanced that it could trick the brain into thinking the invented images it is responding to are real—and human emotions would follow accordingly. Avatars will cause people to feel love, hate, jealousy, etc. And as haptic technologies improve, our abilities to respond physically to our virtual partners will also improve: Sexual pleasure may be routinely available without any inter-human stimulation at all.

If it becomes possible to connect virtual reality programs directly to the brain, thoughts and emotions may also be digitized, rendered binary and reduced to 0s and 1s. Feelings of satisfaction and pleasure (two key components in any relationship) could be created between avatars without any "real" stimulus at all. But would they be real or mimetic?

Once humans begin to perceive virtual social interactions as actually having occurred, it will greatly impact individuals, relationships, communities, and society as a whole.

—Arnold Brown

deeper and a shallower social capital. Someone with more than 3,000 Facebook friends probably has more than 2,000 shallow friendships, but there's a tremendous amount of variety in that number; some of these friendships are viable clients, others may be service providers, others may be long-term friend prospects, or secret crushes, or members of a social circle to which the person with 3,000 friendships wants access; some of them will be annoying people encountered only once at a party, begrudgingly given the status of "friend" to avoid seeming rude. All of these friendships have their own unique value. But Facebook sees little difference among them outside of how they are designated in privacy settings (some people can see more private posts than others). Outside institutions don't recognize any distinction among these virtual friendships, if they recognize such friendships at all.

Sociologist Richard Ling has labeled the new communication phenomenon *micro-coordination*—as people are constantly planning, coordinating, and changing plans because their cyberconnections are always on. University of Southern California sociologist Manuel Castells says that adolescents today build and rebuild social networks via constant messaging. This is helped by the fact that they have what he calls "a safe autonomous pattern," in that their parents are only a speed dial away.

Sociologists describe two kinds of social ties: strong ties of family members and those with shared values, beliefs, and identities; and weak ties to acquaintances and other people with shallower connections. According to some researchers, the Internet and, in particular, mobile devices are enabling the strong community ties to be reinforced, often at the expense of the weak ties. At a time when technology is being lauded for encouraging diversity and facilitating cross-cultural communication, there is, consequently, a strong and growing countertrend: digital tribalism. Aside from strengthening ties to family and close friends, people are using the technology to find others with whom they share important affinities, ranging from genomes to beliefs to lifestyle choices. This digital form of tribalism is an unexpectedly strong trend, as observed by social critics such as Christine Rosen.

Information—including product and service information—spreads electronically with speed and power. Effectively getting a positive message on a tribal network could well be tomorrow's best marketing strategy. Although the tribal identity can be deep and solid, brand connections may not necessarily be so. Maintaining the connection will require constant monitoring of the electronic tribal village and quickness to reposition or reinforce when required.

Bridal showers, for instance, can be attended by distant guests through Skype, and e-registries allow gift givers to view what others have bought. There is much room for innovation here, in terms of bringing people together who would not otherwise be in the same place for business meetings, financial planning, meal sharing, celebrations, and more. Associations might capitalize on online events for far-flung and numerous businesses, professionals, and friends and families of members. Employers might do the same for their employees' personal networks, perhaps offering discounts, education, job postings, and new products to all "friends of friends."

Expat workers and members of the armed forces might be more easily enabled to stay in touch with their families if their employers organized better around online communications and communities. This would ease the burden on relocated personnel, improve morale, attract more people, increase productivity, and spin the sale of products and service to these populations. This could also be true for alumni networks and other diaspora groups.

The Identity Industry

Social scientists make the distinction between a found identity and a made identity. The found identity is one created by your circumstances—who your parents were, your ethnic background, your religion, your sex, where you went to school, your profession, and all the other external factors that people use to categorize and describe you. The made identity, on the other hand, is the one you create for yourself. It is how you wish to see yourself and how you want others to see you.

In the past, people who wanted to escape what they saw as the trap of their found identity did such things as change their name or appearance. They moved somewhere else. Now, and increasingly in the future, technology will let you make and remake your identity at will—virtually. This extraordinary, even revolutionary, development will profoundly affect fundamental societal values such as trust and reliability.

In addition to engaging directly online with other individuals, you can also interact with them through avatars, the images that represent you (or an idealized version of yourself) in virtual worlds. Each virtual world requires a separate avatar, so in effect you can be as many different people as there are virtual worlds. In the future, you will be able to create avatars that will literally take on lives of their own. They will, once created, be able to "think" on their own, without further input from you. They may be able to perform intensive research tasks for you, start and even manage online companies, maintain your social relationships by reading your Facebook updates and blog posts and analyzing them for significant news so you don't have to.

Increasingly, over time, distinctions between real and virtual identity will become less sharply defined, particularly for people who spend substantial amounts of time in the virtual world—or some enhanced combination of the real and the virtual. A company called Total Immersion combines 3-D and augmented reality technology on the Internet, inserting people and physical objects into live video feeds. According to the company's website, "this digital processing mixes real and virtual worlds together, in real time."

All this could lead to growing confusion about identity. We will go from "Who am I?" to "Who, when, and where am I?" What in the twentieth century was seen as a problem that needed treatment—multiple personalities—will increasingly be seen in the twenty-first century as a coping mechanism, greatly affecting the evolving economy, as multiple personas split their expenditures in multiple ways.

> ## "All this could lead to growing confusion about identity. We will go from 'Who am I?' to 'Who, when, and where am I?'"

Companies that provide such services will be a great growth industry as we move further into the "Who are you, really?" era.

Critical Thinking

1. Is community declining in America?
2. What impacts do the new communication technologies have on relationships and community?

ARNOLD BROWN is the chairman of Weiner, Edrich, Brown, Inc., and the coauthor (with Edie Weiner) of *FutureThink: How to Think Clearly in a Time of Change* (Pearson Prentice Hall, 2006).

What Isn't for Sale?

Market thinking so permeates our lives that we barely notice it anymore. A leading philosopher sums up the hidden costs of a price-tag society.

MICHAEL J. SANDEL

There are some things money can't buy—but these days, not many. Almost everything is up for sale. For example:

- *A prison-cell upgrade: $90 a night.* In Santa Ana, California, and some other cities, nonviolent offenders can pay for a clean, quiet jail cell, without any non-paying prisoners to disturb them.
- *Access to the carpool lane while driving solo: $8.* Minneapolis, San Diego, Houston, Seattle, and other cities have sought to ease traffic congestion by letting solo drivers pay to drive in carpool lanes, at rates that vary according to traffic.
- *The services of an Indian surrogate mother: $8,000.* Western couples seeking surrogates increasingly outsource the job to India, and the price is less than one-third the going rate in the United States.
- *The right to shoot an endangered black rhino: $250,000.* South Africa has begun letting some ranchers sell hunters the right to kill a limited number of rhinos, to give the ranchers an incentive to raise and protect the endangered species.
- *Your doctor's cellphone number: $1,500 and up per year.* A growing number of "concierge" doctors offer cellphone access and same-day appointments for patients willing to pay annual fees ranging from $1,500 to $25,000.
- *The right to emit a metric ton of carbon dioxide into the atmosphere: $10.50.* The European Union runs a carbon-dioxide-emissions market that enables companies to buy and sell the right to pollute.
- *The right to immigrate to the United States: $500,000.* Foreigners who invest $500,000 and create at least 10 full-time jobs in an area of high unemployment are eligible for a green card that entitles them to permanent residency.

Not everyone can afford to buy these things. But today there are lots of new ways to make money. If you need to earn some extra cash, here are some novel possibilities:

- *Sell space on your forehead to display commercial advertising: $10,000.* A single mother in Utah who needed money for her son's education was paid $10,000 by an online casino to install a permanent tattoo of the casino's Web address on her forehead. Temporary tattoo ads earn less.
- *Serve as a human guinea pig in a drug-safety trial for a pharmaceutical company: $7,500.* The pay can be higher or lower, depending on the invasiveness of the procedure used to test the drug's effect and the discomfort involved.
- *Fight in Somalia or Afghanistan for a private military contractor: up to $1,000 a day.* The pay varies according to qualifications, experience, and nationality.
- *Stand in line overnight on Capitol Hill to hold a place for a lobbyist who wants to attend a congressional hearing: $15–$20 an hour.* Lobbyists pay line-standing companies, who hire homeless people and others to queue up.
- *If you are a second-grader in an underachieving Dallas school, read a book: $2.* To encourage reading, schools pay kids for each book they read.

We live in a time when almost everything can be bought and sold. Over the past three decades, markets—and market values—have come to govern our lives as never before. We did not arrive at this condition through any deliberate choice. It is almost as if it came upon us.

As the Cold War ended, markets and market thinking enjoyed unrivaled prestige, and understandably so. No other mechanism for organizing the production and distribution of goods had proved as successful at generating affluence and prosperity. And yet even as growing numbers of countries around the world embraced market mechanisms in the operation of their economies, something else was happening. Market values were coming to play a greater and greater role in social life. Economics was becoming an imperial domain. Today, the logic of buying and selling no longer applies to material goods alone. It increasingly governs the whole of life.

The years leading up to the financial crisis of 2008 were a heady time of market faith and deregulation—an era of market triumphalism. The era began in the early 1980s, when Ronald Reagan and Margaret Thatcher proclaimed their conviction that markets, not government, held the key to prosperity and freedom. And it continued into the 1990s with the market-friendly liberalism of Bill Clinton and Tony Blair, who moderated but consolidated the faith that markets are the primary means for achieving the public good.

Today, that faith is in question. The financial crisis did more than cast doubt on the ability of markets to allocate risk efficiently. It also prompted a widespread sense that markets have become detached from morals, and that we need to somehow reconnect the two. But it's not obvious what this would mean, or how we should go about it.

Some say the moral failing at the heart of market triumphalism was greed, which led to irresponsible risk-taking. The solution, according to this view, is to rein in greed, insist on greater integrity and responsibility among bankers and Wall Street executives, and enact sensible regulations to prevent a similar crisis from happening again.

This is, at best, a partial diagnosis. While it is certainly true that greed played a role in the financial crisis, something bigger was and is at stake. The most fateful change that unfolded during the past three decades was not an increase in greed. It was the reach of markets, and of market values, into spheres of life traditionally governed by nonmarket norms. To contend with this condition, we need to do more than inveigh against greed; we need to have a public debate about where markets belong—and where they don't.

Consider, for example, the proliferation of for-profit schools, hospitals, and prisons, and the outsourcing of war to private military contractors. (In Iraq and Afghanistan, private contractors have actually outnumbered United States military troops.) Consider the eclipse of public police forces by private security firms—especially in the United States and the U.K., where the number of private guards is almost twice the number of public police officers.

Or consider the pharmaceutical companies' aggressive marketing of prescription drugs directly to consumers, a practice now prevalent in the United States but prohibited in most other countries. (If you've ever seen the television commercials on the evening news, you could be forgiven for thinking that the greatest health crisis in the world is not malaria or river blindness or sleeping sickness but an epidemic of erectile dysfunction.)

Consider too the reach of commercial advertising into public schools, from buses to corridors to cafeterias; the sale of "naming rights" to parks and civic spaces; the blurred boundaries, within journalism, between news and advertising, likely to blur further as newspapers and magazines struggle to survive; the marketing of "designer" eggs and sperm for assisted reproduction; the buying and selling, by companies and countries, of the right to pollute; a system of campaign finance in the U.S. that comes close to permitting the buying and selling of elections.

These uses of markets to allocate health, education, public safety, national security, criminal justice, environmental protection, recreation, procreation, and other social goods were for the most part unheard-of 30 years ago. Today, we take them largely for granted.

Why worry that we are moving toward a society in which everything is up for sale?

For two reasons. One is about inequality, the other about corruption. First, consider inequality. In a society where everything is for sale, life is harder for those of modest means. The more money can buy, the more affluence—or the lack of it—matters. If the only advantage of affluence were the ability to afford yachts, sports cars, and fancy vacations, inequalities of income and wealth would matter less than they do today. But as money comes to buy more and more, the distribution of income and wealth looms larger.

The second reason we should hesitate to put everything up for sale is more difficult to describe. It is not about inequality and fairness but about the corrosive tendency of markets. Putting a price on the good things in life can corrupt them. That's because markets don't only allocate goods; they express and promote certain attitudes toward the goods being exchanged. Paying kids to read books might get them to read more, but might also teach them to regard reading as a chore rather than a source of intrinsic satisfaction. Hiring foreign mercenaries to fight our wars might spare the lives of our citizens, but might also corrupt the meaning of citizenship.

Economists often assume that markets are inert, that they do not affect the goods being exchanged. But this is untrue. Markets leave their mark. Sometimes, market values crowd out nonmarket values worth caring about.

When we decide that certain goods may be bought and sold, we decide, at least implicitly, that it is appropriate to treat them as commodities, as instruments of profit and use. But not all goods are properly valued in this way. The most obvious example is human beings. Slavery was appalling because it treated human beings as a commodity, to be bought and sold at auction. Such treatment fails to value human beings as persons, worthy of dignity and respect; it sees them as instruments of gain and objects of use.

Something similar can be said of other cherished goods and practices. We don't allow children to be bought and sold, no matter how difficult the process of adoption can be or how willing impatient prospective parents might be. Even if the prospective buyers would treat the child responsibly, we worry that a market in children would express and promote the wrong way of valuing them. Children are properly regarded not as consumer goods but as beings worthy of love and care. Or consider the rights and obligations of citizenship. If you are called to jury duty, you can't hire a substitute to take your place. Nor do we allow citizens to sell their votes, even though others might be eager to buy them. Why not? Because we believe that civic duties are not private property but public responsibilities. To outsource them is to demean them, to value them in the wrong way.

These examples illustrate a broader point: some of the good things in life are degraded if turned into commodities. So to decide where the market belongs, and where it should be kept at a distance, we have to decide how to value the goods in question—health, education, family life, nature, art, civic duties, and so on. These are moral and political questions, not merely economic ones. To resolve them, we have to debate, case by case, the moral meaning of these goods, and the proper way of valuing them.

This is a debate we didn't have during the era of market triumphalism. As a result, without quite realizing it—without ever deciding to do so—we drifted from having a market economy to being a market society.

The difference is this: A market economy is a tool—a valuable and effective tool—for organizing productive activity. A market society is a way of life in which market values seep into every aspect of human endeavor. It's a place where social relations are made over in the image of the market.

> **A market society is a way of life in which market values seep into every aspect of human endeavor. It's a place where social relations are made over in the image of the market.**

The great missing debate in contemporary politics is about the role and reach of markets. Do we want a market economy, or a market society? What role should markets play in public life and personal relations? How can we decide which goods should be bought and sold, and which should be governed by nonmarket values? Where should money's writ not run?

Even if you agree that we need to grapple with big questions about the morality of markets, you might doubt that our public discourse is up to the task. It's a legitimate worry. At a time when political argument consists mainly of shouting matches on cable television, partisan vitriol on talk radio, and ideological food fights on the floor of Congress, it's hard to imagine a reasoned public debate about such controversial moral questions as the right way to value procreation, children, education, health, the environment, citizenship, and other goods. I believe such a debate is possible, but only if we are willing to broaden the terms of our public discourse and grapple more explicitly with competing notions of the good life.

In hopes of avoiding sectarian strife, we often insist that citizens leave their moral and spiritual convictions behind when they enter the public square. But the reluctance to admit arguments about the good life into politics has had an unanticipated consequence. It has helped prepare the way for market triumphalism, and for the continuing hold of market reasoning.

In its own way, market reasoning also empties public life of moral argument. Part of the appeal of markets is that they don't pass judgment on the preferences they satisfy. They don't ask whether some ways of valuing goods are higher, or worthier, than others. If someone is willing to pay for sex, or a kidney, and a consenting adult is willing to sell, the only question the economist asks is "How much?" Markets don't wag fingers. They don't discriminate between worthy preferences and unworthy ones. Each party to a deal decides for him- or herself what value to place on the things being exchanged.

This nonjudgmental stance toward values lies at the heart of market reasoning, and explains much of its appeal. But our reluctance to engage in moral and spiritual argument, together with our embrace of markets, has exacted a heavy price: it has drained public discourse of moral and civic energy, and contributed to the technocratic, managerial politics afflicting many societies today.

A debate about the moral limits of markets would enable us to decide, as a society, where markets serve the public good and where they do not belong. Thinking through the appropriate place of markets requires that we reason together, in public, about the right way to value the social goods we prize. It would be folly to expect that a more morally robust public discourse, even at its best, would lead to agreement on every contested question. But it would make for a healthier public life. And it would make us more aware of the price we pay for living in a society where everything is up for sale.

Critical Thinking

1. What does Sandel mean by the commodification of modern life?
2. What are the shortcomings of market values?
3. What does society loose when market values dominate all other values?

MICHAEL J. SANDEL, a political philosopher at Harvard, is the author of *What Money Can't Buy: The Moral Limits of Markets,* from which this article is adapted.

UNIT 2
Problems of the Political Economy

Unit Selections

Learning Outcomes

- Present your view of how the political decision-making process could be made more fair and democratic. Indicate how the influence of money on politics can be reduced.

- Describe the best way to handle welfare. What problems does welfare cause?

- Explain what has recently happened to the American economy and specifically to jobs.

- Describe the strengths and weaknesses of American capitalism. Describe some of the major problems that now face American businesses and workers and how can they be solved.

- Discuss the prospects of cities, suburbs, and rural areas given current and future demographics.

- Present the pros and cons of immigration today. What should our immigration policy be?

Student Website

www.mhhe.com/cls

Internet References

National Center for Policy Analysis
www.ncpa.org
Penn Library: Sociology
www.library.upenn.edu

Since the political system and the economy interpenetrate each other to a high degree, it is now common to study them together under the label political economy. The political economy is the most basic aspect of society, and it should be studied first. The way it functions affects how problems in other areas can or cannot be addressed. Here we encounter issues of power, control, and influence. It is in this arena that society acts corporately to address the problems that are of public concern. It is important, therefore, to ascertain the degree to which the economic elite control the political system. The answer determines how democratic America is. Next, we want to know how effective the American political economy is. Can government agencies be effective? Can government regulations be effective? Can the economy be effective? Can the economy make everyone, and not just the owners and top administrators, prosper and be happy?

The first subsection of Unit 2 includes three articles on the political system. In the first article Bill Moyers presents his power elite theory. Owners and top administrators in large corporations have overwhelming influence over the government on matters that concern them and this influence results in losses for most Americans. Moyers tells stories about how much their for-profit actions can hurt workers and others. The next article by Andy Kroll exposes many methods that powerful groups use to get special benefits including PACs, direct campaign financing, giving money to government officials (corruption), participating in the drafting of legislation, adroitly finding ways around the laws, disobeying laws and getting away with it, etc. The next article by Diana Spatz examines the present state of welfare. The 1996 welfare law ended welfare as we knew it and has been celebrated because it pushed many people off of welfare and into jobs. However, there is another side of this story, and Spatz presents it with bitterness. She received welfare, which helped her complete college and become a professional worker. Now that path has been largely cut off in most states. Her main complaint is that many of those who were dropped should not have been. She points out that "States were given bonuses for reducing their caseloads rather than reducing poverty."

The second subsection deals with major problems and issues of the economy. The first article by Robert J. Samuelson deals with the poor economic prospects for young people. They will not live better than their parents. The overall economy will recover and grow slowly due to new technologies but necessary transfers to older needy citizens will hold back young people and the economy. Samuelson analyzes many aspects of the economy and demography to support his pessimistic prediction for the young. The next article by James H. Lee is also pessimistic about America's economic future because he predicts a shortage of jobs for many years into the future due to automation. First automation replaced many blue-collar jobs, but it is increasingly replacing white-collar and professional jobs. Furthermore, job trends are disappointing both in numbers and in quality. Job characteristics are changing and antiquating many job skills. For example, future workers will have to be able to operate in a Results Only Work Environment. The many

© Lars A. Niki

other changes in the future job picture that Lee discusses may be interesting to analysts but worrisome to workers.

The last subsection of Unit 2 looks at cities and communities. The first article by Joel Kotkin presents the dominant view that cities are the wave of the future. In 1990 14 percent of the world lived in cities. That shot up to 50 percent in 2008 and could become 70 percent in 2050. Kotkin cites Saskia Sassan who argues that megacities will dominate the global economy. Kotkin, however, thinks otherwise. He argues that large centralized cities are not well suited to the technological age. He envisions a trend toward more dispersed vibrant smaller cities, suburbs and towns that operate on a more human scale. In the second article Steven J. Gold argues that immigration benefits America even though many immigrants today come from quite different cultures. Economists calculate that the economic benefits of immigrants exceed the costs and sociologists show that immigrants do not weaken our culture but strengthen it.

The Rule of the Rich

Bill Moyers

Howard Zinn helped us see how big change can start with small acts. He championed grassroots social change and famously chronicled its story as played out over the course of our nation's history. More, those stirring sagas have inspired and continue to inspire countless people to go out and make a difference. The last time we met, I told him that the stories in *A People's History of the United States* remind me of the fellow who turned the corner just as a big fight broke out down the block. Rushing up to an onlooker he shouted, "Is this a private fight, or can anyone get in it?" For Howard, democracy was one big public fight and everyone should plunge into it. That's the only way, he said, for everyday folks to get justice—by fighting for it.

So let's begin with some everyday folks.

When she heard the news, Connie Brasel cried like a baby. For years she had worked at minimum-wage jobs, until seventeen years ago, when she was hired by the Whirlpool refrigerator factory in Evansville, Indiana. She was making $18.44 an hour when Whirlpool announced in early 2010 that it was closing the operation and moving it to Mexico. She wept. I'm sure many of the other eleven hundred workers who lost their jobs wept, too; they had seen their ticket to the middle class snatched from their hands. The company defended its decision by claiming high costs, underused capacity, and the need to stay competitive. Those excuses didn't console Connie Brasel. "I was becoming part of something bigger than me," she told Steven Greenhouse of *The New York Times*. "Whirlpool was the best thing that ever happened to me."

She was not only sad, she was mad. "They didn't get world-class quality because they had the best managers. They got world-class quality because of the United States and because of their workers."

Among those workers were Natalie Ford, her husband, and her son; all three lost their jobs. "It's devastating," she told the *Times*. Her father had worked at Whirlpool before them. Now "there aren't any jobs here. How is this community going to survive?"

And what about the country? Between 2001 and 2008, about 40,000 U.S. manufacturing plants closed. Six million factory jobs have disappeared over the past dozen years, representing one in three manufacturing jobs. Natalie Ford said to the *Times* what many of us are wondering: "I don't know how without any good-paying jobs here in the United States people are going to pay for their health care, put their children through school."

In polite circles, among our political and financial classes, this is known as "the free market at work." No, it's "wage repression," and it's been happening in our country since around 1980. Economists Thomas Piketty and Emmanuel Saez have found that from 1950 through 1980, the share of all income in America going to everyone but the rich increased from 64 percent to 65 percent. Because the nation's economy was growing handsomely, the average income for nine out of ten Americans was growing, too: from $17,719 to $30,941. That's a 75 percent increase in income in constant 2008 dollars. But then it stopped. Since 1980 the economy has also continued to grow handsomely, but only a fraction at the top have benefitted. The line flattens for the bottom 90 percent of Americans. Average income went from that $30,941 in 1980 to $31,244 in 2008. Think about that: the average income of Americans increased just $303 in twenty-eight years.

Another story in the *Times* caught my eye a few weeks after the one about Connie Brasel and Natalie Ford. The headline read: "Industries Find Surging Profits in Deeper Cuts." Nelson Schwartz reported that despite falling motorcycle sales, Harley-Davidson profits are soaring—with a second quarter profit of $71 million, more than triple what it earned the previous year. Yet Harley-Davidson has announced plans to cut 1,400 to 1,600 more jobs by the end of 2011—this on top of the 2,000 jobs cut in 2009.

The story noted: "This seeming contradiction—falling sales and rising profits—is one reason the mood on Wall Street is so much more buoyant than in households, where pessimism runs deep and unemployment shows few signs of easing."

There you see the two Americas: a buoyant Wall Street; a doleful Main Street. The Connie Brasels and Natalie Fords—left to sink or swim on their own. There were no bailouts for them.

Or, as the chief economist at Bank of America Merrill Lynch, Ethan Harris, told the *Times:* "There's no question that there is an income shift going on in the economy. Companies are squeezing their labor costs to build profits."

Yes, Virginia, there is a Santa Claus. But he's run off with all the toys.

Late in August, I clipped another story from *The Wall Street Journal.* Above an op-ed piece by Robert Frank the headline asked: "Do the Rich Need the Rest of America?" The author didn't seem ambivalent about the answer. He wrote that as stocks have boomed, "the wealthy bounced back. And while the Main Street economy" [where the Connie Brasels and Natalie Fords and most Americans live] "was wracked by high unemployment and the real-estate crash, the wealthy—whose financial fates were more tied to capital markets than jobs and houses—picked themselves up, brushed themselves off, and started buying luxury goods again."

Citing the work of Michael Lind at the Economic Growth Program of the New America Foundation, the article went on to describe how the super-rich earn their fortunes with overseas labor, selling to overseas consumers and managing financial transactions that have little to do with the rest of America, "while relying entirely or almost entirely on immigrant servants at one of several homes around the country."

So the answer to the question "Do the Rich Need the Rest of America?" is as stark as it is ominous: Many don't. As they form their own financial culture increasingly separated from the fate of everyone else, it is "hardly surprising," Frank and Lind concluded, "that so many of them should be so hostile to paying taxes to support the infrastructure and the social programs that help the majority of the American people."

When Howard came down to New York last December for what would be my last interview with him, I showed him this document published in the spring of 2005 by the Wall Street giant Citigroup, setting forth an "Equity Strategy" under the title (I'm not making this up) "Revisiting Plutonomy: The Rich Getting Richer."

Now, most people know what plutocracy is: the rule of the rich, political power controlled by the wealthy. Plutocracy is not an American word and wasn't meant to become an American phenomenon—some of our founders deplored what they called "the veneration of wealth." But plutocracy is here, and a pumped up Citigroup even boasted of coining a variation on the word—"plutonomy," which describes an economic system where the privileged few make sure the rich get richer and that government helps them do it. Five years ago, Citigroup decided the time had come to "bang the drum on plutonomy."

And bang they did. Here are some excerpts from the document "Revisiting Plutonomy":

"Asset booms, a rising profit share, and favorable treatment by market-friendly governments have allowed the rich to prosper . . . [and] take an increasing share of income and wealth over the last twenty years. . . . The top 10 percent, particularly the top 1 percent of the United States—the plutonomists in our parlance—have benefited disproportionately from the recent productivity surge in the U.S. . . . [and] from globalization and the productivity boom, at the relative expense of labor. . . . [And they] are likely to get even wealthier in the coming years. Because the dynamics of plutonomy are still intact."

I'll repeat that: *"The dynamics of plutonomy are still intact."*

That was the case before the Great Collapse of 2008, and it's the case today, two years after the catastrophe. But the plutonomists are doing just fine. Even better in some cases, thanks to our bailout of the big banks. (To see just how our system was rigged by the financial, political, and university elites, run, don't walk, to the theater nearest you showing Charles Ferguson's new film, *Inside Job.* Take a handkerchief because you'll weep for the republic.)

As for the rest of the country, listen to this summary in *The Economist*—no Marxist journal—of a study by Pew Research: "More than half of all workers today have experienced a spell of unemployment, taken a cut in pay or hours or been forced to go part-time. . . . Fewer than half of all adults expect their children to have a higher standard of living than theirs, and more than a quarter say it will be lower. For many Americans, the Great Recession has been the sharpest trauma since the Second World War, wiping out jobs, wealth, and hope itself."

Let that sink in: For millions of garden-variety Americans, the audacity of hope has been replaced by a paucity of hope.

Time for a confession. The legendary correspondent Edward R. Murrow told his generation of journalists that bias is OK as long as you don't try to hide it. Here is mine: Plutocracy and democracy don't mix. Plutocracy too long tolerated leaves democracy on the auction block, subject to the highest bidder.

Socrates said to understand a thing, you must first name it. The name for what's happening to our political system is corruption: a deep, systemic corruption. The former editor of *Harper's,* Roger D. Hodge, brilliantly dissects how democracy has gone on sale in America. Today, he says, voters still "matter," but only as raw material to be shaped by the actual form of political influence—money. Hodge's new book, *The Mendacity of Hope,* describes how America's founding generation especially feared the kind of corruption that occurs when the private ends of a narrow faction succeed in capturing the engines of government. James Madison and many of his contemporaries knew this kind of corruption could consume the republic. So they attempted to erect safeguards against it, hoping to prevent private and narrow personal interests from overriding those of the general public.

They failed. Hardly a century passed after the ringing propositions of 1776 before America was engulfed in the gross materialism and political corruption of the First Gilded Age, when Big Money bought the government right out from under the voters. In their magisterial work, *The Growth of the American Republic,* the historians Morison, Commager, and Leuchtenburg describe how in that era "privilege controlled politics," and "the purchase of votes, the corruption of election officials, the bribing of legislatures, the lobbying of special bills, and the flagrant disregard of laws" threatened the very foundations of the country.

As one of the plutocrats crowed: "We are rich. We own America. We got it, God knows how, but we intend to keep it."

And they have never given up. The Gilded Age returned with a vengeance in our time. It slipped in quietly at first, back in the early 1980s, when Ronald Reagan began a "massive decades-long transfer of national wealth to the rich."

As Roger Hodge makes clear, under Bill Clinton the transfer was even more dramatic, as the top 10 percent captured an ever-growing share of national income.

The trend continued under George W. Bush—those huge tax cuts for the rich, remember, which are now about to be extended because both parties have been bought off by the wealthy—and by 2007 the wealthiest 10 percent of Americans were taking in 50 percent of the national income.

Today, a fraction of people at the top earns more than the bottom 120 million Americans.

People say, "Come on, this is the way the world works." No, it's the way the world is *made* to work.

This vast inequality is not the result of Adam Smith's invisible hand; it did not just happen; it was no accident.

As Hodge drives home, it is the result of a long series of policy decisions "about industry and trade, taxation and military spending, by flesh-and-blood humans sitting in concrete-and-steel buildings." And those policy decisions were paid for by the less than 1 percent who participate in our capitalist democracy by making political contributions.

Over the past thirty years, with the complicity of Republicans and Democrats alike, the plutocrats (or plutonomists, as Citigroup calls them) have used their vastly increased wealth to assure that government does their bidding. Looking back, it all seems so clear that it's amazing that we could have ignored the warning signs at the time.

Yet here we are at a moment, says the new chairman of Common Cause and former Labor Secretary Robert Reich, that "threatens American democracy: an unprecedented concentration of income and wealth at the top; a record amount of secret money flooding our democracy; and a public becoming increasingly angry and cynical about a government that's raising its taxes, reducing its services, and unable to get it back to work." We are losing our democracy, Reich says, to an entirely different system, one where political power derives from wealth.

Its ratification came in January 2010, when the five reactionary members of the Supreme Court ruled that corporations are "persons" with the right to speak during elections by funding ads like those now flooding the airwaves. It was the work of legal fabulists. Corporations are not people; they are legal fictions, creatures of the state, born not of the womb, not of flesh and blood. They're not permitted to vote. They don't bear arms (except for the nuclear bombs they can now drop on a Congressional race without anyone knowing where it came from). Yet thanks to five activist conservative judges, they have the privilege of "personhood" to "speak"—and not in their own voice, mind you, but as ventriloquists, through hired puppets.

Our government has been bought off. Welcome to the plutocracy.

Obviously, Howard Zinn would not have us leave it there. Defeat was never his counsel. Look at this headline from one of his articles he published in *The Progressive* prior to *Citizens United:* "It's Not Up to the Supreme Court." The Court was lost long ago, he said. Don't go there looking for justice: "The Constitution gave no rights to working people; no right to work less than twelve hours a day, no right to a living wage, no right to safe working conditions. Workers had to organize, go on strike, defy the law, the courts, the police, create a great movement which won the eight-hour day, and caused such commotion that Congress was forced to pass a minimum wage law, and Social Security, and unemployment insurance. . . . Those rights only come alive when citizens organize, protest, demonstrate, strike, boycott, rebel, and violate the law in order to uphold justice."

So what are we to do about Big Money in politics buying off democracy?

I can almost hear him throwing that question back at us: "What are we to do? ORGANIZE! Yes, organize—and don't count the costs."

Some people already are mobilizing. There's a rumbling in the land. All across the spectrum, people oppose the escalating power of money in politics. Fed-up Democrats. Disillusioned Republicans. Independents. Greens. Even tea partiers, once they wake up to realize they have been sucker-punched by their bankrollers who have no intention of sharing the wealth.

Veteran public interest groups like Common Cause and Public Citizen are aroused. There are the rising voices, from Web-based initiatives such as freespeechforpeople.org to grassroots initiatives such as Democracy Matters on campuses across the country. Moveon.org is looking for a million people to fight back in a many-pronged strategy to counter the Supreme Court decision.

In taking on Big Money, we're talking about something more than a single issue. We're talking about a broad-based coalition to restore American democracy—one that is trying to be smart about the nuts-and-bolts of building a coalition, remembering that it has a lot to do with human nature.

Some will want to march.

Some will want to petition.

Some will want to engage through the Web.

Some will want to go door-to-door: many gifts, but the same spirit. A fighting spirit.

As Howard Zinn would tell us: No fight, no fun, no results.

Let's be clear: Even with most Americans on our side, the odds are long. We learned long ago that power and privilege never give up anything without a struggle. Money fights hard, and it fights dirty. Think Karl Rove, the Chamber of Commerce, the Brothers Koch. And we may lose.

But hear out Baldemar Velasquez on this. He and his Farm Labor Organizing Committee took on the Campbell Soup Company—and won. They took on North Carolina growers—and won. And now they're taking on no less than R. J. Reynolds Tobacco and one of its principal financial sponsors, JPMorgan Chase.

"It's OK if it's impossible," Velasquez says. "It's OK! The object is not to win. The object is to do the right and good thing. If you decide not to do anything, because it's too hard or too impossible, then nothing will be done, and when you're on your deathbed, you're going to say, 'I wish I had done something.' But if you go and do the right thing NOW, and you do it long enough, good things will happen."

Shades of Howard Zinn!

Critical Thinking

1. What is Bill Moyers' theory about elite power? Do you agree?
2. By what methods do the rich rule?
3. What are the consequences for America of rule by the rich?

BILL MOYERS is the veteran PBS broadcaster. This article is adapted from remarks he made on October 29, 2010, at Boston University as he inaugurated the Howard Zinn Lecture Series.

Follow the Dark Money

The down and dirty history of secret spending, PACS gone wild, and the epic four-decade fight over the only kind of political capital that matters.

ANDY KROLL

"There are two things that are important in politics. The first is money and I can't remember what the second one is."
— Mark Hanna, 19th-century mining tycoon
and GOP fundraiser

I. Nixonland

Bill Liedtke was racing against time. His deadline was a little more than a day away. He'd prepared everything—suitcase stuffed with cash, jet fueled up, pilot standing by. Everything but the Mexican money.

The date was April 5, 1972. Warm afternoon light bathed the windows at Pennzoil Company headquarters in downtown Houston. Liedtke, a former Texas wildcatter who'd risen to be Pennzoil's president, and Roy Winchester, the firm's PR man, waited anxiously for $100,000 due to be hand-delivered by a Mexican businessman named José Díaz de León. When it arrived, Liedtke (pronounced LIT-key) would stuff it into the suitcase with the rest of the cash and checks, bringing the total to $700,000. The Nixon campaign wanted the money before Friday, when a new law kicked in requiring that federal campaigns disclose their donors. Maurice Stans, finance chair of the Committee for the Re-Election of the President, or CREEP, had told fundraisers they needed to beat that deadline. Liedtke said he'd deliver.

Díaz de León finally arrived later that afternoon, emptying a large pouch containing $89,000 in checks and $11,000 in cash onto Liedtke's desk. The donation was from Robert Allen, president of Gulf Resources and Chemical Company. Allen—fearing his shareholders would discover that he'd given six figures to Nixon—had funneled it through a Mexico City bank to Díaz de León, head of Gulf Resources' Mexican subsidiary, who carried the loot over the border.

Winchester and another Pennzoil man rushed the suitcase to the Houston airport, where a company jet was waiting on the tarmac. The two men climbed aboard, bound for Washington. They touched down in DC hours later and sped directly to CREEP's office at 1701 Pennsylvania Avenue NW, across the street from the White House. They arrived at 10 p.m.

It was the last gasp of a two-month fund-raising blitz during which CREEP raked in some $20 million before the new disclosure law took effect. A handful of wealthy donors accounted for nearly half of that haul; insurance tycoon W. Clement Stone alone gave $2.1 million, or $11.4 million in today's dollars. Hugh Sloan, CREEP's treasurer, later described an "avalanche" of cash pouring into the group's coffers—all of it secret.

At least it was secret until some of that Mexican money ended up in the bank account of a one-time CIA operative named Bernard Barker, one of the five men whose bungled burglary at the Democratic National Committee headquarters in the Watergate complex lit the fuse on the biggest political scandal in modern American history.

Over the next two years, prosecutors, congressional investigators, and journalists untangled a conspiracy involving a clandestine sabotage campaign against Democrats, hush-hush cash drops for CREEP surrogates in phone booths, and millions in illegal corporate contributions. As the slow drip of revelations continued, public outrage boiled over. Nixon's approval rating sunk below 25 percent, worse than Lyndon Johnson's during the darkest depths of the Vietnam War. Picketers marched on the White House demanding his impeachment. College campuses erupted in protest over the Watergate abuses.

Almost 40 years later, that outrage is back. Mass movements like the tea party and Occupy have channeled popular anger at a political system widely seen as backward and corrupt. In the age of the super-PAC, Americans commonly say there's too much money in politics, that lobbyists have too much power, and that the system is stacked against the average citizen. "Our government," as one Occupy DC protester put it, "has allowed policy, laws, and justice to be for sale to the highest bidder."

For many political observers, it feels like a return to the pre-Watergate years. Rich bankrollers—W. Clement Stone then, Sheldon Adelson now—cut jaw-dropping checks backing their favorite candidates. Political operatives devise ways to hide tens of millions in campaign donations. And protesters have taken to the streets over what they see as a broken system. "We're back to the Nixon era," says Norman Ornstein of the conservative American Enterprise Institute, "the era of undisclosed money, of big cash amounts and huge interests that are small in number dominating American politics." This is the story of how we got here.

"We're back to the Nixon era," says scholar Norman Ornstein, "the era of undisclosed money . . . and huge interests . . . dominating American politics."

Watergate aside, the issue of campaign finance historically has not resonated with Americans. Those few reporters who do concentrate on it—*Mother Jones* has made it a focus since our post-Watergate inception—struggle to breathe life into stories based on government documents and obscure regulations. But the Supreme Court's 2010 *Citizens United v. Federal Election Commission* decision—freeing corporations and unions to spend unlimited outside money on elections—jolted the public, prompting hundreds of protests and inspiring a nationwide grassroots campaign to, as the group Public Citizen puts it, "reclaim our democracy."

We've been here before. The basic pattern emerging from the last century of campaign finance can be summarized as: scandal, then reform. The Tillman Act's ban on corporate donations to candidates passed after Teddy Roosevelt was caught shaking down big New York City businesses. Watergate spurred the historic 1974 amendments to the Federal Election Campaign Act. And the 1996 Democratic fundraising abuses paved the way for the passage of the Bipartisan Campaign Reform Act of 2002, better known as McCain-Feingold. "Congress," says Democratic election lawyer Joseph Sandler, "is always fighting the last war." And whenever new reforms take effect, Washington's brightest minds turn to finding clever new ways to circumvent them.

Political money, campaign finance watchers say, moves much like water, always looking for an opening to flow through—and political operatives are only too eager to muddy those waters with anonymous, untraceable cash. "It's like holes in a dike: You block one hole, it's going to find its way out another way," says Democratic attorney Neil Reiff.

For decades, the campaign finance wars have pitted two ideological foes against each other: one side clamoring to dam the flow while the other seeks to open the floodgates. The self-styled

---

Teddy's Trust Issues

Dark-money disaster: During the 1904 campaign, New York Life Insurance secretly gave $48,000 ($1.25 million today) to the Republicans.
Key figure: President Teddy Roosevelt, who ran as a trustbuster while soliciting corporate cash on the side. "He got down on his knees for us," one tycoon recalled.
Backlash: Reformers howled. TR signed the 1907 Tillman Act, which banned companies from giving directly to candidates.

---

good-government types believe that unregulated political money inherently corrupts. A healthy democracy, they say, needs robust regulation—clear disclosure, tough limits on campaign spending and donations, and publicly financed presidential and congressional elections. The dean of this movement is 73-year-old Fred Wertheimer, the former president of the advocacy outfit Common Cause, who now runs the reform group Democracy 21.

On the other side are conservatives and libertarians who consider laws regulating political money an assault on free markets and free speech. They want to deregulate campaign finance—knock down spending and giving limits and roll back disclosure laws. Their leaders include Senate Minority Leader Mitch McConnell (R-Ky.), conservative lawyer James Bopp Jr., and former FEC commissioner Brad Smith, who now chairs the Center for Competitive Politics, which fights campaign finance regulation.

In this ongoing battle, the upper hand shifts regularly. Wertheimer and his allies scored historic victories in the 1970s in the wake of Watergate and again in the early aughts. Yet more recently, the deregulation camp has won a series of court decisions—*FEC v. Wisconsin Right to Life*, SpeechNow.org *v. FEC*, and, of course, *Citizens United* that have toppled more campaign finance regulations in less time than ever before. Even the Tillman Act's century-old corporate contribution ban is under siege by conservative interest groups.

Meanwhile, money is flooding the political system like never before. This has forced lawmakers, as many of them will forlornly admit, onto an endless fundraising hamster wheel in which they spend more and more time beating the bushes for campaign cash and less and less time actually legislating. In the 2012 election, experts project spending could top a staggering $11 billion—more than double the 2008 total.

What few people realize is how close Wertheimer and Congress came to blocking the deluge.

II. "That Bald-Headed Bastard"

The phone call that launched Fred Wertheimer's four-decade crusade against corruption and corporate money in politics came, of all times, during a nap.

It was May 1971, and Wertheimer, then 32, was unemployed. After four years working for Rep. Silvio Conte (R-Mass.), Wertheimer had quit his job on the Hill and entered into what he now calls "semiretirement." He slept late, browsed the newspapers, took long walks around Washington, and napped each afternoon. Having bills to pay, his wife, Linda, took a job at a fledgling news organization called National Public Radio. (She went on to a long career at NPR as a political correspondent and host of *All Things Considered.*) Wertheimer himself had applied for a handful of jobs, but he hadn't heard back.

Then, one afternoon, he awoke to a phone call. Wertheimer, groggy, reached for the receiver. It was the good-government group Common Cause, where he had applied for a lobbying position. They wound up hiring him to focus on two issues: ending US involvement in the Vietnam War and reforming the nation's weak campaign finance laws.

In a recent interview at his Dupont Circle office, the walls adorned with Mark Rothko prints, framed news clips

("Ethics Watchdog Fred Wertheimer: When He Barks, Congress Listens"), and photos inscribed by the politicians he's worked with (Barack Obama: "Keep fighting the good fight"), Wertheimer, a Brooklyn native with a crown of silver hair, recalled the warning he received from Common Cause founder John Gardner: "Reform is not for the short-winded." Even so, Wertheimer quips, "He never told me it was 41 years and counting."

Luckily for Wertheimer, he had an early taste of victory to keep him going. Watergate and the abuses of the 1972 presidential campaign had left the public agitating for reform, and both Democrats and Republicans in Congress scrambled to introduce new legislation overhauling the nation's campaign finance laws. By 1974, there were five different campaign finance bills bouncing around in the Senate, four with GOP cosponsors. The point man on one of them was none other than the Senate minority leader, Pennsylvania Republican Hugh Scott.

For much of 1974, Wertheimer shuttled around the ornate Russell Senate Office Building, his loafers clicking on the polished marble floors. He was the top lobbyist in the reform push, the broker between lawmakers working on various versions of the historic campaign finance legislation. The five bills were soon boiled down into one that included limits on campaign spending and donations, the creation of a new elections watchdog, and public financing programs for presidential and Senate races. The legislation also left open the possibility of public financing for House campaigns. It was as close to the Common Cause ideal as Wertheimer could've hoped for. The House and Senate passed their own versions of the bill with bipartisan support, then headed into conference to iron out the differences.

Wertheimer's enemies seethed. One was Rep. Wayne Hays (D-Ohio), a sour bull of a politician who chaired the House Administration Committee and loathed campaign finance reform. Like many old-school pols, Hays saw the reforms as a threat to his seat. (Hays would later resign after it was revealed he'd paid his mistress to work in his office.) He'd fought Wertheimer—the "skunk"—every step of the way, stalling or killing campaign finance legislation. One of the 1974 conferees, Hays once spotted Wertheimer lingering outside the meeting room, seemingly twisting lawmakers' arms. Wertheimer says another member of Congress relayed Hays' snarling,

behind-closed-doors reaction: "What's that bald-headed bastard doing here?"

Hays and the other conferees ultimately denied Wertheimer his grand slam of reforms by scrapping congressional public financing. Still, the limits on campaign spending and donations and the creation of the Federal Election Commission made for a stunning victory. In the final vote, 75 percent of House Republicans backed reform, as did 41 percent of Senate Republicans. On October 15, 1974, President Gerald Ford signed into law the amendments to the Federal Election Campaign Act (FECA), the bedrock of modern campaign finance law.

The amendments took effect on January 1, 1975. The very next day, Sen. James Buckley (R-N.Y.)—older brother of conservative icon William F. Buckley—sued the secretary of the Senate, Francis Valeo, in an all-out attack on the constitutionality of FECA. *Buckley v. Valeo* reached the Supreme Court in September 1975, and four months later the high court handed down a bittersweet ruling for Wertheimer. In a complex and at times impenetrable opinion—one thought to have been written by as many as five justices—the court upheld the law's contribution limits, presidential public financing program, and disclosure provisions. But it struck down the limits on spending, including so-called independent expenditures—money spent by individuals or outside groups "totally independent" of campaigns. *Buckley* deemed political money a form of speech and sought to balance two interests: the First Amendment's free speech protections and what the justices termed "corruption and the appearance of corruption." Money given straight to candidates could corrupt, the court argued, but independent expenditures did not and thus couldn't be limited.

Buckley not only wiped out chunks of the 1974 law—it has shaped most major campaign finance court decisions ever since. The Roberts court drew heavily on *Buckley* in its *Citizens United* decision, which opened the door to unlimited third-party spending and radically reshaped the political playing field. "*Buckley*," says Michael Toner, a former chairman of the FEC and onetime chief counsel to the Republican National Committee, "is a seed that has sprouted a thousand blossoms."

III. Pac Attack

"It was reported I once called George McGovern a grossly overeducated SOB." Pause. "I've never called him educated." Laughter filled the Riverview Room at the Watergate Hotel. It was May 18, 1983, and the 200 or so guests, among them congressmen and senators and luminaries of the Reagan Revolution, doubled over their $110-a-plate dinners and glasses of wine. At a roast in his honor, John T. ("Terry") Dolan had stolen the show.

The guests had every reason to celebrate Dolan. A Reagan disciple and brash political operative, Dolan was the founder of the National Conservative Political Action Committee, known as NCPAC (pronounced "nick pack"). Freed by the *Buckley* decision, which shot down fundraising and spending limits on independent groups, Dolan forged NCPAC into a formidable political machine. He raised and spent as much money as he could, and he helped pioneer the dark art of the attack ad. One ad bashing

---

Watergate

Dark-money disaster: President Richard Nixon's 1972 reelection campaign raked in $20 million in secret donations; some went to fund the Watergate break-in. Nixon told his chief of staff to inform donors, "Anybody who wants to be an ambassador must at least give $250,000."

Key figure: Herbert Kalmbach, Nixon's personal attorney and the deputy finance chair for the Committee for the Re-Election of the President, who destroyed evidence of the hushed donations. He was fined $10,000 and served six months in prison.

Backlash: Congress imposed new limits on campaign gifts and set up the Federal Election Commission.

McGovern, the South Dakota senator, showed a basketball player dribbling a ball as an announcer said: "Globetrotter is a great name for a basketball team, but it's a terrible name for a senator. While the energy crisis was brewing, George McGovern was touring Cuba with Fidel Castro."

NCPAC famously spent $1.2 million in the 1980 election relentlessly attacking six Democratic lions of the Senate; four of them—McGovern, Birch Bayh of Indiana, Frank Church of Idaho, and John Culver of Iowa—would lose. On just one day during the '80 campaign, NCPAC ran 150 anti-Church ads on Idaho radio stations. NCPAC also spent $2 million to help Reagan beat President Jimmy Carter. In the 1984 presidential election, it dropped another $2 million hammering Walter Mondale. The country had never seen anything like Dolan's outside attack machine—and he knew it. "We're on the cutting edge of politics," he told the *Washington Post* in 1980.

Dolan made no bones about his brass-knuckles style. "A group like ours," he once said, "could lie through its teeth, and the candidate it helps stays clean." Democrats branded Dolan a lying "extremist," while patrician Republicans sneered at his smashmouth tactics. Yet when they weren't bashing Dolan, his enemies scrambled to catch up. Strategist Peter Fenn urged fellow Democrats to "get down in the gutter with NCPAC" if they wanted to win.

Slim and mustachioed, Dolan loved telling biting jokes and encouraged a loose atmosphere around the NCPAC office, where water gun fights were common and hamsters roamed the halls. Dolan also groomed future Republican operatives, including message guru Frank Luntz, conservative media watchdog L. Brent Bozell III, political strategist Mike Murphy, and PR man and political historian Craig Shirley.

Thanks in part to Dolan's audacious brand of politics, Reagan was twice elected president. Dolan, however, didn't live to see the end of the Reagan era. A closeted gay man, he died from AIDS-related complications in 1986, at the age of 36. His friends, who never spoke of his illness, hailed him as a pillar of the New Right movement and a canny tactician who changed the way politics was played—if not always for the better.

NCPAC, which faded away in the years after Dolan's death, illustrated a larger trend in post-*Buckley* politics: the rise of the political action committee. At the end of 1974, there were 600 registered PACs; nine years later, there were 3,500. PACs spent $23 million on congressional races in 1976; by 1982, it was $80 million.

Pacs came in all varieties: independent committees like NCPAC, trade association PACs, party PACs, and more. There were PACs representing whole industries, like the mighty Business Industry Political Action Committee (BIPAC), formed by the National Association of Manufacturers, which grew so large and cash-flush that in the 1980s it rivaled the parties as the true power broker in Washington.

The presidential candidates started their own committees. Reagan's Citizens for the Republic PAC, for instance, acted as a campaign-in-waiting between his '76 and '80 presidential bids. The group held on to leftover donations and safeguarded valuable mailing lists while quietly laying the groundwork for his successful 1980 election campaign.

The rise of business and corporate PACs—and also innovations like direct mail—helped the Republican Party dominate

---

The Keating Five

Dark-money disaster: After receiving a combined $1.3 million in donations, five Democratic and Republican senators met with banking regulators on behalf of Charles Keating's failing S&L.
Key figure: Mildly rebuked by the Senate Ethics Committee in 1991, a chastened Sen. John McCain (R-Ariz.) said, "I'm sure that my political obituary will always have something about the Keating Five in it."
Backlash: In a roundabout way, the 2002 McCain-Feingold Act.

---

the arms race of the 1970s and 1980s. In the 1980 campaign, for instance, the GOP spent $5 million in support of Senate candidates, compared to the Democratic Party's $590,000. Two years later, the Republican National Senatorial Committee doled out $9 million to candidates, while the Democratic Senatorial Campaign Committee gave just $2.3 million.

Yet the explosion of new PACs soon ended, and though they remain a fixture of electoral politics to this day, their luster faded. As the '80s wore on, a loophole opened by the FEC gave rise to soft money—unregulated, undisclosed, unlimited money given to parties (as opposed to candidates) by unions, corporations, and wealthy individuals. At first, the FEC let the parties raise and spend soft money solely for "party-building activities": building a new office, say, or a TV studio. But election lawyers and savvy strategists soon widened the loophole.

Politicos remember 1988 as the first election when soft money figured in a big way. Joseph Sandler, then a lawyer at the Democratic National Committee (and later its general counsel), recalls soft money from unions and corporations pouring into the party's coffers after Michael Dukakis seized the nomination. "We thought, 'What do we do with it?'" Sandler says. "So we invented new uses for soft money for general party stuff to get out the vote." That included phone banks, surveys, direct mail, and other administrative costs.

The parties raised $45 million in soft money in 1988; in 1992, it was $86 million. By then Wertheimer, the reformers, and newspaper editorial boards around the country were decrying what they saw as a perversion of the campaign finance laws. In May 1993, a newly elected President Bill Clinton paid lip service to banning soft money, but a bill to do just that died in conference, after passing both the House and Senate.

The bill's demise would prove a blessing and a curse for Clinton. Soft money would power his reelection campaign two years later—yet it would also trigger the biggest campaign finance scandal since Watergate.

IV. "The White House Is Like a Subway"

On September 7, 1995, Bill Clinton joined his top aides and advisers for a strategy session in the White House's second-floor Treaty Room. It was here, on a muggy August day in 1898, that William McKinley had presided over the signing of a treaty that had ended hostilities in the Spanish-American War. Now, Clinton and his lieutenants faced a war of a different kind: winning reelection in the face of vicious GOP attacks and a hobbled US economy.

The loudest voice in the room that day belonged to Dick Morris, the charismatic and controversial political strategist. "It's complicated" was the best way to describe the relationship between Clinton and Morris. The president had hired, fired, and rehired Morris throughout his two-decade ascent from obscure Arkansas official to governor to leader of the free world. Shortly after the Democrats' midterm hammering in November 1994, Clinton turned to Morris once again to chart a course to victory in the 1996 election.

Morris, as usual, had a plan.

The party, he said, needed to saturate the airwaves with TV ads starting *now*, 14 months before Election Day, in Colorado, Iowa, Michigan, and other swing states. Advertising early and often, getting out in front of the GOP, was key to winning the '95 budget fight and the '96 election. "If we win now, we'll win later," Morris said at the meeting. "If we lose now, we'll be dead no matter what we do."

The Democrats' weapon of choice were so-called issue ads slamming the GOP and its leader, House Speaker Newt Gingrich, for a budget that cut funding for Medicare, Medicaid, and Head Start. The ads would also tout Clinton's pledge to cut taxes on the middle class, beef up environmental protections, and balance the budget without axing popular programs. In reality, the ads were campaign spots. All that was missing was the "Vote for Bill Clinton" tagline. Why the feint? As long as Democrats claimed they were running issue ads, they could fund them with soft money.

Clinton signed off.

There was just one problem: The DNC was broke. Democrats would need to raise tens of millions of dollars, fast; thankfully, they had the ultimate rainmaker in Clinton. The president hated asking for money, a former aide recalls, yet no one schmoozed a room full of rich people like Clinton. "He was a master at talking to them about what he was doing and where he wanted the country to go—and by the way, we need some money to get there," the aide says.

In the months that followed, the White House and DNC sent a clear message to donors: Bring your checkbooks; we're open for business. Clinton attended more than 230 fundraising events in the 10 months before the election, sometimes five or six a week. "Every minute of my time is spent at these fundraisers," the president griped. Donors, meanwhile, knew access was just a six-figure check away. "The White House is like a subway," said one contributor. "You have to put in coins to open the gates."

"There will be huge scandals," predicts Sen. John McCain, "because there's too much money washing around . . . we don't know who's behind it."

And how those coins added up. The DNC raised more than $122 million in soft money during the '96 cycle. The RNC did even better, raking in $141 million. Together, the two parties unleashed $120 million in soft money on faux issue ads.

Yet Morris' strategy put the Democrats' soft money to far more devastating use. One issue spot, crafted by ad man Marius Penczner, depicted a patient's beeping EKG monitor slowly flatlining as a narrator read the GOP's proposed health care cuts. In another, a little girl played in her crib while the narrator rattled off GOP-backed education cuts. And the ads ran relentlessly: By Election Day of November 1996, the average TV viewer in targeted states saw one Democratic issue ad every three days.

The barrage was later credited with opening a wide lead for Clinton nearly a year before the election. Although the RNC caught on to Morris' strategy and mimicked it, GOP candidate Bob Dole never closed the gap. Looking back on his ad strategy and the '96 election, Morris later wrote, "There has never been anything even remotely like it in the history of presidential elections."

Then, after Election Day, the details of the Democrats' fundraising scheme exploded into a full-blown scandal. Sen. Fred Thompson (R-Tenn.), who had worked on the Senate's Watergate investigation two decades earlier, launched a probe that eventually forced the Clinton administration and the DNC to admit to plying donors with coffee klatches with the president, sleepovers in the White House's Lincoln Bedroom, rides on Air Force One, and other exclusive perks. It emerged that John Huang, a major Democratic fundraiser and the DNC's vice chairman of finance, had laundered nearly a million dollars in illegal foreign contributions to the DNC from an Indonesian conglomerate and a Korean electronics company, among other sources. Democrats also accepted $65,000 in illegal donations at a now-infamous luncheon at a Los Angeles-area Buddhist temple. The DNC would later return about $3 million.

For Fred Wertheimer and the reformers, Clinton's soft money operation marked a return to the dark-money days of Watergate. "Though still on the books, campaign finance laws have been replaced by the law of the jungle," Wertheimer fumed at the time.

The pendulum was swinging back to reform.

The Clinton Years

Dark-money disaster: In 1996, a California Buddhist temple illegally funneled $65,000 to the Democrats at an event attended by Vice President Al Gore. The Dems eventually returned nearly $3 million in illegal donations, some from foreign donors. Meanwhile, big donors were offered Lincoln Bedroom sleepovers, coffees, golf outings, or morning jogs with President Bill Clinton.
Key figure: Fundraisers Charlie Trie, John Huang, Johnny Chung, Maria Hsia, and James Riady, an Indonesian businessman who was fined $8.6 million.
Backlash: Spurred passage of McCain-Feingold in 2002, which banned unregulated soft money to parties.

V. "Legislative Sledgehammer"

A few days after Republicans recaptured the Senate in the 1994 midterm elections, Russ Feingold was driving through Wisconsin in his used, blue, wood-paneled Buick Roadmaster station wagon. Before the "tsunami of '94," Feingold had ranked last in seniority in his party, but at least Democrats controlled the Senate. Now he had even less clout on the Hill. Somewhere outside Madison the wagon's hulking car phone rang. The ensuing conversation changed Feingold's life.

On the line was Arizona's John McCain. The veteran Republican senator praised Feingold's work, his independence, and his determination, and suggested that the two men team up on legislation. Feingold—knowing that McCain had remade himself as a reformer after getting ensnared in the 1989 Keating Five banking scandal—suggested campaign finance.

Thus began one of the unlikeliest yet most influential partnerships in the history of money in politics.

In the decade before, reformers in Congress had introduced new campaign finance laws every session. Each time the legislation perished on the floor or met the veto of the president. McCain and Feingold would face the same pattern until, in the wake of the '96 scandal, a window for reform opened once again.

A pivotal moment came in 1997. The two senators had watched in horror at the explosion of soft money in the previous year's election. At a meeting in Feingold's Senate office, McCain pressed to scrap their existing bill and replace it with a straightforward soft money ban, which he believed held the best hope of passing. Feingold wouldn't hear of it, since doing so would entail jettisoning measures dear to his heart, including one that would abolish PAC contributions. McCain left Feingold's office furious. McCain-Feingold almost died right then and there.

The next day, the two met in the Republican cloakroom just off the Senate floor. Feingold could see that McCain was still unsettled by their argument. "Russ, I was up all night," he said. "I was so upset."

"I think you're right, John," Feingold told him. "We gotta get this. We gotta pass the soft money ban." The men hugged.

Following the '96 election, Wertheimer had predicted that Congress had only a 90-day window to pass a soft money ban before the public's anger dissipated. In fact, it took more than five years, by which point McCain had begun calling himself Sen. Quixote.

McCain and Feingold had plenty of help. Wertheimer, who'd moved on to Democracy 21, lobbied relentlessly. More crucial was a decadelong influx of money from the nation's biggest charities and foundations that started in the mid-'90s—upward of $140 million—to fund reform groups and underwrite new campaign finance research. "The idea was to create an impression that a mass movement was afoot, that everywhere [politicians] looked—in academic institutions, in the business community, in religious groups, in ethnic groups, everywhere—people were talking about reform," Sean Treglia, who led Pew Charitable Trusts' campaign finance program, later said .

But it was serendipity as much as money or momentum that nudged McCain-Feingold over the edge. On May 24, 2001, Jim Jeffords, Vermont's junior senator and a lifelong Republican, defected from the GOP and declared himself an independent. For the first time in history, control of the Senate changed hands without an election. Sen. Trent Lott (R-Miss.), a staunch opponent of McCain-Feingold, relinquished the title of majority leader to Sen. Tom Daschle (D-S.D.). "Jeffords flips, Daschle comes into control, and we can see the finish line," recalls Bob Schiff, Feingold's top lieutenant on campaign finance.

The rest of 2001 saw McCain, Feingold, and their fellow reformers fight off an onslaught of amendments aimed at kneecapping their bill. Finally, in the winter of 2002, after the House passed its version of the legislation by a 51-vote margin, the Senate easily green-lighted the bill. McCain-Feingold headed to the desk of President George W. Bush.

At 7 a.m. on March 27, 2002, the duo's seven-year campaign ended as it began: with a phone call. A Bush White House aide phoned McCain at his home in Arizona to inform him that the president had signed McCain-Feingold into law that morning. There was no signing ceremony, no Rose Garden press conference. A commemorative pen would be delivered shortly to McCain's Capitol Hill office.

That same morning, a few blocks east of the White House, a staffer from a law firm representing the National Rifle Association stood shivering on the front steps of the US District Court and holding a sheaf of papers. The staffer's instructions were to file the NRA's lawsuit challenging the constitutionality of McCain-Feingold the minute the courthouse opened. With the ink still wet on the two senators' crowning achievement, the assault began.

By beating the other challengers to the court that morning, the NRA earned the naming rights to what promised to be a blockbuster case destined for the Supreme Court. *National Rifle Association v. FEC,* the legal textbooks would read.

Then Sen. Mitch McConnell, one of Washington's fiercest foes of campaign finance laws, stepped into the fray.

A stiff, jowly conservative born in Tuscumbia, Alabama, McConnell was known mostly for two things: his encyclopedic knowledge and mastery of congressional procedure, and his First Amendment zealotry. McConnell slammed McCain-Feingold as a "legislative sledgehammer" that would smash the First Amendment's free speech protections to bits. The law, he argued, "constitutes the most threatening frontal assault on core First Amendment values in a generation."

On the day Bush signed McCain-Feingold, McConnell filed a suit of his own challenging the new law's constitutionality. He'd already assembled a murderer's row of lawyers to argue his case, among them then-Stanford Law dean Kathleen Sullivan, First Amendment guru Floyd Abrams, and James Bopp Jr., a shrewd attorney who had built a career out of demolishing campaign finance laws. Though McConnell had filed his suit after the NRA, he wanted his name on the case. And so in a rare move, McConnell brokered a backroom deal with the NRA to swap the group's name for his. The case would be called *McConnell v. FEC.* "He wanted it; he was the leader," recalls Cleta Mitchell, an attorney for the NRA on the *McConnell* case. "The NRA knew it would be foolish to make a mortal enemy of a powerful senator over something like naming rights."

"If you can deregulate money in politics, then you can buy the policy outcomes you prefer," says the Campaign Legal Center's Paul S. Ryan.

It wasn't the first time McConnell had set out to gut the nation's campaign finance laws. Long before he challenged McCain-Feingold, McConnell had trained his sights on the FEC. If he couldn't get rid of campaign finance regulations altogether, he knew defanging the nation's elections watchdog would weaken enforcement.

In 1998, after the FEC launched probes of Newt Gingrich's political slush fund, GOPAC, and Pat Robertson's Christian Coalition, McConnell took aim at the commission's top lawyer, a fast-talking Queens native named Larry Noble. Noble was an FEC lifer who'd joined the commission soon after it opened in 1975. No fan of Noble or his aggressive style, McConnell wrote an amendment essentially firing him and slipped it into a $27 billion funding bill for the Treasury Department, Postal Service, and other federal agencies. Democrats howled in protest; the *New York Times* published four editorials in Noble's defense, calling McConnell's amendment an "attempted lynching." (McConnell denied specifically targeting Noble.)

Republicans on the House side kept up the fight McConnell had started. On the evening of October 1, 1998, their attack on Noble burst into public view on the House floor when Democrats vowed to block the Treasury and postal bill until Noble was safe. Millions in funding for anti-cybercrime efforts, the DARE anti-drug campaign, and an entire fleet of Black Hawk helicopters were in limbo.

Noble watched wide-eyed as this drama played out on his TV back home in Maryland. "Wow, Dad," Noble's 11-year-old son marveled. "I can't believe you're worth 16 Black Hawk helicopters."

Throughout the 2000s, McConnell also reshaped the six-member FEC by exerting control over the nominating process. Former commissioner Brad Smith, whom McConnell tapped for the post, recalls, "He essentially said, 'We need to put Republicans on the FEC who favor our point of view on regulation.'" McConnell leveraged his Senate clout to install ideologues hostile to campaign finance law. One of them, Donald McGahn, later told a group of students at the University of Virginia Law School that he simply would not enforce the laws he'd been hired to uphold. "I plead guilty as charged," he said.

Eventually, McConnell's FEC strategy would pay off. The number of 3-to-3 deadlocks on enforcement actions averaged 1 percent between 2003 and 2007; it shot up to 16 percent in 2009 and was 11 percent in 2010. For much of 2008, the FEC was so tangled that the commission lacked the minimum four-person quorum to even function. Political outfits have capitalized on the commission's hobbled state. The percentage of groups disclosing their donors dropped by more than 43 percent between 2004 and 2010.

But while McConnell succeeded in his behind-the-scenes maneuver, the fight he'd put his name on didn't go so well.

Conventional wisdom suggested the Supreme Court would side with McConnell in the challenge to McCain-Feingold. Instead, the high court's 5-to-4 decision, handed down on December 10, 2003, upheld nearly the entire law, humbling McConnell and his legal team. *McConnell v. FEC* is now remembered as a high-water mark for the reform community.

VI. In the Hands of the Court

James Bopp Jr. read the 300-page *McConnell* decision in disbelief back at his law office in Terre Haute, an old southwest Indiana mining town of 70,000 on the banks of the Wabash River.

An unassuming Hoosier with neatly parted silver hair and a cool, measured demeanor, Bopp was a central figure in the conservative movement to deregulate campaign finance that, in the 2000s, took the fight to Wertheimer and the reformers, brought the *Citizens United* case, and helped usher in super-PACs. Before, conservatives and libertarians had struggled to organize themselves on money in politics. "You had the ACLU, a few cranky libertarian sorts, a stray report from the Cato Institute, and some lackeys in the fight trying to preserve their own interests," Smith says. "That began to change after *McConnell*." At the heart of that pushback was Bopp.

Bopp's crusade dates back to his early childhood. Born into a conservative Midwestern family, the conversation at home often revolved around politics and government, he recalls, and young Jim devoured books on conservative and libertarian philosophy. At Boy Scout camp in rural Indiana, Bopp remembers reading the works of Austrian economist Friedrich Hayek, a founding father of the libertarian movement, by flashlight in his tent. "I never had a heart," Bopp jokes today. "I only had a brain."

Bopp attended Indiana University (he still has basketball season tickets) and law school at the University of Florida, and then, in 1978, he got hired as general counsel for the group National Right to Life. The turning point in his legal career came in 1993. Ten days before a statewide election, a Democratic judge blocked two Virginia anti-abortion groups from distributing voter guides on the basis that the pamphlets violated electioneering laws. Outraged at what he saw as a body block on the organizations' free speech rights, Bopp got the judge to lift the injunction the day before the election. But the damage to their campaign had been done. At the next meeting of National Right to Life's state chapters, Bopp urged the groups' leaders to go on the offensive. "Sue ahead of time," he advised them. "Get rid of these laws so [you're] not victimized like that."

Bopp has been in attack mode ever since. With anti-abortion groups as ready-made standard bearers, he has challenged and defeated more than 150 campaign finance laws. In recent years, he's represented same-sex marriage opponents in California and Washington state in a broader effort to topple donor disclosure laws. (See *Mother Jones'* May/June 2011 issue for an in-depth profile of Bopp.)

Paul S. Ryan, senior counsel at the pro-reform Campaign Legal Center, says Bopp's use of the culture wars to attack political money regulations is central to understanding his

Hammer Time

Dark-money disaster: GOP Majority Leader Tom "The Hammer" DeLay snuck around a ban on corporate donations by funneling them through the Republican National Committee back to Texas Republicans.
Key figure: DeLay, who was convicted of money laundering and sentenced to three years in prison, all while condemning "the criminalization of politics." He's currently out on bail while appealing.
Backlash: DeLay lasted just three weeks on *Dancing With the Stars*.

Citizens United

Dark-money disaster: In a January 2010 decision, the Supreme Court ruled that limits on outside political spending by corporations and unions violate the First Amendment. Paved the way for the creation of super-PACs.
Key figure: Chief Justice John Roberts; justices Samuel Alito, Anthony Kennedy, Antonin Scalia, and Clarence Thomas; and legal mastermind James Bopp.
Backlash: Increasing calls for a constitutional amendment to undo *Citizens United*.

influence and success. "Bopp recognizes something that few on the left recognize: that campaign finance law underlies all other substantive law," Ryan says. "If you can deregulate money in politics, you can buy the policy outcomes you prefer."

In 1997, Bopp created the James Madison Center for Free Speech, which once counted McConnell as an honorary chairman, to give fellow conservatives a platform in the political money trenches. Sometimes that meant battling members of their own party—including Ken Mehlman, who as RNC chairman called for a ban on outside 527 groups during the 2004 election. Elected as an RNC delegate in 2005, Bopp pressed the party to embrace a deregulatory position on campaign finance. Freedom to raise and spend campaign money without restrictions, he says, should be "a central part of our philosophy."

Bopp brushes aside questions about the wisdom of wanting more cash sloshing around politics when most of the public wants *less* of it. He doesn't buy the argument that more campaign giving erodes public trust in government—and if it did, he says, that would be a good thing: "People should rely less on government anyway. The less government there is, the better off we all are."

By the mid-2000s, the campaign finance deregulation movement had fully blossomed. Brad Smith had left the FEC and formed the Center for Competitive Politics, a rival to Common Cause and Wertheimer's campaign finance reform group Democracy 21. The Institute for Justice, a libertarian law firm, waded into campaign finance legal fights in hopes of knocking down regulations. And Bopp was plowing ahead with his right-to-life cases and other election-related lawsuits. "All of this created a new esprit de corps," Smith says. "For the first time, it was okay to walk around Washington and say it's respectable to oppose campaign finance reform."

Bopp and his allies also saw their fortunes radically improve with the arrival of John Roberts and Samuel Alito to the Supreme Court during George W. Bush's second term. Reformers and legal experts argue, in fact, that the switch from Sandra Day O'Connor to Alito marked the single most crucial moment in the past decade of the money wars. In an instant, the key fifth vote in *McConnell* was replaced by Alito, a reliable conservative with a libertarian streak.

The effect was near-instantaneous. In 2007, Bopp argued in *FEC v. Wisconsin Right to Life* that McCain-Feingold's ban on running issue ads 30 days before a primary and 60 days before an election was unconstitutional. The court had upheld this very provision four years earlier; the Roberts court killed it. Then, in January 2010, the court ruled 5-to-4 in *Citizens United*—another case brought by Bopp (though he didn't argue it before the court)—that corporations and labor unions are entitled to the same free speech protections as people and so can spend directly from their general treasuries on unlimited independent expenditures. *Citizens United* had arrived at the court as a minor case with few implications for campaign finance. But Roberts and his fellow conservative justices used the case to issue a ground-shaking decision that demolished decades of precedent. (Later that year, a DC appeals court relied on *Citizens United* in a case called SpeechNow.org v. *FEC*, argued by Brad Smith's Center for Competitive Politics, which ushered in super-PACs.)

Wertheimer called *Citizens United* "a disaster for the American people" and "the most radical and destructive campaign finance decision in Supreme Court history." The American Enterprise Institute's Norman Ornstein says the decision was as misguided as the 1857 *Dred Scott v. Sandford* ruling denying slaves the right to citizenship. "The Roberts court is going to go down in history in the same way [Chief Justice] Roger Taney and his court went down in history with *Dred Scott*," Ornstein says. In his 2010 State of the Union, President Obama himself lambasted the high court for having "reversed a century of law that I believe will open the floodgates for special interests."

The Roberts court's hostility to limiting money in politics has forced the reformers to overhaul their strategy. The Campaign Legal Center's Paul S. Ryan says groups like his now struggle to fund legal defenses of what's left of campaign finance law. Donors see any legal strategy dead-ending at the Supreme Court—and Ryan agrees. "With the Supreme Court the way it is," he says, "why bother?"

The reformers have instead taken the fight to Congress with legislation bolstering disclosure in campaign giving and political ads, but they have little to show for it. The 2010 DISCLOSE Act died in the Senate after Republicans, led by McConnell, filibustered the bill. A slimmed-down version of the legislation, introduced in March, faces similarly long odds. It's a tough time, Wertheimer admits, to be a reformer in Washington.

Stymied in the courts and in Congress, the fight against super-PACs and dark money in politics is now being waged in the streets. Buoyed by the Occupy movement, activists nationwide are knocking on doors, lobbying state lawmakers, and rallying at courthouses in an effort to ensure campaign finance is not a back-burner issue.

On December 15, in 83 towns and cities, from Burlington, Vermont, to Anchorage, Alaska, people gathered in living rooms and kitchens to discuss *Citizens United* and a constitutional amendment to neutralize its effects. In a recent poll, 6 in 10 people said they disagreed with *Citizens United;* 8 in 10 said there was "too much big money" in politics.

After condemning the decision, President Obama bent to the post-*Citizens United* reality and urged supporters to give to the super-PAC backing him.

Reformers know the success of their long-shot campaign means tapping into that sentiment. Short of a constitutional convention, passing an amendment, for example, requires the support of two-thirds of the House and Senate and the assent of 38 state legislatures. "The challenge is overcoming that skepticism about the amendment," says Robert Weissman, president of Public Citizen. "The only way to do that is to build a movement."

At the same time, Bopp and his allies continue their push to dismantle the remaining campaign finance laws. Their latest target: the century-old Tillman Act, which bans corporations from donating directly to candidates. Should Tillman fall, companies won't need PACs, super-PACs, or shadowy nonprofits;

they'd simply hand checks to the candidates themselves and could theoretically create innumerable shell companies to skirt the existing $2,500 donation cap.

Absent from this struggle is President Obama. After condemning super-PACs, he bent to the post-*Citizens United* political reality and urged his supporters to give not only to his campaign but to the super-PAC supporting him, Priorities USA Action. (Despite Obama's blessing, Priorities has come nowhere close to raising as much money as the pro-Romney super-PAC Restore Our Future or Karl Rove's American Crossroads.) And with his decision to rely solely on private donations in 2008 and 2012 in order to get a leg up on his opponent, Obama has undercut the public financing system created in Watergate's aftermath. To compete with Obama and appease Republican allies during the last presidential race, John McCain also backtracked on his campaign finance convictions (but ultimately ended up accepting public financing).

Super-PACs, seven-figure checks, billionaire bankrollers, shadowy nonprofits: This is the state of play in what will be the first presidential election since Watergate to be fully privately funded. Faced with this money-drenched system, reformers respond: It won't last. The pendulum is poised to swing once again. "I promise you, there will be huge scandals," McCain said in March, "because there's too much money washing around, too much of it we don't know who's behind it, and too much corruption associated with that kind of money." Russ Feingold, McCain's longtime legislative partner, agrees. "When this kind of money is changing hands secretly, it's almost automatic that there will be a scandal," Feingold says. "And this scandal could be the mother of all scandals."

Critical Thinking

1. How do powerful groups get their way in Washington?
2. How do the powerful get around laws that attempt to constrain them?

The End of Welfare as I Knew It

How Temporary Assistance for Needy Families failed the test of the Great Recession.

DIANA SPATZ

I'll always remember the day President Clinton signed Temporary Assistance to Needy Families (TANF), or welfare reform, into law. It was August 1996, and I was reading the morning paper in Barstow, California, completing the last leg of a cross-country road trip I'd taken with my daughter to celebrate my finishing school. Having just earned my bachelor's degree from the University of California, Berkeley, I would finally earn enough to get my family off welfare—and out of poverty—for good. As I read the news that the Personal Responsibility and Work Opportunity Reconciliation Act had become law, I hung my head and cried. I felt like I'd crossed a bridge just as it collapsed behind me, and worried what would become of mothers who remained trapped on the other side.

Since 1996, politicians have bragged about passing welfare reform. Even House Speaker John Boehner recently praised TANF as a bipartisan success. But successful at what? If kicking low-income children and their families off welfare is the measure, then TANF was a huge success. States were given bonuses for reducing their caseloads rather than reducing poverty. As long as families were off the rolls, it didn't matter how or why. Studies show that parents were ten times more likely to get cut off welfare because of punitive sanctions than because they got jobs paying enough to "income off." In many states, "full family" sanctions cut low-income children off welfare along with their parents. Under the "work first" mantra, TANF caseloads plummeted by almost 70 percent, as nearly 9 million low-income parents and children were purged from the national welfare rolls by 2008. Given the four goals of TANF—promoting low-wage work, encouraging marriage, reducing caseloads and curtailing out-of-wedlock births—these outcomes are no surprise. But if the measure of success is poverty reduction, TANF has failed.

To start, its restrictions on postsecondary education and training—the most effective pathway out of poverty for parents on welfare—make earning a bachelor's degree nearly impossible. Even earning an associate degree is difficult. "Any job is a good job" was the slogan emblazoned on the walls of county welfare agencies across the country, as tens of thousands of low-income mothers were made to quit college to do up to thirty-five hours per week of unpaid "workfare": sweeping streets, picking up trash in parks and cleaning public restrooms in exchange for benefits as low as $240 a month.

9 Number, in millions, purged from the welfare rolls by 2008.
$\frac{1}{5}$ proportion of poor children served by TANF today.

Contrary to "welfare queen" stereotypes, like most welfare mothers, I worked first. Work wasn't the problem; it was the nature of the work—low-wage, dead-end jobs with no benefits and little chance for advancement—that kept families like mine on the welfare rolls. Investing in my education enabled me to break that cycle and earn a solid upper-middle-class income. I now pay three times more in taxes than I used to earn working full time in a low-wage, dead-end job.

This trajectory is what motivated mothers like Rya Frontera and Melissa Johnson to pursue nursing degrees, despite being sanctioned: having their families' cash grants cut off and losing childcare and transportation assistance when they refused to quit school. Whereas mothers in "work first" programs earn less than $9,000 a year, after completing her BS in nursing Melissa graduated off welfare to a career-path job as a registered nurse making $90,000 a year. Similarly, Rya is now a full-time nurse with full benefits working for Kaiser. Not only are they off welfare permanently; both women are filling a crucial labor market need, as our nation faces a nursing shortage with no end in sight. Isn't that how welfare should work?

It is also time to end the arbitrary rules under TANF that imposed a lifetime limit of sixty months for receiving benefits, and that allowed states to enact shorter time limits. It took me ten years to overcome a lifetime of physical, emotional and sexual abuse; depression; and post-traumatic stress disorder, one or more of which have been experienced by most mothers on welfare as girls or adults—or in my case, both. In to one-third of welfare families nationally—the experience of "timed off" families clearly challenges the notion that five years is enough; TANF's work-first emphasis relegated many parents to low-wage jobs that didn't pay enough to get their families off welfare, let alone out of poverty. Consequently, in 2003 the vast majority of parents in California's CalWORKs program who reached their sixty-month limit were working and playing by the rules when they timed off welfare for the rest of their lives. And this year, like many states, California shortened its lifetime limit to forty-eight months in response to budget shortfalls, despite having the second-highest unemployment rate in the country. As a result, 22,500 parents were permanently cut off the welfare rolls on July 1.

22,500 Number of parents cut off in July after California shortened its lifetime limit to forty-eight months.
80 percent of mothers in California's welfare system who are victims of domestic violence.

Ashley Proctor, a young single mother in Oakland, was doing her thirty-two-hour weekly work requirement when she timed off. Her benefits were cut to a "child only" grant of $320 per month. "My son and I are sleeping on a friend's sofa," she says. "On the weekends I take him to our storage unit so he can play with his toys." That's better than what mothers faced in other states, where time limits as short as twenty-one months were enacted. How unfortunate that Congress, in its infinite wisdom, didn't put a time limit on poverty instead.

While states like California curtailed much-needed benefits, under welfare reform billions in federal funds were invested in unproven "marriage promotion" programs to marry poor women off the welfare rolls. Never mind that in some of California's most populous counties in 2003, most timed-off parents were already in two-parent families where one was working. And in a cruel twist, while billions were spent on marriage promotion programs that were mandatory for the states, the Family Violence Option let states choose whether to provide domestic violence services in their TANF programs, including waivers of time limits and welfare-to-work rules. Furthermore, although research shows that women who receive welfare experience domestic violence at double the rate of all American women, not a dime in federal funding was provided for family violence services. Even in California, which adopted the FVO, studies show that as many as 80 percent of CalWORKs mothers are domestic violence victims. Of these, less than 1 percent get family violence counseling and services, and less than one-quarter of 1 percent get waivers from welfare work requirements that could save their lives.

This includes mothers like Felicia Jones, whom my agency, Low-Income Families' Empowerment Through Education, or LIFETIME, was helping when she went into hiding after her ex threatened to kill her and their children. While on the run, Felicia got a notice of a mandatory welfare-to-work appointment, which had been scheduled on the same day and time as the hearing for her restraining order. When she called to say she couldn't make the appointment, her caseworker said she couldn't help

her and hung up the phone, and later sanctioned Felicia for missing that appointment. Despite my urging, Felicia was too afraid to request a state appeals hearing and later disappeared. To this day, I don't know what happened to her and her children.

Fifteen years of welfare reform, and what do we have to show for it? Poverty is at its highest level in nearly twenty years. The number of children living in deep poverty—in families with income less than 50 percent of the poverty line—is at its highest level in thirty-five years. The unemployment rate for single mothers, who represent 90 percent of parents in the welfare system, has nearly doubled, to a twenty-five-year high. Welfare rolls are rising for the first time since TANF was passed, despite efforts by states to tighten time limits and make it harder for families to get help. In Georgia, for example, families applying for TANF have faced "wait periods" before they can get cash assistance—the welfare equivalent of a poll tax or literacy test—with caseworkers offering to send children into foster care or put them up for adoption to ease the burden. Consequently, since 2002 Georgia increased TANF spending on child welfare–related services by 245 percent. According to Clare Richie, a senior policy analyst with the Georgia Budget and Policy Institute, the state now spends more on adoption services and foster care (58 percent) than it does on assistance to families.

This trend is alarming to people like Georgia State Senator Donzella James, who has been getting calls from constituents whose children are being taken away by the Department of Family and Child Services, the state's welfare agency. "One woman told me, 'I'm not a bad mother. I'm just unemployed,'" she said. Similarly, Arizona, Rhode Island and Texas spend nearly half their TANF block grants on child welfare–related services. One has to wonder if this was the plan all along, given the proposal by Newt Gingrich, who was House speaker when TANF was created, to use orphanages to reduce the welfare rolls.

The Great Recession was the first true test of welfare reform during an economic downturn, and TANF failed the grade miserably. The proof is in the numbers: in 1995 the old welfare program served at least eight out of every ten low-income children, including mine. Today TANF serves only two out of every ten poor children nationwide. In passing TANF, Congress and Bill Clinton made good on their promise to "end welfare as we know it." It's time to end welfare reform as we know it instead.

Critical Thinking

1. What were the benefits of traditional welfare that were taken away?
2. Is the current welfare system reasonably fair?
3. How would you reform welfare?

Diana Spatz is executive director of LIFETIME, a statewide organization of low-income parents in California who are pursuing postsecondary education and training as their pathway out of poverty.

The Withering of the Affluent Society

Though Americans see upward mobility as their birthright, that assumption faces growing challenges, with consequences not just for the size of our wallets but for the tenor of our politics.

ROBERT J. SAMUELSON

The future of affluence is not what it used to be. Americans have long believed—it's part of our national character—that our economic well-being will constantly increase. We see ourselves as a striving, inventive, and pragmatic people destined for higher living standards. History is a continuum of progress, from Robert Fulton's steamboat to Henry Ford's assembly line to Bill Gates' software. Every generation will live better than its predecessors.

Well, maybe not.

For millions of younger Americans—say, those 40 and under—living better than their parents is a pipe dream. They won't. The threat to their hopes does not arise from an impending collapse of technological gains of the sort epitomized by the creations of Fulton, Ford, and Gates. These advances will almost certainly continue, and per capita income—the average for all Americans and a conventional indicator of living standards—will climb. Statistically, American progress will resume. The Great Recession will be a bump, not a dead end.

The trouble is that many of these gains will bypass the young. The increases that might have fattened their paychecks will be siphoned off to satisfy other groups and other needs. Today's young workers will have to finance Social Security and Medicare for a rapidly growing cohort of older Americans. Through higher premiums for employer-provided health insurance, they will subsidize care for others. Through higher taxes and fees, they will pay to repair aging infrastructure (roads, bridges, water systems) and to support squeezed public services, from schools to police.

The hit to their disposable incomes would matter less if the young were major beneficiaries of the resultant spending. In some cases—outlays for infrastructure and local services—they may be. But these are exceptions. By 2025 Social Security and Medicare will simply reroute income from the nearly four-fifths of the population that will be under 65 to the older one-fifth. And health care spending at all age levels is notoriously skewed: Ten percent of patients account for 65 percent of medical costs, reports the Kaiser Family Foundation. Although insurance provides peace of mind, the money still goes from young to old: Average health spending for those 45 to 64 is triple that for those 18 to 24.

The living standards of younger Americans will almost certainly suffer in comparison to those of their parents in a second crucial way. Our notion of economic progress is tied to financial security, but the young will have less of it. What good are higher incomes if they're abruptly revoked? Though it wasn't a second Great Depression, the Great Recession was a close call, shattering faith that modern economic policies made broad collapses impossible. Except for the savage 1980–82 slump, post-World War II recessions had been modest. Only minorities of Americans had suffered. By contrast, the Great Recession hurt almost everyone, through high unemployment, widespread home foreclosures, huge wealth losses in stocks and real estate—and fears of worse. A 2012 Gallup poll found that 68 percent of Americans knew someone who had lost a job.

The prospect of downward mobility is not just dispiriting. It assails the whole post–World War II faith in prosperity. Beginning in the 1950s, commentators celebrated the onrush of abundance as marking a new era in human progress. In his 1958 bestseller *The Affluent Society,* Harvard economist John Kenneth Galbraith announced the arrival of a "great and unprecedented affluence" that had eradicated the historical "poverty of the masses."

Economic growth became a secular religion that was its own reward. Perhaps its chief virtue was that it dampened class conflict. In *The Great Leap: The Past Twenty-Five Years in America* (1966), John Brooks observed, "The middle class was enlarging itself and ever encroaching on the two extremes"—the very rich and the very poor. Business and labor could afford to reconcile because both could now share the fruits of expanding production. We could afford more spending on public services (education, health, environmental protection, culture) without depressing private incomes. Indeed, that was Galbraith's main theme: Our prosperity could and should support both.

To be sure, there were crises of faith, moments when economic progress seemed delayed or doomed. The longest lapse occurred in the 1970s, when double-digit inflation spawned pessimism and frequent recessions, culminating in the 1980–82 downturn. Monthly unemployment peaked at 10.8 percent. But after Federal Reserve chairman Paul Volcker and President Ronald Reagan took steps to suppress high inflation, faith returned.

Now, it's again imperiled. A 2011 Gallup poll found that 55 percent of Americans didn't think their children would live as well as they did, the highest rate ever. We may face a crimped and contentious future.

Let's be clear: The prospect is not national impoverishment; it is of relative deprivation. Even if disposable per capita incomes fell 10 percent—an extreme outcome—Americans would remain wealthy by any historical standard. Such a change would entail a decline in the annual disposable income from $37,000 to $33,300 (in 2011 inflation-adjusted dollars), probably over many years. People might adjust in ways that barely affected daily routines. They might live in slightly smaller houses, drive more fuel-efficient vehicles, or eat out a bit less. These are inconveniences, not tragedies.

But popular expectations would be dashed. Even assuming a full recovery from the Great Recession—possible, though not certain—the resulting prosperity will be qualified by greater competition for scarce economic resources. Massive federal budget deficits are only the most conspicuous sign of a society that has promised itself more than it can afford. To resurrect a familiar metaphor: A more slowly growing economic pie will face more claimants for slices. Some will receive bigger slices, others smaller.

Generally speaking, there are two types of economic mobility, though they're often confused. The first is intergenerational mobility (also called "relative mobility"). It involves children moving up or down the economic ladder from their parents' position—do they rise to the top, stay where they started, or fall toward the bottom? Call the second type "national" mobility (specialists refer to it as "absolute mobility"). It concerns whether or not most members of each succeeding generation live better than their predecessors. If they do, then the whole society can be upwardly mobile even if all children occupy the same position relative to others as their parents on the social ladder. To take an obvious example, the poorest third of Americans lived much better in 1980 than in 1930.

In the United States, both types of mobility abound. For starters, birth is not fate. Americans do not automatically match their parents' position on the economic ladder. A report by the Pew Economic Mobility Project finds that 61 percent of children born to parents in the richest fifth of Americans fall from that stratum, while 58 percent of children born in the poorest fifth rise above to a higher stratum. There's not much movement from the very

bottom to the very top. Only six percent of children make that journey. But in between, there's much shifting.

Similarly, economic growth since World War II has allowed most Americans to live better than their parents did—even if they haven't moved up the economic ladder. In the first two postwar decades, household incomes roughly doubled. Despite slower growth since then, about two-thirds of today's Americans have higher incomes than their parents at a similar age, Pew finds. Even this understates the extent of the achievement, because some of those who lost ground still have relatively high incomes. They're children of well-to-do families who don't match their parents' status, but their fall has been modest. Among the poorest fifth of Americans, about four-fifths have incomes higher than their parents'.

Both types of mobility have contributed to America's success. Although studies suggest that intergenerational mobility—again, children moving up or down the economic ladder—is greater in some other countries, the United States has enough of it to foster the bedrock belief that striving and talent are rewarded. That is important because societies in which economic status is rigid discriminate against individual ability and effort and discourage parents from striving to help their children succeed. As for national (or "absolute") mobility, it affects social peace and satisfaction, because intergenerational mobility is a zero-sum game. For everyone who climbs the ladder into a higher stratum, someone else must fall down into a lower one. By contrast, a rising tide does lift all boats.

Even if the United States fully recovers from the Great Recession, Americans will endure greater competition for scarce economic resources.

But there's a rub: Upward national mobility requires strong economic growth—and U.S. growth is weakening. Growth comes from two sources: more labor (more workers or longer hours) and improved efficiency (or labor productivity, measured in output per hour). Unfortunately, slower labor force expansion virtually guarantees a decline in overall U.S. economic growth.

As economist Brink Lindsey of the Kauffman Foundation notes, two powerful trends boosted labor force growth for many years: the influx of baby boomers from the late 1960s to the mid-1980s, and the flood of married women into jobs starting in the

U.S. Economic Growth, 1950–2040

	1950–2011	2002–2011	2012–2022	2023–2040
Annual GDP growth (%) due to:				
Labor force increases	1.5	0.8	0.7	0.5
Productivity increases	1.8	1.4	1.7	1.7
Total annual growth	**3.3**	**2.3**	**2.3**	**2.2**

Note: Some numbers do not add due to rounding
Sources: Congressional Budget Office, Social Security Administration

late 1950s. Both trends have ended. Baby boomers are retiring; the oldest ones, born in 1946, turned 65 in 2011. And women's participation ebbed a decade ago, well before the recession, with some women deciding to stay home or retire early. (From 1960 to 1999, the labor force participation rate of women 16 and over rose from 38 percent to 60 percent; in 2011, it was 58 percent.)

As a result of these trends, the number of new workers barely exceeds the number of those retiring. Barring major pleasant surprises, the slower labor force increases reduce projections of overall economic growth from a postwar average of slightly more than three percent to slightly more than two percent, as the table below shows. (The table shows "potential" economic growth under assumed conditions of "full employment," but actual results are also affected by business cycles.)

Ideally, we would raise productivity to offset slower labor force growth. Realistically, we don't know how to do this. What creates higher productivity is a murky mixture of new technologies, industry organization, government policies, management competence, worker abilities, and market pressures. Economists don't fully understand the process and can't manipulate it. Future rates of productivity growth could as easily fall as rise. In the table, the assumed annual gains average 1.7 percent, near the post–World War II rate of 1.8 percent. But gains might be two percent, one percent, or who knows what. Large deficits and higher taxes may crowd out investment or discourage risk taking, slowing productivity increases. That would further trim future economic growth, making it even harder for the young to achieve upward mobility.

It's already hard enough. The mounting number of retirees increases pressure to move money from workers to the elderly. Consider that in 1960 the worker-to-retiree ratio was 5:1; in 2010 it was 3:1, and the projection for 2025 is nearly 2:1. At the federal level, the pressures stem from higher spending on Social Security, Medicare, and Medicaid. At the state and local levels, they stem from Medicaid (states pay about 40 percent of its costs) and pensions for government workers. In *The Predictable Surprise: The Unraveling of the U.S. Retirement System* (2012), Sylvester Schieber, an actuary and former chairman of the Social Security Advisory Board, estimates that state and local public employee pensions are 20 to 25 percent underfunded.

Higher taxes to pay for Social Security and Medicare will undermine after-tax wages. So will mounting employer costs for health insurance and pensions; these expenses limit what companies would otherwise pay in wage increases. Schieber estimates that all these factors could absorb two-thirds of compensation growth from 2015 to 2030. Other studies reach similar conclusions. Economist David Auerbach and physician Arthur Kellermann, both of the Rand Corporation, find that 80 percent of median-family income gains from 1999 to 2009 went to higher health spending in the form of employer-paid premiums, out-of-pocket costs, and taxes. And these studies don't count the cost of infrastructure repair.

The future of today's young has been heavily mortgaged. The grimmest prospect is a death spiral for the welfare state. That could happen if we continue to pay for promised benefits by increasing taxes or deficits, further retarding economic growth and thus spurring still more tax and deficit increases to sustain benefits. But to all of these unsettling possibilities,

there's a ritualistic, upbeat response: We shall overcome. We're a can-do people. The U.S. economy adapts to change. It creates new technologies and industries. Its long-term resilience is incontestable. As Vice President Joseph Biden once put it, "No one's ever made money betting against America."

Unfortunately, that isn't true. Many people have made money betting against America: those who sold stocks in August 1929 or sold the dollar in the late 1970s, and those who bet against the U.S. mortgage market in 2006. The list goes on. It's true that over long stretches—decades—the U.S. economy has generated higher living standards for most citizens. But even this truth is selective. Banking panics occurred regularly in the 1800s. In the mid- to late 19th century, disease and poor diets lowered living standards of urban workers. Then came the Great Depression, the Great Inflation, and now the Great Recession.

So: America is not entitled to economic success. What actually happens depends on private markets and public policies. To be sure, the future is not etched in stone. Uncertainties abound, as any prediction must acknowledge. Here are three caveats.

First, forecasts of the future as an extension of the present are suspect. Unforeseen events—for good and ill—intervene. History is littered with false prophets. Consider Harvard economist Alvin Hansen (1887–1975). In 1938, when unemployment was still 19 percent, he sought to explain why the U.S. economy couldn't shake the Depression. His answer was "secular stagnation." There was no engine of expansion. Slower population growth meant fewer new consumers and less reason for businesses to invest. Technology was not advancing, dampening investment in new industry. And decades earlier the "frontier" had effectively ceased to exist, so there was no longer any spending on new settlements to boost the economy.

It was all plausible—and wrong. After World War II, the baby boom created a population explosion. Countless technologies spawned new industries in television, aviation, synthetic fibers, and plastics, to name a few. And there was a new frontier to settle—suburbia.

The second caveat is that economic progress may be overrated. Younger Americans may be less obsessed with material goods as the be all and end all of a satisfying life. Moreover, many Americans will enjoy rising incomes over their lifetimes, reflecting experience and seniority. In 2009, for example, the median income of working men aged 45 to 54 was 40 percent higher than for their counterparts aged 25 to 34. Viewing their own lives, most Americans might feel upwardly mobile. The difference would be that tomorrow's 45-year-olds might have less than today's.

Finally, we are not helpless. We might mitigate the forces that assail a broad-based affluence. Just because health spending hasn't been tamed in the past doesn't mean it won't be tamed in the future. As society ages, Americans may recognize that longer life expectancies justify longer working lives and that wealthier retirees deserve fewer (or no) subsidies from less affluent younger workers. That could lead to steps that would reduce the burdens of the old on the young.

Though the future will doubtlessly differ from how anyone now imagines it, the trends fostering downward mobility are insistent, because they are rooted in demographics, politics, and global economics.

We are at a symbolic turning point. The coincidence of the Great Recession with baby boomers' retirements marks the eclipse of the post—World War II social compact, formed in the 1950s and '60s. That arrangement promised that business cycles would be mild, because economic policy could moderate booms and busts. Technological change would be gradual, because dominant firms such as General Electric, AT&T, and General Motors controlled it and had a stake in gradual change. Large institutions were mostly benign. Major corporations provided career jobs and generous fringe benefits (health insurance, pensions) for most of their workers. There were reciprocal loyalties and obligations between employee and employer. Greater wealth enabled government to create a safety net for the old, the disabled, and the poor.

The props underlying this unspoken compact have been weakening since 1980. Technological changes are no longer gradual; they're abrupt and disruptive, driven largely by computer hardware and software companies, or Web-based enterprises such as Google and Facebook. Career jobs still exist but are dwindling in number. The reciprocal loyalties between workers and their employers have weakened. The promise of overall economic stability seems hollow. The fundamental lesson of the 2007–09 financial crisis is that economists overestimated their ability to prevent calamitous boom-bust cycles. Globalization has increased economic complexity faster than economists' capacity to keep up. The social safety net—actually, the welfare state—is popular, but huge government deficits put its affordability in doubt.

The premise of the post–World War II affluent society, that we were or would soon become so rich that we could afford almost anything, was never true, but we often acted as if it were. We avoided unpleasant choices, especially in government, accepting routine federal budget deficits (46 out of 51 years since 1961). Now, limits are painfully evident. There are more promises than can be fulfilled. Meeting all of government's spending commitments would require higher, broad-based taxes, which both liberals and conservatives reject, or perpetually large deficits, which both parties consider unsustainable and undesirable.

What looms is a future of more distributional struggles between young and old, rich and poor, different regions, and many interest groups. Each will defend subsidies, work to avoid tax increases, and maneuver for regulatory advantage.

The role of economic growth in advanced nations is less to make people richer than to reduce conflict. If most people feel that they're "getting ahead," they're less resentful of others who are doing better or hold different views. "Periods of economic expansion in America and elsewhere, during which most citizens had reason to be optimistic, have also witnessed greater openness, tolerance, and democracy," writes Harvard economist Benjamin Friedman in *The Moral Consequences of Economic Growth* (2005). If, however, people fall behind—or fear they will—they become more resentful. Until the Great Recession, three decades of growing economic inequality had inspired little popular backlash. This changed after unemployment rose. The Tea Party and Occupy Wall Street movements reflect the fallout of feared downward mobility.

Lower economic growth will have broad consequences. Already, defense spending is headed toward claiming the lowest share of GDP since 1940. In effect, the welfare state is defeating the Pentagon. Some will cheer, others complain. Either way, America's global role will change.

The prospect of downward mobility could discourage younger Americans from marrying and having families—a development that would accelerate America's aging. Although people marry and have children for many reasons, their economic outlook is an important influence. Low-income men are not prime candidates for marriage. Birthrates collapsed in the 1930s because families worried that they could not support new offspring. It is surely no coincidence that in the wake of the Great Recession the number of marriages fell five percent in 2010 and births three percent.

As it is, the generations are in an undeclared war. Americans in their late forties, fifties, and sixties believe that the contract made with them should be kept. They want their Social Security and Medicare benefits. They are angry when what they thought were career jobs are unexpectedly terminated; corporate buy-outs and firings weren't part of the bargain. Meanwhile, their children and grandchildren are befuddled and frustrated. Their unemployment rates are high, and their wage levels—compared to those of the past—are low. Yet they feel guilty advocating trims to Social Security and Medicare, even when the transfers go from the struggling young to the comfortable old.

The Affluent Society was more a state of mind than an explicit economic target or threshold level of income. It announced the arrival of an era when traditional economic concerns were being overwhelmed by a seemingly unstoppable flood of abundance. Prosperity was a panacea. We could afford a decent society as well as a wealthy society. Many traditional social, political, and economic choices could, with a little patience, be evaded. There was enough for almost everything. We have been, in historian David Potter's apt phrase, a "people of plenty." What happens when there is less plenty than we expected? We are about to find out.

Critical Thinking

1. Why does Samuelson believe that even after the recovery America's economic growth will be small? Can anything be done to change this?

2. What are the massive transfers that will slow down the economy?

ROBERT J. SAMUELSON, a columnist for *The Washington Post,* is the author most recently of *The Great Inflation and Its Aftermath: The Past and Future of American Affluence* (2008).

Hard at Work in the Jobless Future

JAMES H. LEE

Futurists have long been following the impacts of automation on jobs—not just in manufacturing, but also increasingly in white-collar work. Those in financial services, for example, are being lost to software algorithms, intelligent computers, and robotics.

Terms used for this phenomenon include "off-peopling" and "other-sourcing." As Jared Weiner of Weiner, Edrich, Brown recently observed, "Those jobs are not going to return—they can be done more efficiently and error-free by intelligent software."

In the investment business (in which I work), we are seeing the replacement of financial analysts with quantitative analytic systems, and floor traders with trading algorithms. Mutual funds and traditional portfolio managers now compete against ETFs (exchange-traded funds), many of which offer completely automated strategies.

Industries that undergo this transformation don't disappear, but the number of jobs that they support changes drastically. Consider the business of farming, which employed half the population in the early 1900s but now provides just 3% of all jobs. The United States is still a huge exporter of food; it is simply a far more efficient food producer now in terms of total output per farm worker.

In an ideal world, jobs would be plentiful, competitive, and pay well. Most job opportunities have two of these qualities but not all three.

Medicine, law, and finance are jobs that are both competitive and pay well. Retail, hospitality, and personal services are competitive but pay low wages. Unions often ensure that jobs pay well and are plentiful, only to later find that those jobs and related industries are no longer competitive.

Since 1970, manufacturing jobs as a percentage of total employment have declined from a quarter of payrolls to less than 10%. Some of this decline is from outsourcing, some is a result of other-sourcing. Those looking for a rebound in manufacturing jobs will likely be disappointed. These jobs will probably not be replaced—not in the United States and possibly not overseas, either.

This is all a part of the transition toward a postindustrial economy.

Jeff Dachis, Internet consulting legend and founder of Razorfish, coined the phrase "everything that can be digital, will be." To the extent that the world becomes more digital, it will also become more global. To the extent that the economy remains physical, business may become more local.

The question is, what is the future of work, and what can we do about it? Here are some ideas.

The Future of Work: Emerging Trends

Work will always be about finding what other people want and need, and then creating practical solutions to fulfill those desires. Our basic assumptions about how work gets done are what's changing. It's less about having a fixed location and schedule and more about thoughtful and engaged activity. Increasingly, this inspiration can happen anytime, anyplace.

Jobs are disappearing, but there's still a future for work. An investment manager looks at how automation and information technology are changing the economic landscape and forcing workers to forge new career paths beyond outdated ideas about permanent employment.

There is a blurring of distinctions among work, play, and professional development. The ways that we measure productivity will be less focused on time spent and more about the value of the ideas and the quality of the output. People are also going to have a much better awareness of when good work is being done.

The old model of work provided an enormous level of predictability. In previous eras, people had a sense of job security and knew how much they would earn on a monthly basis. This gave people a certain sense of confidence in their ability to maintain large amounts of debt. The consumer economy thrived on this system for more than half a century. Location-based and formal jobs will continue to exist, of course, but these will become smaller slices of the overall economy.

The new trends for the workplace have significantly less built-in certainty. We will all need to rethink, redefine, and broaden our sources of economic security. To the extent that people are developing a broader range of skills, we will also become more resilient and capable of adapting to change.

Finally, we can expect that people will redefine what they truly need in a physical sense and find better ways of fulfilling their needs. This involves sharing and making smarter use of the assets we already have. Businesses are doing the same.

The outcome could be an economy that balances the needs between economic efficiency and human values.

Multitasking Careers

In Escape from Cubicle Nation (Berkley Trade, 2010), career coach Pamela Slim encourages corporate employees to start a "side hustle" to try out new business ideas. She also recommends having a side hustle as a backup plan in the event of job loss. This strategy is not just for corporate types, and Slim says that "it can also be a great backup for small business owners affected by shifting markets and slow sales."

She says that an ideal side hustle is money-making activity that is doable, enjoyable, can generate quick cash flow, and does not require significant investment. Examples that she includes are businesses such as Web design, massage, tax preparation, photography, and personal training.

The new norm is for people to maintain and develop skill sets in multiple simultaneous careers. In this environment, the ability to learn is something of a survival skill. Education never stops, and the line between working and learning becomes increasingly blurred.

After getting her PhD in gastrointestinal medicine, Helen Samson Mullen spent years working for a pharmaceutical company—first as a medical researcher and then as an independent consultant. More recently, she has been getting certifications for her career transition as a life coach. Clinical project management is now her "side hustle" to bring in cash flow while she builds her coaching business. Meanwhile, she's also writing a book and manages her own website. Even with so many things happening at once, Helen told me that "life is so much less crazy now than it was when I was consulting. I was always searching for life balance and now feel like I'm moving into harmony." Her husband, Rob, is managing some interesting career shifts of his own, and is making a lateral move from a 22-year career in pharmaceuticals to starting his own insurance agency with State Farm.

Fixed hours, fixed location, and fixed jobs are quickly becoming a thing of the past for many industries, as opportunities become more fluid and transient. The 40-hour workweek is becoming less relevant as we see more subcontractors, temps, freelancers, and self-employed. The U.S. Government Accountability Office estimates that these "contingent workers" now make up a third of the workforce. Uncertain economics make long-term employment contracts less realistic, while improvements in communications make it easier to subcontract even complex jobs to knowledge workers who log in from airports, home offices, and coffee shops.

Results-Only Workplace Environments

Imagine an office where meetings are optional. Nobody talks about how many hours they worked last week. People have an unlimited amount of vacation and paid time off. Work is done anytime and anywhere, based entirely on individual needs and preferences. Finally, employees at all levels are encouraged to stop doing anything that is a waste of their time, their customers' time, or the company's time.

There is a catch: Quality work needs to be completed on schedule and within budget.

Sound like a radical utopia? These are all basic principles of the Results Only Work Environment (ROWE), as pioneered by Cali Ressler and Jody Thompson while they were human resource managers for Best Buy.

It's "management by objective" taken to a whole new level, Ressler and Thompson write in their book, Why Work Sucks and How to Fix It (Portfolio, 2008).

Best Buy's headquarters was one of the first offices to implement the ROWE a little over five years ago, according to Ressler and Thompson. The movement is small, but growing. The Gap Outlet, Valspar, and a number of Minneapolis-based municipal departments have implemented the strategy. Today, 10,000 employees now work in some form of ROWE.

Employees don't even know if they are working fewer hours (they no longer count them), but firms that have adopted the practice have often shown significant improvements in productivity.

"Thanks to ROWE, people at Best Buy are happier with their lives and their work," Ressler and Thompson write in their book. "The company has benefited, too, with increases in productivity averaging 35% and sharp decreases in voluntary turnover rates, as much as 90% in some divisions."

Interestingly enough, the process tends to reveal workers who do not produce results, causing involuntary terminations to creep upward. ROWE managers learn how to treat their employees like responsible grown-ups. There is no time tracking or micromanagement.

"The funny thing is that once employees experience a ROWE they don't want to work any other way," they write. "So employees give back. They get smarter about their work because they want to make sure they get results. They know that if they can deliver results then in exchange they will get trust and control over their time."

Co-Working

There are now more alternatives to either working at home alone or being part of a much larger office. Co-working spaces are shared work facilities where people can get together in an officelike environment while telecommuting or starting up new businesses.

"We provide space and opportunity for people that don't have it," Wes Garnett, founder of The coIN Loft, a co-working space in Wilmington, Delaware, told me.

Getting office space in the traditional sense can be an expensive proposition—with multiyear leases, renovation costs, monthly utilities. "For $200 [a month], you can have access to presentation facilities, a conference room, and a dedicated place to work." And coIN Loft offers day rates for people with less-frequent space needs.

According to Garnett, more people are going to co-working spaces as "community centers for people with ideas and entrepreneurial inclinations." He explains that co-working spaces provide a physical proximity that allows people to develop natural networks and exchange ideas on projects.

"We all know that we're happier and more productive together, than alone" is the motto for nearby Independents Hall in Philadelphia.

Co-working visas enable people to choose from among 200 locations across the United States and in three dozen other countries.

Silicon Colleagues

Expert systems such as IBM's Watson are now "smarter" than real people—at least on the game show Jeopardy. It was a moment in television history when Watson decimated previous human champions Ken Jennings and Brad Rutter on trivia questions, which included categories such as "Chicks Dig Me."

IBM's Watson is a software-based knowledge system with unusually robust voice recognition. IBM has stated that its initial markets for the technology are health care, financial services, and customer relations. In the beginning, these systems will work side-by-side with human agents, whispering in their ear to prompt them with appropriate questions and answers that they might not have considered otherwise. In the next decade, they may replace people altogether in jobs that require simple requests for information.

"It's a way for America to get back its call centers," **futurist** Garry Golden told me. He sees such expert systems reaching the workplace in the next two to three years.

Opting Out

A changing economy is causing people to rethink their priorities. In a recent survey by Ogilvy and Mather, 76% of respondents reported that they would rather spend more time with their families than make more money.

Similarly, the Associated Press has reported that less than half of all Americans say they are happy with their jobs.

Given the stresses of the modern workplace, it is not surprising that more people are simply "opting out" of the workforce. Since 1998, there has been a slight decline in the labor force participation rate—about 5% for men and 3% for women. This trend may accelerate once extensions to unemployment benefits expire. Some of these people are joining the DIY movement, and others are becoming homesteaders.

A shift back toward one-income households can happen when the costs of taxes, commuting, and child care consume a large portion of earnings. People who opt out are not considered unemployed, as they are no longer actively looking for paid work. Their focus often reflects a shift in values toward other activities, such as raising kids, volunteer work, or living simply. This type of lifestyle is often precarious and carries risks, two factors that can be mitigated through public policy that extends the social safety net to better cover informal working as well as formal employment. But this way of life also carries rewards and is becoming a more and more attractive option for millions of people.

The Future of Work, Personified

Justin Caggiano is a laid-back rock-climbing guide whom my wife and I met during our last vacation in the red canyons of Moab, Utah. He's also been guiding rafters, climbers, and hikers for the past six years.

We watched Justin scramble up the side of a hundred-foot natural wall called The Ice Cream Parlor, a nearby climbing destination that earned its name from keeping shaded and cool in the morning despite the surrounding desert. His wiry frame allowed him to navigate the canyon cliffs and set up the safety ropes in a fraction of the time that it took us to make the same climb later that day.

Justin's rock-climbing skills easily translated into work as an arborist during the off-season, climbing up trees and then cutting them from the top down to prevent damage to nearby buildings. Since graduating from college six years ago, he has also worked as an artisanal baker, a carpenter, and a house painter. This makes him something of a down-to-earth renaissance man.

His advice is "to be as flexible as you can—and work your tail off."

It's an itinerant lifestyle for Justin, who frequently changes his location based on the season, work, and nearby climbing opportunities. Rather than committing to a single employer, he pieces together jobs wherever he can find them. His easygoing personality enables him to connect with people and find new opportunities when they become available.

In the winter, he planned to stay with a friend who is building a house, trading help with carpentry and wiring in exchange for free rent. He's been living on a shoestring for a while now, putting away money every year. Longer term, he'd like to develop all of the skills that he needs to build his own home and then pay for land and materials entirely with savings from his bank account. He plans to grow fruit trees and become somewhat self-sufficient. After that time, he says, "I'll work when I'm needed, and live the debt-free, low-cost lifestyle when I'm older."

Our concept of work is getting reworked. A career used to be a ladder of opportunities within a single company. For the postwar generation, the concept of "lifetime employment" was a realistic expectation. My father worked for 40 years at DuPont as a research scientist and spent almost all of that time at a sprawling complex called the Experimental Station. Most of my friends' parents had similar careers. Over time, they were gradually promoted and moved up the corporate ladder. At best, it was a steady progression. At worst, they found their careers stuck in neutral.

The baby boomers had a somewhat different career trajectory. They still managed to have a single career, but it more closely resembled a lattice than a ladder. After working for an employer for five to 10 years, they might find a better opportunity elsewhere and continue their climb. The successful ones cultivated networks at related businesses and continually found better opportunities for themselves.

The career path for younger generations more closely resembles a patchwork quilt, as people attempt to stitch together multiple jobs into something that is flexible and works for them. In today's environment, they sometimes can't find a single job that is big enough to cover all of their expenses, so, like Justin, they find themselves working multiple jobs simultaneously. Some of these jobs might match and be complementary to existing skills, while others may be completely unrelated.

The future of work is less secure and less stable than it was. For many of us, our notions of employment were formed by the labor environment of the later twentieth century. But the reality of jobless working may be more in line with our values. If we can build support systems to benefit workers, wherever they are and whether they be formally employed or not, then we may be able to view the changes sweeping across society as opportunities to return to a fuller, more genuine, and more honest way of life.

Justin's lesson is applicable to all of us; there's a difference between earning a living and making a life.

Justin Caggiano, a rock climber who shows how flexibility and hard work can lead to success even without a steady job.

Critical Thinking

1. What are causes of the shrinking number of jobs relative to job seekers in America?
2. What are the ramifications of less jobs in the future?

JAMES H. LEE is an investment manager in Wilmington, Delaware, and a blogger for *The Futurist* magazine.

Urban Legends

Why Suburbs, Not Cities, Are the Answer

JOEL KOTKIN

The human world is fast becoming an urban world— and according to many, the faster that happens and the bigger the cities get, the better off we all will be. The old suburban model, with families enjoying their own space in detached houses, is increasingly behind us; we're heading toward heavier reliance on public transit, greater density, and far less personal space. Global cities, even colossal ones like Mumbai and Mexico City, represent our cosmopolitan future, we're now told; they will be nerve centers of international commerce and technological innovation just like the great metropolises of the past—only with the Internet and smart phones.

According to Columbia University's Saskia Sassen, mega-cities will inevitably occupy what Vladimir Lenin called the "commanding heights" of the global economy, though instead of making things they'll apparently be specializing in high-end "producer services"—advertising, law, accounting, and so forth—for worldwide clients. Other scholars, such as Harvard University's Edward Glaeser, envision universities helping to power the new "skilled city," where high wages and social amenities attract enough talent to enable even higher-cost urban meccas to compete.

The theory goes beyond established Western cities. A recent World Bank report on global megacities insists that when it comes to spurring economic growth, denser is better: "To try to spread out economic activity," the report argues, is to snuff it. Historian Peter Hall seems to be speaking for a whole generation of urbanists when he argues that we are on the cusp of a "coming golden age" of great cities.

The only problem is, these predictions may not be accurate. Yes, the percentage of people living in cities is clearly growing. In 1975, Tokyo was the largest city in the world, with over 26 million residents, and there were only two other cities worldwide with more than 10 million residents. By 2025, the U.N. projects that there may be 27 cities of that size. The proportion of the world's population living in cities, which has already shot up from 14 percent in 1900 to about 50 percent in 2008, could be 70 percent by 2050. But here's what the boosters don't tell you: It's far less clear whether the extreme centralization and concentration advocated by these new urban utopians is inevitable—and it's not at all clear that it's desirable.

Not all Global Cities are created equal. We can hope the developing-world metropolises of the future will look a lot like the developed-world cities of today, just much, much larger— but that's not likely to be the case. Today's Third World megacities face basic challenges in feeding their people, getting them to and from work, and maintaining a minimum level of health. In some, like Mumbai, life expectancy is now at least seven years less than the country as a whole. And many of the world's largest advanced cities are nestled in relatively declining economies—London, Los Angeles, New York, Tokyo. All suffer growing income inequality and outward migration of middle-class families. Even in the best of circumstances, the new age of the megacity might well be an era of unparalleled human congestion and gross inequality.

Perhaps we need to consider another approach. As unfashionable as it might sound, what if we thought less about the benefits of urban density and more about the many possibilities for proliferating more human-scaled urban centers; what if healthy growth turns out to be best achieved through dispersion, not concentration? Instead of overcrowded cities rimmed by hellish new slums, imagine a world filled with vibrant smaller cities, suburbs, and towns: Which do you think is likelier to produce a higher quality of life, a cleaner environment, and a lifestyle conducive to creative thinking?

So how do we get there? First, we need to dismantle some common urban legends.

Perhaps the most damaging misconception of all is the idea that concentration by its very nature creates wealth. Many writers, led by popular theorist Richard Florida, argue that centralized urban areas provide broader cultural opportunities and better access to technology, attracting more innovative, plugged-in people (Florida's "creative class") who will in the long term produce greater economic vibrancy. The hipper the city, the mantra goes, the richer and more successful it will be— and a number of declining American industrial hubs have tried to rebrand themselves as "creative class" hot spots accordingly.

But this argument, or at least many applications of it, gets things backward. Arts and culture generally do not fuel economic growth by themselves; rather, economic growth tends to create the preconditions for their development. Ancient Athens and Rome didn't start out as undiscovered artist neighborhoods. They were metropolises built on imperial wealth—largely collected by force from their colonies—that funded a new class of patrons and consumers of the arts. Renaissance Florence and Amsterdam established themselves as trade centers first and only then began to nurture great artists from their own middle classes and the surrounding regions.

Even modern Los Angeles owes its initial ascendancy as much to agriculture and oil as to Hollywood. Today, its port and related industries employ far more people than the entertainment business does. (In any case, the men who built Hollywood were hardly cultured aesthetes by middle-class American standards; they were furriers, butchers, and petty traders, mostly from hardscrabble backgrounds in the czarist *shtetls* and back streets of America's tough ethnic ghettos.) New York, now arguably the world's cultural capital, was once dismissed as a boorish, money-obsessed town, much like the contemporary urban critique of Dallas, Houston, or Phoenix.

Sadly, cities desperate to reverse their slides have been quick to buy into the simplistic idea that by merely branding themselves "creative" they can renew their dying economies; think of Cleveland's Rock and Roll Hall of Fame, Michigan's bid to market Detroit as a "cool city," and similar efforts in the washed-up industrial towns of the British north. Being told you live in a "European Capital of Culture," as Liverpool was in 2008, means little when your city has no jobs and people are leaving by the busload.

Even legitimate cultural meccas aren't insulated from economic turmoil. Berlin—beloved by writers, artists, tourists, and romantic expatriates—has cultural institutions that would put any wannabe European Capital of Culture to shame, as well as a thriving underground art and music scene. Yet for all its bohemian spirit, Berlin is also deeply in debt and suffers from unemployment far higher than Germany's national average, with rates reaching 14 percent. A full quarter of its workers, many of them living in wretched immigrant ghettos, earn less than 900 euros a month; compare that with Frankfurt, a smaller city more known for its skyscrapers and airport terminals than for any major cultural output, but which boasts one of Germany's lowest unemployment rates and by some estimates the highest per capita income of any European city. No wonder Berlin Mayor Klaus Wowereit once described his city as "poor but sexy."

Culture, media, and other "creative" industries, important as they are for a city's continued prosperity, simply do not spark an economy on their own. It turns out to be the comparatively boring, old-fashioned industries, such as trade in goods, manufacturing, energy, and agriculture, that drive the world's fastest-rising cities. In the 1960s and 1970s, the industrial capitals of Seoul and Tokyo developed their economies far faster than Cairo and Jakarta, which never created advanced industrial bases. China's great coastal urban centers, notably Guangzhou, Shanghai, and Shenzhen, are replicating this pattern with big business in steel, textiles, garments,

and electronics, and the country's vast interior is now poised to repeat it once again. Fossil fuels—not art galleries—have powered the growth of several of the world's fastest-rising urban areas, including Abu Dhabi, Houston, Moscow, and Perth.

It's only after urban centers achieve economic success that they tend to look toward the higher-end amenities the creative-classers love. When Abu Dhabi decided to import its fancy Guggenheim and Louvre satellite museums, it was already, according to *Fortune* magazine, the world's richest city. Beijing, Houston, Shanghai, and Singapore are opening or expanding schools for the arts, museums, and gallery districts. But they paid for them the old-fashioned way.

Nor is the much-vaunted "urban core" the only game in town. Innovators of all kinds seek to avoid the high property prices, overcrowding, and often harsh anti-business climates of the city center. Britain's recent strides in technology and design-led manufacturing have been concentrated not in London, but along the outer reaches of the Thames Valley and the areas around Cambridge. It's the same story in continental Europe, from the exurban Grand-Couronne outside of Paris to the "edge cities" that have sprung up around Amsterdam and Rotterdam. In India, the bulk of new tech companies cluster in campus-like developments around—but not necessarily in—Bangalore, Hyderabad, and New Delhi. And let's not forget that Silicon Valley, the granddaddy of global tech centers and still home to the world's largest concentration of high-tech workers, remains essentially a vast suburb. Apple, Google, and Intel don't seem to mind. Those relative few who choose to live in San Francisco can always take the company-provided bus.

In fact, the suburbs are not as terrible as urban boosters frequently insist.

Consider the environment. We tend to associate suburbia with carbon dioxide-producing sprawl and urban areas with sustainability and green living. But though it's true that urban residents use less gas to get to work than their suburban or rural counterparts, when it comes to overall energy use the picture gets more complicated. Studies in Australia and Spain have found that when you factor in apartment common areas, second residences, consumption, and air travel, urban residents can easily use more energy than their less densely packed neighbors. Moreover, studies around the world—from Beijing and Rome to London and Vancouver—have found that packed concentrations of concrete, asphalt, steel, and glass produce what are known as "heat islands," generating 6 to 10 degrees Celsius more heat than surrounding areas and extending as far as twice a city's political boundaries.

When it comes to inequality, cities might even be the problem. In the West, the largest cities today also tend to suffer the most extreme polarization of incomes. In 1980, Manhattan ranked 17th among U.S. counties for income disparity; by 2007 it was first, with the top fifth of wage earners earning 52 times what the bottom fifth earned. In Toronto between 1970 and 2001, according to one recent study, middle-income neighborhoods shrank by half, dropping from two-thirds of the city to one-third, while poor districts more than doubled to 40 percent. By 2020, middle-class neighborhoods could fall to about 10 percent.

Cities often offer a raw deal for the working class, which ends up squeezed by a lethal combination of chronically high housing costs and chronically low opportunity in economies dominated by finance and other elite industries. Once the cost of living is factored in, more than half the children in inner London live in poverty, the highest level in Britain, according to a Greater London Authority study. More than 1 million Londoners were on public support in 2002, in a city of roughly 8 million.

The disparities are even starker in Asia. Shenzhen and Hong Kong, for instance, have among the most skewed income distributions in the region. A relatively small number of skilled professionals and investors are doing very well, yet millions are migrating to urban slums in places like Mumbai not because they've all suddenly become "knowledge workers," but because of the changing economics of farming. And by the way, Mumbai's slums are still expanding as a proportion of the city's overall population—even as India's nationwide poverty rate has fallen from one in three Indians to one in five over the last two decades. Forty years ago, slum dwellers accounted for one in six Mumbaikars. Now they are a majority.

To their credit, talented new urbanists have had moderate success in turning smaller cities like Chattanooga and Hamburg into marginally more pleasant places to live. But grandiose theorists, with their focus on footloose elites and telecommuting technogeniuses, have no practical answers for the real problems that plague places like Mumbai, let alone Cairo, Jakarta, Manila, Nairobi, or any other 21st-century megacity: rampant crime, crushing poverty, choking pollution. It's time for a completely different approach, one that abandons the long-held assumption that scale and growth go hand in hand.

Throughout the long history of urban development, the size of a city roughly correlated with its wealth, standard of living, and political strength. The greatest and most powerful cities were almost always the largest in population: Babylon, Rome, Alexandria, Baghdad, Delhi, London, or New York.

But bigger might no longer mean better. The most advantaged city of the future could well turn out to be a much smaller one. Cities today are expanding at an unparalleled rate when it comes to size, but wealth, power, and general well-being lag behind. With the exception of Los Angeles, New York, and Tokyo, most cities of 10 million or more are relatively poor, with a low standard of living and little strategic influence. The cities that do have influence, modern infrastructure, and relatively high per capita income, by contrast, are often wealthy small cities like Abu Dhabi or hard-charging up-and-comers such as Singapore. Their efficient, agile economies can outpace lumbering megacities financially, while also maintaining a high quality of life. With almost 5 million residents, for example, Singapore isn't at the top of the list in terms of population. But its GDP is much higher than that of larger cities like Cairo, Lagos, and Manila. Singapore boasts a per capita income of almost $50,000, one of the highest in the world, roughly the same as America's or Norway's. With one of the world's three largest ports, a zippy and safe subway system, and an impressive skyline, Singapore is easily the cleanest, most efficient big city in all of Asia. Other smaller-scaled cities like Austin, Monterrey, and Tel Aviv have enjoyed similar success.

It turns out that the rise of the megacity is by no means inevitable—and it might not even be happening. Shlomo Angel, an adjunct professor at New York University's Wagner School, has demonstrated that as the world's urban population exploded from 1960 to 2000, the percentage living in the 100 largest megacities actually declined from nearly 30 percent to closer to 25 percent. Even the widely cited 2009 World Bank report on megacities, a staunchly pro-urban document, acknowledges that as societies become wealthier, they inevitably begin to deconcentrate, with the middle classes moving to the periphery. Urban population densities have been on the decline since the 19th century, Angel notes, as people have sought out cheaper and more appealing homes beyond city limits. In fact, despite all the "back to the city" hype of the past decade, more than 80 percent of new metropolitan growth in the United States since 2000 has been in suburbs.

And that's not such a bad thing. Ultimately, dispersion—both city to suburb and megacity to small city—holds out some intriguing solutions to current urban problems. The idea took hold during the initial golden age of industrial growth—the English 19th century—when suburban "garden cities" were established around London's borders. The great early 20th-century visionary Ebenezer Howard saw this as a means to create a "new civilization" superior to the crowded, dirty, and congested cities of his day. It was an ideal that attracted a wide range of thinkers, including Friedrich Engels and H.G. Wells.

More recently, a network of smaller cities in the Netherlands has helped create a smartly distributed national economy. Amsterdam, for example, has low-density areas between its core and its corporate centers. It has kept the great Dutch city both livable and competitive. American urbanists are trying to bring the same thinking to the United States. Delore Zimmerman, of the North Dakota-based Praxis Strategy Group, has helped foster high-tech-oriented development in small towns and cities from the Red River Valley in North Dakota and Minnesota to the Wenatchee region in Washington State. The outcome has been promising: Both areas are reviving from periods of economic and demographic decline.

But the dispersion model holds out even more hope for the developing world, where an alternative to megacities is an even more urgent necessity. Ashok R. Datar, chairman of the Mumbai Environmental Social Network and a longtime advisor to the Ambani corporate group, suggests that slowing migration to urban slums represents the most practical strategy for relieving Mumbai's relentless poverty. His plan is similar to Zimmerman's: By bolstering local industries, you can stanch the flow of job seekers to major city centers, maintaining a greater balance between rural areas and cities and avoiding the severe overcrowding that plagues Mumbai right now.

Between the 19th century, when Charles Dickens described London as a "sooty spectre" that haunted and deformed its inhabitants, and the present, something has been lost from our discussion of cities: the human element. The goal of urban planners should not be to fulfill their own grandiose visions of megacities on a hill, but to meet the needs of the people living in them, particularly those people suffering from overcrowding, environmental misery, and social inequality. When it comes to exporting our notions to the rest of the globe, we must be aware of our own susceptibility to fashionable theories in urban design—because while the West may be able to live with its mistakes, the developing world doesn't enjoy that luxury.

Critical Thinking

1. Why do some analysts think that megacities are the wave of the future?

2. Why does Kotkin think that smaller cities, suburbs, and towns are the best prospects for the future?

3. What size places sustain the best quality of life?

Immigration Benefits America

Steven J. Gold

David Stoll suggests that because contemporary immigrants are non-European, uneducated, poor, motivated by financial gain and uninterested in joining the moral community of American society, their presence threatens national unity, obscures American citizens' obligations to one another and will shortly change the US into a minority–majority society.

Since immigrants tend to be poor and powerless, their burgeoning existence can be attributed to the endorsement it receives from coastal elites who, Stoll contends, are motivated by either economic self-interest (they seek to exploit the low-cost labor of immigrants), naive idealism (they assume that immigrants will both benefit themselves and the country) or both.

According to Stoll, social transformations brought on by immigrants and their allies will ultimately replace the long-standing bases of American identity—ones rooted in nationalism, shared origins and mutual obligation among citizens—with the hazy concepts of transnationalism and globalism. The economic outcome of this will allow the well-heeled to grow more affluent while everyone else becomes poorer.

Given the negative consequences of contemporary immigration, Stoll encourages Americans to reject this "post national" vision of American society. Instead, we should strive to retain ethnic and nationalistic forms of moral community that emphasize our obligations to the well-being of our fellow citizens before concerning ourselves with the fate of those from elsewhere.

Stoll's characterization of migration's impact on the United States raises several important and controversial issues. However, before we accept his conclusions, it is worthwhile to evaluate the grounds upon which he calculates the negative impact of immigration—economically, socially and morally—on American society.

Students of American history will find a familiar ring to Stoll's warnings. For over 100 years, some members of established factions have worried that immigrants would reduce wages, erode social solidarity and remain loyal to their family, religion or country of origin rather than to the US. While immigration does pose many challenges for the US, there is every reason to believe that it will also provide numerous benefits to the country just as it has in the past. To paraphrase Mark Twain, both historical and contemporary reports of American society's demise as a consequence of the arrival of impoverished and culturally dissimilar immigrants have been greatly exaggerated.

To begin with, I question the author's contentions about the existence of a growing community of scholars and immigration supporters who foresee or desire the end of nations. During the 1980s and 1990s, a few theorists speculated that forms of regional and global governance coupled with free-flowing migration might result in the diminution of the nation state. However, the overwhelming consensus of research, especially that conducted since the events of September 11, 2001, has affirmed the continued importance of nation states as locations of political and economic power as well as national identity.

Stoll's assertions about the economic impact of immigrants on the US have been well-studied, and a preponderance of resulting data would appear to contradict them. First, although he fails to mention it, a considerable fraction of contemporary immigrants to the US are not members of a low-wage migration stream. On the contrary, they are highly educated professionals. These newcomers find employment in well-paid occupations for which there is considerable demand. In 2006, 27% of the foreign-born population age 25 or older had a BA or higher degree, a fraction nearly identical to that of the US population at large. [At the same time, it is true that a larger portion of immigrants have only a high school degree or less than is the case among the native-born US population (Terrazas et al. 2007)].

Such educated migrants work as scientists, technicians, engineers, economists, professors, physicians, nurses and entrepreneurs. Their activities are vital to the most advanced, innovative and profitable sectors in the US economy. Since the US economy demands many more persons with these skills than exist among the native-born, immigrants provide a considerable fraction of the human capital that allows American companies to function and generate good jobs. 40% of PhD scientists working in the US are foreign born. Indeed, according to Duke University scholar Vivek Wadhwa, 52% of the technology start-ups in Silicon Valley, one of the US's greatest engines of recent economic growth, had a CEO or chief engineer born overseas (Bernstein 2009).

The work of these skilled immigrants is also vital to the provision of a wide range of services including healthcare, transportation and public works associated with the standard of living and quality of life that Americans have come to expect.

When highly educated persons come to the US, natives reap the benefits of their costly skills without having to pay for their training. In addition to those who arrive in the US upon the completion of their schooling, immigrant students increase their education here. Accordingly, a significant fraction of the science and technology PhD degrees awarded by American universities go to foreign-born students. Between 70% and 96% of these students stay on to work in the US for at least 5 years after their graduation (Executive Office of the President 2007).

Over and above their professional know-how, foreign-born workers often possess linguistic, cultural, and technical skills and contacts that permit American companies to sell goods and services abroad. In this way, their presence fosters American firms' access to global markets.

Less-skilled immigrants also contribute to Americans' economic well-being. They perform a wide array of essential jobs that few native-born workers are interested in taking, including food service, domestic jobs, meat packing, farm work, construction, light manufacturing and hospitality. Immigrants are disproportionately represented among proprietors of the small businesses that generate employment while making our lives more convenient and communities more lively (Light and Gold 2000).

While opponents to immigration have long claimed that newcomers drive down wages, a significant body of research reveals that the economic impact of immigrants on American life has been highly positive (Fix and Passell 1994). For example, a comprehensive study of the economic impact of immigrants on American society conducted by the National Research Council concluded that immigration delivers a "significant positive gain" of $1 billion to $10 billion each year to native-born Americans (Smith and Edmonston 1997). President George W. Bush's Council of Economic Advisors determined that 90% of the US-born population benefited economically from the presence of immigrants (Executive Office of the President 2007). Findings like these suggest that rather than constituting an economic threat to most American workers, immigrants are an asset.

In addition to these short-term economic benefits, immigrants and their children also contribute to America's long-term population growth. Countries such as Japan, Spain and Italy, which have low birth rates, aging populations and relatively low levels of immigration, face demographic crises, including labor shortages and a demographic crunch in which a relatively small number of workers will be expected to pay for the retirement and health care needs of a sizeable elderly population. The presence of immigrants and their children helps the US population remain comparatively youthful and stave off such troubling scenarios (Wiseman 2005).

The consequences of overpopulation, including high real estate prices, overburdened social services, congested transportation systems and environmental pollution are widely reported in coastal cities and Sunbelt regions of the US. Other parts of the country, however, confront the opposite problem of population loss, which yields labor shortages, declining real estate values and an insufficient level of consumer demand and tax revenue to sustain basic services, schools, and businesses.

Immigrants and refugees are often willing to live in small towns and accept unglamorous but essential jobs in agriculture and other industries. They play critical roles in delivering needed commodities, and allow smaller communities to survive. For this reason, cities like Lansing, Michigan, Fort Wayne, Indiana, Littleton, Colorado and Boise, Idaho have established programs to attract, welcome and assist refugees and immigrants (Migration Policy Institute 2009).

Stoll observes with some alarm that America will soon become a minority–majority society. However, the historical record shows that over time, a number of groups that were initially thought to be inassimilable have found their place in the American mosaic. Accordingly, there is reason to believe that the most recent wave of immigrants will, like those of earlier cohorts, prove to be good citizens and valuable assets to their adopted country.

A century ago, leading intellectuals of the progressive era including Madison Grant, University of Wisconsin sociologist E.A. Ross, Harvard psychologist William MacDougall and patrician author Henry Adams endorsed the eugenics movement. They warned that "alien races" including the Irish, Italians, Greeks, Jews and Poles were incapable of functioning in American society and, through their limited intelligence, base urges and flawed ethics, would pollute the national gene pool while bringing about the downfall of the American way of life. In 1911, the Dillingham Commission of the US Congress reported that new immigrants were "racially inferior, inclined toward violent crime, resisted assimilation" and likely to drive native-born citizens out of work (Pedraza 1996: 8). Such views were incorporated into the Immigration Act of 1924, which placed stringent restrictions on the arrival of immigrants who did not originate in Northern Europe and completely excluded those from Asia. Its quotas were not fully rescinded until 1965.

In retrospect, the concerns of these professors and pundits now seem unfounded. Not only do we celebrate the countless contributions of these populations to the American way of life, but further no longer regard such nationalities as racially distinct from other European Americans. Based on this record, it appears quite likely that the descendents of today's immigrant minorities will be regarded as equally American as those whose forebears came from Europe.

David Stoll suggests that immigrants do not share American notions of civic nationalism. However, various indicators suggest otherwise. In a detailed study of immigration and crime, Rubén G. Rumbaut and Walter Ewing found that immigrants, including those lacking legal documentation, have much lower rates of criminality than the native born.

Another indicator of immigrants' willingness to honor established notions of American nationality is through their military service. According to the Department of Defense, as of February 2008, more than 65,000 immigrants (non-US citizens and naturalized citizens) were serving on active duty in the US Armed Forces. This accounts for about 5% of all active duty personnel. Since September 2001, the US Citizenship and Immigration Services has naturalized more than 37,250 foreign-born members of the US Armed Forces and granted posthumous citizenship to 111 service members who were killed in the line of duty (Batalova 2008).

The fact that so many immigrants are willing to serve in the American armed forces during a war that is both dangerous and internationally unpopular demonstrates their patriotism and willingness to literally put their lives on the line to further the goals and values of their new nation.

In conclusion, this brief review of contemporary and historical patterns of immigration presents a far more positive image of the impact of immigrants on American society than does Stoll's essay. While the presence of immigrants will certainly challenge both the native-born population as well as newcomers, such evidence suggests that immigrants will continue to make life in the US more affluent, more fulfilling and more inclusive for both natives and new arrivals than it would be without them.

Further Reading

Batalova, J. 2008. Immigrants in the US Armed Forces, Migration Information Source. www.migrationinformation.org. Accessed 7 May 2009.

Bernstein, R. 2009. Letter from America: Don't Deny Benefit of Foreigners, *New York Times,* May, 6.

Executive Office of the President, Council of Economic Advisors 2007. *Immigration's economic impact.* Washington DC: The White House, June 20.

Fix, M., & Passel, J. S. 1994. *Immigration and immigrants: Setting the record straight.* Washington D.C.: The Urban Institute.

Light, I., & Gold, S. J. 2000. *Ethnic economies.* San Diego: Academic Press.

Migration Policy Institute. 2009. E Pluribus Unum Prizes. http://www.migrationinformation.org/integrationawards/ Accessed 7 May 2009.

Pedraza, S. 1996. Origins and destinies: Immigration, race and ethnicity in American history. In S. Pedraza, & R. G. Rumbaut (Eds.), *Origins and destinies: Immigration, race and ethnicity in America* (pp. 1–20). Belmont, CA: Wadsworth Publishing.

Rumbaut, R. G., & Ewing, W. 2007. *The myth of immigrant criminality and the paradox of assimilation: Incarceration rates among native and foreign-born men.* Washington DC: American Immigration Law Foundation, Spring.

Smith, J. P., & Edmonston, B. (Eds.) 1997. *The new Americans: Economic, demographic, and fiscal effects of immigration.* Washington, DC: National Academy Press.

Terrazas, A., Batalova, J., & Fan, V. 2007. Frequently requested statistics on immigrants in the United States. Migration Information Source. www.migrationinformation.org. Accessed 7 May 2009.

Weisman, J. 2005. Aging population poses global challenges. Washingtonpost.com, Page A01. Accessed 7 May 2009.

Critical Thinking

1. How does immigration benefit America and how does it harm America?

2. How is immigration viewed in public opinion?

3. Are most immigrants a good fit with American values?

S. J. GOLD is professor, associate chair and graduate program director in the Department of Sociology at Michigan State University. He is past chair of the International Migration Section of the American Sociological Association and author, co-author or co-editor of five books, most recently, *The Israeli Diaspora* (Routledge/University of Washington Press 2002). Together with Rubén G. Rumbaut, he is the editor of *The New Americans* book series from LFB Publishers.

The Invisible Ones

Ms. undertook an investigation into the shadow world of sex and labor trafficking in the United States, and learned not just the dimensions of the problem but the startling inadequacy of the federal response.

REBECCA CLARREN

We like to think of slavery in America as something consigned to history books, a dark chapter set in Southern cotton plantations and the hulls of ships set sail from Africa. Florencia Molina wishes this were true.

For part of the year in 2002, Molina, a 30-year-old Mexican, was held against her will and forced to work in a factory in Southern California, making dresses from 5:30 in the morning until 11 at night, seven days a week. She was not allowed to take a shower or leave the factory, at night sharing a small bed with another woman. She received one meal of beans and rice a day. If she didn't sew fast enough, her boss would pull her hair, pinch and slap her. Though she often worked 17 hours a day, her time card only gave credit for three.

Molina wasn't physically chained to her sewing machine; she wasn't shackled to the floor of the factory. Even so, she says she was in bondage. The factory doors were locked during the day and at night a watchman prevented her from leaving.

"If we wouldn't do what she [her boss] said, she told us somebody who we love would pay the consequences," says Molina, a small woman with steady dark eyes and black hair that falls below her waist. "She told me she could kill me and no one would ask her for me. She told me dogs have more rights than I have in this country."

Molina is one of the estimated tens of thousands of people trafficked into the U.S. from other countries and forced to work against their will. Large numbers are from El Salvador, Mexico, Korea, Vietnam and China, but in any country where people are desperate for jobs, they're prey to the allure of a mythic, prosperous U.S. It's hard to find an incontrovertible estimate of the numbers, because trafficking operates in a shadow world, but the CIA estimated in 1999 that as many as 50,000 women and children were trafficked into the U.S. each year. More recent estimates by the Bush administration have lowered this figure— to between 14,500 and 17,500. Polaris Project, an international anti-trafficking group, thinks there are likely more than 100,000 trafficking victims currently enslaved in the U.S., and those include, unbelievably, an undetermined number of enslaved U.S. residents as well.

Whatever the tally of victims, all modern-day slavery, or human trafficking, operates on coercion, fear, psychological abuse, torture or rape. About 80 percent of those enslaved are women and girls, pawns in the fastest-growing and one of the largest criminal industries in the world, second only to the drug trade, and tied with the arms trade. With an estimated 800,000 people trafficked across all international borders each year, the shadow industry is estimated to generate $31.6 billion in profits annually.

Molina's story is not unusual. Desperate times had prompted her to leave Mexico, after her ex-husband kicked her and their young children out of the house. She seized a chance to work in a U.S. factory owned by a woman from her town, planning to return to Mexico in six months with enough money to open her own sewing shop.

However, when she arrived in Southern California, the boss confiscated her birth certificate and ID and told her that if she tried to run away and go to the police, she would be jailed. Without knowing English, and with a fear of police based on the corrupt law enforcement of her hometown, Molina believed her.

"When I came to this country, I came with a lot of dreams," she says. "But when I arrived I realized that my dreams were dead. I was in the darkness with no hope and no light."

There is a perception, propagated in large part by mainstream media, that slavery in the U.S. occurs mostly in the guise of forced prostitution. But sex trafficking constitutes only about half of slavery in the U.S., according to a report by the Berkeley Human Rights Center and the nonprofit Free the Slaves based on surveys of trafficking service providers, newspaper articles and government reports.

The majority of trafficking victims are people who may be sewing our clothes, picking our crops, washing dishes in our restaurants, cleaning our motel rooms and building our homes and office buildings. They may be enslaved as domestic servants in our neighbors' homes. And they're everywhere in the U.S. While trafficking victims are most prevalent in New York,

Texas, Florida and California, investigations have been opened in 48 states and all U.S. territories.

Due in large part to the efforts of feminist groups, in 2000 Congress passed the Trafficking Victims Protection Act (TVPA), which created a special "T visa" that enables victims of sex and labor trafficking to remain temporarily in the United States—if they agree to assist in the investigation or prosecution of their traffickers and if they would suffer severe harm if removed from the U.S. After three years, the attorney general can admit them for permanent residency—though a process for doing so has yet to be worked out. Previously, trafficking victims were often deported as "illegal" aliens.

Under the TVPA, trafficking victims also become eligible to receive federally and state-funded services just as if they were refugees. These include cash assistance, housing, food stamps, health care, and educational and job services.

According to President George W. Bush, human trafficking is an issue that his administration cares about deeply. "We're beginning to make good, substantial progress," said Bush in 2004. "The message is getting out: We're serious. And when we catch you, you'll find out we're serious. We're staying on the hunt."

But, in fact, seven years after the passage of what was hailed as a very innovative law that created powerful new tools to prosecute and punish traffickers, the Bush administration has failed to fund and implement its provisions in a truly meaningful way. There has been a shocking lack of trafficking investigations—just 639 were opened by the Department of Justice between fiscal years 2001 and 2006. Only 360 defendants have been charged, resulting in 238 convictions. And, as of January, the federal government has provided refugee-type benefits to just over 1,100 people who had been trafficked.

"Here we have this crime that is often rape plus torture plus assault, and yet we have very little enforcement," says Kevin Bales, president of the Washington, D.C.-based Free the Slaves, which works to end slavery worldwide. "Think of it this way: Roughly 17,000 people were murdered in America last year—about the same number as the State Department claims were trafficked. Imagine if we only prosecuted, as we do with slavery, a little over 100 of those cases. People would freak out; it would be on the cover of *Time*. So far we've heard plenty of talk and [had] very little walk."

Furthermore, the regulations that the federal government was supposed to write enabling victims of trafficking to gain permanent residency status have yet to be completed, so those who have been released from enslavement are left in limbo. A spokesperson for the Department of Homeland Security says that the rules remain in draft form and there is no pending date for their release.

Hope for victims of trafficking has an address; it's just very hard to find. In Los Angeles, off a busy street near apartment buildings and convenience stores, hidden away behind oodles of security, is a confidential shelter. In the backyard, bright flowers and fruit trees line a vegetable garden where survivors of trafficking plant not only vegetables and herbs, but also the seeds of their own recovery.

"Our clients planted this garden as a place of refuge and meditation to help them start to take control of their lives again. It's about trying to re-create a normal life," says Kay Buck, executive director of the Coalition to Abolish Slavery & Trafficking (CAST), a nonprofit that runs the shelter and provides other social services for trafficking victims.

"Here we have this crime that is often rape plus torture plus assault, yet we have very little enforcement."

—Kevin Bales

In the entire U.S., there are only a handful of shelters devoted entirely to victims of trafficking, and the situation is unlikely to improve in the near future. CAST has seen its budget sliced by over 50 percent since the federal Office of Refugee Resettlement, under the Department of Health and Human Services, restructured its funding stream in 2006. Now, over half the federal money available for victim services no longer goes directly to nonprofit service providers, but instead is given to intermediaries, primarily the U.S. Conference of Catholic Bishops' Migration and Refugee Services. The Conference, which receives up to $6 million per year under a five-year contract, then subcontracts with individual groups like CAST, reimbursing groups on a per-victim basis—at an initial maximum of $600 per victim per month—to pay for such needs as food, rent and health care. The groups are only guaranteed these funds, individual by individual, for a few months at a time before they must reapply, thus hindering long-term service plans. The U.S. Conference of Catholic Bishops also requires that service providers stipulate that they won't hand out condoms or provide referral for abortion.

"We are being nickeled and dimed to the point where we do not have time to provide much-needed services to trafficked individuals," says Joy Zarembka, director of Break the Chain Campaign, a Washington, D.C.-based group that helps victims of domestic servitude. "Because organizations have no way of knowing how many cases they will have or how much money they will receive, they cannot guarantee that there is funding for staff. How can you predict a budget that is predicated on the amount of trafficked individuals who may escape in your jurisdiction over the course of a year? This is not what the Trafficking Act intended."

For women like Eyam (not her real name), 37, a former slave of an Indonesian family living in Beverly Hills, this failure to create a process for permanent residency has prevented her from feeling truly free. Enslaved for 17 years, Eyam was beaten with hangers, raped and often fed only noodles or rice. She was paid nothing to clean, cook and wait on the family 24 hours a day.

"I was living in a hell," she says in her heavily accented voice. "They make me really hurt in my life. I don't trust any more with men. Only thing they didn't do to me was to take my spirit out of my body."

Eyam escaped in 2000, using a knife to open a lock while her captors were out of town. She is worried that she will not receive permanent residency and will be forced to return to Indonesia. Returning to Indonesia permanently, where her U.S. captor has many connections and where she fears retaliation for cooperating with U.S. law-enforcement authorities, isn't an option. Eyam is desperate to visit her family—poor farmers in rural Indonesia—but immigration attorneys warn her and others not to travel outside the U.S. until their permanent residency status is approved.

The requirement that trafficking victims must cooperate with law enforcement to prosecute their traffickers in order to receive a T visa can put women or their families at tremendous risk, says Kamala D. Harris, district attorney of San Francisco. Harris was one of the driving forces behind state legislation to make human trafficking a felony in California and to provide additional funds for trafficking survivors to receive social services.

"We have to do everything we can to make sure women and girls don't face retaliation, even death, for testifying," she says. "First and foremost our guiding approach should be protecting victims. Then, in the process, if victims want to come forward and lend their voices, that's all the better."

Trafficked women don't easily trust law enforcement anyway, according to Mario Estrada, a 32-year veteran with the Los Angeles County Sheriff's Department. As he passes through Hacienda Heights, a middle-class community east of the city of Los Angeles, he recalls a raid at an ordinary-looking beige house six months before. There, behind the boarded-up windows, seven Korean women, the youngest aged 15, were forced to work as prostitutes.

"The girls kept saying they were OK," says Estrada. "They're so afraid of law enforcement, they won't help us, they won't open up. It's the hardest thing to convince them that [they're] not suspects, [they're] victims."

While Estrada suspects there could be over 100 similar operations in Los Angeles County, he isn't optimistic about uncovering too many of them. There are 9,000 law enforcement officers in the Sheriff's Department, but only Estrada and three others have experience and training in human trafficking. In the past year, they've busted just five human trafficking operations.

And Los Angeles—where county sheriff's department and city police personnel are now being educated on human trafficking—is better at dealing with trafficking than most jurisdictions. While 34 states have passed some form of anti-trafficking law, only California and a few other states mandate that law enforcement be trained in recognizing and apprehending traffickers. On the federal level, as of May the U.S. Department of Justice had given only 42 grants to cities and states to train local law enforcement. That means that while agents at the FBI and at Immigration and Customs Enforcement offices throughout the country may understand human trafficking, many local law enforcement officers—who are most likely to be the first to come in contact with trafficking victims—remain clueless.

"In the absence of training, the concern is that trafficking cases may be misdiagnosed," says Katherine Chon, executive director of Polaris Project, a Washington, D.C.-based nonprofit. "For example, in the Asian massage-parlor network, women are transported to the parlor by taxis that are controlled by traffickers. An untrained observer might assume that the woman was free to walk to a street corner and hail a cab, not realizing she was a trafficking victim."

Aside from federal and local law enforcement identifying trafficking victims, the federal Department of Labor (DOL) also plays a role, as it's charged with monitoring labor conditions to ensure that slavery doesn't occur. The DOL's already understaffed Wage and Hour Division, which interfaces with victims of trafficking in farm fields and factories, saw its staff cut further between 2001 and 2005. And it shows. At the DOL office in Fort Myers, Fla., for example, which serves an estimated 100,000 Spanish-speaking migrant workers, there is no full-time staff and the office is open just a half-day a week.

Within the next year, Congress will very likely reauthorize the Trafficking Victims Protection Act for the next two years. It's an opportunity, say advocates, to reform the law. Aside from trying to untangle T visas from the requirement that victims cooperate with law enforcement, a coalition of antitrafficking advocates wants U.S. and international agencies to establish a database on patterns of trafficking.

At the state level, says Jessica Neuwirth, founder of the international human-rights-for-women organization Equality Now, the need remains for anti-trafficking legislation to authorize local prosecutions and provide more money for shelters, victim services and law-enforcement training. Neuwirth helped draft stronger anti-trafficking legislation for New York—which passed this June—to separate sex and labor trafficking into separate categories, placing sex-trafficking crimes under the existing laws against prostitution and pimping. The law also works to stop sex trafficking at the demand end by increasing penalties for johns.

"We have to shift the burden of responsibility to the people who go out and buy a woman for sex," says Neuwirth. "Hopefully other states will use the New York law as a model."

Clearly, better training for law enforcement will be a key to victim identification. Groups such as the National Center for Women & Policing (NCWP), a Washington, D.C.-based division of the Feminist Majority Foundation (publisher of *Ms.*), have brokered meetings between nonprofit social service providers and federal law enforcement authorities to increase outreach and education about trafficking. In addition, NCWP has brought together law-enforcement officials from various foreign embassies to share their country's experiences with trafficking and attempt to coordinate international responses to trafficking. More models such as this are needed, says Margie Moore, director of the NCWP.

Ultimately ending labor slavery will take more than good laws and trained law enforcement. Corporations that profit from cheap labor must be held accountable, says Julie A. Su, co-founder of Sweatshop Watch in Los Angeles and litigation director of the Asian Pacific American Legal Center. Those corporations often subcontract labor, then claim ignorance of worker enslavement by their subcontractors. That's no excuse, says Su: "If they claim they don't know the conditions in which workers labor, they're willfully ignorant. A primary reason trafficking exists is the demand by companies for the cheapest, most vulnerable workers."

While Su and others have filed lawsuits over the past several years to ensure that companies pay legal wages, she suggests the situation won't improve greatly until the public becomes aware and outraged by the conditions under which a pair of pants was sewn, or produce was picked. Laws that require "sweatshop free" labeling in garments and on food products would increase consumer awareness and pressure for change.

Trafficking survivors such as Molina and Eyam are instigating change, and reclaiming their lives. They have joined a 10-member advisory caucus created by CAST to advocate for local and national policy, empower other survivors and become leaders in the fight to end modern-day slavery.

Today, Eyam lives in her own apartment, and cooks and cleans at a local homeless shelter. When she talks about her job, her face breaks into a wide smile, exposing brand-new braces on her teeth.

Molina works as a security guard in Los Angeles; she's completed English classes and is working toward her GED. But she has not yet been able to bring her sons from Mexico to the U.S.

"Not being with my children is the hardest part. I know some days they might have pain and feel sad and I'm not there to console them," she says, tears streaking her cheeks. Then she swallows hard and talks about her hopes: She wants to become a sheriff to help other victims of trafficking.

> **"If [corporations] claim they don't know the conditions in which workers labor, they're willfully ignorant. A primary reason for trafficking is demand for the cheapest workers."**
> —Julie Su

"I want to be for my children somebody who can inspire them to be a good person. I want to be a voice for those who are in fear, who don't have the power or the courage to come forward. There were a lot of people who helped me; I call them my angels. I want to be one of them for someone else."

Critical Thinking

1. What do you know about slavery in America today? How large is it?

2. Describe sex slavery in America. How are people forced into sex slavery?

REBECCA CLARREN writes about labor issues for a variety of national magazines. She lives in Portland, Ore. *Ms.* research associate Jennifer Hahn contributed to this article. For ways to help stop trafficking, see www.msmagazine.com.

UNIT 3
Problems of Poverty and Inequality

Unit Selections

Learning Outcomes

After reading this unit, you should be able to:

- How has globalization affected the economic situation of Americans?

- Explain the increase of inequality over the past three decades. How might increased inequality adversely impact American society?

- Compare the lives of people at the bottom rung of the social ladder with the people at the top.

- Discuss why people are poor. Are people poor mainly because they lack ambition and willingness to work or because their opportunities are very constrained?

- How extensive is discrimination between racial and ethnic groups in the United States today?

- Describe the situation of Muslims in the United States today.

- How different is the world of men from the world of women in American society today? Compare the treatment of women in the United States with their treatment around the world.

- Americans believe in tolerance, but what should be tolerated and what should not be tolerated? Explain.

- What is your view on gay marriage? Should it be legalized?

- Are men disadvantaged? If so, how?

Student Website
www.mhhe.com/cls

Internet References

grass-roots.org
www.grass-roots.org

Immigration Facts
www.immigrationforum.org

Joint Center for Poverty Research
www.jcpr.org

SocioSite
www.pscw.uva.nl/sociosite/TOPICS/Women.html

William Davidson Institute
www.wdi.bus.umich.edu

WWW Virtual Library: Demography & Population Studies
http://demography.anu.edu.au/VirtualLibrary

America is famous as the land of opportunity, and people from around the world have come to its shores in pursuit of the American dream. But how is America living up to this dream today? It is still a place for people to get rich, but it is also a place where people are trapped in poverty. This unit tells a number of stories of Americans dealing with advantages and disadvantages, opportunities and barriers, power and powerlessness. The first subsection of this unit deals with income inequality and the hardships of the poor. In the first article, Michael Spence analyzes the impact of globalization on American income and employment and the impacts are negative. Everyone understands that American industrial labor has difficulty competing with cheap foreign labor. On the other hand, everyone benefits as consumers because our goods are cheaper. The results have been good for the developing countries. Thirteen countries, including China, have economic growth rates exceeding 7 percent for 25 years or more. Until a decade ago, developed countries also grew at modest rates as high end jobs increased. Now the developing countries are competing in the high-end sectors and seriously threatening the American economy.

In the next article Peter Edelman focuses on poverty in America. There are two major problems: the lack of jobs and the low pay for many jobs. Low-wage work applies to 103 million workers. The persistence of poverty is not due to lack of political effort. Various public policies have kept about 40 million from falling into poverty (mainly due to social security). Numerous trends have adversely affected the poor, including the increase of single-parent families, disappearance of industrial jobs, increase in temps, foreign competition, and the cutback in social programs, including welfare. The final article in this subsection by Paul Gorski attacks the culture of poverty myth that the poverty of the poor is their own fault because they have the wrong values, beliefs, and behaviors. The truth is that most of the poor want to work, value education, and are willing to try. The main problem is their lack of real opportunities.

The three articles in the next subsection present various aspects of intergroup conflicts, including the cultural and attitudinal foundations of negative racial and ethnic relations. Lawrence Bobo comments on the racial divide that still exists in America. The next article is the speech given by Barack Obama precipitated by the inflammatory words of his pastor, Reverend Wright. He begins with the Constitutional Convention in 1787 then points to slavery, which mocked the precepts of the Constitution. Then he positioned his campaign as a further step in the long march to close the gap between the American creed and the reality. Then he tells his own story and how his view of America differs from that of Reverend Wright. His speech is inspiring, patriotic, and hopeful. That and his election will become a marker in American history. In the next article, the author demonstrates the prevalence of prejudice in America and how quickly hatred toward a group can evolve. Since September 11, 2001, hatred toward Muslims has erupted despite calls for tolerance by President George W. Bush and other public leaders. False stories circulate like wildfire and self-identified prophets preach hatred and fear. Sixty-two percent of Americans say they have never met

© Ingram Publishing / AGE Fotootook

a Muslim, so the absence of personal knowledge makes one susceptible to wild stories from talk radio, the Internet, and other media that frequently peddles falsehood. Fortunately, there is also a lot of support for American Muslims in many quarters.

The final subsection focuses on gender inequality and related issues. In the first article Anne-Marie Slaughter means exactly what her title says "Women still can't have it all." She tried and found it impossible. She has had a fabulous career but regrets what she had to miss out in her family life. Why can she not have it all? The system is not set up for that. She discusses at length how the system could be changed so that women could have it all. The next article is by two assistant state's attorneys who describe how widespread human sex trafficking is in the United States. The painful story of worldwide sex trafficking is well known, but its extent in America is vastly underestimated because prostitution in America is seen as freely chosen by the prostitutes. For some this is true, but the authors try to show that most of them are sex slaves. Some are totally controlled like slaves, others are apparently free but are manipulated and threatened to the point that they are really captives. Crime syndicates are often involved, and it is dangerous to disobey them. The next article is a speech given by Secretary of State Hillary Rodham Clinton on international Human Rights Day in 2011. In it she throws her support for LGBT rights. She starts with the United Nations passage of the Declaration of Human Rights in 1948, which declared that all human beings are born free and equal in dignity and rights. These are a birthright of all peoples even if governments deny them. Increasingly races, ethnic groups, and women have gained most of these rights. Now gays and lesbians are claiming these rights, and Hillary Clinton supports their cause. In doing so she has to raise and counter many objections to LGBT rights. Finally, Hanna Rosen develops a surprising theme, i.e., that men are disadvantaged today in many ways. Women outnumber men in the labor force, managerial jobs, and college graduations. Women exceed men on many performance measures . She asks whether life and job demands now favor women and their skills.

The Impact of Globalization on Income and Employment: The Downside of Integrating Markets

MICHAEL SPENCE

Globalization is the process by which markets integrate worldwide. Over the past 60 years, it has accelerated steadily as new technologies and management expertise have reduced transportation and transaction costs and as tariffs and other man-made barriers to international trade have been lowered. The impact has been stunning. More and more developing countries have been experiencing sustained growth rates of 7–10 percent; 13 countries, including China, have grown by more than 7 percent per year for 25 years or more. Although this was unclear at the outset, the world now finds itself just past the midpoint in a century-long process in which income levels in developing countries have been converging toward those in developed countries. Now, the emerging economies' impact on the global economy and the advanced economies is rising rapidly. Until about a decade ago, the effects of globalization on the distribution of wealth and jobs were largely benign. On average, advanced economies were growing at a respectable rate of 2.5 percent, and in most of them, the breadth and variety of employment opportunities at various levels of education seemed to be increasing. With external help, even the countries ravaged by World War II recovered. Imported goods became cheaper as emerging markets engaged with the global economy, benefiting consumers in both developed and developing countries.

But as the developing countries became larger and richer, their economic structures changed in response to the forces of comparative advantage: they moved up the value-added chain. Now, developing countries increasingly produce the kind of high-value-added components that 30 years ago were the exclusive purview of advanced economies. This climb is a permanent, irreversible change. With China and India—which together account for almost 40 percent of the world's population—resolutely moving up this ladder, structural economic changes in emerging countries will only have more impact on the rest of the world in the future.

By relocating some parts of international supply chains, globalization has been affecting the price of goods, job patterns, and wages almost everywhere. It is changing the structure of individual economies in ways that affect different groups within those countries differently. In the advanced economies, it is redistributing employment opportunities and incomes.

For most of the postwar period, U.S. policymakers assumed that growth and employment went hand in hand, and the U.S. economy's performance largely confirmed that assumption. But the structural evolution of the global economy today and its effects on the U.S. economy mean that, for the first time, growth and employment in the United States are starting to diverge. The major emerging economies are becoming more competitive in areas in which the U.S. economy has historically been dominant, such as the design and manufacture of semiconductors, pharmaceuticals, and information technology services. At the same time, many job opportunities in the United States are shifting away from the sectors that are experiencing the most growth and to those that are experiencing less. The result is growing disparities in income and employment across the U.S. economy, with highly educated workers enjoying more opportunities and workers with less education facing declining employment prospects and stagnant incomes. The U.S. government must urgently develop a long-term policy to address these distributional effects and their structural underpinnings and restore competitiveness and growth to the U.S. economy.

Jobless in the U.S.

Between 1990 and 2008, the number of employed workers in the United States grew from about 122 million to about 149 million. Of the roughly 27 million jobs created during that period, 98 percent were in the so-called nontradable sector of the economy, the sector that produces goods and services that must be consumed domestically. The largest employers in the U.S. nontradable sector were the government (with 22 million jobs in 2008) and the health-care industry (with 16 million jobs in 2008). Together, the two industries created ten million new jobs between 1990 and 2008, or just under 40 percent of total additions. (The retail, construction, and hotel and restaurant industries also contributed significantly to job growth.) Meanwhile, employment barely grew in the tradable sector of the U.S. economy, the sector that produces goods and services that can be consumed anywhere, such as manufactured products, engineering, and consulting services. That sector, which accounted for more than 34 million jobs in 1990, grew by a negligible 600,000 jobs between 1990 and 2008.

Dramatic, new labor-saving technologies in information services eliminated some jobs across the whole U.S. economy. But employment in the United States has been affected even more by the fact that many manufacturing activities, principally their lower-value-added components, have been moving to emerging economies. This trend is causing employment to fall in virtually all of the U.S. manufacturing sector, except at the high end of the value-added chain. Employment is growing, however, in other parts of the tradable sector—most prominently, finance, computer design and engineering, and top management at multinational enterprises. Like the top end of the manufacturing chain, these expanding industries and positions generally employ highly educated people, and they are the areas in which the U.S. economy continues to have a comparative advantage and can successfully compete in the global economy.

In other words, the employment structure of the U.S. economy has been shifting away from the tradable sector, except for the upper end of the value-added chain, and toward the nontradable sector. This is a problem, because the nontradable sector is likely to generate fewer jobs than is expected of it in the future. Moreover, the range of employment opportunities available in the tradable sector is declining, which is limiting choices for U.S. workers in the middle-income bracket. It would be unwise to assume that under present circumstances, employment in the government and health care in the United States will continue to grow as much as it had been growing before the recent economic crisis. If anything, it is remarkable that the U.S. economy did not have much of an employment problem until the recent economic crisis. If the nontradable sector continues to lose its capacity to absorb labor, as it has in recent years, and the tradable sector does not become an employment engine, the United States should brace itself for a long period of high unemployment.

For What It's Worth

One way to measure the size of a company, industry, or economy is to determine its output. But a better way is to determine its added value—namely, the difference between the value of its outputs, that is, the goods and services it produces, and the costs of its inputs, such as the raw materials and energy it consumes. (Value added comes from the capital and labor that turn the inputs into outputs.) Goods and services themselves are often purchased as intermediate inputs by other companies or industries, legal services purchased by a corporation being one example. The value added produced by all the industries in all the sectors of an economy adds up to that country's GDP. Unlike employment, value added in the tradable and nontradable parts of the U.S. economy has increased at a similar rate since 1990. In the nontradable sector, which experienced rapid employment growth, this means that value added grew slightly faster than employment: value added per employee increased modestly, by an annual average of 0.7 percent since

1990. On the tradable side of the U.S. economy, where employment levels barely increased, both value added overall and value added per employee rose very swiftly as the U.S. tradable sector moved up the value-added chain and grew in sync with the global economy. Whereas in the nontradable sector, value added per employee grew from $72,000 to over $80,000 between 1990 and 2008, in the tradable sector it grew from $79,000 to $120,000—in other words, it grew by just about 12 percent in the nontradable sector but by close to 52 percent in the tradable sector.

Most striking are the trends within the tradable sector. Value added rose across that sector, including in finance, where employment increased, and in manufacturing industries, where employment mostly declined. In fact, at the upper end of the manufacturing chain, value added increased so much that it outweighed the losses at the lower end caused by the movement of economic activity from the United States to other countries.

Value added represents income for someone. For employed people, it means personal income; for shareholders and other owners of capital, profit or returns on investment; for the government, tax revenues. Generally, the incomes of workers are closely correlated with value added per employee (this is not the case in the mining industry and utilities, however, where value added per employee is much higher than wages because these activities are very capital intensive and most value added is a return on capital). Since value added in the nontradable part of the U.S. economy did not rise much, neither did average incomes in that sector. In the tradable sector, on the other hand, incomes rose rapidly along with value added per employee thanks both to rising productivity gains in some industries and the movement of lower-income jobs to other countries. And since most new jobs were created in the nontradable part of the economy, in which wages grew little, the distribution of income in the U.S. economy became more uneven. The overall picture is clear: employment opportunities and incomes are high, and rising, for the highly educated people at the upper end of the tradable sector of the U.S. economy, but they are diminishing at the lower end. And there is every reason to believe that these trends will continue. As emerging economies continue to move up the value-added chain—and they must in order to keep growing—the tradable sectors of advanced economies will require less labor and the more labor-intensive tasks will shift to emerging economies.

Highly educated U.S. workers are already gravitating toward the high-value-added parts of the U.S. economy, particularly in the tradable sector. As labor economists have noted, the return on education is rising. The highly educated, and only them, are enjoying more job opportunities and higher incomes. Competition for highly educated workers in the tradable sector spills over to the nontradable sector, raising incomes in the high-value-added part of that sector as well. But with fewer jobs in the lower-value-added part of the tradable sector, competition for similar jobs in the nontradable sector is increasing. This, in turn, further depresses income growth in the lower-value-added part of the nontradable sector. Thus, the evolving structure of the global economy has diverse effects on different groups of people in the United States. Opportunities are expanding for the highly educated throughout the economy: they are expanding in the tradable sector because the global economy is growing and in the nontradable sector because that job market must remain competitive with the tradable sector. But opportunities are shrinking for the less well educated.

Faced with an undesirable economic outcome, economists tend to assume that its cause is a market failure. Market failures come in many forms, from inefficiencies caused by information gaps to the unpriced impacts of externalities such as the environment. But the effects on the U.S. economy of the global economy's structural evolution is not a market failure: it is not an economically inefficient outcome. (If anything, the global economy is generally becoming more efficient.) But it is nonetheless a cause for concern in that it is creating a distributional problem in the advanced economies. Not everyone is gaining in those countries, and some may be losing.

Although everyone does benefit from lower-priced goods and services, people also care greatly about the chance to be productively employed and the quality of their work. Declining employment opportunities feel real and immediate; the rise in real incomes brought by lower prices does not. For example, according to recent surveys, a substantial number of Americans believe that their children will have fewer opportunities than they have had. The slow recovery from the recent economic crisis may be affecting these perceptions, which means that they might dissipate as the situation improves and growth returns. But the long-term structural evolution of the U.S. and global economies suggests that distributional issues will remain. These must be taken seriously.

Making It Work

Analysts have been quick to point out that not all the structural changes under way in the U.S. economy should be attributed to greater openness in the global economy. Some important changes in employment patterns and income distribution are the result of labor-saving information technology and the automation of transactions. Automation has undoubtedly cut jobs in the information- and transaction-intensive parts of value-added chains throughout the U.S. economy, in both the tradable and the nontradable sectors. But if that were the only trend, why would employment decline so much more in manufacturing than in other industries?

One answer might be that information processing and automation occupy a more significant fraction of the value-added chain in manufacturing. But this is not true. Information-processing technology, for example, has eliminated jobs throughout the U.S. economy, including in finance, retail, and the government —all areas in which employment has grown. The structural trends affecting the U.S. economy cannot be explained by changes in technology alone. To think otherwise tends to yield the misleading conclusions that technology, not the global economy, is the principal cause of the United States' employment challenge and that the most important forces operating on the structure of the U.S. economy are internal, not external. In fact, all these factors are relevant, with some more significant in some sectors of the economy than in others.

If giving technology as the preferred explanation for the U.S. economy's distributional problems is a way to ignore the structural changes of the global economy, invoking multinational companies (MNCs) as the preferred explanation is a way to overstate their impact. MNCs are said to underpay and otherwise exploit poor people in developing countries, exporting jobs that should have stayed in the United States.

MNCs do, indeed, play a central role in managing the evolution of the global economy. They are the principal architects of global supply chains, and they move the production of goods and services around the world in response to supply-chain and market opportunities that are constantly changing. MNCs have generated growth and jobs in developing countries, and by moving to those countries some lower-value-added parts of their supply chains, they have increased growth and competitiveness in advanced economies such as the United States. A June 2010 report by the McKinsey Global Institute estimated that U.S.-based MNCs accounted for 31 percent of GDP growth in the United States since 1990.

With ample labor available in various skill and educational categories throughout the tradable sector globally, companies have little incentive to invest in technologies that save on labor or otherwise increase the competitiveness of the labor-intensive value-added activities in advanced economies. In short, companies' private interest (profit) and the public's interest (employment) do not align perfectly. These conditions might not last: if growth continues to be high in emerging economies, in two or three decades there will be less cheap labor available there. But two or three decades is a long time.

In the meantime, even though public and private interests are not perfectly aligned today, they are not perfectly opposed either. Relatively modest shifts at the margin could bring them back in sync. Given the enormous size of the global labor force, the dial would not need to be moved very much to restore employment growth in the tradable sector of the U.S. economy. Specifically, the right combination of productivity-enhancing technology and competitive wage levels could keep some manufacturing industries, or at least some value-added pieces of their production chains, in the United States and other advanced countries. But accomplishing this will require more than a decision from the market; it must also involve labor, business, and governments. Germany, for one, has managed to retain its advanced manufacturing activities in industrial machinery by removing rigidities in the labor market and making a conscious effort to privilege employment over rapid rises in incomes. Wages may have increased only modestly in Germany over the past decade, but income inequality is markedly flatter there than in the United States, where it is higher than in most other industrial countries and rising steadily.

Conditioning access to the domestic market on domestic production is a form of protectionism and a way to try to limit the movement out of the country of jobs and of value-added components in the supply chain. This is more common than might be supposed. It exists in the aerospace industry; and in the 1970s and 1980s, in the car industry, quotas on Japanese imports to the United States led to an expansion of the manufacture of Japanese cars in the United States. However, if the large economies—such as China, the European Union, Japan, or the United States—pursue protectionist measures on a broad front, the global economy will be undermined. Yet that may be exactly what happens if employment challenges such as the ones affecting the United States are not tackled differently. With pressure on government budgets at all levels, rapidly rising health-care costs, a fragile housing market, the post-crisis effort to curb excess consumption and boost savings, and the risk of a second economic downturn, it is highly unlikely that net employment in the nontradable sector of the U.S. economy will continue to grow as rapidly as it has been.

The drop in domestic consumption in the United States has left the country with a shortage of aggregate demand. More public-sector investment would help, but the fiscal consolidation currently under way may make expanding government investment difficult. Meanwhile, because private-sector investment responds to demand and currently there is a shortfall in demand caused by the economic crisis and increased savings by households, such investment will not return until domestic consumption or exports increase. Therefore, the United States will need to focus on increasing job growth in the tradable sector. Some growth will naturally come from the high-value-added part of that sector. The question is whether there will be enough growth and whether the educational attainment of U.S. workers will keep pace with rising job requirements at that level. There are reasons to be skeptical.

The Big Tradeoff

It is a common view that the market will solve the disparities in employment and incomes once the economic crisis recedes and growth is restored. Warren Buffett and other very smart, experienced, and influential opinion-makers say so clearly. But as this analysis suggests, they may not be right. And as long as their view dominates U.S. public policy and opinion, it will be difficult to address the issues related to structural change and employment in the United States in a systematic way.

What is needed instead of benign neglect is, first, an agreement that restoring rewarding employment opportunities for a full spectrum of Americans should be a fundamental goal. With that objective as a starting point, it will then be necessary to develop ways to increase both the competitiveness and the inclusiveness of the U.S. economy. This is largely uncharted territory: distributional issues are difficult to solve because they require correcting outcomes on the global market without doing too much damage to its efficiency and openness. But admitting that not all the answers are known is a good place to begin. With considerable uncertainty about the efficacy of various policy options, a multistakeholder, multipronged approach to addressing these distributional problems is best. The relevant knowledge about promising new technologies and market opportunities is dispersed among business, the government, labor, and universities, and it needs to be assembled and turned into initiatives. President Barack Obama has already appointed a commission, led by Jeffrey Immelt, the CEO of General Electric, to focus on competitiveness and employment issues in the U.S. economy. This is an important step forward. But it will be hugely difficult to invest in human capital, technology, and infrastructure as much as is necessary at a time of fiscal distress and declining government employment. And yet restoring opportunities for future generations requires making sacrifices in the present.

Given the structural changes under way in the U.S. economy—especially the growing premium on highly educated workers at the top end of the value-added chain—education should be boosted. As many people as possible should be able to compete in that part of the economy. But if this goal is clear, the ways to achieve it are less so. Improving the performance of the educational system has been a priority for some years, yet the results are in doubt. For example, the Organization for Economic Cooperation and Development administers a set of standardized tests, the Program for International Student Assessment, across more than 60 countries, advanced and developing, to measure the cognitive skills of teenage students. The United States ranks close to the average in reading and science and well behind most countries in math.

The problems in the quality and effectiveness of parts of the U.S. educational system have been recognized for some time. Numerous attempts to improve matters, including administering national standardized tests and providing merit-based compensation, have thus far yielded inconclusive results. And the problem extends beyond the school system. A lack of commitment to education in families and in communities makes the entire field of education seem unattractive, demoralizing dedicated teachers and turning off talented students from teaching. That, in turn, reduces the incentives of communities to value the primacy of education. To break this pattern, it will be necessary to shift communities'—and the country's—values about education through moral leadership, at both the community and the national levels. Creating attractive employment opportunities conditional on educational success is another important incentive. One comes full circle, in other words: increased educational effectiveness is needed for the United States to be competitive, and the promise of rewarding employment is a necessary incentive for committing to improving education.

As important as education is, it cannot be the whole solution; the United States will not educate its way out of its problems. Both the federal and state governments must pursue complementary lines of attack. They should invest in infrastructure, which would create jobs in the short term and raise the return on private-sector investment in the medium to longer term. They should also invest in technologies that could expand employment opportunities in the tradable sector of the U.S. economy at income levels other than the very top. The private sector will have to help guide these investments because it has much of the relevant knowledge about where these opportunities might lie. But this effort will also require the participation of the public sector. The U.S. government already invests heavily in science and technology but not with job creation as its primary focus; that has generally been viewed only as a beneficial side effect. It is time to devote public funding to developing infrastructure and the technological base of the U.S. economy with the specific goal of restoring competitiveness and expanding employment in the tradable sector. The tax structure also needs to be reformed. It should be simplified and reconfigured to promote competitiveness, investment, and employment. And both loopholes and distorting incentives should be eliminated. For example, corporate tax rates and tax rates on investment returns should be lowered in order to make the United States more attractive for business and investment. MNCs with earnings outside the United States currently have a strong incentive to keep their earnings abroad and reinvest them abroad because earnings are taxed both where they are earned and also in the United States if they are repatriated. Lower tax rates would mean a loss in revenue for the U.S. government, but that could be replaced by taxes on consumption, which would have the added benefit of helping shift the composition of demand from domestic to foreign—a necessary move if the United States wants to avoid high unemployment and an unsustainable current account deficit.

But even these measures may not be sufficient. Globalization has redefined the competition for employment and incomes in the United States. Tradeoffs will have to be made between the two. Germany clearly chose to protect employment in the industries of its tradable sector that came under competitive threat. Now, U.S. policymakers must choose, too.

Some will argue that global market forces should simply be allowed to operate without interference. Tampering with market outcomes, the argument goes, risks distorting incentives and reducing efficiency and innovation. But this is not the only approach, nor is it the best one. The distribution of income across many advanced economies (and major emerging economies) differs markedly. For example, the ratio of the average income of the top 20 percent of the population to the average income of the bottom 20 percent is four to one in Germany and eight to one in the United States. Many other advanced countries have flatter income distributions than the United States, suggesting that tradeoffs between market forces and equity are possible. The U.S. government needs to face up to them.

Experimenting the Way Forward

The massive changes in the global economy since World War II have had overwhelmingly positive effects. Hundreds of millions of people in the developing world have escaped poverty, and more will in the future. The global economy will continue to grow—probably at least threefold over the next 30 years. One person's gain is not necessarily another's loss; global growth is not even close to a zero-sum game. But globalization hurts some subgroups within some countries, including the advanced economies.

The late American economist Paul Samuelson once said, "Every good cause is worth some inefficiency." Surely, equity and social cohesion are among them. The challenge for the U.S. economy will be to find a place in the rapidly evolving global economy that retains its dynamism and openness while providing all Americans with rewarding employment opportunities and a reasonable degree of equity. This is not a problem to which there are easy answers. As the issue becomes more pressing, ideology and orthodoxy must be set aside, and creativity, flexibility, and pragmatism must be encouraged. The United States will not be able to deduce its way toward the solutions; it will have to experiment its way forward.

Source

Spence, Michael. "The impact of globalization on income and employment: the downside of integrating markets." *Foreign Affairs* 90.4 (2011): 28. *General OneFile*. Web. 20 Dec. 2011.

Critical Thinking

1. How does globalization affect income and employment in America?
2. How does globalization increase inequality?
3. Why does Spence believe that the American economy will be in serious trouble for a long time?

MICHAEL SPENCE is Distinguished Visiting Fellow at the Council on Foreign Relations and the author of *The Next Convergence: The Future of Economic Growth in a Multispeed World*. He received the Nobel Prize in Economics in 2001.

The State of Poverty in America

PETER EDELMAN

The problem is worse than we thought, but we can solve it.

We have two basic poverty problems in the United States. One is the prevalence of low-wage work. The other concerns those who have almost no work.

The two overlap.

Most people who are poor work as much as they can and go in and out of poverty. Fewer people have little or no work on a continuing basis, but they are in much worse straits and tend to stay poor from one generation to the next.

The numbers in both categories are stunning.

Low-wage work encompasses people with incomes below twice the poverty line—not poor but struggling all the time to make ends meet. They now total 103 million, which means that fully one-third of the population has an income below what would be $36,000 for a family of three.

In the bottom tier are 20.5 million people—6.7 percent of the population—who are in deep poverty, with an income less than half the poverty line (below $9,000 for a family of three). Some 6 million people out of those 20.5 million have no income at all other than food stamps.

These dire facts tempt one to believe that there may be some truth to President Ronald Reagan's often-quoted declaration that "we fought a war against poverty and poverty won." But that is not the case. Our public policies have been remarkably successful. Starting with the Social Security Act of 1935, continuing with the burst of activity in the 1960s, and on from there, we have made great progress.

We enacted Medicaid and the Children's Health Insurance Program, and many health indicators for low-income people improved. We enacted food stamps, and the near-starvation conditions we saw in some parts of the country were ameliorated. We enacted the Earned Income Tax Credit and the Child Tax Credit, and the incomes of low-wage workers with children were lifted. We enacted Pell grants, and millions of people could afford college who otherwise couldn't possibly attend. We enacted Supplemental Security Income and thereby raised the income floor for elderly and disabled people whose earnings from work didn't provide enough Social Security. There is much more—housing vouchers, Head Start, child-care assistance, and legal services for the poor, to name a few. The Obama administration and Congress added 16 million

people to Medicaid in the Affordable Care Act, appropriated billions to improve the education of low-income children, and spent an impressive amount on the least well-off in the Recovery Act.

All in all, our various public policies kept a remarkable 40 million people from falling into poverty in 2010—about half because of Social Security and half due to the other programs just mentioned. To assert that we fought a war against poverty and poverty won because there is still poverty is like saying that the Clean Air and Clean Water acts failed because there is still pollution.

Nonetheless, the level of poverty in the nation changed little between 1970 and 2000 and is much worse now. It was at 11.1 percent in 1973—the lowest level achieved since we began measuring—and after going up sharply during the Reagan and George H. W. Bush years, went back down during the 1990s to 11.3 percent in 2000, as President Bill Clinton left office.

Why didn't it fall further? The economics have been working against us for four decades, exacerbated by trends in family composition. Well-paying industrial jobs disappeared to other countries and to automation. The economy grew, but the fruits of the growth went exclusively to those at the top. Other jobs replaced the ones lost, but most of the new jobs paid much less. The wage of the median-paying job barely grew—by one measure going up only about 7 percent over the 38 years from 1973 to 2011. Half the jobs in the country now pay less than $33,000 a year, and a quarter pay less than the poverty line of $22,000 for a family of four. We have become a low-wage economy to a far greater extent than we realize.

Households with only one wage-earner—typically those headed by single mothers—have found it extremely difficult to support a family. The share of families with children headed by single mothers rose from 12.8 percent in 1970 to 26.2 percent in 2010 (and from 37.1 percent in 1971 to 52.8 percent in 2010 among African Americans). In 2010, 46.9 percent of children under 18 living in households headed by a single mother were poor.

The percentage of people in deep poverty has doubled since 1976. A major reason for this rise is the near death of cash assistance for families with children. Welfare has shrunk from 14 million recipients (too many, in my view) before the Temporary Assistance for Needy Families law (TANF) was enacted in 1996 to 4.2 million today, just 1.5 percent of the population.

At last count, Wyoming had 607 people on TANF, or just 2.7 percent of its poor children. Twenty-six states have less than 20 percent of their poor children on TANF. The proportion of poor families with children receiving welfare has shrunk from 68 percent before TANF was enacted to 27 percent today.

What's the agenda going forward? The heart of it is creating jobs that yield a living income. Restoring prosperity, ensuring that the economy functions at or near full employment, is our most powerful anti-poverty weapon. We need more, though—a vital union sector and a higher minimum wage, for two. We also need work supports—health care, child care, and help with the cost of housing and postsecondary education. These are all income equivalents—all policies that will contribute to bringing everyone closer to having a living income.

There's a gigantic problem here, however: We look to be headed to a future of too many low-wage jobs. Wages in China, India, and other emerging economies may be rising, but we can't foresee any substantial increase in the prevailing wage for many millions of American jobs. That means we better start talking about wage supplements that are much bigger than the Earned Income Tax Credit. We need a dose of reality about the future of the American paycheck.

The second big problem is the crisis—and it is a crisis—posed by the 20 million people at the bottom of the economy. We have a huge hole in our safety net. In many states, TANF and food stamps combined don't even get people to half of the poverty line, and a substantial majority of poor families don't receive TANF at all.

Even worse, we have destroyed the safety net for the poorest children in the country. Seven million women and children are among the 20.5 million in deep poverty. One in four children in a household headed by a single mother is in deep poverty. We have to restore the safety net for the poorest of the poor.

Getting serious about investing in our children—from prenatal care and early-childhood assistance on through education at all levels—is also essential if we are to achieve a future without such calamitous levels of poverty. In addition, we must confront the destruction being wrought by the criminal-justice system. These are poverty issues and race issues as well. The schools and the justice system present the civil-rights challenges of this century.

Combining all of the problems in vicious interaction is the question of place—the issues that arise from having too many poor people concentrated in one area, whether in the inner city, Appalachia, the Mississippi Delta, or on Indian reservations. Such places are home to a minority of the poor, but they include a hugely disproportionate share of intergenerational and persistent poverty. Our most serious policy failing over the past four-plus decades has been our neglect of this concentrated poverty. We have held our own in other respects, but we have lost ground here.

Finally, we need to be much more forthright about how much all of this has to do with race and gender. It is always important to emphasize that white people make up the largest number of the poor, to counter the stereotype that the face of poverty is one of color. At the same time, though, we must face more squarely that African Americans, Latinos, and Native Americans are all poor at almost three times the rate of whites and ask why that continues to be true. We need as a nation to be more honest about who it is that suffers most from terrible schools and the way we lock people up. Poverty most definitely cuts across racial lines, but it doesn't cut evenly.

There's a lot to do.

Critical Thinking

1. What are the main sources of poverty in America?
2. What are the prospects for poverty reduction in the future?
3. Explain why so many working people are poor.

The Myth of the "Culture of Poverty"

Instead of accepting myths that harm low-income students, we need to eradicate the systemwide inequities that stand in their way.

PAUL GORSKI

As the students file out of Janet's classroom, I sit in the back corner, scribbling a few final notes. Defeat in her eyes, Janet drops into a seat next to me with a sigh.

"I love these kids," she declares, as if trying to convince me. "I adore them. But my hope is fading."

"Why's that?" I ask, stuffing my notes into a folder.

"They're smart. I know they're smart, but . . . "

And then the deficit floodgates open: "They don't care about school. They're unmotivated. And their parents—I'm lucky if two or three of them show up for conferences. No wonder the kids are unprepared to learn."

At Janet's invitation, I spent dozens of hours in her class-room, meeting her students, observing her teaching, helping her navigate the complexities of an urban midwestern elementary classroom with a growing percentage of students in poverty. I observed powerful moments of teaching and learning, caring and support. And I witnessed moments of internal conflict in Janet, when what she wanted to believe about her students collided with her prejudices.

Like most educators, Janet is determined to create an environment in which each student reaches his or her full potential. And like many of us, despite overflowing with good intentions, Janet has bought into the most common and dangerous myths about poverty.

Chief among these is the "culture of poverty" myth—the idea that poor people share more or less monolithic and predictable beliefs, values, and behaviors. For educators like Janet to be the best teachers they can be for all students, they need to challenge this myth and reach a deeper understanding of class and poverty.

Roots of the Culture of Poverty Concept

Oscar Lewis coined the term *culture of poverty* in his 1961 book *The Children of Sanchez*. Lewis based his thesis on his ethnographic studies of small Mexican communities. His studies uncovered approximately 50 attributes shared within these communities: frequent violence, a lack of a sense of history, a neglect of planning for the future, and so on. Despite studying very small communities, Lewis extrapolated his findings to suggest a universal culture of poverty. More than 45 years later, the premise of the culture of poverty paradigm remains the same: that people in poverty share a consistent and observable "culture."

Lewis ignited a debate about the nature of poverty that continues today. But just as important—especially in the age of data-driven decision making—he inspired a flood of research. Researchers around the world tested the culture of poverty concept empirically (see Billings, 1974; Carmon, 1985; Jones & Luo, 1999). Others analyzed the overall body of evidence regarding the culture of poverty paradigm (see Abell & Lyon, 1979; Ortiz & Briggs, 2003; Rodman, 1977).

These studies raise a variety of questions and come to a variety of conclusions about poverty. But on this they all agree: *There is no such thing as a culture of poverty.* Differences in values and behaviors among poor people are just as great as those between poor and wealthy people.

In actuality, the culture of poverty concept is constructed from a collection of smaller stereotypes which, however false, seem to have crept into mainstream thinking as unquestioned fact. Let's look at some examples.

Myth: Poor people are unmotivated and have weak work ethics.

The Reality: Poor people do not have weaker work ethics or lower levels of motivation than wealthier people (Iversen & Farber, 1996; Wilson, 1997). Although poor people are often stereotyped as lazy, 83 percent of children from low-income families have at least one employed parent; close to 60 percent have at least one parent who works full-time and year-round (National Center for Children in Poverty, 2004). In fact, the severe shortage of living-wage jobs means that many poor adults must work two, three, or four jobs. According to the Economic Policy Institute (2002), poor working adults spend more hours working each week than their wealthier counterparts.

Myth: Poor parents are uninvolved in their children's learning, largely because they do not value education.

The Reality: Low-income parents hold the same attitudes about education that wealthy parents do (Compton-Lilly, 2003; Lareau & Horvat, 1999; Leichter, 1978). Low-income parents are less likely to attend school functions or volunteer in their children's classrooms (National Center for Education Statistics, 2005)—not because they care less about education, but because they have less access to school involvement than their wealthier peers. They are more likely to work multiple jobs, to work evenings, to have jobs without paid leave, and to be unable to afford child care and public transportation. It might be said more accurately that schools that fail to take these considerations into account do not value the involvement of poor families as much as they value the involvement of other families.

Myth: Poor people are linguistically deficient.

The Reality: All people, regardless of the languages and language varieties they speak, use a full continuum of language registers (Bomer, Dworin, May, & Semingson, 2008). What's more, linguists have known for decades that all language varieties are highly structured with complex grammatical rules (Gee, 2004; Hess, 1974; Miller, Cho, & Bracey, 2005). What often are assumed to be *deficient* varieties of English—Appalachian varieties, perhaps, or what some refer to as Black English Vernacular—are no less sophisticated than so-called "standard English."

Myth: Poor people tend to abuse drugs and alcohol.

The Reality: Poor people are no more likely than their wealthier counterparts to abuse alcohol or drugs. Although drug sales are more visible in poor neighborhoods, drug use is equally distributed across poor, middle class, and wealthy communities (Saxe, Kadushin, Tighe, Rindskopf, & Beveridge, 2001). Chen, Sheth, Krejci, and Wallace (2003) found that alcohol consumption is significantly higher among upper middle class white high school students than among poor black high school students. Their finding supports a history of research showing that alcohol abuse is far more prevalent among wealthy people than among poor people (Diala, Muntaner, & Walrath, 2004; Galea, Ahern, Tracy, & Vlahov, 2007). In other words, considering alcohol and illicit drugs together, wealthy people are more likely than poor people to be substance abusers.

The Culture of Classism

The myth of a "culture of poverty" distracts us from a dangerous culture that does exist—the culture of classism. This culture continues to harden in our schools today. It leads the most well intentioned of us, like my friend Janet, into low expectations for low-income students. It makes teachers fear their most powerless pupils. And, worst of all, it diverts attention from what people in poverty *do* have in common: inequitable access to basic human rights.

The most destructive tool of the culture of classism is deficit theory. In education, we often talk about the deficit perspective—defining students by their weaknesses rather than their strengths. Deficit theory takes this attitude a step further, suggesting that poor people are poor because of their own moral and intellectual deficiencies (Collins, 1988). Deficit theorists use two strategies for propagating this world view: (1) drawing on well-established stereotypes, and (2) ignoring systemic conditions, such as inequitable access to high-quality schooling, that support the cycle of poverty.

The implications of deficit theory reach far beyond individual bias. If we convince ourselves that poverty results not from gross inequities (in which we might be complicit) but from poor people's own deficiencies, we are much less likely to support authentic antipoverty policy and programs. Further, if we believe, however wrongly, that poor people don't value education, then we dodge any responsibility to redress the gross education inequities with which they contend. This application of deficit theory establishes the idea of what Gans (1995) calls the *undeserving poor*—a segment of our society that simply does not deserve a fair shake.

If the goal of deficit theory is to justify a system that privileges economically advantaged students at the expense of working-class and poor students, then it appears to be working marvelously. In our determination to "fix" the mythical culture of poor students, we ignore the ways in which our society cheats them out of opportunities that their wealthier peers take for granted. We ignore the fact that poor people suffer disproportionately the effects of nearly every major social ill. They lack access to health care, living-wage jobs, safe and affordable housing, clean air and water, and so on (Books, 2004)—conditions that limit their abilities to achieve to their full potential.

Perhaps most of us, as educators, feel powerless to address these bigger issues. But the question is this: Are we willing, at the very least, to tackle the classism in our own schools and classrooms?

The myth of a "culture of poverty" distracts us from a dangerous culture that does exist—the culture of classism.

This classism is plentiful and well documented (Kozol, 1992). For example, compared with their wealthier peers, poor students are more likely to attend schools that have less funding (Carey, 2005); lower teacher salaries (Karoly, 2001); more limited computer and Internet access (Gorski, 2003); larger class sizes; higher student-to-teacher ratios; a less-rigorous curriculum; and fewer experienced teachers (Barton, 2004). The National Commission on Teaching and America's Future (2004) also found that low-income schools were more likely to suffer from cockroach or rat infestation, dirty or inoperative student bathrooms, large numbers of teacher vacancies and substitute teachers, more teachers who are not licensed in their subject areas, insufficient or outdated classroom materials, and inadequate or nonexistent learning facilities, such as science labs.

Here in Minnesota, several school districts offer universal half-day kindergarten but allow those families that can afford to do so to pay for full-day services. Our poor students scarcely make it out of early childhood without paying the price for our culture of classism. Deficit theory requires us to ignore these inequities—or worse, to see them as normal and justified.

What does this mean? Regardless of how much students in poverty value education, they must overcome tremendous inequities to learn. Perhaps the greatest myth of all is the one that dubs education the "great equalizer." Without considerable change, it cannot be anything of the sort.

What Can We Do?

The socioeconomic opportunity gap can be eliminated only when we stop trying to "fix" poor students and start addressing the ways in which our schools perpetuate classism. This includes destroying the inequities listed above as well as abolishing such practices as tracking and ability grouping, segregational redistricting, and the privatization of public schools. We must demand the best possible education for all students—higher-order pedagogies, innovative learning materials, and holistic teaching and learning. But first, we must demand basic human rights for all people: adequate housing and health care, living-wage jobs, and so on.

Of course, we ought not tell students who suffer today that, if they can wait for this education revolution, everything will fall into place. So as we prepare ourselves for bigger changes, we must

- Educate ourselves about class and poverty.
- Reject deficit theory and help students and colleagues unlearn misperceptions about poverty.
- Make school involvement accessible to all families.
- Follow Janet's lead, inviting colleagues to observe our teaching for signs of class bias.
- Continue reaching out to low-income families even when they appear unresponsive (and without assuming, if they are unresponsive, that we know why).
- Respond when colleagues stereotype poor students or parents.
- Never assume that all students have equitable access to such learning resources as computers and the Internet, and never assign work requiring this access without providing in-school time to complete it.
- Ensure that learning materials do not stereotype poor people.
- Fight to keep low-income students from being assigned unjustly to special education or low academic tracks.
- Make curriculum relevant to poor students, drawing on and validating their experiences and intelligences.
- Teach about issues related to class and poverty—including consumer culture, the dissolution of labor unions, and environmental injustice—and about movements for class equity.
- Teach about the antipoverty work of Martin Luther King Jr., Helen Keller, the Black Panthers, César Chávez,

and other U.S. icons—and about why this dimension of their legacies has been erased from our national consciousness.
- Fight to ensure that school meal programs offer healthy options.
- Examine proposed corporate-school partnerships, rejecting those that require the adoption of specific curriculums or pedagogies.

Most important, we must consider how our own class biases affect our interactions with and expectations of our students. And then we must ask ourselves, Where, in reality, does the deficit lie? Does it lie in poor people, the most disenfranchised people among us? Does it lie in the education system itself—in, as Jonathan Kozol says, the savage inequalities of our schools? Or does it lie in us—educators with unquestionably good intentions who too often fall to the temptation of the quick fix, the easily digestible framework that never requires us to consider how we comply with the culture of classism.

References

Abell, T., & Lyon, L. (1979). Do the differences make a difference? An empirical evaluation of the culture of poverty in the United States. *American Anthropologist, 6*(3), 602–621.

Barton, R. E. (2004). Why does the gap persist? *Educational Leadership, 62*(3), 8–13.

Billings, D. (1974). Culture and poverty in Appalachia: A theoretical discussion and empirical analysis. *Social Forces, 53*(2), 315–323.

Bomer, R., Dworin, J. E., May, L., & Semingson, R. (2008). Miseducating teachers about the poor: A critical analysis of Ruby Payne's claims about poverty. *Teachers College Record, 110*(11). Available: www.tcrecord.org/PrintContent .asp?ContentID=14591

Books, S. (2004). *Poverty and schooling in the U.S.: Contexts and consequences.* Mahway, NJ: Erlbaum.

Carey, K. (2005). *The funding gap 2004: Many states still shortchange low-income and minority students.* Washington, DC: Education Trust.

Carmon, N. (1985). Poverty and culture. *Sociological Perspectives, 28*(4), 403–418.

Chen, K., Sheth, A., Krejci, J., & Wallace, J. (2003, August). *Understanding differences in alcohol use among high school students in two different communities.* Paper presented at the annual meeting of the American Sociological Association, Atlanta, GA.

Collins, J. (1988). Language and class in minority education. *Anthropology and Education Quarterly, 19*(4), 299–326.

Compton-Lilly, C. (2003). *Reading families: The literate lives of urban children.* New York: Teachers College Press.

Diala, C. C., Muntaner, C., & Walrath, C. (2004). Gender, occupational, and socioeconomic correlates of alcohol and drug abuse among U.S. rural, metropolitan, and urban residents. *American Journal of Drug and Alcohol Abuse, 30*(2), 409–428.

Economic Policy Institute. (2002). *The state of working class America* 2002–03. Washington, DC: Author.

Galea, S., Ahern, J., Tracy, M., & Vlahov, D. (2007). Neighborhood income and income distribution and the use of cigarettes, alcohol, and marijuana. *American Journal of Preventive Medicine, 32*(6), 195–202.

Gans, H. J. (1995). *The war against the poor: The underclass and antipoverty policy.* New York: BasicBooks.

Gee, J. R (2004). *Situated language and learning: A critique of traditional schooling.* New York: Routledge.

Gorski, R. C. (2003). Privilege and repression in the digital era: Rethinking the sociopolitics of the digital divide. *Race, Gender and Class,* 10(4), 145–176.

Hess, K. M. (1974). The nonstandard speakers in our schools: What should be done? *The Elementary School Journal,* 74(5), 280–290.

Iversen, R. R., & Farber, N. (1996). Transmission of family values, work, and welfare among poor urban black women. *Work and Occupations,* 23(4), 437–460.

Jones, R. K., & Luo, Y. (1999). The culture of poverty and African-American culture: An empirical assessment. *Sociological Perspectives,* 42(3), 439–458.

Karoly, L. A. (2001). Investing in the future: Reducing poverty through human capital investments. In S. Danzinger & R. Haveman (Eds.), *Undemanding poverty* (pp. 314–356). New York: Russell Sage Foundation.

Kozol, J. (1992). *Savage inequalities. Children in America's schools.* New York: Harper-Collins.

Lareau, A., & Horvat, E. (1999). Moments of social inclusion and exclusion: Race, class, and cultural capital in family-school relationships. *Sociology of Education,* 72, 37–53.

Leichter, H. J. (Ed.). (1978). *Families and communities as educators.* New York: Teachers College Press.

Lewis, O. (1961). *The children of Sanchez: Autobiography of a Mexican family.* New York: Random House.

Miller, R. J., Cho, G. E., & Bracey, J. R. (2005). Working-class children's experience through the prism of personal story-telling. *Human Development,* 48, 115–135.

National Center for Children in Poverty. (2004). *Parental employment in low-income families.* New York: Author.

National Center for Education Statistics. (2005). *Parent and family involvement in education:* 2002–03. Washington, DC: Author.

National Commission on Teaching and America's Future. (2004). *Fifty years after* Brown v. Board of Education: *A two-tiered education system.* Washington, DC: Author.

Ortiz, A. T., & Briggs, L. (2003). The culture of poverty, crack babies, and welfare cheats: The making of the "healthy white baby crisis." *Social Text,* 21(3), 39–57.

Rodman, R. (1977). Culture of poverty: The rise and fall of a concept. *Sociological Review,* 25(4), 867–876.

Saxe, L., Kadushin, C., Tighe, E., Rindskopf, D., & Beveridge, A. (2001). *National evaluation of the fighting back program: General population surveys, 1995–1999.* New York: City University of New York Graduate Center.

Wilson, W. J. (1997). *When work disappears.* New York: Random House.

Critical Thinking

1. What is the culture of poverty theory?

2. Why does Gorski believe that the culture of poverty theory is a myth?

3. Do most of the poor have middle-class values?

PAUL GORSKI is Assistant Professor in the Graduate School of Education, Hamline University, St. Paul, Minnesota, and the founder of EdChange (www.edchange.org).

Somewhere between Jim Crow & Post-Racialism

Reflections on the Racial Divide in America Today

LAWRENCE D. BOBO

In assessing the results of the Negro revolution so far, it can be concluded that Negroes have established a foothold, no more. We have written a Declaration of Independence, itself an accomplishment, but the effort to transform the words into a life experience still lies ahead.

—Martin Luther King, Jr.,
Where Do We Go From Here? (1968)

By the middle of the twentieth century, the color line was as well defined and as firmly entrenched as any institution in the land. After all, it was older than most institutions, including the federal government itself. More important, it informed the content and shaped the lives of those institutions and the people who lived under them.

—John Hope Franklin,
The Color Line (1993)

This is where we are right now. It's a racial stalemate we've been stuck in for years. Contrary to the claims of some of my critics, black and white, I have never been so naive as to believe that we can get beyond our racial divisions in a single election cycle, or with a single candidacy—particularly a candidacy as imperfect as my own.

—Barack H. Obama,
"A More Perfect Union" (May 18, 2008)[1]

The year 1965 marked an important inflection point in the struggle for racial justice in the United States, underscoring two fundamental points about race in America.[2] First, that racial inequality and division were not only Southern problems attached to Jim Crow segregation. Second, that the nature of those inequalities and divisions was a matter not merely of formal civil status and law, but also of deeply etched economic arrangements, social and political conditions, and cultural outlooks and practices. Viewed in full, the racial divide was a challenge of truly national reach, multilayered in its complexity and depth. Therefore, the achievement of basic citizenship rights in the South was a pivotal but far from exhaustive stage of the struggle.

The positive trend of the times revolved around the achievement of voting rights. March 7, 1965, now known as Bloody Sunday, saw police and state troopers attack several hundred peaceful civil rights protestors at the Edmund Pettus Bridge in Selma, Alabama. The subsequent march from Selma to Montgomery, participated in by tens of thousands, along with other protest actions, provided the pressure that finally compelled Congress to pass the Voting Rights Act of 1965. A triumphant Reverend Martin Luther King, Jr., and other activists attended the signing in Washington, D.C., on August 6, 1965. It was a moment of great triumph for civil rights.

The long march to freedom seemed to be at its apex, inspiring talk of an era of "Second Reconstruction." A decade earlier, in the historic *Brown v. Board of Education* decision of 1954, the U.S. Supreme Court repudiated the "separate but equal" doctrine. Subsequently, a major civil rights movement victory was achieved with the passage of the Civil Rights Act of 1964, which forbade discrimination in employment and in most public places. With voting rights now protected as well, and the federal government authorized to intervene directly to assure those rights, one might have expected 1965 to stand as a moment of shimmering and untarnished civil rights progress. Yet the mood of optimism and triumph did not last for long.

The negative trend of the times was epitomized by deep and explosive inequalities and resentments of race smoldering in many Northern, urban ghettos. The extent to which the "race problem" was not just a Southern problem of civil rights, but a national problem of inequality woven deep into our economic and cultural fabric, would quickly be laid bare following passage of the Voting Rights Act. Scarcely five days after then-President Johnson signed the bill into law, the Los Angeles community of Watts erupted into flames. Quelling the disorder, which raged for roughly six days, required the mobilization of the National Guard and nearly fifteen thousand troops. When disorder finally subsided, thirty-four people had died, more than one thousand had been injured, well over three thousand were arrested, and approximately $35 million in property damage had been done. Subsequent studies and reports revealed patterns of police abuse, political marginalization, intense poverty, and myriad forms of economic, housing, and social discrimination as contributing to the mix of conditions that led to the riots.

It was thus more than fitting that in 1965, *Dædalus* committed two issues to examining the conditions of "The Negro American." The essays were wide-ranging. The topics addressed spanned questions of power, demographic change, economic conditions, politics and civil status, religion and the church, family and community dynamics, as well as group identity, racial attitudes, and the future of race relations. Scholars from most social scientific fields, including anthropology, economics, history, law, political science, psychology, and sociology, contributed to the volumes. No single theme or message dominated these essays. Instead, the volumes wrestled with the multidimensional and complex patterns of a rapidly changing racial terrain.

Some critical observations stand out from two of those earlier essays, which have been amplified and made centerpieces of much subsequent social science scholarship. Sociologist and anthropologist St. Clair Drake drew a distinction between what he termed *primary victimization* and *indirect victimization.* Primary victimization involved overt discrimination in the labor market that imposed a job ceiling on the economic opportunities available to blacks alongside housing discrimination and segregation that relegated blacks to racially distinct urban ghettos. Indirect or secondary victimization involved the multidimensional and cumulative disadvantages resulting from primary victimization. These consequences included poorer schooling, poor health, and greater exposure to disorder and crime. In a related vein, sociologist Daniel Patrick Moynihan stressed the central importance of employment prospects in the wake of the civil rights victories that secured the basic citizenship rights of African Americans. Both Drake and Moynihan expressed concern about a black class structure marked by signs of a large and growing economically marginalized segment of the black community. Drake went so far as to declare, "If Negroes are not to become a permanent lumpen-proletariat within American society as a result of social forces already at work and increased automation, deliberate planning by governmental and private agencies will be necessary." Striking a similar chord, Moynihan asserted: "[T]here would also seem to be no question that opportunities for a large mass of Negro workers in the lower ranges of training and education have not been improving, that in many ways the circumstances of these workers relative to the white work force have grown worse." This marginalized economic status, both scholars suggested, would have ramifying effects, including weakening family structures in ways likely to worsen the challenges faced by black communities.[3]

If the scholarly assessments of 1965 occurred against a backdrop of powerful and transformative mass-based movement for civil rights and an inchoate sense of deep but imminent change, the backdrop for most scholarly assessments today is the election of Barack Obama as president of the United States, the rise of a potent narrative of post-racialism, and a sense of stalemate or stagnation in racial change. Many meanings or interpretations can be attached to the term *post-racial.* In its simplest and least controversial form, the term is intended merely to signal a hopeful trajectory for events and social trends, not an accomplished fact of social life. It is something toward which we as a nation still strive and remain guardedly hopeful about fully achieving. Three other meanings of post-racialism are filled with more grounds for dispute and controversy. One of these meanings attaches to the waning salience of what some have portrayed as a "black victimology" narrative. From this perspective, black complaints and grievances about inequality and discrimination are well-worn tales, at least passé if not now pointedly false assessments of the main challenges facing blacks in a world largely free of the dismal burdens of overt racial divisions and oppression.[4]

A second and no less controversial view of post-racialism takes the position that the level and pace of change in the demographic makeup and the identity choices and politics of Americans are rendering the traditional black-white divide irrelevant. Accordingly, Americans increasingly revere mixture and hybridity and are rushing to embrace a decidedly "beige" view of themselves and what is good for the body politic. Old-fashioned racial dichotomies pale against the surge toward flexible, deracialized, and mixed ethnoracial identities and outlooks.[5]

A third, and perhaps the most controversial, view of post-racialism has the most in common with the well-rehearsed rhetoric of color blindness. To wit, American society, or at least a large and steadily growing fraction of it, has genuinely moved beyond race—so much so that we as a nation are now ready to transcend the disabling racial divisions of the past. From this perspective, nothing symbolizes better the moment of transcendence than Obama's election as president. This transcendence is said to be especially true of a younger generation, what *New Yorker* editor David Remnick has referred to as "the Joshua Generation." More than any other, this generation is ready to cross the great river of racial identity, division, and acrimony that has for so long defined American culture and politics.

It is in this context of the first African American president of the United States and the rise to prominence of the narrative of post-racialism that a group of social scientists were asked to examine, from many different disciplinary and intellectual vantage points, changes in the racial divide since the time of the *Dædalus* issues focusing on race in 1965 and 1966.

The context today has points of great discontinuity and of great similarity to that mid-1960s inflection point. From the viewpoint of 1965, the election of Obama as the first African American president of the United States, as well as the expansion and the cultural prominence and success of the black middle class of which Obama is a member, speak to the enormous and enduring successes of the civil rights era. Yet also from the standpoint of 1965, the persistence of deep poverty and joblessness for a large fraction of the black population, slowly changing rates of residential segregation by race, continued evidence of antiblack discrimination in many domains of life, and historically high rates of black incarceration signal a journey toward racial justice that remains, even by superficial accounting, seriously incomplete.

I n order to set a context for the essays contained in this volume, I address three key questions in this introduction. The first concerns racial boundaries. In an era of widespread talk of having achieved the post-racial society, do we have real evidence that attention to and the meaning of basic race categories are fundamentally breaking down? The second set of questions concerns the extent of economic inequality along the racial divide. Has racial economic inequality narrowed to a point where we need no longer think or talk of black disadvantage? Or have the bases of race-linked economic inequality changed so much that, at the least, the dynamics of discrimination and prejudice no longer need concern us? The third question is, how have racial attitudes changed in the period since the mid-1960s *Dædalus* issues?

To foreshadow a bit, I will show that basic racial boundaries are not quickly and inevitably collapsing, though they are changing and under great pressure. Racial economic inequality is less extreme today, there is a substantial black middle class, and inequality *within* the black population itself has probably never been greater. Yet there remain large and durable patterns of black-white economic inequality as well, patterns that are not overcome or eliminated even for

the middle class and that still rest to a significant degree on discriminatory social processes. In addition, I maintain that we continue to witness the erosion and decline of Jim Crow racist attitudes in the United States. However, in their place has emerged a new pattern of attitudes and beliefs, variously labeled *symbolic racism, modern racism, color-blind racism,* or as I prefer it, *laissez-faire racism.* The new form of racism is a more covert, sophisticated, culture-centered, and subtle racist ideology, qualitatively less extreme and more socially permeable than Jim Crow racism with its attendant biological foundations and calls for overt discrimination. But this new racism yields a powerful influence in our culture and politics.[6]

Consider first the matter of group boundaries. The 2000 Census broke new ground by allowing individuals to mark more than one box in designating racial background. Indeed, great political pressure and tumult led to the decision to move the Census in a direction that more formally and institutionally acknowledged the presence of increasing mixture and heterogeneity in the American population with regard to racial background. Nearly seven million people exercised that option in 2000. The successful rise of Obama to the office of president, the first African American to do so, as a child of a white American mother and a black Kenyan father, has only accelerated the sense of the newfound latitude and recognition granted to those who claim more than one racial heritage.[7]

Despite Obama's electoral success and the press attention given to the phenomenon, some will no doubt find it surprising that the overwhelming majority of Americans identify with only one race. Less than 2 percent of the population marked more than one box on the 2000 Census in designating their racial background. Fully 98 percent marked just one. I claim no deep-rootedness or profound personal salience for these identities. Rather, my point is that we should be mindful that the level of "discussion" and contention around mixture is far out of proportion to the extent to which most Americans actually designate and see themselves in these terms.

Moreover, even if we restrict attention to just those who marked more than one box, two-thirds of these respondents designated two groups other than blacks (namely, Hispanic-white, Asian-white, or Hispanic and Asian mixtures). Some degree of mixture with black constituted just under a third of mixed race identifiers in 2000. Given the historic size of the black population and the extended length of contact with white Americans, this remarkable result says something powerful about the potency and durability of the historic black-white divide.

It is worth recalling that sexual relations and childbearing across the racial divide are not recent phenomena. The 1890 U.S. Census contained categories for not only "Negro" but also "Mulatto," "Quadroon," and even "Octoroon"; these were clear signs of the extent of "mixing" that had taken place in the United States. Indeed, well over one million individuals fell into one of the mixed race categories at that time. In order to protect the institution of slavery and to prevent the offspring of white slave masters and exploited black slave women from having a claim on freedom as well as on the property of the master, slave status, as defined by law, followed the mother's status, not the father's. For most of its history, the United States legally barred or discouraged racial mixing and intermarriage. At the time of the *Loving v. Virginia* case in 1967, seventeen states still banned racial intermarriage.[8]

Formal, legal definitions of who was black, and especially the development of rules of "hypodescent," or the one-drop rule, have a further implication that is often lost in discussions of race: these practices tended to fuse together race and class, in effect making blackness synonymous with the very bottom of the class structure. As historian David Hollinger explains:

The combination of hypodescent with the denial to blacks residing in many states with large black populations of any opportunity for legal marriage to whites ensured that the color line would long remain to a very large extent a property line. Hence the dynamics of race formation and the dynamics of class formation were, in this most crucial of all American cases, largely the same. This is one of the most important truths about the history of the United States brought into sharper focus when that history is viewed through the lens of the question of ethnoracial mixture.[9]

Still, we know that today the ethnoracial landscape in the United States is changing. As of the 2000 Census, whites constituted just 69 percent of the U.S. population, with Hispanics and blacks each around 12 percent. This distribution represents a substantial decline in the percentage of whites from twenty or, even more so, forty years ago.

With continued immigration, differential group fertility patterns, and the continued degree of intermarriage and mixing, these patterns will not remain stable. . . .

Does that pressure for change foretell the ultimate undoing of the black-white divide? At least three lines of research raise doubts about such a forecast. First, studies of the perceptions of and identities among those of mixed racial backgrounds point to strong evidence of the cultural persistence of the one-drop rule. Systematic experiments by sociologists and social psychologists are intriguing in this regard. For example, sociologist Melissa Herman's recent research concluded that "others' perceptions shape a person's identity and social understandings of race. My study found that part-black multiracial youth are more likely to be seen as black by observers and to define themselves as black when forced to choose one race."[10]

Second, studies of patterns in racial intermarriage point to a highly durable if somewhat less extreme black-white divide today. A careful assessment of racial intermarriage

patterns in 1990 by demographer Vincent Kang Fu found that "one key feature of the data is overwhelming endogamy for blacks and whites. At least 92 percent of white men, white women, black women and black men are married to members of their own group."[11] Rates of intermarriage rose for blacks and whites over the course of the 1990s. However, subsequent analysts continued to stress the degree to which a fundamental black-white divide persists. As demographers Zhenchao Qian and Daniel Lichter conclude in their analyses of U.S. Census data from 1990 and 2000:

[O]ur results also highlight a singularly persistent substantive lesson: African Americans are least likely of all racial/ethnic minorities to marry whites. And, although the pace of marital assimilation among African Americans proceeded more rapidly over the 1990s than it did in earlier decades, the social boundaries between African American and whites remain highly rigid and resilient to change. The "one-drop" rule apparently persists for African Americans.[12]

Third, some key synthetic works argue for an evolving racial scheme in the United States, but a scheme that nonetheless preserves a heavily stigmatized black category. A decade ago, sociologist Herbert Gans offered the provocative but well-grounded speculation that the United States would witness a transition from a society defined by a great white–non-white divide to one increasingly defined by a black–non-black fissure, with an in-between or residual category for those granted provisional or "honorary white" status. As Gans explained: "If current trends persist, today's multiracial hierarchy could be replaced by what I think of as a dual or bimodal one consisting of 'nonblack' and 'black' population categories, with a third 'residual' category for the groups that do not, or do not yet, fit into the basic dualism." Most troubling, this new dualism would, in Gans's expectations, continue to bring a profound sense of undeservingness and stigma for those assigned its bottom rung.[13]

Gans's remarks have recently received substantial support from demographer Frank Bean and his colleagues. Based on their extensive analyses of population trends across a variety of indicators, Bean and colleagues write: "A black-nonblack divide appears to be taking shape in the United States, in which Asians and Latinos are closer to whites. Hence, America's color lines are moving toward a new demarcation that places many blacks in a position of disadvantage similar to that resulting from the traditional black-white divide."

If basic racial categories and identities are not soon to dissolve, then let me now address that second set of questions, concerning the degree of racial economic inequality. I should begin by noting that there has been considerable expansion in the size, security, and, arguably, salience and influence of the black middle class. . . .[14]

The official black poverty rate has fluctuated between two to three times the poverty rate for whites. Recent trend analyses suggest that this disparity declined during the economic boom years of the 1990s but remained substantial. As public policy analyst Michael Stoll explains: "Among all black families, the poverty rate declined from a 20 year high of about 40 percent in 1982 and 1993 to 25 percent in 2000. During this period, the poverty rate for white families remained fairly constant, at about 10 percent." That of 25 percent remains true through more recent estimates. In addition, the Great Recession has taken a particularly heavy toll on minority communities, African Americans perhaps most of all. As the Center for American Progress declared in a recent report: "Economic security and losses during the recession and recovery exacerbated the already weak situation for African Americans. They experienced declining employment rates, rising poverty rates, falling home-ownership rates, decreasing health insurance and retirement coverage during the last business cycle from 2001 to 2007. The recession that followed made a bad situation much worse."[15]

Overall trends in poverty, however, do not fully capture the cumulative and multidimensional nature of black economic disadvantage. Sociologist William Julius Wilson stresses how circumstances of persistently weak employment prospects and joblessness, particularly for low-skilled black men, weaken the formation of stable two-parent households and undermine other community structures. Persistent economic hardship and weakened social institutions then create circumstances that lead to rising rates of single-parent households, out-of-wedlock childbearing, welfare dependency, and greater risk of juvenile delinquency and involvement in crime. Harvard sociologist Robert Sampson points to an extraordinary circumstance of exposure to living in deeply disadvantaged communities for large segments of the African American population. This disadvantage involves living in conditions that expose residents to high surrounding rates of unemployment, family breakup, individuals and families reliant on welfare, poor-performing schools, juvenile delinquency, and crime. As Sampson explains:

[A]lthough we knew that the average national rate of family disruption and poverty among blacks was two to four times higher than among whites, the number of distinct ecological contexts in which blacks achieve equality to whites is striking. In not one city of 100,000 or more in the United States do blacks live in ecological equality with whites when it comes to these basic features of economic and family organization. Accordingly, racial differences in poverty and family disruption are so strong that the "worst" urban contexts in which whites reside are considerably better than the average context of black communities.[16]

Recent work published by sociologist Patrick Sharkey assesses race differences in the chances of mobility out of impoverished neighborhoods. The result is a very depressing one. He finds evidence of little upward social mobility for disadvantaged blacks and a fragile capacity to maintain advantaged status among even the most well-off African Americans. He writes: "[M]ore than 70% of black children who are raised in the poorest quarter of American neighborhoods will continue to live in the poorest quarter of neighborhoods as adults. Since the 1970s, more than half of black families have lived in the poorest quarter of neighborhoods in consecutive generations, compared to just 7% of white families." Discussing the upper end, Sharkey writes: "Among the small number of black families who live in the top quartile, only 35% remain there in the second generation. By themselves, these figures reveal the striking persistence of neighborhood disadvantage among black families." This figure of 35 percent remaining in the top quartile across generations for blacks contrasts to 63 percent among whites. Thus, "White families exhibit a high rate of mobility out of the poorest neighborhoods and a low rate of mobility out of the most affluent neighborhoods, and the opposite is true among black families."[17]

The general labor market prospects of African Americans have undergone key changes in the last several decades. Three patterns loom large. There is far more internal differentiation and inequality within the black population than was true at the close of World War II, or even during our baseline of the mid-1960s. The fortunes of men and women have recently diverged within the black community. Black women have considerably narrowed the gap between themselves and white women in terms of educational attainment, major occupational categories, and earnings. Black men have faced a growing problem of economic marginalization. Importantly, this is contingent on levels of education; education has become a far sharper dividing line, shaping life chances more heavily than ever before in the black community.[18]

Several other dimensions of socioeconomic status bear mentioning. Even by conservative estimates, the high school dropout rate among blacks is twice that of whites, at 20 percent versus 11 percent. Blacks also have much lower college completion rates (17 percent versus 30 percent) and lower advanced degree completion rates (6 percent versus 11 percent). These differences are enormously consequential. As the essays in this volume by economist James Heckman and social psychologist Richard Nisbett emphasize, educational attainment and achievement increasingly define access to the good life, broadly defined. Moreover, some scholars make a strong case that important inequalities in resources still plague the educational experiences of many black school children, involving such factors as fewer well-trained teachers and less access to AP courses and other curriculum-enriching materials and experiences.[19]

One of the major social trends affecting African Americans over the past several decades has been the sharply punitive and incarceration-focused turn in the American criminal justice system. Between 1980 and 2000, the rate of black incarceration nearly tripled. The black-to-white incarceration ratio increased to above eight to one during this time period. Actuarial forecasts, or lifetime estimates, of the risk of incarceration for black males born in the 1990s approach one in three, as compared to below one in ten for non-Hispanic white males. A recent major study by the Pew Foundation reported that as of 2007, one in fifteen black males age eighteen and above was in jail or prison, and one in nine black males between the ages of twenty and thirty-four was in jail or prison. Blacks constitute a hugely disproportionate share of those incarcerated relative to their numbers in the general population.[20]

The reach of mass incarceration has risen to such levels that some analysts view it as altering normative life-course experiences for blacks in low-income neighborhoods. Indeed, the fabric of social life changes in heavily policed, low-income urban communities. The degree of incarceration has prompted scholars to describe the change as ushering in a new fourth stage of racial oppression, "the carceral state," constituted by the emergence of "the new Jim Crow" or, more narrowly, racialized mass incarceration. Whichever label one employs, there is no denying that exposure to the criminal justice system touches the lives of a large fraction of the African American population, especially young men of low education and skill levels. These low levels of education and greater exposure to poverty, along with what many regard as the racially biased conduct of the War on Drugs, play a huge role in black over-representation in jails or federal and state prisons.[21]

Processes of racial residential segregation are a key factor in contemporary racial inequality. Despite important declines in overall rates of segregation over the past three decades and blacks' increasing suburbanization, blacks remain highly segregated from whites. Some have suggested that active self-segregation on the part of blacks is now a major factor sustaining residential segregation. A number of careful investigations of preferences for neighborhood characteristics and makeup and of the housing search process strongly challenge such claims. Instead, there is substantial evidence that, particularly among white Americans, neighborhoods and social spaces are strongly racially coded, with negative racial stereotypes playing a powerful role in shaping the degree of willingness to enter (or remain) in racially integrated living spaces. Moreover, careful auditing studies continue to show lower, but still significant, rates of antiblack discrimination on the part of real estate agents, homeowners, and landlords.[22]

Lastly, I want to stress that wealth inequality between blacks and whites remains enormous. Recent scholarship has convincingly argued that wealth (or accumulated assets) is a crucial determinant of quality of life. Blacks at all levels of the class hierarchy typically possess far less wealth than otherwise comparable whites. Moreover, the composition of black wealth is more heavily based in homes and automobiles as compared to white wealth, which includes a more even spread across savings, stocks and bonds, business ownership, and other more readily liquidated assets. Whereas approximately 75 percent of whites own their homes, only 47 percent of blacks do. Looking beyond homeownership to the full range of financial assets, analyses from sociologists Melvin Oliver and Tom Shapiro put the black-to-white wealth gap ratio in the range of ten or eleven to one. Other estimates, such as those based on Panel Study of Income Dynamics data, are lower but still represent gaping disparities. . . .[23]

In many respects, these sizable gaps in wealth associated with race are one of the principal ways in which the cumulative and "sedimentary" impact of a long history of racial oppression manifests itself. Research has shown that black and white families do not differ substantially in the extent to which they try to save income. Much wealth is inherited; it is not the product of strictly individual merit or achievement. Furthermore, social policy in many ways played a direct role in facilitating the accumulation of wealth for many generations of white Americans while systematically constraining or undermining such opportunities for African Americans. For example, Oliver and Shapiro and political scientist Ira Katznelson both point to federal home mortgage lending guidelines and practices, which were once openly discriminatory, as playing a crucial role in this process.[24]

What do we know about changes in racial attitudes in the United States? The first and most consistent finding of the major national studies of racial attitudes in the United States has been a steady repudiation of the outlooks that supported the Jim Crow social order. Jim Crow racism once reigned in American society, particularly in the South. Accordingly, blacks were understood as inherently inferior to whites, both intellectually and temperamentally. As a result, society was to be expressly ordered in terms of white privilege, with blacks relegated to secondary status in education, access to jobs, and in civic status such as the right to vote. Above all, racial mixture was to be avoided; hence, society needed to be segregated. The best survey data on American public opinion suggest that this set of ideas has been in steady retreat since the 1940s.[25]

There is one telling illustration of this trend. It shows the percentage of white Americans in national surveys who said that they would *not* be willing to vote for a qualified black candidate for president if nominated by their own party. When first asked in 1958, nearly two out of three white Americans endorsed such an openly discriminatory posture. That trend has undergone unabated decline, reaching the point where roughly only one in five white Americans expressed this view by the time the Reverend Jesse Jackson launched his first bid for the Democratic presidential nomination in 1984. It declined to fewer than one in ten by the time of Obama's campaign in 2008.

In broad sweep, though not necessarily in exact levels, the aforementioned trend is true of most questions on racial attitudes from national surveys that deal with broad principles of whether American society should be integrated or segregated, discriminatory or nondiscriminatory on the basis of race. Whether the specific domain involved school integration, residential integration, or even racial intermarriage, the level of endorsement of discriminatory, segregationist responses has continued to decline. To an important degree, these changes have been led by highly educated whites and those outside the South. African Americans have never endorsed elements of the Jim Crow outlook to any substantial degree, though many of these questions were not initially asked of black respondents out of fear that the questions would be regarded as an insult, or to the assumption that their responses were predictable.

This picture of the repudiation of Jim Crow is complicated somewhat by evidence of significant social distance preferences. To be sure, low and typically declining percentages of whites objected when asked about entering into integrated social settings—neighborhoods or schools—where one or just a small number of blacks might be present. But as the number of blacks involved increased, and as one shifts from more impersonal and public domains of life (workplaces, schools, neighborhoods) to more intimate and personal domains (intermarriage), expressed levels of white resistance rise and the degree of positive change is not as great.

The notion of the 1960s as an inflection point in the struggle for racial change is reinforced by the growing preoccupation of studies of racial attitudes in the post-1960 period with matters of public policy. These studies consider levels of support or opposition to public policies designed to bring about greater racial equality (antidiscrimination laws and various forms of affirmative action) and actual integration (open housing laws and methods of school desegregation such as school busing). The picture that results is complex but has several recurrent features. Blacks are typically far more supportive of social-policy intervention on matters of race than are whites. In general, support for policy or governmental intervention to bring about greater integration or to reduce racial inequality lags well behind endorsement of similar broad principles or ideals. This finding has led many scholars to note a "principle-implementation gap." Some policies, however, have wider appeal than others. Efforts to enhance or improve the human capital attributes of blacks and other minority group members are more popular than policies that call for group preferences. Forms of affirmative action

that imply quotas or otherwise disregard meritocratic criteria of reward are deeply unpopular.

One important line of investigation seeking to understand the principle-implementation gap involved assessments of perceptions and causal attributions for racial inequality. To the extent that many individuals do not perceive much racial inequality, or explain it in terms of individual dispositions and choices (as opposed to structural constraints and conditions such as discrimination), then there is little need seen for government action. Table 1 shows responses to a series of questions on possible causes of black-white economic inequality that included "less inborn ability," "lack of motivation and willpower," "no chance for an education," and "mainly due to discrimination." The questions thus span biological basis (ability), cultural basis (motivation), a weak form of structural constraint (education), and finally, a strong structural constraint (discrimination).[26]

There is low and decreasing support among whites for the overtly racist belief that blacks have less inborn ability. The most widely endorsed account among whites points to a lack of motivation or willpower on the part of blacks as a key factor in racial inequality, though this attribution declines over time. Attributions to discrimination as well as to the weaker structural account of lack of a chance for education also decline among whites. Blacks are generally far more likely than whites to endorse structural accounts of racial inequality, particularly the strongest attribution of discrimination. However, like their white counterparts, a declining number of blacks point to discrimination as the key factor, and there is actually a rise in the percentage of African Americans attributing racial inequality to a lack of motivation or willpower on the part of blacks themselves. More detailed multivariate analyses suggest that there has been growth in cultural attributions for racial inequality. Among African Americans this growth seems most prominent among somewhat younger, ideologically conservative, and less well-educated individuals. . . .[27]

We can see trends in whites' stereotype trait ratings of whites as compared to blacks on the dimensions of being hardworking or lazy and intelligent or unintelligent. In 1990, when these trait-rating stereotype questions were first posed in national surveys, more than 60 percent of whites rated whites as more likely to be hardworking than blacks, and just under 60 percent rated blacks as less intelligent. A variety of other trait dimensions were included in this early assessment, such as welfare dependency, involvement in drugs and gangs, and levels of patriotism. Whites usually expressed a substantially negative image of blacks relative to how they rated whites across this array of traits. The trends suggest some slight reduction in negative stereotyping over the past two decades, but such negative images of blacks still remain quite commonplace. To the extent that unfavorable beliefs about the behavioral characteristics of blacks have a bearing on levels of support for policies designed to benefit blacks, these data imply, and much evidence confirms, that negative beliefs about blacks' abilities and behavioral choices contribute to low levels of white support for significant social-policy interventions to ameliorate racial inequality.[28]

A third and perhaps most vigorously considered resolution of the principle-implementation gap involves the hypothesis that a new form of antiblack racism is at the root of much white opposition to policies aimed at reducing racial inequality. This scholarship has focused largely on the emergence of attitudes of resentment toward the demands or grievances voiced by African Americans and the expectation of governmental redress for those demands and grievances. In trends for one question frequently used to tap such sentiments; respondents are asked to agree or disagree with the statement, "Irish, Italian, Jewish and many other minorities overcame prejudice and worked their way up. Blacks should do the same without special favors." Throughout the 1994 to 2008 time span, roughly three-fourths of white Americans agreed with this assertion. There is no meaningful trend, despite a slight dip in 2004: the lopsided view among whites is that blacks need to make it all on their own.[29]

Throughout the fourteen-year time span, whites were always substantially more likely to endorse this viewpoint than blacks; however, not only did a non-trivial number of blacks agree with it (about 50 percent), but the black-white gap actually narrowed slightly over time. The meaning and effects of this type of outlook vary in important ways depending on race, usually carrying less potent implications for policy views among blacks than among whites. Indeed, one reason for focusing on this type of attitude is that it and similar items are found to correlate with a wide range of social-policy outlooks. And some evidence suggests that how attitudes and outlooks connect with partisanship and voting behavior may be strengthening and growing.[30]

Judged by the trends considered here and in the essays in this volume, declarations of having arrived at the post-racial moment are premature. Much has changed—and unequivocally for the better—in light of where the United States stood in 1965. Indeed, I will speculate that none of the contributors to the 1965/1966 *Dædalus* volumes would have considered likely changes that have now, a mere four or so decades later, been realized, including the election of an African American President of the United States, the appointment of the first black Chair of the Joint Chiefs of Staff, and the appointment of two different African American Secretaries of State. Similarly, the size and reach of today's black middle class were not easy to forecast from the scholarly perch of mid-1960s data and understandings. At the same time, troublingly entrenched patterns of poverty, segregation, gaps in educational attainment and achievement, racial identity formation, and disparaging racial stereotypes

all endure into the present, even if in somewhat less extreme forms. And the scandalous rise in what is now termed racialized mass incarceration was not foreseen but now adds a new measure of urgency to these concerns.

The very complex and contradictory nature of these changes cautions against the urge to make sweeping and simple declarations about where we now stand. But our nation's "mixed" or ambiguous circumstance—suspended uncomfortably somewhere between the collapse of the Jim Crow social order and a post-racial social order that has yet to be attained—gives rise to many intense exchanges over whether or how much "race matters." This is true of scholarly discourse, where many see racial division as a deeply entrenched and tragic American flaw and many others see racial division as a waning exception to the coming triumph of American liberalism.[31]

Average Americans, both black and white, face and wage much of the same debate in their day-to-day lives. One way of capturing this dynamic is illustrated . . . in a 2009 national survey that asked, "Do you think that blacks have achieved racial equality, will soon achieve racial equality, will not achieve racial equality in your lifetime, or will never achieve racial equality?" Fielded after the 2008 election and the inauguration of Obama in early 2009, these results are instructive. Almost two out of three white Americans (61.3 percent) said that blacks have achieved racial equality. Another 21.5 percent of whites endorse the view that blacks will soon achieve racial equality. Thus, the overwhelming fraction of white Americans see the post-racial moment as effectively here (83.8 percent). Fewer than one in five blacks endorsed the idea that they have already achieved racial equality. A more substantial fraction, 36.2 percent, believe that they will soon achieve racial equality. African Americans, then, are divided almost evenly between those doubtful that racial equality will soon be achieved (with more than one in ten saying that it will never be achieved) and those who see equality as within reach, at 46.6 percent versus 53.6 percent.[32]

These results underscore why discussions of race so easily and quickly become polarized and fractious along racial lines. The central tendencies of public opinion on these issues, despite real increasing overlap, remain enormously far apart between black and white Americans. When such differences in perception and belief are grounded in, or at least reinforced by, wide economic inequality, persistent residential segregation, largely racially homogeneous family units and close friendship networks, and a popular culture still suffused with negative ideas and images about African Americans, then there should be little surprise that we still find it enormously difficult to have sustained civil discussions about race and racial matters. Despite growing much closer together in recent decades, the gaps in perspective between blacks and whites are still sizable.

The ideas and evidence marshaled in this *Dædalus* issue should help sharpen our focus and open up productive new lines of discourse and inquiry. Four of the essays directly engage central, but changing, features of racial stratification in the United States. Sociologist Douglas S. Massey provides a trenchant, broad map of change in the status of African Americans. Sociologist William Julius Wilson reviews and assesses his field-defining argument about the "declining significance of race." The core framework is sustained, he maintains, by much subsequent careful research; but Wilson stresses now the special importance of employment in the government sector to the economic well-being of many African Americans. Economist James J. Heckman focuses on education, building the case for enhancing the capacities of families and communities to prepare children to get the most out of schooling. Social psychologist Richard E. Nisbett looks closely at the types of early intervention strategies that evidence suggests are most likely to improve ultimate educational attainment and achievement.

Three essays put the changing status of African Americans in more explicit political, policy-related, and legal perspectives. Political scientist Rogers M. Smith and his colleagues identify the pivotal role played by agents of competing racial policy coalitions, pointing to the differing agendas and degrees of political success and influence of those pursuing a color-blind strategy and those pursuing a color-conscious strategy. Legal scholar Michael J. Klarman challenges the presumption that the U.S. Supreme Court has been a special ally or supporter of African American interests and claims. He suggests that the Court has often, particularly in a string of recent rulings, tilted heavily in the direction of a color-blind set of principles that do little to advance the interests of black communities. Political scientist Daniel Sabbagh traces the impetus for affirmative action and its evolution in the United States and compares that to how affirmative action is now pursued in a number of other countries.

Several essays examine the cultural dynamics of race and racial identities. Anthropologists Marcyliena Morgan and Dionne Bennett examine the remarkable dynamism, worldwide spread, and influence of hip-hop music. Social psychologists Jennifer A. Richeson and Maureen A. Craig examine the psychological dynamics of identity choices facing minority communities and individuals in this era of rapid population change. Political scientist Jennifer L. Hochschild and her colleagues assess how younger cohorts of Americans are bringing different views of race and its importance to politics and social life.

Three essays pivot off the 2008 presidential election. Political scientist Taeku Lee examines the complex role of race, group identity, and immigrant status in forging new political identities, coalitions, and voting behavior. Political scientist Cathy J. Cohen shows the continuing racial consciousness and orientations of black youth. Sociologist Alford A. Young, Jr., examines the special meaning of Obama's candidacy and success for young black men.

Two final essays push in quite different directions. Sociologist Roger Waldinger argues that even as the black-white divide remains an important problem, we as a nation are facing deep contradictions in how we deal with immigration and immigrants themselves, particularly those coming from Latin America. Historian Martha Biondi muses on continuities with and departures from past traditions in recent discourse surrounding the mission of African American studies programs and departments.

This issue is a companion volume to the Winter 2011 issue of *Dædalus,* Race in the Age of Obama, guest edited by Gerald Early, the Merle Kling Professor of Modern Letters and Director of the Center for the Humanities at Washington University in St. Louis. It has been my privilege to work with Gerald on this project, and I am grateful to the contributors to this volume for their informed analyses.

This essay's epigraphs from Martin Luther King, Jr., John Hope Franklin, and Barack Obama, each in its own fashion, remind us of the depth and complexity of race in the United States. Although it is tempting to seek quick and simple assessments of where we have been and where we are going, it is wise, instead, to wrestle with taking stock of all the variegated and nuanced circumstances underlying the black-white divide and its associated phenomena. Just as 1965 seemed a point of inflection, of contradictory lines of development, future generations may look back and regard 2011 as a similarly fraught moment. At the same time that a nation celebrates the historic election of an African American president, the cultural production of demeaning antiblack images—postcards featuring watermelons on the White House lawn prior to the annual Easter egg roll, Obama featured in loincloth and with a bone through his nose in ads denouncing the health care bill, a cartoon showing police officers shooting an out-of-control chimpanzee under the heading "They'll have to find someone else to write the next stimulus bill"—are ugly reminders of some of the more overtly racialized reactions to the ascendancy of an African American to the presidency of the United States.

As a result of complex and contradictory indicators, no pithy phrase or bold declaration can possibly do justice to the full body of research, evidence, and ideas reviewed here. One optimistic trend is that examinations of the status of blacks have moved to a place of prominence and sophistication in the social sciences that probably was never imagined by founding figures of the tradition, such as W.E.B. Du Bois. That accumulating body of knowledge and theory, including the new contributions herein, deepens our understanding of the experience of race in the United States. The configuration and salience of the color line some fifty or one hundred years from now, however, cannot be forecast with any measure of certainty. Perhaps the strongest general declaration one can make at present is that we stand somewhere between a Jim Crow past and the aspiration of a post-racial future.

Notes

1. Martin Luther King, Jr., *Where Do We Go From Here: Chaos or Community?* (New York: Bantam, 1968), 19; John Hope Franklin, *The Color Line: Legacy for the 21st Century* (Columbia: University of Missouri Press, 1993), 36; Barack H. Obama, "A More Perfect Union," speech delivered at the National Constitution Center, Philadelphia, May 18, 2008.

2. I wish to thank Alicia Simmons, Victor Thompson, and Deborah De Laurell for their invaluable assistance in preparing this essay. I am responsible for any remaining errors or shortcomings.

3. St. Clair Drake, "The Social and Economic Status of the Negro in the United States," *Dædalus* 94 (4) (Fall 1965): 3–46; Daniel Patrick Moynihan, "Employment, Income, and the Ordeal of the Negro Family," *Dædalus* 94 (4) (Fall 1965): 134–159.

4. See John McWhorter, *Losing the Race: Self-Sabotage in Black America* (New York: Free Press, 2000); and Charles Johnson, "The End of the Black American Narrative," *The American Scholar* 77 (3) (Summer 2008).

5. See Hua Hsu, "The End of White America?" *The Atlantic,* January/February 2009; and Susan Saulny, "Black? White? Asian? More Young Americans Choose All of the Above," *The New York Times,* January 29, 2011.

6. On laissez-faire racism, see Lawrence D. Bobo, James R. Kluegel, and Ryan A. Smith, "Laissez-Faire Racism: The Crystallization of a Kinder, Gentler, Antiblack Ideology," in *Racial Attitudes in the 1990s: Continuity and Change,* ed. Steven A. Tuch and Jack K. Martin (Greenwood, Conn.: Praeger, 1997), 15–44; on modern or symbolic racism, see David O. Sears, "Symbolic Racism," in *Eliminating Racism: Profiles in Controversy,* ed. Phyllis A. Katz and Dalmas A. Taylor (New York: Plenum Press, 1988), 53–84; and on color-blind racism, see Eduardo Bonilla-Silva, *Racism without Racists: Colorblind Racism and Racial Inequality in Contemporary America* (Boulder, Colo.: Rowman and Littlefield, 2010).

7. See C. Matthew Snipp, "Defining Race and Ethnicity: The Constitution, the Supreme Court, and the Census," in *Doing Race: 21 Essays for the 21st Century,* ed. Hazel R. Markus and Paula M.L. Moya (New York: W.W. Norton, 2010), 105–122. It is noteworthy that Obama himself checked only the "Black" category rather than marking more than one race on his 2010 Census form.

8. On the history of "mixing" in the United States, see Gary B. Nash, "The Hidden History of Mestizo America," *Journal of American History* 82 (1995): 941–964; and Victor Thompson, "The Strange Career of Racial Science: Racial Categories and African American Identity," in *The Oxford Handbook of African American Citizenship,* ed. Henry Louis Gates, Jr., et al. (New York: Oxford University Press, forthcoming).

9. David A. Hollinger, "Amalgamation and Hypodescent: The Question of Ethnoracial Mixture in the History of the United States," *American Historical Review* 108 (December 2003): 1305–1390.

10. Melissa R. Herman, "Do You See Who I Am?: How Observers' Background Affects the Perceptions of Multiracial Faces," *Social Psychology Quarterly* 73 (2010): 58–78; see also Arnold K. Ho, Jim Sidanius, Daniel T. Levin, and Mahzarin R. Banaji,

"Evidence for Hypo-descent and Racial Hierarchy in the Categorization and Perception of Biracial Individuals," *Journal of Personality and Social Psychology* 94 (2010): 1–15.

11. Vincent Kang Fu, "How Many Melting Pots?: Intermarriage, Panethnicity, and the Black/Non-Black Divide in the United States," *Journal of Comparative Family Studies* 38 (2007): 215–237. On the point of a racial preference hierarchy, see Vincent Kang Fu, "Racial Intermarriage Pairings," *Demography* 38 (2001): 147–159.

12. Zenchao Qian and Daniel T. Lichter, "Social Boundaries and Marital Assimilation: Interpreting Trends in Racial and Ethnic Intermarriage," *American Sociological Review* 72 (2007): 68–94. See also Zenchao Qian, "Breaking the Last Taboo: Interracial Marriage in America," *Contexts* 4 (2005): 33–37.

13. Herbert J. Gans, "The Possibility of a New Racial Hierarchy in the Twenty-First Century United States," in *The Cultural Territories of Race: Black and White Boundaries,* ed. Michèle Lamont (New York: Russell Sage, 1999), 371–390; and Frank D. Bean et al., "The New U.S. Immigrants: How Do They Affect Our Understanding of the African American Experience?" *Annals of the American Academy of Political and Social Science* 621 (2009): 202–220. For closely related discussions, see Mary C. Waters, *Black Identities: West Indian Immigrant Dreams and American Realities* (Cambridge, Mass.: Harvard University Press, 1999); and Milton Vickerman, "Recent Immigration and Race: Continuity and Change," *Du Bois Review* 4 (2007): 141–165.

14. See Bart Landry, *The New Black Middle Class* (Berkeley: University of California Press, 1987); Karyn Lacy, *Blue Chip Black: Race, Class and Status in the New Black Middle Class* (Berkeley: University of California Press, 2007); and Mary Pattillo, *Black on the Block: The Politics of Race and Class in the City* (Chicago: University of Chicago Press, 2007).

15. Christian E. Weller, Jaryn Fields, and Folayemi Agbede, "The State of Communities of Color in the U.S. Economy" (Washington, D.C.: Center for American Progress, January 21, 2011), http://www.americanprogress.org/issues/2011/01/coc_snapshot.html/print.html (accessed January 23, 2011).

16. William Julius Wilson, *The Truly Disadvantaged: The Inner City, the Underclass, and Public Policy* (Chicago: University of Chicago Press, 1987); William Julius Wilson, *When Work Disappears: The World of the New Urban Poor* (New York: Knopf, 1996); and Robert J. Sampson, "Urban Black Violence: The Effect of Male Joblessness and Family Disruption," *American Journal of Sociology* 93 (1987): 348–382.

17. Patrick Sharkey, "The Intergenerational Transmission of Context," *American Journal of Sociology* 113 (4): 931–969. See also Tom Hertz, "Rags, Riches, and Race: The Intergenerational Economic Mobility of Black and White Families in the United States," in *Unequal Chances: Family Background and Economic Success,* ed. Samuel Bowles, Herbert Gintis, and Melissa Osborne Groves (Princeton, N.J.: Princeton University Press, 2005).

18. See Michael B. Katz, Mark J. Stern, and Jamie J. Fader, "The New African American Inequality," *The Journal of American History* 92 (1) (2005): 75–108.

19. Linda Darling Hammond, "The Color Line in American Education: Race, Resources, and Student Achievement,"

Du Bois Review 1 (2004): 213–246; and Linda Darling Hammond, "Structured for Failure: Race, Resources, and Student Achievement," in *Doing Race,* ed. Markus and Moya, 295–321.

20. Alfred Blumstein, "Race and Criminal Justice," in *America Becoming: Racial Trends and Their Consequences, Volume II,* ed. Neil J. Smelser, William Julius Wilson, and Faith Mitchell (Washington, D.C.: National Academies Press, 2001), 21–31; and Pew Center on the States, "One in 100: Behind Bars in America 2008" (Washington, D.C.: Pew Charitable Trusts, 2008).

21. Generally, see Bruce Western, *Punishment and Inequality in America* (New York: Russell Sage, 2006). On changes in the normative life trajectories, see Becky Pettit and Bruce Western, "Mass Imprisonment and the Life-Course: Race and Class Inequality in U.S. Incarceration," *American Sociological Review* 69 (2004): 151–169. On the social costs of heavy police scrutiny of poor neighborhoods, see Loïc Wacquant, "Deadly Symbiosis: When Ghetto and Prison Meet and Mesh," *Punishment and Society* 3 (2001): 95–135; and Alice Goffman, "On the Run: Wanted Men in a Philadelphia Ghetto," *American Sociological Review* 74 (2009): 339–357. On the rising incarceration rates for blacks more broadly, see Lawrence D. Bobo and Victor Thompson, "Racialized Mass Incarceration: Poverty, Prejudice, and Punitiveness," in *Doing Race,* ed. Markus and Moya, 322–355; and Michelle Alexander, *The New Jim Crow: Mass Incarceration in the Age of Colorblindness* (New York: The New Press, 2010).

22. Generally, see Douglas S. Massey and Nancy A. Denton, *American Apartheid: Segregation and the Making of the Underclass* (Cambridge, Mass.: Harvard University Press, 1993); Camille Z. Charles, *Won't You Be My Neighbor?: Race Class, and Residence in Los Angeles* (New York: Russell Sage, 2006); Robert J. Sampson, "Seeing Disorder: Neighborhood Stigma and the Social Construction of 'Broken Windows,'" *Social Psychology Quarterly* 67 (2004): 319–342; Maria Krysan, Mick Couper, Reynolds Farley, and Tyrone A. Forman, "Does Race Matter in Neighborhood Preferences? Results from a Video Experiment," *American Journal of Sociology* 115 (2) (2009): 527–559; and Devah Pager and Hana Shepherd, "The Sociology of Discrimination: Racial Discrimination in Employment, Housing, Credit, and Consumer Markets," *Annual Review of Sociology* 34 (2008): 181–209.

23. Melvin L. Oliver and Thomas M. Shapiro, *Black Wealth/White Wealth: A New Perspective on Racial Inequality* (New York: Routledge, 1995); Dalton Conley, *Being Black, Living in the Red: Race, Wealth, and Social Policy in America* (Berkeley: University of California Press, 1999); and Thomas M. Shapiro, *The Hidden Cost of Being African American: How Wealth Perpetuates Inequality* (New York: Oxford University Press, 2004).

24. See Ira Katznelson, *When Affirmative Action Was White: An Untold Story of Racial Inequality in Twentieth-Century America* (New York: W.W. Norton, 2005).

25. I owe much of this discussion of racial attitudes to Howard Schuman, Charlotte Steeh, Lawrence D. Bobo, and Maria Krysan, *Racial Attitudes in America: Trends and Interpretations* (Cambridge, Mass.: Harvard University Press, 1997). See also Lawrence D. Bobo, "Racial Attitudes and Relations at the Close of the Twentieth Century," in *America Becoming: Racial Trends and Their Consequences, Volume 1,* ed. Neil J. Smelser,

William Julius Wilson, and Faith Mitchell (Washington, D.C.: National Academies Press, 2001), 264–301; and Maria Krysan, "From Color Caste to Color Blind?: Racial Attitudes Since World War II," in *The Oxford Handbook of African American Citizenship,* ed. Gates.

26. Important early work on attributions for racial inequality appears in Howard Schuman, "Sociological Racism," *Society 7* (1969): 44–48; Richard Apostle et al., *The Anatomy of Racial Attitudes* (Berkeley: University of California Press, 1983); James R. Kluegel and Eliot R. Smith, *Beliefs About Inequality: Americans' Views of What Is and What Ought to Be* (New York: Aldine de Gruyter, 1986); Paul M. Sniderman and Michael G. Hagen, *Race and Inequality: A Study in American Values* (Chatham, N.J.: Chatham House, 1985); and James R. Kluegel "Trends in Whites' Explanations of the Black-White Gap in Socioeconomic Status, 1977–1989," *American Sociological Review* 55 (1990): 512–525.

27. Matthew O. Hunt, "African-American, Hispanic, and White Beliefs about Black/White Inequality, 1977–2004," *American Sociological Review* 72 (2007): 390–415; Lawrence D. Bobo et al., "The Real Record on Racial Attitudes," in *Social Trends in the United States 1972–2008: Evidence from the General Social Survey,* ed. Peter V. Marsden (Princeton, N.J.: Princeton University Press, forthcoming).

28. On the stereotype measures, see Tom W. Smith, "Ethnic Images," GSS Technical Report No. 19 (Chicago: National Opinion Research Center, 1990); and Lawrence D. Bobo and James R. Kluegel, "Status, Ideology, and Dimensions of Whites' Racial Beliefs and Attitudes: Progress and Stagnation," in *Racial Attitudes in the 1990s,* ed. Tuch and Martin, 93–120. On the stereotype connection to public policy views, see Martin I. Gilens, *Why Americans Hate Welfare: Race, Media, and the Politics of Antipoverty Policy* (Chicago: University of Chicago Press, 1999); Lawrence D. Bobo and James R. Kluegel, "Opposition to Race-Targeting: Self-Interest, Stratification Ideology, or Racial Attitudes?" *American Sociological Review* 58 (1993): 443–464; and Steven A. Tuch and Michael Hughes, "Whites' Racial Policy Attitudes," *Social Science Quarterly* 77 (1996): 723–745.

29. For one excellent empirical report, see David O. Sears, Collette van Larr, Mary Carillo, and Rick Kosterman, "Is It Really Racism?: The Origins of White American Opposition to Race-Targeted Policies," *Public Opinion Quarterly* 61 (1997): 16–53. For a careful review and assessment of debates regarding the new racism hypothesis, see Maria Krysan, "Prejudice, Politics, and Public Opinion: Understanding the Sources of Racial Policy Attitudes," *Annual Review of Sociology* 26 (2000): 135–168.

30. For a discussion of the growing role of such resentments in partisan outlooks and political behavior, see Nicholas A. Valentino and David O. Sears, "Old Times There Are Not Forgotten: Race and Partisan Realignment in the Contemporary South," *American Journal of Political Science* 49 (2005): 672–688. For differential effects by race, see Lawrence D. Bobo and Devon Johnson, "A Taste for Punishment: Black and White Americans' Views on the Death Penalty and the War on Drugs," *Du Bois Review* 1 (2004): 151–180.

31. Those representative of the "deeply rooted racial flaw" camp would include Derrick Bell, *Faces at the Bottom of the Well: The Permanence of Racism* (New York: Basic Books, 1992);

Andrew Hacker, *Two Nations: Black and White: Separate, Hostile, Unequal* (New York: Scribner, 1992); Donald R. Kinder and Lynn M. Sanders, *Divided by Color: Racial Politics and Democratic Ideals* (Chicago: University of Chicago Press, 1996); Charles W. Mills, *The Racial Contract* (Ithaca, N.Y.: Cornell University Press, 1997); Joe R. Feagin, *Racist America: Roots, Current Realities, and Future Reparations* (New York: Routledge, 2000); Michael K. Brown et al., *White-Washing Race: The Myth of a Color-Blind Society* (Berkeley: University of California Press, 2003); and Douglas S. Massey, *Categorically Unequal: The American Stratification System* (New York: Russell Sage, 2006). Those representative of the "triumph of American liberalism" camp would include Nathan Glazer, "The Emergence of an American Ethnic Pattern," in *From Different Shores: Perspectives on Race and Ethnicity in America,* ed. Ronald Takaki (New York: Oxford University Press, 1987), 11–23; Orlando Patterson, *The Ordeal of Integration: Progress and Resentment in America's "Racial" Crisis* (Washington, D.C.: Basic Civitas, 1997); Paul M. Sniderman and Edward G. Carmines, *Reaching Beyond Race* (Cambridge, Mass.: Harvard University Press, 1997); Abigail Thernstrom and Stephan Thern-strom, *America in Black and White: One Nation, Indivisible* (New York: Simon & Schuster, 1997); and Richard D. Alba, *Blurring the Color Line: The New Chance for a More Integrated America* (Cambridge, Mass.: Harvard University Press, 2009).

32. These numbers point to a sharp rise in the percentage of white Americans endorsing the view that we have or will soon achieve racial equality; the figure rose from about 66 percent in 2000 to over 80 percent in 2009. A similar increase occurred among blacks: while 27 percent endorsed this view in 2000, the figure rose to 53 percent in 2009; thus, it nearly doubled. The 2000 survey allowed respondents to answer, "Don't know"; the 2009 survey did not. These percentages are calculated without the "don't know" responses. The 2000 results are reported in Lawrence D. Bobo, "Inequalities that Endure? Racial Ideology, American Politics, and the Peculiar Role of the Social Sciences," in *The Changing Terrain of Race and Ethnicity,* ed. Maria Krysan and Amanda E. Lewis (New York: Russell Sage, 2004), 13–42.

Critical Thinking

1. Can you list evidences of a racial divide in your own town? Explain your answer.

2. Do you see differences among races regarding expectations of government programs?

3. What can be done to close up the racial divide?

LAWRENCE D. BOBO, a Fellow of the American Academy since 2006, is the W.E.B. Du Bois Professor of the Social Sciences at Harvard University and a founding editor of the *Du Bois Review*. His publications include *Racialized Politics: The Debate about Racism in America* (with David O. Sears and James Sidanius, 2000), *Urban Inequality: Evidence from Four Cities* (with Alice O'Connor and Chris Tilly, 2001), and *Prejudice in Politics: Group Position, Public Opinion, and the Wisconsin Treaty Rights Dispute* (with Mia Tuan, 2006).

A More Perfect Union

BARACK OBAMA

Two hundred and twenty one years ago, in a hall that still stands across the street, a group of men gathered and, with these simple words, launched America's improbable experiment in democracy. Farmers and scholars; statesmen and patriots who had traveled across an ocean to escape tyranny and persecution finally made real their declaration of independence at a Philadelphia convention that lasted through the spring of 1787.

The document they produced was eventually signed but ultimately unfinished. It was stained by this nation's original sin of slavery, a question that divided the colonies and brought the convention to a stalemate until the founders chose to allow the slave trade to continue for at least twenty more years, and to leave any final resolution to future generations.

Of course, the answer to the slavery question was already embedded within our Constitution—a Constitution that had at is very core the ideal of equal citizenship under the law; a Constitution that promised its people liberty, and justice, and a union that could be and should be perfected over time.

And yet words on a parchment would not be enough to deliver slaves from bondage, or provide men and women of every color and creed their full rights and obligations as citizens of the United States. What would be needed were Americans in successive generations who were willing to do their part—through protests and struggle, on the streets and in the courts, through a civil war and civil disobedience and always at great risk—to narrow that gap between the promise of our ideals and the reality of their time.

This was one of the tasks we set forth at the beginning of this campaign—to continue the long march of those who came before us, a march for a more just, more equal, more free, more caring and more prosperous America. I chose to run for the presidency at this moment in history because I believe deeply that we cannot solve the challenges of our time unless we solve them together—unless we perfect our union by understanding that we may have different stories, but we hold common hopes; that we may not look the same and we may not have come from the same place, but we all want to move in the same direction—towards a better future for of children and our grandchildren.

This belief comes from my unyielding faith in the decency and generosity of the American people. But it also comes from my own American story.

I am the son of a black man from Kenya and a white woman from Kansas. I was raised with the help of a white grandfather who survived a Depression to serve in Patton's Army during World War II and a white grandmother who worked on a bomber assembly line at Fort Leavenworth while he was overseas. I've gone to some of the best schools in America and lived in one of the world's poorest nations. I am married to a black American who carries within her the blood of slaves and slaveowners—an inheritance we pass on to our two precious daughters. I have brothers, sisters, nieces, nephews, uncles and cousins, of every race and every hue, scattered across three continents, and for as long as I live, I will never forget that in no other country on Earth is my story even possible.

It's a story that hasn't made me the most conventional candidate. But it is a story that has seared into my genetic makeup the idea that this nation is more than the sum of its parts—that out of many, we are truly one.

Throughout the first year of this campaign, against all predictions to the contrary, we saw how hungry the American people were for this message of unity. Despite the temptation to view my candidacy through a purely racial lens, we won commanding victories in states with some of the whitest populations in the country. In South Carolina, where the Confederate Flag still flies, we built a powerful coalition of African Americans and white Americans.

This is not to say that race has not been an issue in the campaign. At various stages in the campaign, some commentators have deemed me either "too black" or "not black enough." We saw racial tensions bubble to the surface during the week before the South Carolina primary. The press has scoured every exit poll for the latest evidence of racial polarization, not just in terms of white and black, but black and brown as well.

And yet, it has only been in the last couple of weeks that the discussion of race in this campaign has taken a particularly divisive turn.

On one end of the spectrum, we've heard the implication that my candidacy is somehow an exercise in affirmative action; that it's based solely on the desire of wide-eyed liberals to purchase racial reconciliation on the cheap. On the other end, we've heard my former pastor, Reverend Jeremiah Wright, use incendiary language to express views that have the potential not only to widen the racial divide, but views that denigrate both the greatness and the goodness of our nation; that rightly offend white and black alike.

I have already condemned, in unequivocal terms, the statements of Reverend Wright that have caused such controversy. For some, nagging questions remain. Did I know him to be an occasionally fierce critic of American domestic and foreign policy? Of course. Did I ever hear him make remarks that could be considered controversial while I sat in church? Yes. Did I strongly disagree with many of his political views? Absolutely—just as I'm sure many of you have heard remarks from your pastors, priests, or rabbis with which you strongly disagreed.

But the remarks that have caused this recent firestorm weren't simply controversial. They weren't simply a religious leader's effort to speak out against perceived injustice. Instead, they expressed a profoundly distorted view of this country—a view that sees white racism as endemic, and that elevates what is wrong with America above all that we know is right with America; a view that sees the conflicts in the Middle East as rooted primarily in the actions of stalwart allies like Israel, instead of emanating from the perverse and hateful ideologies of radical Islam.

As such, Reverend Wright's comments were not only wrong but divisive, divisive at a time when we need unity; racially charged at a time when we need to come together to solve a set of monumental problems—two wars, a terrorist threat, a falling economy, a chronic health care crisis and potentially devastating climate change; problems that are neither black or white or Latino or Asian, but rather problems that confront us all.

Given my background, my politics, and my professed values and ideals, there will no doubt be those for whom my statements of condemnation are not enough. Why associate myself with Reverend Wright in the first place, they may ask? Why not join another church? And I confess that if all that I knew of Reverend Wright were the snippets of those sermons that have run in an endless loop on the television and You Tube, or if Trinity United Church of Christ conformed to the caricatures being peddled by some commentators, there is no doubt that I would react in much the same way.

But the truth is, that isn't all that I know of the man. The man I met more than twenty years ago is a man who helped introduce me to my Christian faith, a man who spoke to me about our obligations to love one another; to care for the sick and lift up the poor. He is a man who served his country as a U.S. Marine; who has studied and lectured at some of the finest universities and seminaries in the country, and who for over thirty years led a church that serves the community by doing God's work here on Earth—by housing the homeless, ministering to the needy, providing day care services and scholarships and prison ministries, and reaching out to those suffering from HIV/AIDS.

In my first book, *Dreams from My Father,* I described the experience of my first service at Trinity:

> People began to shout, to rise from their seats and clap and cry out, a forceful wind carrying the reverend's voice up into the rafters....And in that single note—hope!—I

heard something else; at the foot of that cross, inside the thousands of churches across the city, I imagined the stories of ordinary black people merging with the stories of David and Goliath, Moses and Pharaoh, the Christians in the lion's den, Ezekiel's field of dry bones. Those stories—of survival, and freedom, and hope—became our story, my story; the blood that had spilled was our blood, the tears our tears; until this black church, on this bright day, seemed once more a vessel carrying the story of a people into future generations and into a larger world. Our trials and triumphs became at once unique and universal, black and more than black; in chronicling our journey, the stories and songs gave us a means to reclaim memories that we didn't need to feel shame about... memories that all people might study and cherish—and with which we could start to rebuild.

That has been my experience at Trinity. Like other predominantly black churches across the country, Trinity embodies the black community in its entirety—the doctor and the welfare mom, the model student and the former gangbanger. Like other black churches, Trinity's services are full of raucous laughter and sometimes bawdy humor. They are full of dancing, clapping, screaming and shouting that may seem jarring to the untrained ear. The church contains in full the kindness and cruelty, the fierce intelligence and the shocking ignorance, the struggles and successes, the love and yes, the bitterness and bias that make up the black experience in America.

And this helps explain, perhaps, my relationship with Reverend Wright. As imperfect as he may be, he has been like family to me. He strengthened my faith, officiated my wedding, and baptized my children. Not once in my conversations with him have I heard him talk about any ethnic group in derogatory terms, or treat whites with whom he interacted with anything but courtesy and respect. He contains within him the contradictions—the good and the bad—of the community that he has served diligently for so many years.

I can no more disown him than I can disown the black community. I can no more disown him than I can my white grandmother—a woman who helped raise me, a woman who sacrificed again and again for me, a woman who loves me as much as she loves anything in this world, but a woman who once confessed her fear of black men who passed by her on the street, and who on more than one occasion has uttered racial or ethnic stereotypes that made me cringe.

These people are a part of me. And they are a part of America, this country that I love.

Some will see this as an attempt to justify or excuse comments that are simply inexcusable. I can assure you it is not. I suppose the politically safe thing would be to move on from this episode and just hope that it fades into the woodwork. We can dismiss Reverend Wright as a crank or a demagogue, just as some have dismissed Geraldine Ferraro, in the aftermath of her recent statements, as harboring some deep-seated racial bias.

But race is an issue that I believe this nation cannot afford to ignore right now. We would be making the same mistake that

Reverend Wright made in his offending sermons about America—to simplify and stereotype and amplify the negative to the point that it distorts reality.

The fact is that the comments that have been made and the issues that have surfaced over the last few weeks reflect the complexities of race in this country that we've never really worked through—a part of our union that we have yet to perfect. And if we walk away now, if we simply retreat into our respective corners, we will never be able to come together and solve challenges like health care, or education, or the need to find good jobs for every American.

Understanding this reality requires a reminder of how we arrived at this point. As William Faulkner once wrote, "The past isn't dead and buried. In fact, it isn't even past." We do not need to recite here the history of racial injustice in this country. But we do need to remind ourselves that so many of the disparities that exist in the African-American community today can be directly traced to inequalities passed on from an earlier generation that suffered under the brutal legacy of slavery and Jim Crow.

Segregated schools were, and are, inferior schools; we still haven't fixed them, fifty years after *Brown v. Board of Education*, and the inferior education they provided, then and now, helps explain the pervasive achievement gap between today's black and white students.

Legalized discrimination—where blacks were prevented, often through violence, from owning property, or loans were not granted to African-American business owners, or black homeowners could not access FHA mortgages, or blacks were excluded from unions, or the police force, or fire departments—meant that black families could not amass any meaningful wealth to bequeath to future generations. That history helps explain the wealth and income gap between black and white, and the concentrated pockets of poverty that persists in so many of today's urban and rural communities.

A lack of economic opportunity among black men, and the shame and frustration that came from not being able to provide for one's family, contributed to the erosion of black families—a problem that welfare policies for many years may have worsened. And the lack of basic services in so many urban black neighborhoods—parks for kids to play in, police walking the beat, regular garbage pick-up and building code enforcement—all helped create a cycle of violence, blight and neglect that continue to haunt us.

This is the reality in which Reverend Wright and other African-Americans of his generation grew up. They came of age in the late fifties and early sixties, a time when segregation was still the law of the land and opportunity was systematically constricted. What's remarkable is not how many failed in the face of discrimination, but rather how many men and women overcame the odds; how many were able to make a way out of no way for those like me who would come after them.

But for all those who scratched and clawed their way to get a piece of the American Dream, there were many who didn't make it—those who were ultimately defeated, in one way or another, by discrimination. That legacy of defeat was passed on to future generations—those young men and increasingly young women who we see standing on street corners or languishing in our prisons, without hope or prospects for the future. Even for those blacks who did make it, questions of race, and racism, continue to define their worldview in fundamental ways. For the men and women of Reverend Wright's generation, the memories of humiliation and doubt and fear have not gone away; nor has the anger and the bitterness of those years. That anger may not get expressed in public, in front of white co-workers or white friends. But it does find voice in the barbershop or around the kitchen table. At times, that anger is exploited by politicians, to gin up votes along racial lines, or to make up for a politician's own failings.

And occasionally it finds voice in the church on Sunday morning, in the pulpit and in the pews. The fact that so many people are surprised to hear that anger in some of Reverend Wright's sermons simply reminds us of the old truism that the most segregated hour in American life occurs on Sunday morning. That anger is not always productive; indeed, all too often it distracts attention from solving real problems; it keeps us from squarely facing our own complicity in our condition, and prevents the African American community from forging the alliances it needs to bring about real change. But the anger is real; it is powerful; and to simply wish it away, to condemn it without understanding its roots, only serves to widen the chasm of misunderstanding that exists between the races.

In fact, a similar anger exists within segments of the white community. Most working- and middle-class white Americans don't feel that they have been particularly privileged by their race. Their experience is the immigrant experience—as far as they're concerned, no one's handed them anything, they've built it from scratch. They've worked hard all their lives, many times only to see their jobs shipped overseas or their pension dumped after a lifetime of labor. They are anxious about their futures, and feel their dreams slipping away; in an era of stagnant wages and global competition, opportunity comes to be seen as a zero sum game, in which your dreams come at my expense. So when they are told to bus their children to a school across town; when they hear that an African American is getting an advantage in landing a good job or a spot in a good college because of an injustice that they themselves never committed; when they're told that their fears about crime in urban neighborhoods are somehow prejudiced, resentment builds over time.

Like the anger within the black community, these resentments aren't always expressed in polite company. But they have helped shape the political landscape for at least a generation. Anger over welfare and affirmative action helped forge the Reagan Coalition. Politicians routinely exploited fears of crime for their own electoral ends. Talk show hosts and conservative commentators built entire careers unmasking bogus claims of racism while dismissing legitimate discussions of racial injustice and inequality as mere political correctness or reverse racism.

Just as black anger often proved counterproductive, so have these white resentments distracted attention from the real culprits of the middle class squeeze—a corporate culture rife with inside dealing, questionable accounting practices, and short-term greed; a Washington dominated by lobbyists and special interests; economic policies that favor the few over the many. And yet, to wish away the resentments of white Americans, to label them as misguided or even racist, without recognizing they are grounded in legitimate concerns—this too widens the racial divide, and blocks the path to understanding.

This is where we are right now. It's a racial stalemate we've been stuck in for years. Contrary to the claims of some of my critics, black and white, I have never been so naïve as to believe that we can get beyond our racial divisions in a single election cycle, or with a single candidacy—particularly a candidacy as imperfect as my own.

But I have asserted a firm conviction—a conviction rooted in my faith in God and my faith in the American people—that working together we can move beyond some of our old racial wounds, and that in fact we have no choice is we are to continue on the path of a more perfect union.

For the African-American community, that path means embracing the burdens of our past without becoming victims of our past. It means continuing to insist on a full measure of justice in every aspect of American life. But it also means binding our particular grievances—for better health care, and better schools, and better jobs—to the larger aspirations of all Americans—the white woman struggling to break the glass ceiling, the white man whose been laid off, the immigrant trying to feed his family. And it means taking full responsibility for own lives—by demanding more from our fathers, and spending more time with our children, and reading to them, and teaching them that while they may face challenges and discrimination in their own lives, they must never succumb to despair or cynicism; they must always believe that they can write their own destiny.

Ironically, this quintessentially American—and yes, conservative—notion of self-help found frequent expression in Reverend Wright's sermons. But what my former pastor too often failed to understand is that embarking on a program of self-help also requires a belief that society can change.

The profound mistake of Reverend Wright's sermons is not that he spoke about racism in our society. It's that he spoke as if our society was static; as if no progress has been made; as if this country—a country that has made it possible for one of his own members to run for the highest office in the land and build a coalition of white and black; Latino and Asian, rich and poor, young and old—is still irrevocably bound to a tragic past. But what we know—what we have seen—is that America can change. That is true genius of this nation. What we have already achieved gives us hope—the audacity to hope—for what we can and must achieve tomorrow.

In the white community, the path to a more perfect union means acknowledging that what ails the African-American community does not just exist in the minds of black people; that the legacy of discrimination—and current incidents of discrimination, while less overt than in the past—are real and must be addressed. Not just with words, but with deeds—by investing in our schools and our communities; by enforcing our civil rights laws and ensuring fairness in our criminal justice system; by providing this generation with ladders of opportunity that were unavailable for previous generations. It requires all Americans to realize that your dreams do not have to come at the expense of my dreams; that investing in the health, welfare, and education of black and brown and white children will ultimately help all of America prosper.

In the end, then, what is called for is nothing more, and nothing less, than what all the world's great religions demand—that we do unto others as we would have them do unto us.Let us be our brother's keeper, Scripture tells us. Let us be our sister's keeper. Let us find that common stake we all have in one another, and let our politics reflect that spirit as well.

For we have a choice in this country. We can accept a politics that breeds division, and conflict, and cynicism. We can tackle race only as spectacle—as we did in the OJ trial—or in the wake of tragedy, as we did in the aftermath of Katrina—or as fodder for the nightly news. We can play Reverend Wright's sermons on every channel, every day and talk about them from now until the election, and make the only question in this campaign whether or not the American people think that I somehow believe or sympathize with his most offensive words. We can pounce on some gaffe by a Hillary supporter as evidence that she's playing the race card, or we can speculate on whether white men will all flock to John McCain in the general election regardless of his policies.

We can do that.

But if we do, I can tell you that in the next election, we'll be talking about some other distraction. And then another one. And then another one. And nothing will change.

That is one option. Or, at this moment, in this election, we can come together and say, "Not this time." This time we want to talk about the crumbling schools that are stealing the future of black children and white children and Asian children and Hispanic children and Native American children. This time we want to reject the cynicism that tells us that these kids can't learn; that those kids who don't look like us are somebody else's problem. The children of America are not those kids, they are our kids, and we will not let them fall behind in a 21st century economy. Not this time.

This time we want to talk about how the lines in the Emergency Room are filled with whites and blacks and Hispanics who do not have health care; who don't have the power on their own to overcome the special interests in Washington, but who can take them on if we do it together.

This time we want to talk about the shuttered mills that once provided a decent life for men and women of every race, and the homes for sale that once belonged to Americans from every religion, every region, every walk of life. This time we want to talk about the fact that the real problem is not that someone who doesn't look like you might take your job; it's that the corporation you work for will ship it overseas for nothing more than a profit.

This time we want to talk about the men and women of every color and creed who serve together, and fight together, and bleed together under the same proud flag. We want to talk about how to bring them home from a war that never should've been authorized and never should've been waged, and we want to talk about how we'll show our patriotism by caring for them, and their families, and giving them the benefits they have earned.

I would not be running for President if I didn't believe with all my heart that this is what the vast majority of Americans want for this country. This union may never be perfect, but generation after generation has shown that it can always be perfected. And today, whenever I find myself feeling doubtful or cynical about this possibility, what gives me the most hope is the next generation—the young people whose attitudes and beliefs and openness to change have already made history in this election.

There is one story in particularly that I'd like to leave you with today—a story I told when I had the great honor of speaking on Dr. King's birthday at his home church, Ebenezer Baptist, in Atlanta.

There is a young, twenty-three year old white woman named Ashley Baia who organized for our campaign in Florence, South Carolina. She had been working to organize a mostly African-American community since the beginning of this campaign, and one day she was at a roundtable discussion where everyone went around telling their story and why they were there.

And Ashley said that when she was nine years old, her mother got cancer. And because she had to miss days of work, she was let go and lost her health care. They had to file for bankruptcy, and that's when Ashley decided that she had to do something to help her mom.

She knew that food was one of their most expensive costs, and so Ashley convinced her mother that what she really liked and really wanted to eat more than anything else was mustard and relish sandwiches. Because that was the cheapest way to eat.

She did this for a year until her mom got better, and she told everyone at the roundtable that the reason she joined our campaign was so that she could help the millions of other children in the country who want and need to help their parents too.

Now Ashley might have made a different choice. Perhaps somebody told her along the way that the source of her mother's problems were blacks who were on welfare and too lazy to work, or Hispanics who were coming into the country illegally. But she didn't. She sought out allies in her fight against injustice.

Anyway, Ashley finishes her story and then goes around the room and asks everyone else why they're supporting the campaign. They all have different stories and reasons. Many bring up a specific issue. And finally they come to this elderly black man who's been sitting there quietly the entire time. And Ashley asks him why he's there. And he does not bring up a specific issue. He does not say health care or the economy. He does not say education or the war. He does not say that he was there because of Barack Obama. He simply says to everyone in the room, "I am here because of Ashley."

"I'm here because of Ashley." By itself, that single moment of recognition between that young white girl and that old black man is not enough. It is not enough to give health care to the sick, or jobs to the jobless, or education to our children.

But it is where we start. It is where our union grows stronger. And as so many generations have come to realize over the course of the two-hundred and twenty one years since a band of patriots signed that document in Philadelphia, that is where the perfection begins.

Critical Thinking

1. How does Barack Obama trace the evolution of civil rights to the Constitution?

2. What does the election of Obama signify for the progress of civil rights in the United States?

Obama, Barack. From a speech to supporters in Philadelphia, PA, on March 18, 2008.

Fear and Loathing of Islam

A decade after 9/11, ordinary life for American Muslims is enough to arouse suspicion.

MOUSTAFA BAYOUMI

Something's gone terribly wrong. In August 2007 the New York Police Department released a report called "Radicalization in the West: The Homegrown Threat," claiming that the looming danger to the United States was from "unremarkable" Muslim men under 35 who visit "extremist incubators." The language sounds ominous, conjuring up *Clockwork Orange*–style laboratories of human reprogramming, twisting average Muslims into instruments of evil. And yet what are these "incubators"? The report states that they are mosques, "cafes, cab driver hangouts, flophouses, prisons, student associations, non-governmental organizations, hookah (water pipe) bars, butcher shops and book stores"—in other words, precisely the places where ordinary life happens.

But the report wasn't based on any independent social science research, and actual studies clearly refuted the very claims made by the NYPD. The Rand Corporation found that the number of homegrown radicals here is "tiny." "There are more than 3 million Muslims in the United States, and few more than 100 have joined jihad—about one out of every 30,000—suggesting an American Muslim population that remains hostile to jihadist ideology and its exhortations to violence," Rand's 2010 report found. "A mistrust of American Muslims by other Americans seems misplaced," it concluded. This year, an analysis by the Triangle Center on Terrorism and Homeland Security also described the number of American Muslims involved in domestic terrorism since 2001 as "tiny." "This study's findings challenge Americans to be vigilant against the threat of homegrown terrorism while maintaining a responsible sense of proportion," it said. And a 2011 Gallup survey found that American Muslims were the least likely of any major US religious group to consider attacks on civilians justified.

Every group has its loonies. And yet the idea that American Muslim communities are foul nests of hatred, where dark-skinned men plot Arabic violence while combing one another's beards, persists. In fact, it's worse than that. In the past few years, another narrative about American Muslims has come along, which sows a different kind of paranoia. While the old story revolves around security, portraying American Muslims as potential terrorists or terrorist sympathizers, the new narrative operates more along the axis of culture. Simple acts of religious or cultural expression and the straightforward activities of Muslim daily life have become suspicious. Building a mosque in Lower Manhattan or in Sheepshead Bay, Brooklyn, or in Murfreesboro, Tennessee, becomes an act of "stealth jihad." Muslims filing for divorce invokes the bizarre charge of "creeping Sharia." A dual-language Arabic-English high school in New York is demonized as a "madrassa." The State Board of Education in Texas determines that reading about Islam is not education but indoctrination. Changing your Muslim-sounding name to one with a more Anglophone tenor triggers an NYPD investigation, according to the Associated Press. Even the fact that some Butterball turkeys are "halal" was enough to fire up the bigotry last Thanksgiving, the most American of holidays.

What happens when ordinary life becomes grounds for suspicion without a hint of wrongdoing; when law enforcement premises its work on spying on the quotidian and policing the unremarkable; and when the everyday affairs of American Muslim life can so easily be transformed into nefarious intent? Something has gone terribly wrong for American Muslims when, more than a decade after the terrorist attacks of September 11, anti-Muslim sentiment in the United States continues to grow.

A *Washington Post*/ABC News poll taken in October 2001 found that 39 percent of Americans held unfavorable opinions of Islam. After dipping for a few years, the number rose to 46 percent in 2006 and reached 49 percent—basically half the population—in 2010, the last year the question was asked. (Other recent polls show similar results.) Such anti-Muslim attitudes are not merely absorbed by law enforcement and the military or reflected on the airwaves and in the words of our politicians. Rather, the idea that American Muslims are to be feared or loathed or excluded from the United States is being actively promoted.

Absent personal contact, most Americans get their views of Islam through TV, talk-radio, the Internet and really bad action movies.

This past September, *Wired* broke the story that the FBI tells its counterterrorism agents in training that mainstream American Muslims are probably terrorist sympathizers, that the Prophet Muhammad was a "cult leader" and that the religiously mandated practice of giving charity in Islam is no more than a "funding mechanism for combat." The training materials, which stated that FBI agents had the "ability to bend or suspend the law and impinge on freedoms of others," identify other insidious techniques Muslims use for promoting jihad, including "immigration" and "law suits"—in other words, the ordinary uses of the American political system. The revelations forced the FBI to remove 876 pages from its manuals.

Another egregious example that recently came to light is that the NYPD, as part of its training, screened *The Third Jihad,* a film that claims "the true agenda of much of Islam in America" is "a strategy to infiltrate and dominate" the country. The film ran on a continuous loop for somewhere between three months and a year of training and was viewed by at least 1,489 officers. Yet another example involved Army Lt. Col. Matthew Dooley, who taught a course at the Pentagon's Joint Forces Staff College that informed senior officers that the United States would have to fight a "total war" against the world's Muslims, including abandoning the international laws of war that protect civilians (deemed "no longer relevant"), and possibly applying "the historical precedents of Dresden, Tokyo, Hiroshima, Nagasaki" to destroy Islam's holy cities of Mecca and Medina. Claiming "Islam is an ideology rather than solely a religion," the class taught that the United States was "culturally vulnerable" to this threat because of its "'judeo-christian' [*sic*] ethic of reason and tolerance." The Pentagon canceled the course in the wake of the revelations, and Dooley maintains a nonteaching position, pending an investigation.

The consequences of these efforts to promote anti-Muslim beliefs and sentiments influence how American Muslims practice their faith, engage with their neighbors, cooperate with law enforcement, work at their jobs and study at school. Anti-mosque activity, according to the ACLU, has taken place in more than half the states in the country. And American Muslims, who make up 1–2 percent of the population, account for more than 20 percent of religion-based filings with the Equal Employment Opportunity Commission.

There is legitimate concern about future acts of terrorism in the United States. But there is also plenty of reason to be skeptical of many of the plots that the FBI has disrupted, which are usually scripted by a paid informant, often with a criminal record himself [see Petra Bartosiewicz, "The FBI Stings Muslims,"]. Yet the publicity these "plots" receive feeds the anti-Muslim fervor.

Media coverage plays a major role in ramping up anti-Muslim attitudes, for a very simple reason: 62 percent of Americans, according to a 2010 *Time* magazine poll, say they have never met a Muslim. (If you do know a Muslim, you're less likely to harbor anti-Muslim feelings, polls also show.) Absent ordinary personal contact, most Americans will get their views of Islam through television, cable news, talk-radio, the Internet and really bad action movies. Because the counterweight of personal contact is missing, Muslim attitudes are easily ventriloquized and distorted, and Muslims themselves often rendered mute or suspect. The myth that American Muslims haven't spoken out against terrorism, for example, continues to haunt the community, even though they do so loudly and repeatedly.

Then there's the myth, promulgated by Representative Peter King in his radicalization hearings last year, of American Muslim noncooperation with law enforcement. In reality, around 40 percent of Muslim domestic terrorism suspects since September 11, 2001, have been turned in by fellow Muslims, who have sometimes discovered later that the FBI was directing the operation.

Republican politicians, meanwhile, have been falling all over themselves to vilify Muslims, especially during the presidential primary. Herman Cain proclaimed that "a majority of Muslims share the extremist views," initially vowing not to appoint any Muslims to his cabinet. Rick Santorum endorsed religious profiling, saying that "obviously Muslims would be someone [*sic*] you'd look at." Newt Gingrich compared Muslims to Nazis in 2010, when he opposed building an Islamic center in Lower Manhattan. "Nazis don't have the right to put up a sign next to the Holocaust museum in Washington," he said. And, in 2007, Mitt Romney said, "Based on the numbers of American Muslims [as a percentage] in our population, I cannot see that a cabinet position would be justified. But of course, I would imagine that Muslims could serve at lower levels of my administration." Whatever happened to the matter of qualifications? But hey, if you're a Muslim, that's all you'll ever be. Romney has hired Walid Phares, part of the active anti-Muslim network, as a foreign policy adviser, and GOP voters continue to consider that President Obama is a Muslim in large numbers (52 percent of Mississippi GOP members thought so in March).

It gets stranger still. When media portrayals of everyday American Muslim life are produced, the very ordinariness is attacked as a lie. TLC's show *All-American Muslim* premiered in November to favorable reviews. The show, which focused on five Lebanese-American Shiite Muslim families in the Dearborn, Michigan, area, was a bit of a yawner for racy reality TV, but it was a useful kind of ethnography for Americans unfamiliar with the stuff of daily American Muslim life. Immediately, the organized anti-Muslim network kicked into gear. The Florida Family Association, basically a one-man show run by David Caton, led a boycott of the show via e-mail that was quickly picked up by the extreme right-wing anti-Islamic blogosphere, and led to Lowe's and Kayak.com pulling their ads. Caton's e-mail read, "The show profiles only Muslims that appear to be ordinary folks while excluding many Islamic believers whose agenda poses a clear and present danger to liberties and traditional values that the majority of Americans cherish."

Follow the logic. The only thing accepted as "normal" for a Muslim is to act like an extremist. Ordinary Muslim folk appearing to live ordinary Muslim lives? That's just plain suspicious.

The same belief drives the NYPD's surveillance of American Muslim communities. Police Commissioner Raymond Kelly informed American Muslim audiences in 2007 that the radicalization report of that year was "never intended to be a policy prescriptive for law enforcement actions," but we now know he was lying. In its Pulitzer Prize–winning series published beginning in August 2011, the Associated Press has reported on how American Muslims who were not suspected of any wrongdoing were spied on in New York and beyond by the NYPD, with the CIA's help. The NYPD catalogued the locations of barbershops, cafes and restaurants, noting where the undercover officers— dubbed "rakers"—heard "political and inflammatory rhetoric," though what that means, and the fact that it's free speech, is never stated. Undercover officers chatted up bookstore owners, played cricket with Muslims and uncovered such unsavory things as a travel agency on Atlantic Avenue in Brooklyn, where an officer "observed a female named 'Rasha' working in the travel agency, she recommended the 'Royal Jordanian Airline.'"

The department also spied on Muslim college students throughout the Tri-State area, including at Brooklyn College, where I teach. Soheeb Amin, president of the college's Islamic Society, told me that the AP reports were more of a confirmation than a revelation. "We know that there are people who are looking for excuses to get you in trouble for your religion," he noted, and so he has adjusted. "I don't talk about politics. I don't talk about anything controversial. I don't do anything that can raise suspicion." Like many American Muslims, he feels his rights to practice his religion and express his ideas have been compromised. He told me he prays the mandatory five daily prayers, "but now I know that there are NYPD reports that mention that people prayed four times a day, and I guess five is worse than that," he added, only half-jokingly. Muslims from New Jersey, including a decorated soldier, recently filed suit against the NYPD for violating their constitutional rights.

D oes this mean that the United States is an Islamophobic country? Of course not. Large support for American Muslims exists in many quarters. Polls may suggest that about half the population is anti-Muslim, but that leaves half that isn't. In many quarters of the country, there is genuine, not suspicious, interest in American Muslims and the realities they face, as evidenced by the fact that TLC produced *All-American Muslim*. Aasif Mandvi's contributions to *The Daily Show* routinely deflate the power of this contemporary prejudice, and libraries, museums, classrooms and houses of worship across the country now regularly include Muslims and Islam in their programming in an attempt to further understanding and combat bigotry.

American Muslims have responded to events over the past decade and the expansion of an anti-Muslim network largely by being more, not less, visible. The number of mosques grew 74 percent over the past decade, despite the opposition Muslims sometimes confront in their construction. Even if a 2011 poll found that 48 percent of American Muslims reported experiencing discrimination in the previous twelve months, they also showed more optimism than other Americans in the poll that their lives would be better in five years (perhaps, in part, because of today's discrimination). The guiding belief in the American Muslim community today is that the country will recognize that Muslims have always been and will continue to be a part of America.

An ordinary life is more meaningful than it sounds. It signifies being able to live your life as you define yourself, not as others define you, and being able to assume a life free of unwarranted government prying. In fact, ordinariness is the foundation of an open society, because it endows citizens with a private life and demands that the government operate openly—not the other way around, which is how closed societies operate.

There is a real danger that the same tools that enable today's Islamophobia will continue to migrate and expand with little or no public outcry. The FBI deploys a strategy of sting operations against Occupy protesters that is eerily familiar to American Muslims, to little outrage. The president enacts a law that allows for the indefinite detention of American citizens, and after a federal judge strikes it down as unconstitutional, Congress rushes in two days later to try to keep it on the books. American citizens can be assassinated by presidential decree, making a mockery of due process. Forget the Muslims. This mission creep is as good a reason as any to pay attention to Islamophobia today—because when the ordinary affairs of the United States include such actions, the stakes are nothing less than extraordinary.

Critical Thinking

1. How have Muslims been treated in the United States since 9/11?

2. Why are beliefs about Arab Americans so false?

MOUSTAFA BAYOUMI, *a professor of English at Brooklyn College, CUNY, is the author of* How Does It Feel to Be a Problem?: Being Young and Arab in America *(Penguin), which won an American Book Award and the Arab American Book Award for Non-Fiction. He is the editor of* Midnight on the Mavi Marmara *(O/R Books and Haymarket Books) and co-editor of* The Edward Said Reader *(Vintage).*

Why Women Still Can't Have It All

It's time to stop fooling ourselves, says a woman who left a position of power: the women who have managed to be both mothers and top professionals are superhuman, rich, or self-employed. If we truly believe in equal opportunity for all women, here's what has to change.

ANNE-MARIE SLAUGHTER

EIGHTEEN MONTHS INTO my job as the first woman director of policy planning at the State Department, a foreign-policy dream job that traces its origins back to George Kennan, I found myself in New York, at the United Nations' annual assemblage of every foreign minister and head of state in the world. On a Wednesday evening, President and Mrs. Obama hosted a glamorous reception at the American Museum of Natural History. I sipped champagne, greeted foreign dignitaries, and mingled. But I could not stop thinking about my 14-year-old son, who had started eighth grade three weeks earlier and was already resuming what had become his pattern of skipping homework, disrupting classes, failing math, and tuning out any adult who tried to reach him. Over the summer, we had barely spoken to each other—or, more accurately, he had barely spoken to me. And the previous spring I had received several urgent phone calls—invariably on the day of an important meeting—that required me to take the first train from Washington, D.C., where I worked, back to Princeton, New Jersey, where he lived. My husband, who has always done everything possible to support my career, took care of him and his 12-year-old brother during the week; outside of those midweek emergencies, I came home only on weekends.

As the evening wore on, I ran into a colleague who held a senior position in the White House. She has two sons exactly my sons' ages, but she had chosen to move them from California to D.C. when she got her job, which meant her husband commuted back to California regularly. I told her how difficult I was finding it to be away from my son when he clearly needed me. Then I said, "When this is over, I'm going to write an op-ed titled 'Women Can't Have It All.'"

She was horrified. "You *can't* write that," she said. "You, of all people." What she meant was that such a statement, coming from a high-profile career woman—a role model—would be a terrible signal to younger generations of women. By the end of the evening, she had talked me out of it, but for the remainder of my stint in Washington, I was increasingly aware that the feminist beliefs on which I had built my entire career were shifting under my feet. I had always assumed that if I could get a foreign-policy job in the State Department or the White House while my party was in power, I would stay the course as long as I had the opportunity to do work I loved. But in January 2011, when my two-year public-service leave from Princeton University was up, I hurried home as fast as I could.

A rude epiphany hit me soon after I got there. When people asked why I had left government, I explained that I'd come home not only because of Princeton's rules (after two years of leave, you lose your tenure), but also because of my desire to be with my family and my conclusion that juggling high-level government work with the needs of two teenage boys was not possible. I have not exactly left the ranks of full-time career women: I teach a full course load; write regular print and online columns on foreign policy; give 40 to 50 speeches a year; appear regularly on TV and radio; and am working on a new academic book. But I routinely got reactions from other women my age or older that ranged from disappointed ("It's such a pity that you had to leave Washington") to condescending ("I wouldn't generalize from your experience. *I've* never had to compromise, and *my* kids turned out great").

The first set of reactions, with the underlying assumption that my choice was somehow sad or unfortunate, was irksome enough. But it was the second set of reactions—those implying that my parenting and/or my commitment to my profession were somehow substandard—that triggered a blind fury. Suddenly, finally, the penny dropped. All my life, I'd been on the other side of this exchange. I'd been the woman smiling the faintly superior smile while another woman told me she had decided to take some time out or pursue a less competitive career track so that she could spend more time with her family. I'd been the woman congratulating herself on her unswerving commitment to the feminist cause, chatting smugly with her dwindling number of college or law-school friends who had reached and maintained their place on the highest rungs of their profession. I'd been the one telling young women at my lectures that you *can* have it all and do it all, regardless of what field you are in. Which means I'd been part, albeit unwittingly, of making millions of women feel that *they* are to blame if they cannot manage to rise up the ladder as fast as men and also have a family and an active home life (and be thin and beautiful to boot).

Last spring, I flew to Oxford to give a public lecture. At the request of a young Rhodes Scholar I know, I'd agreed to talk to the Rhodes community about "work-family balance." I ended up speaking to a group of about 40 men and women in their mid-20s. What poured out of me was a set of very frank reflections on how unexpectedly hard it was to do the kind of job I wanted to do as a high government official and be the kind of parent I wanted to be, at a demanding time for my children (even though my husband, an academic, was willing to take on the lion's share of parenting for the two years I was in Washington). I concluded by saying that my time in office had convinced me that further government service would be very unlikely while my sons were still at home. The audience was rapt, and asked many thoughtful questions. One of the first was from a young woman who began by thanking me for "not giving just one more fatuous 'You can have it all' talk." Just about all of the women in that room planned to combine careers and family in some way. But almost all assumed and accepted that they would have to make compromises that the men in their lives were far less likely to have to make.

The striking gap between the responses I heard from those young women (and others like them) and the responses I heard from my peers and associates prompted me to write this article. Women of my generation have clung to the feminist credo we were raised with, even as our ranks have been steadily thinned by unresolvable tensions between family and career, because we are determined not to drop the flag for the next generation. But when many members of the younger generation have stopped listening, on the grounds that glibly repeating "you can have it all" is simply airbrushing reality, it is time to talk.

I still strongly believe that women can "have it all" (and that men can too). I believe that we can "have it all at the same time." But not today, not with the way America's economy and society are currently structured. My experiences over the past three years have forced me to confront a number of uncomfortable facts that need to be widely acknowledged—and quickly changed.

Before my service in government, I'd spent my career in academia: as a law professor and then as the dean of Princeton's Woodrow Wilson School of Public and International Affairs. Both were demanding jobs, but I had the ability to set my own schedule most of the time. I could be with my kids when I needed to be, and still get the work done. I had to travel frequently, but I found I could make up for that with an extended period at home or a family vacation.

I knew that I was lucky in my career choice, but I had no idea how lucky until I spent two years in Washington within a rigid bureaucracy, even with bosses as understanding as Hillary Clinton and her chief of staff, Cheryl Mills. My workweek started at 4:20 on Monday morning, when I got up to get the 5:30 train from Trenton to Washington. It ended late on Friday, with the train home. In between, the days were crammed with meetings, and when the meetings stopped, the writing work began—a never-ending stream of memos, reports, and comments on other people's drafts. For two years, I never left the office early enough to go to any stores other than those open 24 hours, which meant that everything from dry cleaning to hair appointments to Christmas shopping had to be done on weekends, amid

children's sporting events, music lessons, family meals, and conference calls. I was entitled to four hours of vacation per pay period, which came to one day of vacation a month. And I had it better than many of my peers in D.C.; Secretary Clinton deliberately came in around 8 a.m. and left around 7 p.m., to allow her close staff to have morning and evening time with their families (although of course she worked earlier and later, from home).

In short, the minute I found myself in a job that is typical for the vast majority of working women (and men), working long hours on someone else's schedule, I could no longer be both the parent and the professional I wanted to be—at least not with a child experiencing a rocky adolescence. I realized what should have perhaps been obvious: having it all, at least for me, depended almost entirely on what type of job I had. The flip side is the harder truth: having it all was not possible in many types of jobs, including high government office—at least not for very long.

I am hardly alone in this realization. Michèle Flournoy stepped down after three years as undersecretary of defense for policy, the third-highest job in the department, to spend more time at home with her three children, two of whom are teenagers. Karen Hughes left her position as the counselor to President George W. Bush after a year and a half in Washington to go home to Texas for the sake of her family. Mary Matalin, who spent two years as an assistant to Bush and the counselor to Vice President Dick Cheney before stepping down to spend more time with her daughters, wrote: "Having control over your schedule is the only way that women who want to have a career and a family can make it work."

Yet the decision to step down from a position of power—to value family over professional advancement, even for a time—is directly at odds with the prevailing social pressures on career professionals in the United States. One phrase says it all about current attitudes toward work and family, particularly among elites. In Washington, "leaving to spend time with your family" is a euphemism for being fired. This understanding is so ingrained that when Flournoy announced her resignation last December, *The New York Times* covered her decision as follows:

> Ms. Flournoy's announcement surprised friends and a number of Pentagon officials, but all said they took her reason for resignation at face value and not as a standard Washington excuse for an official who has in reality been forced out. "I can absolutely and unequivocally state that her decision to step down has nothing to do with anything other than her commitment to her family," said Doug Wilson, a top Pentagon spokesman. "She has loved this job and people here love her.

Think about what this "standard Washington excuse" implies: it is so unthinkable that an official would *actually* step down to spend time with his or her family that this must be a cover for something else. How could anyone voluntarily leave the circles of power for the responsibilities of parenthood? Depending on one's vantage point, it is either ironic or maddening that this view abides in the nation's capital, despite the ritual commitments to "family values" that are part of every political campaign. Regardless, this sentiment makes true work-life balance exceptionally difficult. But it cannot change unless top women speak out.

Only recently have I begun to appreciate the extent to which many young professional women feel under assault by women my age and older. After I gave a recent speech in New York, several women in their late 60s or early 70s came up to tell me how glad and proud they were to see me speaking as a foreign-policy expert. A couple of them went on, however, to contrast my career with the path being traveled by "younger women today." One expressed dismay that many younger women "are just not willing to get out there and do it." Said another, unaware of the circumstances of my recent job change: "They think they have to choose between having a career and having a family."

A similar assumption underlies Facebook Chief Operating Officer Sheryl Sandberg's widely publicized 2011 commencement speech at Barnard, and her earlier TED talk, in which she lamented the dismally small number of women at the top and advised young women not to "leave before you leave." When a woman starts thinking about having children, Sandberg said, "she doesn't raise her hand anymore...She starts leaning back." Although couched in terms of encouragement, Sandberg's exhortation contains more than a note of reproach. We who have made it to the top, or are striving to get there, are essentially saying to the women in the generation behind us: "What's the matter with you?"

They have an answer that we don't want to hear. After the speech I gave in New York, I went to dinner with a group of 30-somethings. I sat across from two vibrant women, one of whom worked at the UN and the other at a big New York law firm. As nearly always happens in these situations, they soon began asking me about work-life balance. When I told them I was writing this article, the lawyer said, "I look for role models and can't find any." She said the women in her firm who had become partners and taken on management positions had made tremendous sacrifices, "many of which they don't even seem to realize . . . They take two years off when their kids are young but then work like crazy to get back on track professionally, which means that they see their kids when they are toddlers but not teenagers, or really barely at all." Her friend nodded, mentioning the top professional women she knew, all of whom essentially relied on round-the-clock nannies. Both were very clear that they did not want that life, but could not figure out how to combine professional success and satisfaction with a real commitment to family.

I realize that I am blessed to have been born in the late 1950s instead of the early 1930s, as my mother was, or the beginning of the 20th century, as my grandmothers were. My mother built a successful and rewarding career as a professional artist largely in the years after my brothers and I left home—and after being told in her 20s that she could not go to medical school, as her father had done and her brother would go on to do, because, of course, she was going to get married. I owe my own freedoms and opportunities to the pioneering generation of women ahead of me—the women now in their 60s, 70s, and 80s who faced overt sexism of a kind I see only when watching *Mad Men*, and who knew that the only way to make it as a woman was to act exactly like a man. To admit to, much less act on, maternal longings would have been fatal to their careers.

But precisely thanks to their progress, a different kind of conversation is now possible. It is time for women in leadership positions to recognize that although we are still blazing trails and breaking ceilings, many of us are also reinforcing a falsehood: that "having it all" is, more than anything, a function of personal determination. As Kerry Rubin and Lia Macko, the authors of *Midlife Crisis at 30,* their cri de coeur for Gen-X and Gen-Y women, put it:

> What we discovered in our research is that while the empowerment part of the equation has been loudly celebrated, there has been very little honest discussion among women of our age about the real barriers and flaws that still exist in the system despite the opportunities we inherited.

I am well aware that the majority of American women face problems far greater than any discussed in this article. I am writing for my demographic—highly educated, well-off women who are privileged enough to have choices in the first place. We may not have choices about whether to do paid work, as dual incomes have become indispensable. But we have choices about the type and tempo of the work we do. We are the women who could be leading, and who should be equally represented in the leadership ranks.

Millions of other working women face much more difficult life circumstances. Some are single mothers; many struggle to find any job; others support husbands who cannot find jobs. Many cope with a work life in which good day care is either unavailable or very expensive; school schedules do not match work schedules; and schools themselves are failing to educate their children. Many of these women are worrying not about having it all, but rather about holding on to what they do have. And although women as a group have made substantial gains in wages, educational attainment, and prestige over the past three decades, the economists Justin Wolfers and Betsey Stevenson have shown that women are less happy today than their predecessors were in 1972, both in absolute terms and relative to men.

The best hope for improving the lot of all women, and for closing what Wolfers and Stevenson call a "new gender gap"—measured by well-being rather than wages—is to close the leadership gap: to elect a woman president and 50 women senators; to ensure that women are equally represented in the ranks of corporate executives and judicial leaders. Only when women wield power in sufficient numbers will we create a society that genuinely works for all women. That will be a society that works for everyone.

The Half-Truths We Hold Dear

Let's briefly examine the stories we tell ourselves, the clichés that I and many other women typically fall back on when younger women ask us how we have managed to "have it all." They are not necessarily lies, but at best partial truths. We must clear them out of the way to make room for a more honest and productive discussion about real solutions to the problems faced by professional women.

It's possible if you are just committed enough.

Our usual starting point, whether we say it explicitly or not, is that having it all depends primarily on the depth and intensity of a woman's commitment to her career. That is precisely the sentiment behind the dismay so many older career women feel about the younger generation. *They are not committed enough,* we say, to make the trade-offs and sacrifices that the women ahead of them made.

Yet instead of chiding, perhaps we should face some basic facts. Very few women reach leadership positions. The pool of female candidates for any top job is small, and will only grow smaller if the women who come after us decide to take time out, or drop out of professional competition altogether, to raise children. That is exactly what has Sheryl Sandberg so upset, and rightly so. In her words, "Women are not making it to the top. A hundred and ninety heads of state; nine are women. Of all the people in parliament in the world, 13 percent are women. In the corporate sector, [the share of] women at the top—C-level jobs, board seats—tops out at 15, 16 percent."

Can "insufficient commitment" even plausibly explain these numbers? To be sure, the women who do make it to the top are highly committed to their profession. On closer examination, however, it turns out that most of them have something else in common: they are genuine superwomen. Consider the number of women recently in the top ranks in Washington—Susan Rice, Elizabeth Sherwood-Randall, Michelle Gavin, Nancy-Ann Min DeParle—who are Rhodes Scholars. Samantha Power, another senior White House official, won a Pulitzer Prize at age 32. Or consider Sandberg herself, who graduated with the prize given to Harvard's top student of economics. These women cannot possibly be the standard against which even very talented professional women should measure themselves. Such a standard sets up most women for a sense of failure.

What's more, among those who have made it to the top, a balanced life still is more elusive for women than it is for men. A simple measure is how many women in top positions have children compared with their male colleagues. Every male Supreme Court justice has a family. Two of the three female justices are single with no children. And the third, Ruth Bader Ginsburg, began her career as a judge only when her younger child was almost grown. The pattern is the same at the National Security Council: Condoleezza Rice, the first and only woman national-security adviser, is also the only national-security adviser since the 1950s not to have a family.

The line of high-level women appointees in the Obama administration is one woman deep. Virtually all of us who have stepped down have been succeeded by men; searches for women to succeed men in similar positions come up empty. Just about every woman who could plausibly be tapped is already in government. The rest of the foreign-policy world is not much better; Micah Zenko, a fellow at the Council on Foreign Relations, recently surveyed the best data he could find across the government, the military, the academy, and think tanks, and found that women hold fewer than 30 percent of the senior foreign-policy positions in each of these institutions.

These numbers are all the more striking when we look back to the 1980s, when women now in their late 40s and 50s were coming out of graduate school, and remember that our classes were nearly 50-50 men and women. We were sure then that by now, we would be living in a 50-50 world. Something derailed that dream.

Sandberg thinks that "something" is an "ambition gap"—that women do not dream big enough. I am all for encouraging young women to reach for the stars. But I fear that the obstacles that keep women from reaching the top are rather more prosaic than the scope of their ambition. My longtime and invaluable assistant, who has a doctorate and juggles many balls as the mother of teenage twins, e-mailed me while I was working on this article: "You know what would help the vast majority of women with work/family balance? MAKE SCHOOL SCHEDULES MATCH WORK SCHEDULES." The present system, she noted, is based on a society that no longer exists—one in which farming was a major occupation and stay-at-home moms were the norm. Yet the system hasn't changed.

Consider some of the responses of women interviewed by Zenko about why "women are significantly underrepresented in foreign policy and national security positions in government, academia, and think tanks." Juliette Kayyem, who served as an assistant secretary in the Department of Homeland Security from 2009 to 2011 and now writes a foreign-policy and national-security column for *The Boston Globe,* told Zenko that among other reasons,

> the basic truth is also this: the travel sucks. As my youngest of three children is now 6, I can look back at the years when they were all young and realize just how disruptive all the travel was. There were also trips I couldn't take because I was pregnant or on leave, the conferences I couldn't attend because (note to conference organizers: weekends are a bad choice) kids would be home from school, and the various excursions that were offered but just couldn't be managed.

Jolynn Shoemaker, the director of Women in International Security, agreed: "Inflexible schedules, unrelenting travel, and constant pressure to be in the office are common features of these jobs."

These "mundane" issues—the need to travel constantly to succeed, the conflicts between school schedules and work schedules, the insistence that work be done in the office—cannot be solved by exhortations to close the ambition gap. I would hope to see commencement speeches that finger America's social and business policies, rather than women's level of ambition, in explaining the dearth of women at the top. But changing these policies requires much more than speeches. It means fighting the mundane battles—every day, every year—in individual workplaces, in legislatures, and in the media.

It's possible if you marry the right person.

Sandberg's second message in her Barnard commencement address was: "The most important career decision you're going to make is whether or not you have a life partner and who that partner is." Lisa Jackson, the administrator of the Environmental Protection Agency, recently drove that message home to an audience of Princeton students and alumni gathered to hear her acceptance speech for the James Madison Medal. During the Q&A session, an audience member asked her how she managed her career and her family. She laughed and pointed to her husband in the front row, saying: "There's my work-life balance." I could never have had the career I have had without my husband, Andrew Moravcsik, who is a tenured professor of politics and international affairs at Princeton. Andy has spent more time with our sons than I have, not only on homework, but also on baseball, music lessons, photography, card games, and more. When each of them had to bring in a foreign dish for his fourth-grade class dinner, Andy made his grandmother's Hungarian *palacsinta;* when our older son needed to memorize his lines for a lead role in a school play, he turned to Andy for help.

Still, the proposition that women can have high-powered careers as long as their husbands or partners are willing to share the parenting load equally (or disproportionately) assumes that most women will *feel* as comfortable as men do about being away from their children, as long as their partner is home with them. In my experience, that is simply not the case.

Here I step onto treacherous ground, mined with stereotypes. From years of conversations and observations, however, I've come to believe that men and women respond quite differently when problems at home force them to recognize that their absence is hurting a child, or at least that their presence would likely help. I do not believe fathers love their children any less than mothers do, but men do seem more likely to choose their job at a cost to their family, while women seem more likely to choose their family at a cost to their job.

Many factors determine this choice, of course. Men are still socialized to believe that their primary family obligation is to be the breadwinner; women, to believe that their primary family obligation is to be the caregiver. But it may be more than that. When I described the choice between my children and my job to Senator Jeanne Shaheen, she said exactly what I felt: "There's really no choice." She wasn't referring to social expectations, but to a maternal imperative felt so deeply that the "choice" is reflexive.

Men and women also seem to frame the choice differently. In *Midlife Crisis at 30,* Mary Matalin recalls her days working as President Bush's assistant and Vice President Cheney's counselor:

> Even when the stress was overwhelming—those days when I'd cry in the car on the way to work, asking myself "Why am I doing this??"—I always knew the answer to that question: I believe in this president.

But Matalin goes on to describe her choice to leave in words that are again uncannily similar to the explanation I have given so many people since leaving the State Department:

> I finally asked myself, "Who needs me more?" And that's when I realized, it's somebody else's turn to do this job.

I'm indispensable to my kids, but I'm not close to indispensable to the White House.

To many men, however, the choice to spend more time with their children, instead of working long hours on issues that affect many lives, seems selfish. Male leaders are routinely praised for having sacrificed their personal life on the altar of public or corporate service. That sacrifice, of course, typically involves their family. Yet their children, too, are trained to value public service over private responsibility. At the diplomat Richard Holbrooke's memorial service, one of his sons told the audience that when he was a child, his father was often gone, not around to teach him to throw a ball or to watch his games. But as he grew older, he said, he realized that Holbrooke's absence was the price of saving people around the world—a price worth paying.

It is not clear to me that this ethical framework makes sense for society. Why should we want leaders who fall short on personal responsibilities? Perhaps leaders who invested time in their own families would be more keenly aware of the toll their public choices—on issues from war to welfare—take on private lives. (Kati Marton, Holbrooke's widow and a noted author, says that although Holbrooke adored his children, he came to appreciate the full importance of family only in his 50s, at which point he became a very present parent and grandparent, while continuing to pursue an extraordinary public career.) Regardless, it is clear which set of choices society values more today. Workers who put their careers first are typically rewarded; workers who choose their families are overlooked, disbelieved, or accused of unprofessionalism.

In sum, having a supportive mate may well be a necessary condition if women are to have it all, but it is not sufficient. If women feel deeply that turning down a promotion that would involve more travel, for instance, is the right thing to do, then they will continue to do that. Ultimately, it is society that must change, coming to value choices to put family ahead of work just as much as those to put work ahead of family. If we really valued those choices, we would value the people who make them; if we valued the people who make them, we would do everything possible to hire and retain them; if we did everything possible to allow them to combine work and family equally over time, then the choices would get a lot easier.

It's possible if you sequence it right.

Young women should be wary of the assertion "You can have it all; you just can't have it all at once." This 21st-century addendum to the original line is now proffered by many senior women to their younger mentees. To the extent that it means, in the words of one working mother, "I'm going to do my best and I'm going to keep the long term in mind and know that it's not always going to be this hard to balance," it is sound advice. But to the extent that it means that women can have it all if they just find the right sequence of career and family, it's cheerfully wrong.

The most important sequencing issue is when to have children. Many of the top women leaders of the generation just ahead of me—Madeleine Albright, Hillary Clinton, Ruth

Bader Ginsburg, Sandra Day O'Connor, Patricia Wald, Nannerl Keohane—had their children in their 20s and early 30s, as was the norm in the 1950s through the 1970s. A child born when his mother is 25 will finish high school when his mother is 43, an age at which, with full-time immersion in a career, she still has plenty of time and energy for advancement.

Yet this sequence has fallen out of favor with many high-potential women, and understandably so. People tend to marry later now, and anyway, if you have children earlier, you may have difficulty getting a graduate degree, a good first job, and opportunities for advancement in the crucial early years of your career. Making matters worse, you will also have less income while raising your children, and hence less ability to hire the help that can be indispensable to your juggling act.

When I was the dean, the Woodrow Wilson School created a program called Pathways to Public Service, aimed at advising women whose children were almost grown about how to go into public service, and many women still ask me about the best "on-ramps" to careers in their mid-40s. Honestly, I'm not sure what to tell most of them. Unlike the pioneering women who entered the workforce after having children in the 1970s, these women are competing with their younger selves. Government and NGO jobs are an option, but many careers are effectively closed off. Personally, I have never seen a woman in her 40s enter the academic market successfully, or enter a law firm as a junior associate, Alicia Florrick of *The Good Wife* notwithstanding.

These considerations are why so many career women of my generation chose to establish themselves in their careers first and have children in their mid-to-late 30s. But that raises the possibility of spending long, stressful years and a small fortune trying to have a baby. I lived that nightmare: for three years, beginning at age 35, I did everything possible to conceive and was frantic at the thought that I had simply left having a biological child until it was too late.

And when everything does work out? I had my first child at 38 (and counted myself blessed) and my second at 40. That means I will be 58 when both of my children are out of the house. What's more, it means that many peak career opportunities are coinciding precisely with their teenage years, when, experienced parents advise, being available as a parent is just as important as in the first years of a child's life.

Many women of my generation have found themselves, in the prime of their careers, saying no to opportunities they once would have jumped at and hoping those chances come around again later. Many others who have decided to step back for a while, taking on consultant positions or part-time work that lets them spend more time with their children (or aging parents), are worrying about how long they can "stay out" before they lose the competitive edge they worked so hard to acquire.

Given the way our work culture is oriented today, I recommend establishing yourself in your career first but still trying to have kids before you are 35—or else freeze your eggs, whether you are married or not. You may well be a more mature and less frustrated parent in your 30s or 40s; you are also more likely to have found a lasting life partner. But the truth is, neither sequence is optimal, and both involve trade-offs that men do not have to make.

You should be able to have a family if you want one—however and whenever your life circumstances allow—and still have the career you desire. If more women could strike this balance, more women would reach leadership positions. And if more women were in leadership positions, they could make it easier for more women to stay in the workforce. The rest of this essay details how.

Changing the Culture of Face Time

Back in the Reagan administration, a *New York Times* story about the ferociously competitive budget director Dick Darman reported, "Mr. Darman sometimes managed to convey the impression that he was the last one working in the Reagan White House by leaving his suit coat on his chair and his office light burning after he left for home." (Darman claimed that it was just easier to leave his suit jacket in the office so he could put it on again in the morning, but his record of psychological manipulation suggests otherwise.)

The culture of "time macho"—a relentless competition to work harder, stay later, pull more all-nighters, travel around the world and bill the extra hours that the international date line affords you—remains astonishingly prevalent among professionals today. Nothing captures the belief that more time equals more value better than the cult of billable hours afflicting large law firms across the country and providing exactly the wrong incentives for employees who hope to integrate work and family. Yet even in industries that don't explicitly reward sheer quantity of hours spent on the job, the pressure to arrive early, stay late, and be available, always, for in-person meetings at 11 a.m. on Saturdays can be intense. Indeed, by some measures, the problem has gotten worse over time: a study by the Center for American Progress reports that nationwide, the share of all professionals—women and men—working more than 50 hours a week has increased since the late 1970s.

But more time in the office does not always mean more "value added"—and it does not always add up to a more successful organization. In 2009, Sandra Pocharski, a senior female partner at Monitor Group and the head of the firm's Leadership and Organization practice, commissioned a Harvard Business School professor to assess the factors that helped or hindered women's effectiveness and advancement at Monitor. The study found that the company's culture was characterized by an "always on" mode of working, often without due regard to the impact on employees. Pocharski observed:

Clients come first, always, and sometimes burning the midnight oil really does make the difference between success and failure. But sometimes we were just defaulting to behavior that overloaded our people without improving results much, if at all. We decided we needed managers to get better at distinguishing between these categories, and to recognize the hidden costs of assuming that "time is cheap." When that time doesn't add a lot of value and comes at a high cost to talented employees, who will leave when the personal cost becomes unsustainable—well, that is clearly a bad outcome for everyone.

I have worked very long hours and pulled plenty of all-nighters myself over the course of my career, including a few nights on my office couch during my two years in D.C. Being willing to put the time in when the job simply has to get done is rightfully a hallmark of a successful professional. But looking back, I have to admit that my assumption that I would stay late made me much less efficient over the course of the day than I might have been, and certainly less so than some of my colleagues, who managed to get the same amount of work done and go home at a decent hour. If Dick Darman had had a boss who clearly valued prioritization and time management, he might have found reason to turn out the lights and take his jacket home.

Long hours are one thing, and realistically, they are often unavoidable. But do they really need to be spent at the office? To be sure, being in the office *some* of the time is beneficial. In-person meetings can be far more efficient than phone or e-mail tag; trust and collegiality are much more easily built up around the same physical table; and spontaneous conversations often generate good ideas and lasting relationships. Still, armed with e-mail, instant messaging, phones, and videoconferencing technology, we should be able to move to a culture where the office is a base of operations more than the required locus of work.

Being able to work from home—in the evening after children are put to bed, or during their sick days or snow days, and at least some of the time on weekends—can be the key, for mothers, to carrying your full load versus letting a team down at crucial moments. State-of-the-art videoconferencing facilities can dramatically reduce the need for long business trips. These technologies are making inroads, and allowing easier integration of work and family life. According to the Women's Business Center, 61 percent of women business owners use technology to "integrate the responsibilities of work and home"; 44 percent use technology to allow employees "to work off-site or to have flexible work schedules." Yet our work culture still remains more office-centered than it needs to be, especially in light of technological advances.

One way to change that is by changing the "default rules" that govern office work—the baseline expectations about when, where, and how work will be done. As behavioral economists well know, these baselines can make an enormous difference in the way people act. It is one thing, for instance, for an organization to allow phone-ins to a meeting on an ad hoc basis, when parenting and work schedules collide—a system that's better than nothing, but likely to engender guilt among those calling in, and possibly resentment among those in the room. It is quite another for that organization to declare that its policy will be to schedule in-person meetings, whenever possible, during the hours of the school day—a system that might normalize call-ins for those (rarer) meetings still held in the late afternoon.

One real-world example comes from the British Foreign and Commonwealth Office, a place most people are more likely to associate with distinguished gentlemen in pinstripes than with progressive thinking about work-family balance. Like so many other places, however, the FCO worries about losing talented members of two-career couples around the world, particularly women. So it recently changed its basic policy from a default rule that jobs have to be done on-site to one that assumes that some jobs might be done remotely, and invites workers to make the case for remote work. Kara Owen, a career foreign-service officer who was the FCO's diversity director and will soon become the British deputy ambassador to France, writes that she has now done two remote jobs. Before her current maternity leave, she was working a London job from Dublin to be with her partner, using teleconferencing technology and timing her trips to London to coincide "with key meetings where I needed to be in the room (or chatting at the pre-meeting coffee) to have an impact, or to do intensive 'network maintenance.'" In fact, she writes, "I have found the distance and quiet to be a real advantage in a strategic role, providing I have put in the investment up front to develop very strong personal relationships with the game changers." Owen recognizes that not every job can be done this way. But she says that for her part, she has been able to combine family requirements with her career.

Changes in default office rules should not advantage parents over other workers; indeed, done right, they can improve relations among co-workers by raising their awareness of each other's circumstances and instilling a sense of fairness. Two years ago, the ACLU Foundation of Massachusetts decided to replace its "parental leave" policy with a "family leave" policy that provides for as much as 12 weeks of leave not only for new parents, but also for employees who need to care for a spouse, child, or parent with a serious health condition. According to Director Carol Rose, "We wanted a policy that took into account the fact that even employees who do not have children have family obligations." The policy was shaped by the belief that giving women "special treatment" can "backfire if the broader norms shaping the behavior of all employees do not change." When I was the dean of the Wilson School, I managed with the mantra "Family comes first"—any family—and found that my employees were both productive and intensely loyal.

None of these changes will happen by themselves, and reasons to avoid them will seldom be hard to find. But obstacles and inertia are usually surmountable if leaders are open to changing their assumptions about the workplace. The use of technology in many high-level government jobs, for instance, is complicated by the need to have access to classified information. But in 2009, Deputy Secretary of State James Steinberg, who shares the parenting of his two young daughters equally with his wife, made getting such access at home an immediate priority so that he could leave the office at a reasonable hour and participate in important meetings via videoconferencing if necessary. I wonder how many women in similar positions would be afraid to ask, lest they be seen as insufficiently committed to their jobs.

Revaluing Family Values

While employers shouldn't privilege parents over other workers, too often they end up doing the opposite, usually subtly, and usually in ways that make it harder for a primary caregiver to get ahead. Many people in positions of power seem to place a low value on child care in comparison with other outside activities. Consider the following proposition: An employer has two equally talented and productive employees. One trains for and runs marathons when he is not working. The other takes care of two children. What assumptions is the employer likely to make about the marathon runner? That he gets up in the dark every day and logs an hour or two running before even coming into the office, or drives himself to get out there even after a long day. That he is ferociously disciplined and willing to push himself through distraction, exhaustion, and days when nothing seems to go right in the service of a goal far in the distance. That he must manage his time exceptionally well to squeeze all of that in.

Be honest: Do you think the employer makes those same assumptions about the parent? Even though she likely rises in the dark hours before she needs to be at work, organizes her children's day, makes breakfast, packs lunch, gets them off to school, figures out shopping and other errands even if she is lucky enough to have a housekeeper—and does much the same work at the end of the day. Cheryl Mills, Hillary Clinton's indefatigable chief of staff, has twins in elementary school; even with a fully engaged husband, she famously gets up at four every morning to check and send e-mails before her kids wake up. Louise Richardson, now the vice chancellor of the University of St. Andrews, in Scotland, combined an assistant professorship in government at Harvard with mothering three young children. She organized her time so ruthlessly that she always keyed in 1:11 or 2:22 or 3:33 on the microwave rather than 1:00, 2:00, or 3:00, because hitting the same number three times took less time.

Elizabeth Warren, who is now running for the U.S. Senate in Massachusetts, has a similar story. When she had two young children and a part-time law practice, she struggled to find enough time to write the papers and articles that would help get her an academic position. In her words:

> I needed a plan. I figured out that writing time was when Alex was asleep. So the minute I put him down for a nap or he fell asleep in the baby swing, I went to my desk and started working on something—footnotes, reading, outlining, writing...I learned to do everything else with a baby on my hip.

The discipline, organization, and sheer endurance it takes to succeed at top levels with young children at home is easily comparable to running 20 to 40 miles a week. But that's rarely how employers see things, not only when making allowances, but when making promotions. Perhaps because people *choose* to have children? People also choose to run marathons.

One final example: I have worked with many Orthodox Jewish men who observed the Sabbath from sundown on Friday until sundown on Saturday. Jack Lew, the two-time director of the Office of Management and Budget, former deputy secretary of state for management and resources, and now White House chief of staff, is a case in point. Jack's wife lived in New York when he worked in the State Department, so he would leave the office early enough on Friday afternoon to take the shuttle to New York and a taxi to his apartment before sundown. He would not work on Friday after sundown or all day Saturday. Everyone who knew him, including me, admired his commitment to his faith and his ability to carve out the time for it, even with an enormously demanding job.

It is hard to imagine, however, that we would have the same response if a mother told us she was blocking out mid-Friday afternoon through the end of the day on Saturday, every week, to spend time with her children. I suspect this would be seen as unprofessional, an imposition of unnecessary costs on co-workers. In fact, of course, one of the great values of the Sabbath—whether Jewish or Christian—is precisely that it carves out a family oasis, with rituals and a mandatory setting-aside of work.

Our assumptions are just that: things we believe that are not necessarily so. Yet what we assume has an enormous impact on our perceptions and responses. Fortunately, changing our assumptions is up to us.

Redefining the Arc of a Successful Career

The American definition of a successful professional is someone who can climb the ladder the furthest in the shortest time, generally peaking between ages 45 and 55. It is a definition well suited to the mid-20th century, an era when people had kids in their 20s, stayed in one job, retired at 67, and were dead, on average, by age 71.

It makes far less sense today. Average life expectancy for people in their 20s has increased to 80; men and women in good health can easily work until they are 75. They can expect to have multiple jobs and even multiple careers throughout their working life. Couples marry later, have kids later, and can expect to live on two incomes. They may well retire *earlier*—the average retirement age has gone down from 67 to 63—but that is commonly "retirement" only in the sense of collecting retirement benefits. Many people go on to "encore" careers.

Assuming the priceless gifts of good health and good fortune, a professional woman can thus expect her working life to stretch some 50 years, from her early or mid-20s to her mid-70s. It is reasonable to assume that she will build her credentials and establish herself, at least in her first career, between 22 and 35; she will have children, if she wants them, sometime between 25 and 45; she'll want maximum flexibility and control over her time in the 10 years that her children are 8 to 18; and she should plan to take positions of maximum authority and demands on her time after her children are out of the house. Women who have children in their late 20s can expect to immerse themselves completely in their careers in their late 40s, with plenty of time still to rise to the top in their late 50s and early 60s. Women who make partner, managing director, or senior vice president; get tenure; or establish a medical practice before having children in their late 30s should be coming back on line for the most demanding jobs at almost exactly the same age.

Along the way, women should think about the climb to leadership not in terms of a straight upward slope, but as irregular stair steps, with periodic plateaus (and even dips) when they turn down promotions to remain in a job that works for their family situation; when they leave high-powered jobs and spend a year or two at home on a reduced schedule; or when they step off a conventional professional track to take a consulting position or project-based work for a number of years. I think of these plateaus as "investment intervals." My husband and I took a sabbatical in Shanghai, from August 2007 to May 2008, right in the thick of an election year when many of my friends were advising various candidates on foreign-policy issues. We thought of the move in part as "putting money in the family bank," taking advantage of the opportunity to spend a close year together in a foreign culture. But we were also investing in our children's ability to learn Mandarin and in our own knowledge of Asia.

Peaking in your late 50s and early 60s rather than your late 40s and early 50s makes particular sense for women, who live longer than men. And many of the stereotypes about older workers simply do not hold. A 2006 survey of human-resources professionals shows that only 23 percent think older workers are less flexible than younger workers; only 11 percent think older workers require more training than younger workers; and only 7 percent think older workers have less drive than younger workers.

Whether women will really have the confidence to stair-step their careers, however, will again depend in part on perceptions. Slowing down the rate of promotions, taking time out periodically, pursuing an alternative path during crucial parenting or parent-care years—all have to become more visible and more noticeably accepted as a pause rather than an opt-out. (In an encouraging sign, *Mass Career Customization,* a 2007 book by Cathleen Benko and Anne Weisberg arguing that "today's career is no longer a straight climb up the corporate ladder, but rather a combination of climbs, lateral moves, and planned descents," was a *Wall Street Journal* best seller.)

Institutions can also take concrete steps to promote this acceptance. For instance, in 1970, Princeton established a tenure-extension policy that allowed female assistant professors expecting a child to request a one-year extension on their tenure clocks. This policy was later extended to men, and broadened to include adoptions. In the early 2000s, two reports on the status of female faculty discovered that only about 3 percent of assistant professors requested tenure extensions in a given year. And in response to a survey question, women were much more likely than men to think that a tenure extension would be detrimental to an assistant professor's career.

So in 2005, under President Shirley Tilghman, Princeton changed the default rule. The administration announced that all assistant professors, female and male, who had a new child would *automatically* receive a one-year extension on the tenure clock, with no opt-outs allowed. Instead, assistant professors could request early consideration for tenure if they wished. The number of assistant professors who receive a tenure extension has tripled since the change.

One of the best ways to move social norms in this direction is to choose and celebrate different role models. New Jersey Governor Chris Christie and I are poles apart politically, but he went way up in my estimation when he announced that one reason he decided against running for president in 2012 was the impact his campaign would have had on his children. He reportedly made clear at a fund-raiser in Louisiana that he

didn't want to be away from his children for long periods of time; according to a Republican official at the event, he said that "his son [missed] him after being gone for the three days on the road, and that he needed to get back." He may not get my vote if and when he does run for president, but he definitely gets my admiration (providing he doesn't turn around and join the GOP ticket this fall).

If we are looking for high-profile female role models, we might begin with Michelle Obama. She started out with the same résumé as her husband, but has repeatedly made career decisions designed to let her do work she cared about and also be the kind of parent she wanted to be. She moved from a high-powered law firm first to Chicago city government and then to the University of Chicago shortly before her daughters were born, a move that let her work only 10 minutes away from home. She has spoken publicly and often about her initial concerns that her husband's entry into politics would be bad for their family life, and about her determination to limit her participation in the presidential election campaign to have more time at home. Even as first lady, she has been adamant that she be able to balance her official duties with family time. We should see her as a full-time career woman, but one who is taking a very visible investment interval. We should celebrate her not only as a wife, mother, and champion of healthy eating, but also as a woman who has had the courage and judgment to invest in her daughters when they need her most. And we should expect a glittering career from her after she leaves the White House and her daughters leave for college.

Rediscovering the Pursuit of Happiness

One of the most complicated and surprising parts of my journey out of Washington was coming to grips with what I really wanted. I had opportunities to stay on, and I could have tried to work out an arrangement allowing me to spend more time at home. I might have been able to get my family to join me in Washington for a year; I might have been able to get classified technology installed at my house the way Jim Steinberg did; I might have been able to commute only four days a week instead of five. (While this last change would have still left me very little time at home, given the intensity of my job, it might have made the job doable for another year or two.) But I realized that I didn't just *need* to go home. Deep down, I *wanted* to go home. I wanted to be able to spend time with my children in the last few years that they are likely to live at home, crucial years for their development into responsible, productive, happy, and caring adults. But also irreplaceable years for me to enjoy the simple pleasures of parenting—baseball games, piano recitals, waffle breakfasts, family trips, and goofy rituals. My older son is doing very well these days, but even when he gives us a hard time, as all teenagers do, being home to shape his choices and help him make good decisions is deeply satisfying.

The flip side of my realization is captured in Macko and Rubin's ruminations on the importance of bringing the different parts of their lives together as 30-year-old women:

If we didn't start to learn how to integrate our personal, social, and professional lives, we were about five years away from morphing into the angry woman on the other side of a mahogany desk who questions her staffs work ethic after standard 12-hour workdays, before heading home to eat moo shoo pork in her lonely apartment.

Women have contributed to the fetish of the one-dimensional life, albeit by necessity. The pioneer generation of feminists walled off their personal lives from their professional personas to ensure that they could never be discriminated against for a lack of commitment to their work. When I was a law student in the 1980s, many women who were then climbing the legal hierarchy in New York firms told me that they never admitted to taking time out for a child's doctor appointment or school performance, but instead invented a much more neutral excuse.

Today, however, women in power can and should change that environment, although change is not easy. When I became dean of the Woodrow Wilson School, in 2002, I decided that one of the advantages of being a woman in power was that I could help change the norms by deliberately talking about my children and my desire to have a balanced life. Thus, I would end faculty meetings at 6 p.m. by saying that I had to go home for dinner; I would also make clear to all student organizations that I would not come to dinner with them, because I needed to be home from six to eight, but that I would often be willing to come back after eight for a meeting. I also once told the Dean's Advisory Committee that the associate dean would chair the next session so I could go to a parent-teacher conference.

After a few months of this, several female assistant professors showed up in my office quite agitated. "You *have* to stop talking about your kids," one said. "You are not showing the gravitas that people expect from a dean, which is particularly damaging precisely because you are the first woman dean of the school." I told them that I was doing it deliberately and continued my practice, but it is interesting that gravitas and parenthood don't seem to go together.

Ten years later, whenever I am introduced at a lecture or other speaking engagement, I insist that the person introducing me mention that I have two sons. It seems odd to me to list degrees, awards, positions, and interests and *not* include the dimension of my life that is most important to me—and takes an enormous amount of my time. As Secretary Clinton once said in a television interview in Beijing when the interviewer asked her about Chelsea's upcoming wedding: "That's my real life." But I notice that my male introducers are typically uncomfortable when I make the request. They frequently say things like "And she particularly wanted me to mention that she has two sons"—thereby drawing attention to the unusual nature of my request, when my entire purpose is to make family references routine and normal in professional life.

This does not mean that you should insist that your colleagues spend time cooing over pictures of your baby or listening to the prodigious accomplishments of your kindergartner. It does mean that if you are late coming in one week, because it is your turn to drive the kids to school, that you be honest about what you are doing. Indeed, Sheryl Sandberg recently acknowledged not only that she leaves work at 5:30 to have dinner with her family, but also that for many years she did not dare make this admission, even though she would of course make up the work time later in the evening. Her willingness to speak out now is a strong step in the right direction.

Seeking out a more balanced life is not a women's issue; balance would be better for us all. Bronnie Ware, an Australian blogger who worked for years in palliative care and is the author of the 2011 book *The Top Five Regrets of the Dying,* writes that the regret she heard most often was "I wish I'd had the courage to live a life true to myself, not the life others expected of me." The second-most-common regret was "I wish I didn't work so hard." She writes: "This came from every male patient that I nursed. They missed their children's youth and their partner's companionship."

Juliette Kayyem, who several years ago left the Department of Homeland Security soon after her husband, David Barron, left a high position in the Justice Department, says their joint decision to leave Washington and return to Boston sprang from their desire to work on the *"happiness project,"* meaning quality time with their three children. (She borrowed the term from her friend Gretchen Rubin, who wrote a best-selling book and now runs a blog with that name.)

It's time to embrace a national happiness project. As a daughter of Charlottesville, Virginia, the home of Thomas Jefferson and the university he founded, I grew up with the Declaration of Independence in my blood. Last I checked, he did not declare American independence in the name of life, liberty, and professional success. Let us rediscover the pursuit of happiness, and let us start at home.

Innovation Nation

As I write this, I can hear the reaction of some readers to many of the proposals in this essay: It's all fine and well for a tenured professor to write about flexible working hours, investment intervals, and family-comes-first management. But what about the real world? Most American women cannot demand these things, particularly in a bad economy, and their employers have little incentive to grant them voluntarily. Indeed, the most frequent reaction I get in putting forth these ideas is that when the choice is whether to hire a man who will work whenever and wherever needed, or a woman who needs more flexibility, choosing the man will add more value to the company.

In fact, while many of these issues are hard to quantify and measure precisely, the statistics seem to tell a different story. A seminal study of 527 U.S. companies, published in the *Academy of Management Journal* in 2000, suggests that "organizations with more extensive work-family policies have higher perceived firm-level performance" among their industry peers. These findings accorded with a 2003 study conducted by Michelle Arthur at the University of New Mexico. Examining 130 announcements of family-friendly policies in *The Wall Street Journal,* Arthur found that the announcements alone significantly improved share prices. In 2011, a study on flexibility in the workplace by Ellen Galinsky, Kelly Sakai, and Tyler Wigton of the Families and Work Institute showed that increased flexibility correlates positively with job engagement, job satisfaction, employee retention, and employee health.

This is only a small sampling from a large and growing literature trying to pin down the relationship between family-friendly policies and economic performance. Other scholars have concluded that good family policies attract better talent, which in turn raises productivity, but that the policies themselves have no impact on productivity. Still others argue that results attributed to these policies are actually a function of good management overall. What is evident, however, is that many firms that recruit and train well-educated professional women are aware that when a woman leaves because of bad work-family balance, they are losing the money and time they invested in her.

Even the legal industry, built around the billable hour, is taking notice. Deborah Epstein Henry, a former big-firm litigator, is now the president of Flex-Time Lawyers, a national consulting firm focused partly on strategies for the retention of female attorneys. In her book *Law and Reorder,* published by the American Bar Association in 2010, she describes a legal profession "where the billable hour no longer works"; where attorneys, judges, recruiters, and academics all agree that this system of compensation has perverted the industry, leading to brutal work hours, massive inefficiency, and highly inflated costs. The answer—already being deployed in different corners of the industry—is a combination of alternative fee structures, virtual firms, women-owned firms, and the outsourcing of discrete legal jobs to other jurisdictions. Women, and Generation X and Y lawyers more generally, are pushing for these changes on the supply side; clients determined to reduce legal fees and increase flexible service are pulling on the demand side. Slowly, change is happening.

At the core of all this is self-interest. Losing smart and motivated women not only diminishes a company's talent pool; it also reduces the return on its investment in training and mentoring. In trying to address these issues, some firms are finding out that women's ways of working may just be better ways of working, for employees and clients alike.

Experts on creativity and innovation emphasize the value of encouraging nonlinear thinking and cultivating randomness by taking long walks or looking at your environment from unusual angles. In their new book, *A New Culture of Learning: Cultivating the Imagination for a World of Constant Change,* the innovation gurus John Seely Brown and Douglas Thomas write, "We believe that connecting play and imagination may be the single most important step in unleashing the new culture of learning."

Space for play and imagination is exactly what emerges when rigid work schedules and hierarchies loosen up. Skeptics should consider the "California effect." California is the cradle of American innovation—in technology, entertainment, sports, food, and lifestyles. It is also a place where people take leisure as seriously as they take work; where companies like Google deliberately encourage play, with Ping-Pong tables, light sabers, and policies that require employees to spend one day a week working on whatever they wish. Charles Baudelaire wrote: "Genius is nothing more nor less than childhood recovered at will." Google apparently has taken note.

No parent would mistake child care for childhood. Still, seeing the world anew through a child's eyes can be a powerful source of stimulation. When the Nobel laureate Thomas Schelling wrote *The Strategy of Conflict,* a classic text applying game theory to conflicts among nations, he frequently drew on child-rearing for examples of when deterrence might succeed or fail. "It may be easier to articulate the peculiar difficulty of constraining [a ruler] by the use of threats," he wrote, "when one is fresh from a vain attempt at using threats to keep a small child from hurting a dog or a small dog from hurting a child."

The books I've read with my children, the silly movies I've watched, the games I've played, questions I've answered, and people I've met while parenting have broadened my world. Another axiom of the literature on innovation is that the more often people with different perspectives come together, the more likely creative ideas are to emerge. Giving workers the ability to integrate their non-work lives with their work— whether they spend that time mothering or marathoning—will open the door to a much wider range of influences and ideas.

Enlisting Men

Perhaps the most encouraging news of all for achieving the sorts of changes that I have proposed is that men are joining the cause. In commenting on a draft of this article, Martha Minow, the dean of the Harvard Law School, wrote me that one change she has observed during 30 years of teaching law at Harvard is that today many young men are asking questions about how they can manage a work-life balance. And more systematic research on Generation Y confirms that many more men than in the past are asking questions about how they are going to integrate active parenthood with their professional lives.

Abstract aspirations are easier than concrete trade-offs, of course. These young men have not yet faced the question of whether they are prepared to give up that more prestigious clerkship or fellowship, decline a promotion, or delay their professional goals to spend more time with their children and to support their partner's career.

Yet once work practices and work culture begin to evolve, those changes are likely to carry their own momentum. Kara Owen, the British foreign-service officer who worked a London job from Dublin, wrote me in an e-mail:

I think the culture on flexible working started to change the minute the Board of Management (who were all men at the time) started to work flexibly—quite a few of them started working one day a week from home.

Men have, of course, become much more involved parents over the past couple of decades, and that, too, suggests broad support for big changes in the way we balance work and family. It is noteworthy that both James Steinberg, deputy secretary of state, and William Lynn, deputy secretary of defense, stepped down two years into the Obama administration so that they could spend more time with their children (for real).

Going forward, women would do well to frame work-family balance in terms of the broader social and economic issues that affect both women and men. After all, we have a new generation of young men who have been raised by full-time working mothers. Let us presume, as I do with my sons, that they will understand "supporting their families" to mean more than earning money.

I have been blessed to work with and be mentored by some extraordinary women. Watching Hillary Clinton in action makes me incredibly proud—of her intelligence, expertise, professionalism, charisma, and command of any audience. I get a similar rush when I see a frontpage picture of Christine Lagarde, the managing director of the International Monetary Fund, and Angela Merkel, the chancellor of Germany, deep in conversation about some of the most important issues on the world stage; or of Susan Rice, the U.S. ambassador to the United Nations, standing up forcefully for the Syrian people in the Security Council.

These women are extraordinary role models. If I had a daughter, I would encourage her to look to them, and I want a world in which they are extraordinary but not unusual. Yet I also want a world in which, in Lisa Jackson's words, "to be a strong woman, you don't have to give up on the things that define you as a woman." That means respecting, enabling, and indeed celebrating the full range of women's choices. "Empowering yourself," Jackson said in her speech at Princeton, "doesn't have to mean rejecting motherhood, or eliminating the nurturing or feminine aspects of who you are."

I gave a speech at Vassar last November and arrived in time to wander the campus on a lovely fall afternoon. It is a place infused with a spirit of community and generosity, filled with benches, walkways, public art, and quiet places donated by alumnae seeking to encourage contemplation and connection. Turning the pages of the alumni magazine (Vassar is now coed), I was struck by the entries of older alumnae, who greeted their classmates with *Salve* (Latin for "hello") and wrote witty remembrances sprinkled with literary allusions. Theirs was a world in which women wore their learning lightly; their news is mostly of their children's accomplishments. Many of us look back on that earlier era as a time when it was fine to joke that women went to college to get an "M.R.S." And many women of my generation abandoned the Seven Sisters as soon as the formerly all-male Ivy League universities became coed. I would never return to the world of segregated sexes and rampant discrimination. But now is the time to revisit the assumption that women must rush to adapt to the "man's world" that our mothers and mentors warned us about.

I continually push the young women in my classes to speak more. They must gain the confidence to value their own insights and questions, and to present them readily. My husband agrees, but he actually tries to get the young men in his classes to act more like the women—to speak less and listen more. If women are ever to achieve real equality as leaders, then we have to stop accepting male behavior and male choices as the default and the ideal. We must insist on changing social policies and bending career tracks to accommodate *our* choices, too. We have the power to do it if we decide to, and we have many men standing beside us.

We'll create a better society in the process, for *all* women. We may need to put a woman in the White House before we are able to change the conditions of the women working at Walmart. But when we do, we will stop talking about whether women can have it all. We will properly focus on how we can help all Americans have healthy, happy, productive lives, valuing the people they love as much as the success they seek.

Critical Thinking

1. What are the strains faced by most American women today?
2. What factors explain why women can't have it all?
3. Should women be able to have it all?

Human Sex Trafficking

AMANDA WALKER-RODRIGUEZ, JD AND RODNEY HILL, JD

H uman sex trafficking is the most common form of modern-day slavery. Estimates place the number of its domestic and international victims in the millions, mostly females and children enslaved in the commercial sex industry for little or no money.[1] The terms *human trafficking* and *sex slavery* usually conjure up images of young girls beaten and abused in faraway places, like Eastern Europe, Asia, or Africa. Actually, human sex trafficking and sex slavery happen locally in cities and towns, both large and small, throughout the United States, right in citizens' backyards.

Appreciating the magnitude of the problem requires first understanding what the issue is and what it is not. Additionally, people must be able to identify the victim in common trafficking situations.

Human Sex Trafficking

Many people probably remember popular movies and television shows depicting pimps as dressing flashy and driving large fancy cars. More important, the women—adults—consensually and voluntarily engaged in the business of prostitution without complaint. This characterization is extremely inaccurate, nothing more than fiction. In reality, the pimp *traffics* young women (and sometimes men) completely against their will by force or threat of force; this is human sex trafficking.

The Scope

Not only is human sex trafficking slavery but it is big business. It is the fastest-growing business of organized crime and the third-largest criminal enterprise in the world.[2] The majority of sex trafficking is international, with victims taken from such places as South and Southeast Asia, the former Soviet Union, Central and South America, and other less developed areas and moved to more developed ones, including Asia, the Middle East, Western Europe, and North America.[3]

Unfortunately, however, sex trafficking also occurs domestically.[4] The United States not only faces an influx of international victims but also has its own homegrown problem of interstate sex trafficking of minors.[5]

The United States not only faces an influx of international victims but also has its own homegrown problem of interstate sex trafficking of minors.

Although comprehensive research to document the number of children engaged in prostitution in the United States is lacking, an estimated 293,000 American youths currently are at risk of becoming victims of commercial sexual exploitation.[6] The majority of these victims are runaway or thrown-away youths who live on the streets and become victims of prostitution.[7] These children generally come from homes where they have been abused or from families who have abandoned them. Often, they become involved in prostitution to support themselves financially or to get the things they feel they need or want (like drugs).

Other young people are recruited into prostitution through forced abduction, pressure from parents, or through deceptive agreements between parents and traffickers. Once these children become involved in prostitution, they often are forced to travel far from their homes and, as a result, are isolated from their friends and family. Few children in this situation can develop new relationships with peers or adults other than the person victimizing them. The lifestyle of such youths revolves around violence, forced drug use, and constant threats.[8]

Among children and teens living on the streets in the United States, involvement in commercial sex activity is a problem of epidemic proportion. Many girls living on the street engage in formal prostitution, and some become entangled in nationwide organized crime networks where they are trafficked nationally. Criminal networks transport these children around the United States by a variety of means—cars, buses, vans, trucks, or planes—and often provide them counterfeit identification to use in the event of arrest. The average age at which girls first become victims of prostitution is 12 to 14. It is not only the girls on the streets who are affected; boys and transgender youth enter into prostitution between the ages of 11 and 13 on average.[9]

The Operation

Today, the business of human sex trafficking is much more organized and violent. These women and young girls are sold to traffickers, locked up in rooms or brothels for weeks or months, drugged, terrorized, and raped repeatedly.[10] These continual abuses make it easier for the traffickers to control their victims. The captives are so afraid and intimidated that they rarely speak out against their traffickers, even when faced with an opportunity to escape.

Today, the business of human sex trafficking is much more organized and violent.

Generally, the traffickers are very organized. Many have a hierarchy system similar to that of other criminal organizations. Traffickers who have more than one victim often have a "bottom," who sits atop the hierarchy of prostitutes. The bottom, a victim herself, has been with the trafficker the longest and has earned his trust. Bottoms collect the money from the other girls, discipline them, seduce unwitting youths into trafficking, and handle the day-to-day business for the trafficker.

Traffickers represent every social, ethnic, and racial group. Various organizational types exist in trafficking. Some perpetrators are involved with local street and motorcycle gangs, others are members of larger nationwide gangs and criminal organizations, and some have no affiliation with any one group or organization. Traffickers are not only men—women run many established rings.

Traffickers represent every social, ethnic, and racial group.

Traffickers use force, drugs, emotional tactics, and financial methods to control their victims. They have an especially easy time establishing a strong bond with young girls. These perpetrators may promise marriage and a lifestyle the youths often did not have in their previous familial relationships. They claim they "love" and "need" the victim and that any sex acts are for their future together. In cases where the children have few or no positive male role models in their lives, the traffickers take advantage of this fact and, in many cases, demand that the victims refer to them as "daddy," making it tougher for the youths to break the hold the perpetrator has on them.

Sometimes, the traffickers use violence, such as gang rape and other forms of abuse, to force the youths to work for them and remain under their control. One victim, a runaway from Baltimore County, Maryland, was gang raped by a group of men associated with the trafficker, who subsequently staged a "rescue." He then demanded that she repay him by working for him as one of his prostitutes. In many cases, however, the victims simply are beaten until they submit to the trafficker's demands.

In some situations, the youths have become addicted to drugs. The traffickers simply can use their ability to supply them with drugs as a means of control.

Traffickers often take their victims' identity forms, including birth certificates, passports, and drivers' licenses. In these cases, even if youths do leave they would have no ability to support themselves and often will return to the trafficker.

These abusive methods of control impact the victims both physically and mentally. Similar to cases involving Stockholm Syndrome, these victims, who have been abused over an extended period of time, begin to feel an attachment to the perpetrator.[11] This paradoxical psychological phenomenon makes it difficult for law enforcement to breach the bond of control, albeit abusive, the trafficker holds over the victim.

National Problem with Local Ties

The Federal Level

In 2000, Congress passed the Trafficking Victims Protection Act (TVPA), which created the first comprehensive federal law to address trafficking, with a significant focus on the international dimension of the problem. The law provides a three-pronged approach: *prevention* through public awareness programs overseas and a State Department-led monitoring and sanctions program; *protection* through a new T Visa and services for foreign national victims; and *prosecution* through new federal crimes and severe penalties.[12]

As a result of the passing of the TVPA, the Office to Monitor and Combat Trafficking in Persons was established in October 2001. This enabling legislation led to the creation of a bureau within the State Department to specifically address human trafficking and exploitation on all levels and to take legal action against perpetrators.[13] Additionally, this act was designed to enforce all laws within the 13th Amendment to the U.S. Constitution that apply.[14]

U.S. Immigration and Customs Enforcement (ICE) is one of the lead federal agencies charged with enforcing the TVPA. Human trafficking represents significant risks to homeland security. Would-be terrorists and criminals often can access the same routes and use the same methods as human traffickers. ICE's Human Smuggling and Trafficking Unit works to identify criminals and organizations involved in these illicit activities.

The FBI also enforces the TVPA. In June 2003, the FBI, in conjunction with the Department of Justice Child Exploitation and Obscenity Section and the National Center for Missing and Exploited Children, launched the Innocence Lost National Initiative. The agencies' combined efforts address the growing problem of domestic sex trafficking of children in the United States. To date, these groups have worked successfully to rescue nearly 900 children. Investigations successfully have led to the conviction of more than 500 pimps, madams, and their associates who exploit children through prostitution. These convictions have resulted in lengthy sentences, including multiple 25-year-to-life sentences and the seizure of real property, vehicles, and monetary assets.[15]

Both ICE and the FBI, along with other local, state, and federal law enforcement agencies and national victim-based advocacy groups in joint task forces, have combined resources and expertise on the issue. Today, the FBI participates in approximately 30 law enforcement task forces and about 42 Bureau of Justice Assistance (BJA)-sponsored task forces around the nation.[16]

In July 2004, the Human Smuggling Trafficking Center (HSTC) was created. The HSTC serves as a fusion center for information on human smuggling and trafficking, bringing together analysts, officers, and investigators from such agencies as the CIA, FBI, ICE, Department of State, and Department of Homeland Security.

The Local Level

With DOJ funding assistance, many jurisdictions have created human trafficking task forces to combat the problem. BJA's 42 such task forces can be demonstrated by several examples.[17]

- In 2004, the FBI's Washington field office and the D.C. Metropolitan Police Department joined with a variety of nongovernment organizations and service providers to combat the growing problem of human trafficking within Washington, D.C.
- In January 2005, the Massachusetts Human Trafficking Task Force was formed, with the Boston Police Department serving as the lead law enforcement entity. It uses a two-pronged approach, addressing investigations focusing on international victims and those focusing on the commercial sexual exploitation of children.
- The New Jersey Human Trafficking Task Force attacks the problem by training law enforcement in the methods of identifying victims and signs of trafficking, coordinating statewide efforts in the identification and provision of services to victims of human trafficking, and increasing the successful interdiction and prosecution of trafficking of human persons.
- Since 2006, the Louisiana Human Trafficking Task Force, which has law enforcement, training, and victim services components, has focused its law enforcement and victim rescue efforts on the Interstate 10 corridor from the Texas border on the west to the Mississippi border on the east. This corridor, the basic northern border of the hurricane-ravaged areas of Louisiana, long has served as a major avenue of illegal immigration efforts. The I-10 corridor also is the main avenue for individuals participating in human trafficking to supply the labor needs in the hurricane-damaged areas of the state.

- In 2007, the Maryland Human Trafficking Task Force was formed. It aims to create a heightened law enforcement and victim service presence in the community. Its law enforcement efforts include establishing roving operations to identify victims and traffickers, deputizing local law enforcement to assist in federal human trafficking investigations, and providing training for law enforcement officers.

Anytown, USA

In December 2008, Corey Davis, the ringleader of a sex-trafficking ring that spanned at least three states, was sentenced in federal court in Bridgeport, Connecticut, on federal civil rights charges for organizing and leading the sex-trafficking operation that exploited as many as 20 females, including minors. Davis received a sentence of 293 months in prison followed by a lifetime term of supervised release. He pleaded guilty to multiple sex-trafficking charges, including recruiting a girl under the age of 18 to engage in prostitution. Davis admitted that he recruited a minor to engage in prostitution; that he was the organizer of a sex-trafficking venture; and that he used force, fraud, and coercion to compel the victim to commit commercial sex acts from which he obtained the proceeds.

According to the indictment, Davis lured victims to his operation with promises of modeling contracts and a glamorous lifestyle. He then forced them into a grueling schedule of dancing and performing at strip clubs in Connecticut, New York, and New Jersey. When the clubs closed, Davis forced the victims to walk the streets until 4 or 5 A.M. propositioning customers. The indictment also alleged that he beat many of the victims to force them to work for him and that he also used physical abuse as punishment for disobeying the stringent rules he imposed to isolate and control them.[18]

As this and other examples show, human trafficking cases happen all over the United States. A few instances would represent just the "tip of the iceberg" in a growing criminal enterprise. Local and state criminal justice officials must understand that these cases are not isolated incidents that occur infrequently. They must remain alert for signs of trafficking in their jurisdictions and aggressively follow through on the smallest clue. Numerous websites openly (though they try to mask their actions) advertise for prostitution. Many of these sites involve young girls victimized by sex trafficking. Many of the pictures are altered to give the impression of older girls engaged in this activity freely and voluntarily. However, as prosecutors, the authors both have encountered numerous cases of suspected human trafficking involving underage girls.

Local and state criminal justice officials must understand that these cases are not isolated incidents that occur infrequently.

The article "The Girls Next Door" describes a conventional midcentury home in Plainfield, New Jersey, that sat in a nice middle-class neighborhood. Unbeknownst to the neighbors, the house was part of a network of stash houses in the New York area where underage girls and young women from dozens of countries were trafficked and held captive. Acting on a tip, police raided the house in February 2002, expecting to find an underground brothel. Instead, they found four girls between the ages of 14 and 17, all Mexican nationals without documentation.

However, they were not prostitutes; they were sex slaves. These girls did not work for profit or a paycheck. They were captives to the traffickers and keepers who controlled their every move. The police found a squalid, land-based equivalent of a 19th-century slave ship. They encountered rancid, doorless bathrooms; bare, putrid mattresses; and a stash of penicillin, "morning after" pills, and an antiulcer medication that can induce abortion. The girls were pale, exhausted, and malnourished.[19]

Human sex trafficking warning signs include, among other indicators, streetwalkers and strip clubs. However, a jurisdiction's lack of streetwalkers or strip clubs does not mean that it is immune to the problem of trafficking. Because human trafficking involves big money, if money can be made, sex slaves can be sold. Sex trafficking can happen anywhere, however unlikely a place. Investigators should be attuned to reading the signs of trafficking and looking closely for them.

Investigation of Human Sex Trafficking

ICE aggressively targets the global criminal infrastructure, including the people, money, and materials that support human trafficking networks. The agency strives to prevent human trafficking in the United States by prosecuting the traffickers and rescuing and protecting the victims. However, most human trafficking cases start at the local level.

Strategies

Local and state law enforcement officers may unknowingly encounter sex trafficking when they deal with homeless and runaway juveniles; criminal gang activity; crimes involving immigrant children who have no guardians; domestic violence calls; and investigations at truck stops, motels, massage parlors, spas, and strip clubs. To this end, the authors offer various suggestions and indicators to help patrol officers identify victims of sex trafficking, as well as tips for detectives who investigate these crimes.

Patrol Officers

- Document suspicious calls and complaints on a police information report, even if the details seem trivial.

- Be aware of trafficking when responding to certain call types, such as reports of foot traffic in and out of a house. Consider situations that seem similar to drug complaints.

- Look closely at calls for assaults, domestic situations, verbal disputes, or thefts. These could involve a trafficking victim being abused and disciplined by a trafficker, a customer having a dispute with a victim, or a client who had money taken during a sex act.

- Locations, such as truck stops, strip clubs, massage parlors, and cheap motels, are havens for prostitutes forced into sex trafficking. Many massage parlors and strip clubs that engage in sex trafficking will have cramped living quarters where the victims are forced to stay.

- When encountering prostitutes and other victims of trafficking, do not display judgment or talk down to them. Understand the violent nature in how they are forced into trafficking, which explains their lack of cooperation. Speak with them in a location completely safe and away from other people, including potential victims.

- Check for identification. Traffickers take the victims' identification and, in cases of foreign nationals, their travel information. The lack of either item should raise concern.

Detectives/Investigators

- Monitor websites that advertise for dating and hooking up. Most vice units are familiar with the common sites used by sex traffickers as a means of advertisement.

- Conduct surveillance at motels, truck stops, strip clubs, and massage parlors. Look to see if the girls arrive alone or with someone else. Girls being transported to these locations should raise concerns of trafficking.

- Upon an arrest, check cell phone records, motel receipts, computer printouts of advertisements, and tollbooth receipts. Look for phone calls from the jailed prostitute to the pimp. Check surveillance cameras at motels and toll facilities as evidence to indicate the trafficking of the victim.

- Obtain written statements from the customers; get them to work for you.

- Seek assistance from nongovernmental organizations involved in fighting sex trafficking. Many of these entities have workers who will interview these victims on behalf of the police.

- After executing a search warrant, photograph everything. Remember that in court, a picture may be worth a thousand words: nothing else can more effectively describe a cramped living quarter a victim is forced to reside in.

- Look for advertisements in local newspapers, specifically the sports sections, that advertise massage parlors. These businesses should be checked out to ensure they are legitimate and not fronts for trafficking.
- Contact your local U.S. Attorney's Office, FBI field office, or ICE for assistance. Explore what federal resources exist to help address this problem.

Other Considerations

Patrol officers and investigators can look for many other human trafficking indicators as well.[20] These certainly warrant closer attention.

General Indicators

- People who live on or near work premises
- Individuals with restricted or controlled communication and transportation
- Persons frequently moved by traffickers
- A living space with a large number of occupants
- People lacking private space, personal possessions, or financial records
- Someone with limited knowledge about how to get around in a community

Physical Indicators

- Injuries from beatings or weapons
- Signs of torture (e.g., cigarette burns)
- Brands or scarring, indicating ownership
- Signs of malnourishment

Financial/Legal Indicators

- Someone else has possession of an individual's legal/travel documents
- Existing debt issues
- One attorney claiming to represent multiple illegal aliens detained at different locations
- Third party who insists on interpreting. Did the victim sign a contract?

Brothel Indicators

- Large amounts of cash and condoms
- Customer logbook or receipt book ("trick book")
- Sparse rooms
- Men come and go frequently

Conclusion

This form of cruel modern-day slavery occurs more often than many people might think. And, it is not just an international or a national problem—it also is a local one. It is big business, and it involves a lot of perpetrators and victims.

Agencies at all levels must remain alert to this issue and address it vigilantly. Even local officers must understand the problem and know how to recognize it in their jurisdictions. Coordinated and aggressive efforts from all law enforcement organizations can put an end to these perpetrators' operations and free the victims.

Notes

1. www.routledgesociology.com/books/Human-Sex-Trafficking -isbn9780415576789 (accessed July 19, 2010).
2. www.unodc.org/unodc/en/human-trafficking/what-is-human -trafficking.html (accessed July 19, 2010).
3. www.justice.gov/criminal/ceos/trafficking.html (accessed July 19, 2010).
4. Ibid.
5. www.justice.gov/criminal/ceos/prostitution.html (accessed July 19, 2010).
6. Richard J. Estes and Neil Alan Weiner, *Commercial Sexual Exploitation of Children in the U.S., Canada, and Mexico* (University of Pennsylvania, Executive Summary, 2001).
7. Ibid.
8. http://fpc.state.gov/documents/organization/9107.pdf (accessed July 19, 2010).
9. Estes and Weiner.
10. www.womenshealth.gov/violence/types/human-trafficking.cfm (accessed July 19, 2010).
11. For additional information, see Nathalie De Fabrique, Stephen J. Romano, Gregory M. Vecchi, and Vincent B. Van Hasselt, "Understanding Stockholm Syndrome," *FBI Law Enforcement Bulletin*, July 2007, 10–15.
12. Trafficking Victims Protection Act, Pub. L. No. 106–386 (2000), codified at 22 U.S.C. § 7101, et seq.
13. Ibid.
14. U.S. CONST. amend. XIII, § 1: "Neither slavery nor involuntary servitude, except as a punishment for crime whereof the party shall have been duly convicted, shall exist within the United States, or any place subject to their jurisdiction."
15. U.S. Department of Justice, "U.S. Army Soldier Sentenced to Over 17 Years in Prison for Operating a Brothel from Millersville Apartment and to Drug Trafficking," www.justice .gov/usao/md/Public-Affairs/press_releases/press10a.htm (accessed September 30, 2010).
16. www.fbi.gov/hq/cid/civilrights/trafficking_initiatives.htm (accessed September 30, 2010).
17. www.ojp.usdoj.gov/BJA/grant/42HTTF.pdf (accessed September 30, 2010).

18. http://actioncenter.polarisproject.org/the-frontlines/recent -federal-cases/435-leader-of-expansive-multi-state-sex -trafficking-ring-sentenced (accessed July 19, 2010).

19. www.nytimes.com/2004/01/25/magazine/25SEXTRAFFIC .html (accessed July 19, 2010).

20. http://httf.wordpress.com/indicators/ (accessed July 19, 2010).

Critical Thinking

1. Are most American prostitutes totally free or are they completely or practically enslaved?

2. How are most prostitutes enslaved or prevented from leaving prostitution until they are useless for making profits on sex services?

From *FBI Law Enforcement Bulletin* by Amanda Walker-Rodriguez and Rodney Hill, March 2011. Published by Federal Bureau of Investigation. www.fbi.gov

Free and Equal in Dignity and LGBT Rights

"Be on the right side of history"

H ILLARY R ODHAM C LINTON

G ood evening, and let me express my deep honor and pleasure at being here. I want to thank Director General Tokayev and Ms. Wyden along with other ministers, ambassadors, excellencies, and UN partners. This weekend, we will celebrate Human Rights Day, the anniversary of one of the great accomplishments of the last century.

Beginning in 1947, delegates from six continents devoted themselves to drafting a declaration that would enshrine the fundamental rights and freedoms of people everywhere In the aftermath of World War II, many nations pressed for a statement of this kind to help ensure that we would prevent future atrocities and protect the inherent humanity and dignity of all people. And so the delegates went to work. They discussed, they wrote, they revisited, revised, rewrote, for thousands of hours. And they incorporated suggestions and revisions from governments, organizations and individuals around the world.

At three o'clock in the morning on December 10th, 1948, after nearly two years of drafting and one last long night of debate, the president of the UN General Assembly called for a vote on the final text. Forty-eight nations voted in favor; eight abstained; none dissented. And the Universal Declaration of Human Rights was adopted. It proclaims a simple, powerful idea: All human beings are born free and equal in dignity and rights. And with the declaration, it was made clear that rights are not conferred by government; they are the birthright of all people. It doe not matter what country we live in, who our leaders are, or even who we are. Because we are human, we therefore have rights. And because we have rights, governments are bound to protect them.

In the 63 years since the declaration was adopted, many nations have made great progress in making human rights a human reality. Step by step, barriers that once prevented people from enjoying the full measure of liberty, the full experience of dignity, and the full benefits of humanity have fallen away. In many places, racist laws have been repealed legal and social practices that relegated women to second-class status have been abolished, the ability of religious minorities to practice their faith freely has been secured.

In most cases, this progress was not easily won. People fought and organized and campaigned in public squares and private spaces to change not only laws, but hearts and minds. And thanks to that work of generations, for millions of individuals whose lives were once narrowed by injustice, they are now able to live more freely and to participate more fully in the political, economic, and social lives of their communities.

Now, there is still, as you all know, much more to be done to secure that commitment, that reality, and progress for all people. Today, I want to talk about the work we have left to do to protect one group of people whose human rights are still denied in too many parts of the world today. In many ways, they are an invisible minority. They are arrested, beaten, terrorized, even executed. Many are treated with contempt and violence by their fellow citizens while authorities empowered to protect them look the other way or, too often, even join in the abuse. They are denied opportunities to work and learn, driven from their homes and countries, and forced to suppress or deny who they are to protect themselves from harm.

I am talking about gay, lesbian, bisexual, and transgender people, human beings born free and given bestowed equality and dignity, who have a right to claim that, which is now one of the remaining human rights challenges of our time. I speak about this subject knowing that my own country's record on human rights for gay people is far from perfect.Until 2003, it was still a crime in parts of our country. Many LGBT Americans have endured violence and harassment in their own lives, and for some, including many young people, bullying and exclusion are daily experiences. So we, like all nations, have more work to do to protect human rights at home.

Now, raising this issue, I know, is sensitive for many people and that the obstacles standing in the way of protecting the human rights of LGBT people rest on deeply held personal, political, cultural, and religious beliefs. So I come here before you with respect, understanding, and humility. Even though progress on this front is not easy, we cannot delay acting. So in that spirit, I want to talk about the difficult and important issues we must address together to reach a global consensus that recognizes the human rights of LGBT citizens everywhere.

The first issue goes to the heart of the matter. Some have suggested that gay rights and human rights are separate and distinct; but, in fact, they are one and the same. Now, of course, 60 years ago, the governments that drafted and passed the Universal Declaration of Human Rights were not thinking about how it applied to the LGBT community. They also weren't thinking about how it applied to indigenous people or children or people with disabilities or other marginalized groups. Yet in the past 60 years, we have come to recognize that members of these groups are entitled to the full measure of dignity and rights, because, like all people, they share a common humanity.

This recognition did not occur all at once. It evolved over time. And as it did, we understood that we were honoring rights that people always had, rather than creating new or special rights for them. Like being a woman, like being a racial, religious, tribal, or ethnic minority, being LGBT does not make you less human. And that is why gay rights are human rights, and human rights are gay rights.

It is violation of human rights when people are beaten or killed because of their sexual orientation, or because they do not conform to cultural norms about how men and women should look or behave. It is a violation of human rights when governments declare it illegal to be gay, or allow those who harm gay people to go unpunished. It is a violation of human rights when lesbian or transgendered women are subjected to so-called corrective rape, or forcibly subjected to hormone treatments, or when people are murdered after public calls for violence toward gays, or when they are forced to flee their nations and seek asylum in other lands to save their lives. And it is a violation of human rights when life-saving care is withheld from people because they are gay, or equal access to justice is denied to people because they are gay, or public spaces are out of bounds to people because they are gay. No matter what we look like, where we come from, or who we are, we are all equally entitled to our human rights and dignity.

The second issue is a question of whether homosexuality arises from a particular part of the world. Some seem to believe it is a Western phenomenon, and therefore people outside the West have grounds to reject it. Well, in reality, gay people are born into and belong to every society in the world. They are all ages, all races, all faiths; they are doctors and teachers, farmers and bankers, soldiers and athletes; and whether we know it, or whether we acknowledge it, they are our family, our friends, and our neighbors.

Being gay is not a Western invention; it is a human reality. And protecting the human rights of all people, gay or straight, is not something that only Western governments do. South Africa's constitution, written in the aftermath of Apartheid, protects the equality of all citizens, including gay people. In Colombia and Argentina, the rights of gays are also legally protected. In Nepal, the supreme court has ruled that equal rights apply to LGBT citizens. The Government of Mongolia has committed to pursue new legislation that will tackle anti-gay discrimination.

Now, some worry that protecting the human rights of the LGBT community is a luxury that only wealthy nations can afford. But in fact, in all countries, there are costs to not protecting these rights, in both gay and straight lives lost to disease and violence, and the silencing of voices and views that would strengthen communities, in ideas never pursued by entrepreneurs who happen to be gay. Costs are incurred whenever any group is treated as lesser than the other, whether they are women, racial, or religious minorities, or the LGBT. Former President Mogae of Botswana pointed out recently that for as long as LGBT people are kept in the shadows, there cannot be an effective public health program to tackle HIV and AIDS. Well, that holds true for other challenges as well.

The third, and perhaps most challenging, issue arises when people cite religious or cultural values as a reason to violate or not to protect the human rights of LGBT citizens. This is not unlike the justification offered for violent practices towards women like honor killings, widow burning, or female genital mutilation. Some people still defend those practices as part of a cultural tradition. But violence toward women isn't cultural; it's criminal. Likewise with slavery, what was once justified as sanctioned by God is now properly reviled as an unconscionable violation of human rights.

In each of these cases, we came to learn that no practice or tradition trumps the human rights that belong to all of us. And this holds true for inflicting violence on LGBT people, criminalizing their status or behavior, expelling them from their families and communities, or tacitly or explicitly accepting their killing.

Of course, it bears noting that rarely are cultural and religious traditions and teachings actually in conflict with the protection of human rights. Indeed, our religion and our culture are sources of compassion and inspiration toward our fellow human beings. It was not only those who've justified slavery who leaned on religion, it was also those who sought to abolish it. And let us keep in mind that our commitments to protect the freedom of religion and to defend the dignity of LGBT people emanate from a common source. For many of us, religious belief and practice is a vital source of meaning and identity, and fundamental to who we are as people. And likewise, for most of us, the bonds of love and family that we forge are also vital sources of meaning and identity. And caring for others is an expression of what it means to be fully human. It is because the human experience is universal that human rights are universal and cut across all religions and cultures.

The fourth issue is what history teaches us about how we make progress towards rights for all. Progress starts with honest discussion. Now, there are some who say and believe that all gay people are pedophiles, that homosexuality is a disease that can be caught or cured, or that gays recruit others to become gay. Well, these notions are simply not true. They are also unlikely to disappear if those who promote or accept them are dismissed out of hand rather than invited to share their fears and concerns. No one has ever abandoned a belief because he was forced to do so.

Universal human rights include freedom of expression and freedom of belief, even if our words or beliefs denigrate the humanity of others. Yet, while we are each free to believe whatever we choose, we cannot do whatever we choose, not in a world where we protect the human rights of all.

Reaching understanding of these issues takes more than speech. It does take a conversation. In fact, it takes a constellation of conversations in places big and small. And it takes a willingness to see stark differences in belief as a reason to begin the conversation, not to avoid it.

But progress comes from changes in laws. In many places, including my own country, legal protections have preceded, not followed, broader recognition of rights. Law have a teaching effect. Laws that discriminate validate other kinds of discrimination. Laws that require equal protections reinforce the moral imperative of equality. And practically speaking, it is often the case that laws must change before fears about change dissipate.

Many in my country thought that President Truman was making a grave error when he ordered the racial desegregation of our military. They argued that it would undermine unit cohesion. And it wasn't until he went ahead and did it that we saw how it strengthened our social fabric in ways even the supporters of the policy could not foresee. Likewise, some worried in my country that the repeal of "Don't Ask, Don't Tell" would have a negative effect on our armed forces. Now, the Marine Corps Commandant, who was one of the strongest voices against the repeal, says that his concerns were unfounded and that the Marines have embraced the change.

Finally, progress comes from being willing to walk a mile in someone else's shoes. We need to ask ourselves, "How would it feel if it were a crime to love the person I love? How would it feel to be discriminated against for something about myself that I cannot change?" This challenge applies to all of us as we reflect upon deeply held beliefs, as we work to embrace tolerance and respect for the dignity of all persons, and as we engage humbly with those with whom we disagree in the hope of creating greater understanding.

A fifth and final question is how we do our part to bring the world to embrace human rights for all people including LGBT people. Yes, LGBT people must help lead this effort, as so many of you are. Their knowledge and experiences are invaluable and their courage inspirational. We know the names of brave LGBT activists who have literally given their lives for this cause, and there are many more whose names we will never know. But often those who are denied rights are least empowered to bring about the changes they seek. Acting alone, minorities can never achieve the majorities necessary for political change.

So when any part of humanity is sidelined, the rest of us cannot sit on the sidelines. Every time a barrier to progress has fallen, it has taken a cooperative effort from those on both sides of the barrier. In the fight for women's rights, the support of men remains crucial. The fight for racial equality has relied on contributions from people of all races. Combating Islamophobia or anti-Semitism is a task for people of all faiths. And the same is true with this struggle for equality.

Conversely, when we see denials and abuses of human rights and fail to act, that sends the message to those deniers and abusers that they won't suffer any consequences for their actions, and so they carry on. But when we do act we send a powerful moral message. Right here in Geneva, the international community acted this year to strengthen a global consensus around the human rights of LGBT people. At the Human Rights Council in March, 85 countries from all regions supported a statement calling for an end to criminalization and violence against people because of their sexual orientation and gender identity.

At the following session of the Council in June, South Africa took the lead on a resolution about violence against LGBT people. The delegation from South Africa spoke eloquently about their own experience and struggle for human equality and its indivisibility. When the measure passed, it became the irst-ever UN resolution recognizing the human rights of gay people worldwide. In the Organization of American States this year, the Inter-American Commission on Human Rights created a unit on the rights of LGBT people, a step toward what we hope will be the creation of a special rapporteur.

Now, we must go further and work here and in every region of the world to galvanize more support for the human rights of the LGBT community. To the leaders of those countries where people are jailed, beaten, or executed for being gay, I ask you to consider this: Leadership, by definition, means being out in front of your people when it is called for. It means standing up for the dignity of all your citizens and persuading your people to do the same. It also means ensuring that all citizens are treated as equals under your laws, because let me be clear—I am not saying that gay people can't or don't commit crimes. They can and they do, just like straight people. And when they do, they should be held accountable, but it should never be a crime to be gay.

And to people of all nations, I say supporting human rights is your responsibility too. The lives of gay people are shaped not only by laws, but by the treatment they receive every day from their families, from their neighbors. Eleanor Roosevelt, who did so much to advance human rights worldwide, said that these rights begin in the small places close to home—the streets where people live, the schools they attend, the factories, farms, and offices where they work. These places are your domain. The actions you take, the ideals that you advocate, can determine whether human rights flourish where you are.

And finally, to LGBT men and women worldwide, let me say this: Wherever you live and whatever the circumstances of your life, whether you are connected to a network of support or feel isolated and vulnerable, please know that you are not alone. People around the globe are working hard to support you and to bring an end to the injustices and dangers you face. That is certainly true for my country. And you have an ally in the United States of America and you have millions of friends among the American people.

The Obama Administration defends the human rights of LGBT people as part of our comprehensive human rights policy and as a priority of our foreign policy. In our embassies, our diplomats are raising concerns about specific cases and laws, and working with a range of partners to strengthen human rights protections for all. In Washington, we have created a task force at the State Department to support and coordinate this work. And in the coming months, we will provide every embassy with a toolkit to help improve their efforts. And we have created a program that offers emergency support to defenders of human rights for LGBT people.

This morning, back in Washington, President Obama put into place the first U.S. Government strategy dedicated to combating human rights abuses against LGBT persons abroad. Building on efforts already underway at the State Department and across the government, the President has directed all U.S. Government agencies engaged overseas to combat the criminalization of LGBT status and conduct, to enhance efforts to protect vulnerable LGBT refugees and asylum seekers, to ensure that our foreign assistance promotes the protection of LGBT rights, to enlist international organizations in the fight against discrimination, and to respond swiftly to abuses against LGBT persons.

I am also pleased to announce that we are launching a new Global Equality Fund that will support the work of civil society organizations working on these issues around the world. This fund will help them record facts so they can target their advocacy, learn how to use the law as a tool, manage their budgets, train their staffs, and forge partnerships with women's organizations and other human rights groups. We have committed more than $3 million to start this fund, and we have hope that others will join us in supporting it.

The women and men who advocate for human rights for the LGBT community in hostile places, some of whom are here today with us, are brave and dedicated, and deserve all the help we can give them. We know the road ahead will not be easy. A great deal of work lies before us. But many of us have seen firsthand how quickly change can come. In our lifetimes, attitudes toward gay people in many places have been transformed. Many people, including myself, have experienced a deepening of our own convictions on this topic over the years, as we have devoted more thought to it, engaged in dialogues and debates, and established personal and professional relationships with people who are gay.

This evolution is evident in many places. To highlight one example, the Delhi High Court decriminalized homosexuality in India two years ago, writing, and I quote, "If there is one tenet that can be said to be an underlying theme of the Indian constitution, it is inclusiveness." There is little doubt in my mind that support for LGBT human rights will continue to climb. Because for many young people, this is simple: All people deserve to be treated with dignity and have their human rights respected, no matter who they are or whom they love.

There is a phrase that people in the United States invoke when urging others to support human rights: "Be on the right side of history." The story of the United States is the story of a nation that has repeatedly grappled with intolerance and inequality. We fought a brutal civil war over slavery. People from coast to coast joined in campaigns to recognize the rights of women, indigenous peoples, racial minorities, children, people with disabilities, immigrants, workers, and on and on. And the march toward equality and justice has continued. Those who advocate for expanding the circle of human rights were and are on the right side of history, and history honors them. Those who tried to constrict human rights were wrong, and history reflects that as well.

I know that the thoughts I've shared today involve questions on which opinions are still evolving. As it has happened so many times before, opinion will converge once again with the truth, the immutable truth, that all persons are created free and equal in dignity and rights. We are called once more to make real the words of the Universal Declaration. Let us answer that call. Let us be on the right side of history, for our people, our nations, and future generations, whose lives will be shaped by the work we do today. I come before you with great hope and confidence that no matter how long the road ahead, we will travel it successfully together. Thank you very much.

Critical Thinking

1. Should human rights arguments apply to lesbians and gays?
2. What arguments are made against LGBT demands for equality?
3. How does Hillary Clinton justify her support for LGBT rights?

From speech delivered at Palais des Nations, Geneva, Switzerland, December 6, 2011.

The End of Men

Earlier this year, women became the majority of the workforce for the first time in U.S. history. Most managers are now women too. And for every two men who get a college degree this year, three women will do the same. For years, women's progress has been cast as a struggle for equality. But what if equality isn't the end point? What if modern, postindustrial society is simply better suited to women? A report on the unprecedented role reversal now under way—and its vast cultural consequences.

HANNA ROSIN

In the 1970s the biologist Ronald Ericsson came up with a way to separate sperm carrying the male-producing Y chromosome from those carrying the X. He sent the two kinds of sperm swimming down a glass tube through ever-thicker albumin barriers. The sperm with the X chromosome had a larger head and a longer tail, and so, he figured, they would get bogged down in the viscous liquid. The sperm with the Y chromosome were leaner and faster and could swim down to the bottom of the tube more efficiently. Ericsson had grown up on a ranch in South Dakota, where he'd developed an Old West, cowboy swagger. The process, he said, was like "cutting out cattle at the gate." The cattle left flailing behind the gate were of course the X's, which seemed to please him. He would sometimes demonstrate the process using cartilage from a bull's penis as a pointer.

In the late 1970s, Ericsson leased the method to clinics around the U.S., calling it the first scientifically proven method for choosing the sex of a child. Instead of a lab coat, he wore cowboy boots and a cowboy hat, and doled out his version of cowboy poetry. (*People* magazine once suggested a TV mini-series based on his life called *Cowboy in the Lab*.) The right prescription for life, he would say, was "breakfast at five-thirty, on the saddle by six, no room for Mr. Limp Wrist." In 1979, he loaned out his ranch as the backdrop for the iconic "Marlboro Country" ads because he believed in the campaign's central image—"a guy riding on his horse along the river, no bureaucrats, no lawyers," he recalled when I spoke to him this spring. "He's the boss." (The photographers took some 6,500 pictures, a pictorial record of the frontier that Ericsson still takes great pride in.)

Feminists of the era did not take kindly to Ericsson and his Marlboro Man veneer. To them, the lab cowboy and his sperminator portended a dystopia of mass-produced boys. "You

have to be concerned about the future of all women," Roberta Steinbacher, a nun-turned-social-psychologist, said in a 1984 *People* profile of Ericsson. "There's no question that there exists a universal preference for sons." Steinbacher went on to complain about women becoming locked in as "second-class citizens" while men continued to dominate positions of control and influence. "I think women have to ask themselves, 'Where does this stop?'" she said. "A lot of us wouldn't be here right now if these practices had been in effect years ago."

Ericsson, now 74, laughed when I read him these quotes from his old antagonist. Seldom has it been so easy to prove a dire prediction wrong. In the '90s, when Ericsson looked into the numbers for the two dozen or so clinics that use his process, he discovered, to his surprise, that couples were requesting more girls than boys, a gap that has persisted, even though Ericsson advertises the method as more effective for producing boys. In some clinics, Ericsson has said, the ratio is now as high as 2 to 1. Polling data on American sex preference is sparse, and does not show a clear preference for girls. But the picture from the doctor's office unambiguously does. A newer method for sperm selection, called MicroSort, is currently completing Food and Drug Administration clinical trials. The girl requests for that method run at about 75 percent.

Even more unsettling for Ericsson, it has become clear that in choosing the sex of the next generation, *he* is no longer the boss. "It's the women who are driving all the decisions," he says—a change the MicroSort spokespeople I met with also mentioned. At first, Ericsson says, women who called his clinics would apologize and shyly explain that they already had two boys. "Now they just call and [say] outright, 'I want a girl.' These mothers look at their lives and think their daughters will have a bright future their mother and grandmother didn't have, brighter than their sons, even, so why wouldn't you choose a girl?"

Why wouldn't you choose a girl? That such a statement should be so casually uttered by an old cowboy like Ericsson—or by anyone, for that matter—is monumental. For nearly as long as civilization has existed, patriarchy—enforced through the rights of the firstborn son—has been the organizing principle, with few exceptions. Men in ancient Greece tied off their left testicle in an effort to produce male heirs; women have killed themselves (or been killed) for failing to bear sons. In her iconic 1949 book, *The Second Sex,* the French feminist Simone de Beauvoir suggested that women so detested their own "feminine condition" that they regarded their newborn daughters with irritation and disgust. Now the centuries-old preference for sons is eroding—or even reversing. "Women of our generation want daughters precisely because we like who we are," breezes one woman in *Cookie* magazine. Even Ericsson, the stubborn old goat, can sigh and mark the passing of an era. "Did male dominance exist? Of course it existed. But it seems to be gone now. And the era of the firstborn son is totally gone."

Ericsson's extended family is as good an illustration of the rapidly shifting landscape as any other. His 26-year-old granddaughter—"tall, slender, brighter than hell, with a take-no-prisoners personality"—is a biochemist and works on genetic sequencing. His niece studied civil engineering at the University of Southern California. His grandsons, he says, are bright and handsome, but in school "their eyes glaze over. I have to tell 'em: 'Just don't screw up and crash your pickup truck and get some girl pregnant and ruin your life.'" Recently Ericsson joked with the old boys at his elementary-school reunion that he was going to have a sex-change operation. "Women live longer than men. They do better in this economy. More of 'em graduate from college. They go into space and do everything men do, and sometimes they do it a whole lot better. I mean, hell, get out of the way—these females are going to leave us males in the dust."

Man has been the dominant sex since, well, the dawn of mankind. But for the first time in human history, that is changing—and with shocking speed. Cultural and economic changes always reinforce each other. And the global economy is evolving in a way that is eroding the historical preference for male children, worldwide. Over several centuries, South Korea, for instance, constructed one of the most rigid patriarchal societies in the world. Many wives who failed to produce male heirs were abused and treated as domestic servants; some families prayed to spirits to kill off girl children. Then, in the 1970s and '80s, the government embraced an industrial revolution and encouraged women to enter the labor force. Women moved to the city and went to college. They advanced rapidly, from industrial jobs to clerical jobs to professional work. The traditional order began to crumble soon after. In 1990, the country's laws were revised so that women could keep custody of their children after a divorce and inherit property. In 2005, the court ruled that women could register children under their own names. As recently as 1985, about half of all women in a national survey said they "must have a son." That percentage fell slowly until 1991 and then plummeted to just over 15 percent by 2003. Male preference in South Korea "is over," says Monica Das Gupta, a demographer and Asia expert at the World Bank. "It happened so fast. It's hard to believe it, but it is." The same shift is now beginning in other rapidly industrializing countries such as India and China.

Up to a point, the reasons behind this shift are obvious. As thinking and communicating have come to eclipse physical strength and stamina as the keys to economic success, those societies that take advantage of the talents of all their adults, not just half of them, have pulled away from the rest. And because geopolitics and global culture are, ultimately, Darwinian, other societies either follow suit or end up marginalized. In 2006, the Organization for Economic Cooperation and Development devised the Gender, Institutions and Development Database, which measures the economic and political power of women in 162 countries. With few exceptions, the greater the power of women, the greater the country's economic success. Aid agencies have started to recognize this relationship and have pushed to institute political quotas in about 100 countries, essentially forcing women into power in an effort to improve those countries' fortunes. In some war-torn states, women are stepping in as a sort of maternal rescue team. Liberia's president, Ellen Johnson Sirleaf, portrayed her country as a sick child in need of her care during her campaign five years ago. Postgenocide Rwanda elected to heal itself by becoming the first country with a majority of women in parliament.

In feminist circles, these social, political, and economic changes are always cast as a slow, arduous form of catch-up in a continuing struggle for female equality. But in the U.S., the world's most advanced economy, something much more remarkable seems to be happening. American parents are beginning to choose to have girls over boys. As they imagine the pride of watching a child grow and develop and succeed as an adult, it is more often a girl that they see in their mind's eye.

What if the modern, postindustrial economy is simply more congenial to women than to men? For a long time, evolutionary psychologists have claimed that we are all imprinted with adaptive imperatives from a distant past: men are faster and stronger and hardwired to fight for scarce resources, and that shows up now as a drive to win on Wall Street; women are programmed to find good providers and to care for their offspring, and that is manifested in more-nurturing and more-flexible behavior, ordaining them to domesticity. This kind of thinking frames our sense of the natural order. But what if men and women were fulfilling not biological imperatives but social roles, based on what was more efficient throughout a long era of human history? What if that era has now come to an end? More to the point, what if the economics of the new era are better suited to women?

Once you open your eyes to this possibility, the evidence is all around you. It can be found, most immediately, in the wreckage of the Great Recession, in which three-quarters of the 8 million jobs lost were lost by men. The worst-hit industries were overwhelmingly male and deeply identified with macho: construction, manufacturing, high finance. Some of these jobs will come back, but the overall pattern of dislocation is neither temporary nor random. The recession merely revealed—and accelerated—a profound economic shift that has been going on for at least 30 years, and in some respects even longer.

Earlier this year, for the first time in American history, the balance of the workforce tipped toward women, who now hold a majority of the nation's jobs. The working class, which has long defined our notions of masculinity, is slowly turning into a matriarchy, with men increasingly absent from the home and women making all the decisions. Women dominate today's colleges and professional schools—for every two men who will receive a B.A. this year, three women will do the same. Of the 15 job categories projected to grow the most in the next decade in the U.S., all but two are occupied primarily by women. Indeed, the U.S. economy is in some ways becoming a kind of traveling sisterhood: upper-class women leave home and enter the workforce, creating domestic jobs for other women to fill.

The postindustrial economy is indifferent to men's size and strength. The attributes that are most valuable today—social intelligence, open communication, the ability to sit still and focus—are, at a minimum, not predominantly male. In fact, the opposite may be true. Women in poor parts of India are learning English faster than men to meet the demands of new global call centers. Women own more than 40 percent of private businesses in China, where a red Ferrari is the new status symbol for female entrepreneurs. Last year, Iceland elected Prime Minister Johanna Sigurdardottir, the world's first openly lesbian head of state, who campaigned explicitly against the male elite she claimed had destroyed the nation's banking system, and who vowed to end the "age of testosterone."

Yes, the U.S. still has a wage gap, one that can be convincingly explained—at least in part—by discrimination. Yes, women still do most of the child care. And yes, the upper reaches of society are still dominated by men. But given the power of the forces pushing at the economy, this setup feels like the last gasp of a dying age rather than the permanent establishment. Dozens of college women I interviewed for this story assumed that they very well might be the ones working while their husbands stayed at home, either looking for work or minding the children. Guys, one senior remarked to me, "are the new ball and chain." It may be happening slowly and unevenly, but it's unmistakably happening: in the long view, the modern economy is becoming a place where women hold the cards.

Dozens of college women I interviewed assumed that they very well might be the ones working while their husbands stayed at home. Guys, one senior remarked to me, "are the new ball and chain."

In his final book, *The Bachelors' Ball,* published in 2007, the sociologist Pierre Bourdieu describes the changing gender dynamics of Béarn, the region in southwestern France where he grew up. The eldest sons once held the privileges of patrimonial loyalty and filial inheritance in Béarn. But over the decades, changing economic forces turned those privileges into

curses. Although the land no longer produced the impressive income it once had, the men felt obligated to tend it. Meanwhile, modern women shunned farm life, lured away by jobs and adventure in the city. They occasionally returned for the traditional balls, but the men who awaited them had lost their prestige and become unmarriageable. This is the image that keeps recurring to me, one that Bourdieu describes in his book: at the bachelors' ball, the men, self-conscious about their diminished status, stand stiffly, their hands by their sides, as the women twirl away.

The role reversal that's under way between American men and women shows up most obviously and painfully in the working class. In recent years, male support groups have sprung up throughout the Rust Belt and in other places where the postindustrial economy has turned traditional family roles upside down. Some groups help men cope with unemployment, and others help them reconnect with their alienated families. Mustafaa El-Scari, a teacher and social worker, leads some of these groups in Kansas City. El-Scari has studied the sociology of men and boys set adrift, and he considers it his special gift to get them to open up and reflect on their new condition. The day I visited one of his classes, earlier this year, he was facing a particularly resistant crowd.

None of the 30 or so men sitting in a classroom at a downtown Kansas City school have come for voluntary adult enrichment. Having failed to pay their child support, they were given the choice by a judge to go to jail or attend a weekly class on fathering, which to them seemed the better deal. This week's lesson, from a workbook called *Quenching the Father Thirst,* was supposed to involve writing a letter to a hypothetical estranged 14-year-old daughter named Crystal, whose father left her when she was a baby. But El-Scari has his own idea about how to get through to this barely awake, skeptical crew, and letters to Crystal have nothing to do with it.

Like them, he explains, he grew up watching Bill Cosby living behind his metaphorical "white picket fence"—one man, one woman, and a bunch of happy kids. "Well, that check bounced a long time ago," he says. "Let's see," he continues, reading from a worksheet. What are the four kinds of paternal authority? Moral, emotional, social, and physical. "But you ain't none of those in that house. All you are is a paycheck, and now you ain't even that. And if you try to exercise your authority, she'll call 911. How does that make you feel? You're supposed to be the authority, and she says, 'Get out of the house, bitch.' She's calling you 'bitch'!"

The men are black and white, their ages ranging from about 20 to 40. A couple look like they might have spent a night or two on the streets, but the rest look like they work, or used to. Now they have put down their sodas, and El-Scari has their attention, so he gets a little more philosophical. "Who's doing what?" he asks them. "What is our role? Everyone's telling us we're supposed to be the head of a nuclear family, so you feel like you got robbed. It's toxic, and poisonous, and it's setting us up for failure." He writes on the board: $85,000. "This is her salary." Then: $12,000. "This is your salary. Who's the damn man? Who's the man now?" A murmur rises. "That's right. She's the man."

Judging by the men I spoke with afterward, El-Scari seemed to have pegged his audience perfectly. Darren Henderson was making $33 an hour laying sheet metal, until the real-estate crisis hit and he lost his job. Then he lost his duplex—"there's my little piece of the American dream"—then his car. And then he fell behind on his child-support payments. "They make it like I'm just sitting around," he said, "but I'm not." As proof of his efforts, he took out a new commercial driver's permit and a bartending license, and then threw them down on the ground like jokers, for all the use they'd been. His daughter's mother had a $50,000-a-year job and was getting her master's degree in social work. He'd just signed up for food stamps, which is just about the only social-welfare program a man can easily access. Recently she'd seen him waiting at the bus stop. "Looked me in the eye," he recalled, "and just drove on by."

The men in that room, almost without exception, were casualties of the end of the manufacturing era. Most of them had continued to work with their hands even as demand for manual labor was declining. Since 2000, manufacturing has lost almost 6 million jobs, more than a third of its total workforce, and has taken in few young workers. The housing bubble masked this new reality for a while, creating work in construction and related industries. Many of the men I spoke with had worked as electricians or builders; one had been a successful real-estate agent. Now those jobs are gone too. Henderson spent his days shuttling between unemployment offices and job interviews, wondering what his daughter might be doing at any given moment. In 1950, roughly one in 20 men of prime working age, like Henderson, was not working; today that ratio is about one in five, the highest ever recorded.

Men dominate just two of the 15 job categories projected to grow the most over the next decade: janitor and computer engineer. Women have everything else—nursing, home health assistance, child care, food preparation. Many of the new jobs, says Heather Boushey of the Center for American Progress, "replace the things that women used to do in the home for free." None is especially high-paying. But the steady accumulation of these jobs adds up to an economy that, for the working class, has become more amenable to women than to men.

The list of growing jobs is heavy on nurturing professions, in which women, ironically, seem to benefit from old stereotypes and habits. Theoretically, there is no reason men should not be qualified. But they have proved remarkably unable to adapt. Over the course of the past century, feminism has pushed women to do things once considered against their nature—first enter the workforce as singles, then continue to work while married, then work even with small children at home. Many professions that started out as the province of men are now filled mostly with women—secretary and teacher come to mind. Yet I'm not aware of any that have gone the opposite way. Nursing schools have tried hard to recruit men in the past few years, with minimal success. Teaching schools, eager to recruit male role models, are having a similarly hard time. The range of acceptable masculine roles has changed comparatively little, and has

perhaps even narrowed as men have shied away from some careers women have entered. As Jessica Grose wrote in *Slate,* men seem "fixed in cultural aspic." And with each passing day, they lag further behind.

As we recover from the Great Recession, some traditionally male jobs will return—men are almost always harder-hit than women in economic downturns because construction and manufacturing are more cyclical than service industries—but that won't change the long-term trend. When we look back on this period, argues Jamie Ladge, a business professor at Northeastern University, we will see it as a "turning point for women in the workforce."

When we look back at this period, we will see it as a "turning point for women in the workforce."

The economic and cultural power shift from men to women would be hugely significant even if it never extended beyond working-class America. But women are also starting to dominate middle management, and a surprising number of professional careers as well. According to the Bureau of Labor Statistics, women now hold 51.4 percent of managerial and professional jobs—up from 26.1 percent in 1980. They make up 54 percent of all accountants and hold about half of all banking and insurance jobs. About a third of America's physicians are now women, as are 45 percent of associates in law firms—and both those percentages are rising fast. A white-collar economy values raw intellectual horsepower, which men and women have in equal amounts. It also requires communication skills and social intelligence, areas in which women, according to many studies, have a slight edge. Perhaps most important—for better or worse—it increasingly requires formal education credentials, which women are more prone to acquire, particularly early in adulthood. Just about the only professions in which women still make up a relatively small minority of newly minted workers are engineering and those calling on a hard-science background, and even in those areas, women have made strong gains since the 1970s.

Office work has been steadily adapting to women—and in turn being reshaped by them—for 30 years or more. Joel Garreau picks up on this phenomenon in his 1991 book, *Edge City,* which explores the rise of suburbs that are home to giant swaths of office space along with the usual houses and malls. Companies began moving out of the city in search not only of lower rent but also of the "best educated, most conscientious, most stable workers." They found their brightest prospects among "underemployed females living in middle-class communities on the fringe of the old urban areas." As Garreau chronicles the rise of suburban office parks, he places special emphasis on 1978, the peak year for women entering the workforce. When brawn was off the list of job requirements, women often measured up better than men. They were smart, dutiful, and, as long as employers could make the jobs more convenient for them, more reliable. The 1999 movie *Office Space* was maybe the first to capture how alien and dispiriting the office park can be for men. Disgusted by their jobs and their boss, Peter and his two friends embezzle money and start sleeping through their alarm clocks. At the movie's end, a male co-worker burns down the office park, and Peter abandons desk work for a job in construction.

Near the top of the jobs pyramid, of course, the upward march of women stalls. Prominent female CEOs, past and present, are so rare that they count as minor celebrities, and most of us can tick off their names just from occasionally reading the business pages: Meg Whitman at eBay, Carly Fiorina at Hewlett-Packard, Anne Mulcahy and Ursula Burns at Xerox, Indra Nooyi at PepsiCo; the accomplishment is considered so extraordinary that Whitman and Fiorina are using it as the basis for political campaigns. Only 3 percent of *Fortune* 500 CEOs are women, and the number has never risen much above that.

But even the way this issue is now framed reveals that men's hold on power in elite circles may be loosening. In business circles, the lack of women at the top is described as a "brain drain" and a crisis of "talent retention." And while female CEOs may be rare in America's largest companies, they are highly prized: last year, they outearned their male counterparts by 43 percent, on average, and received bigger raises.

Even around the delicate question of working mothers, the terms of the conversation are shifting. Last year, in a story about breastfeeding, I complained about how the early years of child rearing keep women out of power positions. But the term *mommy track* is slowly morphing into the gender-neutral *flex time*, reflecting changes in the workforce. For recent college graduates of both sexes, flexible arrangements are at the top of the list of workplace demands, according to a study published last year in the *Harvard Business Review*. And companies eager to attract and retain talented workers and managers are responding. The consulting firm Deloitte, for instance, started what's now considered the model program, called Mass Career Customization, which allows employees to adjust their hours depending on their life stage. The program, Deloitte's website explains, solves "a complex issue—one that can no longer be classified as a woman's issue."

"Women are knocking on the door of leadership at the very moment when their talents are especially well matched with the requirements of the day," writes David Gergen in the introduction to *Enlightened Power: How Women Are Transforming the Practice of Leadership*. What are these talents? Once it was thought that leaders should be aggressive and competitive, and that men are naturally more of both. But psychological research has complicated this picture. In lab studies that simulate negotiations, men and women are just about equally assertive and competitive, with slight variations. Men tend to assert themselves in a controlling manner, while women tend to take into account the rights of others, but both styles are equally effective, write the psychologists Alice Eagly and Linda Carli, in their 2007 book, *Through the Labyrinth*.

Over the years, researchers have sometimes exaggerated these differences and described the particular talents of women in crude gender stereotypes: women as more empathetic, as better consensus-seekers and better lateral thinkers; women as bringing a superior moral sensibility to bear on a cutthroat business world. In the '90s, this field of feminist business theory seemed to be forcing the point. But after the latest financial crisis, these ideas have more resonance. Researchers have started looking into the relationship between testosterone and excessive risk, and wondering if groups of men, in some basic hormonal way, spur each other to make reckless decisions. The picture emerging is a mirror image of the traditional gender map: men and markets on the side of the irrational and over-emotional, and women on the side of the cool and levelheaded.

We don't yet know with certainty whether testosterone strongly influences business decision-making. But the perception of the ideal business leader is starting to shift. The old model of command and control, with one leader holding all the decision-making power, is considered hidebound. The new model is sometimes called "post-heroic," or "transformational" in the words of the historian and leadership expert James MacGregor Burns. The aim is to behave like a good coach, and channel your charisma to motivate others to be hardworking and creative. The model is not explicitly defined as feminist, but it echoes literature about male-female differences. A program at Columbia Business School, for example, teaches sensitive leadership and social intelligence, including better reading of facial expressions and body language. "We never explicitly say, 'Develop your feminine side,' but it's clear that's what we're advocating," says Jamie Ladge.

A 2008 study attempted to quantify the effect of this more-feminine management style. Researchers at Columbia Business School and the University of Maryland analyzed data on the top 1,500 U.S. companies from 1992 to 2006 to determine the relationship between firm performance and female participation in senior management. Firms that had women in top positions performed better, and this was especially true if the firm pursued what the researchers called an "innovation intensive strategy," in which, they argued, "creativity and collaboration may be especially important"—an apt description of the future economy.

It could be that women boost corporate performance, or it could be that better-performing firms have the luxury of recruiting and keeping high-potential women. But the association is clear: innovative, successful firms are the ones that promote women. The same Columbia-Maryland study ranked America's industries by the proportion of firms that employed female executives, and the bottom of the list reads like the ghosts of the economy past: shipbuilding, real estate, coal, steelworks, machinery.

If you really want to see where the world is headed, of course, looking at the current workforce can get you only so far. To see the future—of the workforce, the economy, and the culture—you need to spend some time at America's colleges and professional schools, where a quiet revolution is under way. More than ever, college is the gateway to economic success, a necessary precondition for moving into the upper-middle class—and increasingly even the middle class. It's this broad, striving middle class that defines our society. And demographically, we can see with absolute clarity that in the coming decades the middle class will be dominated by women.

We've all heard about the collegiate gender gap. But the implications of that gap have not yet been fully digested. Women now earn 60 percent of master's degrees, about half of all law and medical degrees, and 42 percent of all M.B.A.s. Most important, women earn almost 60 percent of all bachelor's degrees—the minimum requirement, in most cases, for an affluent life. In a stark reversal since the 1970s, men are now more likely than women to hold only a high-school diploma. "One would think that if men were acting in a rational way, they would be getting the education they need to get along out there," says Tom Mortenson, a senior scholar at the Pell Institute for the Study of Opportunity in Higher Education. "But they are just failing to adapt."

This spring, I visited a few schools around Kansas City to get a feel for the gender dynamics of higher education. I started at the downtown campus of Metropolitan Community College. Metropolitan is the kind of place where people go to learn practical job skills and keep current with the changing economy, and as in most community colleges these days, men were conspicuously absent. One afternoon, in the basement cafeteria of a nearly windowless brick building, several women were trying to keep their eyes on their biology textbook and ignore the text messages from their babysitters. Another crew was outside the ladies' room, braiding each other's hair. One woman, still in her medical-assistant scrubs, looked like she was about to fall asleep in the elevator between the first and fourth floors.

When Bernard Franklin took over as campus president in 2005, he looked around and told his staff early on that their new priority was to "recruit more boys." He set up mentoring programs and men-only study groups and student associations. He made a special effort to bond with male students, who liked to call him "Suit." "It upset some of my feminists," he recalls. Yet, a few years later, the tidal wave of women continues to wash through the school—they now make up about 70 percent of its students. They come to train to be nurses and teachers—African American women, usually a few years older than traditional college students, and lately, working-class white women from the suburbs seeking a cheap way to earn a credential. As for the men? Well, little has changed. "I recall one guy who was really smart," one of the school's counselors told me. "But he was reading at a sixth-grade level and felt embarrassed in front of the women. He had to hide his books from his friends, who would tease him when he studied. Then came the excuses. 'It's spring, gotta play ball.' 'It's winter, too cold.' He didn't make it."

It makes some economic sense that women attend community colleges—and in fact, all colleges—in greater numbers than men. Women ages 25 to 34 with only a high-school diploma currently have a median income of $25,474, while men in the same position earn $32,469. But it makes sense only up to a point. The well-paid lifetime union job has been disappearing for at least 30 years. Kansas City, for example, has shifted from steel manufacturing to pharmaceuticals and information technologies. "The economy isn't as friendly to men as it once was," says Jacqueline King, of the American Council on Education. "You would think men and women would go to these colleges at the same rate." But they don't.

In 2005, King's group conducted a survey of lower-income adults in college. Men, it turned out, had a harder time committing to school, even when they desperately needed to retool. They tended to start out behind academically, and many felt intimidated by the schoolwork. They reported feeling isolated and were much worse at seeking out fellow students, study groups, or counselors to help them adjust. Mothers going back to school described themselves as good role models for their children. Fathers worried that they were abrogating their responsibilities as breadwinner.

The student gender gap started to feel like a crisis to some people in higher-education circles in the mid-2000s, when it began showing up not just in community and liberal-arts colleges but in the flagship public universities—the UCs and the SUNYS and the UNCs. Like many of those schools, the University of Missouri at Kansas City, a full research university with more than 13,000 students, is now tipping toward 60 percent women, a level many admissions officers worry could permanently shift the atmosphere and reputation of a school. In February, I visited with Ashley Burress, UMKC's student-body president. (The other three student-government officers this school year were also women.) Burress, a cute, short, African American 24-year-old grad student who is getting a doctor-of-pharmacy degree, had many of the same complaints I heard from other young women. Guys high-five each other when they get a C, while girls beat themselves up over a B-minus. Guys play video games in each other's rooms, while girls crowd the study hall. Girls get their degrees with no drama, while guys seem always in danger of drifting away. "In 2012, I will be Dr. Burress," she said. "Will I have to deal with guys who don't even have a bachelor's degree? I would like to date, but I'm putting myself in a really small pool."

UMKC is a working- and middle-class school—the kind of place where traditional sex roles might not be anathema. Yet as I talked to students this spring, I realized how much the basic expectations for men and women had shifted. Many of the women's mothers had established their careers later in life, sometimes after a divorce, and they had urged their daughters to get to their own careers more quickly. They would be a campus of Tracy Flicks, except that they seemed neither especially brittle nor secretly falling apart.

Victoria, Michelle, and Erin are sorority sisters. Victoria's mom is a part-time bartender at a hotel. Victoria is a biology major and wants to be a surgeon; soon she'll apply to a bunch of medical schools. She doesn't want kids for a while, because she knows she'll "be at the hospital, like, 100 hours a week," and when she does have kids, well, she'll "be the hotshot surgeon, and he"—a nameless he—"will be at home playing with the kiddies."

Michelle, a self-described "perfectionist," also has her life mapped out. She's a psychology major and wants to be a family therapist. After college, she will apply to grad school and look for internships. She is well aware of the career-counseling resources on campus. And her fiancé?

Michelle: He's changed majors, like, 16 times. Last week he wanted to be a dentist. This week it's environmental science.

Erin: Did he switch again this week? When you guys have kids, he'll definitely stay home. Seriously, what does he want to do?

Michelle: It depends on the day of the week. Remember last year? It was bio. It really is a joke. But it's not. It's funny, but it's not.

Among traditional college students from the highest-income families, the gender gap pretty much disappears. But the story is not so simple. Wealthier students tend to go to elite private schools, and elite private schools live by their own rules. Quietly, they've been opening up a new frontier in affirmative action, with boys playing the role of the underprivileged applicants needing an extra boost. In 2003, a study by the economists Sandy Baum and Eban Goodstein found that among selective liberal-arts schools, being male raises the chance of college acceptance by 6.5 to 9 percentage points. Now the U.S. Commission on Civil Rights has voted to investigate what some academics have described as the "open secret" that private schools "are discriminating in admissions in order to maintain what they regard as an appropriate gender balance."

Jennifer Delahunty, the dean of admissions and financial aid at Kenyon College, in Ohio, let this secret out in a 2006 *New York Times* op-ed. Gender balance, she wrote back then, is the elephant in the room. And today, she told me, the problem hasn't gone away. A typical female applicant, she said, manages the process herself—lines up the interviews, sets up a campus visit, requests a visit with faculty members. But the college has seen more than one male applicant "sit back on the couch, sometimes with their eyes closed, while their mom tells them where to go and what to do. Sometimes we say, 'What a nice essay his mom wrote,'" she said, in that funny-but-not vein.

To avoid crossing the dreaded 60 percent threshold, admissions officers have created a language to explain away the boys' deficits: "Brain hasn't kicked in yet." "Slow to cook." "Hasn't quite peaked." "Holistic picture." At times Delahunty has become so worried about "overeducated females" and "undereducated males" that she jokes she is getting conspiratorial. She once called her sister, a pediatrician, to vet her latest theory: "Maybe these boys are genetically like canaries in a coal mine, absorbing so many toxins and bad things in the environment that their DNA is shifting. Maybe they're like those frogs—they're more vulnerable or something, so they've gotten deformed."

Clearly, some percentage of boys are just temperamentally unsuited to college, at least at age 18 or 20, but without it, they have a harder time finding their place these days. "Forty years ago, 30 years ago, if you were one of the fairly constant fraction of boys who wasn't ready to learn in high school, there were ways for you to enter the mainstream economy," says Henry Farber, an economist at Princeton. "When you woke up, there were jobs. There were good industrial jobs, so you could have a good industrial, blue-collar career. Now those jobs are gone."

Since the 1980s, as women have flooded colleges, male enrollment has grown far more slowly. And the disparities start before college. Throughout the '90s, various authors and researchers agonized over why boys seemed to be failing at every level of education, from elementary school on up, and identified various culprits: a misguided feminism that treated normal boys as incipient harassers (Christina Hoff Sommers); different brain chemistry (Michael Gurian); a demanding, verbally focused curriculum that ignored boys' interests (Richard Whitmire). But again, it's not all that clear that boys have become more dysfunctional—or have changed in any way. What's clear is that schools, like the economy, now value the self-control, focus, and verbal aptitude that seem to come more easily to young girls.

Researchers have suggested any number of solutions. A movement is growing for more all-boys schools and classes, and for respecting the individual learning styles of boys. Some people think that boys should be able to walk around in class, or take more time on tests, or have tests and books that cater to their interests. In their desperation to reach out to boys, some colleges have formed football teams and started engineering programs. Most of these special accommodations sound very much like the kind of affirmative action proposed for women over the years—which in itself is an alarming flip.

Whether boys have changed or not, we are well past the time to start trying some experiments. It is fabulous to see girls and young women poised for success in the coming years. But allowing generations of boys to grow up feeling rootless and obsolete is not a recipe for a peaceful future. Men have few natural support groups and little access to social welfare; the men's-rights groups that do exist in the U.S. are taking on an angry, antiwoman edge. Marriages fall apart or never happen at all, and children are raised with no fathers. Far from being celebrated, women's rising power is perceived as a threat.

Wh? hat would a society in which women are on top look like? We already have an inkling. This is the first time that the cohort of Americans ages 30 to 44 has more college-educated women than college-educated men, and the effects are upsetting the traditional Cleaver-family dynamics. In 1970, women contributed 2 to 6 percent of the family income. Now the typical working wife brings home 42.2 percent, and four in 10 mothers—many of them single mothers—are the primary breadwinners in their families. The whole question of whether mothers should work is moot, argues Heather Boushey of the Center for American Progress, "because they just do. This idealized family—he works, she stays home—hardly exists anymore."

The terms of marriage have changed radically since 1970. Typically, women's income has been the main factor in determining whether a family moves up the class ladder or stays stagnant. And increasing numbers of women—unable to find men with a similar income and education—are forgoing marriage altogether. In 1970, 84 percent of women ages 30 to 44 were married; now 60 percent are. In 2007, among American women without a high-school diploma, 43 percent were married. And yet, for all the hand-wringing over the lonely spinster, the real loser in society—the only one to have made just slight financial gains since the 1970s—is the single man, whether poor or rich, college-educated or not. Hens rejoice; it's the bachelor party that's over.

The sociologist Kathryn Edin spent five years talking with low-income mothers in the inner suburbs of Philadelphia. Many of these neighborhoods, she found, had turned into matriarchies, with women making all the decisions and dictating what the men should and should not do. "I think something feminists have missed," Edin told me, "is how much power women have" when they're not bound by marriage. The women, she explained, "make every important decision"—whether to have a baby, how to raise it, where to live. "It's definitely 'my way or the highway,'" she said. "Thirty years ago, cultural norms were such that the fathers might have said, 'Great, catch me if you can.' Now they are desperate to father, but they are pessimistic about whether they can meet her expectations." The women don't want them as husbands, and they have no steady income to provide. So what do they have?

"Nothing," Edin says. "They have nothing. The men were just annihilated in the recession of the '90s, and things never got better. Now it's just awful."

The situation today is not, as Edin likes to say, a "feminist nirvana." The phenomenon of children being born to unmarried parents "has spread to barrios and trailer parks and rural areas and small towns," Edin says, and it is creeping up the class ladder. After staying steady for a while, the portion of American children born to unmarried parents jumped to 40 percent in the past few years. Many of their mothers are struggling financially; the most successful are working and going to school and hustling to feed the children, and then falling asleep in the elevator of the community college.

Still, they are in charge. "The family changes over the past four decades have been bad for men and bad for kids, but it's not clear they are bad for women," says W. Bradford Wilcox, the head of the University of Virginia's National Marriage Project.

Over the years, researchers have proposed different theories to explain the erosion of marriage in the lower classes: the rise of welfare, or the disappearance of work and thus of marriageable men. But Edin thinks the most compelling theory is that marriage has disappeared because women are setting the terms—and setting them too high for the men around them to reach. "I want that white-picket-fence dream," one woman told Edin, and the men she knew just didn't measure up, so she had become her own one-woman mother/father/nurturer/provider. The whole country's future could look much as the present does for many lower-class African Americans: the mothers pull themselves up, but the men don't follow. First-generation college-educated white women may join their black counterparts in a new kind of middle class, where marriage is increasingly rare.

As the traditional order has been upended, signs of the profound disruption have popped up in odd places. Japan is in a national panic over the rise of the "herbivores," the cohort of young men who are rejecting the hard-drinking salaryman life of their fathers and are instead gardening, organizing dessert parties, acting cartoonishly feminine, and declining to have sex. The generational young-women counterparts are known in Japan as the "carnivores," or sometimes the "hunters."

American pop culture keeps producing endless variations on the omega male, who ranks even below the beta in the wolf pack. This often-unemployed, romantically challenged loser can show up as a perpetual adolescent (in Judd Apatow's *Knocked Up* or *The 40-Year-Old Virgin*), or a charmless misanthrope (in Noah Baumbach's *Greenberg*), or a happy couch potato (in a Bud Light commercial). He can be sweet, bitter, nostalgic, or cynical, but he cannot figure out how to be a man. "We call each other 'man,'" says Ben Stiller's character in *Greenberg,* "but it's a joke. It's like imitating other people." The American male novelist, meanwhile, has lost his mojo and entirely given up on sex as a way for his characters to assert macho dominance, Katie Roiphe explains in her essay "The Naked and the Conflicted." Instead, she writes, "the current sexual style is more childlike; innocence is more fashionable than virility, the cuddle preferable to sex."

At the same time, a new kind of alpha female has appeared, stirring up anxiety and, occasionally, fear. The cougar trope started out as a joke about desperate older women. Now it's gone mainstream, even in Hollywood, home to the 50-some-thing producer with a starlet on his arm. Susan Sarandon and Demi Moore have boy toys, and Aaron Johnson, the 19-year-old star of *Kick-Ass,* is a proud boy toy for a woman 24 years his senior. The *New York Times* columnist Gail Collins recently wrote that the cougar phenomenon is beginning to look like it's not about desperate women at all but about "desperate young American men who are latching on to an older woman who's a good earner." *Up in the Air,* a movie set against the backdrop of recession-era layoffs, hammers home its point about the shattered ego of the American man. A character played by George Clooney is called too old to be attractive by his younger female colleague and is later rejected by an older woman whom he falls in love with after she sleeps with him—and who turns out to be married. George Clooney! If the sexiest man alive can get twice rejected (and sexually played) in a movie, what hope is there for anyone else? The message to American men is summarized by the title of a recent offering from the romantic-comedy mill: *She's Out of My League.*

In fact, the more women dominate, the more they behave, fittingly, like the dominant sex. Rates of violence committed by middle-aged women have skyrocketed since the 1980s, and no one knows why. High-profile female killers have been showing up regularly in the news: Amy Bishop, the homicidal Alabama professor; Jihad Jane and her sidekick, Jihad Jamie; the latest generation of Black Widows, responsible for suicide bombings in Russia. In Roman Polanski's *The Ghost Writer,* the traditional political wife is rewritten as a cold-blooded killer at the heart of an evil conspiracy. In her recent video *Telephone,* Lady Gaga, with her infallible radar for the cultural edge, rewrites *Thelma and Louise* as a story not about elusive female empowerment but about sheer, ruthless power. Instead of killing themselves, she and her girlfriend (played by Beyoncé) kill a bad boyfriend and random others in a homicidal spree and then escape in their yellow pickup truck, Gaga bragging, "We did it, Honey B."

The Marlboro Man, meanwhile, master of wild beast and wild country, seems too farfetched and preposterous even for advertising. His modern equivalents are the stunted men in the Dodge Charger ad that ran during this year's Super Bowl in February. Of all the days in the year, one might think, Super Bowl Sunday should be the one most dedicated to the cinematic celebration of macho. The men in Super Bowl ads should be throwing balls and racing motorcycles and doing whatever it is men imagine they could do all day if only women were not around to restrain them.

Instead, four men stare into the camera, unsmiling, not moving except for tiny blinks and sways. They look like they've been tranquilized, like they can barely hold themselves up against the breeze. Their lips do not move, but a voice-over explains their predicament—how they've been beaten silent by the demands of tedious employers and enviro-fascists and women. Especially women. "I will put the seat down, I will separate the recycling, I will carry your lip balm." This last one—lip balm—is expressed with the mildest spit of emotion, the only hint of the suppressed rage against the dominatrix. Then the commercial abruptly cuts to the fantasy, a Dodge Charger vrooming toward the camera punctuated by bold all caps: MAN'S LAST STAND. But the motto is unconvincing. After that display of muteness and passivity, you can only imagine a woman—one with shiny lips—steering the beast.

Critical Thinking

1. How are women and girls advantaged over men and boys?
2. Since men have income and job advantages over women, are the genders more or less equal?
3. Do the demands of modern life favor women?

HANNA ROSIN is an *Atlantic* contributing editor and the co-editor of *DoubleX*.

UNIT 4
Institutional Problems

Unit Selections

Learning Outcomes

After reading this unit, you should be able to:

- What changes in the family in the past half century do you think are good, and what changes do you think are bad? What can be done about the bad changes?

- What are the forces behind high divorce rates? Will these forces decline or increase? Defend your answer.

- What are the secrets of successful parenting?

- How are work life and careers affecting family life?

- What type of marriage relationship do you think is ideal?

- What are some major principles of good parenting?

- What is wrong with America's education system, and how can it be improved?

- What are some of the major problems with the health care system today?

Student Website
www.mhhe.com/cls

Internet References

Go Ask Alice!
www.goaskalice.columbia.edu
National Council on Family Relations (NCFR)
www.ncfr.com
National Institute on Aging (NIA)
www.nih.gov/nia
National Institute on Drug Abuse (NIDA)
www.nida.nih.gov
National Institutes of Health (NIH)
www.nih.gov

Parenting and Families
www.cyfc.umn.edu/features/index.html
The Center for Education Reform
http://edreform.com/school_choice
The National Academy for Child Development (NACD)
www.nacd.org
World Health Organization (WHO)
www.who.int/home-page

This unit looks at the problems in three institutional areas: family, education, and health care. The family is the basic institution in society. Politicians and preachers are earnestly preaching this message today as though most people need to be convinced, but everyone already agrees. Nevertheless, families are having real problems, and sociologists should be as concerned as are preachers. Unlike the preachers who blame the couples who divorce for shallow commitment, sociologists point to additional causes such as the numerous changes in society that have had an impact on the family. For example, women have to work because many men do not make enough income to support a family adequately. So, women are working not only to enjoy a career but also out of necessity. Working women are often less dependent on their husbands. As a result, divorce can be an option for badly treated wives.

In the first article, Kate Bolick makes a shocking observation: Increasingly, women's marriage options are between "deadbeats (whose numbers are rising) and playboys (whose power is growing)." She reviews the history of marriage and current trends like later age of marriage, more casual views of marriage, greater sexual freedom, gender changes in the workplace, higher expectations for intimacy and companionship, and greater options for women. These undermine the permanence and success of marriage. In the next article Nancie L Gonzalez reports on the great worldwide variety in cultural norms about appropriate marriages and practices. In light of this variety she accuses the religiously based traditional view of the family as narrow minded and intolerant when its backers try to impose it on others. This leads the reader to ask what "family values [are appropriate] in the postindustrial, individualistic, global society in which we now live?" In the next article, Nancy Schute reports on the research findings about good and bad parenting practices. Some common parenting mistakes are overindulging children on the one hand and nagging or lecturing them on the other hand. Parents must set limits but not micromanage their children. Not surprisingly, research shows that loving them is essential to good parenting.

The second subsection deals with education, a perennial problem area. In the first article Paul Glastris argues that No Child Left Behind is now seen as a deeply flawed school reform policy and in need of a massive overhaul. Glastris, however, views this critique of standards-and-testing-based education as premature. He predicts that it will soon be attached to a core curriculum approach that will genuinely improve education. It will involve three stages. First, most states will institute "common core standards" that will define what students should know and replace the jumbled standards now in place. Second, the development of new high-stakes tests based on these new standards. Third, the development and implementation of new computer-based learning software that will work wonders. This transition has already begun. In the next article Peter W. Cookson Jr. also focuses on school improvement. Money is not the answer. National per pupil expenditures have doubled since 1970 without improving performance. The answer is new technology that cuts costs while improving learning. New technologies will customize students' learning so that each student will have an individualized program with frequent testing and revision to boost weak areas. The program will be designed to create interest and excitement.

© Mark Bowden/Getty Images

The last subsection deals with healthcare issues, and this sphere is also in turmoil and plagued with problems. In the first article Aubrey de Gray advocates a war against aging. Possible medical and biochemical innovations could eventually enable us to live for a millennium. Continuous repair treatments would stop our bodies and minds from wearing down so we would not really grow old. Currently, our bodies continually experience damage but are not immediately repaired. Therefore, damage accumulates until it causes serious problems. Change that and we will live much longer. In the final article Frank W. Maletz recommends a major overhaul of the healthcare system. Costs are two high and results are disappointing. He proposes that the emphasis be shifted from treatment to preventive care to save a lot of money and make the nation much healthier. He wants an integrated, holistic health-delivery system. It would involve much greater retrievable information, sophisticated data security systems, and considerable monitoring. Unfortunately, he must also identify the barriers to his progressive plans.

All the Single Ladies

Recent years have *seen an explosion of male joblessness and a steep decline in men's life prospects that have disrupted the "romantic market" in ways that narrow a marriage-minded woman's options: increasingly, her choice is between deadbeats (whose numbers are rising) and playboys (whose power is growing). But this strange state of affairs also presents an opportunity: as the economy evolves, it's time to embrace new ideas about romance and family—and to acknowledge the end of "traditional" marriage as society's highest ideal.*

KATE BOLICK

In 2001, when I was 28, I broke up with my boyfriend. Allan and I had been together for three years, and there was no good reason to end things. He was (and remains) an exceptional person, intelligent, good-looking, loyal, kind. My friends, many of whom were married or in marriage-track relationships, were bewildered. I was bewildered. To account for my behavior, all I had were two intangible yet undeniable convictions: something was missing; I wasn't ready to settle down.

The period that followed was awful. I barely ate for sobbing all the time. (A friend who suffered my company a lot that summer sent me a birthday text this past July: "A decade ago you and I were reuniting, and you were crying a lot.") I missed Allan desperately—his calm, sure voice; the sweetly fastidious way he folded his shirts. On good days, I felt secure that I'd done the right thing. Learning to be alone would make me a better person, and eventually a better partner. On bad days, I feared I would be alone forever. Had I made the biggest mistake of my life?

Ten years later, I occasionally ask myself the same question. Today I am 39, with too many ex-boyfriends to count and, I am told, two grim-seeming options to face down: either stay single or settle for a "good enough" mate. At this point, certainly, falling in love and getting married may be less a matter of choice than a stroke of wild great luck. A decade ago, luck didn't even cross my mind. I'd been in love before, and I'd be in love again. This wasn't hubris so much as naïveté; I'd had serious, long-term boyfriends since my freshman year of high school, and simply couldn't envision my life any differently.

Well, there was a lot I didn't know 10 years ago. The decision to end a stable relationship for abstract rather than concrete reasons ("something was missing"), I see now, is in keeping with a post-Boomer ideology that values emotional fulfillment above all else. And the elevation of independence over coupling ("I wasn't ready to settle down") is a second-wave feminist idea I'd acquired from my mother, who had embraced it, in part, I suspect, to correct for her own choices.

I was her first and only recruit, marching off to third grade in tiny green or blue T-shirts declaring: A WOMAN WITHOUT A MAN IS LIKE A FISH WITHOUT A BICYCLE, or: A WOMAN'S PLACE IS IN THE HOUSE—AND THE SENATE, and bellowing along to Gloria Steinem & Co.'s feminist-minded children's album, *Free to Be . . . You and Me* (released the same year Title IX was passed, also the year of my birth). Marlo Thomas and Alan Alda's retelling of "Atalanta," the ancient Greek myth about a fleet-footed princess who longs to travel the world before finding her prince, became the theme song of my life. Once, in high school, driving home from a family vacation, my mother turned to my boyfriend and me cuddling in the backseat and said, "Isn't it time you two started seeing other people?" She adored Brian—he was invited on family vacations! But my future was to be one of limitless possibilities, where getting married was something I'd do when I was ready, to a man who was in every way my equal, and she didn't want me to get tied down just yet.

This unfettered future was the promise of my time and place. I spent many a golden afternoon at my small New England liberal-arts college debating with friends the merits of leg-shaving and whether or not we'd take our husband's surname. (Even then, our concerns struck me as retro; hadn't the women's libbers tackled all this stuff already?) We took for granted that we'd spend our 20s finding ourselves, whatever that meant, and save marriage for after we'd finished graduate school and launched our careers, which of course would happen at the magical age of 30.

That we would marry, and that there would always be men we wanted to marry, we took on faith. How could we not? One of the many ways in which our lives differed from our mothers' was in the variety of our interactions with the opposite sex. Men were our classmates and colleagues, our bosses and professors, as well as, in time, our students and employees and subordinates—an entire universe of prospective friends, boyfriends, friends with benefits, and even ex-boyfriends-turned-friends. In this brave new world, boundaries were fluid, and roles constantly changing. Allan and I had met when we worked together at a magazine in Boston (full disclosure: this one), where I was an assistant and he an editor; two years later, he quit his job to follow me to New York so that I could go to graduate school and he could focus on his writing.

After the worst of our breakup, we eventually found our way to a friendship so deep and sustaining that several years ago, when he got engaged, his fiancée suggested that I help him buy his wedding suit. As he and I toured through Manhattan's men's-wear ateliers, we enjoyed explaining to the confused tailors and salesclerks that no, no, *we* weren't getting married. Isn't life funny that way?

I retell that moment as an aside, as if it's a tangent to the larger story, but in a way, it is the story. In 1969, when my 25-year-old mother, a college-educated high-school teacher, married a handsome lawyer-to-be, most women her age were doing more or less the same thing. By the time she was in her mid-30s, she was raising two small children and struggling to find a satisfying career. She'd never had sex with anyone but my father. Could she have even envisioned herself on a shopping excursion with an ex-lover, never mind one who was getting married while she remained alone? And the ex-lover's fiancée being so generous and open-minded as to suggest the shopping trip to begin with?

What my mother could envision was a future in which I made my own choices. I don't think either of us could have predicted what happens when you multiply that sense of agency by an entire generation.

But what transpired next lay well beyond the powers of everybody's imagination: as women have climbed ever higher, men have been falling behind. We've arrived at the top of the staircase, finally ready to start our lives, only to discover a cavernous room at the tail end of a party, most of the men gone already, some having never shown up—and those who remain are leering by the cheese table, or are, you know, the ones you don't want to go out with.

In the 1990s, Stephanie Coontz, a social historian at Evergreen State College in Washington, noticed an uptick in questions from reporters and audiences asking if the institution of marriage was falling apart. She didn't think it was, and was struck by how everyone believed in some mythical Golden Age of Marriage and saw mounting divorce rates as evidence of the dissolution of this halcyon past. She decided to write a book discrediting the notion and proving that the ways in which we think about and construct the legal union between a man and a woman have always been in flux.

What Coontz found was even more interesting than she'd originally expected. In her fascinating *Marriage, a History: From Obedience to Intimacy, or How Love Conquered Marriage,* she surveys 5,000 years of human habits, from our days as hunters and gatherers up until the present, showing our social arrangements to be more complex and varied than could ever seem possible. She'd long known that the *Leave It to Beaver*–style family model popular in the 1950s and '60s had been a flash in the pan, and like a lot of historians, she couldn't understand how people had become so attached to an idea that had developed so late and been so short-lived.

For thousands of years, marriage had been a primarily economic and political contract between two people, negotiated and policed by their families, church, and community. It took more than one person to make a farm or business thrive, and

so a potential mate's skills, resources, thrift, and industriousness were valued as highly as personality and attractiveness. This held true for all classes. In the American colonies, wealthy merchants entrusted business matters to their landlocked wives while off at sea, just as sailors, vulnerable to the unpredictability of seasonal employment, relied on their wives' steady income as domestics in elite households. Two-income families were the norm.

Not until the 18th century did labor begin to be divided along a sharp line: wage-earning for the men and unpaid maintenance of household and children for the women. Coontz notes that as recently as the late 17th century, women's contributions to the family economy were openly recognized, and advice books urged husbands and wives to share domestic tasks. But as labor became separated, so did our spheres of experience—the marketplace versus the home—one founded on reason and action, the other on compassion and comfort. Not until the post-war gains of the 1950s, however, were a majority of American families able to actually afford living off a single breadwinner.

All of this was intriguing, for sure—but even more surprising to Coontz was the realization that those alarmed reporters and audiences might be onto something. Coontz still didn't think that marriage was falling apart, but she came to see that it was undergoing a transformation far more radical than anyone could have predicted, and that our current attitudes and arrangements are without precedent. "Today we are experiencing a historical revolution every bit as wrenching, far-reaching, and irreversible as the Industrial Revolution," she wrote.

A smaller proportion of American women in their early 30s are married than at any point since the 1950s, if not earlier.

Last summer I called Coontz to talk to her about this revolution. "We are without a doubt in the midst of an extraordinary sea change," she told me. "The transformation is momentous—immensely liberating and immensely scary. When it comes to what people actually want and expect from marriage and relationships, and how they organize their sexual and romantic lives, all the old ways have broken down."

For starters, we keep putting marriage off. In 1960, the median age of first marriage in the United States was 23 for men and 20 for women; today it is 28 and 26. Today, a smaller proportion of American women in their early 30s are married than at any other point since the 1950s, if not earlier. We're also marrying less—with a significant degree of change taking place in just the past decade and a half. In 1997, 29 percent of my Gen X cohort was married; among today's Millennials that figure has dropped to 22 percent. (Compare that with 1960, when more than half of those ages 18 to 29 had already tied the knot.) These numbers reflect major attitudinal shifts. According to the Pew Research Center, a full 44 percent of Millennials and 43 percent of Gen Xers think that marriage is becoming obsolete.

Even more momentously, we no longer need husbands to have children, nor do we have to have children if we don't want to. For those who want their own biological child, and haven't found the right man, now is a good time to be alive. Biological parenthood in a nuclear family need not be the be-all and end-all of womanhood—and in fact it increasingly is not. Today 40 percent of children are born to single mothers. This isn't to say all of these women preferred that route, but the fact that so many upper-middle-class women are choosing to travel it—and that gays and lesbians (married or single) and older women are also having children, via adoption or in vitro fertilization—has helped shrink the stigma against single motherhood. Even as single motherhood is no longer a disgrace, motherhood itself is no longer compulsory. Since 1976, the percentage of women in their early 40s who have not given birth has nearly doubled. A childless single woman of a certain age is no longer automatically perceived as a barren spinster.

Of course, between the diminishing external pressure to have children and the common misperception that our biology is ours to control, some of us don't deal with the matter in a timely fashion. Like me, for instance. Do I want children? My answer is: I don't know. But somewhere along the way, I decided to not let my biology dictate my romantic life. If I find someone I really like being with, and if he and I decide we want a child together, and it's too late for me to conceive naturally, I'll consider whatever technological aid is currently available, or adopt (and if he's not open to adoption, he's not the kind of man I want to be with).

Do I realize that this further narrows my pool of prospects? Yes. Just as I am fully aware that with each passing year, I become less attractive to the men in my peer group, who have plenty of younger, more fertile women to pick from. But what can I possibly do about that? Sure, my stance here could be read as a feint, or even self-deception. By blithely deeming biology a nonissue, I'm conveniently removing myself from arguably the most significant decision a woman has to make. But that's only if you regard motherhood as the defining feature of womanhood—and I happen not to.

Foremost among the reasons for all these changes in family structure are the gains of the women's movement. Over the past half century, women have steadily gained on—and are in some ways surpassing—men in education and employment. From 1970 (seven years after the Equal Pay Act was passed) to 2007, women's earnings grew by 44 percent, compared with 6 percent for men. In 2008, women still earned just 77 cents to the male dollar—but that figure doesn't account for the difference in hours worked, or the fact that women tend to choose lower-paying fields like nursing or education. A 2010 study of single, childless urban workers between the ages of 22 and 30 found that the women actually earned 8 percent *more* than the men. Women are also more likely than men to go to college: in 2010, 55 percent of all college graduates ages 25 to 29 were female.

B y themselves, the cultural and technological advances that have made my stance on childbearing plausible would be enough to reshape our understanding of the modern family—but, unfortunately, they happen to be dovetailing with another set of developments that can be summed up as: the deterioration of the male condition. As Hanna Rosin laid out in these pages last year ("The End of Men," July/August 2010), men have been rapidly declining—in income, in educational attainment, and in future employment prospects—relative to women. As of last year, women held 51.4 percent of all managerial and professional positions, up from 26 percent in 1980. Today women outnumber men not only in college but in graduate school; they earned 60 percent of all bachelor's and master's degrees awarded in 2010, and men are now more likely than women to hold only a high-school diploma.

No one has been hurt more by the arrival of the post-industrial economy than the stubbornly large pool of men without higher education. An analysis by Michael Greenstone, an economist at MIT, reveals that, after accounting for inflation, male median wages have fallen by 32 percent since their peak in 1973, once you account for the men who have stopped working altogether. The Great Recession accelerated this imbalance. Nearly three-quarters of the 7.5 million jobs lost in the depths of the recession were lost by men, making 2010 the first time in American history that women made up the majority of the workforce. Men have since then regained a small portion of the positions they'd lost—but they remain in a deep hole, and most of the jobs that are least likely ever to come back are in traditionally male-dominated sectors, like manufacturing and construction.

The implications are extraordinary. If, in all sectors of society, women are on the ascent, and if gender parity is actually within reach, this means that a marriage regime based on men's overwhelming economic dominance may be passing into extinction. As long as women were denied the financial and educational opportunities of men, it behooved them to "marry up"—how else would they improve their lot? (As Maureen Dowd memorably put it in her 2005 book, *Are Men Necessary?*, "Females are still programmed to look for older men with resources, while males are still programmed to look for younger women with adoring gazes.") Now that we can pursue our own status and security, and are therefore liberated from needing men the way we once did, we are free to like them more, or at least more idiosyncratically, which is how love ought to be, isn't it?

My friend B., who is tall and gorgeous, jokes that she could have married an NBA player, but decided to go with the guy she can talk to all night—a graphic artist who comes up to her shoulder. C., the editorial force behind some of today's most celebrated novels, is a modern-day Venus de Milo—with a boyfriend 14 years her junior. Then there are those women who choose to forgo men altogether. Sonia Sotomayor isn't merely a powerful woman in a black robe—she's also a stellar example of what it can mean to exercise authority over every single aspect of your personal life. When Gloria Steinem said, in the 1970s, "We're becoming the men we wanted to marry," I doubt even she realized the prescience of her words.

But while the rise of women has been good for everyone, the decline of males has obviously been bad news for men—and bad news for marriage. For all the changes the institution has undergone, American women as a whole have never been confronted with such a radically shrinking pool of what are traditionally considered to be "marriageable" men—those who are better educated and earn more than they do. So women are now contending with what we might call the new scarcity. Even as women have seen their range of options broaden in recent years—for instance, expanding the kind of men it's culturally acceptable to be with, and making it okay not to marry at all—the new scarcity disrupts what economists call the "marriage market" in a way that in fact narrows the available choices, making a good man harder to find than ever. At the rate things are going, the next generation's pool of good men will be significantly smaller. What does this portend for the future of the American family?

Every so often, society experiences a "crisis in gender" (as some academics have called it) that radically transforms the social landscape.

Take the years after the Civil War, when America reeled from the loss of close to 620,000 men, the majority of them from the South. An article published last year in *The Journal of Southern History* reported that in 1860, there were 104 marriageable white men for every 100 white women; in 1870, that number dropped to 87.5. A generation of Southern women found themselves facing a "marriage squeeze." They could no longer assume that they would become wives and mothers—a terrifying prospect in an era when women relied on marriage for social acceptability and financial resources.

Instead, they were forced to ask themselves: Will I marry a man who has poor prospects ("marrying down," in sociological parlance)? Will I marry a man much older, or much younger? Will I remain alone, a spinster? Diaries and letters from the period reveal a populace fraught with insecurity. As casualties mounted, expectations dropped, and women resigned themselves to lives without husbands, or simply lowered their standards. (In 1862, a Confederate nurse named Ada Bacot described in her diary the lamentable fashion "of a woman marring a man younger than herself.") Their fears were not unfounded—the mean age at first marriage did rise—but in time, approximately 92 percent of these Southern-born white women found someone to partner with. The anxious climate, however, as well as the extremely high levels of widowhood—nearly one-third of Southern white women over the age of 40 were widows in 1880—persisted.

Or take 1940s Russia, which lost some 20 million men and 7 million women to World War II. In order to replenish the population, the state instituted an aggressive pro-natalist policy to support single mothers. Mie Nakachi, a historian at Hokkaido University, in Japan, has outlined its components: mothers were given generous subsidies and often put up in special sanatoria during pregnancy and childbirth; the state day-care system expanded to cover most children from infancy; and penalties were brandished for anyone who perpetuated the stigma against conceiving out of wedlock. In 1944, a new Family Law was passed, which essentially freed men from responsibility for illegitimate children; in effect, the state took on the role of "husband." As a result of this policy—and of the general dearth of males—men moved at will from house to house, where they were expected to do nothing and were treated like kings; a generation of children were raised without reliable fathers, and women became the "responsible" gender. This family pattern was felt for decades after the war.

Indeed, Siberia today is suffering such an acute "man shortage" (due in part to massive rates of alcoholism) that both men and women have lobbied the Russian parliament to legalize polygamy. In 2009, *The Guardian* cited Russian politicians' claims that polygamy would provide husbands for "10 million lonely women." In endorsing polygamy, these women, particularly those in remote rural areas without running water, may be less concerned with loneliness than with something more pragmatic: help with the chores. Caroline Humphrey, a Cambridge University anthropologist who has studied the region, said women supporters believed the legalization of polygamy would be a "godsend," giving them "rights to a man's financial and physical support, legitimacy for their children, and rights to state benefits."

Our own "crisis in gender" isn't a literal imbalance—America as a whole currently enjoys a healthy population ratio of 50.8 percent females and 49.2 percent males. But our shrinking pool of traditionally "marriageable" men is dramatically changing our social landscape, and producing startling dynamics in the marriage market, in ways that aren't immediately apparent.

In their 1983 book, *Too Many Women? The Sex Ratio Question,* two psychologists developed what has become known as the Guttentag-Secord theory, which holds that members of the gender in shorter supply are less dependent on their partners, because they have a greater number of alternative relationships available to them; that is, they have greater "dyadic power" than members of the sex in oversupply. How this plays out, however, varies drastically between genders.

Siberia today is suffering such a "man shortage" that both men and women are lobbying for polygamy.

In societies where men heavily outnumber women—in what's known as a "high-sex-ratio society"—women are valued and treated with deference and respect and use their high dyadic power to create loving, committed bonds with their partners and raise families. Rates of illegitimacy and divorce are low. Women's traditional roles as mothers and homemakers are held in high esteem. In such situations, however, men also use the power of their greater numbers to limit women's economic and political strength, and female literacy and labor-force participation drop.

One might hope that in low-sex-ratio societies—where women outnumber men—women would have the social and sexual advantage. (After all, didn't the mythical all-female nation of Amazons capture men and keep them as their sex slaves?) But that's not what happens: instead, when confronted with a surplus of women, men become promiscuous and unwilling to commit to a monogamous relationship. (Which, I suppose, might explain the Amazons' need to keep men in slave quarters.) In societies with too many women, the theory holds, fewer people marry, and those who do marry do so later in life. Because men take advantage of the variety of potential partners available to them, women's traditional roles are not valued, and because these women can't rely on their partners to stick around, more turn to extrafamilial ambitions like education and career.

In 1988, the sociologists Scott J. South and Katherine Trent set out to test the Guttentag-Secord theory by analyzing data from 117 countries. Most aspects of the theory tested out. In each country, more men meant more married women, less divorce, and fewer women in the workforce. South and Trent also found that the Guttentag-Secord dynamics were more pronounced in developed rather than developing countries. In other words—capitalist men are pigs.

I kid! And yet, as a woman who spent her early 30s actively putting off marriage, I have had ample time to investigate, if you will, the prevailing attitudes of the high-status American urban male. (Granted, given my taste for brainy, creatively ambitious men—or "scrawny nerds," as a high-school friend describes them—my sample is skewed.) My spotty anecdotal findings have revealed that, yes, in many cases, the more successful a man is (or thinks he is), the less interested he is in commitment.

Take the high-powered magazine editor who declared on our first date that he was going to spend his 30s playing the field. Or the prominent academic who announced on our fifth date that he couldn't maintain a committed emotional relationship but was very interested in a physical one. Or the novelist who, after a month of hanging out, said he had to get back out there and tomcat around, but asked if we could keep having sex anyhow, or at least just one last time. Or the writer (yes, another one) who announced after six months together that he had to end things because he "couldn't continue fending off all the sexual offers." And those are just the honest ones.

To be sure, these men were the outliers—the majority of my personal experience has been with commitment-minded men with whom things just didn't work out, for one reason or another. Indeed, another of my anecdotal-research discoveries is of what an ex calls "marriage o'clock"—when a man hits 35 and suddenly, desperately, wants a wife. I'll never forget the post-first-date e-mail message reading: "I wanted to marry you last night, just listening to you." Nor the 40-ish journalist who, on our second date, driving down a long country road, gripped the steering wheel and asked, "Are you The One? Are you The One?" (Can you imagine a woman getting away with this kind of behavior?) Like zealous lepidopterists, they swoop down with their butterfly nets, fingers aimed for the thorax, certain that just because they are ready for marriage and children, I must be, too.

But the non-committers are out there in growing force. If dating and mating is in fact a marketplace—and of course it is—today we're contending with a new "dating gap," where marriage-minded women are increasingly confronted with either deadbeats or players. For evidence, we don't need to look to the past, or abroad—we have two examples right in front of us: the African American community, and the college campus.

In August I traveled to Wilkinsburg, Pennsylvania, a small, predominantly African American borough on the eastern ledge of Pittsburgh. A half-century ago, it was known as "The Holy City" for its preponderance of churches. Today, the cobblestoned streets are lined with defeated clapboard houses that look as if the spirit's been sucked right out of them.

I was there to spend the afternoon with Denean, a 34-year-old nurse who was living in one such house with three of her four children (the eldest is 19 and lived across town) and, these days, a teenage niece. Denean is pretty and slender, with a wry, deadpan humor. For 10 years she worked for a health-care company, but she was laid off in January. She is twice divorced; no two of her children share a father. In February, when she learned (on Facebook) that her second child, 15-year-old Ronicka, was pregnant, Denean slumped down on her enormous slate-gray sofa and didn't get up for 10 hours.

"I had done everything I could to make sure she didn't end up like me, and now this," she told me.

It was a clear, warm day, and we were clustered on the front porch—Denean, Ronicka, and I, along with Denean's niece, Keira, 18, and Denean's friend Chantal, 28, a single mother whose daughter goes to day care with Denean's youngest. The affection between these four high-spirited women was light and infectious, and they spoke knowingly about the stigmas they're up against. "That's right," Denean laughed, "we're your standard bunch of single black moms!"

Given the crisis in gender it has suffered through for the past half century, the African American population might as well be a separate nation. An astonishing 70 percent of black women are unmarried, and they are more than twice as likely as white women to remain that way. Those black women who do marry are more likely than any other group of women to "marry down." This is often chalked up to high incarceration rates—in 2009, of the nearly 1.5 million men in prison, 39 percent were black—but it's more than that. Across all income levels, black men have dropped far behind black women professionally and educationally; women with college degrees outnumber men 2-to-1. In August, the unemployment rate among black men age 20 or older exceeded 17 percent.

In his book, *Is Marriage for White People?*, Ralph Richard Banks, a law professor at Stanford, argues that the black experience of the past half century is a harbinger for society at large. "When you're writing about black people, white people may assume it's unconnected to them," he told me when I got him on the phone. It might seem easy to dismiss Banks's theory that what holds for blacks may hold for nonblacks, if only because no other group has endured such a long history of racism, and racism begets singular ills. But the reality is that what's happened to the black family is already beginning to happen to the white family. In 1950, 64 percent of African American women were married—roughly the same percentage as white women. By 1965, African American marriage rates had declined precipitously, and Daniel Patrick Moynihan was famously declaring black families a "tangle of pathology." Black marriage rates have fallen drastically in the years since—but then, so have white marriage rates. In 1965, when Moynihan wrote with such concern about the African American family, fewer than 25 percent of black children were born out of wedlock; in 2011, considerably more than 25 percent of white children are.

This erosion of traditional marriage and family structure has played out most dramatically among low-income groups, both black and white. According to the sociologist William Julius Wilson, inner-city black men struggled badly in the 1970s, as manufacturing plants shut down or moved to distant suburbs. These men naturally resented their downward mobility, and had trouble making the switch to service jobs requiring a very different style of self-presentation. The joblessness and economic insecurity that resulted created a host of problems, and made many men altogether unmarriable. Today, as manufacturing jobs disappear nationwide (American manufacturing shed about a third of its jobs during the first decade of this century), the same phenomenon may be under way, but on a much larger scale.

Just as the decline of marriage in the black underclass augured the decline of marriage in the white underclass, the decline of marriage in the black middle class has prefigured the decline of marriage in the white middle class. In the 1990s, the author Terry McMillan climbed the bestseller list (and box-office charts) with novels like *Waiting to Exhale* and *How Stella Got Her Groove Back,* which provided incisive glimpses of life and frustrated romance among middle-class black women, where the prospect of marrying a black man often seemed more or less hopeless. (As she writes in *Waiting to Exhale:* "[Successful black men have] taken these stupid statistics about *us* to heart and are having the time of their lives. They do not hold themselves accountable to anybody for anything, and they're getting away with murder . . . They lie to us without a conscience, they fuck as many of us at a time as they want to.") Today, with the precipitous economic and social decline of men of *all* races, it's easy to see why women of any race would feel frustrated by their romantic prospects. (Is it any wonder marriage rates have fallen?) Increasingly, this extends to the upper-middle class, too: early last year, a study by the Pew Research Center reported that professionally successful, college-educated women were confronted with a shrinking pool of like-minded marriage prospects.

"If you're a successful black man in New York City, one of the most appealing and sought-after men around, your options are plentiful," Banks told me. "Why marry if you don't have to?" (Or, as he quotes one black man in his book, "If you have four quality women you're dating and they're in a rotation, who's going to rush into a marriage?") Banks's book caused a small stir by suggesting that black women should expand their choices by marrying outside their race—a choice that the women of Terry McMillan's novels would have found at best unfortunate and at worst an abhorrent betrayal. As it happens, the father of Chantal's child is white, and Denean has dated across the color line. But in any event, the decline in the economic prospects of white men means that marrying outside their race can expand African American women's choices only so far. Increasingly, the new dating gap—where women are forced to choose between deadbeats and players—trumps all else, in all socioeconomic brackets.

The early 1990s witnessed the dawn of "hookup culture" at universities, as colleges stopped acting in loco parentis, and undergraduates, heady with freedom, started throwing themselves into a frenzy of one-night stands.

Depending on whom you ask, this has either liberated young women from being ashamed of their sexual urges, or forced them into a promiscuity they didn't ask for. Young men, apparently, couldn't be happier.

According to Robert H. Frank, an economist at Cornell who has written on supply and demand in the marriage market, this shouldn't be surprising. When the available women significantly outnumber men, which is the case on many campuses today, "courtship behavior changes in the direction of what men want," he told me recently. If women greatly outnumber men, he says, social norms against casual sex will weaken. He qualifies this by explaining that no matter how unbalanced the overall sex ratio may become (in either direction), "there will always be specific men and women who are in high demand as romantic partners—think Penélope Cruz and George Clooney." But even Cruz and Clooney, Frank says, will be affected by changing mores. The likelihood increases "that even a highly sought-after woman will engage in casual sex, even though she would have sufficient market power to defy prevailing norms." If a woman with the "market power" of a Penelope Cruz is affected by this, what are the rest of us to do?

Whether the sexual double standard is cultural or biological, it's finding traction in the increasingly lopsided sexual marketplace that is the American college campus, where women outnumber men, 57 percent to 43 percent. In 2010, *The New York Times* ran a much-discussed article chronicling this phenomenon. "If a guy is not getting what he wants, he can quickly and abruptly go to the next one, because there are so many of us," a University of Georgia co-ed told *The Times,* reporting that at college parties and bars, she will often see two guys being fawned over by six provocatively dressed women. The alternative is just to give up on dating and romance because "there are no guys," as a University of North Carolina student put it.

Last year, a former management consultant named Susan Walsh tried to dig a little deeper. She applied what economists call the Pareto principle—the idea that for many events, roughly 20 percent of the causes create 80 percent of the effects—to the college dating market, and concluded that only 20 percent of the men (those considered to have the highest status) are having 80 percent of the sex, with only 20 percent of the women (those with the greatest sexual willingness); the remaining 80 percent, male and female, sit out the hookup dance altogether. (Surprisingly, a 2007 study commissioned by the Justice Department suggested that male virgins outnumber female virgins on campus.) As Walsh puts it, most of the leftover men are "have nots" in terms of access to sex, and most of the women—both those who are hooking up and those who are not— are "have nots" in terms of access to male attention that leads to commitment. (Of course, plenty of women are perfectly happy with casual, no-strings sex, but they are generally considered to be in the minority.) Yet the myth of everyone having sex all the time is so pervasive that it's assumed to be true, which distorts how young men and women relate. "I think the 80/20 principle is the key to understanding the situation we find ourselves in—one in which casual sex is the cultural norm, despite the fact that most people would actually prefer something quite different," Walsh told me.

My findings have revealed that, yes, the more successful a man is, the less interested he is in commitment.

I became aware of Walsh this past summer when I happened upon her blog, HookingUpSmart.com, and lost an evening to one of those late-night Internet binges, each link leading to the next, drawn into a boy-girl conversation to end all boy-girl conversations. A frumpy beige Web-site palette and pragmatic voice belie a refreshingly frank, at times even raunchy, dialogue; postings in the comments section can swell into the high hundreds—interestingly, the majority of them from men. I felt as if I'd stumbled into the online equivalent of a (progressive) school nurse's office.

A Wharton M.B.A. and stay-at-home mother of two, Walsh began her career as a relationship adviser turned blogger six years ago, when her daughter, then a student at an all-girls high school, started dating. She began seeking counsel from Walsh, and liked what she heard, as did her friends when she told them; in time, the girls were regularly gathering around Walsh's kitchen table to pick her brain. Soon enough, a childhood friend's daughter, a sophomore at Boston University, started coming over with her friends. Walsh started thinking of these '70s-style rap sessions as her own informal "focus groups," the members of one still in high school, those of the other in college, but all of them having similar experiences. In 2008, after the younger group had left home, Walsh started the blog so they could all continue the conversation.

In July, I traveled to Walsh's home, a handsome 19th-century Victorian hidden behind tall hedges in a quiet corner of Brookline, Massachusetts, to sit in on one of these informal roundtables. I came of age with hookup culture, but not of it, having continued through college my high-school habit of serial long-term relationships, and I wanted to hear from the front lines. What would these sexual buccaneers be like? Bold and provocative? Worn-out and embittered?

When Walsh opened the door, I could immediately see why young women find her so easy to talk to; her brunette bob frames bright green eyes and a warm, easy smile. Once everyone had arrived—five recent college graduates, all of them white and upper middle class, some employed and some still looking for work, all unmarried— we sat down to a dinner of chicken and salad in Walsh's high-ceilinged, wood-paneled dining room to weigh in on one of the evening's topics: man whores.

"How do you all feel about guys who get with a ton of girls?," Walsh asked. "Do you think they have 'trash dick'?" She'd run across this term on the Internet.

One of Walsh's pet observations pertains to what she calls the "soft harem," where high-status men (i.e., the football captain) maintain an "official" girlfriend as well as a rotating roster of neo-concubines, who service him in the barroom bathroom or wherever the beer is flowing. "There used to be more assortative mating," she explained, "where a five would date a five. But now every woman who is a six and above wants the hottest guy on campus, and she can have him—for one night."

As I'd expected, these denizens of hookup culture were far more sexually experienced than I'd been at their age. Some had had many partners, and they all joked easily about sexual positions and penis size ("I was like, 'That's a pinkie, not a penis!'") with the offhand knowledge only familiarity can breed. Most of them said that though they'd had a lot of sex, none of it was particularly sensual or exciting. It appears that the erotic promises of the 1960s sexual revolution have run aground on the shoals of changing sex ratios, where young women and men come together in fumbling, drunken couplings fueled less by lust than by a vague sense of social conformity. (I can't help wondering: Did this de-eroticization of sex encourage the rise of pornography? Or is it that pornography endows the inexperienced with a toolbox of socially sanctioned postures and tricks, ensuring that one can engage in what amounts to a public exchange according to a pre-approved script?) For centuries, women's sexuality was repressed by a patriarchal marriage system; now what could be an era of heady carnal delights is stifled by a new form of male entitlement, this one fueled by demographics.

Most striking to me was the innocence of these young women. Of these attractive and vivacious females, only two had ever had a "real" boyfriend—as in, a mutually exclusive and satisfying relationship rather than a series of hookups— and for all their technical know-how, they didn't seem to be any wiser than I'd been at their age. This surprised me; I'd assumed that growing up in a jungle would give them a more matter-of-fact or at least less conventional worldview. Instead, when I asked if they wanted to get married when they grew up, and if so, at what age, to a one they answered "yes" and "27 or 28."

"That's only five or six years from now," I pointed out. "Doesn't that seem—not far off?"

They nodded.

"Take a look at me," I said. "I've never been married, and I have no idea if I ever will be. There's a good chance that this will be your reality, too. Does that freak you out?"

Again they nodded.

"I don't think I can bear doing this for that long!" whispered one, with undisguised alarm.

I remember experiencing that same panicked exhaustion around the time I turned 36, at which point I'd been in the dating game for longer than that alarmed 22-year-old had, and I wanted out. (Is there an expiration date on the fun, running-around period of being single captured so well by movies and television?) I'd spent the past year with a handsome, commitment-minded man, and these better qualities, along with our having several interests in common, allowed me to overlook our many thundering incompatibilities. In short, I was creeping up on marriage o'clock, and I figured, *Enough already*—I had to make something work. When it became clear that sheer will wasn't going to save us, I went to bed one night and had a rare dream about my (late) mother.

"Mom," I said. "Things aren't working out. I'm breaking up with him tomorrow."

"Oh, honey," she said. "I am so sorry. We were rooting for this one, weren't we? When something doesn't work, though, what can you do?"

This, I found irritating. "Mom. I am getting old."

"Pwhah!" she scoffed. "You're fine. You've got six more years."

Six more years. I woke up. In six more years, I'd be 42. All this time, I'd been regarding my single life as a temporary interlude, one I had to make the most of—or swiftly terminate, depending on my mood. Without intending to, by actively rejecting our pop-culture depictions of the single woman—you know the ones—I'd been terrorizing myself with their specters. But now that 35 had come and gone, and with yet another relationship up in flames, all bets were off. It might never happen. Or maybe not until 42. Or 70, for that matter. Was that so bad? If I stopped seeing my present life as provisional, perhaps I'd be a little . . . happier. Perhaps I could actually get down to the business of what it means to be a real single woman.

It's something a lot of people might want to consider, given that now, by choice or by circumstance, more and more of us (women and men), across the economic spectrum, are spending more years of our adult lives unmarried than ever before. The numbers are striking: The Census Bureau has reported that in 2010, the proportion of married households in America dropped to a record low of 48 percent. Fifty percent of the adult population is single (compared with 33 percent in 1950)—and that portion is very likely to keep growing, given the variety of factors that contribute to it. The median age for getting married has been rising, and for those who are affluent and educated, that number climbs even higher. (Indeed, Stephanie Coontz told me that an educated white woman of 40 is more than twice as likely to marry in the next decade as a less educated woman of the same age.) Last year, nearly twice as many single women bought homes as did single men. And yet, what are our ideas about single people? Perverted misanthropes, crazy cat ladies, dating-obsessed shoe shoppers, etc.—all of them some form of terribly lonely. (In her 2008 memoir, *Epilogue,* a 70-something Anne Roiphe muses: "There are millions of women who live alone in America. Some of them are widows. Some of them are divorced and between connections, some of them are odd, loners who prefer to keep their habits undisturbed." That's a pretty good representation of her generation's notions of unmarried women.)

One recent study found a 40 percent increase in men who are shorter than their wives.

Famous Bolick family story: When I was a little girl, my mother and I went for a walk and ran into her friend Regina. They talked for a few minutes, caught up. I gleaned from their conversation that Regina wasn't married, and as soon as we made our goodbyes, I bombarded my mother with questions. "No husband? How could that be? She's a grownup! Grown-ups have husbands!" My mother explained that not all grown-ups get married. "Then who opens the pickle jar?" (I was 5.)

Thus began my lifelong fascination with the idea of the single woman. There was my second-grade teacher, Mrs. Connors, who was, I believe, a former nun, or seemed like one. There was the director of my middle-school gifted-and-talented program,

who struck me as wonderfully remote and original. (Was she a lesbian?) There was a college poetry professor, a brilliant single woman in her 40s who had never been married, rather glamorously, I thought. Once, I told her I wanted to be just like her. "Good God," she said. "I've made a mess of my life. Don't look to me." Why did they all seem so mysterious, even marginalized?

Back when I believed my mother had a happy marriage—and she did for quite a long time, really—she surprised me by confiding that one of the most blissful moments of her life had been when she was 21, driving down the highway in her VW Beetle, with nowhere to go except wherever she wanted to be. "I had my own car, my own job, all the clothes I wanted," she remembered wistfully. Why couldn't she have had more of that?

When I embarked on my own sojourn as a single woman in New York City—talk about a timeworn cliché!—it wasn't dating I was after. I was seeking something more vague and, in my mind, more noble, having to do with finding my own way, and independence. And I found all that. Early on, I sometimes ached, watching so many friends pair off—and without a doubt there has been loneliness. At times I've envied my married friends for being able to rely on a spouse to help make difficult decisions, or even just to carry the bills for a couple of months. And yet I'm perhaps inordinately proud that I've never depended on anyone to pay my way (today that strikes me as a quaint achievement, but there you have it). Once, when my father consoled me, with the best of intentions, for being so unlucky in love, I bristled. I'd gotten to know so many interesting men, and experienced so much. Wasn't that a form of luck?

All of which is to say that the single woman is very rarely seen for who she is—whatever that might be—by others, or even by the single woman herself, so thoroughly do most of us internalize the stigmas that surround our status.

Bella DePaulo, a Harvard-trained social psychologist who is now a visiting professor at the University of California at Santa Barbara, is America's foremost thinker and writer on the single experience. In 2005, she coined the word *singlism,* in an article she published in *Psychological Inquiry.* Intending a parallel with terms like *racism* and *sexism,* DePaulo says singlism is "the stigmatizing of adults who are single [and] includes negative stereotyping of singles and discrimination against singles." In her 2006 book, *Singled Out,* she argues that the complexities of modern life, and the fragility of the institution of marriage, have inspired an unprecedented glorification of coupling. (Laura Kipnis, the author of *Against Love,* has called this "the tyranny of two.") This marriage myth—"matrimania," DePaulo calls it—proclaims that the only route to happiness is finding and keeping one all-purpose, all-important partner who can meet our every emotional and social need. Those who don't have this are pitied. Those who don't want it are seen as threatening. Singlism, therefore, "serves to maintain cultural beliefs about marriage by derogating those whose lives challenge those beliefs."

In July, I visited DePaulo in the improbably named Summerland, California, which, as one might hope, is a charming outpost overlooking a glorious stretch of the Pacific Ocean. DePaulo, a warm, curious woman in her late 50s, describes herself as "single at heart"—meaning that she's always been single and always will be, and that's just the way she wants it. Over lunch at a seafood restaurant, she discussed how the cultural fixation on the couple blinds us to the full web of relationships that sustain us on a daily basis. We are far more than whom we are (or aren't) married to: we are also friends, grandparents, colleagues, cousins, and so on. To ignore the depth and complexities of these networks is to limit the full range of our emotional experiences.

Personally, I've been wondering if we might be witnessing the rise of the aunt, based on the simple fact that my brother's two small daughters have brought me emotional rewards I never could have anticipated. I have always been very close with my family, but welcoming my nieces into the world has reminded me anew of what a gift it is to care deeply, even helplessly, about another. There are many ways to know love in this world.

This is not to question romantic love itself. Rather, we could stand to examine the ways in which we think about love; and the changing face of marriage is giving us a chance to do this. "Love comes from the motor of the mind, the wanting part that craves that piece of chocolate, or a work promotion," Helen Fisher, a biological anthropologist and perhaps this country's leading scholar of love, told me. *That* we want is enduring; *what* we want changes as culture does.

O ur cultural fixation on the couple is actually a relatively recent development. Though "pair-bonding" has been around for 3.5 million years, according to Helen Fisher, the hunters and gatherers evolved in egalitarian groups, with men and women sharing the labor equally. Both left the camp in the morning; both returned at day's end with their bounty. Children were raised collaboratively. As a result, women and men were sexually and socially more or less equals; divorce (or its institution-of-marriage-preceding equivalent) was common. Indeed, Fisher sees the contemporary trend for marriage between equals as us "moving forward into deep history"—back to the social and sexual relationships of millions of years ago.

It wasn't until we moved to farms, and became an agrarian economy centered on property, that the married couple became the central unit of production. As Stephanie Coontz explains, by the Middle Ages, the combination of the couple's economic interdependence and the Catholic Church's success in limiting divorce had created the tradition of getting married to one person and staying that way until death do us part. It was in our personal and collective best interest that the marriage remain intact if we wanted to keep the farm afloat.

That said, being too emotionally attached to one's spouse was discouraged; neighbors, family, and friends were valued just as highly in terms of practical and emotional support. Even servants and apprentices shared the family table, and sometimes slept in the same room with the couple who headed the household, Coontz notes. Until the mid-19th century, the word *love* was used to describe neighborly and familial feelings more often than to describe those felt toward a mate, and same-sex friendships were conducted with what we moderns would consider a romantic intensity. When honeymoons first started, in the 19th century, the newlyweds brought friends and family along for the fun.

But as the 19th century progressed, and especially with the sexualization of marriage in the early 20th century, these older social ties were drastically devalued in order to strengthen the bond between the husband and wife—with contradictory results. As Coontz told me, "When a couple's relationship is strong, a marriage can be more fulfilling than ever. But by overloading marriage with more demands than any one individual can possibly meet, we unduly strain it, and have fewer emotional systems to fall back on if the marriage falters."

Some even believe that the pair bond, far from strengthening communities (which is both the prevailing view of social science and a central tenet of social conservatism), weakens them, the idea being that a married couple becomes too consumed with its own tiny nation of two to pay much heed to anyone else. In 2006, the sociologists Naomi Gerstel and Natalia Sarkisian published a paper concluding that unlike singles, married couples spend less time keeping in touch with and visiting their friends and extended family, and are less likely to provide them with emotional and practical support. They call these "greedy marriages." I can see how couples today might be driven to form such isolated nations—it's not easy in this age of dual-career families and hyper-parenting to keep the wheels turning, never mind having to maintain outside relationships as well. And yet we continue to rank this arrangement above all else!

Now that women are financially independent, and marriage is an option rather than a necessity, we are free to pursue what the British sociologist Anthony Giddens termed the "pure relationship," in which intimacy is sought in and of itself and not solely for reproduction. (If I may quote the eminently quotable Gloria Steinem again: "I can't mate in captivity.") Certainly, in a world where women can create their own social standing, concepts like "marrying up" and "marrying down" evaporate—to the point where the importance of conventional criteria such as age and height, Coontz says, has fallen to an all-time low (no pun intended) in the United States.

Everywhere I turn, I see couples upending existing norms and power structures, whether it's women choosing to be with much younger men, or men choosing to be with women more financially successful than they are (or both at once). My friend M., a successful filmmaker, fell in love with her dog walker, a man 12 years her junior; they stayed together for three years, and are best friends today. As with many such relationships, I didn't even know about their age difference until I became a member of their not-so-secret society. At a rooftop party last September, a man 11 years my junior asked me out for dinner; I didn't take him seriously for one second—and then the next thing I knew, we were driving to his parents' house for Christmas. (When I mentioned what I considered to be this scandalous age difference to the actress Julianne Moore after a newspaper interview that had turned chatty and intimate, she e-mailed me to say, "In terms of scandalously young—I have been with my 9-years-younger husband for 15 years now—so there you go!") The same goes for couples where the woman is taller. Dalton Conley, the dean for the social sciences at New York University, recently analyzed data from the Panel Study of Income Dynamics and found a 40 percent increase, between 1986 and 2003, in men who are shorter than their wives. (Most research confirms casual observation: when it comes to judging a prospective mate on the basis of looks, women are the more lenient gender.)

128

Perhaps true to conservative fears, the rise of gay marriage has helped heterosexuals think more creatively about their own conventions. News stories about polyamory, "ethical non-monogamy," and the like pop up with increasing frequency. Gay men have traditionally had a more permissive attitude toward infidelity; how will this influence the straight world? Coontz points out that two of the hallmarks of contemporary marriage are demands for monogamy on an equal basis, and candor. "Throughout history, there was a fairly high tolerance of [men's] extramarital flings, with women expected to look the other way," she said. "Now we have to ask: Can we be more monogamous? Or understand that flings happen?" (She's also noticed that an unexpected consequence of people's marrying later is that they skip right over the cheating years.) If we're ready to rethink, as individuals, the ways in which we structure our arrangements, are we ready to do this as a society?

In her new book, *Unhitched*, Judith Stacey, a sociologist at NYU, surveys a variety of unconventional arrangements, from gay parenthood to polygamy to—in a mesmerizing case study—the Mosuo people of southwest China, who eschew marriage and visit their lovers only under cover of night. "The sooner and better our society comes to terms with the inescapable variety of intimacy and kinship in the modern world, the fewer unhappy families it will generate," she writes.

"We are not designed, as a species, to raise children in nuclear families."

—Christopher Ryan

The matrilineal Mosuo are worth pausing on, as a reminder of how complex family systems can be, and how rigid ours are—and also as an example of women's innate libidinousness, which is routinely squelched by patriarchal systems, as Christopher Ryan and Cacilda Jethá point out in their own analysis of the Mosuo in their 2010 book, *Sex at Dawn*. For centuries, the Mosuo have lived in households that revolve around the women: the mothers preside over their children and grandchildren, and brothers take paternal responsibility for their sisters' offspring.

Sexual relations are kept separate from family. At night, a Mosuo woman invites her lover to visit her *babahuago* (flower room); the assignation is called *sese* (walking). If she'd prefer he not sleep over, he'll retire to an outer building (never home to his sisters). She can take another lover that night, or a different one the next, or sleep every single night with the same man for the rest of her life—there are no expectations or rules. As Cai Hua, a Chinese anthropologist, explains, these relationships, which are known as *açia*, are founded on each individual's autonomy, and last only as long as each person is in the other's company. Every goodbye is taken to be the end of the *açia* relationship, even if it resumes the following night. "There is no concept of *açia* that applies to the future," Hua says.

America has a rich history of its own sexually alternative utopias, from the 19th-century Oneida Community (which encouraged postmenopausal women to introduce teenage males to sex) to the celibate Shakers, but real change can seldom take hold when economic forces remain static. The extraordinary economic flux we're in is what makes this current moment so distinctive.

In the months leading to my breakup with Allan, my problem, as I saw it, lay in wanting two incompatible states of being—autonomy and intimacy—and this struck me as selfish and juvenile; part of growing up, I knew, was making trade-offs. I was too ashamed to confide in anyone, and as far as I could tell, mine was an alien predicament anyhow; apparently women everywhere wanted exactly what I possessed: a good man; a marriage-in-the-making; a "we."

So I started searching out stories about those who had gone off-script with unconventional arrangements. I had to page back through an entire century, down past the riot grrrls, then the women's libbers, then the flappers, before I found people who talked about love in a way I could relate to: the free-thinking adventurers of early-1900s Greenwich Village. Susan Glaspell, Neith Boyce, Edna St. Vincent Millay—they investigated the limits and possibilities of intimacy with a naive audacity, and a touching decorum, that I found familiar and comforting. I am not a bold person. To read their essays and poems was to perform a shy ideological striptease to the sweetly insistent warble of a gramophone.

"We are not designed, as a species, to raise children in nuclear families," Christopher Ryan, one of the *Sex at Dawn* co-authors, told me over the telephone late last summer. Women who try to be "super-moms," whether single or married, holding down a career and running a household simultaneously, are "swimming upstream." Could we have a modernization of the Mosuo, Ryan mused, with several women and their children living together—perhaps in one of the nation's many foreclosed and abandoned McMansions—bonding, sharing expenses, having a higher quality of life? "In every society where women have power—whether humans or primates—the key is female bonding," he added.

Certainly letting men off the hook isn't progress. But as we talked, I couldn't help thinking about the women in Wilkinsburg—an inadvertent all-female coalition—and how in spite of it all, they derived so much happiness from each other's company. That underprivileged communities are often forced into matrilineal arrangements in the absence of reliable males has been well documented (by the University of Virginia sociologist W. Bradford Wilcox, among others), and I am not in anyway romanticizing these circumstances. Nor am I arguing that we should discourage marriage—it's a tried-and-true model for raising successful children in a modern economy. (Evidence suggests that American children who grow up amidst the disorder that is common to single-parent homes tend to struggle.) But we would do well to study, and to endorse, alternative family arrangements that might provide strength and stability to children as they grow up. I am curious to know what could happen if these de facto female support systems of the sort I saw in Wilkinsburg were recognized as an adaptive response, even an evolutionary stage, that women could be proud to build and maintain.

I definitely noticed an increase in my own contentment when I began to develop and pay more attention to friendships with women who, like me, have never been married. Their worldviews feel relaxingly familiar, and give me the space to sort through my own ambivalence. That's an abstract benefit. More concretely, there's what my brother terms our "immigrant bucket brigade"—my peer group's habit of jumping to the ready to help each other with matters practical and emotional. This isn't to say that my married friends aren't as supportive—some of my best friends are married!—it's just that, with families of their own, they can't be as available.

Indeed, my single friends housed me as I flew around the world to research this article; by the end, I had my own little (unwritten) monograph on the very rich lives of the modern-day single woman. Deb gave me the use of her handsome mid-century apartment in Chelsea when she vacated town for a meditation retreat; Courtney bequeathed her charming Brooklyn aerie while she traveled alone through Italy; Catherine put me up at her rambling Cape Cod summer house; when my weekend at Maria's place on Shelter Island unexpectedly ballooned into two weeks, she set me up in my own little writing room; when a different Courtney needed to be nursed through an operation, I stayed for four days to write paragraphs between changing bandages.

The sense of community we create for one another puts me in mind of the 19th-century availability of single-sex hotels and boarding houses, which were a necessity when women were discouraged from living alone, and then became an albatross when they finally weren't. So last year, inspired by visions of New York's "women only" Barbizon Hotel in its heyday, I persuaded my childhood friend Willamain to take over the newly available apartment in my building in Brooklyn Heights. We've known each other since we were 5, and I thought it would be a great comfort to us both to spend our single lives just a little less atomized. It's worked. These days, I think of us as a mini-neo-single-sex residential hotel of two. We collect one another's mail when necessary, share kitchenware, tend to one another when sick, fall into long conversations when we least expect it—all the benefits of dorm living, without the gross bathrooms.

Could we create something bigger, and more intentional? In August, I flew to Amsterdam to visit an iconic medieval bastion of single-sex living. The Begijnhof was founded in the mid-12th century as a religious all-female collective devoted to taking care of the sick. The women were not nuns, but nor were they married, and they were free to cancel their vows and leave at any time. Over the ensuing centuries, very little has changed. Today the religious trappings are gone (though there is an active chapel on site), and to be accepted, an applicant must be female and between the ages of 30 and 65, and commit to living alone. The institution is beloved by the Dutch, and gaining entry isn't easy. The waiting list is as long as the turnover is low.

I'd heard about the Begijnhof through a friend, who once knew an American woman who lived there, named Ellen. I contacted an old boyfriend who now lives in Amsterdam to see if he knew anything about it (thank you, Facebook), and he put

me in touch with an American friend who has lived there for 12 years: the very same Ellen.

The Begijnhof is big—106 apartments in all—but even so, I nearly pedaled right past it on my rented bicycle, hidden as it is in plain sight: a walled enclosure in the middle of the city, set a meter lower than its surroundings. Throngs of tourists sped past toward the adjacent shopping district. In the wall is a heavy, rounded wood door. I pulled it open and walked through.

Inside was an enchanted garden: a modest courtyard surrounded by classic Dutch houses of all different widths and heights. Roses and hydrangea lined walkways and peeked through gates. The sounds of the city were indiscernible. As I climbed the narrow, twisting stairs to Ellen's sun-filled garret, she leaned over the railing in welcome—white hair cut in a bob, smiling red-painted lips. A writer and producer of avant-garde radio programs, Ellen, 60, has a chic, minimal style that carries over into her little two-floor apartment, which can't be more than 300 square feet. Neat and efficient in the way of a ship, the place has large windows overlooking the courtyard and rooftops below. To be there is like being held in a nest.

We drank tea and talked, and Ellen rolled her own cigarettes and smoked thoughtfully. She talked about how the Dutch don't regard being single as peculiar in any way—people are as they are. She feels blessed to live at the Begijnhof and doesn't ever want to leave. Save for one or two friends on the premises, socially she holds herself aloof; she has no interest in being ensnared by the gossip on which a few of the residents thrive—but she loves knowing that they're there. Ellen has a partner, but since he's not allowed to spend the night, they split time between her place and his nearby home. "If you want to live here, you have to adjust, and you have to be creative," Ellen said. (When I asked her if starting a relationship was a difficult decision after so many years of pleasurable solitude, she looked at me meaningfully and said, "It wasn't a choice—it was a certainty.")

When an American woman gives you a tour of her house, she leads you through all the rooms. Instead, this expat showed me her favorite window views: from her desk, from her (single) bed, from her reading chair. As I perched for a moment in each spot, trying her life on for size, I thought about the years I'd spent struggling against the four walls of my apartment, and I wondered what my mother's life would have been like had she lived and divorced my father. A room of one's own, for each of us. A place where single women can live and thrive as themselves.

Critical Thinking

1. What factors are making successful marriages more difficult?
2. Explain the role of work family relations in weakening marriages.
3. How are changing gender roles impacting marriages?

KATE BOLICK, *a writer based in Los Angeles and Brooklyn, is the culture editor for* Veranda *magazine.*

Matches Made on Earth

Why Family Values Are Human Values

NANCIE L. GONZALEZ

The term "family values," the importance of which fundamentalist Christians have been preaching for decades, continues to permeate religious and political printed matter and discussions in the United States today. The conservatives' concept of family values is generally characterized by abstinence from sex until marriage, which is then entered into with a like-minded individual of the opposite sex and is thereafter permanent and free from adultery. It is also expected that children will ensue, either through birth or adoption. In line with these prescriptions, proponents of traditional family values foment prejudice and activism against divorce, abortion, homosexuality, single-parent families, and even the choice not to have children. The fact that their efforts have become more intensive and intrusive lately can be explained, I believe, by the increasingly tolerant and diverse sexual, racial, and religious views and behavior of the American public at large.

The problem isn't that some people espouse conservative ideals of family, but that they promulgate them as the only way to live, looking down upon and often demonizing those with other values. Indeed, the family values crowd often refers to any who oppose its agenda as having no values at all. They support their ideals as based upon divine "truth" by quoting the Bible and rejecting scientific evidence that supports a different set of explanations for the existence and history of humankind. They repeatedly argue that more general social acceptance of other ways to live will endanger their own. This fear has inspired efforts for decades to influence our school boards and our local, state, and national governments to change text books, curricula, and the law to reflect socially conservative views. When these fail, parents turn to private schools or home schooling, and later enroll their offspring in one of the several conservative Christian colleges whose faculties and administrative personnel are vetted to make sure their values are religiously and politically "correct." The fact that some of these schools are admittedly training their graduates to seek public office or employment in state and national venues is further evidence of their intolerance, and their misunderstanding of the nature of society and culture.

Most of the idealistic family values held by conservative Christians today are not now nor have they ever been characteristic of the world at large. Statistics, as well as more informal evidence suggest that the so-called nontraditional behaviors they condemn are now common throughout the United States and much of the industrialized world, often despite laws forbidding them. Furthermore, such behaviors have existed in many parts of the world for centuries. The problem I see for humanists is to convince much of the conservative American public that these prejudices and fears are unwarranted on at least two grounds: 1) family values are the products of human sociocultural conditions, and cannot be attributed to either divine or biological imperatives, and 2) pluralism in marriage and family values should be expected in any large twenty-first century society as a result of technological advances that have made globalization both possible and perhaps inevitable.

If neither a deity nor our genes are wholly determinative, we must ask our conservative counterparts: what accounts for the vast panorama of intimate human bonding practices, either in the past, or today?

It may be useful to consider what social and biological scientists have concluded about the origin and nature of marriage and the family. All animals must struggle for self and species survival, which demands food, defense, reproduction, and care of newborns until they can care for themselves. Both genetics and learning are involved for all species, but only humans have created *social institutions* to help themselves in these endeavors. By social, I mean any kind of bonding with other humans to share in the food quest; to ward off environmental and other dangers; to reproduce, nurture, and educate the young; and to provide physical and psychological well-being for themselves, their children, and their neighbors. The specific characteristics of these institutions vary with the society; trial and error must have occurred over time, and some societies failed to persist. But those institutions that worked well became customary, "traditional," and thus value-laden. Children would be taught by example and by experience. But traditions change as cultural evolution occurs and as societies grow, develop new technologies, and increasingly influence each other. The young and the most pragmatically minded are likely to change with the times, yet there are always some who cling to the older ways—not that this is, in itself, dysfunctional, for the "old ways" still serve some purposes, and sometimes are reinstated or reinterpreted by succeeding generations.

Although marriage and the family have existed in all human societies and form the primary roots of all the particulars of family values everywhere, different societies have constructed their own definitions of incest; permissible marriage partners; appropriate sexual behavior before, during, and after marriage; "normal" and alternate sexual orientations; ideal post-marital residence; and composition of the ideal family and household, including what to do if too many children "appear," or if conception occurs at an inconvenient time. For example, marriages that we likely consider incestuous but others don't include marriage between first cousins, especially patrilateral parallel cousin marriage (where the children of two brothers marry) seen in some parts of the Middle East and Africa. Among some Bedouin cultures, there was even a stated preference for such a marriage. Similarly, cross-cousin marriage is widespread in many "tribal" societies, including the Yanomamo in South America.

Different societies have constructed their own definitions of incest appropriate sexual behavior, "normal" and alternate sexual orientations, and ideal post-marital residence.

Formal bonding or marriage rituals probably developed in very early human societies, since it was important then as now to confer legitimacy of the children in relation to membership in whatever social unit was pertinent (tribe, clan, patrilineage, matrilineage, nation-state, religious group, and so forth). Formal marriage also establishes rights of inheritance of property, as well as social position. In many societies, including our own, women, and to a lesser extent, men, are treated like adolescents until they marry.

Neither religious nor biological explanations for conservative family values take into account the fact that even the notion of two sexes is not, and probably never has been, biologically correct. We have no way to know whether prehistoric societies recognized inborn sexual variations, what the frequency of such variations might have been, or whether "different" newborns would even have been allowed to live. However, colonial travelers to America noted that some native cultures recognized the existence of some among them whose bodies, psyches, or both weren't comfortable living in either of the two primary gender roles of male or female. They called these people "two spirits" and provided a socially acceptable niche for them.

Homosexuality of different types has been documented throughout Western civilization since at least the ancient Greeks. However, only in the current century has the recognition developed in Western societies that sexual orientation is not merely a matter of differences in genitalia, and that it isn't

a mere matter of choice. The growing acceptance of the idea that sexuality and sexual identity should not alter one's basic humanity and civil rights has led to changes in the laws in many countries, including the decriminalization of certain sex practices and the legalization of same-sex marriage. At the time of this writing, five U.S. states as well as the District of Columbia now allow gay and lesbian couples to marry, and in three more states same-sex marriages are recognized but not performed legally. Nine other states recognize certain legal rights of same-sex couples through civil unions, domestic partnerships, or reciprocal beneficiary laws. Still, these arrangements are only gradually becoming acceptable to the general public, and since same-sex marriage hasn't been documented as legal in any society in history, we shouldn't be surprised that it is and will remain controversial for some time. Nevertheless, it should now be added to the evidence we have for different kinds of marriage and family institutions.

Studies of pre-agricultural and pre-industrial societies, as well as continuing historical research over the past century have documented such a variety of marriage customs and rules that a God hypothesis would almost have to suggest an anthropological deity who understood that no single practice should be imposed upon all. However, the following discussion focuses not on the supernatural, but the natural ways in which human pair bonding and family formation have occurred. These include *monogamy* as the permanent or lifetime union of two persons, usually, but not always, of opposite sex. This was probably the most common marriage form for Paleolithic foragers, as was the nuclear family. However, that small unit had affinal relatives (we call them in-laws), some of whom lived together in what anthropologists call a band. As the noted nineteenth-century anthropologist Edward B. Tylor suggested, early societies had to "marry out or die out." Institutions promoting reproduction and care of the young were crucial to social survival.

Polygamy is often confused with *polygyny—the* union of one man with several wives—but polygamy also includes *polyandry—one* woman with several husbands. All of these forms, especially polygyny, were more typical of larger, more advanced societies based upon pastoralism, agriculture, or both. The advantages were to enlarge the family unit by drawing in more nubile and fertile women, while at the same time providing care for those who might no longer have been able to bear children. If the sex ratio, for whatever reason, was unbalanced, as it was among early converts to the Church of the Latter Day Saints, polygyny also was a way for new single young women to be immediately drawn in to an existing family. The custom was formally abolished by the Mormons in the early part of the twentieth century, but the family values created more than one hundred years earlier have held on for some.

Polyandry has been fairly rare, practiced primarily in the Himalayan regions of Nepal, Tibet, India, and Bhutan. It has also occurred in the Canadian Arctic, Nigeria, and Sri Lanka, and is known to have been present in some pre-contact Polynesian societies, though probably only among higher caste women. Some forms of polyandry appear to be associated with a perceived need to retain aristocratic titles or agricultural lands within kin groups, and/or because of the frequent absence, for long periods, of a man from the household. In Tibet the practice is particularly popular among the priestly Skye class but also among poor small farmers who can ill afford to divide their small holdings. As to the latter variety, as some males return to the household, others leave for a long time, so that there is usually one husband present. Fraternal polyandry occurs when multiple brothers share a common wife. This occurs in the pastoral Toda community in Southern India. Similarly, among the Tibetan Nyinba, anthropologist Nancy Levine described the strong bond between brothers as essential in creating a strong sense of family unity and keeping land holdings intact, thus preserving socioeconomic standing.

Group marriage involving multiple members of both sexes has sometimes been averred to have existed; however, there appears to be no reputable description of it in the anthropological or historical literature. In recent years a movement has arisen that produces something very similar to the idea of group marriage; the term *polyamory* has been offered to describe plural simultaneous attachments between and among people, including lesbian, gay, bisexual, and transgendered individuals (LGBTs). From the perspective of this writing, this may or may not be new under the sun, but it doesn't (yet?) constitute marriage.

Serial monogamy is perhaps the most common type of marriage known in much of the world today. Individuals in such unions may have only one spouse but, shedding that one, they may contract any number later—again, usually only one at a time, except in those societies that still accept and approve polygyny. Serial monogamy depends on the existence of easy divorce laws or more informal practices, such as what is generally called "living together." *Domestic partnerships* by law may or may not be considered marriages. In the United States persons of both the same and opposite sex have for some time entered into such unions, but those of opposite sex partners have generally received greater social acceptance, even without the legal protections, status, or financial benefits society offers to married couples.

Why do some people choose not to abide by the marriage rules of their own society? Obviously, reasons vary. Some think a trial marriage to be a good idea; others simply don't care about rules of any kind. A few may be prohibited from marrying because one or the other is already bound by a previous, legitimate union which can't be formally dissolved. And while others have simply adopted a more individualized lifestyle, some are still convinced of the values of marriage in a previous age (as in polygyny). In short, the choice of whether and whom to marry has increasingly been seen as a personal, individual decision, and it is no longer important to the functioning of the modern industrial state that all persons marry, unless they wish the state to adjudicate property or child custody rights.

Co-residence of the partners and the creation of a household are usually, but not always, typical in any kind of marriage. Yet households vary enormously in both size and composition, and usually, but not always, include some kind of family. In societies in which men must find work through short or long term emigration, *consanguineal households* have arisen that contain no married pair. Such a household is most often headed by an elderly woman, together with some of her sons and daughters and their children. The marital partners of these co-residential adults live elsewhere—often with their own mothers. The United States today is also seeing an increase in extended families moving in together due to economic constraints, as well as "single" parents who live with a partner.

A study by the Pew Research Center released in November, titled, "The Decline of Marriage and Rise of New Families," revealed changing attitudes about what constitutes a family. Among survey respondents, 86 percent said a single parent and child constitute a family; 80 percent considered an unmarried couple living together with a child a family; and 63 percent said a gay or lesbian couple raising a child is a family.

Obviously, the "traditional family" so highly valued by the religious right can't be considered as the typical American household today. Instead, the term "family" has taken on a much broader meaning to incorporate various combinations of persons of different genders, sexual orientations, and familial

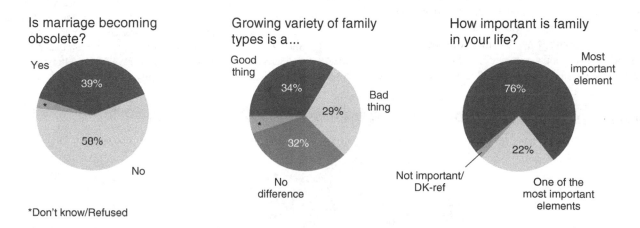

Data from the Pew Research Center's 2010 survey, "The Decline of Marriage and Rise of New Families"

or non-familial relationships living together, as in the refrigerator magnet that proclaims, "Friends Are the Family You Choose for Yourself."

We still, and always will, value the need to bond with others. Kinship remains one major way to do so, but social and geographical mobility have lessened its role as the most important tie that binds. Today it may be similar age groups, vocations, or philosophical views on the nature of the universe or of the hereafter that form the basis of relationships. People will continue to find or invent ways to get together, live together, and share what is important in life with others.

Does this mean that marriage and the family as we know it will likely disappear in the near future as Focus on the Family fears? Does the fact that many young people of various genders and sexual identities choose not to marry or stay married, nor to form traditional households augur the demise, or even the diminution in value of these institutions in our society? Should the legal sanctioning of same-sex marriage in any way affect the dignity of opposite-sex couples joined by similar ceremonies? I think not. Society has, for the most part, already accepted the newer bonding patterns described above—at least for persons of opposite sex.

Taking away any social stigma, LGBT couples will likely experience the same joys and struggles in marriage as straight couples do, thus proving that sexual orientation is irrelevant when it comes to pair-bonding. Although the ethnographic and historical evidence doesn't confirm that true marriages were ever legally sanctioned between persons thought to be of the same sex, present-day reminiscences and folklore suggest that love, sex, and companionship were known and accepted among them, and that untold numbers of people have lived in happy unions with persons perceived to be of the same sex for perhaps hundreds of years.

Finally, what about love and companionship? It is only in modern Western society that these have become the very most important components of marriage. There is no evidence that these occur only between spouses of opposing sex or gender. The idea that sexual activity is only appropriate between members of the opposite sex is a product of our cultural conditioning, born of the thousands of years when it was important to keep people focused on finding a mate of the opposite sex to ensure continued reproduction. The need for population control, rather than survival of the species or of any specific society, makes this value irrelevant today, as it does for the idea that all marriages should produce children. Also, the extended family of yore is no longer functional in industrial society—today one does indeed marry the individual, not the whole family.

Sex is no longer seen as a major reward for contracting marriage, regardless of one's sexual orientation. Tests of virginity have disappeared as premarital sex with more than one partner has become more common and seems to be a largely irrelevant factor for many marriages, including the first. Yet, the fact that homosexual and lesbian partners engage in sexual activities without marriage is always seen as a disgrace, even for many of them who may share the traditional religious notion that unmarried sex is a sin.

As we continue to consider the nature and causes of the diversity of family values in the post-industrial, individualistic, global society in which we now live, I hope that the single set of specific rules of behavior promulgated by Focus on the Family and other such organizations comes to be seen as outmoded, even by the so-called moral majority. As the U.S. Constitution has always insisted, all citizens should have equal rights, so for those who find the "old ways" to their taste, we should wish them well, but plead with them not to damage the lives of those who choose to live or even to think differently, nor to forget that our nation was founded by outsiders and has continually accepted those from other cultures, and that we have, in fact, valued and profited by our diversity.

Critical Thinking

1. Describe some of the many variations in family values throughout the world.
2. Do you agree with Gonzalez that it is right for Americans to feel strongly about their family values but wrong for them to force their values on others?

NANCIE L. GONZALEZ is Professor Emeritus of Anthropology at the University of Maryland. She has conducted ethnographic and ethnohistorical research on marriage and family patterns in a number of societies, including the American Southwest, the Caribbean, Central America, China, and the West Bank and has published widely since the 1960s. She is presently working on a memoir dealing with changes in marriage and family patterns as revealed in letters and diaries from five generations of her own family. She lives in Richmond, Virginia.

From *The Humanist*, January/February 2011, pp. 14–17. Copyright © 2011 by Nancie L. Gonzalez. Reprinted by permission of the author.

Good Parents, Bad Results

Science is providing proof of where Mom and Dad go wrong.

NANCY SHUTE

Does your 3-year-old throw a five-alarm tantrum every time you drop him off at day care? Does "you're so smart!" fail to inspire your 8-year-old to turn off *Grand Theft Auto IV* and tackle his math homework? Do the clothes remain glued to your teenager's bedroom floor, along with your antisocial teenager, no matter how much you nag or cajole? Being a parent has never been easy—just ask your own. But in this day of two-earner couples and single parents, when 9-year-olds have cellphones, 12-year-olds are binge drinking and having oral sex, and there is evidence that teens are more fearful and depressed than ever, the challenges of rearing competent and loving human beings are enough to make a parent seek help from Supernanny. Actually, there is something better: science.

Researchers have spent decades studying what motivates children to behave and can now say exactly what discipline methods work and what don't: Call it "evidence-based parenting." Alas, many of parents' favorite strategies are scientifically proven to fail. "It's intuitive to scream at your child to change their behavior, even though the research is unequivocal that it won't work," says Alan Kazdin, a psychologist who directs the Yale Parenting Center and Child Conduct Clinic. Other examples:

- Yelling and reasoning are equally ineffective; kids tune out both.
- Praise doesn't spoil a child; it's one of the most powerful tools that parents can use to influence a child's actions. But most parents squander praise by using it generically—"you're so smart" or "good job!"—or skimping.
- Spanking and other harsh punishments ("You're grounded for a month!") do stop bad behavior but only temporarily. Punishment works only if it's mild, and it is far outweighed by positive reinforcement of good behavior.

As yet, few of the bestselling books and videos that promise to turn surly brats into little buttercups make use of this knowledge. That may be because the research goes on in academia—at Yale, at Vermont's Behavior Therapy and Psychotherapy Center, and at the University of Washington's Parenting Clinic, for example. Surprisingly, many family therapists and parenting educators aren't up to speed on the research, either, so that parents who seek professional help won't necessarily get the most proven advice. Case in point: Just 16 programs designed for treating kids with disruptive behavior have been proven "well established" in randomized clinical trials, according to a review led by Sheila Eyberg at the University of Florida and published in the January *Journal of Clinical Child and Adolescent Psychology*. Kazdin, who for years has pushed clinical psychologists to adopt evidence-based methods, published a book for parents earlier this year: *The Kazdin Method for Parenting the Defiant Child*. Other lab-tested tomes include *Parenting the Strong-Willed Child* by Rex Forehand and Nicholas Long and *The Incredible Years* by Carolyn Webster-Stratton.

These discipline programs are grounded in classical behavioral psychology—the positive reinforcement taught in Psych 101. Researchers have run randomized controlled trials on all the nuances of typical parent-child interactions and thus can say just how long a timeout should last to be effective or how to praise a 13-year-old so that he beams when he takes out the trash. Who knew that effectively praising a child in order to motivate her has three essential steps? They are: 1) Praise effusively, with the enthusiasm of a Powerball winner. 2) Say exactly what the child did right. 3) Finish with a touch or hug.

What else can parents learn from the science? Researchers say these are the biggest common boo-boos:

1. Parents Fail at Setting Limits

It would be hard to find a parent who doesn't agree that setting and enforcing rules are an essential part of the job description. Yet faced with whining, pouting, and tantrums, many parents cave. "The limited time you have with your kids, you want to make it ideal for them," says Forehand, a professor of psychology at the University of Vermont whose evidence-based program is outlined in his book. "As a result, we end up overindulging our kids."

Faced with whining and pouting, many parents cave. Result: domestic inferno.

A Good Parent's Dilemma: Is It Bad to Spank?

Plenty of people argue for an occasional swat

Last year, the California Legislature considered criminalizing the spanking of toddlers. But at least half of parents, and according to some surveys as many as 94 percent, consider a swat on the bottom to be an appropriate form of discipline. "spanking has worked very well for us," says Tim Holt, a 45-year-old insurance agent and the father of four children, ages 4 to 13, in Simpsonville, S.C., who notes that he and his wife spank very rarely. He recalls spanking his 7-year-old son, Scott, after Scott hit his brother in the head with a shoe and then lied to his father about it. "I pulled Scott aside. We discussed what he had done: Why is it wrong? What does God's law say? That we don't take our anger out on others." Then Holt put Scott over his knee and smacked him on his pants with a plastic glue stick. "It's something that gets his attention and provides a little bit of pain to his bottom."

Proponents include James Dobson, a psychologist and founder of Focus on the Family, who likens squeezing a child's shoulder or spanking his behind to discomfort that "works to shape behavior in the physical world." He writes in *The New Dare to Discipline:* "The minor pain that is associated with this deliberate misbehavior tends to inhibit it. . . . A boy or girl who knows love abounds at home will not resent a well-deserved spanking." But the subject generates more heat than just about any other child-rearing issue. Sweden banned spanking in 1979. The United Nations Committee on the Rights of the Child has been seeking a ban on corporal punishment worldwide since 1996.

The evidence. The debate roils academia, too. Murray Straus, a professor of sociology at the University of New Hampshire, says 110 studies have linked spanking to increased misbehavior in childhood as well as adult problems such as increased spousal abuse and depression. In February, Straus published research linking being spanked in childhood with an adult preference for sadomasochistic sex. Straus acknowledges that most of today's parents were themselves spanked as children but says that since spanking is no more effective than other discipline methods and can cause harm it's not worth the misery. Other researchers, including Diana Baumrind, a psychologist at the University of California-Berkeley, have found that children who were spanked occasionally had no more behavior problems than children who were never spanked. But Baumrind says regular reliance on physical punishment, as well as "impulsive and reactive spanking," causes harm to a child. The bottom line: Proponents of either position can come up with enough evidence to support their belief—but not enough to convince the other side.

Demonizing spanking may leave some parents feeling they must avoid *any* discipline that makes a child feel bad, says Lawrence Diller, a developmental pediatrician in Walnut Creek, Calif., who works with children with attention deficit hyperactivity disorder. He speculates that a more coherent disciplinary approach that includes an occasional well-timed swat can make the overall system more effective and could "make the difference in whether your child will be on Ritalin or not. You don't have to spank. But if you're using spanking as one of array of tools to get control of your kid, you're not hurting them in the long term."

—N.S.

But, paradoxically, not having limits has been proven to make children *more* defiant and rebellious, because they feel unsafe and push to see if parents will respond. Research since the 1960s on parenting styles has found that a child whose mom and dad are permissive is more likely to have problems in school and abuse drugs and alcohol as teenagers. "Parents ask their 1-year-olds what they want for dinner now," says Jean Twenge, an associate professor of psychology at San Diego State University and author of *Generation Me.* "No one ever said that a generation or two ago." Using surveys dating back to the 1930s, Twenge has found significant increases in reported symptoms of depression and anxiety among today's children and teenagers, compared with earlier generations. Suniya Luthar, a psychologist at Columbia University Teachers College, reported in 2003 that children who are showered with advantages are more likely to be depressed and anxious and to abuse drugs and alcohol than the norm. Luthar says that's probably because those children are under a lot of pressure to achieve at school and think that their parents value their achievements more than themselves. They also feel isolated from their parents.

Rule-setting works best when parents give simple, clear commands and discuss the family rules with kids well in advance of a conflict, according to Robert Hendren, a professor of psychiatry at the Medical Investigation of Neurodevelopmental Disorders Institute at the University of California-Davis and president of the American Academy of Child and Adolescent Psychiatry. A common recommendation for parents who fear coming off as a meanie: Let the child choose between two options when either choice is acceptable to the parent. A half-hour of Nintendo right after school, then homework? All homework before game time?

Consistency is also key. "I have to be very strict with myself and go over and tell him the rules and walk away," says Lauren Jordan, a stay-at-home mom in Essex Junction, Vt., whose 4-year-old son, Peter, would scream and hit Jordan and her husband, Sean, then kick the wall during timeout. "It felt out of control." Jordan signed up with Vermont's Behavior Therapy and Psychotherapy Center to learn Forehand's five-week process.

The first week was spent just "attending" to Peter, watching him play and commenting without telling the preschooler what to do. "He *loved* it," says Jordan, whose older son has autism and has required an outsize share of her energy. "I realized at that point that he needs this one-on-one attention." Jordan then had to learn to ignore Peter's minor bad behavior (such as screaming for attention while Mom is on the phone) and to not rush in to scold him during a timeout. "Consistency is the key. It's not easy," Jordan says. "But it's made our home a much happier place."

2. They're Overprotective

Teachers, coaches, and psychotherapists alike have noticed that parents today can't stand to see their children struggle or suffer a setback. So they're stepping in to micromanage everything from playground quarrels to baseball team positions to grades. Even bosses aren't immune. One owner of a New York public relations firm says he has gotten E-mails from parents telling him that's he's making their child work too much. The child in question is in his 20s.

"Many well-meaning parents jump in too quickly," says Robert Brooks, a clinical psychologist in Needham, Mass., and coauthor of *Raising Resilient Children.* "Resilient children realize that sometimes they will fail, make mistakes, have setbacks. They will attempt to learn from them." When parents intercede, Brooks says, "it communicates to the kid that 'I don't think you're capable of dealing with it.' We have to let kids experience the consequences of their behavior."

Otherwise, they may grow afraid to try. "I see a lot of kids who seem really unmotivated," says Kristen Gloff, 36, a clinical and school social worker in the Chicago area. "It's not that they're lazy. They don't want to fail."

3. They Nag. Lecture. Repeat. Then Yell.

If one verbal nudge won't get a kid to come to dinner, 20 surely will. Right? In fact, there's abundant evidence that humans tune out repeated commands. "So many parents think they have to get very emotionally upset, yell, threaten, use sarcasm," says Lynn Clark, a professor emeritus of psychology at Western Kentucky University and author of *SOS Help for Parents.* "The child imitates that behavior, and you get sassy talk."

Nagging also gives children "negative reinforcement," or an incentive—parental attention—to keep misbehaving. "I was kind of ignoring the good behavior, and every time he did something wrong, I would step in and give him attention," says Nancy Ailes, a 46-year-old stay-at-home mom in East Haven, Conn. She was frustrated with her 9-year-old son, Nick, who would melt down and throw things if the day's schedule changed, drag his feet about cleaning his room or doing homework, and call her "bad Mommy" if she complained.

Parent management training this spring at the Yale Child Conduct Center taught Ailes and her husband how to use positive reinforcement instead—to praise Nick immediately and enthusiastically. Now, when Nick is picking up his toys in the family room, she sits down, watches, and says: "Wow, that looks really nice!"

Ailes and her husband, David, also learned how to set up a reward system with points that Nick can cash in for Yu-Gi-Oh cards and Game Boy time and to back up the system with timeouts for bad behavior. Within three weeks, Ailes says, Nick had made

a complete turnaround. "Instead of doing things that make people unhappy," she says, "you do things that make them happy!"

4. They Praise Too Much— and Badly

It seems like a truism that praising children would make them feel good about themselves and motivate them to do better. But parents don't give children attaboys as often as they think, Kazdin says. And when they do, it's all too often either generic ("good job!") or centered on the person, not the task ("you're so smart!"). This kind of praise actually makes children less motivated and self-confident. In one experiment by Carol Dweck, a psychologist now at Stanford University, fifth graders who were praised for being intelligent, rather than making a good effort, actually made less of an effort on tests and had a harder time dealing with failure.

"It's so common now for parents to tell children that they're special," says Twenge. That fosters narcissism, she says, not self-esteem. Twenge thinks parents tell a child "You're special" when they really mean "You're special to me." Much better in every way, she says, to just say: "I love you."

5. They Punish Too Harshly

Although spanking has been deplored by child-development experts since the days of Dr. Spock in the 1940s, as many as 90 percent of parents think it's OK to spank young children, according to research by Murray Straus, a professor of sociology at the University of New Hampshire (more on the spanking controversy in the box). Kazdin and other behavioral researchers say parents commonly punish far more harshly than they need to.

After all, it's not supposed to be about payback, though that's often what's going on, says Jamila Reid, codirector of the Parenting Clinic at the University of Washington. The clinic's "The Incredible Years" program has been found in seven studies to improve children's behavior. "Often parents come looking for bigger sticks. We tell parents the word discipline means 'teach.' It's something to teach a child that there's a better way to respond."

Consider the fine art of the timeout. Parents often sabotage timeouts by lecturing or by giving hugs, according to Sheila Eyberg, a professor of psychology at the University of Florida. Her Parent-Child Interaction Therapy is used in many mental health clinics. Forehand and other researchers have spent many hours observing the use of timeout as a disciplinary strategy to determine exactly what makes it effective. The key finding: Discipline works best when it's immediate, mild, and brief, because it's then associated with the transgression and doesn't breed more anger and resentment. A timeout should last for just a few minutes, usually one minute for each year of age of the child.

Teenagers who have outgrown timeouts shouldn't lose a privilege for more than a day. Beyond that, the child's attitude shifts from regretting bad behavior to resenting the parent. "The punishment business isn't just ineffective," Kazdin says. "It leads to avoidance and escape. It puts a little wedge in the relationship between parent and child." Long groundings also make it more likely that the parents will relent after a few days. Better,

Kazdin says, to ask the child to practice good behavior, such as fixing something he damaged, in order to win privileges back.

6. They Tell Their Child How to Feel

Most parenting books focus on eradicating bad behavior. But in study after study, empathy for other people leads the list of qualities that people need to successfully handle relationships at school, at work, and in the family. Children need to think about how their own feelings will be affected by what they do, as well as the feelings of others, says Myrna Shure, a developmental psychologist at Drexel University and author of *Raising a Thinking Child.* "That is what will inhibit a child from hurting others, either physically or emotionally."

And parents, by telling children "you're fine" or "don't cry," deny children the chance to learn those lessons. "The child learns empathy through being empathized with," says Stanley Greenspan, a child psychiatrist in Chevy Chase, MD, whose most recent book, *Great Kids,* tells parents how to help their child develop 10 essential qualities for a happy life. Empathy, creativity, and logical thinking top the list. A simple "We're so sorry, we know how it feels" is enough.

"Modeling empathic behavior is really very important," says James Windell, a counselor with the juvenile court system in Oakland County, Mich., and author of *8 Weeks to a Well-Behaved Child.* "How you respond to your children's needs sets the stage. It's really easy to be a supportive parent when they bring home a straight-A report card. When they get a bad grade, that's when they really need our support."

7. They Put Grades and SATs Ahead of Creativity

An overemphasis on good grades can also distort the message about how and what children should learn. "We like kids to learn rules, and we want them to learn facts," says Greenspan. "We're impressed when they can read early or identify their shapes. It's much harder for us to inspire them to come up with a creative idea." Children who can think creatively are more likely to be able to bounce back if their first idea doesn't work. They also know it can take time and patience to come up with a good solution. The goal, says Greenspan, is not to have a child who knows how to answer questions but one who will grow up to ask the important questions.

Parents can help their children become independent thinkers by asking open-ended questions like: Can you think of another way to solve the problem with your teammate? Or ask a whining preschooler: Can you think of a different way to tell me what you want?

8. They Forget to Have Fun

"When I talk to families that aren't functioning so well, and I ask, how often do you laugh together, they say: We haven't laughed together for a long time," says Hendren. Those little signs of love and connection—a laugh, a song shared in the car—are, he says, signs of health.

Critical Thinking

1. What are the best ways to raise children?
2. Explain why parents must set limits but not micromanage their children.

From *U.S. News & World Report,* June 23, 2008, pp. 59–62,64. Copyright © 2008 by U.S. News & World Report, LP. Reprinted by permission via Wright's Media.

Introduction: The Next Wave of School Reform

PAUL GLASTRIS

The school reform movement—the decades-old bipartisan drive to improve public education with standards and high-stakes tests—might seem, on the surface at least, to be running out of steam. Its crowning achievement, George W. Bush's No Child Left Behind Act (NCLB), which shook up public schools after it was passed in 2001, is now widely seen as flawed and in need of a massive overhaul. Yet efforts to do so have been stalled for years on Capitol Hill because of political disagreements over how to proceed. With reform in limbo, the Obama administration has been reduced to passing out Get Out of Jail Free cards to countless school districts that face penalties for failing to meet the law's strict targets for improvement. Meanwhile, liberals who were always uncomfortable with using standardized tests to judge student and teacher performance are increasingly in revolt against the whole school reform movement. And conservatives who never liked the increased federal role in education brought by NCLB are agitating for a return to local control.

Yet looks can be deceiving. The truth is that the standards-and-testing model of school reform is far from dead. In fact, it's about to kick into a new high gear, in ways that will alter what happens in the nation's classrooms as fundamentally as NCLB did, and probably more so. Unlike previous waves of school reform, which were debated in Congress and covered in depth by the press, this next one is the product of compacts among states and a quiet injection of federal money—and has therefore garnered almost no national attention. Consequently, few Americans have any idea about the profound changes that are about to hit their children's schools.

The reforms will unfold in three stages, each of which is explored by an article in this report.

In the first stage, already well under way, almost every state is instituting something called the "common core standards," a demanding new set of shared benchmarks that define what students should know and be able to do at the end of each grade. These benchmarks will replace a jumble of widely varying and often weak state standards that have hitherto guided America's schools.

The second stage, hard on the heels of the first, is the development of a new set of high-stakes tests based on these new standards. These tests are already being crafted by university and state education department experts across the country, and are scheduled to be rolled out beginning in 2014. They will be fully computerized and far more demanding than anything most American schoolchildren have ever experienced.

The third stage, now being dreamed up in university and corporate labs, will see the rise of new kinds of computer-based learning software, often in the form of games, in which testing happens automatically as students play and work. When this software becomes available for classrooms a decade or more from now, learning and assessment will meld into a single process, and high-stakes testing as we know it will virtually disappear.

All three of these efforts are attempts to fix the flaws in the current standards-and-testing regime—the chief flaw being that it creates incentives for schools to aim too low. Existing state standards tend to force teachers to cover too much material shallowly. And existing tests tend to be cheap multiple-choice exams focused on assessing basic skills rather than higher-order thinking.

Of course, an alarming number of students lack those basic skills, especially poor and minority students. And the current standards-and-testing system can claim some credit for putting a significant dent in that problem. Since 1992, when states first started seriously imposing standards and high-stakes tests, African American eighth graders have gained 26 points, and Hispanic eighth graders 22 points, on the math portion of the federal National Assessment of Educational Progress (NAEP) test. That means both groups are roughly two and a half grade levels above where they were in 1992, a stunning if seldom-acknowledged improvement. Reading scores haven't risen as much: 12 points for black eighth graders, 13 for Hispanics. Still, that's more than a grade level higher than where these groups were twenty years ago—real progress.

The problem is that teaching and testing for basic skills also tends to lead to a dumbing down of the curriculum and to endless drilling for tests, which frustrates teachers, parents, and students alike. It also does little to improve students' ability to think critically and independently, solve complex problems, apply knowledge to novel situations, work in teams, and communicate effectively—abilities that students must have to succeed in college and, increasingly, the modern-day workplace.

Getting schools to impart these "deeper learning" capacities is precisely what the new wave of school reform aims to achieve. And there is good reason to hope the reforms work, because in many ways the competitiveness of the U.S. economy depends on it. On the Programme for International Student Assessment (PISA), a widely used international test that measures higher-order thinking and problem-solving skills, the United States falls in the middle of the pack among thirty-four developed countries in reading and science, and ranks below the average in math.

In a sense, this is nothing new. As far back as 1964, United States students scored relatively poorly in math and science compared to those in other nations. But we made up for deficiencies in quality with volume: for decades, America graduated a far larger percentage of its citizens from high school and college than did any other country. That advantage in degree attainment, however, has disappeared as other countries have caught up. The U.S. now ranks twelfth in the world in the percentage of its twenty-five- to thirty-four-year-olds with post-secondary degrees. We've fallen behind not because United States high school graduates aren't going on to college—that number has risen consistently—but because the percentage completing college has hardly budged. That's a sign, in part, that too many U.S. students are leaving high school ill-prepared academically. All of this is happening, notes labor economist Anthony Carnevale of Georgetown University, at a time when the globalization of labor markets and the elimination of routine jobs—even reasonably skilled ones—by digital technology means that more and more jobs in the future will require creativity and higher-order-thinking skills.

Is it possible for a large, highly developed nation to make the kinds of changes necessary to boost the critical-thinking skills of its students? Consider the case of Germany. In 2000, Germans learned that their schools, which were long assumed to be first rate, ranked below the average when compared to other countries on the PISA, largely because of the poor quality of schooling offered to less-advantaged citizens. The shock of that news led to a series of reforms, including common national academic standards and new assessments tied to those standards. The result: from 2003 to 2009 Germany added 10 points to its math scores and 6 points to its reading scores on the PISA—on a scale in which 500 is the international average.

That may not seem like much, but over time such progress can deliver huge economic gains. In a 2010 study, economists Eric A. Hanushek of Stanford University and Ludger Woessmann of the University of Munich found that differences in PISA scores and similar measures of cognitive skills explain a great deal of the difference in growth rates among advanced economies from 1960 to 2000. They further calculated that if the United States could raise its average PISA score 25 points by 2030, it could increase its GDP by $45 trillion over the lifespan of children born in 2010.

Could the new tests and common core standards be the secrets to achieving results like this? Obviously it's too early to say. But it's hard to think of another set of government policies already in the pipeline that could more dramatically impact the long-term strength of the U.S. economy. So it's all the more curious that the new tests and standards have garnered almost no press attention, especially in a presidential election year in which the future of the economy is front and center. That's a testament not only to the way these policies slipped in under the political radar, but also to the fact that writing about abstruse subjects like norm-referenced testing and PISA scores is hard to do (believe me). But as **Washington Monthly** contributing editor James Fallows once wrote, the mission of serious journalism is "to make what's important interesting." By that definition, the authors of the three pieces in this report—Robert Rothman, Susan Headden, and Bill Tucker—have produced very good journalism indeed.

Critical Thinking

1. Why are American schools failing?

2. How should American schools be reformed?

3. Do you believe that Glastris has the right answer? Explain.

PAUL GLASTRIS is the editor in chief of the **Washington Monthly.**

Is $600 Billion Enough?

Peter W. Cookson Jr.

Today's new austerity may have an upside if it prods schools to embrace new technologies that cut costs and improve learning.

It is crunch time for public education. Several storms are converging to create a hurricane of educational instability: sharply declining revenues, intense international competition, outdated approaches to teaching and learning, and a significant achievement gap between white students and their African-American and Hispanic peers. Seemingly unable to get to the root causes of what is plaguing the schools, we keep spinning our policy wheels while also spending a great deal of money—$600 billion a year.

The National Center for Education Statistics reports that the nation's per pupil expenditures have doubled in inflation-adjusted terms since 1970, while scores on standardized assessments of student achievement have remained essentially flat. In 1971 the average reading score for nine-year-olds on the National Assessment of Educational Progress was 208 (on a scale of 0 to 500); in 2009 it was 221, an improvement, yes, but still mediocre at best. Moreover, it appears that the longer students stay in school, the smaller the learning gains. Seventeen-year-olds averaged a score of 285 on the NAEP reading test in 1971; nearly 40 years later, they scored only three points better.

Today, the average yearly cost of educating a public school student is more than $10,000. Topping the expenditure scale is New York State, at $17,000, and at the bottom is Utah, at $6,000. Yet on average, Utah students do as well as their New York counterparts on standardized tests. To be sure, interstate and intradistrict funding inequities are sometimes glaring and very likely contribute to achievement gaps between whites and blacks and between other groups. Few policymakers advocate abandoning the goal of finance equity. But on the whole, simply spending more money is not likely to produce greater student learning.

In any case, money is going to be increasingly hard to come by. Nearly every state and school district is grappling with budget shortfalls, and there is little reason to expect much relief in the foreseeable future. Financial constraints have caused states and districts to experiment with a variety of cost-cutting strategies, including bigger classes, shorter school days, fewer school days per year, and reduced extracurricular and after-school programs. We don't know yet how these measures will affect student learning, but we can be certain of one thing: They are not going to usher in the era of breakthrough achievement we desperately need.

Today's climate of austerity is forcing us to grapple with the reality that a good deal of our current education spending is ill directed. We keep investing in 19th-century classrooms even though today's students are 21st-century learners. One promising alternative to business as usual is the creation of cost-effective 21st-century classrooms in which new communication technologies are blended with traditional face-to-face instruction. Teachers will always be the key to unlocking students' imaginations, but standing in front of a 21st-century class and lecturing is neither pedagogically sound nor economically efficient.

Integrating technology into the classroom does not mean putting kids in front of computers all day or turning schools into academic call centers where teachers are technicians and students are "end users." Technology can be a trap. In the 1990s, media scholar Neil Postman of New York University warned against "technopoly," a state of mind that "consists in the deification of technology, finds its satisfactions in technology, and takes its orders from technology." But if we treat technology as a partner, it can facilitate individualized learning and thus stimulate intellectual curiosity and academic ambition. We know that students have different learning styles, skills, abilities, and dispositions, and that they progress and mature at different rates. Common sense and research tell us that if we can customize students' educational experiences, achievement will increase. Truly individualized instruction is the age-old dream of education; technology puts it within our grasp.

In the current industrial-era model of education, all students are exposed to the same (or nearly the same) educational treatment, as if they were identical units moving along an assembly line. At the end of the treatment, they are tested competitively in a yearly exercise of what passes for quality control. This is the system that is failing us, as well as the young people it is supposed to prepare for productive and meaningful lives.

Imagine a middle school student named Alicia. She is about to enter the eighth grade and encounter algebra for the first time. Algebra is not just another subject in Alicia's academic career; it is a gatekeeper course. Failure to master the subject means exclusion from advanced mathematics courses and reduces her chances of admission to a selective college.

Let's assume that Alicia is an average math student. In most situations, she would have only two possible pathways: placement in a "real" algebra class with other mathematically competent students or in a general math class, a kind of "algebra for dummies." Tests largely determine which path Alicia will find herself on. If she is placed in the "real" class, she has a good shot at succeeding in high school; if she is placed in the general class, there is a high probability that her academic career will go nowhere. And students placed in lower academic tracks can see the writing on the wall. That is one reason why nearly 50 percent of teenagers in urban areas leave school before graduation, choosing, however unwisely, to look for work rather than see their rather empty education through.

So the stakes are high for Alicia and for us, because in the era of global competition the wasting of talent is not only a personal tragedy, it is a national security issue. We cannot expect to successfully compete internationally if many of our students fail to complete high school while others fail to achieve their full potential even as they hang on to earn a diploma.

What if we had a different approach? It might look like this: When Alicia is about to enter eighth grade, she is given a battery of diagnostic tests to assess her preparedness for the conceptual thinking required by algebra. The results are not used to slot Alicia into column A or column B. Rather, a computer program is able to integrate data about her aptitudes and abilities to create a unique learning profile. Teachers, with the assistance of intelligent software, are then able to create a customized, individualized algebra curriculum for Alicia by drawing on a wide variety of digitized resources, some from online education companies, universities, and other outside sources, and some developed by teachers at her school.

Alicia's individualized algebra course is dynamic; after she completes her assignments every day she takes a short quiz, perhaps in the form of a game, which gauges her level of comprehension. This allows her teacher to adjust Alicia's next lesson in order to address those areas where she needs more work or a different approach. Her teacher has a large library of digitized alternatives from which to choose, and Alicia's program allows her to make certain choices herself. She is participating in the creation of her own education. Unlike weekly tests that have little diagnostic utility.

Alicia's daily quizzes and games are adaptive; that is, they adjust themselves to her strengths and weaknesses and prescribe a course of study to address her specific learning needs. None of this means that students like Alicia are no longer part of a classroom community or that their only learning comes through a computer. Teachers in "blended" classrooms such as these, like police officers using modern community policing methods, do spend more time than their counterparts of old managing and analyzing data, focusing on problem areas, and carefully charting progress. This is what enables them to use their time more effectively on the "street," talking and listening to flesh-and-blood students and guiding them in their education.

Recently I visited Intermediate School 228 in Brooklyn, New York, where an experimental blended math program called the School of One is being implemented. Just outside the big white doors that lead to the School of One wing, an old-fashioned classroom with battered chairs and heavy desks has been preserved as a kind of case study of what the School of One is not. It is a bit unsettling, since such traditional classrooms served generations of earlier students well, and indeed some of their principles still animate places like the School of One.

Beyond the white doors, however, is a classroom that would have been unrecognizable to a teacher or student of 50 years ago. I.S. 228 students come to this classroom only for their math classes. Kids move around, talk, listen to teachers, occasionally talk back to teachers, and, yes, even hack around a little in the open and airy space. Gone are the rows of desks facing the teacher and blackboard. Movable bookshelves create flexible spaces where students can work together or with instructors in groups of various sizes. Some students collaborate, others work alone on computers. A teacher circulates, spending a few minutes with one student, perhaps a larger block of time instructing a group.

Journalist Ta-Nehisi Coates wrote about his visit to a School of One campus in the Bronx in The Atlantic last year, remembering his own experience as a young man who had struggled mightily in school. "By the time I was in high school, we were using the computer lab once a week for math. But we were using it the same way we used pen and paper—a teacher at the front of the class and all of us following along. The computer lab bored me as much as the chalkboard. . . . I thought I was lazy (and maybe I was) and lacking the will to learn. But as I watched the kids at I.S. 339 working at their own pace and in their own way, I wondered if all I had ever really needed was the equivalent of a warm hug from a cold algorithm."

One of the notable experiments in blended learning is Rocketship Education, a nonprofit charter school network that opened its first school in San Jose, California, in 2007. The five Rocketship elementary schools were designed from the ground up to support customized learning. They are hardly enclaves of privilege. Ninety percent of the students qualify for free or reduced-price lunches, and 75 percent speak English as a second language. With an explicit mission of closing the achievement gap, Rocketship has already seen two of its sites ranked among the 15 top-performing schools serving high-poverty areas in California.

Experiments in blended learning have caught the eye of policymakers and private-sector innovators. President Barack Obama paid a highly publicized visit earlier this year to TechBoston Academy, a blended curriculum public school for grades 6–12 in Boston. The United States Department of Education's 2010 National Education Technology Plan calls for bringing "state-of-the-art technology into learning to enable, motivate, and inspire all students." Education entrepreneur Chris Whittle and his partners are planning to open the first in a planned international network of private schools using a blended curriculum in 2012.

Integrating technology into classrooms will be no easier than it has been in offices and factories. Finding the right ways to shape human-computer interactions is a delicate task, especially when the humans are children. Different approaches will be needed for children of different ages. There will be—and already have been—disappointments and mistakes.

No comprehensive research exists on the impact of computers on education, and those studies that have been conducted yielded conflicting results. That is no surprise. We are only in the early stages of learning how to create effective blended classrooms, and there are many pitfalls—from techno-utopianism and our weakness for thinking that complex problems can be solved with easy technological fixes, to the challenge of identifying the useful technologies amid the mountains of ill-conceived and simply shoddy software and edu-gadgets being peddled by eager companies.

Can we afford such experiments in a time of increasing austerity? Up-front investments will be needed. But over the longer term, blended schools can produce considerable economies. Textbooks are an obvious place to begin. They cost billions of dollars every year. Texas alone budgeted more than $800 million for textbooks in 2010. Information technology, meanwhile, gets radically cheaper every year. Additional savings can be realized through the use of open-source curricula, shared lesson plans, online tutoring, and other measures. In time, fewer teachers will be required as large, unmanageable, industrially organized classrooms disappear. Even in today's classrooms, research shows that teachers with the right training and support can lead quite large classrooms without diminishing student achievement. (Reducing class size, a perennial favorite reform in public opinion surveys, does not automatically improve student performance. The only consistent evidence of a positive effect indicates that kindergarten and primary-level students do better in classrooms that do not exceed 15 students.)

Exploring how blended classrooms can individualize teaching and learning while saving money is a reform strategy that has several virtues. New technologies coupled with new thinking about education can expand students' opportunities to learn, enable implementation of new forms of teaching more in keeping with the learning styles of today's students, and squeeze much better results from our education funds. Six hundred billion dollars is a lot of money; cutting back spending on nonessentials and investing in innovative teaching and learning may be one way to reduce costs and boost achievement at the same time. Perhaps we can turn the energy of the hurricane that is engulfing public education to positive ends by redirecting that energy toward the future.

A School of One program in New York City is one of many efforts to find effective ways to bring technology into the classroom.

Critical Thinking

1. Is spending more money critical to improving our schools?
2. How will new technologies help improve our schools?

PETER W. COOKSON JR., a sociologist and educational consultant, is the former president of TC Innovations at Teachers College, Columbia University, and the author of several books, including *School Choice: The Struggle for the Soul of American Education* (1994) and *Sacred Trust: A Children's Education Bill of Rights,* published earlier this year.

From *Washington Monthly*, Autumn 2011. Copyright © 2011 by Washington Monthly Publishing, LLC, 1319 F St. NW, Suite 710, Washington DC 20004. (202)393-5155. Reprinted by permission. www.washingtonmonthly.com

A Thousand Years Young

AUBREY DE GREY

An "anti-aging activist" identifies the medical and biochemical advances that could eventually eliminate all the wear and tear that our bodies and minds suffer as we grow old. Those who undergo continuous repair treatments could live for millennia, remain healthy throughout, and never fear dying of old age.

Let me first say very explicitly: I don't work on longevity. I work on health. People are going to live longer as a result of the therapies I will describe, but extended longevity is a side effect—a consequence of keeping people healthy. There is no way in hell that we are going to keep people alive for a long time in a frail state. People will live longer only if we succeed in keeping them healthy longer.

The problem of aging is unequivocally humanity's worst medical problem. Roughly 100,000 people worldwide die every day of it, and there's an awful lot of suffering that happens before you die. But I feel that the defeat of aging in the foreseeable future is a realistic proposition. We will have medicine that will get aging under control to the same level that we now have most infectious diseases under control.

This article will describe what aging is, what regenerative medicine is, and what the various alternative approaches are to combat aging and postpone the ill health of old age. I'll then go into the details of the approach that I feel we need to take and what my expectations are for the future.

Regenerative medicine is any medical intervention that seeks to restore some part of the body—or the whole body—to how it was before it suffered some kind of damage. It could be damage that happened as the result of an acute injury, such as spinal cord damage. But it could also be damage that accumulated as a chronic condition over a long period of time.

Aging is a side effect of being alive in the first place. *Metabolism* is the word that biologists use to encompass all the aspects of being alive—all the molecular and cellular and systemic processes that keep us going from one day to the next and from one year to the next.

Ongoing lifelong side effects of metabolism—i.e., *damages*—are created throughout life. For whatever reason, damage is not repaired when it occurs. So damage accumulates. For a long time, the amount of damage is tolerable, and the metabolism just carries on. But eventually, damage becomes sufficiently extensive that it gets in the way of metabolism. Then metabolism doesn't work so well, and *pathologies*—all the things that go wrong late in life, all the aspects of age-related ill health—emerge and progress.

Geriatrics Versus Gerontology

Traditionally, there have been two themes within the study of aging that aim to actually do something about this process. One is the *geriatrics* approach, which encompasses pretty much everything that we have today in terms of medical treatments for the elderly.

The geriatrics approach is all about the pathology. It focuses on old people in whom the pathologies are already emerging, and strives to slow down their progression so that it takes longer for those pathologies to reach a life-threatening stage.

The *gerontology* approach, on the other hand, says that prevention is better than cure. This approach assumes that it will be more effective to dive in at an earlier point in the chain of events and clean up metabolism so that it creates these various types of damage at a slower rate than it naturally would. The effect would be to postpone the age at which damage reaches the level of abundance that is pathogenic.

The two approaches both sound pretty promising, but they're really not. The problem with the geriatrics approach is that aging is awfully chaotic, miserable, and complicated. There are many things that go wrong with people as they get older, and they tend to happen at much the same time. These problems interact, exacerbating each other, and damage accumulates. Even later in life, as damage continues to accumulate, the pathologies of old age become progressively more and more difficult to combat.

The geriatric approach is thus intervening too late in the chain of events. It's better than nothing, but it's not much better than nothing.

So that leaves us with the gerontology approach. Unfortunately, the gerontology approach has its own problem: Metabolism is complicated. What we know about how metabolism works is completely dwarfed by the utterly astronomical amount that we *don't* know about how metabolism works. We have no prospect whatsoever of being able to interfere in this process in a way that does not simply do more harm than good.

A Maintenance Approach

There are some Volkswagen Bugs that are 50 years old or more and still running. And the reason is because those VW Bugs have been extraordinarily well maintained. If you maintain your car only as well as the law requires, then it will only last 15 years or so. But if you do a lot more, then you can do a lot better. Maintenance works.

Now what does that tell us about the human body? Well, quite a lot, because the human body is a machine. It's a really complicated machine, but it's still a machine. So there is a third way of combating aging by postponing age-related ill health. This is the *maintenance* approach. We go in and periodically repair the damage that metabolism creates, so as to prevent that damage from accumulating and reaching the level that causes the pathology of old age to emerge and to progress.

Maintenance is a much more promising approach than either geriatrics or gerontology. First, the maintenance approach is preemptive, so it doesn't have this problem of this downward spiral of the geriatrics approach.

Second, the maintenance approach avoids the problem of the gerontology approach because it does not attempt to intervene with metabolism; we merely fix up the consequences. In other words, we let metabolism create these various types of damage at the rate that it naturally does, and then repair the damages before they cause pathology. We can get away with not understanding very much at all about how metabolism creates damage. We just have to characterize the damage itself and figure out ways to repair it.

That's pretty good news, but it gets better. It also turns out that damage is simpler than its causes or its consequences. All the phenomena that qualify as damage can be classified into one of seven major categories:

- Junk inside cells.
- Junk outside cells.
- Too few cells.
- Too many cells.
- Chromosome mutations.
- Mitochondria mutations.
- Protein cross-links.

By "junk inside cells," I am referring to the molecular byproducts of normal biologic processes that are created in the cell and that the cell, for whatever reason, does not have the machinery to break down or to excrete. Those byproducts simply accumulate, and eventually the cell doesn't work so well. That turns out to be the main cause of cardiovascular disease and of macular degeneration.

"Junk outside cells" means things like senile plaques in Alzheimer's disease. This creates the same molecular damage, but in this case it is in the spaces between cells.

"Too few cells" simply means cells are dying and not being automatically replaced by the division of other cells. This is the cause of Parkinson's disease, the particular part of the brain in which neurons happen to die more rapidly than in most parts of the brain and they're not replaced. When there are too few of them, that part of the brain doesn't work so well.

But here's the really good news. We actually have a pretty good idea how to fix all of these types of damage. Here is the same list of types of damage, and on the right is the set of approaches that I feel are very promising for fixing them:

Damage	Treatment
Junk inside cells	transgenic microbial hydrolases
Junk outside cells	Phagocytosis by immune stimulation
Too few cells (cell loss)	cell therapy
Too many cells (death-resistant cells)	suicide genes and immune stimulation
Chromosome mutations	telomerase/ALT gene deletion plus periodic stem-cell reseeding
Mitochondria mutations	allotopic expression of 13 proteins
Protein cross-links	AGE-breaking molecules and enzymes

Stem-cell therapy replaces those cells that the body cannot replace on its own. That includes joint degeneration and muscular-skeletal problems. For example, arthritis ultimately comes from the degeneration of the collagen and other extracellular material in the joints, which happens as a result of insufficient regeneration of that tissue.

For some other medical conditions, such as Alzheimer's, we need to restore the functions of those cells that are already there by getting rid of the garbage accumulating outside them. Toward that purpose, there are phase-three clinical trials for the elimination of senile plaques in the brains of Alzheimer's patients. This is a technology using vaccination that we at the SENS Foundation are extending to the elimination of other types of extracellular garbage.

In fact, we now have an enormous amount of detail about how we're going to reverse each of the seven categories of age-related damage, so that's why I feel that my estimates of how long it's going to take to get there are likely to be borne out accurately.

The SENS Foundation: Doing Something About Aging

I'm the chief officer of a 501 (c) 3 public charity based in California. The mission of the SENS Foundation is to develop, promote, and enable widespread access to regenerative medicine as solutions to the disabilities and diseases of aging.

Is there any competition in this work? Are other people trying other things? The short answer is, Not really. There are other people, of course, looking at ways to postpone aging and age-related ill health. But regenerative medicine is really the only game in town when we're talking about serious postponement of age-related ill health. And SENS Foundation really is the hub of that concept.

We are a charity, so if you are a billionaire, please see me! But of course it's not just money we need. We need people's time and expertise. If you're a biologist, work on relevant things. Write to us and ask us for advice about what to work on, because we need more manpower in this area. If you're a conference organizer, have me to speak. If you're a journalist, come and interview me. It's all about getting the word out.

—Aubrey de Grey

Details: The SENS Foundation, www.sens.org; e-mail foundation @ sens.org.

Case in Point: Cleaning the Cellular Garbage

I'm going to talk about one example: the garbage that accumulates inside cells. I'm going to explain what *transgenic microbial hydrolases* are.

White blood cells, called macrophages, sweep along a healthy adult's artery walls to clean up miscellaneous detritus, typically lipo- protein particles that were transporting cholesterol around the body from one place to another and that got stuck in the artery wall. Macrophages are very good at coping with cholesterol, but they are not so good at coping with certain derivatives of cholesterol, such as oxysterols. These contaminants end up poisoning macrophages. The macrophages become unable even to cope with native cholesterol, and then they themselves break down, lodging in the artery walls. This is the beginning of an atherosclerotic plaque. The results are cardiovascular disease, heart attacks, or strokes. In the eye, this phenomenon causes macular degeneration.

To combat this problem, we might adapt bioremediation technology from environmental decontamination. The technology that is used to break down pollutants in the environment could be adapted for biomedical purposes, breaking down the body's contaminants.

If we could apply this bioremediation process to our own cells, we could combat the initial process that turns young people into old people in the first place. A very simple idea. The question is, does it work? Bioremediation for getting rid of pollutants works really well: It's a thriving commercial discipline.

There are a number of oxidized derivatives of cholesterol, but the nastiest in abundance and toxicity is 7-ketocholesterol—public enemy number one in atherosclerosis. We have tried "feeding" it to many different strains of bacteria. Most of them can't do anything with it, but we've found two strains of bacteria that gorge themselves on it. After only 10 days, the material is completely gone.

The next step is to figure out how these bacteria are able to do this from a genetic basis. From there, we could try to turn 7-ketocholesterol back into native cholesterol. But there are other steps that we can use—remember that I said we're looking to avoid the problem of things neither being broken down nor excreted. There are modifications that we can make to compounds that are toxic that simply promote their excretion rather than promoting their degradation.

So that's all pretty good news. But don't get me wrong. This is really hard. This is a very ambitious, long-term project. The processes we hope to develop must work in vivo. What we are seeking is a truly definitive, complete cure for cardiovascular disease and for other pathologies caused by the accumulation of molecular garbage inside cells.

Escape Velocity: From Longevity to Immortality?

I do not claim that any of the work I've just described is going to be a "cure" for aging. I claim, rather, that it's got a good chance of adding 30 years of extra healthy life to people's lives. I call that *robust human rejuvenation*. And 30 years is better than nothing, but it sure does not equate to defeating aging completely. So what's the rest of my story?

The rest of the story is that it's not something that's going to work just on people who haven't been conceived yet. It's stuff that is going to work on people who are already middle-aged or older when the therapies arrive.

This is fundamentally what it all comes down to. The maintenance approach is so cool because repairing damage buys time.

At age zero, people start off with not much damage. Time goes on, they age, damage accumulates, reserve is depleted, and eventually, they get down to a certain point—the frailty threshold—and that's when pathologies start to happen. Then they're not long for this world.

Now take someone who is in middle age. You have therapies that are pretty good, but not perfect, at fixing the damage. They can be rejuvenated, but not all the way. These therapies do not reduce the rate at which damage is created. Aging happens at the normal rate.

Then we reapply the same therapies again and again. But consider that the interval between the first and second applications of these therapies to some particular individual may be 15 to 20 years. That's a long time in biomedical technology, and it means that the person is going to get new and improved therapies that will not only fix the types of damage that they could fix 15 years previously, but also fix some types of damage that they could not fix 15 years previously.

So after the second rejuvenation, our hero is not only more thoroughly rejuvenated than he would be if he'd gotten the old therapies, but he's actually more rejuvenated than he was when he got the old therapies, even though at that point he was chronologically younger. Now we see this phenomenon where we don't hit diminishing returns on additional therapies. People over the long term will be getting progressively younger as they're getting chronologically older. They'll remain far away from reaching the frailty threshold, however long that they live. They will only be subjected to the risks of death and ill health that affect young adults. They never become more susceptible to ill health simply as a result of having been born a long time ago.

There's some minimum rate at which we have to improve the comprehensiveness of these therapies in order for the general trend in increased life span to be upwards rather than downwards. And that minimum rate is what I call *longevity escape velocity*. It's the rate at which these rejuvenation therapies need to be improved in terms of comprehensiveness following that first step—the first-generation therapies that give robust human regeneration—in order to stay one step ahead of the problem and to outpace the accumulation of damage that they cannot yet repair.

So is it realistic? Are we likely actually to reach longevity escape velocity and to maintain it? We are. Consider powered flight as an illustrated example: There are very big differences between fundamental breakthroughs and incremental refinements of those breakthroughs. Fundamental breakthroughs are very hard to predict. Mostly people think they're not going to happen right up until they already have happened.

Incremental refinements, meanwhile, are very much more predictable. Leonardo da Vinci probably thought he was only a couple of decades away from getting off the ground. He was wrong. But once the Wright brothers got there, progress was ridiculously rapid. It only took 24 years for someone to fly solo across the Atlantic (that was Lindbergh), 22 more years until the first commercial jet liner, and 20 more years until the first supersonic airlines.

Can we actually give more direct evidence that we are likely to achieve longevity escape velocity? I believe that we can.

An Age-Busting Virtuous Cycle

A few years ago I worked with others on a computer simulation of the aging process to see what the impact would be of these interventions coming in at a realistic schedule. We started by imagining a population of adults who were all born in 1999. Everyone is alive at age zero and almost everyone survives until age 50 or 60, at which point they start dropping like flies; hardly anyone gets beyond 100.

Next, we imagined another population whose intrinsic risk of death at any given age is the same as for the first, but who are receiving these therapies. But they only start receiving them when they are already 80 years old. That population's survival rate will actually mostly coincide with the first population's survival rate, because obviously half the population or so is dead by age 80 and those who are still living are already in a reasonably bad way.

But what if population number two started getting these therapies 10 years earlier, when they're only 70? Initially, the same story is the case—there is not a lot of benefit. But gradually, the therapies get the upper hand. They start to impose genuine rejuvenation on these people so that they become biologically younger and less likely to die. Some of them reach 150, by which time they have very little chance of dying of *any* age-related cause. Eventually, there is exactly no such risk.

And if they're 60 years old when the therapies begin? Then almost half of them will get to that point. So we calculated, group by group.

Here's the real kicker: I was ludicrously over-pessimistic in the parameters that I chose for this simulation. I said that we would assume that the therapy would only be doubled in their efficacy every 42 years. Now, 42 years: That's the difference between Lindbergh's *Spirit of St. Louis* and the *Concorde!* But even then, we unambiguously see longevity escape velocity.

So it's inescapable. If and when we do succeed in developing these rejuvenation therapies that give us those first couple of decades more of health and the postponement of age-related ill health, then we will have done the hard part. The sky is the limit after that.

Here is what it means. At the moment, the world record for life span is 122. We won't be getting anyone who is 150 until such time as we do develop these technologies that give us robust human rejuvenation. But we will have done the hard part, so people not much younger than that will be able to escape aging indefinitely, living even to age 1,000.

A thousand is not pulled out of the air. It's simply the average age—plus or minus a factor of two—that people would live to if we already didn't have aging, if the only risks of death were the same risks that currently afflict young adults in the Western world today.

Should we be developing these therapies? We are ignorant about the circumstances within which humanity of the future will be deciding whether to use these technologies or not. It could actually be a no-brainer that they will want to use them. And if we have prevented them from using them by not developing them in time, then future generations won't be very happy. So it seems to me that we have a clear moral obligation to develop these technologies so as to give humanity of the future the choice. And the sooner, the better.

Critical Thinking

1. Explain how future technologies will be able to overcome the aging process and keep us young.

2. What moral and social questions would such technologies raise?

AUBREY DE GREY is a biomedical gerontologist and chief science officer of the SENS Foundation (www.sens.org). He is the author (with Michael Rae) of *Ending Aging* (St. Martin's Press, 2007) and editor-in-chief of the journal *Rejuvenation Research*. This article draws from his presentation at WorldFuture 2011 in Vancouver.

From Hospital to "Healthspital"

A Better Paradigm for Health Care

Hospitals should not simply be places where people go to get well (or, worse, where they go to die). Future hospitals could become wellness information centers and proactive partners in community well-being, says a practicing orthopedic surgeon.

FRANK W. MALETZ

Is health-care delivery in the United States so broken that it cannot be repaired, remediated, rejuvenated, reformed, or reorganized? Should all existing delivery mechanisms be torn down so we can start from scratch?

My unequivocal answer is *no* to creative destruction, but creative rethinking is imperative. Nowhere on the planet is there a "perfect delivery system" for health-care modeling. In the United States, what is currently called a "system" is certainly not one in the sense of an ecosystem—i.e., controlled, sustainable, natural, with known inputs and outputs, with precise and defined resources and resource management, and with holistic feedback loops. There should also be within the ecosystem a balanced and proportionate response to all perturbations. A health-delivery system requires open adjustability.

The current U.S. health-delivery system does have many strengths: strong expertise at universities and other research hubs. Its free-market structure for product development and dissemination is inventive and innovative. Its safety is ensured through oversight by the U.S. Food and Drug Administration and organizations such as the Joint Commission. The robust National Institutes of Health provides funding and research prioritization. We now also have the social networking tools (wikis, Facebook, Twitter, LinkedIn, and the like) to deploy seamless and remarkable change on the magnitude of a paradigm shift.

But the biggest asset of the current system is the network of 5,010 community hospitals that deliver care to unique individuals locally, one provider to one patient in need, day or night, weekend or holiday. Thus, the United States already has the fundamental building blocks for a strong, personalized health-care-delivery system. So what else is needed?

Goals for Health: Elements of a Redesigned Approach

According to the Institute of Medicine report "Cross the Quality Chasm: A New Health System for the 21st Century," the U.S. healthcare system should strive to effect the following changes:

- Redesign care processes.
- Make effective use of information technology (IT).
- Improve knowledge and skills management.
- Develop effective teams.
- Coordinate care across patient condition, service, and settings.
- Use performance and outcome measurement for continuous quality improvement and accountability.

Reforming health care is a ubiquitous topic in the national dialogue because of the amount of resources that health consumes—16% of GDP. For all the ideas and opinions brought forth, however, all we seem to get is more GDP devoted to the problem, with partial solutions that get traction, then fizzle, doing little to improve quality or reduce the chaos in the system. Then the blame game begins: Rising costs are the "fault" of providers, or of insurers, attorneys, pharmaceutical and product companies, patient demands and expectations, for-profit hospitals, or government leaders who lack will.

It is time now for a true health renaissance, with constructive, holistic, integral, paradigm-shifting thinking and action. I believe that, until we can fix the delivery systems, we cannot begin to correct the reimbursement mechanisms.

What we Already know about Health

First, we know that prevention is more cost-effective than treatment. Emergency-room visits are more expensive than routine maintenance. Chronic disorders such as diabetes, hypertension, heart disease, strokes, and renal failure consume an inordinate share of health-care dollars. Smoking cigarettes is bad. Obesity and nutritional deficiencies are epidemic. Fruitless, futile care at the end of life dominates a large proportion of the Medicare allocation. Reckless behaviors are responsible for much loss of productive and functional young lives. Cure and precision diagnosis are much more desired than mere control, maintenance, or palliation.

We also know that waste and redundancy in a paper-based information system have extraordinary costs both in real dollars and in time that could be allocated much more productively. A systematized, constantly updated, searchable, linkable database available at each point of care would reduce waste, repetition, redundancy, and the tendency for hand-off errors. Care could then be coordinated among all providers.

On the positive side, we know that workers who are healthy function more productively. Jobs, income, and reliable, portable health-insurance benefits add to security and productivity. Happy, contented people live longer and better, and many people already spend huge amounts of money on a host of programs to improve their health and well-being.

We know that regular exercise, especially aerobic, improves clarity, mental functioning, and wellness. Having a meaningful, fulfilled, goal-directed life and trying to contribute to society also increase longevity. And meeting our basic needs, including shelter, nutrition, and clothing, and maintaining appropriate levels of stress, balance, and moderation, are essential ingredients for physical and mental well-being.

Thus, the goal is not simply to eliminate sickness or delay death. We must take a much more holistic and expansive view of health care that embraces wellness and enrichment, a view that is flexible and that adopts the best practice from moment to moment.

Hospitals Today

Hospitals and sanitaria were developed to house the sick and treat or quarantine the diseased, deformed, or demented. Today, care is usually delivered locally to one patient by one provider at a time. Community hospitals provide the vast majority of the contact visits. Patients are generally not fluent in health-related matters, and this lack of understanding leads to major compliance failures with best advice and recommendations.

Providers are not infallible. Patient problems are inherently complex, and there are many unknowns. Medicine itself is becoming more complex. Natural healing using biological, biochemical, and immunologic enhancing remedies will function more predictably than artificial implants, prosthetics, xenograft replacements, and the like, but we are on the verge of advanced treatments with nanotechnology, bioengineering, genomics, proteomics, metabolomics, stem cells, and immunomodulation. Such advances bring us closer to cures and disease elimination.

Hospitals could do more to experimentally model an integrated, holistic health-delivery system that effects a real shift. They would collate the best research and brilliant idea production; incorporate the best of wellness, well-being, natural, and alternative options; improve oversight of chronic debilitating conditions; and mobilize and coordinate effective preventive strategies.

We have the tools to craft a better more healthful future and enable more-productive lives for everyone on the planet. The first step does not require much more than a creative paradigm shift in thinking and approach—a paradigm I call *Healthspital 2.0.*™

Elements for Integration

The biggest need is for data and information management. The needs for privacy and confidentiality of health information have not disappeared in the age of social networking, with people's growing desire to be heard, noticed, and connected. Thus, rather than locking down all health information as a matter of privacy, we need to reconstruct laws regarding inappropriate use of data, such as in the discriminatory use of genetic information.

Seamless availability and transfer of health knowledge allows in-depth knowledge of confounding variables, reduces redundancy, and potentially eliminates hand-off errors. A computerized health "passport" would serve as a template and allow interconnectivity, not just benefiting the patient, but also allowing broader public-health research to be performed. This systemization of information would be able to highlight best outcomes and best practices through true tracking and social networking.

The Healthspital model also requires more-effective use of expert systems. With integrated data management, experts could render opinions from afar on questions within the database. Doctors and other practitioners would have access to remote monitoring, enabling them to render remote advice. They could find answers to questions and discover best practices, as well as share their own discoveries, ideas, and best practices. Innovation could be instantly disseminated globally.

Patients and families will more easily engage with extensive information and support networks, and self-education would expand.

Healthspitals in the Community

Each Healthspital would appreciate the norms, mores, and expectations of the community it serves on issues such as end-of-life ministrations. Dialogue could begin in earnest regarding hospice services. Part of the Healthspital's mission could be to celebrate each patient as a life well lived, honoring individual care preferences during life-and-death decision making.

Throughout the community, such openness would reenergize relationships between younger and older generations and promote mutual caring, which would contribute to the curing function across the health-care continuum.

The Healthspitals' integrated delivery system at the community level would allow a much truer triage at emergency departments. As these are often the places of first resort for patients with all levels of care needs, a system-wide approach to triage would help refer all patients to the appropriate (and often less expensive) level of care. This would lessen the issue of "dumping" and allow tracking of referral patterns to provide a feedback mechanism for improving triage throughout the system.

A Healthspital 2.0 approach could proactively intervene against negative health modulators such as smoking, impaired driving, and other reckless behaviors and would promote modifications.

Healthspitals would also assess and promote healthy lifestyles, such as appropriate nutrition and exercise regimens. Using personal monitoring devices for walks would allow people to compile and monitor their health via a database, which would be accessible to their physicians as well as to researchers tracking public-health trends.

Healthspital 2.0 would, by virtue of eliminating redundancy and improving health, allow huge savings from current health-care expenditures. These savings could be reinvested into promoting more healthful programs such as building walking trails, biking areas, parks, and local organic farms. Public health and wellness would thus become self-sustaining.

Once the Healthspital is fully functional, true reform of medical malpractice would be possible, as errors would decline and overall health of the community would be improved. Also, the integration would allow risk sharing across the system, which would require understanding the rights and responsibilities of all stakeholders, from patients to the Healthspital personnel, all of whom are truly invested in providing and maintaining the health of the entire community—the health ecosystem.

Barriers to the Healthspital Paradigm

Professor Randy Pausch, in *The Last Lecture* (Hyperion, 2008), taught that barriers are put in front of us to see how much we want what is beyond them. Here are some of the challenges facing the Healthspital 2.0 paradigm.

- **Legal issues:** Many modifications of current laws will be needed, especially in the areas of information use and availability at point of care. Issues that will need to be addressed include HIPAA (Health Insurance Portability and Accountability Act), patient dumping, conflict of interest, and discrimination. HIPAA, in particular, was originally enacted as a privacy guard. I contend that the American population is more comfortable sharing personal health-care information than current legislation indicates, so long as they have confidence that the information will be used responsibly.

With 500 million people already utilizing Facebook, I believe the vast majority of people (therefore, patients) would make health-related data available to providers and researchers in the interests of preserving health.

- **Financial issues:** Compared with building a new hospital, the Healthspital model offers potentially tremendous cost savings, but care must be taken that these savings are reinvested into more healthful projects rather than shifted to various nonhealth-related special interests.

- **Political issues:** The creation of the Healthspital 2.0 concept will require substantial commitment, investment, and will on the part of politicians. The paradigm shift is monumental, so it is certainly appropriate to work at the experimental project level where results can be analyzed in terms of cost savings and improved health care. However, politicians with appropriate foresight would also be helpful in providing leadership and serving as champions for concepts such as this.

- **Educational issues:** As with all major changes, educational ramifications of a health system paradigm shift are tremendous. Health awareness should be taught at the earliest levels, starting in pre-school. Science and nutritional coursework throughout formal schooling is imperative, as well as example setting. Patients currently receiving treatment in the older delivery model will need tools that the local community Healthspital will provide. Lifelong education could thus enable individuals to become more involved in their own health future, allowing them to assist responsibly in the delivery of care to themselves and family members.

- **Punitive and unconstructive programs:** Bashing and the blame game must be eliminated throughout the health-delivery system. No one—individual or institution—functions well with a stick at the back. The current pay-for-performance model does not allow the raising of all boats toward improvement, but rather widens the gap between the great performers and the health programs and systems that are performing poorly.

Building a Healthspital Model

I currently work at Lawrence & Memorial Hospital in southeastern Connecticut, a 250-bed community hospital. We serve a number of employers and on the continuum of care from birth to death, from neonatal intensive care to skilled nursing facilities, and with a robust hospice presence. We care for patients in 10 counties, and our primary service area includes both the destitute and the wealthy. We are regional, and our facility would be a perfect venue for an experimental design incorporating any and all of the above suggestions.

How would this work? First and foremost, it would be an experiment requiring bright investigators to provide oversight and analysis of data. All elements of health care and wellness should be incorporated. Every member of the community in the

10 primary service areas should be enrolled, and a swipe-card passport developed such that, at any point of care, information is standardized. Any and all good ideas would be welcomed for inclusion in a central repository of ideas and best practices. Through instant messaging, such bright ideas would be disseminated throughout the system for consideration, and this would assure e-quality.

No person requiring care or requesting information would get anything less than the best available. Funding sources would include venture capitalists, information system vendors, federal government pilot project or American Hospital Association new investigator sources.

Pilot projects shown to work effectively would merge databases and coalesce into a national or even global health-delivery ecosystem, addressing the big five issues of waste and redundancy, expensive access, prevention, chronic disease management, and fruitless ministrations at end-of-life.

Critical Thinking

1. What is good about the U.S. health care system and what is bad about it?

2. How would Maletz change the system? How would you?

FRANK W. MALETZ, MD, is an orthopedic surgeon specializing in spine and trauma at the Lawrence & Memorial Hospital in East Lyme, Connecticut. For more information about the Healthspital 2.0™ concept, please contact the author, e-mail malfam5@aol.com. He will also speak on this topic at WorldFuture 2011: Moving from Vision to Action in Vancouver.

Originally published in the March/April 2011, pp. 17–19 issue of *The Futurist*. Copyright © 2011 by World Future Society, Bethesda, MD. Used with permission via Copyright Clearance Center.0

UNIT 5

Crime, Violence, and Law Enforcement

Unit Selections

Learning Outcomes

After reading this unit, you should be able to:

* Explain the high crime rates in the United States. Why has the crime rate dropped recently?

* Identify the law enforcement policies that are most heavily relied upon today. What do you think are the best policies and why?

* Describe how crime affects society and estimate its full costs. What kinds of crimes are the most costly and why?

* Report on recent evidence that many innocent people are incarcerated for crimes that they did not commit. How do you explain cases of the miscarriage of justice?

* Do the "Stand Your Ground" laws give an unwarranted licence to kill?

* Can you explain why the United States incarcerates the highest percentage of its population compared to the rest of the world? Do high incarceration rates reduce crime?

* Explain the recent dramatic increase in right wing extremist groups. How dangerous are they?

* How much of a threat to the United States is terrorism? How can the public be protected from it?

Student Website

www.mhhe.com/cls

Internet References

ACLU Criminal Justice Home Page
www.aclu.org/crimjustice/index.html
Terrorism Research Center
www.terrorism.com

This unit deals with criminal behavior and its control by the law enforcement system. The first line of defense against crime is the socialization of the young to internalize norms against harmful and illegal behavior. Thus families, schools, religious institutions, and social pressure are the major crime fighters, but they do not do a perfect job, and the police have to handle their failures. Over the last half century until recently, crime has increased, signaling for some commentators a decline in morality. If the power of norms to control criminal behavior diminishes, the role of law enforcement must increase, and that is what has happened. The societal response to crime has been threefold: hire more police, build more prisons, and toughen penalties for crimes. These policies by themselves can have only limited success. For example, putting a drug dealer in prison just creates an opportunity for another person to become a drug dealer. Another approach is to give potential criminals alternatives to crime. The key factor in this approach is a healthy economy that provides many job opportunities for unemployed young men. To some extent, this has happened, and the crime rate has dropped. Programs that work with inner-city youth might also help, but budget-tight cities are not funding many programs like this. Amid the policy debates there is one thing we can agree upon: Crime has declined significantly in the past two decades (with a slight increase lately) after rising substantially for a half century.

The first subsection deals with crime; a major concern today because crime and violence seem to be out of control. In the first article, John J. Donohue analyzes crime using economic cost-benefit analysis. His research leads him to recommend that we expand police forces, adopt sensible gun control laws, legalize drugs, and stop building prisons. In the second article on crime, David A. Anderson uses a similar analytical methodology. He tries to put into monetary terms the impacts of various types of crimes in the United States. The results produce some surprises. First, when he includes many costs that are seldom taken into account, such as the costs of law enforcement, security measures, and lost time at work, the total crime bill is over $1 trillion, or over $4,000 per person. Another surprise is the relative costs of white-collar crime versus street crime. Fraud and cheating on taxes cost Americans over twenty times the costs of theft, burglary, and robbery. In the next article Glenn C. Loury provides an introduction to a *Daedalus* issue on crime and punishment in which he summarizes the points of several articles. It is thus packed with ideas that analyze the extremely high imprison rate in the United States, the increasing racial disparity in imprisonment, the high unemployability of ex-prisoners, the adverse consequences of the current judicial system on inner city neighborhoods, and the way that "high incarceration rates in poor communities destabilize the social relationships in these places and help cause crime rather than prevent it. He notes that "Though blacks and whites use and sell drugs at similar rates, blacks are imprisoned at much higher rates". Other issues are also discussed but the bottom line is that there is much injustice in U.S. justice.

The next subsection deals with law enforcement. Radley Balko reports on the considerable number of proven wrongful convictions and suggests that there are many times that number of unexamined or unproven wrongful convictions. By a long process of reasoning he estimates that about 3-5 percent of imprisonments for felony crimes could be innocents. In the process he explains a lot about how the criminal justice system works and its weaknesses. Clearly reforms are needed. In the next article Adam Weinstein reports on the Stand Your Ground law in Florida that George Zimmerman believes justifies his shooting innocent Trayvon Martin to death. Similar laws have been passed in twenty-five states and in those states justified homicides have doubled since the laws were passed. Weinstein presents the

© Brand X Pictures

stories behind these laws and provides the basis for a proper evaluation of their suitability.

The next article discusses an exceptional characteristic of the United States: It has the highest incarceration rate in the world. That leads to the question of whether high incarceration is good or bad for society. Mark A. R. Kleinman tries to answer that question. It actually is a hard question to answer because it requires assessing many issues, some of which are hard to assess. He finds that, has only a minor effect on reducing crime, and many measures, such as increasing the police force incarceration would have much bigger effects. Overall he shows that our high incarceration rate is bad for the United States and that if we reduced incarceration we would reduce crime.

The final subsection deals with terrorism. The first article, by Mark Potok, demonstrates the recent substantial increase in hate groups and extremist ideas. The antigovernment "Patriot" conspiracy-minded organizations have grown dramatically (60%). Others extremist groups are racist and/or anti-immigration. The FBI is very concerned about this trend and so should be the public. The next article explores the horrifying danger of cyber-warfare. Cyber terrorists could cause financial chaos costing trillions, screw up electrical grids, blow up oil refineries and pipelines, mess up air-traffic-control systems, hack major corporations to death, and cripple the Internet. Accordingly, society could soon break down and the economy collapse. Protection from these attacks is extremely difficult. Finally, Davie E. Hoffman raises several frightful concerns: terrorist attacks by biological, chemical, or cyber methods. Technological advances have greatly increased the dangers from these threats and an industry is developing to try to counter future attacks. Cyber attacks are already widespread. This article is a horror story.

Fighting Crime

An Economist's View

JOHN J. DONOHUE

Over the past 40 years, the number of motor vehicle fatalities per mile driven in the United States has dropped an astounding 70 percent. While some of the gains can be attributed to improvements in technology, public policy has made a big difference. The government followed the advice of researchers who had studied auto accidents, improving highway design and instituting a variety of regulations, including mandatory seat belt use and harsher penalties for drunken driving. By contrast, most types of street crime are still above the levels of 40 years ago, despite the impressive drops in the 1990s. A major reason for the difference, I would argue, is that the crime issue has been hijacked by ideologues and special interests, preventing the emergence of a policy consensus driven by research.

Why listen to an economist pontificate on what most people would call criminology? Economists bring a unique perspective to the table—a utilitarian view in which one assumes that behavior can be changed by altering incentives, that the costs of crime can be measured in terms of money and that public policy is best evaluated by comparing costs and benefits. It's hardly the only view, but I would argue that it is a view that provides exceptional insight into limiting the adverse consequences of antisocial behavior.

We know more today than ever how to reduce crime. If we could get past the barriers of ideology and special pleading, we could see reductions in crime rivaling the magnitude of the gains in automobile safety. What follows are a host of measures that would sharply reduce the $400 billion annual toll from street crime in the United States.

Stop the Building Boom in Prisons

Virtually everyone agrees that incarceration must remain a core element of any strategy to fight crime. Locking up more people reduces crime because more criminals are kept off the streets and/or the prospect of time behind bars deters criminal behavior. But you can have too much of a "good" thing. Between 1933 and 1973, incarceration in the United States varied within a narrow band of roughly 100 to 120 prisoners per 100,000 population. Since then, this rate has been increasing by an average of 5 percent annually. As of June 2003, some two million individuals were imprisoned—a rate of almost 500 per 100,000.

Costs of Prison

To determine whether the current level of incarceration makes sense, one must ask whether the benefits at the margin in terms of less crime exceed the costs to society. On the benefit side, the research suggests that the "elasticity" of crime with respect to incarceration is somewhere between 0.1 and 0.4—that is, increasing the prison population by 10 percent reduces crime by 1 to 4 percent. On the other side of the equation, estimates of the cost of locking up another individual run between $32,000 and $57,000 annually.

The most rigorous study on the relevant elasticity was conducted by William Spelman of the University of Texas. He concluded that "we can be 90 percent confident that the true value is between 0.12 and 0.20, with a best single guess of 0.16." Since Spelman's estimates accounted for the incapacitation effect, but ignored any deterrence effect, I rely conservatively on somewhat larger elasticity of 0.2.

The most carefully constructed and comprehensive study on the costs of incarcerating a criminal was a 1990 report prepared for the National Institute of Justice, which produced the high-end estimate ($57,000 annually, in 2003 dollars). I adjust this figure downward (in part because the study probably overstates prison construction costs and exaggerates the social cost of welfare payments to the dependents of the incarcerated) to arrive at a figure of $46,000 per prisoner per year.

With an elasticity of crime with respect to incarceration of 0.2 and an annual cost of housing a prisoner of $46,000, the "optimal" level of incarceration would require imprisoning 300,000 fewer individuals. This is just a ballpark estimate, of course. But, at the very least, it implies that we cannot expect to get much more crime reduction at reasonable cost by increasing the numbers behind bars. It is time to stop making prison construction the major public works project of our day.

Abolish the Death Penalty

In recent years, the death penalty has been meted out an average of 80 times annually. These executions come at a high tangible cost. For while executing an individual does save the money that would have been used for a lifetime in prison, these savings are dwarfed by the costs of death-penalty trials and appeals. The most scholarly research on the topic, by Philip Cook and Donna Slawson Kuniholm of Duke, found that the State of North Carolina spent $2.16 million per execution more than what would be spent if the maximum penalty were life in prison.

Proponents of the death penalty usually justify these costs by invoking its deterrence effect. But Steve Levitt of the University of Chicago has noted that the risk of execution for those who commit murder is typically small compared with the risk of death that violence-prone criminals willingly face in daily life—and this certainly raises questions about the efficacy of threatening them with the death penalty. Currently, the likelihood of a murderer being executed is less than 1 in 200. By way of comparison, Levitt and his colleague Sudhir Venkatesh find 7 percent of street-level drug sellers die each year. Levitt concludes that "it is hard to believe the fear of execution would be a driving force in a rational criminal's calculus in modern America."

Nor is there direct evidence that the death penalty generates gains for society in terms of murders deterred. In an often-cited paper written in the early 1970s, Isaac Ehrlich (then a graduate student at the University of Chicago) estimated that one execution could save eight lives. But research since has showed that minor changes in the way the figure is estimated eliminate the deterrence effect. Indeed, Levitt, working with Lawrence Katz of Harvard and Ellen Shustorovich of the City University of New York, found that the death penalty might even add to the total number of murders. Thus, abolishing the death penalty would save American taxpayers more than $150 million a year at no apparent cost to society.

Expand the Police Force

In the 1990s, a variety of new policing strategies were introduced in New York City and other localities. New York increased enforcement of statutes on petty crimes like graffiti and marijuana possession and made better use of technology and statistics in identifying crime "hot spots." Boston adopted an innovative multi-agency collaboration that took aim at gang violence. And numerous cities, notably San Diego, introduced "community policing," in which police attempted to work as allies with communities, rather than just antagonists to criminals. The results seem impressive: from 1991 to 1998, the cities that experienced the largest decline in murder rates were San Diego (a 76 percent drop), New York City (71 percent) and Boston (69 percent).

Were better policing strategies responsible for these results, and would cities be wise to adopt or expand such programs? A study of Cincinnati found that a "community service model" of policing, in which cops become more familiar with the neighborhoods they served, did not significantly lower crime. Furthermore, community policing did not seem to affect attitudes toward police.

Two New York Factors

Note, too, that New York's experiments are inconclusive—cities without tough policies on minor crime experienced significant crime drops, too. Moreover, New York's substantial crime declines began before 1993, the year in which Mayor Giuliani took office and initiated the policing changes. Indeed, two other factors seem to explain all of the crime drop in New York City: increases in the total number of police officers and its high abortion rate many years earlier, which Levitt and I found to correlate with subsequent declines in crime because of the reduction in unwanted births of children most at risk of becoming criminals.

Another change in the 1990s—one that received far less press attention than changing policing strategies—was the substantial increase in the size of police forces. From 1994 through 1999, the number of police per capita in the United States grew by almost 10 percent. The expansion was even more pronounced in big cities with high crime rates. Much of this increase can be attributed to the Community Oriented Policing Services (COPS) program, which was signed into law by President Clinton in 1994 and is now in the process of being phased out by President Bush. A report commissioned by the Justice Department credits this program with adding more than 80,000 officers to the streets.

The effects of increases in police, as opposed to changes in policing strategies, have been widely studied, with most studies showing that the benefits have exceeded the costs. The most rigorous studies have found elasticities of crime with respect to police of between 0.30 and 0.79—that is, a 10 percent increase in police reduces crime between 3.0 and 7.9 percent. Using a conservative estimate for this elasticity (0.4) and a rather high estimate of the total annual cost of maintaining an extra police officer ($90,000) while assuming that crime costs $400 billion a year, the United States would have to hire 500,000 additional police officers to reach the optimal policing level. According to the FBI, there are some 665,000 police in the United States. So the optimal level is almost double the number we have today. Thus while adding hundreds of thousands of police officers is hardly a political priority these days, simply restoring financing for the COPS program would be a start.

Adopt Sensible Gun Control

In 2002, there were some 11,000 homicide deaths by firearms. The United States' per capita firearm homicide rate is more than eight times that of Canada, France, Germany, Japan, Spain and Britain. Much could be done to reduce gun-related crime. Most such initiatives are off the table, however, because conservatives have garnered enormous electoral benefits from fighting gun control.

What's more, the highly publicized work of the researcher John Lott has confirmed the views of many conservatives that gun control is already excessive—that allowing citizens to carry concealed handguns would drastically *reduce* violent crime. Lott reasons that the threat of these concealed weapons serves as a deterrent to crime. And his research has been cited by many politicians supporting laws allowing concealed weapons, which have been passed by some 30 states.

There are, however, serious flaws in Lott's research. The best guess based on all the empirical evidence is that these "shall issue" laws actually increase crime, albeit by a relatively modest amount. There are a number of possible explanations for this: the guns being carried are easier to steal (more than a million guns are stolen each year, which is a major source of supply to criminals), for one, while the threat of being shot in a confrontation may inspire criminals to shoot first. It is worth noting, moreover, that laws allowing for easier access to guns increase the threats of both accidental death and suicide.

One alternative to "shall issue" laws is "may issue" laws, which allow discretion in handing out permits, with an applicant having to prove a need for protection. These laws, which have been passed in 11 states, could have some of the deterrent benefits Lott speaks of without as many of the harmful effects that plague "shall issue" laws if the licensing discretion is used wisely.

Another much-debated gun law was President Clinton's 1994 assault-weapons ban, which was recently allowed to expire. This law prohibited a specific list of semiautomatic guns deemed useful for criminal purposes but unnecessary for sport or self-defense, and banned ammunition feeding devices that accept more than 10 rounds. According to plausible guesstimates, assault weapons were used in about 2 percent of pre-ban murders, and large-capacity magazines were used in about 20 percent. The secondary goal of the assault weapons ban was to reduce the harm from crime by forcing criminals to employ less dangerous weapons. Jeffrey Roth and Christopher Koper of the Urban Institute in Washington found that those murdered by assault weapons had, on average, more wounds than those killed with other guns. They also found that, in mass murders, those involving assault weapons included more victims.

Was the ban effective? Probably not very. The law was rife with loopholes. For one thing, the law grandfathered assault weapons produced before the ban, which led gun manufacturers to increase production before the law took effect. In addition, gun companies could—and did—produce potent legal guns with little change in performance. Admittedly, a true ban on assault weapons would not have a huge effect on homicide since most criminals would simply use less powerful guns if the desired weapons were unavailable. A strong ban on large capacity magazines, however, which are estimated to be used in 20 percent of homicides, could be very helpful.

David Hemenway, an economist and director of the Harvard Injury Control Research Center, has examined the evidence on the potential impact of other gun-related measures and identifies six that have shown some success in lowering crime:

- preventing police from selling confiscated guns.
- instituting one-gun-purchase-per-month laws.
- plugging secondary-market loopholes.
- tracing all guns used in crime.
- producing guns that can be fired only by their owners.
- registering all handguns.

None of these, alas, is an easy political sell in today's America.

Legalize Drugs

The most effective federal crime-fighting public initiative in American history was the lifting of alcohol prohibition in the early 1930s. Homicides fell by 14 percent in the two years after prohibition ended. In all likelihood, similar benefits would emerge if we ended drug prohibition, although obviously other steps would need to be taken to reduce the societal costs associated with drug use.

The logic behind drug legalization as a crime reducer is twofold. First, a significant number of homicides are caused by drug-related disputes. The FBI has classified about 5 percent of homicides as drug-related. And this number is very conservative since the FBI attributes only one cause to each murder. A fatal dispute about a drug deal may be characterized as an "argument over money" or a "gangland killing" rather than a drug homicide. Paul Goldstein of the University of Illinois at Chicago found that about 9 percent of homicides in New York City were caused by broader "systemic" drug issues.

The major reason so many drug disputes end in violence is the lack of institutional mechanisms to resolve them—buyers and sellers cannot seek redress in court, or complain to the Better Business Bureau. Legalization could also lower crime by freeing crime-fighters for other purposes. About $40 billion is spent annually on the war on drugs.

Decriminalizing drugs would also free space in prisons. Levitt found a substantial "crowding out" effect, meaning that increased incarceration of drug-related criminals decreases incarceration of other criminals. Currently, more than 400,000 individuals are in prison for nonviolent drug crimes, with about 50,000 of them imprisoned for violations involving only marijuana.

Of course, drug legalization is not without risks. Legalization would tend to increase drug consumption, lowering economic productivity and perhaps increasing behavior that is dangerous to nondrug users.

One simple way to restrain drug consumption after legalization would be through taxation. Gary Becker and Kevin Murphy of the University of Chicago along with Michael Grossman of the City University of New York construct a model in which the optimal equilibrium with legalization and taxation can actually lead to higher retail prices—and lower consumption—than the optimal system under prohibition. Such a policy would also raise additional money for the government, which could be used for any number of purposes. It would be substantially easier to enforce a tax on drugs than it is to enforce the current ban on drugs, since most individuals would pay a premium to purchase their drugs legally. Instead of turning the hundreds of thousands of workers in the illegal drug markets (and their customers) into criminals, we could focus law enforcement on the much smaller set of tax evaders to keep consumption no higher than the levels of today.

Given the highly controversial nature of this proposal, a prudent first step might be to adopt this legalization/taxation/demand control scheme for marijuana to illustrate the benefits of shrinking the size of illegal markets while establishing that an increase in drug usage can be avoided. A number of other measures should be adopted to limit demand. Strict age limits could be enforced, advertising could be banned, and some of the money raised by taxes on drugs could be used to market abstinence and treatment of addicts.

Expand Successful Social Programs

In accepting his party's nomination, John Kerry said, "I am determined that we stop being a nation content to spend $50,000 a year to keep a young person in prison for the rest of their life—when we could invest $10,000 to give them Head Start, Early Start, Smart Start, the best possible start in life." He was expressing a belief common on the center-left that early childhood intervention can make children less likely to commit crime and actually save money down the road.

Is this view correct? Studies on Head Start have shown it to have lamentably little effect on participants' outcomes later in life, including their likelihood of committing crimes. Other programs, however, have shown tremendous potential in reducing crime (and enhancing other positive life outcomes), and resources should be shifted away from the unproductive programs toward the few that seem to work.

One of the most notable, the experimental Perry Preschool program, provided preschool classes to a sample of children in Michigan when they were 3 and 4 years old. This program attempted to involve the whole family by having the preschool teacher conduct weekly home visits. By age 19, Perry Preschool graduates were 40 percent less likely to be arrested than a control group, 50 percent less likely to be arrested more than twice, and far less likely to be arrested for major crimes.

While I would not expect a scaled-up program to perform as well as one implemented with a small group, even half the reduction in crime would be cost-effective. Estimates from studies of the program indicate that financial benefits to government, which came in the form of higher taxes from employment, lower welfare utilization and reduced crime, exceeded program costs by as much as seven to one.

Another cost-effective crime-fighting program is the Job Corps, which provides educational and vocational-skills training and counseling to at-risk youths. Each year, Job Corps enrolls some 60,000 kids at a cost of more than $1 billion. Unlike some similar teenage intervention programs, the Job Corps is residential. Like the Perry Preschool Program, Job Corps has proved to pay for itself, generating more revenue in the form of taxes and avoided welfare payments than the costs of training the at-risk teens. Job Corps has also proved effective in lowering crime: a randomized experiment conducted by the research corporation Mathematica estimates that Job Corps participants are 16 percent less likely to be arrested than their peers.

For programs like the Perry Preschool and Job Corps to be successful in lowering crime, they must be targeted at those most likely to commit crimes. Six percent of the population commits more than 50 percent of crimes. While there are moral and legal issues in targeting groups based on race, it should be possible to use such information to expand successful programs so that they cover more high-risk individuals.

Defend *Roe v. Wade*

One often overlooked variable in crime is the legal status of abortion. Levitt and I found that as much as half of the drop in crime in the 1990s can be explained by the legalization of abortion in the early 1970s. There are two reasons that legalized abortion lowers the crime rate. The first is obvious: more abortions mean fewer children, which in turn can mean fewer criminals when those who would have been born would have reached their high-crime years. The second is more important: abortion reduces the number of unwanted births, and unwanted children are at much greater risk of becoming criminals later on. The five states that legalized abortion before the rest of the country experienced significant drops in crime before other states did. What's more, the higher the rate of abortion in a state in the mid 1970s, the greater the drop in crime in the 1990s.

What would be the impact on crime if *Roe v. Wade* were overturned? If the Supreme Court restored the pre-1973 law allowing states to decide for themselves whether to legalize abortion, I suspect most of the blue states would keep abortion legal. Even in the red states, abortion would not disappear entirely because residents could still find safe, out-of-state abortions. But the number of abortions would fall sharply, particularly for poor women.

Suppose that abortion were outlawed in every state that voted for Bush in 2004 and that the abortion rate dropped by 75 percent in these states but remained the same in blue states. Our research suggests that violent crime would eventually increase by about 12 percent and property crime by about 10 percent over the baseline figure.

Reduce Teen Pregnancy

Keeping abortion legal would prevent crime increases, but we can use the insight from the casual link between abortion and crime reduction to achieve the same ends in a better way: reduce the number of unwanted and teen pregnancies. Take the Children's Aid Society-Carrera program, which aims to reduce births to teenagers by changing their incentives. The three-year after-school program for 13-year-olds includes a work component designed to assist participants to find decent jobs, an academic component including tutoring and homework help, an arts component, an individual sports component, and comprehensive family life and sexual education. Program participants have been 70 percent less likely to give birth in the three years after the program ended than members of a control group.

Again, the success of any social program designed to reduce crime requires targeting, in this case at those most likely to give birth in their teens. The groups with the highest rates of teen births are Hispanics, with a rate of 83 births per 1,000 women

15 to 19 years old, and non-Hispanic blacks, with a rate of 68 per thousand—both well above the national rate of 43. Suppose the program was expanded so that it covered half of all Hispanic and black females ages 13 to 15—some two million girls. With a per-person cost of $4,000, the annual outlay would be roughly $4 billion.

Again, one would not expect a large program to be able to replicate the substantial reductions seen in the smaller program. But an initiative only half as effective in reducing teen births would still lower the birth rates of the 15- to 19-year-old participants by 35 percent. Under these assumptions, the expanded program would lead to about 40,000 fewer teen births a year—a 9 percent reduction.

Recent work by Anindya Sen enables us to quantify the expected reduction in crime from this potential drop in teen births. Sen finds that a 1 percent drop in teen births is associated with a 0.589 percent drop in violent crime years later, when the individuals born to teenagers would have reached their high-crime ages. Thus, the 9 percent reduction in teen births would eventually cut violent crime by 5 percent. Assuming two-thirds of crime costs are attributable to violent crime, this 5 percent reduction would eventually save society more than $14 billion per year. In other words, the benefits would be three times greater than the cost.

Expand the DNA Database

While much of the attention on the use of DNA in criminal justice has focused on its potential for establishing the innocence of the wrongly accused, we have not yet tapped the potential of DNA testing to deter crime. Individuals whose DNA is on file with the government know that leaving even a single hair at the scene of a crime is likely to lead to their arrest and conviction, so a major expansion in the DNA database should generate substantial crime reduction benefits. While some are concerned that the government would get information about a person's medical history, the privacy problem can be minimized. It is possible to take someone's DNA and discard all information except for the unique identifying genetic marker.

Currently, every state requires violent criminals and sex offenders to submit to DNA testing. Most states require testing for all felons and juvenile convicts. If a person is found innocent, his or her DNA sample must be discarded. But the United States' DNA crime-fighting system can be expanded and improved. England tests anyone suspected of a "recordable" offense, with the profile remaining on file even if the person is cleared of the crime. This has allowed Britain to build a DNA database with some two million profiles. England's Forensic Science Service estimates that, in a typical year, matches are found linking suspects to 180 murders, 500 rapes and other sexual offenses, and 30,000 motor vehicle, property and drug crimes. In other words, DNA is used to solve fully 20 percent of murders and a significant fraction of other crimes.

A more drastic—and potentially effective—approach was endorsed by Rudolph Giuliani: recording the DNA of every newborn. One way to lower the costs of the project without eliminating much of the gains would be to test only males, who are far more likely to commit crimes.

To improve the effectiveness of the policy, however, it would be necessary to test every male—not just male babies. This would increase the start-up costs to $15 billion (although thought should be given to the appropriate age cutoff—say age 50—as a plausible cost-reduction measure). In every year thereafter, however, it would be necessary to test only newborns. In 2002, there were a little more than 2 million male births in the United States. So testing every male infant would cost about $200 million annually.

One particular crime-deterrent benefit of having the DNA of every male on file is it would be likely to drastically reduce rapes by strangers. Let's assume (conservatively) that half of all such rapes—half of 56,000 a year—would be deterred by the existence of a complete DNA database. Ted Miller, Mark Cohen and Shelli Rossman added the costs of medical bills, lost productivity, mental health trauma and quality of life changes, to estimate that the average rape costs $90,000. Hence, 28,000 of the rapes by strangers in 2002 cost society about $2.5 billion. While the costs of testing every male—$15 billion in the first year—would exceed the $2.5 billion in benefits in reduced rapes from such a plan, the total benefits from rape reduction alone would exceed the costs in roughly seven years (and perhaps less if the initial testing were limited with a judicious age cutoff). Note, moreover, that stranger rapes are only one of many classes of crimes that would see sharp declines with such expansive DNA testing.

What We Are Losing

Few of these proposals seem likely to be adopted any time soon. Former attorney general John Ashcroft stressed incarceration and the death penalty as principal crime-fighting tools, and President Bush's new attorney general, Alberto Gonzalez, appears wed to an even tougher line. Bush seems intent on shrinking the budget for police and early-intervention social programs. The NRA continues to have success in fighting even the most sensible gun control policies. And few in either political party are willing to discuss the legalization of drugs or a major expansion in the DNA database. The politicians in power thus seem stuck on anti-crime policies that guarantee that crime levels will be far higher than can be justified by any reasonable comparison of costs and benefits—let alone respect for life and property.

Adopting the policies set out above would reduce crime in the neighborhood of 50 percent, saving thousands of lives annually and avoiding crime victimization for millions more. Is anybody in Washington, or the state capitals, listening?

Critical Thinking

1. What policies regarding crime and punishment would be forthcoming if all policies were subjected to cost-benefit analysis?

2. Why are we following policies that are so much at variance with the cost-benefit criteria?

JOHN J. DONOHUE teaches law and economics at the Yale Law School. From "Fighting Crime: An Economist's View," *The Milken Institute Review*, First Quarter 2005, pages 47–58.

The Aggregate Burden of Crime

DAVID A. ANDERSON

Introduction

Distinct from previous studies that have focused on selected crimes, regions, or outcomes, this study attempts an exhaustively broad estimation of the crime burden. . . .

Overt annual expenditures on crime in the United States include $47 billion for police protection, $36 billion for corrections, and $19 billion for the legal and judicial costs of state and local criminal cases. (Unless otherwise noted, all figures are adjusted to reflect 1997 dollars using the Consumer Price Index.) Crime victims suffer $876 million worth of lost workdays, and guns cost society $25 billion in medical bills and lost productivity in a typical year. Beyond the costs of the legal system, victim losses, and crime prevention agencies, the crime burden includes the costs of deterrence (locks, safety lighting and fencing, alarm systems and munitions), the costs of compliance enforcement (non-gendarme inspectors and regulators), implicit psychic and health costs (fear, agony, and the inability to behave as desired), and the opportunity costs of time spent preventing, carrying out, and serving prison terms for criminal activity.

This study estimates the impact of crime taking a comprehensive list of the repercussions of aberrant behavior into account. While the standard measures of criminal activity count crimes and direct costs, this study measures the impact of crimes and includes indirect costs as well. Further, the available data on which crime cost figures are typically based is imprecise. Problems with crime figures stem from the prevalence of unreported crimes, inconsistencies in recording procedures among law enforcement agencies, policies of recording only the most serious crime in events with multiple offenses, and a lack of distinction between attempted and completed crimes. This research does not eliminate these problems, but it includes critical crime-prevention and opportunity costs that are measured with relative precision, and thus places less emphasis on the imprecise figures used in most other measures of the impact of crime. . . .

Previous Studies

Several studies have estimated the impact of crime; however, none has been thorough in its assessment of the substantial indirect costs of crime and the crucial consideration of private crime prevention expenditures. The FBI Crime Index provides a measure of the level of crime by counting the acts of murder, rape, robbery, aggravated assault, burglary, larceny, motor vehicle theft, and arson each year. The FBI Index is purely a count of crimes and does not attempt to place weights on various criminal acts based on their severity. If the number of acts of burglary, larceny, motor vehicle theft, or arson decreases, society might be better off, but with no measure of the severity of the crimes, such a conclusion is necessarily tentative. From a societal standpoint what matters is the extent of damage inflicted by these crimes, which the FBI Index does not measure.

Over the past three decades, studies of the cost of crime have reported increasing crime burdens, perhaps more as a result of improved understanding and accounting for the broad repercussions of crime than due to the increase in the burden itself. Table 1 summarizes the findings of eight previous studies. . . .

The Effects of Crime

The effects of crime fall into several categories depending on whether they constitute the allocation of resources due to crime that could otherwise be used more productively, the production of ill-favored commodities, transfers from victims to criminals, opportunity costs, or implicit costs associated with risks to life and health. This section examines the meaning and ramifications of each of these categories of crime costs.

Crime-Induced Production

Crime can result in the allocation of resources towards products and activities that do not contribute to society except in their association with crime. Examples include the production of personal protection devices, the trafficking of drugs, and the operation of correctional facilities. In the absence of crime, the time, money, and material resources absorbed by the provision of these goods and services could be used for the creation of benefits rather than the avoidance of harm. The foregone benefits from these alternatives represent a real cost of crime to society. (Twenty dollars spent on a door lock is twenty dollars that cannot be spent on groceries.) Thus, expenditures on crime-related products are treated as a loss to society.

Crimes against property also create unnecessary production due to the destruction and expenditure of resources, and crimes against persons necessitate the use of medical and psychological care resources. In each of these cases, crime-related purchases bid-up prices for the associated items, resulting in higher prices for all consumers of the goods. In the absence of crime, the dollars currently spent to remedy and recover from crime

Table 1

Previous Study	Focus	Not Included	$ (billions)
Colins (1994)	General	Opportunity Costs, Miscellaneous Indirect Components	728
Cohen, Miller, and Wiersema (1995)	Victim Costs of Violent and Property Crimes	Prevention, Opportunity, and Indirect Costs	472
U.S. News (1974)	General	Opportunity Costs, Miscellaneous Indirect Components	288
Cohen, Miller, Rossman (1994)	Cost of Rape, Robbery, and Assault	Prevention, Opportunity, and Indirect Costs	183
Zedlewski (1985)	Firearms, Guard Dogs, Victim Losses, Commercial Security	Residential Security, Opportunity Costs, Indirect Costs	160
Cohen (1990)	Cost of Personal and Household Crime to Victims	Prevention, Opportunity, and Indirect Costs	113
President's Commission on Law Enforcement (1967)	General	Opportunity Costs, Miscellaneous Indirect Components	107
Klaus (1994)	National Crime and Victimization Survey Crimes	Prevention, Opportunity, and Indirect Costs	19

would largely be spent in pursuit of other goals, bidding-up the prices of alternative categories of goods. For this reason, the *net* impact of price effects is assumed to be zero in the present research.

Opportunity Costs

As the number of incarcerated individuals increases steadily, society faces the large and growing loss of these potential workers' productivity.... Criminals are risk takers and instigators—characteristics that could make them contributors to society if their entrepreneurial talents were not misguided. Crimes also take time to conceive and carry out, and thus involve the opportunity cost of the criminals' time regardless of detection and incarceration. For many, crime is a full-time occupation. Society is deprived of the goods and services a criminal would have produced in the time consumed by crime and the production of "bads" if he or she were on the level. Additional opportunity costs arise due to victims' lost workdays, and time spent securing assets, looking for keys, purchasing and installing crime prevention devices, and patrolling neighborhood-watch areas.

The Value of Risks to Life and Health

The implicit costs of violent crime include the fear of being injured or killed, the anger associated with the inability to behave as desired, and the agony of being a crime victim. Costs associated with life and health risks are perhaps the most difficult to ascertain, although a considerable literature is devoted to their estimation. The implicit values of lost life and injury are included in the list of crime costs below; those not wishing to consider them can simply subtract these estimates from the aggregate figure.

Transfers

One result of fraud and theft is a transfer of assets from victim to criminal. . . .

Numerical Findings

Crime-Induced Production

. . . Crime-induced production accounts for about $400 billion in expenditures annually. Table 2 presents the costs of goods and services that would not have to be produced in the absence of crime. Drug trafficking accounts for an estimated $161 billion in expenditure. With the $28 billion cost of prenatal drug exposure and almost $11 billion worth of federal, state, and local drug control efforts (including drug treatment, education, interdiction, research, and intelligence), the combined cost of drug-related activities is about $200 billion. Findings that over half of the arrestees in 24 cities tested positive for recent drug use and about one-third of offenders reported being under the influence of drugs at the time of their offense suggest that significant portions of the other crime-cost categories may result indirectly from drug use.

About 682,000 police and 17,000 federal, state, special (park, transit, or county) and local police agencies account for $47 billion in expenditures annually. Thirty-six billion dollars is dedicated each year to the 895 federal and state prisons, 3,019 jails, and 1,091 state, county, and local juvenile detention centers. Aside from guards in correctional institutions, private expenditure on guards amounts to more than $18 billion annually. Security guard agencies employ 55 percent of the 867,000 guards in the U.S.; the remainder are employed in-house. While guards are expected and identifiable at banks and military complexes, they have a less conspicuous presence at railroads, ports, golf courses, laboratories, factories, hospitals, retail stores, and other places of business. The figures in this paper do not include receptionists, who often play a duel role of monitoring unlawful entry into a building and providing information and assistance. . . .

Opportunity Costs

In their study of the costs of murder, rape, robbery, and aggravated assault, Cohen, Miller, and Rossman estimate that the average incarcerated offender costs society $5,700 in lost productivity

Table 2

Crime-Induced Production	$ (millions)
Drug Trafficking	160,584
Police Protection	47,129
Corrections	35,879
Prenatal Exposure to Cocaine and Heroin	28,156
Federal Agencies	23,381
Judicial and Legal Services—State & Local	18,901
Guards	17,917
Drug Control	10,951
DUI Costs to Driver	10,302
Medical Care for Victims	8,990
Computer Viruses and Security	8,000
Alarm Systems	6,478
Passes for Business Access	4,659
Locks, Safes, and Vaults	4,359
Vandalism (except Arson)	2,317
Small Arms and Small Arms Ammunition	2,252
Replacements due to Arson	1,902
Surveillance Cameras	1,471
Safety Lighting	1,466
Protective Fences and Gates	1,159
Airport Security	448
Nonlethal weaponry, e.g., Mace	324
Elec. Retail Article Surveillance	149
Theft Insurance (less indemnity)	96
Guard Dogs	49
Mothers Against Drunk Driving	49
Library Theft Detection	28
Total	**397,395**

Table 3

The Value of Risks to Life and Health	$ (millions)
Value of Lost Life	439,880
Value of Injuries	134,515
Total	**574,395**

without dollar or time limits) and lost earnings (within modest bounds, victims or their spouses typically receive about two thirds of lost earnings for life or the duration of the injury). The values do capture perceived risks of pain, suffering, and mental distress associated with the health losses. If the risk of involvement in violent crime evokes more mental distress than the risk of occupational injuries and fatalities, the labor market values represent conservative estimates of the corresponding costs of crime. Similar estimates have been used in previous studies of crime costs. . . .

The average of 27 previous estimates of the implicit value of human life as reported by W. Kip Viscusi is 7.1 million. Removing two outlying estimates of just under $20 million about which the authors express reservation, the average of the remaining studies is $6.1 million. Viscusi points out that the majority of the estimates fall between $3.7 and $8.6 million ($3 and $7 million in 1990 dollars), the average of which is again $6.1 million. The $6.1 million figure was multiplied by the 72,111 crime-related deaths to obtain the $440 billion estimate of the value of lives lost to crime. Similarly, the average of 15 studies of the implicit value of non-fatal injuries, $52,637, was multiplied by the 2,555,520 reported injuries resulting from drunk driving and boating, arson, rape, robbery, and assaults to find the $135 billion estimate for the implicit cost of crime-related injuries.

Transfers

More than $603 billion worth of transfers result from crime. After the $204 billion lost to occupational fraud and the $123 billion in unpaid taxes, the $109 billion lost to health insurance fraud represents the greatest transfer by more than a factor of two, and the associated costs amount to almost ten percent of the nations' health care expenditures. Robberies, perhaps the classic crime, ironically generate a smaller volume of transfers ($775 million) than any other category of crime. The transfers of goods and money resulting from fraud and theft do not necessarily impose a net burden on society, and may in fact increase social welfare to the extent that those on the receiving end value the goods more than those losing them. Nonetheless, as Table 4 illustrates, those on the losing side bear a $603 billion annual burden. . . .

There are additional cost categories that are not included here, largely because measures that are included absorb much of their impact. Nonetheless, several are worth noting. Thaler, Hellman and Naroff, and Rizzo estimate the erosion of property values per crime. An average of their figures, $2,024, can be multiplied by the total number of crimes reported in 1994, 13,992, to estimate an aggregate housing devaluation of $28 billion. Although this figure should reflect the inability to behave

per year. Their estimate was based on the observation that many prisoners did not work in the legal market prior to their offense, and the opportunity cost of those prisoners' time can be considered to be zero. The current study uses a higher estimate of the opportunity cost of incarceration because unlike previous studies, it examines the relative savings from a *crime-free* society. It is likely that in the absence of crime including drug use, some criminals who are not presently employed in the legal workforce would be willing and able to find gainful employment. This assumption is supported by the fact that many criminals are, in a way, motivated entrepreneurs whose energy has taken an unfortunate focus. In the absence of more enticing underground activities, some of the same individuals could apply these skills successfully in the legal sector.

The Value of Risks to Life and Health

Table 3 presents estimates of the implicit costs of violent crime. The value of life and injury estimates used here reflect the amounts individuals are willing to accept to enter a work environment in which their health state might change. The labor market estimates do not include losses covered by workers' compensation, namely health care costs (usually provided

Table 4

Transfers	$ (millions)
Occupational Fraud	203,952
Unpaid Taxes	123,108
Health Insurance Fraud	108,610
Financial Institution Fraud	52,901
Mail Fraud	35,986
Property/Casualty Insurance Fraud	20,527
Telemarketing Fraud	16,609
Business Burglary	13,229
Motor Vehicle Theft	8,913
Shoplifting	7,185
Household Burglary	4,527
Personal Theft	3,909
Household Larceny	1,996
Coupon Fraud	912
Robbery	775
Total	**603,140**

as desired in the presence of crime, it also includes psychic and monetary costs imposed by criminal behavior that are already included in this [article].

Julie Berry Cullen and Stephen D. Levitt discuss urban flight resulting from crime. They report a nearly one-to-one relationship between serious crimes and individuals parting from major cities. The cost component of this is difficult to assess because higher commuting costs must be measured against lower property costs in rural areas, and the conveniences of city living must be compared with the amenities of suburbia. Several other categories of crime costs receive incomplete representation due to insufficient data, and therefore make the estimates here conservative. These include the costs of unreported crimes (although the National Crime Victimization Survey provides information beyond that reported to the police), lost taxes due to the underground economy, and restrictions of behavior due to crime.

When criminals' costs are estimated implicitly as the value of the assets they receive through crime, the gross cost of crime (including transfers) is estimated to exceed $2,269 billion each year, and the net cost is an estimated $1,666 billion. When criminals' costs are assumed to equal the value of time spent planning and committing crimes and in prison, the estimated annual gross and net costs of crime are $1,705 and $1,102 billion respectively. Table 5 presents the aggregate costs of crime based on the more conservative, time-based estimation method. The disaggregation of this and the previous tables facilitates the creation of customized estimates based on the reader's preferred assumptions. Each of the general studies summarized in Table 1 included transfers, so the appropriate comparison is to the gross cost estimate in the current study. As the result of a more comprehensive treatment of repercussions, the cost of crime is now seen to be more than twice as large as previously recognized.

Table 5

The Aggregate Burden of Crime	$ (billions)
Crime-Induced Production	397
Opportunity Costs	130
Risks to Life and Health	574
Transfers	603
Gross Burden	**$1,705**
Net of Transfers	**$1,102**
Per Capita (in dollars)	**$4,118**

Conclusion

Previous studies of the burden of crime have counted crimes or concentrated on direct crime costs. This paper calculates the aggregate burden of crime rather than absolute numbers, includes indirect costs, and recognizes that transfers resulting from theft should not be included in the net burden of crime to society. The accuracy of society's perspective on crime costs will improve with the understanding that these costs extend beyond victims' losses and the cost of law enforcement to include the opportunity costs of criminals' and prisoners' time, our inability to behave as desired, and the private costs of crime deterrence.

As criminals acquire an estimated $603 billion dollars worth of assets from their victims, they generate an additional $1,102 billion worth of lost productivity, crime-related expenses, and diminished quality of life. The net losses represent an annual per capita burden of $4,118. Including transfers, the aggregate burden of crime is $1,705 billion. In the United States, this is of the same order of magnitude as life insurance purchases ($1,680 billion), the outstanding mortgage debt to commercial banks and savings institutions ($1,853 billion), and annual expenditures on health ($1,038 billion).

As the enormity of this negative-sum game comes to light, so, too, will the need for countervailing efforts to redefine legal policy and forge new ethical standards. Periodic estimates of the full cost of crime could speak to the success of national strategies to encourage decorum, including increased expenditures on law enforcement, new community strategic approaches, technological innovations, legal reform, education, and the development of ethics curricula. Economic theory dictates that resources should be devoted to moral enhancement until the benefits from marginal efforts are surpassed by their costs. Programs that decrease the burden of crime by more than the cost of implementation should be continued, while those associated with negligible or positive net increments in the cost of crime should be altered to better serve societal goals.

Critical Thinking

1. What crimes inflict the highest costs on society but are seldom punished?

2. The total costs of all crime may be over $1 trillion. What makes crime so costly?

From *Journal of Law and Economics*, vol. 42, October 1999, pp. 611–642. Copyright © 1999 by David A. Anderson. Reprinted by permission of the author.

Crime, Inequality & Social Justice

GLENN C. LOURY

Crime and punishment are certainly contentious topics, and the authors gathered in this issue do not always agree with one another. For my own part, I must confess to having a personal stake in this issue. As an African American male, a baby boomer born and raised on Chicago's South Side, I can identify with the plight of the urban poor because I have lived among them. I am tied to them by the bonds of social and psychic affiliation. I myself have passed through the courtroom and the jailhouse on my way along life's journey. I have twice been robbed at gunpoint. I have known–personally and intimately–men and women who lived their entire lives with one foot on either side of the law. Whenever I step to a lectern to speak about incarceration, I envision voiceless and despairing people–both offenders and victims–who would have me speak on their behalf. Of course, personal biography has no authority to compel agreement about public policy. Still, I prefer candor in such matters to a false pretense of clinical detachment and scientific objectivity. While I recognize that these revelations will discredit me in some quarters, that is a fate which I can live with. Allow me to share a few critical observations of my own about crime, inequality, and social justice.

One principal point of disagreement among contributors to this volume has to do with how the fact of mass incarceration relates to the social problem of crime. Mark Kleiman claims that mass incarceration is only a partial problem definition; the other part of the problem is crime. This stance is in sharp contrast to that of Loïc Wacquant, who insists that "hyperincarceration" (his preferred term, since only those living in the lower social strata face much risk of imprisonment) isn't really about crime at all. Rather, he says, it's about "managing dispossessed and dishonored populations." There is merit in both viewpoints. There can be no doubt that public ideas about crime–especially fears of violent victimization–have fueled the imprisonment boom. To speak of a crisis of mass imprisonment without reference to crime is, indeed, to address only one part of the problem. After all, declarations of "war" against crime (and, most noticeably, against *criminals*) are a primary means by which political aspirants now signal their bona fides to their electorates. The long upward trend in crime rates from the mid-1960s to the early 1980s "primed the penal pump" by hardening attitudes and discrediting liberal criminal justice policies. It is certainly the case, therefore, that the steep rise of imprisonment in the United States is closely intertwined with the social experience and political salience of crime in American life. We cannot understand the one without thinking carefully about the other. Nor can we persuade voters to undo the one without addressing their concerns about the other.

Yet evidence suggests that changes over time in the scale of incarceration have not been caused in any direct way by changes in the extent of criminal behavior. Indeed, linkages between prisons and crime have been anything but simple and direct. Prison populations have been on the rise steadily for more than three decades. However, crime rates increased in the 1970s; fell, then rose again in the 1980s; and increased before sharply decreasing again in the 1990s. For two generations, crime rates have fluctuated with no apparent relationship to a steady climb in the extent of imprisonment. Today, with prison populations as large as they have ever been in American history, crime rates are about the same as they were in 1970, when a then-falling United States prison population reached its lowest level in a generation. Prisons and crime cannot be rightly understood simply as opposite sides of the same coin. Incarceration does not exhaust the available means of crime control. Nor does criminal offending directly explain the profound *qualitative* institutional transformation that we have witnessed in the United States over the past two generations.[1]

Further, the trend of racial disparity in imprisonment rates cannot be accounted for as a consequence of changes in rates of offending over time. Crime rates, especially for violent offenses, have always been higher among African Americans than whites in the United States. This long-term disparity goes far toward explaining the historical fact of greater imprisonment for African Americans. Certainly there is little doubt that those who commit violent crimes should be punished, regardless of race. If more African Americans commit such offenses, more will be imprisoned, and no issues of impropriety would be raised thereby. Yet it is significant that the racial disparity of imprisonment rates has increased dramatically since the prison boom began, largely because of the "war on drugs." African Americans were vastly overrepresented among persons incarcerated for drug offenses during the 1980s and 1990s, even as African Americans were no more likely to be using or selling drugs than whites. Moreover, despite a sharp drop in violent crime rates, starting in the early 1990s and extending to the present, racial differences in imprisonment rates have begun a slight decline only in the last few years.

As for the links between imprisonment and public safety, the widely held notion that one prevents crime by incapacitating criminals is simplistic. It fails to take account of the fact that for many crimes–selling drugs, for instance–incapacitated criminals are simply replaced by others, there being no shortage of contenders vying for a chance to enter the illicit trade. (It also ignores the reality of criminal victimization within prisons–no small matter.) Furthermore, by adopting a more holistic view of the complex connections between prisons and communities, we can immediately recognize the significance of the fact that almost everyone who goes to prison is eventually released, most after just two or three years. Evidence suggests that for these hundreds of thousands of ex-offenders released each year, time behind bars will have *diminished,* not enhanced, their odds of living crime-free lives: by lowering employability, severing ties to communal supports, and hardening attitudes.

Thus, the impact of high incarceration rates on the sustainable level of public safety over the long term is ambiguous. The fact–amply demonstrated for the case of Chicago by Robert Sampson and Charles Loeffler in this volume–that incarceration in large American cities is so highly concentrated means that the ill effects of having spent time behind bars may diminish the social opportunities of others who reside in the most heavily impacted communities and who themselves have done nothing wrong. Spatial concentration of imprisonment may foster criminality because it undermines the informal social processes of order maintenance, which are the primary means of sustaining pro-social behavior in all communities. In some poor urban neighborhoods, as many as one in five adult men is behind bars on any given day. As the criminologist Todd Clear has written, "[T]he cycling of these young men through the prison system has become a central factor determining the social ecology of poor neighborhoods, where there is hardly a family without a son, an uncle or a father who has done time in prison."[2] This ubiquity of the prison experience in poor, minority urban neighborhoods has left families in these places less effective at inculcating in their children the kinds of delinquency-resistant self controls and pro-social attitudes that typically insulate youths against lawbreaking. As Clear concludes from his review of the evidence, "[D]eficits in informal social controls that result from high levels of incarceration are, in fact, crime-promoting. The high incarceration rates in poor communities destabilize the social relationships in these places and help cause crime rather than prevent it."

The relationship between prison and public safety is complicated in view of the fact that "what happens in San Quentin need not stay in San Quentin." Nor does the evidence afford us much comfort in the thought that, at the very least, a threat of imprisonment will deter future would-be offenders from breaking the law. Among children exposed to an incarcerated parent or sibling–youngsters who can be assumed to have firsthand knowledge of the penalties associated with law-breaking–the likelihood of their eventual incarceration is actually higher, not lower, than is the case for otherwise comparable children with no such exposure, which attests to the weakness of the deterrent effect of the sanction. Furthermore, in a careful review of the econometric evidence on this question, economist Steven Durlauf and public policy expert Daniel Nagin conclude:

The key empirical conclusion of our literature review is that there is relatively little reliable evidence for variation in the severity of punishment having a substantial deterrent effect, but there is relatively strong evidence that variation in the certainty of punishment has a large deterrent effect. . . . One policy-relevant implication of this conclusion is that lengthy prison sentences, particularly in the form of mandatory minimum type statutes such as California's Three Strikes Law, are difficult to justify on a deterrence-based crime prevention basis.[3]

Disparities by social class in this punishment binge are enormous, and they have far-reaching and often deleterious consequences for the families and communities affected. The prisoners come mainly from the most disadvantaged corners of our unequal society; the prisons both reflect and exacerbate this inequality. The factors that lead young people to crime–the "root causes"–have long been known: disorganized childhoods, inadequate educations, child abuse, limited employability, delinquent peers. These are factors that also have long been more prevalent among the poor than the middle classes, though it has for some time been unfashionable to speak of "root causes." Nevertheless, as Bruce Western stresses in his comprehensive empirical survey of this terrain, "punishment" and "inequality" are intimately linked in modern America, and the causality runs in both directions.[4]

Racial disparities in the incidence of incarceration are also huge. The subordinate status of African American ghetto-dwellers–their social deprivation and spatial isolation in America's cities–puts their residents at great risk of embracing the dysfunctional behaviors that lead to incarceration. Also, it is quite clear that punishment policies serve expressive, not merely instrumental, ends. Americans have wanted to "send a message," and have done so with a vengeance. In the midst of such dramaturgy–necessarily so in America–has lurked a potent racial subplot. Inequalities by race in the realm of punishment exceed those found in just about any other arena of American social life: at roughly seven to one, the black-white ratio of male incarceration rates dwarfs the two to one ratio of unemployment rates, the three to one nonmarital child-bearing ratio, the two to one black-white ratio of infant mortality rates, and the one to five ratio of net worth. (The homicide rate is a noteworthy exception to this generalization about racial disproportions. For twenty- to twenty-nine-year-old males, the black-white ratio has been in the neighborhood of ten to one in recent years.) It is of some political significance that, for young African American men, coercion is the most salient feature of their encounters with the American state. In this issue, Bruce Western and Becky Pettit report that more African American male high school dropouts are held in prisons than belong to unions or are enrolled in any (other) state or federal social welfare programs. They estimate that nearly 70 percent of African American male dropouts born between 1975 and 1979 will have spent at least one year in prison before reaching the age of thirty-five.

Given the scale of imprisonment for African American men, and the troubled history of race relations in this country, it can be no surprise that some observers see the advent of mass incarceration as the catalyst for a new front in the long, historic, and still incomplete struggle for racial justice.[5] Because history and political culture matter, considering the factor of race is crucial to a full understanding and evaluation of our current policy regime. It is true that slavery ended a long time ago. But it is also true that an ideology of racial subordination accompanied the institution of African slavery, and this racial ideology has cast a long shadow. Thus, in his recently published history of the entanglement of race with crime in American political culture at the turn of the twentieth century,[6] historian Khalil Muhammad contrasts the treatment of two related, but differently experienced, phenomena: crime by newly arrived European immigrants and crime by African Americans. Looking at the emergent statistical social-science literatures of that period, Muhammad makes clear that the prevailing ideological climate in the United States at that time led analysts and critics to construe the many problems of urbanizing and industrializing America in distinct ways. In essence, poor, white city-dwelling migrants were understood to be committing crimes, but the poor African Americans migrating to those same cities were seen as inherently criminal.

Our unlovely history of race relations is linked to the current situation, both as a matter of social causation—since the structure of our cities, with their massive racial ghettos, is implicated in the production of deviancy among those living there—and as a matter of ethical evaluation—since the decency of our institutions depends on whether they comport with a narrative of national purpose that recognizes and seeks to limit and to reverse the consequences of history's wrongs. It is certainly arguable (take Loïc Wacquant's essay in this volume, for example) that managing social dysfunction via imprisonment has now become the primary instrument for reproducing racial stratification in American society.

What does all this tell us about our purportedly open and democratic society? What manner of people do our punishment policies reveal us Americans to be? Just look at what we have wrought. We have established what, to many an outside observer, looks like a system of social caste in the centers of our great cities. I refer here to millions of stigmatized, feared, and invisible people. The extent of disparity between the children of the middle class and the children of the disadvantaged to achieve their full human potential is virtually unrivaled elsewhere in the industrial, advanced, civilized, free world. And it is a disparity that is apparently taken for granted in America.

I see the broader society as implicated in the creation and maintenance of these damaged, neglected, feared, and despised communities. People who live in these places know that outsiders view them with suspicion and contempt. The plain historical fact is that North Philadelphia, the West Side of Chicago, the East Side of Detroit, or South Central Los Angeles did not come into being by accident or because of some natural processes.

As Wacquant emphasizes in this issue, these social formations are man-made structures that were created and have persisted because the concentration of their residents in such urban enclaves serves the interests of others. The desperate and vile behaviors of some of the people caught in these social structures reflect not merely their personal moral deviance, but also the moral shortcomings of our society as a whole. Yet many Americans have concluded, in effect, that those languishing at the margins of our society are simply reaping what they have sown. Their suffering is seen as having nothing to do with us—as not being evidence of broader, systemic failures that can be corrected through collective action. As a consequence, there is no broadly based demand for reform—no sense of moral outrage, anguished self-criticism, or public reflection—in the face of what is a massive, collective failure. American political culture, it seems, accepts as credible no account of personal malfeasance other than the conclusion that the offending individual is unworthy.

The legal scholar William Stuntz has recently called attention to the close connection in American history between local control, democratic governance, and inequalities of punishment.[7] He suggests, persuasively in my view, that increases in the severity and inequality of American punishment have mainly been due to a shift over the course of the twentieth century in the ways that crime and punishment policies are formulated. Because caseloads have grown alongside reliance on plea bargaining, prosecutors have gained power at the expense of juries; because a thicket of constitutional protections has been elaborated, federal appellate judges exert more influence than trial judges; because of population decentralization trends in large urban areas—with judges now elected mostly on county-wide ballots and police no longer drawn preponderantly from the communities where they make arrests—suburban and exurban voters now have a good deal more to say than do central-city residents about crime control policies, even though they are less affected by those policies.

The law, Stuntz argues, has grown more extensive in its definition of criminality and has left less room for situational discretion. Alienation of urban populations from democratic control over the apparatus of punishment has resulted in more inequality and less leniency. There is too much law and too little (local) politics. Local populations bear the brunt of the misbehavior by the lawbreakers in their midst. Yet, at the same time, they are closely connected to lawbreakers via bonds of social and psychic affiliation. Mass incarceration is a political not a legal crisis, one that arises from a disjunction between the "locus of control" and the "locus of interests" in the formulation of punishment policies.

Following Stuntz, I wish to suggest that punishment, rightly construed, is a communal affair; and that an ambiguity of relationship—involving proximity to both sides of the offender-victim divide and a wealth of local knowledge combined with keen local interests—is essential to doing justice. Viewed in this light, hyperincarceration and the (racial) inequalities that it has bred are more deeply disturbing because urban minority communities, where both the depredations of crime and the enormous costs of its unequal punishment are experienced, have effectively been divorced from any means of influencing the administration of criminal justice.

To the extent that the socially marginal are not seen as belonging to the same general public body as the rest of us, it becomes possible to do just about anything with them. Yet, in my view, a pure ethic of *personal responsibility* could never provide an adequate foundation for justifying the current situation. In making this claim, I am not invoking a "root causes" argument (he did the crime, but only because he had no choice) so much as I am arguing that society as a whole is implicated in the offender's choices. We have acquiesced in structural arrangements that work to our benefit and the offender's detriment and that shape his consciousness and sense of identity such that his choices, which we must condemn, are nevertheless compelling to him.

In his influential treatise, *A Theory of Justice,* the philosopher John Rawls distinguishes between principles that should govern the distribution of primary goods in society and the very different principles that should determine the distribution of the "negative good" of punishment. He explicitly states that justice in the distribution of economic and social advantages is "entirely different" from justice in the realm of criminal punishment. He even refers to "bad character" as relevant to punishment.[8] As I understand Rawls, his famous "difference principle"–arrived at in "reflective equilibrium" from his hypothetical "original position"–presupposes the moral irrelevance of the mechanisms by which inequalities emerge. (For example, Rawls sees "ability" as a morally irrelevant trait, a manifestation of luck. So, unequal individual rewards based on differences in ability cannot be justified on the grounds of desert.) Yet because he does not see the mechanisms that lead to disparities of punishment as being morally irrelevant, he would not apply the difference principle when assessing the (in)justice of such inequalities, since they are linked to wrongdoing.

In my view, justice is complex because the consequences wrought by our responses to wrongdoing also raise questions of justice. The phrase "Let justice be done though the heavens may fall" is, for me, an oxymoron; no concept of justice deserving the name would accept mass suffering simply because of blind adherence to an abstract principle (such as "do the crime, and you'll do the time"). It is common for ethicists to say things such as "social welfare should be maximized subject to deontological constraints," meaning that actions like distributing body parts taken from a healthy person to render ten other persons healthy cannot be morally justified. But this conviction should go both ways: abstract moral goals should be subjected to constraints that weigh the consequences induced by such pursuits. In the realm of punishment, retribution against offenders and notions of deserved punishment exemplify deontological principles. But even if current incarceration policies perfectly embodied these principles (and that is an eminently dubious proposition), it still would not be sufficient to justify such rigid adherence to moral obligation. For the reason that the effects of mass incarceration–on families and communities that may themselves have done nothing wrong–can cause sufficient harm, the principled claims that punishment is deserved should not be allowed to dictate policy at whim. A million criminal cases, each one rightly decided, can still add up to a great and historic wrong.

Endnotes

1. For an illuminating exploration of the deeper roots of this transformation, see David Garland, *The Culture of Control: Crime and Social Order in Contemporary Society* (Chicago: University of Chicago Press, 2001).

2. Todd R. Clear, *Imprisoning Communities: How Mass Incarceration Makes Disadvantaged Neighborhoods Worse* (New York: Oxford University Press, 2009), 10.

3. Steven Durlauf and Daniel Nagin, "The Deterrent Effect of Imprisonment," unpublished working paper (University of Wisconsin-Madison, March 2010).

4. Bruce Western, *Punishment and Inequality in America* (New York: Russell Sage Foundation, 2006).

5. See Michelle Alexander, *The New Jim Crow: Mass Incarceration in the Age of Colorblindness* (New York: New Press, 2010).

6. Khalil Gibran Muhammad, *The Condemnation of Blackness: Race, Crime, and the Making of Modern Urban America* (Cambridge, Mass.: Harvard University Press, 2010).

7. William Stuntz, "Unequal Justice," *Harvard Law Review* 121 (8) (June 2008): 1969–2040.

8. The full quote from Rawls is: "It is true that in a reasonably well-ordered society those who are punished for violating just laws have normally done something wrong. This is because the purpose of the criminal law is to uphold basic natural duties, those which forbid us to injure other persons in their life and limb, or to deprive them of their liberty and property, and punishments are to serve this end. They are not simply a scheme of taxes and burdens designed to put a price on certain forms of conduct and in this way to guide men's conduct for mutual advantage. It would be far better if the acts proscribed by penal statutes were never done. Thus a propensity to commit such acts is a mark of bad character, and in a just society legal punishments will only fall upon those who display these faults"; John Rawls, *A Theory of Justice,* rev. ed. (1971; Cambridge, Mass.: Belknap Press of Harvard University Press, 1999), 314–315.

Critical Thinking

1. Why is there so much injustice in the justice system?

2. Why are imprisonment rates so high in the United States?

3. Discuss the racial biases in the justice system.

Wrongful Convictions

RADLEY BALKO

How many innocent Americans are behind bars? When Paul House was finally released from prison in 2008, he was a specter of the man who had been sentenced to death more than 22 years earlier. When I visit his home in Crossville, Tennessee, in March, House's mother Joyce, who has cared for him since his release, points to a photo of House taken the day he was finally allowed to come home. In that photo and others from his last days in prison, House is all of 150 pounds, ashen and drawn, his fragile frame nearly consumed by his wheelchair. In most of the images he looks days away from death, although in one he wears the broad smile of a man finally escaping a long confinement.

When House's aunt called to congratulate him on his first day back, his mother handed him her cell phone so he could chat. He inspected the phone, gave her a frustrated look, and asked her to find him one that worked. That kind of Rip Van Winkle moment is common among people freed after a long stint in prison. Dennis Fritz, one of the two wrongly convicted men profiled in John Grisham's 2006 book *The Innocent Man,* talks about nearly calling the police upon seeing someone use an electronic key card the first time he found himself in a hotel after his release. He thought he'd witnessed a burglar use a credit card to jimmy open a door.

"Paul's first meal when he got home was chili verde," Joyce House says. "It's his favorite. And I had been waiting a long time to make it for him." And apparently quite a few meals after that. House, now 49, has put on 75 pounds since his release. More important, he has been getting proper treatment for his advanced-stage multiple sclerosis, treatment the Tennessee prison system hadn't given him.

The years of inadequate care have taken a toll. House can't walk, and he needs help with such basic tasks as bathing, feeding himself, and maneuvering around in his wheelchair. His once distinctively deep voice (which had allegedly been heard by a witness at the crime scene) is now wispy and high-pitched. He spends his time playing computer games and watching game shows.

In the hour or so that I visit with House, his mental facilities fade in and out. Communicating with him can be like trying to listen to a baseball game broadcast by a distant radio station. He will give a slurred but lucid answer to one question, then answer the next one with silence, or with the answer to a previous question, or just with a random assortment of words. He frequently falls back on the resigned refrain, "Oh, well," delivered with a shrug. The gesture and phrasing are identical every time he uses them. It's what House says to kill the expectation that he will be able to deliver the words others in the room are waiting for. It's his signal to stop waiting for him and move on.

In 1986 House was convicted of murdering Carolyn Muncey in Union County, Tennessee, a rural part of the state that shoulders Appalachia. He was sentenced to death. His case is a textbook study in wrongful conviction. It includes mishandled evidence, prosecutorial misconduct, bad science, cops with tunnel vision, DNA testing, the near-execution of an innocent man, and an appellate court reluctant to reopen old cases even in the face of new evidence that strongly suggests the jury got it wrong.

House also embodies the tribulations and frustrations that the wrongly convicted encounter once they get out. According to the doctors treating him, his current condition is the direct result of the inadequate care he received in prison. If he is ever granted a formal exoneration—a process that can be as much political as it is judicial—he will be eligible for compensation for his years behind bars, but even then the money comes with vexing conditions and limitations.

Since 1989, DNA testing has freed 268 people who were convicted of crimes they did not commit. There are dozens of other cases, like House's, where DNA strongly suggests innocence but does not conclusively prove it. Convicting and imprisoning an innocent person is arguably the worst thing a government can do to one of its citizens, short of mistakenly executing him. (There's increasing evidence that this has happened too.) Just about everyone agrees that these are unfathomable tragedies. What is far less clear, and still hotly debated, is what these cases say about the way we administer justice in America, what we owe the wrongly convicted, and how the officials who send innocent people to prison should be held accountable.

How Many Are Innocent?

According to the Innocence Project, an advocacy group that provides legal aid to the wrongly convicted, the average DNA exoneree served 13 years in prison before he or she was freed. Seventeen had been sentenced to death. Remarkably, 67 percent of the exonerated were convicted after 2000, the year that marked the onset of modern DNA testing. Each new exoneration adds more urgency to the question that has hovered over these cases since the first convict was cleared by DNA in 1989: How many more innocent people are waiting to be freed?

Given the soundness of DNA testing, we can be nearly certain that the 268 cleared so far didn't commit the crimes for which they were convicted. There are hundreds of other cases where no DNA evidence exists to definitively establish guilt or innocence, but a prisoner has been freed due to lack of evidence, recantation of eyewitness testimony, or police or prosecutorial misconduct. Those convictions were overturned because there was insufficient evidence to overcome reasonable doubt; it does not necessarily mean the defendant didn't commit the crime. It's unclear whether and how those cases should be factored into any attempt to estimate the number of innocent people in prison.

In a country where there are 15,000 to 20,000 homicides each year, 268 exonerations over two decades may seem like an acceptable margin of error. But reform advocates point out that DNA testing is conclusive only in a small percentage of criminal cases. Testing is helpful only in solving crimes where exchange of DNA is common and significant, mostly rape and murder. (And most murder exonerations have come about because the murder was preceded by a rape that produced testable DNA.) Even within this subset of cases, DNA evidence is not always preserved, nor is it always dispositive to the identity of the perpetrator.

Death penalty cases add urgency to this debate. In a 2007 study published in the *Journal of Criminal Law and Criminology,* the Seton Hall law professor Michael Risinger looked at cases of exoneration for capital murder-rapes between 1982 and 1989, compared them to the total number of murder-rape cases over that period for which DNA would be a factor, and estimated from that data that 3 percent to 5 percent of the people convicted of capital crimes probably are innocent. If Risinger is right, it's still unclear how to extrapolate figures for the larger prison population. Some criminologists argue that there is more pressure on prosecutors and jurors to convict someone, anyone, in high-profile murder cases. That would suggest a higher wrongful conviction rate in death penalty cases. But defendants also tend to have better representation in capital cases, and media interest can also mean more scrutiny for police and prosecutors. That could lead to fewer wrongful convictions.

In a study published in the *Journal of Criminal Law and Criminology* in 2005, a team led by University of Michigan law professor Samuel Gross looked at 328 exonerations of people who had been convicted of rape, murder, and other felonies between 1989 and 2003. They found that while those who have been condemned to die make up just 1 percent of the prison population, they account for 22 percent of the exonerated. But does that mean capital cases are more likely to bring a wrongful conviction? Or does it mean the attention and scrutiny that death penalty cases get after conviction—particularly as an execution date nears—make it more likely that wrongful convictions in capital cases will be discovered?

Many states have special public defender offices that take over death penalty cases after a defendant has exhausted his appeals. These offices tend to be well-staffed, with enough funding to hire their own investigators and forensic specialists. That sometimes stands in stark contrast to the public defender offices that handled the same cases at trial. Perversely, this means that in some jurisdictions, a defendant wrongly convicted of murder may be better off with a death sentence than with life in prison.

Even if we were to drop below the floor set in the Risinger study and assume that 2 percent of the 2008 prison population was innocent, that would still mean about 46,000 people have been convicted and incarcerated for crimes they didn't commit. But some skeptics say even that figure is way too high.

Joshua Marquis, the district attorney for Clatsop County, Oregon, is an outspoken critic of the Innocence Project and of academics like Risinger and Gross. He is skeptical of the belief that wrongful convictions are common. "If I thought that 3 to 5 percent of people in prison right now were innocent, I'd quit my job," Marquis says. "I'd become a public defender or something. Maybe an activist. Look, nobody but a fool would say that wrongful convictions don't happen. As a prosecutor, my worst nightmare is not losing a case—I've lost cases; I'll lose cases in the future. My worst nightmare is convicting an innocent person, and I tell my staff that. But the question here is whether wrongful convictions are epidemic or episodic. And I just don't think it's possible that the number could be anywhere near 3 to 5 percent."

Marquis and Gross have been butting heads for several years. In a 2006 *New York Times* op-ed piece, Marquis took the 328 exonerations Gross and his colleagues found between 1989 and 2003, rounded it up to 340, then multiplied it by 10—a charitable act, he wrote, to "give the professor the benefit of the doubt." He then divided that number by 15 million, the total number of felony convictions during the same period, and came up with what he said was an error rate of just 0.027 percent. His column was later quoted in a concurring opinion by U.S. Supreme Court Justice Antonin Scalia in the 2006 case *Kansas v. Marsh,* the same opinion where Scalia made the notorious claim that nothing in the U.S. Constitution prevents the government from executing an innocent person.

Gross responded with a 2008 article in the *Annual Review of Law and Social Science,* pointing out that his original number was by no means comprehensive. Those were merely the cases in which a judicial or political process had exonerated someone. The figure suggested only that wrongful convictions happen. "By [Marquis'] logic we could estimate the proportion of baseball players who've used steroids by dividing the number of major league players who've been caught by the total of all baseball players at all levels: major league, minor league, semipro, college and Little League," Gross wrote, "and maybe throw in football and basketball players as well."

Whatever the total number of innocent convicts, there is good reason to believe that the 268 cases in which DNA evidence has proven innocence don't begin to scratch the surface. For one thing, the pace of these exonerations hasn't slowed down: There were 22 in 2009, making it the second busiest name-clearing year to date. Furthermore, exonerations are expensive in both time and resources. Merely discovering a possible case and requesting testing often isn't enough. With some commendable exceptions . . . prosecutors tend to fight requests for post-conviction DNA testing. (The U.S. Supreme Court held in 2009 that there is no constitutional right to such tests.) So for now, the pace of genetic exonerations appears to be limited primarily by the amount of money and staff that legal advocacy groups have to uncover these cases and argue them in court, the amount of evidence available for testing, and the willingness of courts to allow the process to happen, not by a lack of cases in need of further investigation.

It's notable that one of the few places in America where a district attorney has specifically dedicated staff and resources to seeking out bad convictions—Dallas County, Texas—has produced more exonerations than all but a handful of states. That's partly because Dallas County District Attorney Craig Watkins is more interested in reopening old cases than his counterparts elsewhere, and partly because of a historical quirk: Since the early 1980s the county has been sending biological crime scene evidence to a private crime lab for testing, and that lab has kept the evidence well preserved. Few states require such evidence be preserved once a defendant has exhausted his appeals, and in some jurisdictions the evidence is routinely destroyed at that point.

"I don't think there was anything unique about the way Dallas was prosecuting crimes," Watkins told me in 2008. "It's unfortunate that other places didn't preserve evidence too. We're just in a unique position where I can look at a case, test DNA evidence from that period, and say without a doubt that a person is innocent. . . . But that doesn't mean other places don't have the same problems Dallas had."

If the rest of the country has an actual (but undetected) wrongful conviction rate as high as Dallas County's, the number of innocents in prison for felony crimes could be in the tens of thousands.

The Trial and Conviction of Paul House

As with many wrongful convictions, the case against Paul House once seemed watertight. House was an outsider, having only recently moved to Union County when Carolyn Muncey was murdered in 1985, and he was an ex-con, having served five years in a Utah prison for sexual assault. He got into scuffles with locals, although he considered Muncey and her husband, Hubert, friends. When Muncey turned up dead, House was a natural suspect.

House has claimed he was innocent of the Utah charge. His mother, Joyce, says it was a he said/she said case in which her son pleaded guilty on the advice of his attorney. "He could have been paroled earlier if he had shown some remorse," she says. "But he said, 'I pled guilty the one time, because that's what the lawyer told me I should do. I'm not going to say

again that I did something I didn't do.' He said he'd rather serve more time than admit to the rape again." Joyce House and Mike Pemberton, Paul House's attorney, are hesitant to go into much detail about the Utah case, and public records aren't available due to the plea bargain. But while what happened in Utah certainly makes House less sympathetic, it has no bearing on whether House is the man who killed Carolyn Muncey.

House also didn't do himself any favors during the Muncey investigation. In initial questioning, he lied to the police about where he was the night of the murder, saying he was with his girlfriend all night. But he later admitted he had gone for a walk at one point and had come back without his shoes and with scratches on his arms. He initially lied to police about the scratches too, saying they were inflicted by his girlfriend's cats. House later said he'd been accosted by some locals while on his walk, scuffled with them, then fled through a field, where he lost his shoes. (House would learn years later that his shoes were found by police before his trial. There was no blood or other biological evidence on them, potentially exculpatory information that was never turned over to House's lawyers.)

"I think it was a situation where you're on parole, you're an outsider, and this woman has just been killed near where you live," says Pemberton, House's attorney. "It wasn't smart of him to lie to the police. But it was understandable."

Carolyn Muncey's husband, who House's attorneys would later suspect was her killer, also lied about where he was when she was killed. He would additionally claim, falsely, that he had never physically abused her. Still, House was clearly the early suspect.

The strongest evidence against House was semen found on Muncey's clothing, which an FBI agent testified at trial "could have" belonged to House. DNA testing didn't exist in 1986, but the agent said House was a secretor, meaning he produced blood type secretions in other body fluids, including semen, and that the type secreted in semen found on Muncey's nightgown was a match to House's type A blood. About 80 percent of people are secretors, and about 36 percent of Americans have type A blood. The agent also said the semen found on Muncey's panties included secretions that didn't match House's blood type, but added, inaccurately, that House's secretion could have "degraded" into a match. Muncey's husband was never tested.

The other strong evidence against House was some blood stains on his jeans that matched Muncey's blood type, but not his own. Those stains on House's jeans did turn out to have been Muncey's blood; the question is how they got there.

House was never charged with rape; there were no physical indications that Muncey had been sexually assaulted. But the semen was used to put him at the crime scene, and the state used the possibility of rape as an aggravating circumstance in arguing that House should receive the death penalty.

House was convicted in February 1986. The morning after his conviction, just hours before the sentencing portion of his trial, House slashed his wrists with a disposable razor. He left behind a suicide note in which he professed his innocence. Jail officials rushed him to a hospital in Knoxville, where doctors saved his life and stitched up his wounds. He was then sent back to the courthouse, where a jury sentenced him to death.

It wasn't until more than a decade later, in 1999, that the case against House began to erode. New witnesses came forward with accusations against Hubert Muncey, Carolyn's husband. Several said he was an alcoholic who frequently beat her. At an ensuing evidentiary hearing, two other women said Hubert had drunkenly confessed to killing his wife several months after the murder. When one went to the police with the information the next day, she said at the hearing, the sheriff brushed her off. Another witness testified that Hubert Muncey had asked her to lie to back up his alibi.

But it was the forensic evidence presented at that 1999 hearing that really unraveled the state's case. When House's attorneys were finally able to get DNA testing for the semen found on Carolyn Muncey's clothes, it showed that the semen was a match to Muncey's husband, not House. The state responded that rape was never part of their case against House (though it is why he was initially a suspect, it was the only conceivable motive, and it was presented as evidence in the sentencing portion of his trial). Besides, prosecutors argued, there was still the blood on House's jeans.

Except there were problems with that too. Cleland Blake, an assistant chief medical examiner for the state of Tennessee, testified that while the blood did belong to Muncey, its chemical composition indicated it was blood that had been taken after she had been autopsied. Worse still, three-quarters of a test tube of the blood taken during Muncey's autopsy went missing between the time of the autopsy and the time House's jeans arrived at the FBI crime lab for testing. The test tubes with Muncey's blood and House's jeans were transported in the same Styrofoam box. The blood on House's jeans, his attorneys argued, must have either been planted or spilled because of sloppy handling of the evidence.

It is extraordinarily difficult to win a new trial in a felony case, even in light of new evidence, and House's case was no exception. A federal circuit court judge denied his request for post-conviction relief, and the U.S. Court of Appeals for the 6th Circuit affirmed that decision. Somewhat surprisingly, the U.S. Supreme Court agreed to hear House's case, and in 2006 issued a rare, bitterly divided 5-to-3 ruling granting House a new trial.

The Supreme Court has occasionally thrown out death penalty convictions because of procedural errors or constitutional violations, but it's rare for the Court to methodically review the evidence in a capital case. Writing for the majority, Justice Anthony Kennedy did exactly that, finding in the end that "although the issue is close, we conclude that this is the rare case where—had the jury heard all the conflicting testimony—it is more likely than not that no reasonable juror viewing the record as a whole would lack reasonable doubt."

It was a surprising and significant victory for House. But it would be another three years before he would be released from prison.

How Do Wrongful Convictions Happen?

The most significant consequence of the spate of DNA exonerations has been a much-needed reassessment of what we thought we knew about how justice is administered in America. Consider the chief causes of wrongful convictions:

Bad Forensic Evidence

DNA technology was developed by scientists, and it has been thoroughly peer-reviewed by other scientists. Most of the forensic science used in the courtroom, on the other hand, was either invented in police stations and crime labs or has been refined and revised there to fight crime and obtain convictions. Most forensic evidence isn't peer-reviewed, isn't subject to blind testing, and is susceptible to corrupting bias, both intentional and unintentional. The most careful analysts can fall victim to cognitive bias creeping into their work, particularly when their lab falls under the auspices of a law enforcement agency. Even fingerprint analysis isn't as sound as is commonly believed.

A congressionally commissioned 2009 report by the National Academy of Sciences found that many other forensic specialties that are often presented in court with the gloss of science—hair and carpet fiber analysis, blood spatter analysis, shoe print identification, and especially bite mark analysis—lack the standards, peer review, and testing procedures of genuinely scientific research and analysis. Some are not supported by any scientific literature at all. Moreover, the report found, even the forensic specialties with some scientific support are often portrayed in court in ways that play down error rates and cognitive bias.

According to an Innocence Project analysis of the first 225 DNA exonerations, flawed or fraudulent forensic evidence factored into about half of the faulty convictions.

Eyewitness Testimony

Social scientists have known about the inherent weakness of eyewitness testimony for decades. Yet it continues to be the leading cause of wrongful convictions in America; it was a factor in 77 percent of those first 225 cases. Simple steps, such as making sure police who administer lineups have no knowledge of the case (since they can give subtle clues to witnesses, even unintentionally) and that witnesses are told that the actual perpetrator may not be among the photos included in a lineup, can go a long way toward improving accuracy. But such reforms also make it more difficult to win convictions, so many jurisdictions, under pressure from police and prosecutor groups, have been hesitant to embrace them.

False Confessions

Difficult as it may be to comprehend, people do confess to crimes they didn't commit. It happened in about one-quarter of the first 225 DNA exonerations. Confessions are more common among suspects who are minors or are mentally handicapped, but they can happen in other contexts as well, particularly after intense or abusive police interrogations.

In a candid 2008 op-ed piece for the *Los Angeles Times,* D.C. Police Detective Jim Trainum detailed how he unwittingly coaxed a false confession out of a 34-year-old woman he suspected of murder. She even revealed details about the crime that could only have been known to police investigators and the killer. But Trainum later discovered that the woman couldn't possibly have committed the crime. When he reviewed video of his interrogation, he realized that he had inadvertently provided the woman with those very specific details, which she then repeated back to him when she was ready to confess.

Trainum concluded that all police interrogations should be videotaped, a policy that would not just discourage abusive questioning but also provide an incontrovertible record of how a suspect's confession was obtained. Here too, however, there has been pushback from some police agencies, out of fear that jurors may be turned off even by legitimate forms of questioning.

Jailhouse Informants

If you were to take every jailhouse informant at his word, you'd find that a remarkably high percentage of the people accused of felonies boast about their crimes to the complete strangers they meet in jail and prison cells. Informants are particularly valuable in federal drug cases, where helping a prosecutor obtain more convictions is often the only way to get time cut from a mandatory minimum sentence. That gives them a pretty good incentive to lie.

There is some disagreement over a prosecutor's duty to verify the testimony he solicits from jailhouse informants. In the 2006, Church Point, Louisiana, case of Ann Colomb, for example, Brett Grayson, an assistant U.S. attorney in Louisiana, put on a parade of jailhouse informants whose claims about buying drugs from Colomb and her sons were rather improbable, especially when the sum of their testimony was considered as a whole. According to defense attorneys I spoke with, when one attorney asked him if he actually believed what his informants were telling the jury, Grayson replied that it doesn't matter if he believes his witnesses; it only matters if the jury does. He expressed a similar sentiment in his closing argument.

After indicating that he isn't familiar with the Colomb case and isn't commenting on Grayson specifically, Josh Marquis says that sentiment is wrong. "A prosecutor absolutely has a duty to only put on evidence he believes is truthful," Marquis says. "And that includes the testimony you put on from informants."

In a 2005 study, the Center on Wrongful Convictions in Chicago found that false or misleading informant testimony was responsible for 38 wrongful convictions in death penalty cases.

The professional culture of the criminal justice system. In addition to the more specific causes of wrongful convictions listed above, there is a problem with the institutional culture among prosecutors, police officers, forensic analysts, and other officials. Misplaced incentives value high conviction rates more than a fair and equal administration of justice.

Prosecutors in particular enjoy absolute immunity from civil liability, even in cases where they manufacture evidence that leads to a wrongful conviction. The only time prosecutors can be sued is when they commit misconduct while acting as investigators—that is, while doing something police normally do. At that point they're subject to qualified immunity, which provides less protection than absolute immunity but still makes it difficult to recover damages.

Marquis says this isn't a problem. "Prosecutors are still subject to criminal liability," he says. "In fact, my predecessor here in Oregon was prosecuted for misconduct in criminal cases. State bars will also hold prosecutors accountable."

But criminal charges are few and far between, and prosecutors can make egregious mistakes that still don't rise to the level of criminal misconduct. Professional sanctions are also rare. A 2010 study by the Northern California Innocence Project found more than 700 examples between 1997 and 2009 in which a court had found misconduct on the part of a prosecutor in the state. Only six of those cases resulted in any disciplinary action by the state bar. A 2010 investigation of federal prosecutorial misconduct by *USA Today* produced similar results: Of 201 cases in which federal judges found that prosecutors had committed misconduct, just one resulted in discipline by a state bar association. Prosecutorial misconduct was a factor in about one-quarter of the first 225 DNA exonerations, but none of the prosecutors in those cases faced any significant discipline from the courts or the bar.

There is also a common misconception that appeals courts serve as a check on criminal justice abuse. It is actually rare for an appeals court to review the evidence in a criminal case. Appeals courts make sure trials abide by the state and federal constitutions and by state or federal rules of criminal procedure, but they almost never second-guess the conclusions of juries.

In a 2008 article published in the *Columbia Law Review,* the University of Virginia law professor Brandon L. Garrett looked at the procedural history of the first 200 cases of DNA exoneration. Of those, just 18 convictions were reversed by appellate courts. Another 67 defendants had their appeals denied with no written ruling at all. In 63 cases, the appellate court opinion described the defendant as guilty, and in 12 cases it referred to the "overwhelming" evidence of guilt. Keep in mind these were all cases in which DNA testing later proved actual innocence. In the remaining cases, the appeals courts either found the defendant's appeal without merit or found that the errors in the case were "harmless"—that is, there were problems with the case, but those problems were unlikely to have affected the jury's verdict due to the other overwhelming evidence of guilt.

"We've seen a lot of exoneration cases where, for example, the defendant raised a claim of ineffective assistance of counsel," says Peter Neufeld, co-founder of the Innocence Project of New York. "And in those cases, the appellate courts often found that the defense lawyer provided substandard representation. But they would then say that the poor lawyering didn't prejudice the case because the evidence of guilt was so overwhelming. Well, these people were later proven innocent! If you have a test that is frequently producing erroneous results, there's either something wrong with the test, or there's something wrong with the way it's being implemented."

Life on the Outside

Paul House was diagnosed with multiple sclerosis in 2000, a year after the evidentiary hearing that would eventually lead to his release. But while House was convicted of Carolyn Muncey's murder less than a year after it happened, it took a decade after his conviction was called into serious question for House to get back home to Crossville. During those 10 years, the state's case continued to fall apart. So did House's body.

After the U.S. Supreme Court overturned House's conviction in 2006, Paul Phillips, the district attorney for Tennessee's 8th Judicial District and the man who prosecuted House in 1986, pushed ahead with plans to retry him. In December 2007, after a series of delays, Harry S. Mattice Jr., a U.S. district court judge in Knoxville, finally ordered the state to try House within 180 days or set him free. Those 180 days then came and went without House being freed, thanks to an extension granted by the 6th Circuit.

In another hearing held in May 2008, Phillips argued that House—who by that point couldn't walk or move his wheelchair without assistance—presented a flight risk. Later, Tennessee Associate Deputy Attorney General Jennifer Smith attempted to show that House presented a danger to the public because he was still capable of feeding himself with a fork, which apparently meant he was also capable of stabbing someone with one. House's bail was set at $500,000, later reduced to $100,000. In July 2008, an anonymous donor paid the bail, allowing House to finally leave prison.

That same month, Phillips told the Associated Press that he would send two additional pieces of biological evidence off for DNA testing: a hair found at the crime scene, and blood found under Carolyn Muncey's fingernails. House's defense team had asked to conduct its own testing of any untested biological evidence for years, but had been told that either there was no such evidence or, if there was, the state didn't know where it was. Philips told the A.P. that if the new tests didn't implicate House, he would drop the murder charge and allow House to go home. In February 2009 the results came back. They didn't implicate House, and in fact pointed to a third, unidentified man. In May of that year, Phillips finally dropped the charge. But he still wouldn't clear House's name, telling Knoxville's local TV station WATE, "There is very adequate proof that Mr. House was involved in this crime. We just don't know the degree of culpability beyond a reasonable doubt." (Phillips' office did not respond to my requests for comment.)

By the time House was diagnosed with M.S. in 2000, his symptoms were already severe, although it took his mother, and not a prison doctor, to notice something was wrong. "I was visiting him, and I brought along some microwave popcorn," Joyce House recalls. "He asked me to heat it up, and I said, 'No, you heat it up.' When he got up, he had to prop himself up

and drag along the wall to get to the microwave. He couldn't even stand up straight." According to Joyce House, her son's doctors today say that the Tennessee prison system's failure to diagnose House's M.S. earlier—then treat it properly after it was diagnosed—may have taken years off his life. (M.S. is also exacerbated by stress.) The disease has also significantly diminished the quality of the life House has left.

Under Tennessee's compensation law for the wrongly convicted, if House is formally exonerated—and that's still a big if—he will be eligible for $50,000 for each year he was in prison, up to $1 million. But there's a catch. The compensation is given in annual $50,000 installments over 20 years. If House dies before then, the payments stop.

Most of the 27 states with compensation laws similarly pay the money off in installments. Last October, A.P. ran a story about Victor Burnette, a 57-year-old Virginia man who served eight years for a 1979 rape before he was exonerated by DNA testing in 2006. Burnette actually turned down the $226,500 the state offered in compensation in 2010 because he was offended by the stipulation that it be paid out over 25 years. Even after the DNA test confirmed his innocence, it took another three years for Burnette to officially be pardoned, which finally made him eligible for the money. The installment plans make it unlikely that many exonerees—especially long-timers, who are arguably the most deserving—will ever see full compensation for their years in prison.

Only about half the people exonerated by DNA testing so far have been compensated at all. Most compensation laws require official findings of actual innocence, which eliminates just about any case that doesn't involve DNA. Some states also exclude anyone who played some role in their own conviction, which would disqualify a defendant who falsely confessed, even if the confession was coerced or beaten out of them.

Paul House has yet another predicament ahead of him. Even if he does win an official exoneration, and even if he somehow lives long enough to receive all of his compensation, he'll have to lose his health insurance to accept it. House's medical care is currently covered by TennCare, Tennessee's Medicare program. If he accepts compensation for his conviction, he will be ineligible. His $50,000 per year in compensation for nearly a quarter century on death row will then be offset by a steep increase in what he'll have to pay for his medical care.

These odd, sometimes absurd predicaments aren't intentionally cruel. They just work out that way. Paul House's attorney Mike Pemberton points out that the prosecutors in these cases aren't necessarily evil, either. "Paul Phillips is an honorable man, and an outstanding trial attorney," Pemberton says. "But on this case he was wrong." Pemberton, who was once a prosecutor himself, says the job can lend itself to tunnel vision, especially once a prosecutor has won a conviction. It can be hard to let go. We have a system with misplaced incentives and very little accountability for state actors who make mistakes. That's a system ripe for bad outcomes.

When I ask Paul House why he thinks it has taken so long to clear his name, he starts to answer, then stammers, looks away, and retreats again to Oh well, his cue to move on because he has no answer.

That may be an understandable response from a guy with advanced M.S. who just spent two decades on death row. But for too long our national response to the increasing evidence that our justice system is flawed has been the same sort of resignation. DNA has only begun to show us where some of those flaws lie. It will take a strong public will to see that policymakers address them.

Critical Thinking

1. DNA has proven many convicted murderers innocent. Discuss estimates of the number of wrongful convictions and the reasons for them.

2. Wrongful convictions reveal some of the injustices in the justice system. How should it be reformed?

RADLEY BALKO (rbalko@reason.com) is a senior editor at reason.

From *Reason Magazine*, July 2011, pp. 20–33. Copyright © 2011 by Reason Foundation, 3415 S. Sepulveda Blvd., Suite 400, Los Angeles, CA 90034. www.reason.com

License to Kill

Immunity for Stand Your Ground shooters. Packing heat in bars. Gun permits for wife beaters. How radical gun laws spawned by a band of NRA lobbyists and Florida politicians have spread nationwide.

ADAM WEINSTEIN

The Florida law made infamous this spring by the killing of unarmed teenager Trayvon Martin was conceived during the epic hurricane season of 2004. That November, 77-year-old James Workman moved his family into an RV outside Pensacola after Hurricane Ivan peeled back the roof of their house. One night a stranger tried to force his way into the trailer, and Workman killed him with two shots from a .38 revolver. The stranger turned out to be a disoriented temporary worker for the Federal Emergency Management Agency who was checking for looters and distressed homeowners. Workman was never arrested, but three months went by before authorities cleared him of wrongdoing.

That was three months too long for Dennis Baxley, a veteran Republican representative in Florida's state Legislature. Four hurricanes had hit the state that year, and there was fear about widespread looting (though little took place). In Baxley's view, Floridians who defended themselves or their property with lethal force shouldn't have had to worry about legal repercussions. Baxley, a National Rifle Association (NRA) member and owner of a prosperous funeral business, teamed up with then-GOP state Sen. Durell Peaden to propose what would become known as Stand Your Ground, the self-defense doctrine essentially permitting anyone feeling threatened in a confrontation to shoot their way out.

Or at least that's the popular version of how the law was born. In fact, its genesis traces back to powerful NRA lobbyists and right-wing policy groups like the American Legislative Exchange Council (ALEC). And the law's rapid spread—it now exists in various forms in 25 states—reflects the success of a coordinated strategy, cultivated in Florida, to roll back gun control laws everywhere.

Baxley says he and Peaden lifted the law's language from a proposal crafted by Marion Hammer, a former NRA president and founder of the Unified Sportsmen of Florida, a local NRA affiliate. A 73-year-old dynamo who tops off her 4-foot-11 frame with a brown pageboy, Hammer has been a force in the state capital for more than three decades. "There is no more tenacious presence in Tallahassee," Gov. Jeb Bush's former chief of staff told CNN in April. "You want her on your side in a fight."

Ever since neighborhood watch volunteer George Zimmerman shot Trayvon Martin point-blank in the chest, the term Stand Your Ground has been widely discussed, but what does it really mean? A *Mother Jones* review of dozens of state laws shows that the concept is built on three planks from the pioneering Florida legislation: A person claiming self-defense is not required to retreat from a threat before opening fire; the burden is almost always on prosecutors to prove that a self-defense claim is *not* credible; and finally, the shooter has immunity from civil suits relating to the use of deadly force. While the so-called Castle Doctrine (as in "a man's home is his") has for centuries generally immunized people from homicide convictions if they resorted to deadly force while defending their home, Florida's law was the first to extend such protection to those firing weapons in public spaces-parking lots, parks, city streets.

Stand Your Ground was shepherded through the Legislature with help from then-state Rep. Marco Rubio and signed into law by Bush on April 26, 2005. It was the "first step of a multi-state strategy," Wayne LaPierre, a long-standing NRA official who is now the group's CEO, told the *Washington Post*. "There's a big tail-wind we have, moving from state legislature to state legislature. The South, the Midwest, everything they call 'flyover land.'" The measure was adopted as model legislation by ALEC, a corporate—sponsored national consortium of lawmakers-which is how it ended up passing in states from Mississippi to Wisconsin. "We are not a rogue state," says Baxley, who was bestowed with the NRA's Defender of Freedom Award shortly before his bill passed. "But we may be a leader."

Stand Your Ground, Explained

The three legal concepts that turned a reasonable self-defense law into a recipe for vigilante justice

1. **Hell no, I won't run away.**
   People who believe they are in danger in public spaces are not required to try to retreat from the perceived threat before defending themselves with force.

2. **I'm totally justified in doing this.**
   People acting in self-defense in their homes, vehicles, or other designated areas are assumed to have reasonably believed they were in imminent danger. The burden of proving otherwise falls on the prosecution.

3. **Ha-ha, you can't sue me.**
   People who use justifiable force to defend themselves are protected not only from criminal prosecution but also civil liability. (The former is common in self-defense legislation; the latter is not.)

Supporters of such laws cite the slippery-slope argument: Seemingly reasonable regulations—waiting periods, licenses, limits on assault weapons and high-capacity magazines—inevitably lead to ever-stricter measures, they argue, until citizens' constitutional right to defend themselves against government tyranny has vanished. Hammer suggests that an assault on gun rights motivated her move to Tallahassee from her native South Carolina in 1974: "Florida was seeing what I would call a burst of gun control measures being filed by Northerners who had moved to South Florida," she told a radio interviewer in 2005. "There was so much gun control being filed that it was very difficult for the NRA to deal with it from over 1,000 miles away."

After leaving work late one night in the mid-1980s, Hammer claims, a group of men in a car threatened her, only to be scared off when she pulled a gun on them. No police report was ever filed, but Hammer maintains that shortly after this incident a local police chief told her that she could have been arrested had she shot them. It was a convenient tale. She soon became a driving force behind Florida's "shall issue" legislation, passed in 1987, which stripped authorities of the ability to deny a concealed-weapons permit to someone they consider potentially dangerous. The law would allow thousands of ex-convicts and spouse beaters to pack heat; a Florida state attorney called it "one of the dumbest laws I have ever seen." A 1988 investigation by the *St. Petersburg Times* found permits had been given to two fugitives with outstanding arrest warrants, a disgraced cop who'd been convicted of a DUI and turned down for a county gun license, a man charged with fondling an eight-year-old girl, and a dead man. Florida has since issued more than 2 million concealed-weapons permits.

That same year Hammer called a panel of Florida legislators "a modern-day Gestapo" for considering legislation to keep guns away from violent criminals and the mentally ill. ("This is the lowest standard of integrity I have ever seen for a lobbyist in Tallahassee," one pro-gun Republican responded at the time.)

But Hammer's efforts really picked up steam when she served as the NRA's first female president from 1995 to 1998—by the end of which time Bush had been elected governor and the GOP had taken firm control of the Statehouse. Hammer and her allies have since barred city and county governments from banning guns in public buildings; forced businesses to let employees keep guns in cars parked in company lots; made it illegal for doctors to warn patients about the hazards of gun ownership (this controversial "Docs versus Glocks" law was overturned by a George W. Bush-appointed federal judge); and secured an exemption to Florida's celebrated open—records laws in order to keep gun permit holders' names a secret. (Baxley had cosponsored a similar bill, explaining in its original text that such lists had been used "to confiscate firearms and render the disarmed population helpless in the face of Nazi atrocities" and Fidel Castro's "tyranny.")

As Florida became known to some as the "Gunshine State," it began exporting its laws, with ALEC's help, to other statehouses. This effort was no doubt aided by the fact that the vice president of Hammer's Unified Sportsmen of Florida is John Patronis, cousin to Republican state Rep. Jimmy Patronis—sponsor of the aforementioned bill that kept names of concealed-weapons license holders secret and ALEC's current Florida chairman. The organization would also be instrumental

to spreading Stand Your Ground nationwide. "We definitely brought that bill forward to ALEC," said Baxley, a member of the group. "It's a place where you can share ideas. I don't see anything nefarious about sharing good ideas." The NRA has served as "corporate co-chair" of ALEC's Public Safety and Elections task force, which pushed Stand Your Ground and other gun laws. Since 2005, the year Florida's law was passed, gun manufacturers like Beretta, Remington, and Glock have poured as much as $39 million into the NRA's lobbying coffers.

Hammer Called Lawmakers "A Modern-Day Gestapo" For Wanting To Keep Guns From Violent Criminals And The Mentally Ill.

Baxley defends the NRA's involvement: "They have lots of members who want this statute. They're people who live in my district. They're concerned about turning back this lawless chaos and anarchy in our society." Records show that the NRA's Political Victory Fund has long supported Baxley—from a $500 contribution in 2000 (the state's maximum allowable donation) to $35,000 spent on radio ads in support of his state Senate bid in 2007. Peaden received at least $2,500 from the NRA and allied groups over the years. The NRA also maxed out on direct contributions to Jeb Bush's gubernatorial campaigns in 1998 and 2002, and it gave $125,000 to the Florida GOP between 2004 and 2010—more than it gave to any other state party. According to the Center for Media and Democracy, the NRA spent $729,863 to influence Florida politics in the 2010 election cycle alone.

Once fairly open to speaking with the media, Hammer has proved elusive since the Trayvon Martin killing. When I approached her for this story, explaining that I was a third-generation gun collector with a Florida carry permit, she declined to comment on the record. "Unfortunately," she wrote in an email, "if you did a truly honest article on the law, it would either never be printed in *Mother Jones*, or if they did publish it, it would not be believed by the mag's audience!"

A climate of fear helped spread Stand Your Ground, according to the National District Attorneys Association. In 2007, it conducted the first in-depth study on the expansion of the Castle Doctrine and found that it took root in part because "there was a change in perceptions of public safety after the terrorist attacks of 9/11. Many citizens . . . became concerned that government agencies could not protect every citizen in the event of subsequent terror attacks." Indeed, the NRA used 9/11 to promote its legislative agenda, most notably in its unsuccessful push to let all commercial airline pilots pack heat. "What would have made 9/11 impossible?" LaPierre asked a crowd at the 2002 NRA convention in Reno, Nevada. "If those pilots on those four airplanes had the right to be armed."

Steven Jansen, vice president and CEO of the Association of Prosecuting Attorneys and a former prosecutor in Detroit, was one of the study's authors. He first noticed the Stand Your Ground movement in early 2006 when it spread from Florida to Michigan, sponsored there by Republican state Sen. Rick Jones, an ALEC member. The law was "troublesome to me," Jansen told me. "We didn't really see a public safety need for it, and it could only muddy the legal waters."

With a confrontation like the one between Trayvon Martin and George Zimmerman, cops and prosecutors would now be forced to make judgment calls about which participant felt like he was in more peril. That raised serious questions about whether real-world situations would ever be as clear-cut as the lawmakers assumed. Jansen pointed to scenarios ranging from road rage to scuffles between rival fraternities: "To presume from the outset, as Florida's law arguably

---

Reloaded

Florida enacted Stand Your Ground in 2005. By 2012, with ALEC's help, 24 more states had similar laws on the books.

Safety Off

Since 2005, Florida lawmakers have taken aim at gun control with a barrage of deregulation measures.

- Requiring employers to let employees keep guns in their cars while at work
- Requiring city and county governments to allow guns in public buildings and parks
- Lifting a long-standing ban on guns in national forests and state parks
- Allowing military personnel as young as 17 to get concealed-weapons licenses. (Age limit remains 21 for everyone else.)
- Withholding the names of concealed-carry licensees in public records
- Permitting concealed-carry licensees "to briefly and openly display the firearm to the ordinary sight of another person." (The original bill would have allowed guns on college campuses, but it was amended after a GOP lawmaker's friend's daughter was accidentally killed with an AK-47 at a frat party.)
- Prohibiting doctors from asking patients if they keep guns or ammo in the house unless it's "relevant" to their care or safety. (Overturned by a federal judge.)
- Allowing legislators, school board members, and county commissioners to carry concealed weapons at official meetings. (Didn't pass; another bill to let judges pack heat "at any time and in any place" died in 2009.)
- Designating a day for tax-free gun purchases. (Didn't pass.)
- Exempting guns manufactured in Florida from any federal regulations. (Didn't pass.)—A.W.

does, that a deadly response in these situations is justified would be at best irresponsible; at worst, that assumption could create a new protected set of behaviors that might otherwise be considered hate crimes or vigilantism."

But legislators across the country nevertheless ignored objections from law enforcement. Indeed, stand Your Ground gives armed civilians rights that even cops don't enjoy: "Society hesitates to grant blanket immunity to police officers, who are well-trained in the use of deadly force and require yearly testing of their qualifications to carry a firearm," Jansen has written. "Yet the expansion of the Castle Doctrine has given such immunity to citizens."

Back when Florida passed Stand Your Ground, a few legislators did raise concerns. "This could be two gangs, deciding to have a fight in the street in Miami," said then-Rep. Jack Seiler, a Democrat from South Florida. "They both have a right to be standing on Biscayne Boulevard." It was a prescient warning. In 2006, a Miami man avoided prosecution after spraying a car filled with gang members with 14 bullets. In 2008, a 15-year-old Tallahassee boy was killed in a shoot-out between rival gangs; two of the gang members successfully took refuge behind Stand Your Ground.

The cumulative effect of those cases has been staggering: Two years after Stand Your Ground passed in Florida, the number of "justifiable homicides" by civilians more than doubled, and it nearly tripled by 2011, FBI statistics show a similar national trend: Justifiable homicides doubled in states with Florida-style laws, while they remained flat or fell in states that lacked them. Jansen also notes that research has shown that, when it came to domestic-abuse cases, "the only thing Stand Your Ground did was blur the lines between who was the batterer and who was the victim."

He says the laws have been passed without legislators asking basic questions: What, exacdty, makes a fear of imminent harm reasonable? Do the laws have a disparate negative effect on minorities or juveniles? And, perhaps the simplest question: "Is it worth losing a life over a car radio?"

That's happened, too. In Miami, a man was granted immunity in March for chasing down a burglar and stabbing him after the thief swung a bag of stolen car radios at him. He "was well within his rights to pursue the victim and demand the return of his property," the judge ruled. A state attorney for Miami-Dade County disagreed: "She, in effect, is saying that it's appropriate to chase someone down with a knife to get property back."

For now, Florida has deemed that it is indeed appropriate, and polls taken after the Martin killing show that half of voters agree. But outrage over that case has cost ALEC prime corporate sponsors—including McDonald's, Coca-Cola, Pepsi, Kraft, and Procter & Gamble—and its tax-exempt status has been challenged by Common Cause. In April, ALEC disbanded the panel that pushed Stand Your Ground and redirected funds to "task forces that focus on the economy."

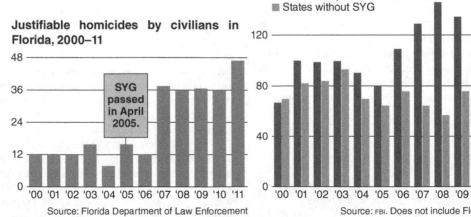

Justifiable homicides by civilians in Florida, 2000–11

SYG passed in April 2005.

Source: Florida Department of Law Enforcement

Justifiable homicides by civilians using firearms in US, 2000–10

■ States that passes SYG,2006-10
■ States without SYG

Source: FBI. Does not include Florida.

Up in Gunsmoke Since 2005, justifiable homicides by civilians in Florida have nearly tripled; they've also shot up in other states that adopted Stand Your Ground.

But Hammer and her allies are still pressing for laxer gun laws. This spring, Hammer got Florida to drop the cost of gun permits and lower the age restriction to 17 for military members, and she's still fighting to allow residents to carry their guns openly. And the NRA is pumping millions into the November elections nationally. "America needs us now more than ever as we gather together as one in the most dangerous times in American history," LaPierre told the NRA's annual convention in St. Louis in April. "By the time I finish this speech, two Americans will be slain, six women will be raped, 27 of us will be robbed, and 50 more will be beaten. That is the harsh reality we face every day." With an unabashed reference to the shooting that brought Stand Your Ground to national attention, LaPierre drove home his point.

"But the media, they don't care. Everyday victims aren't celebrities. They don't draw ratings and sponsors, but sensational reporting from Florida does."

Critical Thinking

1. Explain how George Zimmerman could chase and shoot Trayvon Martin, an innocent person, to death and expect to be exonerated.

2. Why have Stand Your Ground laws been passed in twenty-five states and what have been the results?

Toward Fewer Prisoners and Less Crime

MARK A.R. KLEIMAN

Introduction: Four Ways of Looking at Mass Incarceration

The topic of this volume is mass incarceration. That problem can be approached from (at least) four perspectives: social science, cultural criticism, advocacy, and policy analysis.

The social scientist wants to know about causes and consequences, to use theories to explain events such as the explosion of incarceration in America over the past generation, and to use events to develop new theories. The cultural critic wants to elucidate meanings, asking both what the participants in the social, administrative, and political processes that produce a given set of results intended and intend by their actions and how they justify those actions to themselves and others and what those processes and their results tell us about the character of the social order that produced them. The advocate searches for persuasive means to the end of ameliorating an already-identified evil. The policy analyst tries to figure out what course of action would best serve the public interest, all things considered, trying to take into account unintended as well as intended consequences.

To a policy-analytic eye, "mass incarceration" looks like only a partial problem definition. The other part of the problem is crime. If the crime problem were trivial, or if incarceration had only a trivial effect on crime, the solution to the mass-incarceration problem would trivially obvious: release those currently locked up, and end the practice of sending offenders to jail or prison. The policy analyst's work would then be complete, and the task of persuasion could then be turned over to the advocate, guided by the social scientist and the cultural critic.

But if crime is a real problem and if incarceration can be one means among many to control crime, then the situation looks more complicated. One would need to measure the harms done by crime as well as the harms done by incarceration, ask about the effects of alternative incarceration policies on the rates of different sorts of crime, and consider the likely results of using more of other crime-control measures, including alternative forms of punishment, along with less incarceration.

For example, it seems clear that increasing levels of police activity can reduce victimization rates. Thus it ought to be possible in principle, given some target level of victimization, to "trade off" policing against incarceration, adding police while reducing imprisonment. Whether that would be desirable is a different question. The extremely aggressive style of the New York Police Department, even if we credit it with reductions in crime (and, unusually, reductions in incarceration as well) has profound impacts on the lives of poor young African—American, Dominican, Puerto Rican, and Haitian New Yorkers.

Is it better to live in a city with fewer prisoners but more police surveillance? The answer is not obvious on its face: resolving the question would require both the collection of facts and the assignment of values to different outcomes. But it is the sort of question that a policy analysis starting from the problem of mass incarceration must try to answer, if crime matters and if incarceration is one means of reducing it. So is the question of which prisoners to release, or not admit in the first place.

Thinking about mass incarceration and crime control as twin problems can create two advantages for those whose focus is on how to reduce mass incarceration. First, since many political actors are concerned about crime and do think that incarceration helps control it, advocates of incarceration-reduction will find a better hearing if they are heard as proposing alternative means of crime control rather than as ignoring the crime issue entirely. Second, there is evidence that support for highly punitive approaches to crime varies—albeit with a substantial lag—with the crime rate, so that success in reducing crime will tend to facilitate the project of incarceration reduction. As the crime explosion of 1962–1994 helped produce the problem of mass incarceration, the crime collapse of 1994–2004 might help ameliorate it, especially if victimization rates continue to fall.

The next section of this essay will argue that, even at current levels, crime–especially in poor African-American communities–remains a first-order social problem, comparable to the problem of mass incarceration. The final section will sketch a system of community corrections (probation and parole supervision) that would allow very large reductions in the prison population while not increasing, or perhaps reducing, crime.

The High Cost of Crime

The measurable losses from crime do not seem to be especially large compared to the measurable losses from other sources of risk: surely not large enough to account for the level of public concern over crime. Averaging across households, the average property lost to burglars comes out to about $4 per month, a small fraction of a typical utility bill. Homicide is a horrible event, but also a rare one; three times as many people die on the highways each year as are deliberately killed by others.

Crime—the risk of being victimized—imposes costs on those who are never actually victimized, because of the costly efforts they make to avoid victimization and the "external costs" of victimization-avoidance measures taken by others. Crime, like incarceration, deprives people of liberty; it does so by making them afraid. The deprivation of liberty is, in general, less profound—though there are certainly people who feel trapped in their homes because they are afraid to go outdoors—but it extends to a much larger group of people. The direct and secondary costs of crime avoidance easily swamp the immediate costs of victimization.

If the bulk of crime-related loss is not victimization loss, then the rate of completed victimization—the crime rate—is not a good proxy for the seriousness of the crime problem. A neighborhood abandoned due in part to crime, or where residents stay inside behind locked doors for fear of muggers, or a park that many people are afraid to enter after dark, may have a lower rate of completed crime than a safer neighborhood or park, simply because so many more people are at risk. Even before the spectacular crime decrease of the 1994–2004 period, New York City actually had a relatively low burglary rate compared to other big cities, but the public impression that burglary risk was higher in New York was nonetheless probably correct: as a visitor might easily notice, New Yorkers were habituated to being much more careful about burglary-proofing their homes than was common in cities where burglary was less on residents' minds.

The extent to which the fear of crime reflects mass-media choices about what sort of "news" to emphasize remains an open question. Certainly, there is no strong tendency for measured fear to shift quickly with, or even in the same direction as, measured crime. But this need not indicate that the fear itself is irrational, or insensitive to the actual crime risks prevalent in various social milieux, insofar as victimization might fall precisely as a result of increased precaution.

If the level of precaution tends to risk with the criminal riskiness of the social environment, and if precaution tends to reduce the rate of being victimized, then the measured changes in the rate of completed crime will tend to understate the changes in the underlying risk, especially when crime is increasing: if the number of robberies doubles even as potential victims are taking greater precautions against being robbed, then the rate of robbery per exposed person-hour—imagining that such a quantity could be measured—must have gone up even more. The flow of population away from high-crime urban neighborhoods and into lower-crime suburbs and exurbs means that the measured crime rate could fall even as the level of risk in every area continued to rise.

So the observation that the Great Crime Decline has left the country with "only" 250 percent of the crime rates prevalent in the early 1960s is less reassuring that it would seem. I am not very old, but I am old enough to recall when American storefronts, unlike European storefronts, did not have metal shutters and when middle-class parents did not regard it as imprudent to allow their young teenage children to take busses through tough neighborhoods late at night. If Americans continued to be as careless about the risks of crime as they were forty-five years

ago, the rate of completed crime would no doubt be substantially higher. And the loss of that carelessness—or rather, of a social environment which made that carelessness rational—is not a small loss. Blaming that loss on television news shows rather than on muggers makes it no less of a loss.

The fear of crime deprives the residents of high-crime neighborhoods of economic opportunity by driving jobs away from the places where they live. Whether the "spatial mismatch" between the location of the unemployed and the location of unfilled jobs is an important cause of high minority unemployment remains a contested question, but there can be no doubt that having to commute farther to work is, at best, an inconvenience, especially for teenagers who would be working only part-time in any case and whose attachment to the labor market may be weak. And those disadvantages tend to accumulate, since teenagers with less work experience become less attractive employees as young adults. Worst of all, anything that makes licit employment less attractive will tend to make its illicit alternatives more attractive; and a criminal record can be a very substantial barrier to subsequent employment in the licit economy.

Crime to job loss to poverty to crime is a positive-feedback loop: high-crime neighborhoods tend to be low-opportunity neighborhoods, low-opportunity neighborhoods encourage criminal activity by their residents, and that criminal activity makes the neighborhoods even less attractive places in which to live and do business, and some of the residents less attractive as potential employees. Loss of residents, especially the relatively prosperous residents most likely to be able to afford to move out, makes a neighborhood less attractive to retail businesses, and the loss of retail services in turn makes the neighborhood a less attractive place to live for those who have other options

The economic geography of every metropolitan area provides testimony to the importance of crime as a factor shaping residential and business location decisions. How else could one account for the coexistence of housing abandonment and new housing construction only a few miles apart? There are many reasons for moving to the suburbs, but crime ranks high on the list. The same applies to business-location decisions. It would be unconventional, but it would not be beside the point, to insert a discussion of crime control in a treatise on reducing suburban sprawl.

That poverty is a cause of crime is a commonplace, though the mechanisms involved are complex and poorly understood. That crime is a sustaining cause of poverty is no less true, though in the past it has been much less remarked on. The poor are victimized directly; the probability of criminal victimization rises steadily with income. They are victimized again as a result of crime-avoidance behavior that limits their opportunities and blights their neighborhoods.

The picture is worst for African Americans; even adjusting for overall lower incomes, African Americans suffer much more crime than do members of other ethnic categories. Homicide provides the most dramatic example; representing less than 15 percent of the population, black people suffer more than 50 percent of the murders.

The problem tends to be self-sustaining. Given a constrained criminal-justice system, punishment per crime tends to be lower where crime is more common. Assuming that the threat of punishment has some deterrent effect, growing up where that threat is smaller—and licit economic opportunity less available—should be expected, other things equal, to lead to a higher rate of criminal activity. And indeed that is what we find. African Americans are far more heavily victimized than others, but not as a result of cross-ethnic aggression; crime is overwhelmingly intra-racial.

Paradoxically, then, efforts to reduce the racial disproportion in the prison population are likely to intensify the implicit racial discrimination among victims that results from lower per-crime rates of punishment, leaving African Americans even more exposed to victimization. The critique of the current system in terms of imposing prison terms and the consequent social stigma on a much higher proportion of African Americans than of whites is fully justified by the facts, but the mechanisms involved are far more subtle than conscious, or even systemic, racial discrimination by officials against black perpetrators.

In some ways it would be better if, as is often asserted, systemic racial bias, in the form of more severe punishment for black offenders, lay at the root of problem; then eliminating racial bias could eliminate disproportionate incarceration. But if the actual problem is the positive-feedback loop from high criminal activity to low punishment-per-crime back to high criminal activity, no such fix is available. The standard critique portrays a melodrama; the reality is a tragedy.

Substituting Community Supervision for Incarceration

If crime and mass incarceration are both great evils, then we should look for ways to have less of both at once. One way to do so would be to substitute some other form of punishment for incarceration to serve the twin functions of incapacitation and deterrence. (If, as Useem and Piehl argue, the rising scale of incarceration has brought its marginal crime-control benefits down close to—or in some instances below—zero, then to some extent we could reduce mass incarceration without increasing crime. But the data do not suggest that 50 percent of current incarceration is useless, and cutting our incarceration rate in half would still leave it more than twice its historical norm and more than twice the level in any other advanced polity.)

Probation and parole are the two systems that manage convicted offenders outside the walls. Fines, community service, diversion to drug treatment or mental-health treatment, and "restorative justice" programs all rely on probation and parole supervision as their enforcement mechanism, without which they are no more than helpful hints from the judge. Alas, that enforcement is generally very weak, and compliance with "alternative sanctions" spotty at best. In California's famous Proposition 36 drug-diversion program, only about one entrant in four completed the prescribed course of treatment, and virtually none of them faced any consequence for reneging on the bargain they had made with the court other than the lost opportunity to have their convictions expunged and the risk that an outstanding bench warrant might complicate the course of a future arrest.

That failure does not stem from the laxity or laziness of probation officers—though no doubt some workers in any job are lax and lazy—but from the conditions under which they work. Typically, a big-city probation officer supervises more than 100 clients, and is expected to meet with each of them once a month. That schedule alone largely fills a working week, and the time required to prepare a violation report to send to the supervising judge is measured in hours. So the number of referrals is constrained by the officer's time. The judge and the judge's staff are also busy, and will not thank the probation officer for subjecting them to a flurry of revocation motions.

Short of a revocation motion, the probation officer's leverage over a client is limited. Only the judge can order a term of confinement; the probation officer (generally with the concurrence of supervisor) can only use moral suasion and impose additional requirements, such as more frequent meetings. But what if the client defies those requirements as well?

If a revocation motion is made, the judge, too, has a limited repertoire of sanctions. She can send the offender to prison or jail, usually for a period of months but sometimes for years. She can impose more onerous conditions of supervision (which, again, the probationer may well ignore). She can lengthen the period of supervision, which is a noticeable inconvenience but one that doesn't hit until sometime in the future.

None of these options is attractive. Jails and prisons are crowded, and whatever the probationer did to earn the conviction that underlies his probation term the violation of probation conditions is likely to be relatively trivial: a missed meeting or a "dirty" drug test. To a judge who has just put someone on probation for a burglary, sending someone else away for a mere "technical" violation seems disproportionate, unless that violation comes at the end of a very long string. (Sometimes a new substantive offense is handled as a violation of probation rather than prosecuted afresh; in those cases, a term behind bars is a more likely outcome.)

As a result, the most likely consequence to a probationer of breaking a probation rule is a warning, either by the probation office or (less often) by the judge. If the probationer keeps it up, at some point it will be the case that his previous "last warning" really was the last, and he will be on his way to, or back to, a cell. But such deferred and low-probability risks do little to reduce the violation rate, though they may cumulate to a great deal of punishment. The lack of an immediate and high-probability aversive consequence for a violation helps sustain the high violation rate, and the high violation rate in turn guarantees that most violations will not be sanctioned. This is simply the social trap of the neighborhood with a high crime rate and a low punishment risk per offense, writ small; the community corrections system reproduces the cruel and futile randomized draconianism of the larger criminal-justice system. (Parole supervision is tighter, though it, too over-relies on severe sanctions, but there are about five times as many probationers at any one time as parolees.)

But just as the threat of severe sanctions is largely impotent at controlling behavior if the sanctions are uncertain and deferred, the threat of even a mild sanction can be potent if the consequence follows the act swiftly and certainly. In Hawaii, a judicial warning that the next positive drug test would draw an immediate jail term measured in days succeeded in virtually ending drug use for more than three-quarters of a group of chronically defiant felony probationers, most of them methamphetamine users. The hard part was organizing the judge's staff, the probation department, the sheriff's office, the police, the jail, prosecutors, and defense counsel to actually deliver on that warning when the rules were broken. (That meant, for example, developing a two-page, check-the-box-or-fill-in-the-blank reporting form to replace the elaborate motion-for-revocation paperwork; since only a single violation is in question, very little information is needed.)

Most of the probationers on the program—dubbed HOPE—never faced an actual sanction; the warning alone did the job. On average, the group subjected to tight supervision spent about as many days in jail for probation violations as a comparison group, with more but shorter spells. But they spent only about a third as many days in prison after revocations or new convictions.

The project now covers about 1500 offenders, about one out of five felony probationers on the island of Oahu; the judge plans to expand it to 3000, and intends to manage all of them himself, by contrast with drug-court judge who typically manage caseloads of 50 to 75. Most of the participants are drug users, but by no means all; the process works just as well enforcing a different set of rules on domestic-violence offenders and sex offenders. The process isn't drug-specific; it applies basic principles of behavior change relevant to a wide range of behavior, as long as that behavior can be easily monitored.

Commercial vendors now sell, for $15 per month, a service that tracks the whereabouts of a GPS monitor; parents place them in their young children's backpacks to be able to find them when they stray. One version of that service provides "exception reporting;" after the parent enters a weekly schedule of where the child is supposed to be at given hours of given days, the system sends a text message to the parent's cell phone or email in-box if the child isn't where he is supposed to be.

Now imagine such a unit mounted on an anklet that can't be removed without the GPS unit detecting the change and sending an alert (or merely failing to respond). Put that anklet on a probationer or parolee, and his whereabouts are subject to continuous monitoring. Comparing the position records with the locations of crimes reported to the 9-1-1 system will make it difficult for anyone wearing an anklet to get away with a new predatory offense. Street gangs will not welcome the presence of members whose location is transparent to the police. Such a system makes it feasible to enforce curfews, stay-away orders, "community service" obligations, and requirements to appear as scheduled for employment or therapy. It could even be extended to home confinement, currently used for some sex offenders and for bailees thought to constitute a flight risk.

Unlike the expensive process of monitoring sex offenders, where any straying constitutes a potential emergency and the system must therefore be staffed around the clock, for routine probationers and parolees there would be no urgency about responding to a mere schedule violation; it would suffice for the probation or parole officer to be notified the next morning.

As long as the offender is still wearing the device, finding him would pose no challenge, and the next day is soon enough for a sanction to be effective.

It would be an emergency if the offender removed the device; usually that will mean that he plans either to commit a serious crime or to abscond from supervision. But the police department, already staffed 24/7, could respond to those (presumably rare) events.

The operational challenges would be legion: developing rules about imposing and relaxing restrictions, what to do if the GPS unit loses contact with the satellite (perhaps a cell phone, which also transmits its position, would be required as a back-up); how to deal with false positives; ensuring that the police respond quickly and vigorously to absconding; and managing the sanctions hearings.

But given the results from HOPE, it's a reasonable guess that 80%, perhaps even 90% of probationers and parolees would comply with the system in the sense of not shedding the GPS device, and that they would be highly compliant with rules and commit very few new crimes. They would probably also find it much easier to secure employment, despite their criminal histories, once employers found that they were not only certified drug-free but also showed up for work every day. And as a result, many fewer of them would wind up returning to prison.

Once probation and parole involved that sort of monitoring, only a limited number of cases would justify using incarceration instead: people who commit such heinous crimes that justice demands it (the Bernie Madoffs of the world), people whose demonstrated tendency for assault or sexual predation requires their incarceration to protect potential victims, and those who, in effect, choose incarceration by absconding. Everyone else could be adequately punished and incapacitated from future offending with monitoring alone, backed by brief jail stays. That could both reduce the inflow to prison (by reducing the number of revocations and persuading judges to sentence more felons to probation instead) and increase the outflow from prison by persuading parole boards to make more early-release decisions.

Moreover, converting probation into a real punishment rather than the placeholder for an absent punishment it now largely is would be expected to deter crime, reducing the inflows both to prison and to probation.

How far this process might go is anyone's guess. But it would not be unreasonable to hope that the United States might find itself a decade from now with a European incarceration rate and crime rates resembling those of the 1950s.

The change could not be made overnight; each jurisdiction that adopts such a system will need an operational "shakedown" period, and it is essential that the program not outgrow its capacity to monitor and sanction; once offenders come to believe that the threat of quick incarceration is a bluff, their offending will so swamp the system that it will become a bluff.

But other than the need for shaking down and then phasing in, this approach has no natural upper limit. HOPE costs about $1000 per year on top of routine probation supervision, and most of that excess goes to drug treatment for the minority that cannot comply without professional help. It pays for itself several times over in reduced incarceration cost alone.

The implementation of this idea will vary from jurisdiction to jurisdiction and from population to population. In various ways, it could be applied to juvenile offenders, to probationers, to parolees, and to those released while awaiting trial either on bail or on their own recognizance. For juvenile probationers in particular, "outpatient" supervision under tight monitoring backed with the threat of 48 hours' solitary confinement for each violation, might succeed in squaring the circle of finding a punishment adequately aversive to serve as a deterrent without being so damaging as to push a juvenile who might otherwise have recovered from a period of criminal activity into persistent criminality, by reducing his commitment to, and opportunities within, the world of school and licit work.

This proposal of incarceration on the outpatient plan cannot expect to receive a universally warm welcome. In a criminal-justice-policy debate that sometimes seems to take place between the disciples of Michel Foucault and those of the Marquis de Sade, it will be too intrusive for the foucauldians and not retributive enough for the sadists. But for those not overly reluctant to punish lawbreakers with some months or years of a boring, go-to-bed-early-and-show-up-for-work middle-class lifestyle, and unwilling to accept current levels of incarceration or of crime, the virtual prison cell offers the prospect of having less of both.

With respect to the population not currently in prison, including pre-trial releasees, and those newly placed on probation who would not have gone to prison otherwise, there is no doubt that the proposed system represents a further extension of state control over individuals. Whether that is desirable or not could be debated, with the answer depending in part on the empirical results in terms of crime, days behind bars, and employment, family, and housing status, and in part on the value one assigns to the liberty and privacy of the recently arrested (including their liberty to commit fresh offenses with impunity). In the somewhat longer run—over a period of a few years—the result might be to reduce the scope of direct state control by discouraging offending and thus reducing the total size of the prison-jail-probation-parole-pretrial release population.

Such a happy ending cannot be guaranteed. Such a program has yet to be tried out on a parolee population; it is possible (though I would rate the probability as small) that massive absconsion and consequent return to prison would make it operationally infeasible. It is more plausible that, in some jurisdictions, a combination of haste, under-resourcing, and administrative non-compliance would lead to program breakdown, with the supervised population discovering that, despite the threat, violation did not in fact lead swiftly and predictably to confinement. If that happened, violation rates would surely soar, thus putting the program into a "death spiral" of increasing violation rates and decreasing swiftness and certainty of sanctions. Managing the behavior of offenders is a much more straightforward task than managing the behavior of officials, and most of all of independent officials such as judges.

The other risk is that some offenders who get away with some minor violations under the current loose supervision systems, finish their assigned terms, and then go straight, will instead find tighter supervision intolerable, commit repeated in technical infractions leading to short confinement terms, abscond, and wind up in prison. That risk would be especially grave if the system were applied to misdemeanants in addition to felons, since the misdemeanants start out with a much lower level of prison risk.

But if the application of "outpatient incarceration" can be restricted to those who would otherwise face, with high probability, repeated spells of actual incarceration, then on balance it promotes not only public safety but the liberty and life prospects of the offender population. There are worse fates than being forced to live a law-abiding life.

Critical Thinking

1. Why does Mark Kleinman conclude that the high imprisonment rates in the United States have a net negative impact?

2. What benefits would result from reducing imprisonment?

The Year in Hate & Extremism, 2010

Mark Potok

For the second year in a row, the radical right in America expanded explosively in 2010, driven by resentment over the changing racial demographics of the country, frustration over the government's handling of the economy, and the mainstreaming of conspiracy theories and other demonizing propaganda aimed at various minorities. For many on the radical right, anger is focusing on President Obama, who is seen as embodying everything that's wrong with the country.

Hate groups topped 1,000 for the first time since the Southern Poverty Law Center began counting such groups in the 1980s. Anti-immigrant vigilante groups, despite having some of the political wind taken out of their sails by the adoption of hard-line anti-immigration laws around the country, continued to rise slowly. But by far the most dramatic growth came in the antigovernment "Patriot" movement—conspiracy-minded organizations that see the federal government as their primary enemy—which gained more than 300 new groups, a jump of over 60%.

Taken together, these three strands of the radical right—the hatemongers, the nativists and the antigovernment zealots—increased from 1,753 groups in 2009 to 2,145 in 2010, a 22% rise. That followed a 2008-2009 increase of 40%.

What may be most remarkable is that this growth of right-wing extremism came even as politicians around the country, blown by gusts from the Tea Parties and other conservative formations, tacked hard to the right, co-opting many of the issues important to extremists. Last April, for instance, Arizona Gov. Jan Brewer signed S.B. 1070, the harshest anti-immigrant law in memory, setting off a tsunami of proposals for similar laws across the country. Continuing growth of the radical right could be curtailed as a result of this shift, especially since Republicans, many of them highly conservative, recaptured the U.S. House last fall.

But despite those historic Republican gains, the early signs suggest that even as the more mainstream political right strengthens, the radical right has remained highly energized. In an 11-day period this January, a neo-Nazi was arrested headed for the Arizona border with a dozen homemade grenades; a terrorist bomb attack on a Martin Luther King Jr. Day parade in Spokane, Wash., was averted after police dismantled a sophisticated anti-personnel weapon; and a man who officials said had a long history of antigovernment activities was arrested outside a packed mosque in Dearborn, Mich., and charged with possessing explosives with unlawful intent. That's in addition, the same month, to the shooting of U.S. Rep. Gabrielle Giffords in Arizona, an attack that left six dead and may have had a political dimension.

It's also clear that other kinds of radical activity are on the rise. Since the murder last May 20 of two West Memphis, Ark., police officers by two members of the so-called "sovereign citizens" movement, police from around the country have contacted the Southern Poverty Law Center (SPLC) to report what one detective in Kentucky described as a "dramatic increase" in sovereign activity. Sovereign citizens, who, like militias, are part of the larger Patriot movement, believe that the federal government has no right to tax or regulate them and, as a result, often come into conflict with police and tax authorities. Another sign of their increased activity came early this year, when the Treasury Department, in a report assessing what the

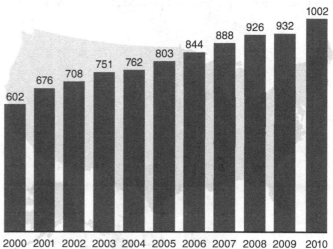

Hate Groups 2000–2010

2000: 602, 2001: 676, 2002: 708, 2003: 751, 2004: 762, 2005: 803, 2006: 844, 2007: 888, 2008: 926, 2009: 932, 2010: 1002

Editor's note: Since the article below was published, authorities have changed their view of an incident in Dearborn, Mich., that is mentioned. Initially, it was believed that the Michigan suspect was planning an attack based on hatred of Muslims. In fact, it turns out that Roger Stockham is an American convert to Sunni Islam, and reportedly was angry at the mosque in question because it was Shi'ite.

IRS faces in 2011, said its biggest challenge will be the "attacks and threats against IRS employees and facilities [that] have risen steadily in recent years."

Extremist ideas have not been limited to the radical right; already this year, state legislators have offered up a raft of proposals influenced by such ideas. In Arizona, the author of the S.B. 1070 law—a man who just became Senate president on the basis of his harshly nativist rhetoric—proposed a law this January that would allow his state to refuse to obey any federal law or regulation it cared to. In Virginia, a state legislator wants to pass a law aimed at creating an alternative currency "in the event of the destruction of the Federal Reserve System's currency"—a longstanding fear of right-wing extremists. And in Montana, a state senator is working to pass a statute called the "Sheriffs First Act" that would require federal law enforcement to ask local sheriffs' permission to act in their counties or face jail. All three laws are almost certainly unconstitutional, legal experts say, and they all originate in ideas that first came from ideologues of the radical right.

There also are new attempts by nativist forces to roll back birthright citizenship, which makes all children born in the United States citizens. Such laws have been introduced this year in Congress, and a coalition of state legislators is promising to do the same in their states. And then there's Oklahoma, where 70% of voters last November approved a measure to forbid judges to consider Islamic law in the state's courtrooms—a completely groundless fear, but one pushed nonetheless by Islamophobes. Since then, lawmakers have promised to pass similar laws in Arizona, Florida, Louisiana, South Carolina, Tennessee and Utah.

After the Giffords assassination attempt, a kind of national dialogue began about the political vitriol that increasingly passes for "mainstream" political debate. But it didn't seem to get very far. Four days after the shooting, a campaign called the Civility Project—a two-year effort led by an evangelical conservative tied to top Republicans—said it was shutting down because of a lack of interest and furious opposition. "The worst E-mails

I received about the Civility Project were from conservatives with just unbelievable language about communists and some words I wouldn't use in this phone call," director Mark DeMoss told *The New York Times*. "This political divide has become so sharp that everything is black and white, and too many conservatives can see no redeeming value in any" opponent.

A *Washington Post*/ABC News poll this January captured the atmosphere well. It found that 82% of Americans saw their country's political discourse as "negative." Even more remarkably, the poll determined that 49% thought that negative tone could or already had encouraged political violence.

Last year's rise in hate groups was the latest in a trend stretching all the way back to the year 2000, when the SPLC counted 602 such groups. Since then, they have risen steadily, mainly on the basis of exploiting the issue of undocumented immigration from Mexico and Central America. Last year, the number of hate groups rose to 1,002 from 932, a 7.5% increase over the previous year and a 66% rise since 2000.

At the same time, what the SPLC defines as "nativist extremist" groups—organizations that go beyond mere advocacy of restrictive immigration policy to actually confront or harass suspected immigrants or their employers—rose slightly, despite the fact that most of their key issues had been taken up by mainstream politicians. There were 319 such groups in 2010, up 3% from 309 in 2009.

But like the year before, it was the antigovernment Patriot groups that grew most dramatically, at least partly on the basis of furious rhetoric from the right aimed at the nation's first black president—a man who has come to represent to at least some Americans ongoing changes in the racial makeup of the country. The Patriot groups, which had risen and fallen once before during the militia movement of the 1990s, first came roaring back in 2009, when they rose 244% to 512 from 149 a year earlier. In 2010, they rose again sharply, adding 312 new groups to reach 824, a 61% increase. The highest prior count of Patriot groups came in 1996, when the SPLC found 858 (see also chart, above).

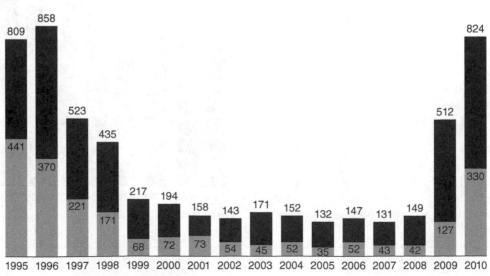

Patriot & Militia Groups 1995–2010

It's hard to predict where this volatile situation will lead. Conservatives last November made great gains and some of them are championing a surprising number of the issues pushed by the radical right—a fact that could help deflate some of the even more extreme political forces. But those GOP electoral advances also left the Congress divided and increasingly lined up against the Democratic president, which is likely to paralyze the country on such key issues as immigration reform.

What seems certain is that President Obama will continue to serve as a lightning rod for many on the political right, a man who represents both the federal government and the fact that the racial make-up of the United States is changing, something that upsets a significant number of white Americans. And that suggests that the polarized politics of this country could get worse before they get better.

Critical Thinking

1. Why have extremist groups suddenly increased in the last few years?
2. What kind of belief do these groups have?
3. Are the right-wing extremist groups dangerous?

From *Intelligence Report*, Spring 2011. Copyright © 2011 by Southern Poverty Law Center. Reprinted by permission by Mark Potok.

War in the Fifth Domain

Are the Mouse and Keyboard the New Weapons of Conflict?

Economist

At the height of the cold war, in June 1982, an American early-warning satellite detected a large blast in Siberia. A missile being fired? A nuclear test? It was, it seems, an explosion on a Soviet gas pipeline. The cause was a malfunction in the computer-control system that Soviet spies had stolen from a firm in Canada. They did not know that the CIA had tampered with the software so that it would "go haywire, after a decent interval, to reset pump speeds and valve settings to produce pressures far beyond those acceptable to pipeline joints and welds," according to the memoirs of Thomas Reed, a former air force secretary. The result, he said, "was the most monumental non-nuclear explosion and fire ever seen from space."

This was one of the earliest demonstrations of the power of a "logic bomb". Three decades later, with more and more vital computer systems linked up to the internet, could enemies use logic bombs to, say, turn off the electricity from the other side of the world? Could terrorists or hackers cause financial chaos by tampering with Wall Street's computerised trading systems? And given that computer chips and software are produced globally, could a foreign power infect high-tech military equipment with computer bugs? "It scares me to death," says one senior military source. "The destructive potential is so great."

After land, sea, air and space, warfare has entered the fifth domain: cyberspace. President Barack Obama has declared America's digital infrastructure to be a "strategic national asset" and appointed Howard Schmidt, the former head of security at Microsoft, as his cyber-security tsar. In May, the Pentagon set up its new Cyber Command (Cybercom) headed by General Keith Alexander, director of the National Security Agency (NSA). His mandate is to conduct "full-spectrum" operations—to defend American military networks and attack other countries' systems. Precisely how, and by what rules, is secret.

Britain, too, has set up a cyber-security policy outfit, and an "operations centre" based in GCHQ, the British equivalent of the NSA. China talks of "winning informationised wars by the mid-21st century". Many other countries are organising for cyberwar, among them Russia, Israel and North Korea. Iran boasts of having the world's second-largest cyber-army.

What will cyberwar look like? In a new book, Richard Clarke, a former White House staffer in charge of counter-terrorism and cyber-security, envisages a catastrophic breakdown within 15 minutes. Computer bugs bring down military e-mail systems; oil refineries and pipelines explode; air-traffic-control systems collapse; freight and metro trains derail; financial data are scrambled; the electrical grid goes down in the eastern United States; orbiting satellites spin out of control. Society soon breaks down as food becomes scarce and money runs out. Worst of all, the identity of the attacker may remain a mystery.

In the view of Mike McConnell, a former spy chief, the effects of full-blown cyberwar are much like a nuclear attack. Cyberwar has already started, he says, "and we are losing it." Not so, retorts Mr Schmidt. There is no cyberwar. Bruce Schneier, an IT industry security guru, accuses securocrats like Mr Clarke of scaremongering. Cyberspace will certainly be part of any future war, he says, but an apocalyptic attack on America is both difficult to achieve technically ("movie-script stuff") and implausible except in the context of a real war, in which case the perpetrator is likely to be obvious.

For the top brass, computer technology is both a blessing and a curse. Bombs are guided by GPS satellites; drones are piloted remotely from across the world; fighter planes and warships are now huge data-processing centres; even the ordinary foot-soldier is being wired up. Yet growing connectivity over an insecure internet multiplies the avenues for e-attack; and growing dependence on computers increases the harm they can cause.

By breaking up data and sending it over multiple routes, the internet can survive the loss of large parts of the network. Yet some of the global digital infrastructure is more fragile. More than nine-tenths of internet traffic travels through undersea fibre-optic cables, and these are dangerously bunched up in a few choke-points, for instance around New York, the Red Sea or the Luzon Strait in the Philippines. Internet traffic is directed by just 13 clusters of potentially vulnerable domain-name servers. Other dangers are coming: weakly governed swathes of Africa are being connected up to fibre-optic cables, potentially creating new havens for cyber-criminals. And the spread of mobile internet will bring new means of attack.

The internet was designed for convenience and reliability, not security. Yet in wiring together the globe, it has merged the garden and the wilderness. No passport is required in cyberspace. And although police are constrained by national borders, criminals roam freely. Enemy states are no longer on the other side of the ocean, but just behind the firewall. The ill-intentioned can mask their identity and location, impersonate others and con their way into the buildings that hold the digitised wealth of the electronic age: money, personal data and intellectual property.

Mr Obama has quoted a figure of $1 trillion lost last year to cybercrime—a bigger underworld than the drugs trade, though such figures are disputed. Banks and other companies do not like to admit how much data they lose. In 2008 alone, Verizon, a telecoms company, recorded the loss of 285m personal-data records, including credit-card and bank-account details, in investigations conducted for clients.

About nine-tenths of the 140 billion e-mails sent daily are spam; of these about 16% contain moneymaking scams, including "phishing" attacks that seek to dupe recipients into giving out passwords or bank details, according to Symantec, a security-software vendor. The amount of information now available online about individuals makes it ever easier to attack a computer by crafting a personalised e-mail that is more likely to be trusted and opened. This is known as "spear-phishing".

The ostentatious hackers and virus-writers who once wrecked computers for fun are all but gone, replaced by criminal gangs seeking to harvest data. "Hacking used to be about making noise. Now it's about staying silent," says Greg Day of McAfee, a vendor of IT security products. Hackers have become wholesale providers of malware—viruses, worms and Trojans that infect computers—for others to use. Websites are now the favoured means of spreading malware, partly because the unwary are directed to them through spam or links posted on social-networking sites. And poorly designed websites often provide a window into valuable databases.

Malware is typically used to steal passwords and other data, or to open a "back door" to a computer so that it can be taken over by outsiders. Such "zombie" machines can be linked up to thousands, if not millions, of others around the world to create a "botnet". Estimates for the number of infected machines range up to 100m. Botnets are used to send spam, spread malware or launch distributed denial-of-service (DDoS) attacks, which seek to bring down a targeted computer by overloading it with countless bogus requests.

The Spy Who Spammed Me

Criminals usually look for easy prey. But states can combine the criminal hacker's tricks, such as spear-phishing, with the intelligence apparatus to reconnoitre a target, the computing power to break codes and passwords, and the patience to probe a system until it finds a weakness—usually a fallible human being. Steven Chabinsky, a senior FBI official responsible for cybersecurity, recently said that "given enough time, motivation and funding, a determined adversary will always—always—be able to penetrate a targeted system."

Traditional human spies risk arrest or execution by trying to smuggle out copies of documents. But those in the cyberworld face no such risks. "A spy might once have been able to take out a few books' worth of material," says one senior American military source, "Now they take the whole library. And if you restock the shelves, they steal it again."

China, in particular, is accused of wholesale espionage, attacking the computers of major Western defence contractors and reputedly taking classified details of the F-35 fighter, the mainstay of future American air power. At the end of 2009, it appears to have targeted Google and more than a score of other IT companies. Experts at a cyber-test-range built in Maryland by Lockheed Martin, a defence contractor (which denies losing the F-35 data), say "advanced persistent threats" are hard to fend off amid the countless minor probing of its networks. Sometimes attackers try to slip information out slowly, hidden in ordinary internet traffic. At other times they have tried to break in by leaving infected memory-sticks in the car park, hoping somebody would plug them into the network. Even unclassified e-mails can contain a wealth of useful information about projects under development.

"Cyber-espionage is the biggest intelligence disaster since the loss of the nuclear secrets [in the late 1940s]," says Jim Lewis of the Centre for Strategic and International Studies, a think-tank in Washington, DC. Spying probably presents the most immediate danger to the West: the loss of high-tech know-how that could erode its economic lead or, if it ever came to a shooting war, blunt its military edge.

Western spooks think China deploys the most assiduous, and most shameless, cyberspies, but Russian ones are probably more skilled and subtle. Top of the league, say the spooks, are still America's NSA and Britain's GCHQ, which may explain why Western countries have until recently been reluctant to complain too loudly about computer snooping.

The next step after penetrating networks to steal data is to disrupt or manipulate them. If military targeting information could be attacked, for example, ballistic missiles would be useless. Those who play war games speak of being able to "change the red and blue dots": make friendly (blue) forces appear to be the enemy (red), and vice versa.

General Alexander says the Pentagon and NSA started cooperating on cyberwarfare in late 2008 after "a serious intrusion into our classified networks". Mr Lewis says this refers to the penetration of Central Command, which oversees the wars in Iraq and Afghanistan, through an infected thumb-drive. It took a week to winkle out the intruder. Nobody knows what, if any, damage was caused. But the thought of an enemy lurking in battle-fighting systems alarms the top brass.

That said, an attacker might prefer to go after unclassified military logistics supply systems, or even the civilian infrastructure. A loss of confidence in financial data and electronic transfers could cause economic upheaval. An even bigger worry is an attack on the power grid. Power companies tend not to keep many spares of expensive generator parts, which can take months to replace. Emergency diesel generators cannot make up for the loss of the grid, and cannot operate indefinitely. Without electricity and other critical services, communications systems and cash-dispensers cease to work. A loss of power lasting just a few days, reckon some, starts to cause a cascade of economic damage.

Experts disagree about the vulnerability of systems that run industrial plants, known as supervisory control and data acquisition (SCADA). But more and more of these are being connected to the internet, raising the risk of remote attack. "Smart" grids, which relay information about energy use to the utilities, are promoted as ways of reducing energy waste. But they also increase security worries about both crime (eg, allowing bills to be falsified) and exposing SCADA networks to attack.

General Alexander has spoken of "hints that some penetrations are targeting systems for remote sabotage". But precisely what is happening is unclear: are outsiders probing SCADA systems only for reconnaissance, or to open "back doors" for future use? One senior American military source said that if any country were found to be planting logic bombs on the grid, it would provoke the equivalent of the Cuban missile crisis.

Estonia, Georgia and WWI

Important thinking about the tactical and legal concepts of cyber-warfare is taking place in a former Soviet barracks in Estonia, now home to NATO's "centre of excellence" for cyber-defence. It was established in response to what has become known as "Web War 1", a concerted denial-of-service attack on Estonian government, media and bank web servers that was precipitated by the decision to move a Soviet-era war memorial in central Tallinn in 2007. This was more a cyber-riot than a war, but it forced Estonia more or less to cut itself off from the internet.

Similar attacks during Russia's war with Georgia the next year looked more ominous, because they seemed to be coordinated with the advance of Russian military columns. Government and media websites went down and telephone lines were jammed, crippling Georgia's ability to present its case abroad. President Mikheil Saakashvili's website had to be moved to an American server better able to fight off the attack. Estonian experts were dispatched to Georgia to help out.

Many assume that both these attacks were instigated by the Kremlin. But investigations traced them only to Russian "hacktivists" and criminal botnets; many of the attacking computers were in Western countries. There are wider issues: did the cyber-attack on Estonia, a member of NATO, count as an armed attack, and should the alliance have defended it? And did Estonia's assistance to Georgia, which is not in NATO, risk drawing Estonia into the war, and NATO along with it?

Such questions permeate discussions of NATO's new "strategic concept", to be adopted later this year. A panel of experts headed by Madeleine Albright, a former American secretary of state, reported in May that cyber-attacks are among the three most likely threats to the alliance. The next significant attack, it said, "may well come down a fibre-optic cable" and may be serious enough to merit a response under the mutual-defence provisions of Article 5.

During his confirmation hearing, senators sent General Alexander several questions. Would he have "significant" offensive cyber-weapons? Might these encourage others to follow suit? How sure would he need to be about the identity of an attacker to "fire back"? Answers to these were restricted to a classified supplement. In public, the general said that the president would be the judge of what constituted cyberwar; if America responded with force in cyberspace it would be in keeping with the rules of war and the "principles of military necessity, discrimination, and proportionality".

General Alexander's seven-month confirmation process is a sign of the qualms senators felt at the merging of military and espionage functions, the militarisation of cyberspace and the fear that it may undermine Americans' right to privacy. Cybercommand will protect only the military ".mil" domain. The government domain, ".gov", and the corporate infrastructure, ".com" will be the responsibility respectively of the Department of Homeland Security and private companies, with support from Cybercom.

One senior military official says General Alexander's priority will be to improve the defences of military networks. Another bigwig casts some doubt on cyber-offence. "It's hard to do it at a specific time," he says. "If a cyber-attack is used as a military weapon, you want a predictable time and effect. If you are using it for espionage it does not matter; you can wait." He implies that cyber-weapons would be used mainly as an adjunct to conventional operations in a narrow theatre.

The Chinese may be thinking the same way. A report on China's cyber-warfare doctrine, written for the congressionally mandated US-China Economic and Security Review Commission, envisages China using cyber-weapons not to defeat America, but to disrupt and slow down its forces long enough for China to seize Taiwan without having to fight a shooting war.

Apocalypse or Asymmetry?

Deterrence in cyber-warfare is more uncertain than, say, in nuclear strategy: there is no mutually assured destruction, the dividing line between criminality and war is blurred and identifying attacking computers, let alone the fingers on the keyboards, is difficult. Retaliation need not be confined to cyberspace; the one system that is certainly not linked to the public internet is America's nuclear firing chain. Still, the more likely use of cyber-weapons is probably not to bring about electronic apocalypse, but as tools of limited warfare.

Cyber-weapons are most effective in the hands of big states. But because they are cheap, they may be most useful to the comparatively weak. They may well suit terrorists. Fortunately, perhaps, the likes of al-Qaeda have mostly used the internet for propaganda and communication. It may be that jihadists lack the ability to, say, induce a refinery to blow itself up. Or it may be that they prefer the gory theatre of suicide-bombings to the anonymity of computer sabotage—for now.

Critical Thinking

1. What kinds of damages can cyberterrorists cause?
2. How can the United States defend against cyberterrorists?
3. Could cyberterrorism cause society to literally break down?

The New Virology

The future of war by other means.

DAVID E. HOFFMAN

Largely unseen by the world, two dangerous germs homed in on their targets in the spring and early summer of 2009. One was made by man to infect computers. The other was made by nature, and could infect man.

The man-made virus could invade a computer running Windows, replicate itself, wreck an industrial process, hide from human operators, and evade anti-virus programs. The natural pathogen could invade human cells, hijack them to replicate billions of copies of itself, and evade the body's immune system. The man-made weapon was Stuxnet, a mysterious piece of computer malware that first appeared in 2009 and was identified more than a year later by Ralph Langner, a Hamburg-based computer security expert, as a worm designed to sabotage Iran's nuclear-enrichment facilities. The natural pathogen was the swine flu virus, which first appeared in Mexico City in March 2009 and touched off a global pandemic.

In the physical world, they have nothing in common. Stuxnet is computer code, bits of binary electronic data. The swine flu virus is a biological organism, a unique remix of genes from older influenza viruses. But they share one fundamental characteristic: They spread themselves and attack before their targets know what is happening. And in that way, they offer a glimpse of a rapidly evolving class of dangerous threats that former U.S. Navy Secretary Richard Danzig once described as instruments of "nonexplosive warfare."

When Danzig first raised the concept in 1998, an Internet bubble was mushrooming, terrorist cult Aum Shinrikyo had attacked the Tokyo subway with sarin gas, and there were fresh disclosures about the vast, illicit biological-weapons program built by the Soviet Union. What has happened since then? Cyberattacks have grown in intensity and sophistication. The technology for manipulating biological organisms is advancing rapidly. But these potentially anonymous weapons continue to perplex and confound our thinking about the future of war and terrorism.

Both cyber and bio threats are embedded in great leaps of technological progress that we would not want to give up, enabling rapid communications, dramatic productivity gains, new drugs and vaccines, richer harvests, and more. But both can also be used to harm and destroy. And both pose a particularly difficult strategic quandary: A hallmark of cyber and bio attacks is their ability to defy deterrence and elude defenses.

Think of it this way: The most sophisticated cyberattacks, like Stuxnet, rarely leave clear fingerprints; bioweapons, too, are famously difficult to trace back to a perpetrator. But the concept of deterrence depends on the threat of certain retaliation that would cause a rational attacker to think twice. So if the attacker can't be found, then the certainty of retaliation dissolves, and deterrence might not be possible.

What would a president of the United States say to the country if thousands of people were dying from a disease or trapped in a massive blackout and he did not know who caused it? A ballistic missile leaves a trajectory that can indicate its origins. An airline hijacker might be caught on video or leave behind a ticket or other telltale clue to his identity. When someone is shot with a weapon, the bullet and firearm can be traced. Not so for many cyber and bio threats.

Moreover, as Danzig pointed out, armies are of little use against such dangers, and neither the production nor delivery of such weapons requires large, expensive systems. They are accessible to small groups or individuals, and can hide under the radar.

So how to think about this? Recently, the Pentagon commissioned one of its most prestigious research advisory groups, JASON, to study the science of cybersecurity. One of the panel's recommendations for dealing with threats: Draw lessons from biology and the functioning of the human body's immune system. When it sees a dangerous pathogen, part of the immune system is adaptive and can resist the invader even if it has never seen the agent before. What computers might need to counter this new warfare is something similar, a "learning algorithm" that would allow them to adapt and resist when a bug like Stuxnet comes sneaking around—as it surely will.

On Feb. 8, 2000, Joshua Lederberg, one of the founders of American microbiology and a Nobel Prize laureate, spoke at a Rand Corp. conference on bioterrorism and homeland defense in Santa Monica, California. Lederberg, a geneticist who had been concerned for years about the United States' vulnerability to the use of biological agents in war and terrorism, told the group there would be no warning of such an attack, no big boom to alert everyone.

"We perhaps put too much stress on an acute incident, an explosion, a compelling notice that something really awful has happened," Lederberg said. "No shrewd user" of a biological weapon "is going to give you that opportunity," he warned. "The 'incident' will be people accumulating illness, disease, death."

Within two years, it happened. In the fall of 2001, at least five envelopes containing anthrax bacteria were mailed to two senators in Washington and media organizations in New York City and Boca Raton, Florida. At least 22 people contracted anthrax as a result; five died. Ten thousand people were given antibiotics as a precaution. With just five envelopes, 35 postal facilities and commercial mailrooms were contaminated. The bacteria were found in seven buildings on Capitol Hill. The U.S. Postal Service closed two heavily contaminated processing centers; one in Washington did not open for two years, and one in New Jersey did not open for four years. More than 1.8 million letters, packages, and magazines were stuck in quarantine at the two centers, which cost roughly $200 million to clean up.

After the attack, the FBI and the U.S. Postal Inspection Service set up a task force to investigate who had done it. In the seven years that followed, more than 10,000 witnesses were interviewed, 5,750 grand jury subpoenas issued, and 6,000 items of evidence collected. In 2007, the FBI determined that the anthrax originated from a batch created and maintained by Bruce E. Ivins, a researcher at the U.S. Army's biodefense laboratory at Fort Detrick, Maryland. Aware that he was under investigation, Ivins committed suicide in July 2008, leaving open the issue of his possible role and motives. There is still some uncertainty about the FBI's microbial forensics, now under review by a committee of the National Academy of Sciences. Regardless, the investigation showed how hard it is to crack such a case.

Amy E. Smithson, a senior fellow at the James Martin Center for Nonproliferation Studies of the Monterey Institute of International Studies, has attempted to investigate and analyze how decision-makers would react to a future biological attack. "The pressures to finger the bad guy are going to be tremendous," Smithson told me. Last year, Smithson assembled three teams of people for simulations of how high-level decision-makers might react. The groups were told they were playing the National Security Council, sitting in the White House Situation Room during the opening of a hypothetical G-8 summit in San Francisco, when a detector signaled the presence of a pathogen, Burkholderia pseudomallei, a bacterium that causes the disease melioidosis, which can be lethal if inhaled. The teams had been given several briefings on microbial forensics and the available intelligence, but still found themselves unsure how to untangle the evidence and how to respond.

Was the pathogen intended to harm the world leaders, or was it just a dispersal into the air, intended to shock? "They were massively frustrated at what microbial forensics and intelligence didn't tell them," Smithson said. "The effort to pinpoint a perpetrator is bound to confound, and the detection systems are not likely to deliver as much data as fast or as clearly as the policymakers want."

So, the conundrum is clear: As Danzig put it a decade ago, "With nonexplosive weapons it may be difficult to tell if an incident is an act of war, the deed of a small terrorist group, a simple crime, or a natural occurrence."

Could such an attack really happen? In the field of biology, much of the debate has centered on the capabilities and intentions of terrorists. While some diseases occur easily in nature and are highly contagious, others require sophisticated processing for use as a weapon, probably well beyond the capability of today's terrorist groups, which in the last decade have preferred explosive weapons—+truck bombs, duffel bags filled with dynamite, exploding airplanes, and old-fashioned guns. By contrast, if the FBI is correct, the anthrax letters were sent by a skilled worker in a sophisticated, well-funded American military laboratory, not someone working out of a safe house or a cave in the Hindu Kush.

New alarms about bioterrorism were sounded in December 2008 by a congressionally mandated commission on weapons of mass destruction, headed by former Senators Bob Graham and Jim Talent. Their report, "World at Risk," concluded that "terrorists are more likely to be able to obtain and use a biological weapon than a nuclear weapon." No terrorist group currently has the ability to carry out a mass-casualty attack using pathogens, the panel reported—weaponizing pathogens and disseminating them in the air is extremely difficult. But, they warned, "the United States should be less concerned that terrorists will

become biologists and far more concerned that biologists will become terrorists." A group of U.S. scientists, however, responded that the commission had exaggerated the threat and that fears of bioterrorism were diverting resources from urgent public health needs for naturally occurring diseases, which have caused far more deaths.

One thing is certain: The technology for probing and manipulating life at the genetic level is accelerating. Advances in sequencing—plotting the genetic blueprint of an organism—have been particularly rapid, leading to great benefits in public health, medicine, and other fields. When swine flu was discovered in two children in Southern California in April 2009, sequencing helped identify it rather quickly as a new type of influenza with genes from pigs as well as birds and humans. That was critical information for launching a response to a looming pandemic. The machines for sequencing, once the size of a mainframe computer, are becoming smaller and cheaper every year.

The obvious question is whether states or terrorists could exploit this technology for malevolent ends. The worry has come up most recently with the rise of synthetic biology, a relatively new field using engineering techniques to create new biological parts, devices, or systems, or redesign existing ones. A U.S. presidential commission concluded last year that synthetic biology should be watched for risks, but did not see the need for more controls. Yet. The panel said that no one had so far created synthetic life, only modified existing, natural hosts. But the inquiry itself highlighted the rapid pace of change in manipulating biology. Will rogue scientists eventually learn how to use the same techniques for evil?

Hostile Cyberattacks have long since left the realm of the theoretical. The Pentagon has said it is hit by "myriad" attacks every day on its 15,000 separate computer networks around the world. Dennis Blair, at the time the director of national intelligence, told Congress in February 2010 that the United States' critical infrastructure—power grids, information networks, and the like—is "severely threatened." He didn't provide statistics but added, "Malicious cyberactivity is occurring on an unprecedented scale with extraordinary sophistication."

Cyberattacks come in different flavors, whether exploitations to steal money or data; disruptions, such as distributed denial-of-service attacks aimed at overloading or paralyzing a website; or thefts, of data or as espionage. Some of the most sophisticated cyberattacks are multistage, in which a piece of malware penetrates a computer to use it as a platform for attacking yet another machine. These can be among the most difficult to trace, and Stuxnet is the most impressive example yet seen. The authors of a dossier produced by Symantec, the antivirus company, found that Stuxnet is "an incredibly large and complex threat." It knew where it was going and how to get there.

The creator of Stuxnet is still unknown, but with the sophistication of the code and the heavy amount of insider knowledge required, all signs point to a state or group of states. The New York Times reported in January that it might have been the result of a collaboration between the United States and Israel, the goal likely being to sabotage Iran's industrial centrifuges, which are used to enrich uranium. It could slow the machines down or speed them up—enough to cause subtle, but crippling, mechanical failures.

What's clear so far is that Stuxnet was written to attack an industrial control system, such as those used for gas pipelines and power plants. At first it was probably brought into a network on a removable flash drive, but once inside, it had the capability to replicate itself over and over again, each time carrying the payload that would be used to do the dirty work. The worm was designed for stealth. Injected into a computer or network, Stuxnet could sidestep anti-virus programs found on Windows computers, conceal itself on removable drives so the user would not know they were infected, and hide from the operators of the industrial equipment. Langner, the Hamburg computer security expert, said Stuxnet works like a sophisticated bank robbery. "During the heist, the observation camera is fed with unsuspicious footage, keeping the guards happy," he wrote.

The Institute for Science and International Security (ISIS), which has closely monitored the Iranian nuclear effort, reported that in late 2009 or early 2010, Iran decommissioned and replaced about 1,000 centrifuges in its uranium-enrichment plant at Natanz. If the goal of Stuxnet was to "set back Iran's progress" while making detection of the malware difficult, an ISIS report stated, "it may have succeeded, at least for a while."

But there are risks of blowback. Langner warns that such malware can proliferate in unexpected ways: "Stuxnet's attack code, available on the Internet, provides an excellent blueprint and jump-start for developing a new generation of cyber warfare weapons." He added, "Unlike bombs, missiles, and guns, cyber weapons can be copied. The proliferation of cyber weapons cannot be controlled. Stuxnet-inspired weapons and weapon technology will soon be in the hands of rogue nation states, terrorists, organized crime, and legions of leisure hackers."

Industrial control systems that were the target of Stuxnet are spread throughout the world and vulnerable to such attacks. In one 11-year-old Australian case, a disenchanted employee of the company that set up the control system at a sewage plant later decided to sabotage it. From his laptop, the worker ordered it to spill 211,337 gallons of raw sewage, and the control system obeyed—polluting parks, rivers, and the grounds of a hotel, killing marine life and turning a creek's water black.

But that attack was rare in another way: It was easy enough to identify the attacker. Stuxnet has been spotted on computer networks for nearly two years, but the world's top computer security experts have yet to pinpoint exactly who created it, or why.

What can be done to prevent catastrophe from nonexplosive warfare? The old arms-control remedies of the Atomic Age may not work. States like China and Russia now encourage groups of freelance hackers to do their dirty work, allowing plausible deniability. It is not clear that treaties could do much to stop them. According to Langner, "such treaties won't be countersigned by rogue nation states, terrorists, organized crime, and hackers. Yet all of these will be able to possess and use such weapons soon."

A major lesson can be drawn from the 1972 global treaty banning germ warfare, which lacked an effective enforcement mechanism from the start and failed to prevent the Soviet Union, South Africa, and Iraq from working on clandestine programs. There are suspicions that Iran, North Korea, and Syria might be harboring germ-warfare research today. The biological-weapons treaty has only 163 signatories, compared with 189 for the Nuclear Non-Proliferation Treaty and 188 for the Chemical Weapons Convention. Two successive U.S. administrations have concluded that biotechnology advances are occurring so swiftly that they probably cannot be policed through an updated legal enforcement protocol in the treaty.

Instead, President Barack Obama in 2009 called for taking alternative measures to avoid risk, such as helping other countries fight infectious disease while keeping an eye out for misuse of biology. Additional attempts are being made in the United States to improve monitoring of research by scientists, companies, and government, but much of it is still voluntary; this is not going to stop a dedicated rogue actor.

As for cyberattacks? Whatever the evidence for possible secret U.S. involvement in using cyberweapons for offensive assaults, it seems probable there will be retaliatory action. And other countries are almost certain to say: If the U.S. program includes offensive operations, why should we refrain? A new arms race beckons. And in this new arms race, there is no road map for disarmament or deterrence. In a shadowy, unaccountable world, we have not yet learned how to name the bad guys—never mind stop them.

Critical Thinking

1. Summarize what is known about biological, chemical, and cyberterrorism.
2. How are new technologies increasing the danger of biological, chemical, and cyberterrorism?
3. How has the United States responded to these threats so far?

DAVID E. HOFFMAN is a contributing editor to **FOREIGN POLICY** and author of *The Dead Hand: The Untold Story of the Cold War Arms Race and Its Dangerous Legacy.*

UNIT 6

Problems of Population, Environment, Resources, and the Future

Unit Selections

Learning Outcomes

After reading this unit, you should be able to:

• Explain why both population growth and population decline are problems.

• Assess the future world food situation.

• Explain how the world's environment is declining and evaluate what it would take to reverse this trend.

• What are the greatest threats to the world's environment?

• Explain why you are optimistic or pessimistic about the long-term results of genetic engineering of humans.

• Summarize the pros and cons of genetically modified foods.

• What are the prospects for democracy in the world? Explain the threats to democracy.

• What does your crystal ball say about the future of the world? Which of the assessments of the future that are reviewed in the readings do you find the most plausible?

Student Website

www.mhhe.com/cls

Internet References

Human Rights and Humanitarian Assistance
www.etown.edu/vl/humrts.html

The Hunger Project
www.thp.org

The previous units have wrestled with many knotty problems within United States society. In this unit the focus is on problems of the future, mostly from a worldwide perspective. Any discussion of the future must begin with a look at present population and environmental trends, which are the focus of the first subsection in this unit. The second subsection looks at the problems of new technologies. The final subsection assesses the prospects for the future in very broad terms.

Some scholars are very concerned about the worsening state of the environment, and others are confident that technological developments will solve most of these problems. Since the debate is about the future, neither view can be proved or disproved. Nevertheless, it is important to look at the factors that are causing environmental decline and increasing the demands on the environment. The first factor is population growth and the first article assesses future demography and its implications. World population is projected by the UN to stabilize at 9.15 billion. The growth will be in the developing countries, while the developed countries will age and decline. This will constrain their economic growth. Most of the world's expected population growth will occur in the poorest, youngest, and heavily Muslim countries that lack education, capital, and employment opportunities. These trends pose alarming challenges to the world's basic governance structures. Instability, violence, terrorism, and even revolutions are, therefore, likely prospects. Greater world integration is needed. In the second article, Lester R. Brown discusses the traumatic impacts of food production limits and very high food prices. The major economic crisis currently affecting most of the world is the food crisis and the future probably will be much worse. Food prices were a major factor in the Arab Spring revolutions. Future food prices are likely to increase significantly (though with some ups and downs). More that half of the world lives in countries where water tables are falling. The ability of America to buffer bad harvests elsewhere has practically disappeared. Soils have been depleting for decades. Deserts are expanding. Cropland is being diverted to ethanol production. Global warming will reduce world food production. Are these addressable problems or do they warn of a major long-term food crisis? Brown argues the latter scenario. Next Phillip Longman is not very concerned about too many people but too many old people. They retire and contribute little to society, but consume a lot, especially healthcare. If there are many young adults contributing a lot to society, the old people can be taken care of without overly burdening young people and holding back society. The balance between producers and withdrawers is quite bad in developed nations. The subtitle of his most recent book is "Why Falling Birthrates Threaten World Prosperity and What to Do about It." The final article in this subsection addresses the problem of anthropomorphic global warming (AGW). Bill McKibben shows that the debate is over. Scientists overwhelming agree on the AGW thesis and the immense dangers it creates for human societies. Time is short. It will change environments worldwide and require economic, policy, and behavioral changes that will greatly stress societies. The costs for addressing the issue will

© Ingram Publishing

be very costly—more than the costs of the two world wars. The costs of not acting will be much greater.

The next subsection looks at technological problems, specifically life-extending and agricultural technologies. The first deals with issues that have been created by DNA research. The beneficial possibilities are enormous; so are the potential dangers and moral questions. For example, society must now decide whether to continue to leave the creation of humans to providence and/or evolution or to genetically engineer our offspring. In the first article in this subsection, several authors debate the issues and options. In the next article, Josh Schonwald examines a highly debated topic: genetic engineering in agriculture or GMO (genetically modified organisms). Schonwald believes GMO crops have gotten a bad name. They are in practically everything we eat since genetically modified soybeans and canola dominate the market. Genetically modified rice could prevent hundred of thousand of children from going blind every year. The industry believes that eventually a life-extending gene will be inserted into vegetables and many other wonderful genetic improvements will be forthcoming. So far, however, fears are winning out against GMOs.

The final subsection assesses the macro prospects for the future. The first article examines a major problem of the economy, the second examines a major problem of the polity, and the third examines the sustainability of the political economy. These are very interesting macro problems. George Packer in the first article more or less says that the United States was a wonderful country in the 1950s and 1960s but now we are not a wonderful country. We are richer and have wonderful toys but are not a good society because the basic social contract that made us great has been broken. In the 1950s and 1960s institutional forces in politics, business, and the media could hold the country together and address our problems. Not so today. The contract between labor, business, and government and between elites and masses is broken and the United States can no longer do the things it needs to do. Next Charles A. Kupchan observes that the developed democratic countries are currently ungovernable and experiencing political breakdown. They cannot deliver what their publics are demanding. Voters want their governments to increase living standards, address the growing inequality, maintain their standing in the world, meet foreign competition, and handle other major issues like AGW. They are failing and losing legitimacy. The old policy tools that worked relatively well decades ago are made less effective by globalization. Furthermore, countries need more consensus than they have today to do what needs to be done. The last article by Francis Fukuyama asks whether liberal democracy can survive the decline of the middle class. He traces the historical development of liberalism, which always emphasized individual rights and private property and eventually included liberal democracy. Now the supports for liberal democracy are being squeezed, especially the strength of the middle class and the role of government to provide for the needs of this class. Many factors are undermining the prospects of the middle class, including technology, ideologies, globalization, trade policies, tax policies, outsourcing, and elite avenues for political influence.

The New Population Bomb: The Four Megatrends That Will Change the World

JACK A. GOLDSTONE

Forty-two years ago, the biologist Paul Ehrlich warned in The Population Bomb that mass starvation would strike in the 1970s and 1980s, with the world's population growth outpacing the production of food and other critical resources. Thanks to innovations and efforts such as the "green revolution" in farming and the widespread adoption of family planning, Ehrlich's worst fears did not come to pass. In fact, since the 1970s, global economic output has increased and fertility has fallen dramatically, especially in developing countries.

The United Nations Population Division now projects that global population growth will nearly halt by 2050. By that date, the world's population will have stabilized at 9.15 billion people, according to the "medium growth" variant of the UN's authoritative population database World Population Prospects: The 2008 Revision. (Today's global population is 6.83 billion.) Barring a cataclysmic climate crisis or a complete failure to recover from the current economic malaise, global economic output is expected to increase by two to three percent per year, meaning that global income will increase far more than population over the next four decades.

But twenty-first-century international security will depend less on how many people inhabit the world than on how the global population is composed and distributed: where populations are declining and where they are growing, which countries are relatively older and which are more youthful, and how demographics will influence population movements across regions.

These elements are not well recognized or widely understood. A recent article in The Economist, for example, cheered the decline in global fertility without noting other vital demographic developments. Indeed, the same UN data cited by The Economist reveal four historic shifts that will fundamentally alter the world's population over the next four decades: the relative demographic weight of the world's developed countries will drop by nearly 25 percent, shifting economic power to the developing nations; the developed countries' labor forces will substantially age and decline, constraining economic growth in the developed world and raising the demand for immigrant workers; most of the world's expected population growth will increasingly be concentrated in today's poorest, youngest, and most heavily Muslim countries, which have a dangerous lack of quality education, capital, and employment opportunities; and, for the first time in history, most of the world's population will become urbanized, with the largest urban centers being in the world's poorest countries, where policing, sanitation, and health care are often scarce. Taken together, these trends will pose challenges every bit as alarming as those noted by Ehrlich. Coping with them will require nothing less than a major reconsideration of the world's basic global governance structures.

Europe's Reversal of Fortunes

At the beginning of the eighteenth century, approximately 20 percent of the world's inhabitants lived in Europe (including Russia). Then, with the Industrial Revolution, Europe's population boomed, and streams of European emigrants set off for the Americas. By the eve of World War I, Europe's population had more than quadrupled. In 1913, Europe had more people than China, and the proportion of the world's population living in Europe and the former European colonies of North America had risen to over 33 percent. But this trend reversed after World War I, as basic health care and sanitation began to spread to poorer countries. In Asia, Africa, and Latin America, people began to live longer, and birthrates remained high or fell only slowly. By 2003, the combined populations of Europe, the United States, and Canada accounted for just 17 percent of the global population. In 2050, this figure is expected to be just 12 percent—far less than it was in 1700. (These projections, moreover, might even understate the reality because they reflect the "medium growth" projection of the UN forecasts, which assumes that the fertility rates of developing countries will decline while those of developed countries will increase. In fact, many developed countries show no evidence of increasing fertility rates.) The West's relative decline is even more dramatic if one also considers changes in income. The Industrial Revolution made Europeans not only more numerous than they had been but also considerably richer per capita than others worldwide. According to the economic historian Angus Maddison, Europe, the United States, and Canada together produced about 32 percent of the world's GDP at the beginning of the nineteenth century. By 1950, that proportion had increased to a remarkable 68 percent of the world's total output (adjusted to reflect purchasing power parity).

This trend, too, is headed for a sharp reversal. The proportion of global GDP produced by Europe, the United States, and Canada fell from 68 percent in 1950 to 47 percent in 2003 and will decline even more steeply in the future. If the growth rate of per capita income (again, adjusted for purchasing power parity) between 2003 and 2050 remains as it was between 1973 and 2003—averaging 1.68 percent annually in Europe, the United States, and Canada and 2.47 percent annually in the rest of the world—then the combined GDP of Europe, the United States, and Canada will roughly double by 2050, whereas the GDP of the rest of the world will grow by a factor of five. The portion of global GDP produced by Europe, the United States, and Canada in 2050 will then be less than 30 percent—smaller than it was in 1820.

These figures also imply that an overwhelming proportion of the world's GDP growth between 2003 and 2050—nearly 80 percent—will occur outside of Europe, the United States, and Canada. By the middle of this century, the global middle class—those capable of purchasing durable consumer products, such as cars, appliances, and electronics—will increasingly be found in what is now considered the developing world. The World Bank has predicted that by 2030 the number of middle-class people in the developing world will be 1.2 billion—a rise of 200 percent since 2005. This means that the developing world's middle class alone will be larger than the total populations of Europe, Japan, and the United States combined. From now on, therefore, the main driver of global economic expansion will be the economic growth of newly industrialized countries, such as Brazil, China, India, Indonesia, Mexico, and Turkey.

Aging Pains

Part of the reason developed countries will be less economically dynamic in the coming decades is that their populations will become substantially older. The European countries, Canada, the United States, Japan, South Korea, and even China are aging at unprecedented rates. Today, the proportion of people aged 60 or older in China and South Korea is 12–15 percent. It is 15–22 percent in the European Union, Canada, and the United States and 30 percent in Japan. With baby boomers aging and life expectancy increasing, these numbers will increase dramatically. In 2050, approximately 30 percent of Americans, Canadians, Chinese, and Europeans will be over 60, as will more than 40 percent of Japanese and South Koreans.

Over the next decades, therefore, these countries will have increasingly large proportions of retirees and increasingly small proportions of workers. As workers born during the baby boom of 1945–65 are retiring, they are not being replaced by a new cohort of citizens of prime working age (15–59 years old).

Industrialized countries are experiencing a drop in their working-age populations that is even more severe than the overall slowdown in their population growth. South Korea represents the most extreme example. Even as its total population is projected to decline by almost 9 percent by 2050 (from 48.3

million to 44.1 million), the population of working-age South Koreans is expected to drop by 36 percent (from 32.9 million to 21.1 million), and the number of South Koreans aged 60 and older will increase by almost 150 percent (from 7.3 million to 18 million). By 2050, in other words, the entire working-age population will barely exceed the 60-and-older population. Although South Korea's case is extreme, it represents an increasingly common fate for developed countries. Europe is expected to lose 24 percent of its prime working-age population (about 120 million workers) by 2050, and its 60-and-older population is expected to increase by 47 percent. In the United States, where higher fertility and more immigration are expected than in Europe, the working-age population will grow by 15 percent over the next four decades—a steep decline from its growth of 62 percent between 1950 and 2010. And by 2050, the United States' 60-and-older population is expected to double.

All this will have a dramatic impact on economic growth, health care, and military strength in the developed world. The forces that fueled economic growth in industrialized countries during the second half of the twentieth century—increased productivity due to better education, the movement of women into the labor force, and innovations in technology—will all likely weaken in the coming decades. College enrollment boomed after World War II, a trend that is not likely to recur in the twenty-first century; the extensive movement of women into the labor force also was a one-time social change; and the technological change of the time resulted from innovators who created new products and leading-edge consumers who were willing to try them out—two groups that are thinning out as the industrialized world's population ages.

Overall economic growth will also be hampered by a decline in the number of new consumers and new households. When developed countries' labor forces were growing by 0.5–1.0 percent per year, as they did until 2005, even annual increases in real output per worker of just 1.7 percent meant that annual economic growth totaled 2.2–2.7 percent per year. But with the labor forces of many developed countries (such as Germany, Hungary, Japan, Russia, and the Baltic states) now shrinking by 0.2 percent per year and those of other countries (including Austria, the Czech Republic, Denmark, Greece, and Italy) growing by less than 0.2 percent per year, the same 1.7 percent increase in real output per worker yields only 1.5–1.9 percent annual overall growth. Moreover, developed countries will be lucky to keep productivity growth at even that level; in many developed countries, productivity is more likely to decline as the population ages.

A further strain on industrialized economies will be rising medical costs: as populations age, they will demand more health care for longer periods of time. Public pension schemes for aging populations are already being reformed in various industrialized countries—often prompting heated debate. In theory, at least, pensions might be kept solvent by increasing the retirement age, raising taxes modestly, and phasing out benefits for the wealthy. Regardless, the number of 80- and 90-year-olds—who are unlikely to work and highly likely to require nursing-home and other expensive care—will rise dramatically. And even if 60- and 70-year-olds remain active and employed, they will require procedures and medications—hip replacements, kidney transplants, blood-pressure treatments—to sustain their health in old age.

All this means that just as aging developed countries will have proportionally fewer workers, innovators, and consumerist young households, a large portion of those countries' remaining economic growth will have to be diverted to pay for the medical bills and pensions of their growing elderly populations. Basic services, meanwhile, will be increasingly costly because fewer young workers will be available for strenuous and labor-intensive jobs. Unfortunately, policymakers seldom reckon with these potentially disruptive effects of otherwise welcome developments, such as higher life expectancy.

Youth and Islam in the Developing World

Even as the industrialized countries of Europe, North America, and Northeast Asia will experience unprecedented aging this century, fast-growing countries in Africa, Latin America, the Middle East, and Southeast Asia will have exceptionally youthful populations. Today, roughly nine out of ten children under the age of 15 live in developing countries. And these are the countries that will continue to have the world's highest birthrates. Indeed, over 70 percent of the world's population growth between now and 2050 will occur in 24 countries, all of which are classified by the World Bank as low income or lower-middle income, with an average per capita income of under $3,855 in 2008.

Many developing countries have few ways of providing employment to their young, fast-growing populations. Would-be laborers, therefore, will be increasingly attracted to the labor markets of the aging developed countries of Europe, North America, and Northeast Asia. Youthful immigrants from nearby regions with high unemployment—Central America, North Africa, and Southeast Asia, for example—will be drawn to those vital entry-level and manual-labor jobs that sustain advanced economies: janitors, nursing-home aides, bus drivers, plumbers, security guards, farm workers, and the like. Current levels of immigration from developing to developed countries are paltry compared to those that the forces of supply and demand might soon create across the world.

These forces will act strongly on the Muslim world, where many economically weak countries will continue to experience dramatic population growth in the decades ahead. In 1950, Bangladesh, Egypt, Indonesia, Nigeria, Pakistan, and Turkey had a combined population of 242 million. By 2009, those six countries were the world's most populous Muslim-majority countries and had a combined population of 886 million. Their populations are continuing to grow and indeed are expected to increase by 475 million between now and 2050—during which time, by comparison, the six most populous developed countries are projected to gain only 44 million inhabitants. Worldwide, of the 48 fastest-growing countries today—those with annual population growth of two percent or more—28 are majority Muslim or have Muslim minorities of 33 percent or more.

It is therefore imperative to improve relations between Muslim and Western societies. This will be difficult given that many Muslims live in poor communities vulnerable to radical appeals and many see the West as antagonistic and militaristic. In the 2009 Pew Global Attitudes Project survey, for example, whereas 69 percent of those Indonesians and Nigerians surveyed reported viewing the United States favorably, just 18 percent of those polled in Egypt, Jordan, Pakistan, and Turkey (all U.S. allies) did. And in 2006, when the Pew survey last asked detailed questions about Muslim-Western relations, more than half of the respondents in Muslim countries characterized those relations as bad and blamed the West for this state of affairs.

But improving relations is all the more important because of the growing demographic weight of poor Muslim countries and the attendant increase in Muslim immigration, especially to Europe from North Africa and the Middle East. (To be sure, forecasts that Muslims will soon dominate Europe are outlandish: Muslims compose just three to ten percent of the population in the major European countries today, and this proportion will at most double by midcentury.) Strategists worldwide must consider that the world's young are becoming concentrated in those countries least prepared to educate and employ them, including some Muslim states. Any resulting poverty, social tension, or ideological radicalization could have disruptive effects in many corners of the world. But this need not be the case; the healthy immigration of workers to the developed world and the movement of capital to the developing world, among other things, could lead to better results.

Urban Sprawl

Exacerbating twenty-first-century risks will be the fact that the world is urbanizing to an unprecedented degree. The year 2010 will likely be the first time in history that a majority of the world's people live in cities rather than in the countryside. Whereas less than 30 percent of the world's population was urban in 1950, according to UN projections, more than 70 percent will be by 2050.

Lower-income countries in Asia and Africa are urbanizing especially rapidly, as agriculture becomes less labor intensive and as employment opportunities shift to the industrial and service sectors. Already, most of the world's urban agglomerations—Mumbai (population 20.1 million), Mexico City (19.5 million), New Delhi (17 million), Shanghai (15.8 million), Calcutta (15.6 million), Karachi (13.1 million), Cairo (12.5 million), Manila (11.7 million), Lagos (10.6 million), Jakarta (9.7 million)—are found in low-income countries. Many of these countries have multiple cities with over one million residents each: Pakistan has eight, Mexico 12, and China more than 100. The UN projects that the urbanized proportion of sub-Saharan Africa will nearly double between 2005 and 2050, from 35 percent (300 million people) to over 67 percent (1 billion). China, which is roughly 40 percent urbanized today, is expected to be 73 percent urbanized by 2050; India, which is less than 30 percent urbanized today, is expected to be 55 percent urbanized by 2050. Overall, the world's urban population is expected to grow by 3 billion people by 2050.

This urbanization may prove destabilizing. Developing countries that urbanize in the twenty-first century will have far lower per capita incomes than did many industrial countries when they first urbanized. The United States, for example, did not reach 65 percent urbanization until 1950, when per capita income was nearly $13,000 (in 2005 dollars). By contrast, Nigeria, Pakistan, and the Philippines, which are approaching similar levels of urbanization, currently have per capita incomes of just $1,800–$4,000 (in 2005 dollars).

According to the research of Richard Cincotta and other political demographers, countries with younger populations are especially prone to civil unrest and are less able to create or sustain democratic institutions. And the more heavily urbanized, the more such countries are likely to experience Dickensian poverty and anarchic violence. In good times, a thriving economy might keep urban residents employed and governments flush with sufficient resources to meet their needs. More often, however, sprawling and impoverished cities are vulnerable to crime lords, gangs, and petty rebellions. Thus, the rapid urbanization of the developing world in the decades ahead might bring, in exaggerated form, problems similar to those that urbanization brought to nineteenth-century Europe. Back then, cyclical employment, inadequate policing, and limited sanitation and education often spawned widespread labor strife, periodic violence, and sometimes—as in the 1820s, the 1830s, and 1848—even revolutions.

International terrorism might also originate in fast-urbanizing developing countries (even more than it already does). With their neighborhood networks, access to the Internet and digital communications technology, and concentration of valuable targets, sprawling cities offer excellent opportunities for recruiting, maintaining, and hiding terrorist networks.

Defusing the Bomb

Averting this century's potential dangers will require sweeping measures. Three major global efforts defused the population bomb of Ehrlich's day: a commitment by governments and nongovernmental organizations to control reproduction rates; agricultural advances, such as the green revolution and the spread of new technology; and a vast increase in international trade, which globalized markets and thus allowed developing countries to export foodstuffs in exchange for seeds, fertilizers, and machinery, which in turn helped them boost production. But today's population bomb is the product less of absolute growth in the world's population than of changes in its age and distribution. Policymakers must therefore adapt today's global governance institutions to the new realities of the aging of the industrialized world, the concentration of the world's economic and population growth in developing countries, and the increase in international immigration.

During the Cold War, Western strategists divided the world into a "First World," of democratic industrialized countries; a "Second World," of communist industrialized countries; and a "Third World," of developing countries. These strategists focused chiefly on deterring or managing conflict between the First and the Second Worlds and on launching proxy wars and diplomatic initiatives to attract Third World countries into the First World's camp. Since the end of the Cold War, strategists have largely abandoned this three-group division and have tended to believe either that the United States, as the sole superpower, would maintain a Pax Americana or that the world would become multipolar, with the United States, Europe, and China playing major roles.

Unfortunately, because they ignore current global demographic trends, these views will be obsolete within a few decades. A better approach would be to consider a different three-world order, with a new First World of the aging industrialized nations of North America, Europe, and Asia's Pacific Rim (including Japan, Singapore, South Korea, and Taiwan, as well as China after 2030, by which point the one-child policy will have produced significant aging); a Second World comprising fast-growing and economically dynamic countries with a healthy mix of young and old inhabitants (such as Brazil, Iran, Mexico, Thailand, Turkey, and Vietnam, as well as China until 2030); and a Third World of fast-growing, very young, and increasingly urbanized countries with poorer economies and often weak governments. To cope with the instability that will likely arise from the new Third World's urbanization, economic strife, lawlessness, and potential terrorist activity, the aging industrialized nations of the new First World must build effective alliances with the growing powers of the new Second World and together reach out to Third World nations. Second World powers will be pivotal in the twenty-first century not just because they will drive economic growth and consume technologies and other products engineered in the First World; they will also be central to international security and cooperation. The realities of religion, culture, and geographic proximity mean that any peaceful and productive engagement by the First World of Third World countries will have to include the open cooperation of Second World countries.

Strategists, therefore, must fundamentally reconsider the structure of various current global institutions. The G-8, for example, will likely become obsolete as a body for making global economic policy. The G-20 is already becoming increasingly important, and this is less a short-term consequence of the ongoing global financial crisis than the beginning of the necessary recognition that Brazil, China, India, Indonesia, Mexico, Turkey, and others are becoming global economic powers. International institutions will not retain their legitimacy if they exclude the world's fastest-growing and most economically dynamic countries. It is essential, therefore, despite European concerns about the potential effects on immigration, to take steps such as admitting Turkey into the European Union. This would add youth and economic dynamism to the EU—and would prove that Muslims are welcome to join Europeans as equals in shaping a free and prosperous future. On the other hand, excluding Turkey from the EU could lead to hostility not only on the part of Turkish citizens, who are expected to number 100 million by 2050, but also on the part of Muslim populations worldwide.

NATO must also adapt. The alliance today is composed almost entirely of countries with aging, shrinking populations and relatively slow-growing economies. It is oriented toward the Northern Hemisphere and holds on to a Cold War structure that cannot adequately respond to contemporary threats. The young and increasingly populous countries of Africa, the Middle East, Central Asia, and South Asia could mobilize insurgents much more easily than NATO could mobilize the troops it would need if it were called on to stabilize those countries. Long-standing NATO members should, therefore—although it would require atypical creativity and flexibility—consider the logistical and demographic advantages of inviting into the alliance countries such as Brazil and Morocco, rather than countries such as Albania. That this seems far-fetched does not minimize the imperative that First World countries begin including large and strategic Second and Third World powers in formal international alliances.

The case of Afghanistan—a country whose population is growing fast and where NATO is currently engaged—illustrates the importance of building effective global institutions. Today, there are 28 million Afghans; by 2025, there will be 45 million; and by 2050, there will be close to 75 million. As nearly 20 million additional Afghans are born over the next 15 years, NATO will have an opportunity to help Afghanistan become reasonably stable, self-governing, and prosperous. If NATO's efforts fail and the Afghans judge that NATO intervention harmed their interests, tens of millions of young Afghans will become more hostile to the West. But if they come to think that NATO's involvement benefited their society, the West will have tens of millions of new friends. The example might then motivate the approximately one billion other young Muslims growing up in low-income countries over the next four decades to look more kindly on relations between their countries and the countries of the industrialized West.

Creative Reforms at Home

The aging industrialized countries can also take various steps at home to promote stability in light of the coming demographic trends. First, they should encourage families to have more children. France and Sweden have had success providing child care, generous leave time, and financial allowances to families with young children. Yet there is no consensus among policymakers—and certainly not among demographers—about what policies best encourage fertility.

More important than unproven tactics for increasing family size is immigration. Correctly managed, population movement can benefit developed and developing countries alike. Given the dangers of young, underemployed, and unstable populations in developing countries, immigration to developed countries can provide economic opportunities for the ambitious and serve as a safety valve for all. Countries that embrace immigrants, such as the United States, gain economically by having willing laborers and greater entrepreneurial spirit. And countries with high levels of emigration (but not so much that they experience so-called brain drains) also benefit because emigrants often send remittances home or return to their native countries with valuable education and work experience.

One somewhat daring approach to immigration would be to encourage a reverse flow of older immigrants from developed to developing countries. If older residents of developed countries took their retirements along the southern coast of the Mediterranean or in Latin America or Africa, it would greatly reduce the strain on their home countries' public entitlement systems. The developing countries involved, meanwhile, would benefit because caring for the elderly and providing retirement and leisure services is highly labor intensive. Relocating a portion of these activities to developing countries would provide employment and valuable training to the young, growing populations of the Second and Third Worlds.

This would require developing residential and medical facilities of First World quality in Second and Third World countries. Yet even this difficult task would be preferable to the status quo, by which low wages and poor facilities lead to a steady drain of medical and nursing talent from developing to developed countries. Many residents of developed countries who desire cheaper medical procedures already practice medical tourism today, with India, Singapore, and Thailand being the most common destinations. (For example, the international consulting firm Deloitte estimated that 750,000 Americans traveled abroad for care in 2008.)

Never since 1800 has a majority of the world's economic growth occurred outside of Europe, the United States, and Canada. Never have so many people in those regions been over 60 years old. And never have low-income countries' populations been so young and so urbanized. But such will be the world's demography in the twenty-first century. The strategic and economic policies of the twentieth century are obsolete, and it is time to find new ones.

Reference

Goldstone, Jack A. "The new population bomb: the four megatrends that will change the world." *Foreign Affairs* 89.1 (2010): 31. *General OneFile*. Web. 23 Jan. 2010. http://0-find.galegroup .com.www.consuls.org/gps/start.do?proId=IPS& userGroupName=a30wc.

Critical Thinking

1. What will be the second-order impacts of future population growth?

2. In the developed countries, population will age and decline relative to developing countries. How will these changes strain world governance structures and generate instability and violence?

From *Foreign Affairs*, vol. 89, no. 1, January/February 2010, pp. 31–43. Copyright © 2010 by Council on Foreign Relations, Inc. Reprinted by permission of Foreign Affairs. www.ForeignAffairs.org

The New Geopolitics of Food

From the Middle East to Madagascar, high prices are spawning land grabs and ousting dictators. Welcome to the 21st-century food wars.

LESTER R. BROWN

In the United States, when world wheat prices rise by 75 percent, as they have over the last year, it means the difference between a $2 loaf of bread and a loaf costing maybe $2.10. If, however, you live in New Delhi, those sky-rocketing costs really matter: A doubling in the world price of wheat actually means that the wheat you carry home from the market to hand-grind into flour for chapatis costs twice as much. And the same is true with rice. If the world price of rice doubles, so does the price of rice in your neighborhood market in Jakarta. And so does the cost of the bowl of boiled rice on an Indonesian family's dinner table.

Welcome to the new food economics of 2011: Prices are climbing, but the impact is not at all being felt equally. For Americans, who spend less than one-tenth of their income in the supermarket, the soaring food prices we've seen so far this year are an annoyance, not a calamity. But for the planet's poorest 2 billion people, who spend 50 to 70 percent of their income on food, these soaring prices may mean going from two meals a day to one. Those who are barely hanging on to the lower rungs of the global economic ladder risk losing their grip entirely. This can contribute—and it has—to revolutions and upheaval.

Already in 2011, the U.N. Food Price Index has eclipsed its previous all-time global high; as of March it had climbed for eight consecutive months. With this year's harvest predicted to fall short, with governments in the Middle East and Africa teetering as a result of the price spikes, and with anxious markets sustaining one shock after another, food has quickly become the hidden driver of world politics. And crises like these are going to become increasingly common. The new geopolitics of food looks a whole lot more volatile—and a whole lot more contentious—than it used to. Scarcity is the new norm.

Until recently, sudden price surges just didn't matter as much, as they were quickly followed by a return to the relatively low food prices that helped shape the political stability of the late 20th century across much of the globe. But now both the causes and consequences are ominously different.

In many ways, this is a resumption of the 2007–2008 food crisis, which subsided not because the world somehow came together to solve its grain crunch once and for all, but because the Great Recession tempered growth in demand even as favorable weather helped farmers produce the largest grain harvest on record. Historically, price spikes tended to be almost exclusively driven by unusual weather—a monsoon failure in India, a drought in the former Soviet Union, a heat wave in the U.S. Midwest. Such events were always disruptive, but thankfully infrequent. Unfortunately, today's price hikes are driven by trends that are both elevating demand and making it more difficult to increase production: among them, a rapidly expanding population, crop-withering temperature increases, and irrigation wells running dry. Each night, there are 219,000 additional people to feed at the global dinner table.

More alarming still, the world is losing its ability to soften the effect of shortages. In response to previous price surges, the United States, the world's largest grain producer, was effectively able to steer the world away from potential catastrophe. From the mid-20th century until 1995, the United States had either grain surpluses or idle cropland that could be planted to rescue countries in trouble. When the Indian monsoon failed in 1965, for example, President Lyndon Johnson's administration shipped one-fifth of the U.S. wheat crop to India, successfully staving off famine. We can't do that anymore; the safety cushion is gone.

That's why the food crisis of 2011 is for real, and why it may bring with it yet more bread riots cum political revolutions. What if the upheavals that greeted dictators Zine el-Abidine Ben Ali in Tunisia, Hosni Mubarak in Egypt, and Muammar al-Qaddafi in Libya (a country that imports 90 percent of its grain) are not the end of the story, but the beginning of it? Get ready, farmers and foreign ministers alike, for a new era in which world food scarcity increasingly shapes global politics.

The doubling of world grain prices since early 2007 has been driven primarily by two factors: accelerating growth in demand and the increasing difficulty of rapidly expanding production. The result is a world that looks strikingly different from the bountiful global grain economy of the last century. What will the geopolitics of food look like in a new era dominated by scarcity? Even at this early stage, we can see at least the broad outlines of the emerging food economy.

On the demand side, farmers now face clear sources of increasing pressure. The first is population growth. Each year the world's farmers must feed 80 million additional people, nearly all of them in developing countries. The world's population has nearly doubled since 1970 and is headed toward 9 billion by midcentury. Some 3 billion people, meanwhile, are also trying to move up the food chain, consuming more meat, milk, and eggs. As more families in China and elsewhere enter the middle class, they expect to eat better. But as global consumption of grain-intensive livestock products climbs, so does the demand for the extra corn and soybeans needed to feed all that livestock. (Grain consumption per person in the United States, for example, is four times that in India, where little grain is converted into animal protein. For now.)

At the same time, the United States, which once was able to act as a global buffer of sorts against poor harvests elsewhere, is now converting massive quantities of grain into fuel for cars, even as world grain consumption, which is already up to roughly 2.2 billion metric tons per year, is growing at an accelerating rate. A decade ago, the growth in consumption was 20 million tons per year. More recently it has risen by 40 million tons every year. But the rate at which the United States is converting grain into ethanol has grown even faster. In 2010, the United States harvested nearly 400 million tons of grain, of which 126 million tons went to ethanol fuel distilleries (up from 16 million tons in 2000). This massive capacity to convert grain into fuel means that the price of grain is now tied to the price of oil. So if oil goes to $150 per barrel or more, the price of grain will follow it upward as it becomes ever more profitable to convert grain into oil substitutes. And it's not just a U.S. phenomenon: Brazil, which distills ethanol from sugar cane, ranks second in production after the United States, while the European Union's goal of getting 10 percent of its transport energy from renewables, mostly biofuels, by 2020 is also diverting land from food crops.

This is not merely a story about the booming demand for food. Everything from falling water tables to eroding soils and the consequences of global warming means that the world's food supply is unlikely to keep up with our collectively growing appetites. Take climate change: The rule of thumb among crop ecologists is that for every 1 degree Celsius rise in temperature above the growing season optimum, farmers can expect a 10 percent decline in grain yields. This relationship was borne out all too dramatically during the 2010 heat wave in Russia, which reduced the country's grain harvest by nearly 40 percent.

While temperatures are rising, water tables are falling as farmers overpump for irrigation. This artificially inflates food production in the short run, creating a food bubble that bursts when aquifers are depleted and pumping is necessarily reduced to the rate of recharge. In arid Saudi Arabia, irrigation had surprisingly enabled the country to be self-sufficient in wheat for more than 20 years; now, wheat production is collapsing because the non-replenishable aquifer the country uses for irrigation is largely depleted. The Saudis soon will be importing all their grain.

Saudi Arabia is only one of some 18 countries with water-based food bubbles. All together, more than half the world's people live in countries where water tables are falling. The politically troubled Arab Middle East is the first geographic region where grain production has peaked and begun to decline because of water shortages, even as populations continue to grow. Grain production is already going down in Syria and Iraq and may soon decline in Yemen. But the largest food bubbles are in India and China. In India, where farmers have drilled some 20 million irrigation wells, water tables are falling and the wells are starting to go dry. The World Bank reports that 175 million Indians are being fed with grain produced by overpumping. In China, overpumping is concentrated in the North China Plain, which produces half of China's wheat and a third of its corn. An estimated 130 million Chinese are currently fed by overpumping. How will these countries make up for the inevitable shortfalls when the aquifers are depleted?

Even as we are running our wells dry, we are also mismanaging our soils, creating new deserts. Soil erosion as a result of overplowing and land mismanagement is undermining the productivity of one-third of the world's cropland. How severe is it? Look at satellite images showing two huge new dust bowls: one stretching across northern and western China and western Mongolia; the other across central Africa. Wang Tao, a leading Chinese desert scholar, reports that each year some 1,400 square miles of land in northern China turn to desert. In Mongolia and Lesotho, grain harvests have shrunk by half or more over the last few decades. North Korea and Haiti are also suffering from heavy soil losses; both countries face famine if they lose international food aid. Civilization can survive the loss of its oil reserves, but it cannot survive the loss of its soil reserves.

Beyond the changes in the environment that make it ever harder to meet human demand, there's an important intangible factor to consider: Over the last half-century or so, we have come to take agricultural progress for granted. Decade after decade, advancing technology underpinned steady gains in raising land productivity. Indeed, world grain yield per acre has tripled since 1950. But now that era is coming to an end in some of the more agriculturally advanced countries, where farmers are already using all available technologies to raise yields. In effect, the farmers have caught up with the scientists. After climbing for a century, rice yield per acre in Japan has not risen at all for 16 years. In China, yields may level off soon. Just those two countries alone account for one-third of the world's rice harvest. Meanwhile, wheat yields have plateaued in Britain, France, and Germany—Western Europe's three largest wheat producers.

In this era of tightening world food supplies, the ability to grow food is fast becoming a new form of geopolitical leverage, and countries are scrambling to secure their own parochial interests at the expense of the common good.

The first signs of trouble came in 2007, when farmers began having difficulty keeping up with the growth in global demand for grain. Grain and soybean prices started to climb, tripling by mid-2008. In response, many exporting countries tried to control the rise of domestic food prices by restricting exports. Among them were Russia and Argentina, two leading wheat exporters. Vietnam, the No. 2 rice exporter, banned exports entirely for several months in early 2008. So did several other smaller exporters of grain.

With exporting countries restricting exports in 2007 and 2008, importing countries panicked. No longer able to rely on the market to supply the grain they needed, several countries took the novel step of trying to negotiate long-term grain-supply agreements with exporting countries. The Philippines, for instance, negotiated a three-year agreement with Vietnam for 1.5 million tons of rice per year. A delegation of Yemenis traveled to Australia with a similar goal in mind, but had no luck. In a seller's market, exporters were reluctant to make long-term commitments.

Fearing they might not be able to buy needed grain from the market, some of the more affluent countries, led by Saudi Arabia, South Korea, and China, took the unusual step in 2008 of buying or leasing land in other countries on which to grow grain for themselves. Most of these land acquisitions are in Africa, where some governments lease cropland for less than $1 per acre per year. Among the principal destinations were Ethiopia and Sudan, countries where millions of people are being sustained with food from the U.N. World Food Program. That the governments of these two countries are willing to sell land to foreign interests when their own people are hungry is a sad commentary on their leadership.

By the end of 2009, hundreds of land acquisition deals had been negotiated, some of them exceeding a million acres. A 2010 World Bank analysis of these "land grabs" reported that a total of nearly 140 million acres were involved—an area that exceeds the cropland devoted to corn and wheat combined in the United States. Such acquisitions also typically involve water rights, meaning that land grabs potentially affect all downstream countries as well. Any water extracted from the upper Nile River basin to irrigate crops in Ethiopia or Sudan, for instance, will now not reach Egypt, upending the delicate water politics of the Nile by adding new countries with which Egypt must negotiate.

The potential for conflict—and not just over water—is high. Many of the land deals have been made in secret, and in most cases, the land involved was already in use by villagers when it was sold or leased. Often those already farming the land were neither consulted about nor even informed of the new arrangements. And because there typically are no formal land titles in many developing-country villages, the farmers who lost their land have had little backing to bring their cases to court. Reporter John Vidal, writing in Britain's Observer, quotes Nyikaw Ochalla from Ethiopia's Gambella region: "The foreign companies are arriving in large numbers, depriving people of land they have used for centuries. There is no consultation with the indigenous population. The deals are done secretly. The only thing the local people see is people coming with lots of tractors to invade their lands."

Local hostility toward such land grabs is the rule, not the exception. In 2007, as food prices were starting to rise, China signed an agreement with the Philippines to lease 2.5 million acres of land slated for food crops that would be shipped home. Once word leaked, the public outcry—much of it from Filipino farmers—forced Manila to suspend the agreement. A similar uproar rocked Madagascar, where a South Korean firm, Daewoo Logistics, had pursued rights to more than 3 million acres of land. Word of the deal helped stoke a political furor that toppled the government and forced cancellation of the agreement. Indeed, few things are more likely to fuel insurgencies than taking land from people. Agricultural equipment is easily sabotaged. If ripe fields of grain are torched, they burn quickly.

Not only are these deals risky, but foreign investors producing food in a country full of hungry people face another political question of how to get the grain out. Will villagers permit trucks laden with grain headed for port cities to proceed when they themselves may be on the verge of starvation? The potential for political instability in countries where villagers have lost their land and their livelihoods is high. Conflicts could easily develop between investor and host countries.

These acquisitions represent a potential investment in agriculture in developing countries of an estimated $50 billion. But it could take many years to realize any substantial production gains. The public infrastructure for modern market-oriented agriculture does not yet exist in most of Africa. In some countries it will take years just to build the roads and ports needed to bring in agricultural inputs such as fertilizer and to export farm products. Beyond that, modern agriculture requires its own infrastructure: machine sheds, grain-drying equipment, silos, fertilizer storage sheds, fuel storage facilities, equipment repair and maintenance services, well-drilling equipment, irrigation pumps, and energy to power the pumps. Overall, development of the land acquired to date appears to be moving very slowly.

So how much will all this expand world food output? We don't know, but the World Bank analysis indicates that only 37 percent of the projects will be devoted to food crops. Most of the land bought up so far will be used to produce biofuels and other industrial crops.

Even if some of these projects do eventually boost land productivity, who will benefit? If virtually all the inputs—the farm equipment, the fertilizer, the pesticides, the seeds—are brought in from abroad and if all the output is shipped out of the country, it will contribute little to the host country's economy. At best, locals may find work as farm laborers, but in highly mechanized operations, the jobs will be few. At worst, impoverished countries like Mozambique and Sudan will be left with less land and water with which to feed their already hungry populations. Thus far the land grabs have contributed more to stirring unrest than to expanding food production.

And this rich country-poor country divide could grow even more pronounced—and soon. This January, a new stage in the scramble among importing countries to secure food began to unfold when South Korea, which imports 70 percent of its grain, announced that it was creating a new public-private entity that will be responsible for acquiring part of this grain. With an initial office in Chicago, the plan is to bypass the large international trading firms by buying grain directly from U.S. farmers. As the Koreans acquire their own grain elevators, they may well sign multiyear delivery contracts with farmers, agreeing to buy specified quantities of wheat, corn, or soybeans at a fixed price.

Other importers will not stand idly by as South Korea tries to tie up a portion of the U.S. grain harvest even before it gets to market. The enterprising Koreans may soon be joined by China, Japan, Saudi Arabia, and other leading importers. Although South Korea's initial focus is the United States, far and away the world's largest grain exporter, it may later consider brokering deals with Canada, Australia, Argentina, and other major exporters. This is happening just as China may be on the verge of entering the U.S. market as a potentially massive importer of grain. With China's 1.4 billion increasingly affluent consumers starting to compete with U.S. consumers for the U.S. grain harvest, cheap food, seen by many as an American birthright, may be coming to an end.

No one knows where this intensifying competition for food supplies will go, but the world seems to be moving away from the international cooperation that evolved over several decades following World War II to an every-country-for-itself philosophy. Food nationalism may help secure food supplies for individual affluent countries, but it does little to enhance world food security. Indeed, the low-income countries that host land grabs or import grain will likely see their food situation deteriorate.

After the carnage of two world wars and the economic missteps that led to the Great Depression, countries joined together in 1945 to create the United Nations, finally realizing that in the modern world we cannot live in isolation, tempting though that might be. The International Monetary Fund was created to help manage the monetary system and promote economic stability and progress. Within the U.N. system, specialized agencies from the World Health Organization to the Food and Agriculture Organization (FAO) play major roles in the world today. All this has fostered international cooperation.

But while the FAO collects and analyzes global agricultural data and provides technical assistance, there is no organized effort to ensure the adequacy of world food supplies. Indeed, most international negotiations on agricultural trade until recently focused on access to markets, with the United States, Canada, Australia, and Argentina persistently pressing Europe and Japan to open their highly protected agricultural markets. But in the first decade of this century, access to supplies has emerged as the overriding issue as the world transitions from an era of food surpluses to a new politics of food scarcity. At the same time, the U.S. food aid program that once worked to fend off famine wherever it threatened has largely been replaced by the U.N. World Food Program (WFP), where the United States is the leading donor. The WFP now has food-assistance operations in some 70 countries and an annual budget of $4 billion. There is little international coordination otherwise. French President Nicolas Sarkozy—the reigning president of the G-20—is proposing to deal with rising food prices by curbing speculation in commodity markets. Useful though this may be, it treats the symptoms of growing food insecurity, not the causes, such as population growth and climate change. The world now needs to focus not only on agricultural policy, but on a structure that integrates it with energy, population, and water policies, each of which directly affects food security.

But that is not happening. Instead, as land and water become scarcer, as the Earth's temperature rises, and as world food security deteriorates, a dangerous geopolitics of food scarcity is emerging. Land grabbing, water grabbing, and buying grain directly from farmers in exporting countries are now integral parts of a global power struggle for food security.

With grain stocks low and climate volatility increasing, the risks are also increasing. We are now so close to the edge that a breakdown in the food system could come at any time. Consider, for example, what would have happened if the 2010 heat wave that was centered in Moscow had instead been centered in Chicago. In round numbers, the 40 percent drop in Russia's hoped-for harvest of roughly 100 million tons cost the world 40 million tons of grain, but a 40 percent drop in the far larger U.S. grain harvest of 400 million tons would have cost 160 million tons. The world's carryover stocks of grain (the amount in the bin when the new harvest begins) would have dropped to just 52 days of consumption. This level would have been not only the lowest on record, but also well below the 62-day carryover that set the stage for the 2007–2008 tripling of world grain prices.

Then what? There would have been chaos in world grain markets. Grain prices would have climbed off the charts. Some grain-exporting countries, trying to hold down domestic food prices, would have restricted or even banned exports, as they did in 2007 and 2008. The TV news would have been dominated not by the hundreds of fires in the Russian countryside, but by footage of food riots in low-income grain-importing countries and reports of governments falling as hunger spread out of control. Oil-exporting countries that import grain would have been trying to barter oil for grain, and low-income grain importers would have lost out. With governments toppling and confidence in the world grain market shattered, the global economy could have started to unravel.

We may not always be so lucky. At issue now is whether the world can go beyond focusing on the symptoms of the deteriorating food situation and instead attack the underlying causes. If we cannot produce higher crop yields with less water and conserve fertile soils, many agricultural areas will cease to be viable. And this goes far beyond farmers. If we cannot move at wartime speed to stabilize the climate, we may not be able to avoid runaway food prices. If we cannot accelerate the shift to smaller families and stabilize the world population sooner rather than later, the ranks of the hungry will almost certainly continue to expand. The time to act is now—before the food crisis of 2011 becomes the new normal.

Critical Thinking

1. Food prices have recently increased substantially, and future prices will go higher according to Brown. What explains these trends?

2. What are some of the major changes in the environment that are affecting food production?

LESTER R. BROWN, president of the Earth Policy Institute, is author of *World on the Edge: How to Prevent Environmental and Economic Collapse.*

Reprinted in entirety by McGraw-Hill with permission from *Foreign Policy,* May/June 2011, pp. 56–58, 61–62. www.foreignpolicy.com. © 2011 Washingtonpost.Newsweek Interactive, LLC.

The World Will Be More Crowded—With Old People

Actually, the children aren't our future.

Phillip Longman

Demography is not destiny, as is sometimes claimed. The human race could be wiped out by a plague or an asteroid, or transformed by some new technology. But no matter what, today's patterns of fertility, migration, and mortality fundamentally determine how much society will or can change for many generations to come.

And what demography tells us is this: The human population will continue to grow, though in a very different way from in the past. The United Nations' most recent "mid-range" projection calls for an increase to 8 billion people by 2025 and to 10.1 billion by century's end.

Until quite recently, such population growth always came primarily from increases in the numbers of young people. Between 1950 and 1990, for example, increases in the number of people under 30 accounted for more than half of the growth of the world's population, while only 12 percent came from increases in the ranks of those over 60.

But in the future it will be the exact opposite. The U.N. now projects that over the next 40 years, more than half (58 percent) of the world's population growth will come from increases in the number of people over 60, while only 6 percent will come from people under 30. Indeed, the U.N. projects that by 2025, the population of children under 5, already in steep decline in most developed countries, will be falling globally—and that's even after assuming a substantial rebound in birth rates in the developing world. A gray tsunami will be sweeping the planet.

Which countries will be aging most rapidly in 2025? They won't be in Europe, where birth rates fell comparatively gradually and now show some signs of ticking up. Instead, they'll be places like Iran and Mexico, which experienced youth bulges that were followed quickly by a collapse in birth rates. In just 35 years, both Iran and Mexico will have a larger percentage of their populations over 60 than France does today. Other places with birth rates now below replacement levels include not just old Europe but also developing countries such as Brazil, Chile, China, Lebanon, Tunisia, South Korea, and Vietnam.

Because of the phenomenon of hyper-aging in the developing world, another great variable is already changing as well: migration. In Mexico, for example, the population of children age 4 and under was 434,000 less in 2010 than it was in 1996. The result? The demographic momentum that fueled huge flows of Mexican migration to the United States has waned, and will wane much more in the future. Already, the net flow of illegal Mexican immigration northward has slowed to a trickle. With fewer children to support and not yet burdened by a huge surge of elders, the Mexican economy is doing much better than in the past, giving people less reason to leave. By 2025, young people on both sides of the border may struggle to understand why their parents' generation built this huge fence.

Despite these trends, most people conclude from their day-to-day lives that overpopulation is a serious problem. One reason is that more than half the world's population is crowded into urban areas. The high cost of raising children in mega-cities is a prime reason that global birth rates continue to fall, yet urbanization also makes the larger trend toward depopulation difficult for most to grasp. If the downward trend in birth rates doesn't moderate and stabilize as the U.N. assumes it will, the world as a whole could be losing population as soon as midcentury. And yet few people will likely see that turning point coming, so long as humans continue to pack into urban areas and increase their consumption of just about everything.

Another related megatrend is the rapid change in the size, structure, and nature of the family. In many countries, such as Germany, Japan, Russia, and South Korea, the one-child family is now becoming the norm. This trend creates a society in which not only do most people have no siblings, but also no aunts, uncles, cousins, nieces, or nephews. Many will lack children of their own as well. Today about one in five people in advanced Western countries, including the United States, remains childless. Huge portions of the world's population will thus have no biological relatives except their parents.

And even where children continue to be born, they are being raised under radically different circumstances, as country after country has seen divorce and out-of-wedlock births surge and the percentage of children living with both of their married parents drop sharply. So not only is the quantity of children in the world poised to shrink rapidly, but on current trends, a near majority of them will be raised in ways that are today strongly associated with negative life outcomes.

Are there signs of any of these trends reversing before 2025? Only a few. The percentage of the world's population raised in religious households is bound to rise, if only because adherents to fundamentalism, whether Christians, Jews, or Muslims, tend to have substantially more children than their secular counterparts. And there are certainly many ways—from increased automation and delayed retirement to health-care reform to the provision of baby bonuses—for societies to at least partially adjust to the tidal shift in global demographics.

But don't count on it. To make such sweeping changes would require a widespread understanding of the century's great paradox: The planet may be bursting, but most of this new population is made up of people who have already been born. So get ready for a planet that's a whole lot more crowded—with old people.

Critical Thinking

1. Why is Longman concerned about an abundance of older people?
2. How will changing demographics affect national economies?

PHILLIP LONGMAN, a fellow at the New America Foundation, is author of *The Empty Cradle: Why Falling Birthrates Threaten World Prosperity and What to Do About It*.

Climate Change

BILL McKIBBEN

"Scientists Are Divided"

No, they're not. In the early years of the global warming debate, there was great controversy over whether the planet was warming, whether humans were the cause, and whether it would be a significant problem. That debate is long since over. Although the details of future forecasts remain unclear, there's no serious question about the general shape of what's to come.

Every national academy of science, long lists of Nobel laureates, and in recent years even the science advisors of President George W. Bush have agreed that we are heating the planet. Indeed, there is a more thorough scientific process here than on almost any other issue: Two decades ago, the United Nations formed the Intergovernmental Panel on Climate Change (IPCC) and charged its scientists with synthesizing the peer-reviewed science and developing broad-based conclusions. The reports have found since 1995 that warming is dangerous and caused by humans. The panel's most recent report, in November 2007, found it is "very likely" (defined as more than 90 percent certain, or about as certain as science gets) that heat-trapping emissions from human activities have caused "most of the observed increase in global average temperatures since the mid-20th century."

If anything, many scientists now think that the IPCC has been too conservative—both because member countries must sign off on the conclusions and because there's a time lag. Its last report synthesized data from the early part of the decade, not the latest scary results, such as what we're now seeing in the Arctic.

In the summer of 2007, ice in the Arctic Ocean melted. It melts a little every summer, of course, but this time was different—by late September, there was 25 percent less ice than ever measured before. And it wasn't a one-time accident. By the end of the summer season in 2008, so much ice had melted that both the Northwest and Northeast passages were open. In other words, you could circumnavigate the Arctic on open water. The computer models, which are just a few years old, said this shouldn't have happened until sometime late in the 21st century. Even skeptics can't dispute such alarming events.

"We Have Time"

Wrong. Time might be the toughest part of the equation. That melting Arctic ice is unsettling not only because it proves the planet is warming rapidly, but also because it will help speed up the warming. That old white ice reflected 80 percent of incoming solar radiation back to space; the new blue water left behind absorbs 80 percent of that sunshine. The process amps up. And there are many other such feedback loops. Another occurs as northern permafrost thaws. Huge amounts of methane long trapped below the ice begin to escape into the atmosphere; methane is an even more potent greenhouse gas than carbon dioxide.

Such examples are the biggest reason why many experts are now fast-forwarding their estimates of how quickly we must shift away from fossil fuel. Indian economist Rajendra Pachauri, who accepted the 2007 Nobel Peace Prize alongside Al Gore on behalf of the IPCC, said recently that we must begin to make fundamental reforms by 2012 or watch the climate system spin out of control; NASA scientist James Hansen, who was the first to blow the whistle on climate change in the late 1980s, has said that we must stop burning coal by 2030. Period.

All of which makes the Copenhagen climate change talks that are set to take place in December 2009 more urgent than they appeared a few years ago. At issue is a seemingly small number: the level of carbon dioxide in the air. Hansen argues that 350 parts per million is the highest level we can maintain "if humanity wishes to preserve a planet similar to that on which civilization developed and to which life on Earth is adapted." But because we're already past that mark—the air outside is currently about 387 parts per million and growing by about 2 parts annually—global warming suddenly feels less like a huge problem, and more like an Oh-My-God Emergency.

"Climate Change Will Help as Many Places as It Hurts"

Wishful thinking. For a long time, the winners-and-losers calculus was pretty standard: Though climate change will cause some parts of the planet to flood or shrivel up, other frigid, rainy regions would at least get some warmer days every year. Or so the thinking went. But more recently, models have begun to show that after a certain point almost everyone on the planet will suffer. Crops might be easier to grow in some places for a few decades as the danger of frost recedes, but over time the threat of heat stress and drought will almost certainly be stronger.

A 2003 report commissioned by the Pentagon forecasts the possibility of violent storms across Europe, megadroughts across the Southwest United States and Mexico, and unpredictable monsoons causing food shortages in China. "Envision Pakistan, India, and China—all armed with nuclear weapons—skirmishing at their borders over refugees, access to shared rivers, and arable land," the report warned. Or Spain and Portugal "fighting over fishing rights—leading to conflicts at sea."

Of course, there are a few places we used to think of as possible winners—mostly the far north, where Canada and Russia could theoretically produce more grain with longer growing seasons, or perhaps explore for oil beneath the newly melted Arctic ice cap. But even those places will have to deal with expensive consequences—a real military race across the high Arctic, for instance.

Want more bad news? Here's how that Pentagon report's scenario played out: As the planet's carrying capacity shrinks, an ancient pattern of desperate, all-out wars over food, water, and energy supplies would reemerge. The report refers to the work of Harvard archaeologist Steven LeBlanc, who notes that wars over resources were the norm until about three centuries ago. When such conflicts broke out, 25 percent of a population's adult males usually died. As abrupt climate change hits home, warfare may again come to define human life. Set against that bleak backdrop, the potential upside of a few longer growing seasons in Vladivostok doesn't seem like an even trade.

"It's China's Fault"

Not so much. China is an easy target to blame for the climate crisis. In the midst of its industrial revolution, China has overtaken the United States as the world's biggest carbon dioxide producer. And everyone has read about the one-a-week pace of power plant construction there. But those numbers are misleading, and not just because a lot of that carbon dioxide was emitted to build products for the West to consume. Rather, it's because China has four times the population of the United States, and per capita is really the only way to think about these emissions. And by that standard, each Chinese person now emits just over a quarter of the carbon dioxide that each American does. Not only that, but carbon dioxide lives in the atmosphere for more than a century. China has been at it in a big way less than 20 years, so it will be many, many years before the Chinese are as responsible for global warming as Americans.

What's more, unlike many of their counterparts in the United States, Chinese officials have begun a concerted effort to reduce emissions in the midst of their country's staggering growth. China now leads the world in the deployment of renewable energy, and there's barely a car made in the United States that can meet China's much tougher fuel-economy standards.

For its part, the United States must develop a plan to cut emissions—something that has eluded Americans for the entire two-decade history of the problem. Although the U.S. Senate voted down the last such attempt, Barack Obama has promised that it will be a priority in his administration. He favors some variation of a "cap and trade" plan that would limit the total amount of carbon dioxide the United States could release, thus putting a price on what has until now been free.

Despite the rapid industrialization of countries such as China and India, and the careless neglect of rich ones such as the United States, climate change is neither any one country's fault, nor any one country's responsibility. It will require sacrifice from everyone. Just as the Chinese might have to use somewhat more expensive power to protect the global environment, Americans will have to pay some of the difference in price, even if just in technology. Call it a Marshall Plan for the environment. Such a plan makes eminent moral and practical sense and could probably be structured so as to bolster emerging green energy industries in the West. But asking Americans to pay to put up windmills in China will be a hard political sell in a country that already thinks China is prospering at its expense. It could be the biggest test of the country's political maturity in many years.

"Climate Change Is an Environmental Problem"

Not really. Environmentalists were the first to sound the alarm. But carbon dioxide is not like traditional pollution. There's no Clean Air Act that can solve it. We must make a fundamental transformation in the most important part of our economies, shifting away from fossil fuels and on to something else. That means, for the United States, it's at least as much a problem for the Commerce and Treasury departments as it is for the Environmental Protection Agency.

And because every country on Earth will have to coordinate, it's far and away the biggest foreign-policy issue we face. (You were thinking terrorism? It's hard to figure out a scenario in which Osama bin Laden destroys Western civilization. It's easy to figure out how it happens with a rising sea level and a wrecked hydrological cycle.)

Expecting the environmental movement to lead this fight is like asking the USDA to wage the war in Iraq. It's not equipped for this kind of battle. It may be ready to save Alaska's Arctic National Wildlife Refuge, which is a noble undertaking but on a far smaller scale. Unless climate change is quickly deghettoized, the chances of making a real difference are small.

"Solving It Will Be Painful"

It depends. What's your definition of painful? On the one hand, you're talking about transforming the backbone of the world's industrial and consumer system. That's certainly expensive. On the other hand, say you manage to convert a lot of it to solar or wind power—think of the money you'd save on fuel.

And then there's the growing realization that we don't have many other possible sources for the economic growth we'll need to pull ourselves out of our current economic crisis. Luckily, green energy should be bigger than IT and biotech combined.

Almost from the moment scientists began studying the problem of climate change, people have been trying to estimate the costs of solving it. The real answer, though, is that it's such a huge transformation that no one really knows for sure. The bottom line is, the growth rate in energy use worldwide could be cut in half during the next 15 years and the steps would, net, save more money than they cost. The IPCC included a cost estimate in its latest five-year update on climate change and looked a little further into the future. It found that an attempt to keep carbon levels below about 500 parts per million would shave a little bit off the world's economic growth—but only a little. As in, the world would have to wait until Thanksgiving 2030 to be as rich as it would have been on January 1 of that year. And in return, it would have a much-transformed energy system.

Unfortunately though, those estimates are probably too optimistic. For one thing, in the years since they were published, the science has grown darker. Deeper and quicker cuts now seem mandatory.

But so far we've just been counting the costs of fixing the system. What about the cost of doing nothing? Nicholas Stern, a renowned economist commissioned by the British government to study the question, concluded that the costs of climate change could eventually reach the combined costs of both world wars and the Great Depression. In 2003, Swiss Re, the world's biggest reinsurance company, and Harvard Medical School explained why global warming would be so expensive. It's not just the infrastructure, such as sea walls against rising oceans, for example. It's also that the increased costs of natural disasters begin to compound. The diminishing time between monster storms in places such as the U.S. Gulf Coast could eventually mean that parts of "developed countries would experience developing nation conditions for prolonged periods." Quite simply, we've already done too much damage and waited too long to have any easy options left.

"We Can Reverse Climate Change"

If only. Solving this crisis is no longer an option. Human beings have already raised the temperature of the planet about a degree Fahrenheit. When people first began to focus on global warming (which is, remember, only 20 years ago), the general consensus was that at this point we'd just be standing on the threshold of realizing its consequences—that the big changes would be a degree or two and hence several decades down the road. But scientists seem to have systematically underestimated just how delicate the balance of the planet's physical systems really is.

The warming is happening faster than we expected, and the results are more widespread and more disturbing. Even that rise of 1 degree has seriously perturbed hydrological cycles: Because warm air holds more water vapor than cold air does, both droughts and floods are increasing dramatically. Just look at the record levels of insurance payouts, for instance. Mosquitoes, able to survive in new places, are spreading more malaria and dengue. Coral reefs are dying, and so are vast stretches of forest.

None of that is going to stop, even if we do everything right from here on out. Given the time lag between when we emit carbon and when the air heats up, we're already guaranteed at least another degree of warming.

The only question now is whether we're going to hold off catastrophe. It won't be easy, because the scientific consensus calls for roughly 5 degrees more warming this century unless we do just about everything right. And if our behavior up until now is any indication, we won't.

Critical Thinking

1. What is the state of scientific opinion on anthropomorphic global warming (AGW)?
2. How is AGW likely to impact the environment?
3. How would AGW impact societies?

Reprinted in entirety by McGraw-Hill with permission from *Foreign Policy,* January/February 2009, pp. 32–38. www.foreignpolicy.com. © 2009 Washingtonpost.Newsweek Interactive, LLC.

Who's Afraid of Human Enhancement?

A *Reason Debate on the Promise, Perils, and Ethics of Human Biotechnology*

On August 25 in Washington, D.C., reason staged a debate about "the promise, perils, and ethics of human biotechnology." Moderated by Editor in Chief Nick Gillespie, the panelists included Ronald Bailey, *Reason*'s science correspondent and author of *Liberation Biology: The Scientific and Moral Case for the Biotech Revolution;* Eric Cohen, director of the Ethics and Public Policy Center's Biotechnology and American Democracy Program and editor of the group's journal, *The New Atlantis*; and Joel Garreau, a reporter and editor for *The Washington Post* and author of *Radical Evolution: The Promise and Peril of Enhancing Our Minds, Our Bodies, and What It Means To Be Human.* What follows is an edited transcript of the event, which was sponsored by the Donald and Paula Smith Family Foundation and the Institute for Humane Studies. Comments can be sent to letters@reason.com.

Nick Gillespie: Our purpose tonight is to hash out questions and issues revolving around human enhancement based on technologies that include cloning; stem-cell research; processes to increase longevity, intelligence, and physical abilities; and many other procedures at various stages of development. What was once the province of science fiction—human beings augmented to such a degree that they become "post-human"—is rapidly becoming fact. Indeed, one of our panelists tonight will even argue that within the next century death itself may become optional. These are the sorts of developments that fill some with hope and others with horror.

Our panelists tonight will not agree on very much, but on this basic point I suspect they're in complete agreement: Forget all the talk about Social Security solvency, income tax rates, blue states, red states, even the war in Iraq. The most fundamental social and political issue facing the world today—and tomorrow—is the question of human enhancement.

Ron Bailey will be kicking off our discussion by giving us a quick overview of his feelings about human enhancement.

Ron Bailey: If I could have given my new book a proper 19th-century descriptive title, it might have been *Liberation*

Biology: The Scientific and Moral Case for the Biotech Revolution, or Why You Should Relax and Enjoy the Brave New World of Immortality, Stem Cells, and Designer Babies.

Of course, I'm not talking about Aldous Huxley's *Brave New World,* which portrays a society of regimented clones in a world run by top-down controllers, the motto of which is "community, identity, and stability." In fact, the biotech revolution I anticipate is the exact opposite of Huxley's *Brave New World.* Let me illustrate by painting you a short vision of what the biotech revolution could bring by the end of this century.

By 2100 the typical American may attend a family reunion in which five generations are playing together. The great-great-great-grandma is 150 years old, and she will be as vital as she was when she was 30 and as vital as her 30-year-old great-great-grandson, with whom she's playing touch football. After the game, she'll enjoy a plate of salad greens filled with not only a full day's worth of nutrients but the medicines she needs to repair the damage to her aging cells. She'll be able to chat about the academic discipline—maybe economics—that she studied in the 1980s with as much acuity and depth of knowledge and memory as her 50-year-old great-granddaughter who is now studying the same thing.

No one in her extended family will have ever caught a cold. They will be immune from birth to the shocks that human flesh has long been heir to: diabetes, cancer, and Alzheimer's disease. Her granddaughter, who recently suffered an unfortunate transport accident, will be sporting new versions of the arm and lung that got damaged in the wreck, and she'll be playing in that game of touch football with the same skill and energy as anyone else in the family. Infectious diseases that terrified us at the beginning of the 21st century, such as HIV-AIDS and the avian flu, will be horrific historical curiosities for the family to chat about over their plates of super-fat farm-raised salmon, which will be as tasty and nutritious as any fish any human has ever eaten: "Grandma, what was it like when people got colds?" Though few of them will actually think much about it, surrounding them will be a world that is greener and cleaner, one more abundant in natural vegetation and with less of an obvious human footprint than the one we live in now.

Not only will this family enjoy all these benefits, but nearly everyone they work with, socialize with, and meet with will enjoy them as well. It will be a remarkably peaceful and pleasant world. Beyond their health and their wealth, they'll be able to control things such as anti-social tendencies and crippling depression. And they'll manage these problems by individual choice, through new biotech pharmaceuticals and personalized genetic treatments.

This idyllic scenario is more than realistic given the reasonably expected breakthroughs and extensions of our knowledge of human, plant, and animal biology and the mastery of the techniques known collectively as biotechnology. We'll be able to manipulate those biologies to meet human needs and desires.

What is astonishing to me is that an extraordinary transideological coalition of left-wing and right-wing bioconservatives has come together to oppose many of the technological advancements that could make that vision real for the whole of humanity. This coalition of biotech opponents consists of some of our leading intellectuals and policy makers. On the left stand bioethicists such as Daniel Callahan, who founded The Hastings Center, arguably the world's first bioethics think tank; George Annas from Boston University; longtime left-wing activists such as Jeremy Rifkin; and environmentalists such as Bill McKibben. On the right stand Leon Kass, [formerly] the chairman of the President's Council on Bioethics, and his fellow council members Francis Fukuyama and Charles Krauthammer, and also people such as William Kristol, the editor of *The Weekly Standard*.

"Forget all the talk about Social Security, income tax rates, blue states, red states, even the war in Iraq. The most fundamental issue facing the world today—and tomorrow—is the question of human enhancement."

—Nick Gillespie

Both sides of this coalition abhor efforts to dramatically extend healthy human life spans by decades and even centuries. Both sides oppose creating stem cells derived from cloned embryos that would serve as perfect transplants to replace damaged, diseased, or worn-out body parts, livers, and nerves. Both sides want to outlaw the efforts of parents to use genetic testing and in vitro fertilization [IVF] and new pharmaceuticals to enhance their children's immune systems, athletic abilities, and intellectual capacities. Both sides of this bioconservative coalition would ban the use of genetically enhanced crops and animals to produce more abundant and more nutritious foods. Astonishingly, they are against heaven. Why? Because they wrongly fear that biotech progress will lead to hell.

In *Liberation Biology,* I thoroughly examine the whole range of bioconservative objections to the biotech revolution. I look forward to addressing them in more detail in the question-and-answer period, but let me note here that the benefits of biotechnology are well-known. The cure of diseases and disabilities for millions of sufferers, the production of more nutritious food with less damage to the natural environment, the enhancement of human physical and intellectual capacities, the retarding of the onset of the ravages of old age—all of these can be easily foreseen.

It is the alleged dangers of biotechnology that are vague, ill-defined, and wholly speculative. While Joel Garreau wonderfully chronicles some of the far-out visions of technological transcendence in *Radical Evolution,* my desires are more modest. All I want to do is dramatically boost people's physical and intellectual capacities, restore the natural environment, and make death optional.

Nick Gillespie: Thank you, Ron. Although I've got to say you've given the opposite side a powerful argument with your vision of a family picnic, especially if you've ever met my cousins. Next up is Eric Cohen.

Eric Cohen: Thanks very much. As a magazine editor, I want to start by simply complimenting Ron's title. I spend a lot of time trying to think of clever titles, which sometimes are the only things people remember about the nice article you publish, and *Liberation Biology* is a very smart title. It's a play, if I understand it correctly, on liberation theology, which is a whole collection of interesting, silly, weird ideas having to do generally with heaven and hell. Ron's title is clever on a couple of levels.

One, it signals that he's breaking from [the concept of heaven and hell]. He's breaking from this whole [religious] mythology, which I suspect in his mind hasn't delivered very much. He's leading us toward the age of flag football with your grandmother and farm-fresh salmon, but he's also signaling that he wants to try to answer some of the same human longings that theology or religion has long answered. So it's an interesting title on that level. I think it's also interesting in [raising the question of] what is it the liberty to do? What is the liberation he's talking about?

It's liberation from all kinds of horrible things in human life—sudden illness, dying children, people who have more ambition than talent, people who have more ideas than time, people who simply don't want to die and want to be a lot more like gods than most human beings are. It's also liberty to do various things, and this brings us to the subject of tonight's panel, which is the question of enhancement.

"By 2100 the typical American may attend a family reunion in which five generations are playing together. The great-great-grandma is 150 years old, and she will be as vital as her 30-year-old great-great-grandson."

—Ronald Bailey

It seems to me that if you take the word *enhancement* at face value, there simply can't be anything wrong with it, right? *Enhancement* means to make things better, so then [all the things Ron talks about are] great. But the question is whether the things that seem like enhancements really are enhancements. The disquiet that some people have with the biotech revolution is [due to our] worry that in trying to make life better in ways we recognize, we're going to make it worse in ways we can't even imagine. That's the set of problems we face.

I should say most biotech is great. I hope the stocks go up. I hope they cure various diseases or at least develop better treatments for them, but some of the more ambitious and more interesting areas of biotechnology give some of us disquiet.

There are two sides to the disquiet. One has to do with the means that we're going to use to supposedly enhance ourselves and the other has to do with the ends. The conventional worry about enhancement has to do with the quality [of improvements] that the rich are going [to be able to afford]. The wealthy are going to become gene rich and the poor are going to become gene poor, and this is going to worsen the inequalities of life. I'm enough of a free market person to believe that if something works in wealthy societies, eventually most people are going to be able to afford it.

The worries about means are a little different though. Here the stem cell debate is paradigmatic. Everybody wants to cure these horrible diseases. It's an end that all sides of the stem cell debate share. The issue is, should we be destroying human embryos to do it? I think you can make a pretty rigorous, rational, and scientific case that embryos are early human lives and that to use them as mere things would make us a lesser society. The worry here is not about the end we're pursuing but about the means that are used to pursue it.

And let me spend some time asking about those ends. What is it that we're trying to enhance? What are the goals here? I think you can break down four different ways of trying to enhance ourselves—and here I follow the definitive discussion in a report by the President's Council on Bioethics called *Beyond Therapy*. The four ways are superior performance in the various activities of life, better children, long lives or even ageless lives, and happiness.

Those are four basic aspirations that are not new, though biotechnology might give us some new ways to pursue them.

If you think it through, there are reasons to at least wonder whether the biotechnologies we're talking about are really going to answer these human longings in any serious way. Obviously everybody's all worked up these days about performance-enhancing drugs in sports, and as Joel tells me, the existing drugs are child's play compared to what's coming. But we have to ask ourselves, is the athlete on steroids a better athlete, a better human athlete? Or has he become more an animal bred for the race? And we might create all kinds of drugs that boost the capacity to, say, remember SAT words. But is that really going to make people smarter, or is it going to narrow their minds in a certain way and make them less able to make the kinds of connections that are essential to real human intelligence and real human wisdom?

The same with the desire for better children. I question whether we would ever be able to design a better child. Can we really make a better musician than Mozart or make a better playwright than Shakespeare? We may be able to make everybody in our wildest dreams as talented as those people, though I doubt it. But there's a deeper issue, which has to do with the nature of the family. It seems to me that parenthood is about not only trying to make your children better but having a welcoming and embracing attitude toward the child that's given to you to raise and given to you to love. I wonder whether embracing full force a kind of designer attitude is really going to make us better parents and better families.

The same with the desire for longevity. There's the worry that we may simply extend debility. It may be that we're going to simply have Alzheimer's disease for 35 years instead of for 10 in the future. I'm not sure that's necessarily progress. In a deeper sense, if we really believed or lived as if we were going to live forever, would we really have the urgency and the aspiration and the ambition to do the things that we do in life? Most of the portraits of immortality that we've seen, or at least many of them, present a less appealing picture than grandma playing flag football. I'm not sure how appealing that is either.

Nick Gillespie: Especially if you're not a Kennedy, right?

Eric Cohen: Right. And let me end with the quintessential aspiration: Everybody wants to be happy. On this much, at least, the ancients and the moderns sort of agreed, although they had different notions of happiness. Will the various interventions in our minds and bodies make us happier? I'm no expert on the future, so we'll have to wait and see, but I think there are real reasons to doubt this. There are reasons to doubt whether our new powers will really make us happy in a genuine human sense. If there were really a pill that simulated love or simulated success or simulated the feeling of playing a great symphony or hitting a great home run, is that really what we aspire to? Simply the simulation? And is there a danger that all these drugs that are supposed to make us happy might just make us more anxious because we're on all these drugs? Everybody's on Prozac, everybody puts a little bit in their coffee, but in fact life still has its hardships and people are still genuinely frustrated and trying to muddle through like most of us do. I wonder whether we'll really be genuinely happy when all the biotech companies promise us happiness in a pill.

These are hard questions. The future's unpredictable, but I think there are at least serious reasons to wonder whether we'll genuinely make ourselves better in all the ways that we hope to by turning to biotech.

Nick Gillespie: Thank you, Eric. I can testify from personal experience, I've already had pills that have made me think I'm as talented as Mozart, but they were not from established pharmaceutical outlets, or FDA-regulated, and I miss them. Joel?

Joel Garreau: Thanks. Eric's journal has made a great impact on me. I'm a paid subscriber to *The New Atlantis,* that's how much I admire his journal. And I've been so dazzled by Ron's work that I've stolen it every chance I've had.

Having been a child of the 1960s, I never anticipated that the most interesting drugs available today [would be] legal and available through prescription. That's the part that really blows my mind. The argument that I make in *Radical Evolution* is that we are at a turning point in history, and there's nothing [that is going to hold that back]. For hundreds of thousands of years, our technologies have been aimed outward at modifying our environment in the fashion of fire, clothes, cities, agriculture, space travel. But now, they are increasingly turned inward at modifying our minds, our memories, our metabolisms, our personalities, our progeny, and possibly our souls. It's not just biotech. It's what I call the GRIN technologies—genetics, robotics, information, and nanotechnology. They are all following a curve of exponential change that is known in the computer industry as Moore's Law. You get regular doublings in capacity every few months.

A doubling is an amazing thing. It means that every few months, every new step is as tall as all of the previous steps combined. The 30 doublings we've had in computer technology since 1959 is an increase of over 400,000 times. We're seeing similar curves in these other technologies, and the significance of this is that it's not going away and it's not science fiction and it's not 100 years from now. It's on our watch, and we have to decide what we're going to do about it in terms of the future of human nature.

This conversation usually gets held in the hall of the technological elite, and the reason I've been typing as fast as I can is that it's time for the conversation to break out into the mainstream. Only in some kind of a bottom-up way are we going to address these issues. I'm not a big fan of top-down hierarchies, just as a practical matter. And the stuff coming online is going to blow our minds.

For example, I spent the better part of a year at DARPA, the Defense Advanced Research Projects Agency, and the stuff that's in their labs is quite remarkable. Up in Boston, there's a human, Matthew Nagel, who was the first to send an e-mail with his thoughts last summer. He can control a robotic arm with his thoughts. Within three years, these memory drugs that are meant to banish the boomers' "senior moments" are going to be coming on the market.

The question that the Educational Testing Service is asking is, what happens if in the very near future you can buy your kids an extra couple of hundred points on their SATs? Think of what parents do now to get their kids into college. Then think of what's happening as these possibilities come online. We're talking about thousands of incremental advances. It's not like we're going to wake up some day and face some big decision. It's one step at a time. How do we handle these advances? And as Ron said, this is really scrambling our politics. Think of how many people love the idea of stem cells who are equally opposed to genetically modified organisms. The distinctions we have now between the left and the right were an Industrial Age reality that is increasingly not part of our future.

It's between the heaven and the hell scenarios that you see the big differences, the optimists vs. the pessimists. On the optimist side, you have the market libertarians and the military right next to some environmentalists and disabled people and even feminists who relish the thought of procreating without men. Then there are the people who fear this: the President's Council on Bioethics hard up against Greenpeace and people who are against the World Bank and Christians who don't believe in Darwin and the Boston Women's Health Collective (which published the feminist classic *Our Bodies, Ourselves*). And Prince Charles. Those are pretty damned strange bedfellows.

The thing about the heaven and the hell scenarios is they basically agree. The heaven scenario says all of these changes are increasing exponentially, and we're going to conquer all the evils of mankind, and it goes straight up and that's terrific. The people who look at the hell scenario also buy this curve of exponential change. But they ask, what happens if this gets into the hands of bumblers or madmen? Their optimistic version of the hell scenario is that we extinguish only the human species in 25 years; the pessimistic version is that we lose all the life on earth. The heaven and hell scenarios are both technodeterminist futures that say technology is moving forward and there's not much we can do about it. Hang on tight. The end. Great summer blockbuster movie, dynamite special effects, not a lot of plot.

The third scenario that I sketch out in *Radical Evolution* is the "prevail" scenario. That's entirely different territory. Prevail [scenarists] don't believe that human history is likely to follow any smooth curves. It's more likely to have hiccups and loops and reverses and belches, as history has in the past. In the prevail scenario, the measure of progress is not how many transistors you can get to talk to each other but how many unpredictable and imaginative humans you can get to talk to each other. The measure of success in prevail is co-evolution. It's child's play to note that if our challenges go up in a curve and if our responses stay flat, we're toast. Stick a fork in us right now. We're done.

But if you get a situation where you can have our responses accelerating as fast as our challenges by bringing humans together in an imaginative way, then you might have a shot. Think of the problems that were facing humanity during the Dark Ages—endless difficulties. Then comes the printing press. All of a sudden you can start collecting and transferring and sharing ideas in a way that had never been possible before. The range of solutions that occurred was beyond the imagination of any one human being or any one country. Global trade, the Enlightenment, the rise of democracy, the rise of science itself.

I'm guardedly hopeful that maybe we're in a period of co-evolution like that now, [where all sorts of new ways of thinking and dealing with things are possible]. Think of 9/11. The fourth airplane never made it to its target. Why? Because the Air Force was quick on the trigger? Uh, no. Because the White House was so smart? Uh, no. What happened was that a bunch of ordinary people like us, empowered by mobile phone technology, figured out, diagnosed, and cured their society's ills in under an hour—and at incredible expense to themselves. That's, I think, an example of co-evolution, and it's a reason why I'm guardedly optimistic about the future.

"I question whether we would ever be able to design a better child. Can we really make a better musician than Mozart or make a better playwright than Shakespeare? I doubt it."

—Eric Cohen

Nick Gillespie: I'll ask each panelist a question before throwing things open to the audience. Ron, tell me one biotechnological development that you actually fear or find troubling.

Ronald Bailey: The possibility of evil people using or creating terrible pathogens and bioterrorism. I'm not at all sure that the current responses that we are trying to develop are going to be successful. The response of our government in developing its new biosecurity system seems geared to shutting down our public knowledge of things, to increasing secrecy. The best way to protect ourselves is to massively support security technologies and hope that they develop so that the defenses that work are widely understood.

Nick Gillespie: Make everything public on some level?

Ronald Bailey: Yes, basically.

Nick Gillespie: Eric, you talk a lot about how "we" have to make decisions about things. That raises what's called the Tonto question: Caught in an ambush, the Lone Ranger turns to his sidekick and says, "Looks like we're surrounded by Indians." And Tonto replies, "Who's we, kemo sabe?" At what level should these decisions be made? I agree these decisions should not be left to "the scientists," but what about the individual's right to choose?

Eric Cohen: A lot of these questions are moral questions and public questions and democratic questions. They're about the kind of society we're going to live in. I think the moral questions presented by the means are easier to deal with in a democratic way. We can have a debate about whether you should kill embryos in order to do research, and we can have an argument about whether we should set limits. I think that's a perfectly legitimate public thing to do. Right now, there are no limits on embryo research. There's not unlimited funding for it, but there are no limits on it at all. Any research scientist in the country can do it.

When you get to the issue of ends, it's a lot more complicated, precisely because these technologies are mixed up with some very desirable things. But in many cases, the means of using them are problematic. There's nothing wrong with developing a pill that you can take to supposedly improve your memory. The question is whether that's actually a good human thing to do. Various people are trying to think about whether you could build a regulatory agency, a kind of hyped-up FDA that dealt with more than just safety issues and dealt with some of the broader issues.

I'm skeptical of the regulatory agency approach. But when it comes to blunt means questions—Should we be engineering children by weeding out the unfit? Should we be using embryos in research?—I think those are questions where there should be a "we." As a society, we should make some collective judgments about the kind of people we want to be.

When you get to some of the more subtle uses of biotech, especially in the enhancement area, then you have smaller levels of "we." Sports teams or leagues are going to set rules about what kinds of drugs are going to be legal in the future. I think these are cultural questions and individual questions. I'm not looking to ban these various drugs. I'm just questioning the wisdom of using many of them and whether they'll actually deliver us the goods we think they will.

Nick Gillespie: Joel, the subtitle of your book mentions "human nature." What is it, and how do we know we're changing it?

Joel Garreau: One of the definitions of human nature that I like the best is that a human is the creature that steals fire from the gods every chance he gets. Or she gets. That's one of the reasons why I don't think these changes are going to go away no matter what country tries to impose some kind of regulatory scheme. This is not just a U.S. question. The superpowers in this regard include India, China, South Korea, and Japan, places that have entirely different ethical and moral takes on what it means to be human than the Judeo-Christian and Western traditions do.

> **"Having been a child of the 1960s, I never anticipated that the most interesting drugs available today [would be] legal and available through prescription. That's the part that really blows my mind."**
>
> —Joel Garreau

In terms of knowing whether we have transcended human nature, I propose the Shakespeare test. Shakespeare knew quite a bit about human nature and he wrote elegantly about it. If you have found somebody who has become so enhanced as to make you wonder whether she's still human, I propose the mental experiment of popping her into your hypothetical time machine and dialing her back to 1605. Present her to Shakespeare and ask him, "What do you think? Is she one of yours? Do you recognize her as human?" I think it would be interesting, for example, if you showed Shakespeare the movie Apollo 13. Once he got past the fact that this was nonfiction and these guys were headed to the moon, he wouldn't have any problem with these guys at all. They're just adventurers who are trying to make it home, like the Greeks of 3,000 years ago.

If you show him the people of the various *Star Trek* series, I don't think he'd have much trouble identifying all of those people as human, although he might stop and scratch his head a little bit about Lt. Comdr. Data [an android]. The guys with the crabs on their foreheads I don't think he'd have any trouble with, but Data, I'd really like to know what kind of take Shakespeare would have on him.

Nick Gillespie: Let's open it up to the audience.

Questioner 1: This is a question for Eric. I agree that we can't know all the effects and impacts of complex changes of the sorts that we're contemplating here. Neither can Ron. The only test we can use to figure out which of you is right has to be the empirical test. Have something of a free market. Probably some people are going to die at 75 or 80. Some people are going to choose to live to be 150 or 200, and then they're going to look back and say, "Gosh, I wish I'd died at 75." Eric wins.

But if you raise the fear of the future being unpredictable but you don't have any kind of empirical testing of it, you can really stop all progress. You can make that argument against progress in any field that we've ever had progress in, whether it's the use of fossil fuels or computing technology or antibiotics.

Eric Cohen: I think there are some basic principles that allow us to be a decent society. Equality is one. We don't treat other people, even weak, disabled, and vulnerable people, as means to our ends. I think that's a better way to live. If you think that principle through, you can set certain kinds of limits on certain technologies. It may be that if we destroyed as many embryos as we wanted to that we would cure 10 diseases. But I think we can come together and say we wouldn't be a better civilization or society if we did that. It's perfectly legitimate to argue for limits on that sort of thing.

We can say the same about some other technologies, especially those dealing with the beginning of life. Think of pre-implantation genetic screening, where you produce 10 embryos, subject them to all kinds of genetic tests, choose the ones that you think are healthy and promising, and discard the ones that aren't. I think we can set limits on those kinds of things.

I'm not sure that's the right way to govern some of the more subtle self-enhancement technologies. If Ron Bailey, in the privacy of his own home, wants to experiment with memory-enhancing drugs, all the power to him. Maybe he'll write 30 books, and they'll all be great, but I'm frankly very skeptical. I think it's a very superficial and simplistic understanding of human excellence and human intelligence that clings or looks longingly at some of these drugs and believes that they're going to make us smarter and better.

At the end of the day the ways that matter most in being good have to do with character anyway. That's an old-fashioned thing, but I think the people that we most admire are generally people not only of ability but people of character. There's no pill that's going to make us better in that way.

Nick Gillespie: Eric, you raise the question of equality and the ways technology might undercut that. During the past 500 years or so, comprising what's considered the modern era, it seems clear that we've increased human enhancement technologies and the treatment of people as equals. More people have political rights than in the past. There's a greater distribution of goods and opportunities across global society now compared to 50, let alone 500, years ago. If we look at the historical record, it's fair to conclude that technology has not only allowed humans to enhance and augment themselves but has also helped them become more equal.

Eric Cohen: In many ways, technology and progress have served the end of equality. I'm in a kind of weird position, right? I'm arguing both for equality and for excellence in a certain sense. On the one hand, I'm worried that these drugs, to put it bluntly, are going to make us sort of pathetic. I mean, yes, we might hit 900 home runs a season, but frankly some of these athletes are sort of pathetic. They're kind of dependent on their drugs, and they all deny it. [Baltimore Orioles slugger] Rafael Palmeiro wouldn't want to be seen shooting his steroids up in the batter's box because he knows that people would think he's less of an athlete. He's less excellent. He's more like the horses we breed.

Nick Gillespie: Would his wife be upset to learn that he's taking Viagra?

Eric Cohen: I don't know. I'll leave that to them.

Nick Gillespie: Palmeiro is a paid spokesman for Viagra, and he's married. That's why I mentioned it. Does taking Viagra—an enhancement drug—make his marital bed less real, less meaningful?

Eric Cohen: Let me bracket the Viagra question for a minute. There's a worry about these enhancements actually undermining the very excellence that they claim to serve. At the same time, I think there are genuine issues with equality. Yes, equality is much better. From the standpoint of equality, it's a heck of a lot better to live today than it was to live 300 years ago in British society. We are more equal, for the most part, but we also treat people in radically unequal ways, both at the beginning of life and at the end of life. And that's another kind of equality that I think has been compromised. If you take that principle seriously and if you take basic biology seriously, then embryos are embryonic human lives, and we're now talking about using them in research. We already abort children with Down syndrome. Those are ways we're saying these people are not good enough. We're not going to welcome them in our society. We're going to eliminate them, and so from that perspective equality has been hurt. Technology has created a mind-set that has made us more inegalitarian even as it's served the cause of equality. I think both things are happening at once.

Questioner 2: I've got two questions, one for Joel and one for Eric. Joel, you've noted that Asian people have an entirely different way of looking at what it is to be a human being than people in the West do. Can you elaborate on that? Eric, isn't it OK if we just sort of relax and let people live a little longer and make some mistakes?

Joel Garreau: I'm not an expert on Hindu philosophy or Confucianism, but I am interested in the facts on the ground in a lot of these cultures. The Chinese have made no secret of the fact that they want to be dominant in the 2008 Olympics. At the University of Pennsylvania Lee Sweeney has been creating genetically altered Schwarzenegger mice. You ought to see his mice. They've got haunches like steers, and their necks are bigger than their heads, and there isn't a day that goes by that he doesn't get a call from an athlete or a coach who is begging him to use them as a human equivalent of this. Lee thinks that the 2004 Olympics were the last ones without genetically engineered humans.

> **"I wonder who the real futurists are—the Catholics who have 10 kids and oppose embryo research, or the libertarians who have no kids and live to 110 and then get hit by a car?"**
>
> —Eric Cohen

An awful lot of the scientists in India have applauded the restrictions on stem cells in this country because they see our [relatively restrictive government policies] as an opportunity to make the great leap forward past the West in these technologies.

This is not some science fiction future. These are decisions that are happening now. That's why I'm so glad that Eric [and others] are asking the questions they are, because they're really good questions. I'm not crazy about some of the answers, but I'm glad they're asking the questions. I'm also glad that the Europeans are trying this business of using governments to control genetically modified organisms. I doubt that it's going to work on a basic practical level, but I like to see humans taking different approaches [to biotechnology] because we've got a long way to go and a short time to get there.

Eric Cohen: If we all relax, we'd have no panel discussions and get all worked up, and then what would we do in Washington? I'm not sure I have an objection to the pursuit of longevity taken in itself. I'm not sure I'm convinced that it's a great idea either, but I think there we'll just have to kind of wait and see. I would just note anecdotally that a lot of the people I know who are obsessed with longevity are also people who don't have children. One way of thinking about the future is to obsessively try to live longer and think about how we can [improve] the world that we want to inhabit. The other way to think about the future is to think about the world we're going to pass down to those who follow us. I wonder who the real futurists are—the Catholics who have 10 kids and oppose embryo research, or the libertarians who have no kids and live to 110 and then get hit by a car?

And there are ethical questions involved here that mean we can't simply relax. Should we be using nascent human life as a tool to develop therapies [that will let us live longer]?

Ronald Bailey: I've suggested to my wife that we'll have children when we're younger. In any case, with regard to treasuring every embryo, nature certainly doesn't do that; 80 percent of all naturally conceived embryos, as far as we know, are not implanted and never become people or babies or anything else. In fact, the results of IVF are better than those of nature.

Questioner 3: In terms of consenting to genetic treatments, do embryos—or children, for that matter—have the ability to give their consent?

Ronald Bailey: I want to remind everybody in the audience that you did not give consent to be born. In fact, you did not give consent to be born with any of the genes that you have. So any embryos that parents decide to modify stand in exactly the same relation that all previous embryos have stood in.

If you think about what people are apt to do, this isn't really an issue. Would you want the person-to-be to be smarter? Well, yeah, that'd be good. Forty IQ points would be good too. Would they like to have a good immune system? Yeah, they'd like that. What about athletic ability? Yeah, OK. I think you can presume consent for most of the things that parents are going to do for their children because they're not going to try to make them worse. They're going to try to make them better.

Critical Thinking

1. What kinds of changes in humans might future technologies achieve?

2. What moral questions would these changes raise?

3. How would you balance the benefits and the risks of human enhancement?

Engineering the Future of Food

JOSH SCHONWALD

Tomorrow's genetically modified food and farmed fish will be more sustainable and far healthier than much of what we eattoday—if we can overcome our fears and embrace it. Here's how one foodie learned to stop worrying and love "frankenfood."

The Plant Transformation Facility at the University of California, Davis, has been the scene of more than 15,000 "transgenic events," which is the term molecular biologists use when they blast DNA from one life form into another. In room 192 of Robbins Hall, a brick building not far from the student union, thousands of microscopic plantlets grow in Petri dishes bathed in pink and fluorescent blue light.

Here, molecular biologists can mix what were previously sexually incompatible species together using a gas-pump-like tool called the Helium Particle Delivery System. Using bullets (literally) made out of gold, they fire genes from one species into another in a bombardment chamber. The Davis lab has given birth to grapes spiked with jellyfish, tomatoes spiked with carp, transgenic squash, transgenic carrots, transgenic tomatoes.

Another important site in genetic engineering history, an innocuous office building about a ten-minute drive from Robbins Hall, is the birthplace of the most audacious plant in the history of high-tech plants. Among biotech people and anti-bio-tech people, this plant, a tomato, needs no introduction. The so-called Flavr Savr was supposed to be the game changer—longer shelf life, better yield, better taste. Calgene, the company that created the Flavr Savr, claimed it could bring "backyard flavor" to the supermarket tomato.

Achieving "backyard flavor" in an industrial-scale, California-grown tomato has long been one of the holy grails of the $4 billion-plus tomato industry. During the pre-tomato launch hype-a-thon, the president of Calgene claimed that genetic engineering could not only bring us the tomato of our childhood dreams, but also remake the taste of the tomato, tailored to our every desire: "Eventually we're going to design acidic tomatoes for the New Jersey palate and sweet tomatoes for the Chicago palate."

The Flavr Savr turned out to be the Edsel of the produce world, a spectacular failure not just for Calgene, but for the whole biotech industry. This purportedly longer-shelf-life tomato became the lightning rod for much of the anti-genetically modified organism (GMO) movement. People learned about other transgenic crops—a potato with a chicken gene, tobacco with a firefly gene, and, perhaps most notoriously, a tomato with an Arctic flounder gene, which provided an image for a Greenpeace anti-GMO campaign. Nongovernmental organizations cried foul. Consumers were alarmed. It was an op-ed about the Flavr Savr where the term Frankenfood first appeared. As for the tomato's taste, most reports said that, far from achieving backyard flavor, it was not that great.

By 1997, supermarkets stopped stocking the bioengineered tomato. The Flavr Savr was a financial disaster for Calgene.

But that was almost fifteen years ago.

One fall day, across campus from the Helium Particle Delivery System, I went to visit Kent Bradford, the director of UC Davis's Seed Biotechnology Center and presumably among the best-positioned people at Davis to answer my burning question: Whatever happened after the Flavr Savr?

The Culinary Potential of Frankenfood

Genetic engineering obviously didn't stop with the Flavr Savr debacle; the use of GMOs has exploded. Many genetically engineered foods can be found throughout our food supply. Genetically modified soybeans and canola dominate the market, which means that most processed food—everything from your spaghetti to your Snickers bar—has GM ingredients. More than 90% of American cotton and 80% of corn crops come from GM seed. All of these crops, though, are what are called "commodity crops." They're not what you pick up at your local greengrocer. They're industrial crops, secondary ingredients. Not what interested me.

What I wanted to know is what was happening with the quest to achieve "backyard flavor"? And what I couldn't get out of my head was this claim that tomatoes could be engineered for precise tastes—"acidic tomatoes for the New Jersey palate and sweet tomatoes for the Chicago palate."

What was going on? Did they just stop working on "sweet tomatoes for the Chicago palate"? Wouldn't the Flavr Savr creators be intent on redemption, going back to the bench to try again? Or did everything just stop?

Strangely, Bradford, a plant geneticist who has been at UC Davis since the early 1980s, shared my curiosity about the post-Flavr Savr world—he just had a different way of explaining it.

"Yes. Where are all these output traits?" he said. (Input traits are breederspeak for what's so often critical to agriculture—disease resistance, insect resistance, adaptability to particular environments. An output trait is breeder parlance for what I was looking for—traits that improve taste and texture, traits that could change the dining experience of the future.)

Bradford had observed that, almost twenty years after the biotech revolution began, there were few signs of any "Second Generation" crops. The First Generation was the commodity crops: soybean, maize, cotton, canola, sugar beets. Most expected that, after the first wave of crops proved their worth, the next wave would be more consumer focused—better tomatoes, tastier lettuce. But biotech specialty crops (that's the crop scientist term for produce) hadn't appeared. In fact, a GMO specialty crop hadn't been commercialized since 1998. Even Bradford, a longtime biotech believer, considered, "Maybe the genes weren't working?"

A few years ago, Bradford and his collaborator Jamie Miller set out to find out "what was going on" with bioengineered specialty crops. They surveyed the leading plant science journals and tracked GM crop field trials—all subject to government regulation—from 2003 to 2008. Searching for citations related to specialty crops, they found that research not only had never stopped but was thriving.

"There was research on 46 different species," says Bradford. "More than 300 traits were being tested." A lot of it was on input traits (disease, weed resistance), but breeders had also experimented with output traits. "It was happening at the research level, but it just didn't move to the next step. It just stopped there."

There was an obvious explanation, Bradford says, sighing. "It was regulatory."

Post Flavr Savr, in response to growing consumer concerns about transgenic breeding, a regulatory process was created that treated genetically modified foods differently from conventionally bred crops. If you have iceberg lettuce, using classic plant-breeding techniques (crossing, back-crossing), the assumption is that the resulting lettuce is safe. There's no requirement for pretesting. You just introduce the product into the market. But with GMOs, Bradford says, the attitude was that "it's guilty until proven innocent."

A genetically engineered crop must pass review by the U.S. Department of Agriculture, the Environmental Protection Agency, and the Food and Drug Administration before it is commercialized. The cost could range from $50,000 to tens of millions of dollars to win regulatory approval. For every "transgenic event," the genetic engineer must show exactly what genes went into the plant and how they function, and then prove how the plant makeup has been altered. That research is costly. So is plant storage. Once a transgenic creation is spawned at the Plant Transformation Facility, it is whisked to the UC Davis Controlled Environment Facility, where it will stay in a tightly secured warehouse. Or it will be airmailed to some other

place, where it'll live out its life in another intensely biosecure environment.

The process is costly and time-consuming, which partly explains why biotech crop development is largely in the hands of the agribusiness giants—the Monsantos, Syngentas, and Bayer Crop Sciences of the world—who have the resources to undertake the process. With such high approval costs, big companies have favored commodity crops with market potential for hundreds of millions of dollars in sales, not tens of millions.

We talked about the reasons for what Bradford calls "the bottleneck" for the biotech specialty crops. It was NGOs such as Greenpeace and the Union of Concerned Scientists that were the bogeymen, in his view. Big Organic, a $20 billion industry, had a vested interested in stopping GMOs. Back in 2000, when the USDA was developing the National Organic Program standards, the first draft did not prohibit genetically modified foods, but then activists launched an anti-GMO campaign, flooding the USDA with a tidal wave of letters—275,026, to be exact. The USDA then determined that genetically modified organisms would not be included under the standard for organic produce. Being deemed un-kosher in the organic world is a hard stigma to overcome.

The anti-GMO movement hasn't lost momentum; the Non-GMO Project has become the fastest-growing food eco-label in North America, with sales eclipsing $1 billion in 2011. As for Europe: After a 12-year moratorium on GMO crops, the European Union greenlighted a GMO potato—but not for human consumption. It would be used to produce higher levels of starch, which is helpful for industries like paper manufacturing. In short, the European market is still overwhelmingly closed for genetically modified foodstuffs.

What If the World Embraced Agricultural Biotechnology?

According to the World Health Organization, 250 million children worldwide, mostly in the developing world, have diets lacking in vitamin A. Between 250,000 and 500,000 of these children go blind every year. Yet, there is a crop, developed more than 13 years ago, that is fortified with vitamin A compounds. If children unable to get vitamin A from other protein sources simply eat this crop, they will not go blind and die. It is named "golden rice" because of its yellowish hue, and every health organization in the world has declared it to be safe to eat.

But golden rice was not bred through traditional means; it was bred in a lab. So golden rice is, by its opponents' definition, Frankenfood, and therefore, like many other GMO crops, it's been ferociously opposed.

Now let's say that golden rice does get approved (as some predict it will in 2013), and let's say it saves millions of children from starvation and blindness in Asia. Or let's say bioengineered crops slow down the creation of algal dead zones in the Gulf of Mexico. Or a low-fat, anti-cancer potato becomes a smash hit at McDonald's. Consumer worries about GMOs evaporate, becoming as anachronistic as fears of microwave ovens causing cancer. The regulatory barriers are gone; transgenic plants are treated the same as any other. The Monsanto juggernaut is over; small, boutique companies and open-source plant breeders in the comfort of a Brooklyn loft have a chance to contribute to the vegetable economy. Then what happens?

- Food will look different. There will almost surely be more varieties. Austrian heirloom lettuce varieties like Forellenschluss and heirloom tomatoes like the Brandywines and Cherokee Purples could become readily available. So many vegetables today aren't commercially viable because of disease vulnerabilities or production inefficiencies. But in a genetically engineered future, all the flaws that make them ill-suited for commercialization become mere speed bumps.

  "You could have disease immunity almost immediately," says Bradford. "And it would be very easy to take care of these other variables. Instead of taking a decade to ready a crop for commercialization, it will take a matter of months."

  It's possible that colors would change. You could find pink lettuce and blue arugula—maybe with a green orange slice for St. Patrick's Day. Color becomes malleable because it's often a single trait.

- Food will taste different. It is also likely, some geneticists say, that in 2035 some lettuces won't taste anything like lettuce. The notion of tomatoes with customized flavor was a reckless ambition in the 1990s when the Flavr Savr debuted; modifying taste is among the most challenging tasks for plant geneticists. You can silence a gene in the potato genome, tuning down the bitterness or acidic quality, but it's still a fractional impact on taste.

  Taste is complex. A tomato, for instance, has between five and twenty compounds that influence flavor. Changing flavor requires not one gene, but packages of genes, and the genes must be placed precisely. Then there is texture, inextricably linked to flavor. Modifying taste eludes technologists today, but in the next ten years, that could change, as bio-engineers will be able to choose from a genetic cassette—stacks of genes that together confer desired traits. With a few mouse clicks, geneticists say, they could choose from a range of flavors, textures, and colors.

  "Think of it like Photoshop," says C. S. Prakash, director of the Center for Plant Biotechnology Research at Tuskegee University. "At some point that won't be a far-fetched metaphor." It will be technologically possible, therefore, to create a Caesar salad without the Caesar dressing; the flavor of the Caesar could be bred into the lettuce.

  Textures would also be far easier to change. You could bite into an apple that has the consistency of a banana. In a biotech-friendly future, fruits and vegetables would merely be another frontier for adventurous and often mind-bending culinary pioneers.

- We'll see produce that doesn't spoil. In a biotech future, the sell-by dates will be different; instead of rushing

to eat your lettuce in a week, looseleaf lettuce could languish, unsealed, for a month or more. One of the huge problems in the produce industry is perishability, with close to one-third of all fresh fruits and vegetables produced lost to overripening or damage during shipment. But bioengineers are already making progress in changing the post-harvest behavior of plants. By having an enzyme shut off, an apple has been modified so that it won't turn brown after it is sliced, and a banana has been engineered to ripen more slowly.

Although small organic farmers are often the most hostile to technologized solutions and may be the least likely group to adopt high-tech crops, it's possible that GMOs could change the farmers' markets in places like Chicago or Buffalo.

"In New York and Illinois, it's pretty hard to grow a lot of crops because they're going to freeze," explains Dennis Miller, a food scientist at Cornell University. "But you could engineer in frost tolerance. You could extend the growing season and bring in more exotic crops into new regions. I don't know if we'll be growing bananas in upstate New York, but it would expand the options for locally grown fruits and vegetables."

How Frankenfood Will Improve Health

Most breeders expect that the biggest change for consumers would be something that's already familiar to any Whole Foods shopper. We already have calcium-fortified orange juice and herbal tea enhanced with antioxidants, but in an agbiotech-friendly world, the produce section would likely be overflowing with health enhancements. Orange potatoes enhanced with beta-carotene., calcium-enhanced carrots, and crops with enhanced antioxidants are already in the pipeline. By the 2030s, vegetables and fruits will be vitamin, nutrient, and beneficial-gene-delivery vehicles.

To illustrate how this would play out, Prakash points to the work of Cynthia Kenyon, a University of California-San Francisco molecular biologist, who extended the life span of a ground worm by six times by changing a gene called "def 2."

While this is in the realm of basic science, Prakash also suggests that, if something like a "fountain of youth" gene is found to benefit humans, it could be bred into vegetables. By combining genetics and plant science, a whole new realm of products would likely appear.

Some geneticists envision a future in which crop development would become a highly collaborative process: Nutritionists, geneticists, physicians, chefs, and marketers would work to develop new fruits and vegetables aimed at various consumer wants.

Another Kind of Foodie Hero

A scientist in a white lab coat doesn't conjure the same feelings as a micro-farmer in a straw hat. Growing fish in a warehouse isn't quite as stirring as pulling them out of a choppy Alaskan sea. A meat-spawning bioreactor doesn't have the same allure as a dew-covered Virginia pasture.

But it's time to broaden the foodie pantheon.

Let's continue to celebrate our heirloom-fava-bean growers and our grass-fed-goat herders. Let's carefully scrutinize the claims of nutritional science and keep a wary eye on new technologies, especially those with panacea-like claims from multinational corporations with monopolistic aims and a history of DDT and Agent Orange production. But let's not be so black-and-white; let's not be reflexively and categorically opposed to any and all technological solutions. Savoring the slowest food and foraging for wild asparagus shouldn't be viewed as at odds with championing lab-engineered vitamin A-enhanced rice that could save children from blindness.

Pairing a locally grown, seasonal mesclun mix from an organic micro-farm with cobia, a saltwater fish grown in an industrial-sized warehouse, is not an incompatible, ethically confused choice.

I make this point because of the rising tide of food-specific neo-Luddism in America. While well intentioned and often beneficial in its impact, this foodie fundamentalism is unfortunately often associated with a dangerous antiscientism. If we're going to meet the enormous challenges of feeding the world's still-growing population, we are going to need all the ingenuity we can bring to bear.

My modest hope: Let's keep an open mind. Let's consider even the fringy, sometimes yucky, maybe kooky ideas. Let's not miss opportunities to build a long-term sustainable future for our planet.

"The proces is costly and time consuming, which partly explains why biotech crop development is largely in the hands of the agribusiness giants."

"With a few mouse clicks, geneticists say, they could choose from a range of flavors, textures, and colors."

Notes

Adapted from the forthcoming book *The Taste of Tomorrow: Dispatches from the Future of Food* by Josh Schonwald. Copyright ©2012 by Josh Schonwald. To be published on April 10, 2012, by Harper, an imprint of HarperCollins Publishers.

AquAdvantage® Salmon includes a gene from the Chinook salmon, which provides the fish with the potential to grow to market size in half the time of conventional salmon, according to maker AquaBounty Technologies.

Critical Thinking

1. The big debate in agriculture concerns genetically modified organisms (GMOs). Present the pro and con arguments.
2. How do you balance the benefits and risks of GMO?

The Broken Contract

Inequality and American Decline

GEORGE PACKER

Iraq was one of those wars where people actually put on pounds. A few years ago, I was eating lunch with another reporter at an American-style greasy spoon in Baghdad's Green Zone. At a nearby table, a couple of American contractors were finishing off their burgers and fries. They were wearing the contractor's uniform: khakis, polo shirts, baseball caps, and Department of Defense identity badges in plastic pouches hanging from nylon lanyards around their necks. The man who had served their food might have been the only Iraqi they spoke with all day. The Green Zone was set up to make you feel that Iraq was a hallucination and you were actually in Normal, Illinois. This narcotizing effect seeped into the consciousness of every American who hunkered down and worked and partied behind its blast walls—the soldier and the civilian, the diplomat and the journalist, the important and the obscure. Hardly anyone stayed longer than a year; almost everyone went home with a collection of exaggerated war stories, making an effort to forget that they were leaving behind shoddy, unfinished projects and a country spiraling downward into civil war. As the two contractors got up and ambled out of the restaurant, my friend looked at me and said, "We're just not that good anymore."

The Iraq war was a kind of stress test applied to the American body politic. And every major system and organ failed the test: the executive and legislative branches, the military, the intelligence world, the for-profits, the nonprofits, the media. It turned out that we were not in good shape at all—without even realizing it. Americans just hadn't tried anything this hard in around half a century. It is easy, and completely justified, to blame certain individuals for the Iraq tragedy. But over the years, I've become more concerned with failures that went beyond individuals, and beyond Iraq—concerned with the growing arteriosclerosis of American institutions. Iraq was not an exceptional case. It was a vivid symptom of a long-term trend, one that worsens year by year. The same ailments that led to the disastrous occupation were on full display in Washington this past summer, during the debt-ceiling debacle: ideological rigidity bordering on fanaticism, an indifference to facts, an inability to think beyond the short term, the dissolution of national interest into partisan advantage.

Was it ever any different? Is it really true that we're just not that good anymore? As a thought experiment, compare your life today with that of someone like you in 1978. Think of an educated, reasonably comfortable couple perched somewhere within the vast American middle class of that year. And think how much less pleasant their lives are than yours. The man is wearing a brown and gold polyester print shirt with a flared collar and oversize tortoiseshell glasses; she's got on a high-waisted, V-neck rayon dress and platform clogs. Their morning coffee is Maxwell House filter drip. They drive an AMC Pacer hatchback, with a nonfunctioning air conditioner and a tape deck that keeps eating their eight-tracks. When she wants to make something a little daring for dinner, she puts together a pasta primavera. They type their letters on an IBM Selectric, the new model with the corrective ribbon. There is only antenna television, and the biggest thing on is Laverne and Shirley. Long-distance phone calls cost a dollar a minute on weekends; air travel is prohibitively expensive. The city they live near is no longer a place where they spend much time: trash on the sidewalks, junkies on the corner, vandalized pay phones, half-deserted subway cars covered in graffiti.

By contemporary standards, life in 1978 was inconvenient, constrained, and ugly. Things were badly made and didn't work very well. Highly regulated industries, such as telecommunications and airlines, were costly and offered few choices. The industrial landscape was decaying, but the sleek information revolution had not yet emerged to take its place. Life before the Android, the Apple Store, FedEx, HBO, Twitter feeds, Whole Foods, Lipitor, air bags, the Emerging Markets Index Fund, and the pre-K Gifted and Talented Program prep course is not a world to which many of us would willingly return.

The surface of life has greatly improved, at least for educated, reasonably comfortable people—say, the top 20 percent, socioeconomically. Yet the deeper structures, the institutions that underpin a healthy democratic society, have fallen into a state of decadence. We have all the information in the universe at our fingertips, while our most basic problems go unsolved year after year: climate change, income inequality, wage stagnation, national debt, immigration, falling educational achievement, deteriorating infrastructure, declining news standards. All around, we see dazzling technological change, but no progress. Last year, a Wall Street company that few people have ever heard of dug an 800-mile trench under farms, rivers, and mountains between Chicago and New York and laid fiber-optic cable connecting the Chicago Mercantile Exchange and the New York Stock Exchange. This feat of infrastructure building, which cost $300 million, shaves three milliseconds off high-speed, high-volume automated trades—a big competitive advantage. But passenger trains between Chicago and New York run barely faster than they did in 1950, and the country no longer seems capable, at least politically, of building faster ones. Just ask people in Florida, Ohio, and Wisconsin, whose governors recently refused federal money for high-speed rail projects.

We can upgrade our iPhones, but we can't fix our roads and bridges. We invented broadband, but we can't extend it to 35 percent of the public. We can get 300 television channels on the iPad, but in the past decade 20 newspapers closed down all their foreign bureaus. We have touch-screen voting machines, but last year just 40 percent of registered voters turned out, and our political system is more polarized, more choked with its own bile, than at any time since the Civil War. There is nothing today like the personal destruction of the McCarthy era or the street fights of the 1960s. But in those periods, institutional forces still existed in politics, business, and the media that could hold the center together. It used to be called the establishment, and it no longer exists. Solving fundamental problems with a can-do practicality—the very thing the world used to associate with America, and that redeemed us from our vulgarity and arrogance—now seems beyond our reach.

The Unwritten Contract

Why and how did this happen? Those are hard questions. A roundabout way of answering them is to first ask, when did this start to happen? Any time frame has an element of arbitrariness, and also contains the beginning of a theory. Mine goes back to that shabby, forgettable year of 1978. It is surprising to say that in or around 1978, American life changed—and changed dramatically. It was, like this moment, a time of widespread pessimism—high inflation, high unemployment, high gas prices. And the country reacted to its sense of decline by moving away from the social arrangement that had been in place since the 1930s and 1940s.

What was that arrangement? It is sometimes called "the mixed economy"; the term I prefer is "middle-class democracy." It was an unwritten social contract among labor, business, and government—between the elites and the masses. It guaranteed that the benefits of the economic growth following World War II were distributed more widely, and with more shared prosperity, than at any time in human history. In the 1970s, corporate executives earned 40 times as much as their lowest-paid employees. (By 2007, the ratio was over 400 to 1.) Labor law and government policy kept the balance of power between workers and owners on an even keel, leading to a

virtuous circle of higher wages and more economic stimulus. The tax code restricted the amount of wealth that could be accumulated in private hands and passed on from one generation to the next, thereby preventing the formation of an inherited plutocracy. The regulatory agencies were strong enough to prevent the kind of speculative bubbles that now occur every five years or so: between the Great Depression and the Reagan era there was not a single systemwide financial crisis, which is why recessions during those decades were far milder than they have since become. Commercial banking was a stable, boring business. (In movies from the 1940s and 1950s, bankers are dull, solid pillars of the community.) Investment banking, cordoned off by the iron wall of the Glass-Steagall Act, was a closed world of private partnerships in which rich men carefully weighed their risks because they were playing with their own money. Partly as a result of this shared prosperity, political participation reached an all-time high during the postwar years (with the exception of those, such as black Americans in the South, who were still denied access to the ballot box).

At the same time, the country's elites were playing a role that today is almost unrecognizable. They actually saw themselves as custodians of national institutions and interests. The heads of banks, corporations, universities, law firms, foundations, and media companies were neither more nor less venal, meretricious, and greedy than their counterparts today. But they rose to the top in a culture that put a brake on these traits and certainly did not glorify them. Organizations such as the Council on Foreign Relations, the Committee for Economic Development, and the Ford Foundation did not act on behalf of a single, highly privileged point of view—that of the rich. Rather, they rose above the country's conflicting interests and tried to unite them into an overarching idea of the national interest. Business leaders who had fought the New Deal as vehemently as the United States. Chamber of Commerce is now fighting healthcare and financial reform later came to accept Social Security and labor unions, did not stand in the way of Medicare, and supported other pieces of Lyndon Johnson's Great Society. They saw this legislation as contributing to the social peace that ensured a productive economy. In 1964, Johnson created the National Commission on Technology, Automation, and Economic Progress to study the effects of these coming changes on the work force. The commission included two labor leaders, two corporate leaders, the civil rights activist Whitney Young, and the sociologist Daniel Bell. Two years later, they came out with their recommendations: a guaranteed annual income and a massive job-training program. This is how elites once behaved: as if they had actual responsibilities.

Of course, the consensus of the postwar years contained plenty of injustice. If you were black or female, it made very little room for you. It could be stifling and conformist, authoritarian and intrusive. Yet those years also offered the means of redressing the very wrongs they contained: for example, strong government, enlightened business, and activist labor were important bulwarks of the civil rights movement. Nostalgia is a useless emotion. Like any era, the postwar years had their costs. But from where we stand in 2011, they look pretty good.

The Rise of Organized Money

Two things happened to this social arrangement. The first was the 1960s. The story is familiar: youth rebellion and revolution, a ferocious backlash now known as the culture wars, and a permanent change in American manners and morals. Far more than political Utopia, the legacy of the 1960s was personal liberation. Some conservatives argue that the social revolution of the 1960s and 1970s prepared the way for the economic revolution of the 1980s, that Abbie Hoffman and Ronald Reagan were both about freedom. But Woodstock was not enough to blow apart the middle-class democracy that had benefited tens of millions of Americans. The Nixon and Ford presidencies actually extended it. In his 2001 book, The Paradox of American Democracy, John Judis notes that in the three decades between 1933 and 1966, the federal government created 11 regulatory agencies to protect consumers, workers, and investors. In the five years between 1970 and 1975, it established another 12, including the Environmental Protection Agency, the Occupational Safety and Health Administration, and the Consumer Product Safety Commission. Richard Nixon was a closet liberal, and today he would be to the left of Senator Olympia Snowe, the moderate Republican.

The second thing that happened was the economic slowdown of the 1970s, brought on by "stagflation" and the oil shock. It eroded Americans' paychecks and what was left of their confidence in the federal government after Vietnam, Watergate, and the disorder of the 1960s. It also alarmed the country's business leaders, and they turned their alarm into action. They became convinced that capitalism itself was under attack by the likes of Rachel Carson and Ralph Nader, and they organized themselves into lobbying groups and think tanks that quickly became familiar and powerful players in United States. politics: the Business Roundtable, the Heritage Foundation, and others. Their budgets and influence soon rivaled those of the older, consensus-minded groups, such as the Brookings Institution. By the mid-1970s, chief executives had stopped believing that they had an obligation to act as disinterested stewards of the national economy. They became a special interest; the interest they represented was their own. The neoconservative writer Irving Kristol played a key role in focusing executives' minds on this narrower and more urgent agenda. He told them, "Corporate philanthropy should not be, and cannot be, disinterested."

Among the non-disinterested spending that corporations began to engage in, none was more interested than lobbying. Lobbying has existed since the beginning of the republic, but it was a sleepy, bourbon-and-cigars practice until the mid- to late 1970s. In 1971, there were only 145 businesses represented by registered lobbyists in Washington; by 1982, there were 2,445. In 1974, there were just over 600 registered political action committees, which raised $12.5 million that year; in 1982, there were 3,371, which raised $83 million. In 1974, a total of $77 million was spent on the midterm elections; in 1982, it was $343 million. Not all this lobbying and campaign spending was done by corporations, but they did more and did it better than anyone else. And they got results.

These changes were wrought not only by conservative thinkers and their allies in the business class. Among those responsible were the high-minded liberals, the McGovernites and Watergate reformers, who created the open primary, clean election laws, and "outsider" political campaigns that relied heavily on television advertising. In theory, those reforms opened up the political system to previously disenfranchised voters by getting rid of the smoke-filled room, the party caucus, and the urban boss—exchanging Richard Daley for Jesse Jackson. In practice, what replaced the old politics was not a more egalitarian new politics. Instead, as the parties lost their coherence and authority, they were overtaken by grass-roots politics of a new type, driven by direct mail, beholden to special interest groups, and funded by lobbyists. The electorate was transformed from coalitions of different blocs—labor, small business, the farm vote—to an atomized nation of television watchers. Politicians began to focus their energies on big dollars for big ad buys. As things turned out, this did not set them free to do the people's work: as Senator Tom Harkin, the Iowa Democrat, once told me, he and his colleagues spend half their free time raising money.

This is a story about the perverse effects of democratization. Getting rid of elites, or watching them surrender their moral authority, did not necessarily empower ordinary people. Once Walter Reuther of the United Auto Workers and Walter Wriston of Citicorp stopped sitting together on Commissions to Make the World a Better Place and started paying lobbyists to fight for their separate interests in Congress, the balance of power tilted heavily toward business. Thirty years later, who has done better by the government—the United Auto Workers or Citicorp?

In 1978, all these trends came to a head. That year, three reform bills were brought up for a vote in Congress. One of the bills was to establish a new office of consumer representation, giving the public a consumer advocate in the federal bureaucracy. A second bill proposed modestly increasing the capital gains tax and getting rid of the three-Martini-lunch deduction. A third sought to make it harder for employers to circumvent labor laws and block union organizing. These bills had bipartisan backing in Congress; they were introduced at the very end of the era when bipartisanship was routine, when necessary and important legislation had support from both parties. The Democrats controlled the White House and both houses of Congress, and the bills were popular with the public. And yet, one by one, each bill went down in defeat. (Eventually, the tax bill passed, but only after it was changed; instead of raising the capital gains tax rate, the final bill cut it nearly in half.)

How and why this happened are explored in Jacob Hacker and Paul Pierson's recent book, Winner-Take-All Politics. Their explanation, in two words, is organized money. Business groups launched a lobbying assault the likes of which Washington had never seen, and when it was all over, the next era in American life had begun. At the end of the year, the midterm elections saw the Republicans gain 15 seats in the House and three in the Senate. The numbers were less impressive than the character of the new members who came to Washington. They were not politicians looking to get along with colleagues and solve problems by passing legislation. Rather, they were movement conservatives who were hostile to the very idea of government. Among them was a history professor from Georgia named Newt Gingrich. The Reagan revolution began in 1978.

Organized money did not foist these far-reaching changes on an unsuspecting public. In the late 1970s, popular anger at government was running high, and President Jimmy Carter was a perfect target. This was not a case of false consciousness; it was a case of a fed-up public. Two years later, Reagan came to power in a landslide. The public wanted him.

But that archetypal 1978 couple with the AMC Pacer was not voting to see its share of the economic pie drastically reduced over the next 30 years. They were not fed up with how little of the national income went to the top one percent or how unfairly progressive the tax code was. They did not want to dismantle government programs such as Social Security and Medicare, which had brought economic security to the middle class. They were not voting to weaken government itself, as long as it defended their interests. But for the next three decades, the dominant political faction pursued these goals as though they were what most Americans wanted. Organized money and the conservative movement seized that moment back in 1978 to begin a massive, generation-long transfer of wealth to the richest Americans. The transfer continued in good economic times and bad, under Democratic presidents and Republican, when Democrats controlled Congress and when Republicans did. For the Democrats, too, went begging to Wall Street and corporate America, because that's where the money was. They accepted the perfectly legal bribes just as eagerly as Republicans, and when the moment came, some of them voted almost as obediently. In 2007, when Congress was considering closing a loophole in the law that allowed hedge fund managers to pay a tax rate of 15 percent on most of their earnings—considerably less than their secretaries—it was New York's Democratic senator Charles Schumer who rushed to their defense and made sure it did not happen. As Bob Dole, then a Republican senator, said back in 1982, "Poor people don't make campaign contributions."

Mocking the American Promise

This inequality is the ill that underlies all the others. Like an odorless gas, it pervades every corner of the United States and saps the strength of the country's democracy. But it seems impossible to find the source and shut it off. For years, certain politicians and pundits denied that it even existed. But the evidence became overwhelming. Between 1979 and 2006, middle-class Americans saw their annual incomes after taxes increase by 21 percent (adjusted for inflation). The poorest Americans saw their incomes rise by only 11 percent. The top one percent, meanwhile, saw their incomes increase by 256 percent. This almost tripled their share of the national income, up to 23 percent, the highest level since 1928. The graph that shows their share over time looks almost flat under Kennedy, Johnson, Nixon, Ford, and Carter, followed by continual spikes under Reagan, the elder Bush, Clinton, and the younger Bush.

Some argue that this inequality was an unavoidable result of deeper shifts: global competition, cheap goods made in China, technological changes. Although those factors played a

part, they have not been decisive. In Europe, where the same changes took place, inequality has remained much lower than in the United States. The decisive factor has been politics and public policy: tax rates, spending choices, labor laws, regulations, campaign finance rules. Book after book by economists and other scholars over the past few years has presented an airtight case: over the past three decades, the government has consistently favored the rich. This is the source of the problem: our leaders, our institutions.

But even more fundamental than public policy is the long-term transformation of the manners and morals of American elites—what they became willing to do that they would not have done, or even thought about doing, before. Political changes precipitated, and in turn were aided by, deeper changes in norms of responsibility and self-restraint. In 1978, it might have been economically feasible and perfectly legal for an executive to award himself a multimillion-dollar bonus while shedding 40 percent of his work force and requiring the survivors to take annual furloughs without pay. But no executive would have wanted the shame and outrage that would have followed—any more than an executive today would want to be quoted using a racial slur or photographed with a paid escort. These days, it is hard to open a newspaper without reading stories about grotesque overcompensation at the top and widespread hardship below. Getting rid of a taboo is easier than establishing one, and once a prohibition erodes, it can never be restored in quite the same way. As Leo Tolstoy wrote, "There are no conditions of life to which a man cannot get accustomed, especially if he sees them accepted by everyone around him."

The persistence of this trend toward greater inequality over the past 30 years suggests a kind of feedback loop that cannot be broken by the usual political means. The more wealth accumulates in a few hands at the top, the more influence and favor the well-connected rich acquire, which makes it easier for them and their political allies to cast off restraint without paying a social price. That, in turn, frees them up to amass more money, until cause and effect become impossible to distinguish. Nothing seems to slow this process down—not wars, not technology, not a recession, not a historic election. Perhaps, out of a well-founded fear that the country is coming apart at the seams, the wealthy and their political allies will finally have to rein themselves in, and, for example, start thinking about their taxes less like Stephen Schwarzman and more like Warren Buffett.

In the meantime, inequality will continue to mock the American promise of opportunity for all. Inequality creates a lopsided economy, which leaves the rich with so much money that they can binge on speculation, and leaves the middle class without enough money to buy the things they think they deserve, which leads them to borrow and go into debt. These were among the long-term causes of the financial crisis and the Great Recession. Inequality hardens society into a class system, imprisoning people in the circumstances of their birth—a rebuke to the very idea of the American dream. Inequality divides us from one another in schools, in neighborhoods, at work, on airplanes, in hospitals, in what we eat, in the condition of our bodies, in what we think, in our children's futures, in how we die. Inequality makes it harder to imagine the lives of others—which is one reason why the fate of over 14 million more or less permanently unemployed Americans leaves so little impression in the country's political and media capitals. Inequality corrodes trust among fellow citizens, making it seem as if the game is rigged. Inequality provokes a generalized anger that finds targets where it can—immigrants, foreign countries, American elites, government in all forms—and it rewards demagogues while discrediting reformers. Inequality saps the will to conceive of ambitious solutions to large collective problems, because those problems no longer seem very collective. Inequality undermines democracy.

Critical Thinking

1. What has changed in the relations between labor, management, and the government?
2. How does the broken contract affect society?
3. What should be the next step between these parties?

GEORGE PACKER is a staff writer at *The New Yorker*. This essay is adapted from a Joanna Jackson Goldman Memorial Lecture on American Civilization and Government that he delivered earlier this year at the New York Public Library's Cullman Center for Scholars & Writers.

The Democratic Malaise

Globalization and the Threat to the West

CHARLES A. KUPCHAN

A crisis of governability has engulfed the world's most advanced democracies. It is no accident that the United States, Europe, and Japan are simultaneously experiencing political breakdown; globalization is producing a widening gap between what electorates are asking of their governments and what those governments are able to deliver. The mismatch between the growing demand for good governance and its shrinking supply is one of the gravest challenges facing the Western world today.

Voters in industrialized democracies are looking to their governments to respond to the decline in living standards and the growing inequality resulting from unprecedented global flows of goods, services, and capital. They also expect their representatives to deal with surging immigration, global warming, and other knock-on effects of a globalized world. But Western governments are not up to the task. Globalization is making less effective the policy levers at their disposal while also diminishing the West's traditional sway over world affairs by fueling the "rise of the rest." The inability of democratic governments to address the needs of their broader publics has, in turn, only increased popular disaffection, further undermining the legitimacy and efficacy of representative institutions.

This crisis of governability within the Western world comes at a particularly inopportune moment. The international system is in the midst of tectonic change due to the diffusion of wealth and power to new quarters. Globalization was supposed to have played to the advantage of liberal societies, which were presumably best suited to capitalize on the fast and fluid nature of the global marketplace. But instead, mass publics in the advanced democracies of North America, Europe, and East Asia have been particularly hard hit—precisely because their countries' economies are both mature and open to the world.

In contrast, Brazil, India, Turkey, and other rising democracies are benefiting from the shift of economic vitality from the developed to the developing world. And China is proving particularly adept at reaping globalization's benefits while limiting its liabilities—in no small part because it has retained control over policy instruments abandoned by its liberal competitors. State capitalism has its distinct advantages, at least for now. As a consequence, it is not just the West's material primacy that is at stake today but also the allure of its version of modernity. Unless liberal democracies can restore their political and economic solvency, the politics, as well as the geopolitics, of the twenty-first century may well be up for grabs.

Deer in the Headlights

Globalization has expanded aggregate wealth and enabled developing countries to achieve unprecedented prosperity. The proliferation of investment, trade, and communication networks has deepened interdependence and its potentially pacifying effects and has helped pry open nondemocratic states and foster popular uprisings. But at the same time, globalization and the digital economy on which it depends are the main source of the West's current crisis of governability. Deindustrialization and outsourcing, global trade and fiscal imbalances, excess capital and credit and asset bubbles—these consequences of globalization are imposing hardships and insecurity not experienced for generations. The distress stemming from the economic crisis that began in 2008 is particularly acute, but the underlying problems began much earlier. For the better part of two decades, middle-class wages in the world's leading democracies have been stagnant, and economic inequality has been rising sharply as globalization has handsomely rewarded its winners but left its many losers behind.

These trends are not temporary byproducts of the business cycle, nor are they due primarily to insufficient regulation of "the financial sector, tax cuts amid expensive wars, or other errant policies. Stagnant wages and rising inequality are, as the economic analysts Daniel Alpert, Robert Hockett, and Nouriel Roubini recently argued in their study "The Way Forward," a consequence of the integration of billions of low-wage workers into the global economy and increases in productivity stemming from the application of information technology to the manufacturing sector. These developments have pushed global capacity far higher than demand, exacting a heavy toll on workers in the high-wage economies of the industrialized West. The resulting dislocation and disaffection among Western electorates have been magnified by globalization's intensification of transnational threats, such as international crime, terrorism, unwanted immigration, and environmental degradation. Adding to this nasty mix is the information revolution; the Internet and the profusion of mass media appear to be fueling ideological polarization more than they are cultivating deliberative debate.

Voters confronted with economic duress, social dislocation, and political division look to their elected representatives for help. But just as globalization is stimulating this pressing demand for responsive governance, it is also ensuring that its provision is in desperately short supply. For three main reasons, governments in the industrialized West have entered a period of pronounced ineffectiveness.

First, globalization has made many of the traditional policy tools used by liberal democracies much blunter instruments. Washington has regularly turned to fiscal and monetary policy to modulate economic performance. But in the midst of global competition and unprecedented debt, the United States. economy seems all but immune to injections of stimulus spending or the Federal Reserve's latest moves on interest rates. The scope and speed of commercial and financial flows mean that decisions and developments elsewhere—Beijing's intransigence on the value of the yuan, Europe's sluggish response to its financial crisis, the actions of investors and ratings agencies, an increase in the quality of Hyundai's latest models—outweigh decisions taken in Washington. Europe's democracies long relied on monetary policy to adjust to fluctuations in national economic performance. But they gave up that option when they joined the eurozone. Japan over the last two decades has tried one stimulus strategy after another, but to no avail. In a globalized world, democracies simply have less control over outcomes than they used to.

Second, many of the problems that Western electorates are asking their governments to solve require a level of international cooperation that is unattainable. The diffusion of power from the West to the rest means that there are today many new cooks in the kitchen; effective action no longer rests primarily on collaboration among like-minded democracies. Instead, it depends on cooperation among a much larger and more diverse circle of states. The United States now looks to the G-20 to rebalance the international economy. But consensus is elusive among nations that are at different stages of development and embrace divergent approaches to economic governance. Challenges such as curbing global warming or effectively isolating Iran similarly depend on a collective effort that is well beyond reach.

Third, democracies can be nimble and responsive when their electorates are content and enjoy a consensus born of rising expectations, but they are clumsy and sluggish when their citizens are downcast and divided. Polities in which governance depends on popular participation, institutional checks and balances, and competition among interest groups appear to be better at distributing benefits than at apportioning sacrifice. But sacrifice is exactly what is necessary to restore economic solvency, which confronts Western governments with the unappetizing prospect of pursuing policies that threaten to weaken their electoral appeal.

One Problem, Three Flavors

In the United States, partisan confrontation is paralyzing the political system. The underlying cause is the poor state of the United States economy. Since 2008, many Americans have lost their houses, jobs, and retirement savings. And these setbacks come on the heels of back-to-back decades of stagnation in middle-class wages. Over the past ten years, the average household income in the United States has fallen by over ten percent. In the meantime, income inequality has been steadily rising, making the United States the most unequal country in the industrialized world. The primary source of the declining fortunes of the American worker is global competition; jobs have been heading overseas. In addition, many of the most competitive companies in the digital economy do not have long coattails. Face-book's estimated value is around $70 billion, and it employs roughly 2,000 workers; compare this with General Motors, which is valued at $35 billion and has 77,000 employees in the United States and 208,000 worldwide. The wealth of the United States' cutting-edge companies is not trickling down to the middle class.

These harsh economic realities are helping revive ideological and partisan cleavages long muted by the nation's rising economic fortunes. During the decades after World War II, a broadly shared prosperity pulled Democrats and Republicans toward the political center. But today, Capitol Hill is largely devoid of both centrists and bipartisanship; Democrats campaign for more stimulus, relief for the unemployed, and taxes on the rich, whereas Republicans clamor for radical cuts in the size and cost of government. Expediting the hollowing out of the center are partisan redistricting, a media environment that provokes more than it informs, and a broken campaign finance system that has been captured by special interests.

The resulting polarization is tying the country in knots. President Barack Obama realized as much, which is why he entered office promising to be a "post-partisan" president. But the failure of Obama's best efforts to revive the economy and restore bipartisan cooperation has exposed the systemic nature of the nation's economic and political dysfunction. His $787 billion stimulus package, passed without the support of a single House Republican, was unable to resuscitate an economy plagued by debt, a deficit of middle-class jobs, and the global slowdown. Since the Republicans gained control of the House in 2010, partisan confrontation has stood in the way of progress on nearly every issue. Bills to promote economic growth either fail to pass or are so watered down that they have little impact. Immigration reform and legislation to curb global warming are not even on the table.

Ineffective governance, combined with daily doses of partisan bile, has pushed public approval of Congress to historic lows. Spreading frustration has spawned the Occupy Wall Street movement—the first sustained bout of public protests since the Vietnam War. The electorate's discontent only deepens the challenges of governance, as vulnerable politicians cater to the narrow interests of the party base and the nation's political system loses what little wind it has in its sails.

Europe's crisis of governability, meanwhile, is taking the form of a renationalization of its politics. Publics are revolting against the double dislocations of European integration and globalization. As a consequence, the EU's member states are busily clawing back the prerogatives of sovereignty, threatening the project of European political and economic integration set in motion after World War II. As in the United States, economic conditions are the root of the problem. Over the past two decades, middle-class incomes in most major European economies have been falling and inequality has been rising. Unemployment in Spain stands at over 20 percent, and even Germany, the EU's premier economy, saw its middle class contract by 13 percent between 2000 and 2008. Those who slip through the cracks find a fraying safety net beneath them; Europe's comfortable welfare systems, which have become unsustainable in the face of global competition, are being dramatically scaled back. The austerity stemming from the ongoing debt crisis in the eurozone has only made matters worse. Greeks are as angry about the EU-enforced belt-tightening as Germans are about having to bail out Europe's economic laggards.

Europe's aging population has made immigration an economic necessity. But the lack of progress in integrating Muslim immigrants into the social mainstream has intensified discomfort over the EU's willingness to accept more outsiders into its midst. Far-right parties have been the beneficiaries of this anxiety, and their hard-edged nationalism targets not only immigrants but also the EU. Generational change is taking its own toll on popular enthusiasm for European integration. Europeans with memories of World War II see the EU as Europe's escape route from its bloody past. But younger Europeans have no past from which to flee. Whereas their elders viewed the European project as an article of faith, current leaders and electorates tend to assess the EU through a cold—and often negative—valuation of costs and benefits.

The collective governance that the EU desperately needs in order to thrive in a globalized world rests uneasily with a political street that is becoming decidedly hostile to the European project. Europe's institutions could descend to the level of its politics, which would effectively reduce the EU to little more than a trade bloc. Alternatively, national politics could again be infused with a European calling, which would breathe new legitimacy into an increasingly hollow union. The latter outcome is much preferable, but it will require leadership and resolve that, at least for now, are nowhere to be found.

Japan, for its part, has been politically adrift since Junichiro Koizumi stepped down as prime minister in 2006. Thereafter, the Liberal Democratic Party (LDP), which had dominated Japanese politics throughout most of the postwar era, stumbled badly, losing power to the Democratic Party of Japan (DPJ) in 2009. The consolidation of a two-party system had the potential to improve governance but instead produced only gridlock and declining public confidence. Japan has cycled through six prime ministers in the last five years. This past summer, public approval of the DPJ stood at 18 percent. The DPJ and the LDP are as internally divided as they are at loggerheads. Policymaking has ground to a halt even on urgent issues; it took over 100 days for the Diet to pass legislation providing relief to the victims of last year's earthquake, tsunami, and nuclear disaster.

The trouble began with the bursting of Japan's asset bubble in 1991, a setback that exposed deeper problems in the country's economy and led to a "lost decade" of recession. Japanese manufacturers suffered as jobs and investment headed to China and the "Asian tigers." The country's traditional social compact, by which corporations provided lifetime employment and comfortable pensions, was no longer sustainable. The past two decades have brought a long slide in middle-class incomes, rising inequality, and a spike in the poverty rate from roughly seven percent in the 1980s to 16 percent in 2009. In 1989, Japan ranked fourth in the world in terms of per capita GDP; by 2010, its rank had plummeted to 24th.

It was to address such problems that Koizumi embarked on ambitious efforts to liberalize the economy and reduce the power of bureaucrats and interest groups. His charisma and ample parliamentary support made for significant progress, but his LDP and DPJ successors have been too weak to keep the process moving forward. Japan is therefore stuck in a no man's land, exposed to the dislocations of a globalized economy yet not liberalized or strategic enough to compete effectively.

Bitter Medicine

It is not by chance that the West's crisis of governability coincides with new political strength among rising powers; economic and political vigor is passing from the core to the periphery of the international system. And while the world's most open states are experiencing a loss of control as they integrate into a globalized world, illiberal states, such as China, are deliberately keeping a much tighter grip on their societies through centralized decision-making, censorship of the media, and state-supervised markets. If the leading democracies continue to lose their luster as developing countries chart their rise, the unfolding transition in global power will be significantly more destabilizing. Conversely, a realignment of the international pecking order would likely be more orderly if the Western democracies recouped and provided purposeful leadership.

What is needed is nothing less than a compelling twenty-first-century answer to the fundamental tensions among democracy, capitalism, and globalization. This new political agenda should aim to reassert popular control over political economy, directing state action toward effective responses to both the economic realities of global markets and the demands of mass societies for an equitable distribution of rewards and sacrifices.

The West should pursue three broad strategies to meet this challenge and thus better equip its democratic institutions for a globalized world. First, when up against state capitalism and the potent force of global markets, the Western democracies have little choice but to engage in strategic economic planning on an unprecedented scale. State-led investment in jobs, infrastructure, education, and research will be required to restore economic competitiveness. Second, leaders should seek to channel electorate discontent toward reformist ends through a progressive brand of populism. By pursuing policies that advantage mass publics rather than the party faithful or special interests, politicians can not only rebuild their popularity but also reinvigorate democratic institutions and the values of citizenship and sacrifice. Third, Western governments must lead their electorates away from the temptation to turn inward. As history makes clear, hard times can stoke protectionism and isolationism. But globalization is here to stay, and retreat is not an option.

None of these strategies will be easy to implement, and embracing all of them together will require extraordinary leadership and the political courage to match. But until such an agenda is devised and realized, the democratic malaise will persist.

Critical Thinking

1. What threatens the viability of democracy in developed societies?
2. Why are developed societies practically "ungovernable"?
3. What are the voters demanding and why can't governments meet their demands?

CHARLES A. KUPCHAN is Professor of International Affairs at Georgetown University and Whitney Shepardson Senior Fellow at the Council on Foreign Relations. This essay is adapted from his forthcoming book *No One's World: The West, the Rising Rest, and the Coming Global Turn* (Oxford University Press, 2012).

From *Foreign Affairs*, vol. 91, no. 1, January/February 2012, pp. 62–67. Copyright © 2012 by Council on Foreign Relations, Inc. Reprinted by permission of Foreign Affairs. www.ForeignAffairs.com

The Future of History: Can Liberal Democracy Survive the Decline of the Middle Class?

FRANCIS FUKUYAMA

Something strange is going on in the world today. The global financial crisis that began in 2008 and the ongoing crisis of the euro are both products of the model of lightly regulated financial capitalism that emerged over the past three decades. Yet despite widespread anger at Wall Street bailouts, there has been no great upsurge of left-wing American populism in response. It is conceivable that the Occupy Wall Street movement will gain traction, but the most dynamic recent populist movement to date has been the right-wing Tea Party, whose main target is the regulatory state that seeks to protect ordinary people from financial speculators. Something similar is true in Europe as well, where the left is anemic and right-wing populist parties are on the move.

There are several reasons for this lack of left-wing mobilization, but chief among them is a failure in the realm of ideas. For the past generation, the ideological high ground on economic issues has been held by a libertarian right. The left has not been able to make a plausible case for an agenda other than a return to an unaffordable form of old-fashioned social democracy. This absence of a plausible progressive counter-narrative is unhealthy, because competition is good for intellectual—debate just as it is for economic activity. And serious intellectual debate is urgently needed, since the current form of globalized capitalism is eroding the middle-class social base on which liberal democracy rests.

The Democratic Wave

Social forces and conditions do not simply "determine" ideologies, as Karl Marx once maintained, but ideas do not become powerful unless they speak to the concerns of large numbers of ordinary people. Liberal democracy is the default ideology around much of the world today in part because it responds to and is facilitated by certain socioeconomic structures. Changes in those structures may have ideological consequences, just as ideological changes may have socioeconomic consequences.

Almost all the powerful ideas that shaped human societies up until the past 300 years were religious in nature, with the important exception of Confucianism in China. The first major secular ideology to have a lasting worldwide effect was liberalism, a doctrine associated with the rise of first a commercial and then an industrial middle class in certain parts of Europe in the seventeenth century. (By "middle class," I mean people who are neither at the top nor at the bottom of their societies in terms of income, who have received at least a secondary education, and who own either real property, durable goods, or their own businesses.)

As enunciated by classic thinkers such as Locke, Montesquieu, and Mill, liberalism holds that the legitimacy of state authority derives from the state's ability to protect the individual rights of its citizens and that state power needs to be limited by the adherence to law. One of the fundamental rights to be protected is that of private property; England's Glorious Revolution of 1688–89 was critical to the development of modern liberalism because it first established the constitutional principle that the state could not legitimately tax its citizens without their consent.

At first, liberalism did not necessarily imply democracy. The Whigs who supported the constitutional settlement of 1689 tended to be the wealthiest property owners in England; the parliament of that period represented less than ten percent of the whole population. Many classic liberals, including Mill, were highly skeptical of the virtues of democracy: they believed that responsible political participation required education and a stake in society—that is, property ownership. Up through the end of the nineteenth century, the franchise was limited by property and educational requirements in virtually all parts of Europe. Andrew

Jackson's election as U.S. president in 1828 and his subsequent abolition of property requirements for voting, at least for white males, thus marked an important early victory for a more robust democratic principle. In Europe, the exclusion of the vast majority of the population from political power and the rise of an industrial working class paved the way for Marxism. The Communist Manifesto was published in 1848, the same year that revolutions spread to all the major European countries save the United Kingdom. And so began a century of competition for the leadership of the democratic movement between communists, who were willing to jettison procedural democracy (multiparty elections) in favor of what they believed was substantive democracy (economic redistribution), and liberal democrats, who believed in expanding political participation while maintaining a rule of law protecting individual rights, including property rights.

At stake was the allegiance of the new industrial working class. Early Marxists believed they would win by sheer force of numbers: as the franchise was expanded in the late nineteenth century, parties such as the United Kingdom's Labour and Germany's Social Democrats grew by leaps and bounds and threatened the hegemony of both conservatives and traditional liberals. The rise of the working class was fiercely resisted, often by nondemocratic means; the communists and many socialists, in turn, abandoned formal democracy in favor of a direct seizure of power.

Throughout the first half of the twentieth century, there was a strong consensus on the progressive left that some form of socialism—government control of the commanding heights of the economy in order to ensure an egalitarian distribution of wealth—was unavoidable for all advanced countries. Even a conservative economist such as Joseph Schumpeter could write in his 1942 book, *Capitalism, Socialism, and Democracy*, that socialism would emerge victorious because capitalist society was culturally self-undermining. Socialism was believed to represent the will and interests of the vast majority of people in modern societies. Yet even as the great ideological conflicts of the twentieth century played themselves out on a political and military level, critical changes were happening on a social level that undermined the Marxist scenario. First, the real living standards of the industrial working class kept rising, to the point where many workers or their children were able to join the middle class. Second, the relative size of the working class stopped growing and actually began to decline, particularly in the second half of the twentieth century, when services began to displace manufacturing in what were labeled "postindustrial" economics. Finally, a new group of poor or disadvantaged people emerged below the industrial working class—a heterogeneous mixture of racial and ethnic minorities, recent immigrants, and socially excluded groups, such as women, gays, and the disabled. As a result of these changes, in most industrialized societies, the old working class has become just another domestic interest group, one using the political power of trade unions to protect the hard-won gains of an earlier era. Economic class, moreover, turned out not to be a great banner under which to mobilize populations in advanced industrial countries for political action. The Second International got a rude wake-up call in 1914, when the working classes of Europe abandoned calls for class warfare and lined up behind conservative leaders preaching nationalist slogans, a pattern that persists to the present day. Many Marxists tried to explain this, according to the scholar Ernest Gellner, by what he dubbed the "wrong address theory":

> Just as extreme Shi'ite Muslims hold that Archangel Gabriel made a mistake, delivering the Message to Mohamed when it was intended for Ali, so Marxists basically like to think that the spirit of history or human consciousness made a terrible boob. The awakening message was intended for classes, but by some terrible postal error was delivered to nations.

Gellner went on to argue that religion serves a function similar to nationalism in the contemporary Middle East: it mobilizes people effectively because it has a spiritual and emotional content that class consciousness does not. Just as European nationalism was driven by the shift of Europeans from the countryside to cities in the late nineteenth century, so, too, Islamism is a reaction to the urbanization and displacement taking place in contemporary Middle Eastern societies. Marx's letter will never be delivered to the address marked "class." Marx believed that the middle class, or at least the capital-owning slice of it that he called the bourgeoisie, would always remain a small and privileged minority in modern societies. What happened instead was that the bourgeoisie and the middle class more generally ended up constituting the vast majority of the populations of most advanced countries, posing problems for socialism. From the days of Aristotle, thinkers have believed that stable democracy rests on a broad middle class and that societies with extremes of wealth and poverty are susceptible either to oligarchic domination or populist revolution. When much of the developed world succeeded in creating middle-class societies, the appeal of Marxism vanished. The only places where leftist radicalism persists as a powerful force are in highly unequal areas of the world, such as parts of Latin America, Nepal, and the impoverished regions of eastern India.

What the political scientist Samuel Huntington labeled the "third wave" of global democratization, which began in southern Europe in the 1970s and culminated in the fall of communism in Eastern Europe in 1989, increased the number of electoral democracies around the world from around 45 in 1970 to more than 120 by the late 1990s. Economic growth has led to the emergence of new middle classes in countries such as Brazil, India, Indonesia, South Africa, and Turkey. As the economist Moises Naim has pointed out, these middle classes are relatively well educated, own property, and are technologically connected to the outside world. They are demanding of their governments and mobilize easily as a result of their access to technology. It should not be surprising that the chief instigators of the Arab Spring uprisings were well-educated Tunisians and Egyptians whose expectations for jobs and political participation were stymied by the dictatorships under which they lived.

Middle-class people do not necessarily support democracy in principle: like everyone else, they are self-interested actors who want to protect their property and position. In countries such as China and Thailand, many middle-class people feel threatened by the redistributive demands of the poor and hence have lined up in support of authoritarian governments that protect their class interests. Nor is it the case that democracies necessarily meet the expectations of their own middle classes, and when they do not, the middle classes can become restive.

The Least Bad Alternative?

There is today a broad global consensus about the legitimacy, at least in principle, of liberal democracy. In the words of the economist Amartya Sen, "While democracy is not yet universally practiced, nor indeed uniformly accepted, in the general climate of world opinion, democratic governance has now achieved the status of being taken to be generally right." It is most broadly accepted in countries that have reached a level of material prosperity sufficient to allow a majority of their citizens to think of themselves as middle class, which is why there tends to be a correlation between high levels of—development and stable democracy.

Some societies, such as Iran and Saudi Arabia, reject liberal democracy in favor of a form of Islamic theocracy. Yet these regimes are developmental dead ends, kept alive only because they sit atop vast pools of oil. There was at one time a large Arab exception to the third wave, but the Arab Spring has shown that Arab publics can be mobilized against dictatorship just as readily as those in Eastern Europe and Latin America were. This does not of course mean that the path to a well-functioning democracy will be easy or straightforward in Tunisia, Egypt, or Libya, but it does suggest that the desire for—political freedom and participation is not a cultural peculiarity of Europeans and Americans.

The single most serious challenge to liberal democracy in the world today comes from China, which has combined authoritarian government with a partially marketized economy. China is heir to a long and proud tradition of high-quality bureaucratic government, one that stretches back over two millennia. Its leaders have managed a hugely complex transition from a centralized, Soviet-style planned economy to a dynamic open one and have done so with remarkable competence—more competence, frankly, than U.S. leaders have shown in the management of their own macroeconomic policy recently. Many people currently admire the Chinese system not just for its economic record but also because it can make large, complex decisions quickly, compared with the agonizing policy paralysis that has struck both the United States and Europe in the past few years. Especially since the recent financial crisis, the Chinese themselves have begun touting the "China model" as an alternative to liberal democracy.

This model is unlikely to ever become a serious alternative to liberal democracy in regions outside East Asia, however. In the first place, the model is culturally specific: the Chinese government is built around a long tradition of meritocratic recruitment, civil service examinations, a high emphasis on education, and deference to technocratic authority. Few developing countries can hope to emulate this model; those that have, such as Singapore and South Korea (at least in an earlier period), were already within the Chinese cultural zone. The Chinese themselves are skeptical about whether their model can be exported; the so-called Beijing consensus is a Western invention, not a Chinese one. It is also unclear whether the model can be sustained. Neither export-driven growth nor the top-down approach to decision-making will continue to yield good results forever. The fact that the Chinese government would not permit open discussion of the disastrous high-speed rail accident last summer and could not bring the Railway Ministry responsible for it to heel suggests that there are other time bombs hidden behind the facade of efficient decision-making.

Finally, China faces a great moral vulnerability down the road. The Chinese government does not force its officials to respect the basic dignity of its citizens. Every week, there are new protests about land seizures, environmental violations, or gross corruption on the part of some official. While the country is growing rapidly, these abuses can be swept under the carpet. But rapid growth will not continue forever, and the government will have to pay a price in pent-up anger. The regime no longer has any guiding ideal around which it is organized; it is run by a Communist Party supposedly committed to equality that presides over a society marked by dramatic and growing inequality.

So the stability of the Chinese system can in no way be taken for granted. The Chinese government argues that its citizens are culturally different and will always prefer benevolent, growth-promoting dictatorship to a messy democracy that threatens social stability. But it is unlikely that a spreading middle class will behave all that differently in China from the way it has behaved in other parts of the world. Other authoritarian regimes may be trying to emulate China's success, but there is little chance that much of the world will look like today's China 50 years down the road.

Democracy's Future

There is a broad correlation among economic growth, social change, and the hegemony of liberal democratic ideology in the world today. And at the moment, no plausible rival ideology looms. But some very troubling economic and social trends, if they continue, will both threaten the stability of contemporary liberal democracies and dethrone democratic ideology as it is now understood. The sociologist Barrington Moore once flatly asserted, "No bourgeois, no democracy." The Marxists didn't get their communist Utopia because mature capitalism generated middle-class societies, not working-class ones. But what if the further development of technology and globalization undermines the middle class and makes it impossible for more than a minority of citizens in an advanced society to achieve middle-class status?

There are already abundant signs that such a phase of development has begun. Median incomes in the United States have been stagnating in real terms since the 1970s. The economic impact of this stagnation has been softened to some extent by the fact that most U.S. households have shifted to two income earners in the past generation. Moreover, as the economist Raghuram Rajan has persuasively argued, since Americans are reluctant to engage in straightforward redistribution, the United States has instead attempted a highly dangerous and inefficient form of redistribution over the past generation by subsidizing mortgages for low-income households. This trend, facilitated by a flood of liquidity pouring in from China and other countries, gave many ordinary Americans the illusion that their standards of living were rising steadily during the past decade. In this respect, the bursting of the housing bubble in 2008–9 was nothing more than a cruel reversion to the mean. Americans may today benefit from cheap cell phones, inexpensive clothing, and Facebook, but they increasingly cannot afford their own homes, or health insurance, or comfortable pensions when they retire.

A more troubling phenomenon, identified by the venture capitalist Peter Thiel and the economist Tyler Cowen, is that the benefits of the most recent waves of technological innovation have accrued disproportionately to the most talented and well-educated members of society. This phenomenon helped cause the massive growth of inequality in the United States over the past generation. In 1974, the top one percent of families took home nine percent of GDP; by 2007, that share had increased to 23.5 percent.

Trade and tax policies may have accelerated this trend, but the real villain here is technology. In earlier phases of industrialization—the ages of textiles, coal, steel, and the internal combustion engine—the benefits of technological changes almost always flowed down in significant ways to the rest of society in terms of employment. But this is not a law of nature. We are today living in what the scholar Shoshana Zuboff has labeled "the age of the smart machine," in which technology is increasingly able to substitute for more and higher human functions. Every great advance for Silicon Valley likely means a loss of low-skill jobs elsewhere in the economy, a trend that is unlikely to end anytime soon. Inequality has always existed, as a result of natural differences in talent and character. But today's technological

world vastly magnifies those differences. In a nineteenth-century agrarian society, people with strong math skills did not have that many opportunities to capitalize on their talent. Today, they can become financial wizards or software engineers and take home ever larger proportions of the national wealth.

The other factor undermining middle-class incomes in developed countries is globalization. With the lowering of transportation and communications costs and the entry into the global work force of hundreds of millions of new workers in developing countries, the kind of work done by the old middle class in the developed world can now be performed much more cheaply elsewhere. Under an economic model that prioritizes the maximization of aggregate income, it is inevitable that jobs will be outsourced.

Smarter ideas and policies could have contained the damage. Germany has succeeded in protecting a significant part of its manufacturing base and industrial labor force even as its companies have remained globally competitive. The United States and the United Kingdom, on the other hand, happily embraced the transition to the postindustrial service economy. Free trade became less a theory than an ideology: when members of the U.S. Congress tried to retaliate with trade sanctions against China for keeping its currency undervalued, they were indignantly charged with protectionism, as if the playing field were already level. There was a lot of happy talk about the wonders of the knowledge economy, and how dirty, dangerous manufacturing jobs would inevitably be replaced by highly educated workers doing creative and interesting things. This was a gauzy veil placed over the hard facts of deindustrialization. It overlooked the fact that the benefits of the new order accrued disproportionately to a very small number of people in finance and high technology, interests that dominated the media and the general political conversation.

The Absent Left

One of the most puzzling features of the world in the aftermath of the financial crisis is that so far, populism has taken primarily a right-wing form, not a left-wing one.

In the United States, for example, although the Tea Party is anti-elitist in its rhetoric, its members vote for conservative politicians who serve the interests of precisely those financiers and corporate elites they claim to despise. There are many explanations for this phenomenon. They include a deeply embedded belief in equality of opportunity rather than equality of outcome and the fact that cultural issues, such as abortion and gun rights, crosscut economic ones.

But the deeper reason a broad-based populist left has failed to materialize is an intellectual one. It has been several decades since anyone on the left has been able to articulate, first, a coherent analysis of what happens to the structure of advanced societies as they undergo economic change and, second, a realistic agenda that has any hope of protecting a middle-class society.

The main trends in left-wing thought in the last two generations have been, frankly, disastrous as either conceptual frameworks or tools for mobilization. Marxism died many years ago, and the few old believers still around are ready for nursing homes. The academic left replaced it with postmodernism, multiculturalism, feminism, critical theory, and a host of other fragmented intellectual trends that are more cultural than economic in focus. Postmodernism begins with a denial of the possibility of any master narrative of history or society, undercutting its own authority as a voice for the majority of citizens who feel betrayed by their elites. Multiculturalism validates the victimhood of virtually every out-group. It is impossible to generate a mass progressive movement on the basis of such a motley coalition: most of the working- and lower-middle-class citizens victimized by the system are culturally conservative and would be embarrassed to be seen in the presence of allies like this.

Whatever the theoretical justifications underlying the left's agenda, its biggest problem is a lack of credibility. Over the past two generations, the mainstream left has followed a social democratic program that centers on the state provision of a variety of services, such as pensions, health care, and education. That model is now exhausted: welfare states have become big, bureaucratic, and inflexible; they are often captured by the very organizations that administer them, through public-sector unions; and, most important, they are fiscally unsustainable given the aging of populations virtually everywhere in the developed world. Thus, when existing social democratic parties come to power, they no longer aspire to be more than custodians of a welfare state that was created decades ago; none has a new, exciting agenda around which to rally the masses.

An Ideology of the Future

Imagine, for a moment, an obscure scribbler today in a garret somewhere trying to outline an ideology of the future that could provide a realistic path toward a world with healthy middle-class societies and robust democracies. What would that ideology look like?

It would have to have at least two components, political and economic. Politically, the new ideology would need to reassert the supremacy of democratic politics over economics and legitimate a new government as an expression of the public interest. But the agenda it put forward to protect middle-class life could not simply rely on the existing mechanisms of the welfare state. The ideology would need to somehow redesign the public sector, freeing it from its dependence on existing stakeholders and using new, technology-empowered approaches to delivering services. It would have to argue forth-rightly for more redistribution

and present a realistic route to ending interest groups' domination of politics.

Economically, the ideology could not begin with a denunciation of capitalism as such, as if old-fashioned socialism were still a viable alternative. It is more the variety of capitalism that is at stake and the degree to which governments should help societies adjust to change. Globalization need be seen not as an inexorable fact of life but rather as a challenge and an opportunity that must be carefully controlled politically. The new ideology would not see markets as an end in themselves; instead, it would value global trade and investment to the extent that they contributed to a flourishing middle class, not just to greater aggregate national wealth.

It is not possible to get to that point, however, without providing a serious and sustained critique of much of the edifice of modern neoclassical economics, beginning with fundamental assumptions such as the sovereignty of individual preferences and that aggregate income is an accurate measure of national well-being. This critique would have to note that people's incomes do not necessarily represent their true contributions to society. It would have to go further, however, and recognize that even if labor markets were efficient, the natural distribution of talents is not necessarily fair and that individuals are not sovereign entities but beings heavily shaped by their surrounding societies.

Most of these ideas have been around in bits and pieces for some time; the scribbler would have to put them into a coherent package. He or she would also have to avoid the "wrong address" problem. The critique of globalization, that is, would have to be tied to nationalism as a strategy for mobilization in a way that defined national interest in a more sophisticated way than, for example, the "Buy American" campaigns of unions in the United States. The product would be a synthesis of ideas from both the left and the right, detached from the agenda of the marginalized groups that constitute the existing progressive movement. The ideology would be populist; the message would begin with a critique of the elites that allowed the benefit of the many to be sacrificed to that of the few and a critique of the money politics, especially in Washington, that overwhelmingly benefits the wealthy.

The dangers inherent in such a movement are obvious: a pullback by the United States, in particular, from its advocacy of a more open global system could set off protectionist responses elsewhere. In many respects, the Reagan-Thatcher revolution succeeded just as its proponents hoped, bringing about an increasingly competitive, globalized, friction-free world. Along the way, it generated tremendous wealth and created rising middle classes all over the developing world, and the spread of democracy in their wake. It is possible that the developed world is on the cusp of a series of technological breakthroughs that will not only increase productivity but also provide meaningful employment to large numbers of middle-class people.

But that is more a matter of faith than a reflection of the empirical reality of the last 30 years, which points in the opposite direction. Indeed, there are a lot of reasons to think that inequality will continue to worsen. The current concentration of wealth in the United States has already become self-reinforcing: as the economist Simon Johnson has argued, the financial sector has used its lobbying clout to avoid more onerous forms of regulation. Schools for the well-off are better than ever; those for everyone else continue to deteriorate. Elites in all societies use their superior access to the political system to protect their interests, absent a countervailing democratic mobilization to rectify the situation. American elites are no exception to the rule.

That mobilization will not happen, however, as long as the middle classes of the developed world remain enthralled by the narrative of the past generation: that their interests will be best served by ever-freer markets and smaller states. The alternative narrative is out there, waiting to be born.

Source

Fukuyama, Francis. "The future of history: can liberal democracy survive the decline of the middle class?" *Foreign Affairs* 91.1 (2012). *General Reference Center GOLD*. Web. 25 Jan. 2012.

Critical Thinking

1. Why is a healthy middle class necessary to the sustainability of liberal democracy?

2. What are the causes of the increasing inequality that threatens democracy?

FRANCIS FUKUYAMA is a Senior Fellow at the Center on Democracy, Development, and the Rule of Law at Stanford University and the author, most recently, of *The Origins of Political Order: From Prehuman Times to the French Revolution.*

Test-Your-Knowledge Form

We encourage you to photocopy and use this page as a tool to assess how the articles in *Annual Editions* expand on the information in your textbook. By reflecting on the articles you will gain enhanced text information. You can also access this useful form on a product's book support website at www.mhhe.com/cls.

NAME: DATE:

_____

TITLE AND NUMBER OF ARTICLE:

_____

BRIEFLY STATE THE MAIN IDEA OF THIS ARTICLE:

_____

LIST THREE IMPORTANT FACTS THAT THE AUTHOR USES TO SUPPORT THE MAIN IDEA:

_____

WHAT INFORMATION OR IDEAS DISCUSSED IN THIS ARTICLE ARE ALSO DISCUSSED IN YOUR TEXTBOOK OR OTHER READINGS THAT YOU HAVE DONE? LIST THE TEXTBOOK CHAPTERS AND PAGE NUMBERS:

_____

LIST ANY EXAMPLES OF BIAS OR FAULTY REASONING THAT YOU FOUND IN THE ARTICLE:

_____

LIST ANY NEW TERMS/CONCEPTS THAT WERE DISCUSSED IN THE ARTICLE, AND WRITE A SHORT DEFINITION: